OCR BIOLOGY 1

A-Level Year 1/AS **Student Workbook**

OCR BIOLOGY 1

A-Level Year 1/AS Student Workbook

Meet the Writing Team

Tracey Greenwood
I have been writing resources for students since 1993. I have a Ph.D in biology, specialising in lake ecology and I have taught both graduate and undergraduate biology.

Tracey
Senior Author

Lissa Bainbridge-Smith
I worked in industry in a research and development capacity for 8 years before joining BIOZONE in 2006. I have an M.Sc from Waikato University.

Lissa
Author

Kent Pryor
I have a BSc from Massey University majoring in zoology and ecology and taught secondary school biology and chemistry for 9 years before joining BIOZONE as an author in 2009.

Kent
Author

Richard Allan
I have had 11 years experience teaching senior secondary school biology. I have a Masters degree in biology and founded BIOZONE in the 1980s after developing resources for my own students.

Richard
Founder & CEO

Thanks to:

The staff at BIOZONE, including Gemma Conn and Julie Fairless for design and graphics support, Paolo Curray for IT support, Debbie Antoniadis and Tim Lind for office handling and logistics, and the BIOZONE sales team.

First edition 2015
Fourth printing with clarifications

ISBN 978-1-927309-13-1

Copyright © 2015 Richard Allan
Published by **BIOZONE International Ltd**

Printed by REPLIKA PRESS PVT LTD using paper produced from renewable and waste materials

Purchases of this workbook may be made direct from the publisher:

BIOZONE Learning Media (UK) Ltd.

Telephone local:	01283 530 366
Telephone international:	+44 1283 530 366
Fax local:	01283 831 900
Fax international:	+44 1283 831 900
Email:	sales@biozone.co.uk

www.**BIOZONE**.co.uk

Cover Photograph

The veiled chameleon (*Chamaeleo calyptratus*) is native to Yemen and southern Saudi Arabia. Its flattened leaf like shape and ability to change colour help it to blend into the background and allow it to both ambush prey and remain undetected by predators. Most exhibit shades of green or brown at rest but can become brightly coloured when disturbed, during courtship, or when defending territory against another chameleon. Veiled chameleons have a casque, a helmet like extension on their head, which is thought to help collect water.

PHOTO: IGOR SIWANOWICZ / BARCROFT MEDIA LTD

Contents

Activity is marked: ▪ to be done;   ✓ when completed

Contents

Activity is marked: ⬛ to be done;   ✓ when completed

Contents

Activity is marked: to be done;   when completed

Using This Workbook

This first edition of OCR Biology 1 has been specifically written to meet the content and skills requirements of AS/A Level OCR Biology. Learning outcomes in the introduction to each chapter provide you with a concise guide to the knowledge and skills requirements for each module. Each learning outcome is matched to the activity or activities addressing it. Practical Activity Groups are identified in the chapter introductions by a code (PAG) and supported by activities designed to provide background and familiarity with apparatus, techniques, experimental design, and interpretation of results. A wide range of activities will help you to build on what you already know, explore new topics, work collaboratively, and practise your skills in data handling and interpretation. We hope that you find the workbook valuable and that you make full use of its features.

▶ The outline of the chapter structure below will help you to navigate through the material in each chapter.

Introduction
- A check list of the knowledge and skills requirements for the chapter.
- A list of key terms.

Activities
- The KEY IDEA provides your focus for the activity.
- Annotated diagrams help you understand the content.
- Questions review the content of the page.

Review
- Create your own summary for review.
- Hints help you to focus on what is important.
- Your summary will consolidate your understanding of the content in the chapter.

Literacy
- Activities are based on, but not restricted to, the introductory key terms list.
- Several types of activities test your understanding of the concepts and biological terms in the chapter.

Linkages are made between ideas in separate activities

Structure of a chapter

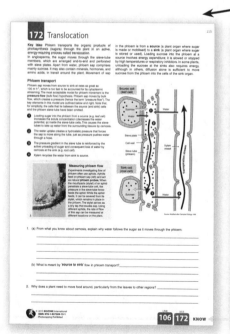

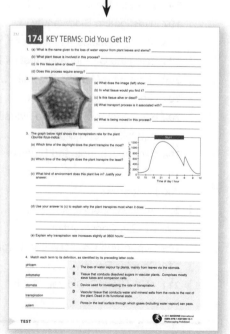

▶ Understanding the activity coding system and making use of the online material identified will enable you to get the most out of this resource. The chapter content is structured to build knowledge and skills but this structure does not necessarily represent a strict order of treatment. Be guided by your teacher, who will assign activities as part of a wider programme of independent and group-based work.

Look out for these features and know how to use them:

The **chapter introduction** provides you with a summary of the knowledge and skills requirements for the topic, phrased as a set of learning outcomes. Use the check boxes to identify and mark off the points as you complete them. The chapter introduction also provides you with a list of key terms for the chapter, from which you can construct your own glossary as you work through the activities.

The **activities** form most of this workbook. They are numbered sequentially and each has a task code identifying the skill emphasised. Each activity has a short introduction with a key idea identifying the main message of the page. Most of the information is associated with pictures and diagrams, and your understanding of the content is reviewed through the questions. Some of the activities involve modelling and group work.

Free response questions allow you to use the information provided to answer questions about the content of the activity, either directly or by applying the same principles to a new situation. In some cases, an activity will assume understanding of prior content.

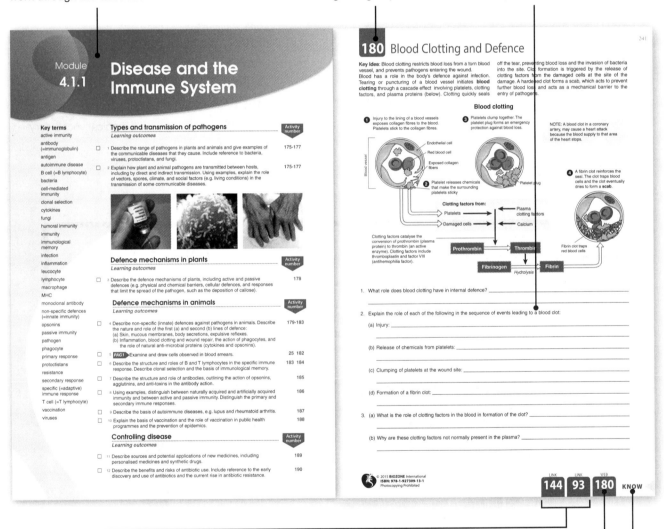

LINK tabs at the bottom of the activity page identify activities that are related in that they build on content or apply the same principles to a new situation.

WEB tabs at the bottom of the activity page alert the reader to the **Weblinks** resource, which provides external, online support material for the activity, usually in the form of an animation, video clip, photo library, or quiz. Bookmark the Weblinks page (see next page) and visit it frequently as you progress through the workbook.

A **TASK CODE** on the page tab identifies the type of activity. For example, is it primarily information-based (KNOW), or does it involve modelling (PRAC) or data handling (DATA)? A full list of codes is given on the following page but the codes themselves are relatively self explanatory.

Using the Tab System

The tab system is a useful system for quickly identifying related content and online support. Links generally refer to activities that build on the information in the activity in depth or extent. In the example below, the weblink 163 provides a photographic overview of plant tissues. Activities 164 and 165 cover xylem and phloem respectively, examining those vascular tissues in more detail. Sometimes, a link will reflect on material that has been covered earlier as a reminder for important terms that have already been defined or for a formula that may be required to answer a question. The weblinks code is always the same as the activity number on which it is cited. On visiting the weblink page (below), find the number and it will correspond to one or more external websites providing a video or animation of some aspect of the activity's content. Occasionally, the weblink may provide a bank of photographs where images are provided in colour, e.g. for plant and animal histology.

Activities are coded

COMP = comprehension of text

DATA = data handling and interpretation

KNOW = content you need to know

PRAC = a paper practical or a practical focus

REFER = reference - use this for information

REVISE = review the material in the section

TEST = test your understanding

VOCAB = learning your biological vocabulary

Link
Connections are made between activities in different sections of the syllabus that are related through content or because they build on prior knowledge.

Weblinks
Bookmark the weblinks page: www.biozone.co.uk/OCR-1-9131

Access the external URL for the activity by clicking the link

www.biozone.co.uk/weblink/OCR-1-9131

This WEBLINKS page provides links to **external websites** with supporting information for the activities. These sites are distinct from those provided in the BIOLINKS area of BIOZONE's web site. For the most part, they are narrowly focussed animations and video clips directly relevant to some aspect of the activity on which they are cited. They provide great support to help your understanding of basic concepts.

Chapter in the workbook

Hyperlink to the external website page.

Activity in the workbook

Bookmark weblinks by typing in the address: it is not accessible directly from BIOZONE's website
Corrections and clarifications to current editions are always posted on the weblinks page

Using BIOZONE's Website

Access the **BIOLINKS** database of web sites directly from the homepage of our website.

Contact us with questions, feedback, ideas, and critical commentary. We welcome your input.

Use Google to search for websites of interest. The more precise your search words are, the better the list of results. Be specific, e.g. "biotechnology medicine DNA uses", rather than "biotechnology".

Biolinks is organised into easy-to-use sub-sections relating to general areas of interest. It's a great way to quickly find out more on topics of interest.

Command Terms

Questions come in a variety of forms. Whether you are studying for an exam or writing an essay, it is important to understand exactly what the question is asking. A question has two parts to it: one part of the question will provide you with information, the second part of the question will provide you with instructions as to how to answer the question. Following these instructions is most important. Often students in examinations know the material but fail to follow instructions and do not answer the question appropriately. Examiners often use certain key words to introduce questions. Look out for them and be clear as to what they mean. Below is a description of terms commonly used when asking questions in biology.

Commonly used terms in biology

The following terms are frequently used when asking questions in examinations and assessments. Students should have a clear understanding of each of the following terms and use this understanding to answer questions appropriately.

Account for: Provide a satisfactory explanation or reason for an observation.

Analyse: Interpret data to reach stated conclusions.

Annotate: Add **brief** notes to a diagram, drawing or graph.

Apply: Use an idea, equation, principle, theory, or law in a new situation.

Appreciate: To understand the meaning or relevance of a particular situation.

Calculate: Find an answer using mathematical methods. Show the working unless instructed not to.

Compare: Give an account of similarities and differences between two or more items, referring to both (or all) of them throughout. Comparisons can be given using a table. Comparisons generally ask for similarities more than differences (see contrast).

Construct: Represent or develop in graphical form.

Contrast: Show differences. Set in opposition.

Deduce: Reach a conclusion from information given.

Define: Give the precise meaning of a word or phrase as concisely as possible.

Derive: Manipulate a mathematical equation to give a new equation or result.

Describe: Give a detailed account, including all the relevant information.

Design: Produce a plan, object, simulation or model.

Determine: Find the only possible answer.

Discuss: Give an account including, where possible, a range of arguments, assessments of the relative importance of various factors, or comparison of alternative hypotheses.

Distinguish: Give the difference(s) between two or more different items.

Draw: Represent by means of pencil lines. Add labels unless told not to do so.

Estimate: Find an approximate value for an unknown quantity, based on the information provided and application of scientific knowledge.

Evaluate: Assess the implications and limitations.

Explain: Give a clear account including causes, reasons, or mechanisms.

Identify: Find an answer from a number of possibilities.

Illustrate: Give concrete examples. Explain clearly by using comparisons or examples.

Interpret: Comment upon, give examples, describe relationships. Describe, then evaluate.

List: Give a sequence of names or other brief answers with no elaboration. Each one should be clearly distinguishable from the others.

Measure: Find a value for a quantity.

Outline: Give a brief account or summary. Include essential information only.

Predict: Give an expected result.

Solve: Obtain an answer using algebraic and/or numerical methods.

State: Give a specific name, value, or other answer. No supporting argument or calculation is necessary.

Suggest: Propose a hypothesis or other possible explanation.

Summarise: Give a brief, condensed account. Include conclusions and avoid unnecessary details.

In conclusion

Students should familiarise themselves with this list of terms and, where necessary throughout the course, they should refer back to them when answering questions. The list of terms mentioned above is not exhaustive and students should compare this list with past examination papers / essays etc. and add any new terms (and their meaning) to the list above. The aim is to become familiar with interpreting the question and answering it appropriately.

Development of Practical Skills in Biology

Module 1.2 is also supported in OCR Biology 2

Key terms

accuracy
assumption
bar graph
chi-squared test
control
controlled variable
correlation
dependent variable
fair test
histogram
hypothesis
independent variable
line graph
mean
median
mode
observation
percentage error
precision
prediction
qualitative data
quantitative data
sample
scatter graph
standard deviation
statistical test
Student's *t* test
variable

1.1 Practical skills assessed in a written examination

Learning outcomes supported as indicated and throughout

Activity number

- ☐ 1 Demonstrate an understanding of science as inquiry. Appreciate that unexpected results may lead to new hypotheses and to new discoveries.   **1 2**
- ☐ 2 Demonstrate an understanding of experimental design including the identification of dependent, independent, and controlled variables, choice of a control, and awareness of assumptions in your design.   **3 4 5**
- ☐ 3 Evaluate experimental methods and procedures according to their ability to meet expected outcomes (e.g. test your predictions).   **5 26**
- ☐ 4 Demonstrate an ability to use a range of apparatus and techniques correctly.   **11**
- ☐ 5 Demonstrate an ability to use appropriate units for measurement and record your data systematically and accurately, e.g. in tables or spreadsheets.   **6 12**
- ☐ 6 Use graphs and tables appropriately to present observations and data.   **13 15-18**
- ☐ 7 Process, analyse, and interpret qualitative and quantitative experimental data.   **4 5 26**
- ☐ 8 Evaluate results and draw valid conclusions based on evidence. Resolve any conflicting evidence based on understanding and logical reasoning. Identify and explain anomalies in experimental measurements.   **26**
- ☐ 9 Identify limitations in experimental procedures and suggest how these could be overcome through improvements to design, apparatus, or technique.   **5 26**
- ☐ 10 Recognise and evaluate the precision and accuracy of collected data, including margins of error, percentage errors and uncertainties in apparatus.   **6 11**

  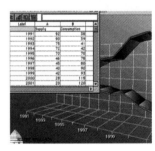

1.2 Practical skills assessed in the practical endorsement

Learning outcomes (PAGs and exemplars throughout OCR Biology 1 & 2)

Activity number

- ☐ 1 Solve problems in a practical context using investigative approaches and methods.   **4 5 26**
- ☐ 2 Use a range of apparatus, materials, and techniques correctly, following written instructions and making and recording observations and measurements.   **4 5 11**
- ☐ 3 Record experimental work and present information and data in a scientific way.   **12**
- ☐ 4 Process data, carry out research and report findings using appropriate software and tools. Use online and offline research and correctly cite information sources.   **1 7-10 13-19 26**
- ☐ 5 Use appropriate apparatus to record a range of quantitative data, including mass, time, volume, temperature, length, and pH.   **11 33**
- ☐ 6 Use appropriate instrumentation, such as a colorimeter or potometer, to record quantitative data.   **65 169**
- ☐ 7 Use laboratory glassware for a range of techniques, including serial dilution.   **11**
- ☐ 8 Use a light microscope (including graticule) at high and low power.   **29 33**
- ☐ 9 Make annotated scientific drawings from observations.   **24 25**

☐ 10 Use qualitative reagents to identify biological molecules. **4 64**

☐ 11 Separate biological compounds using thin layer chromatography or electrophoresis. **66**

☐ 12 Record physiological functions and plant or animal responses safely and ethically. **138 169**

☐ 13 Use aseptic techniques in microbiological investigations. **Book 2**

☐ 14 Use dissection equipment safely. **154**

☐ 15 Use sampling techniques e.g. quadrats, transects, in fieldwork. **Book 2**

☐ 16 Use ICT, e.g in computer modelling or to collect or process data. **229 230**

Mathematical skills

Supported as noted but also throughout OCR Biology 1 & 2

Activity number

M0: Arithmetic and numerical computation

☐ 1 Recognise and use appropriate units in calculations. **6 7**

☐ 2 Recognise and use expressions in both decimal and standard form. **7 10**

☐ 3 Carry out calculations involving fractions, percentages, and ratios. **8 10**

☐ 4 Estimate results to assess if calculated values are appropriate. **7**

☐ 5 Use calculator to find and use power, exponential, and logarithmic functions (AL). **9**

M1: Handling data

☐ 1 Use an appropriate number of significant figures in reporting calculations. **6**

☐ 2 Find arithmetic means for a range of data. **21 26**

☐ 3 Represent and interpret frequency data in the form of bar graphs and histograms. **15 16 23**

☐ 4 Demonstrate an understanding of simple probability, e.g. as in genetic inheritance. **194**

☐ 5 Show understanding of the principles of sampling as applied to scientific data and analyse random data collected by an appropriate sampling method. **23 194 195**

☐ 6 Calculate or compare mean, mode, and median for sample data. **21 23 26**

☐ 7 Plot and interpret scatter graphs to identify correlation between two variables. **18**

☐ 8 Make order of magnitude calculations, e.g. in calculating magnification. **34**

☐ 9 Select and apply appropriate statistical tests to analyse and interpret data, e.g. the chi-squared test, the Student's t test, and Spearman's rank correlation. **20 199 229 230**

☐ 10 Understand and use measures of dispersion, e.g. standard deviation and range. **22 23**

☐ 11 Identify and determine uncertainties in measurements. **11**

M2: Algebra

☐ 1 Demonstrate understanding of the symbols =, <, <<, >>, >, ∝, ~ **7**

☐ 2 Manipulate equations to change the subject. **34**

☐ 3 Substitute numerical values into algebraic equations using appropriate units. **19 104**

☐ 4 Solve algebraic equations. **34 66 137**

☐ 5 Use logarithms in relation to quantities ranging over several orders of magnitude (AL only). **9**

M3: Graphs

☐ 1 Translate information between graphical, numerical, and algebraic forms. **19**

☐ 2 Select an appropriate format to plot two variables from experimental or other data. **14**

☐ 3 Predict or sketch the shape of a graph with a linear relationship ($y = mx + c$). **19**

☐ 4 Determine the intercept of a graph (AL only). **19**

☐ 5 Calculate rate of change from a graph showing a linear relationship. **19 88**

☐ 6 Draw and use the slope of a tangent to a curve as a measure of rate of change. **88**

M4: Geometry and trigonometry

☐ 1 Calculate the circumferences, surface areas, and volumes of regular shapes. **100**

1   How Do We Do Science?

Key Idea: The scientific method is a rigorous process of observation, measurement, and analysis that helps us to explain phenomena and predict changes in a system.
Scientific knowledge is gained through a non-linear, dynamic process called the **scientific method**. The scientific method is not a strict set of rules to be followed, but rather a way of approaching problems in a rigorous, but open-minded way. It involves inspiration and creativity, it is dynamic and context dependent, and usually involves collaboration. The model below is one interpretation of the scientific method.

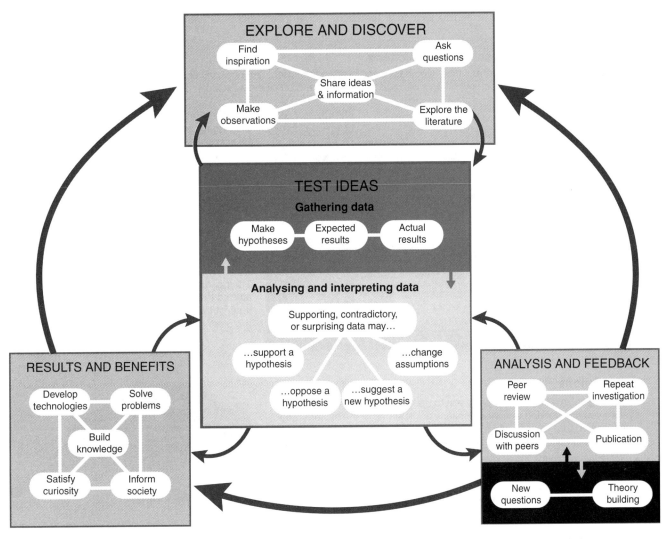

Citation and reference by numbers

Introduction

Hemoglobin is surely the most studied of all proteins. Indeed, the molecular analysis of hemoglobin has been the testing ground for many contemporary ideas and concepts in biology, particularly the understanding of the crystallographic structure and structure-function relationship of proteins, ligand binding, structural transitions between conformers, allosteric interactions, and others (1,2).

The ability of the aerobic metabolism of animals to satisfy the demands for only possible thanks to the role such as hemoglobins, contained or erythrocytes, which facilitate t tion of large quantities of gas and

References

1. Perutz MF. Species adaptation in a protein molecule. *Adv Protein Chem* 1984; 36: 213-244.
2. Berenbrink M. Evolution of vertebrate haemoglobins: Histidine side chains, specific buffer value and Bohr effect. *Respir Physiol Neurobiol* 2006; 154: 165-184.
3. Giardina B, Mosca D, De Rosa MC. The Bohr effect of haemoglobin

Citation and reference by authors

the long-term viability of a population. Individual fitness, resistance to disease and parasites, and the ability of populations to respond to environmental changes may decrease as a con (Lacy 1997). Alt "bottlenecks,"

Author →

Keller. L. F., P. Arcese, J. N. M. Smith, W. M. Hochachka, and S. C. Stearns. 1994. Selection against inbred Song Sparrows during a natural population bottleneck. *Nature* 372:356–357.
Lacy, R. C. 1997. Importance of genetic variation to the viability of mammalian populations. *Journal of Mammalogy* 78:320–335.
Lande, R. 1990. Extinction risks from anthropogenic, ecological and genetic factors. Pages 1–22 in L. F. Landweber and A. P. Dobson,

Year   Title   Publication   Volume and pages

The style you choose is not as important as being consistent, thorough, and honest about drawing on other people's work. All the information needed to locate the reference should be included (above).

Citation and references

All scientific work acknowledges sources of information through citation and a list of references. Citations support the statements made in the text in context, and **all** citations are then listed alphabetically, or identified and referenced sequentially by number. Internet sites are dated and site author acknowledged.

Thorough and accurate citation and referencing shows you have explored the topic, have evidence to support your work, and you are not taking credit for work that is not your own. Each publication sets its own particular referencing style and these can vary widely. In your own work, it is most important to be consistent.

1. What is the role of citation and correct referencing when reporting on scientific investigations? _____

_____

2. Study the diagram and write a paragraph on the scientific process and the role of surprising results in the progression of science. Staple it to this page. At the end of your course, reexamine what you wrote. Have your ideas changed?

LINK LINK LINK LINK LINK
218   217   78   76   28   KNOW

2 Hypotheses and Predictions

Key Idea: A hypothesis is a tentative, testable explanation for an observed phenomenon. An assumption is something that is accepted as true but is not tested.

Scientific hypotheses are tentative testable explanations for observed phenomena. A hypothesis leads to one or more predictions about the way a system will behave so a **research hypothesis** is often written to include a testable prediction, i.e if X is true, then the effect of Y will be Z. For every hypothesis, there is a corresponding **null hypothesis**: a hypothesis of no difference or no effect. A null hypothesis allows a hypothesis to be tested statistically and can be rejected if the experimental results are statistically significant. Hypotheses are not static, but may be modified as more information becomes available.

Observations, hypotheses, and predictions

Observation is the basis for formulating hypotheses and making predictions. An observation may generate a number of plausible hypotheses, and each hypothesis will lead to one or more predictions, which can be tested by further investigation.

Observation 1: Some caterpillar species are brightly coloured and appear to be conspicuous to predators such as insectivorous (insect-eating) birds.

Predators appear to avoid these species. These caterpillars are often found in groups, rather than as solitary animals.

Observation 2: Some caterpillar species are cryptic in their appearance or behaviour.

Their camouflage is so convincing that, when alerted to danger, they are difficult to see against their background. Such caterpillars are often found alone.

Assumptions

Any biological investigation requires you to make assumptions about the system you are working with. Assumptions are features of the system (and investigation) that you assume to be true but do not (or cannot) test. Possible assumptions about the biological system described above include:

- insectivorous birds have colour vision;
- caterpillars that look bright or cryptic to us, also appear that way to insectivorous birds; and
- insectivorous birds can learn about the palatability of prey by tasting them.

1. Study the example above illustrating the features of cryptic and conspicuous caterpillars, then answer the following:

   (a) Generate a hypothesis to explain the observation that some caterpillars are brightly coloured and conspicuous while others are cryptic and blend into their surroundings:

   Hypothesis: _____

   _____

   _____

   (b) State the null form of this hypothesis: _____

   _____

   (c) Describe one of the **assumptions** being made in your hypothesis:_____

   _____

   _____

   (d) Based on your hypothesis, generate a **prediction** about the behaviour of insectivorous birds towards caterpillars:

   _____

   _____

© 2015 **BIOZONE** International
ISBN: 978-1-927309-13-1
Photocopying Prohibited

3 Types of Data

Key Idea: Data is information collected during an investigation. Data may be quantitative, qualitative, or ranked.
Data is information collected during an investigation and it can be quantitative, qualitative, or ranked (below). When planning a biological investigation, it is important to consider the type of data that will be collected. It is best to collect quantitative data, because it is mathematically versatile and easier to analyse it objectively (without bias).

Types of data

Quantitative (interval or ratio)
Characteristics for which measurements or counts can be made, e.g. height, weight, number.
Summary measures: mean, median, standard deviation.

Qualitative (nominal)
Non-numerical and descriptive, e.g. sex, colour, viability (dead/alive), presence or absence of a specific feature.
Summary measures: frequencies and proportions

e.g. Sex of children in a family (male, female)

Ranked (ordinal)
Data are ranked on a scale that represents an order, although the intervals between the orders on the scale may not be equal, e.g. abundance (abundant, common, rare). Summary measures: frequencies and proportions

e.g. Birth order in a family (1, 2, 3)

Discontinuous (discrete)
e.g. Number of children in a family (3, 0, 4)

Continuous
e.g. Height of children in a family (1.5 m, 0.8 m)

Discontinuous or discrete data:
The unit of measurement cannot be split up (e.g. can't have half a child).

Continuous data:
The unit of measurement can be a part number (e.g. 5.25 kg).

1. For each of the photographic examples A-C below, classify the data as quantitative, ranked, or qualitative:

A: Skin colour

B: Eggs per nest

C: Tree trunk diameter

(a) Skin colour: _Qualitative_

(b) Number of eggs per nest: _Quantitative_

(c) Tree trunk diameter: _Quantitative_

2. Why is it best to collect quantitative data where possible in biological studies? _It's easier to compare numerical values than qualititative results_

3. Give an example of data that could not be collected quantitatively and explain your answer: _____
The different genders

4. Students walked a grid on a football field and ranked plant species present as abundant, common, or rare. How might they have collected and expressed this information more usefully?

_____

_____

© 2015 **BIOZONE** International
ISBN: 978-1-927309-13-1
Photocopying Prohibited

LINK 5 LINK 4 WEB 3 **KNOW**

4 Making A Qualitative Investigation

Key Idea: Qualitative data is non-numerical and descriptive. Qualitative data is more difficult to analyse and interpret objectively than quantitative data. It is also more likely to be biased. However, sometimes it is appropriate to collect qualitative data, e.g. when recording colour changes in simple tests for common components of foods. Two common tests for carbohydrates are the iodine/potassium iodide test for starch and the Benedict's test for reducing sugars, such as glucose. These tests indicate the presence of a substance with a colour change. All monosaccharides are reducing sugars as are the disaccharides, lactose and maltose. The monosaccharide fructose is a ketose, but it gives a positive test because it is converted to glucose in the reagent. When a starchy fruit ripens, the starch is converted to reducing sugars.

The aim

To investigate the effect of ripening on the relative content of starch and simple sugars in bananas.

The tests

Iodine-potassium iodide test for starch
The sample is covered with the iodine in potassium iodide solution. The sample turns blue-black if starch is present.

Benedict's test for reducing sugars
The sample is heated with the reagent in a boiling water bath. After 2 minutes, the sample is removed and stirred, and the colour recorded immediately after stirring. A change from a blue to a brick red colour indicates a reducing sugar.

①	②	③	④	⑤	⑥	⑦

Green unripe and hard — Bright yellow ripening but firm with green tip — Mottled yellow/brown ripe and soft

Summary of the method

Two 1 cm thick slices of banana from each of seven stages of ripeness were cut and crushed to a paste. One slice from each stage was tested using the I/KI test for starch, and the other was tested using the Benedict's test.

The colour changes were recorded in a table. Signs (+/−) were used to indicate the intensity of the reaction relative to those in bananas that were either less or more ripe.

Stage of ripeness	Starch-iodine test		Benedict's test	
1	blue-black	+++++	blue clear	−
2	blue-black	++++	blue clear	−
3	blue-black	+++	green	+
4	blue-black	++	yellow cloudy	++
5	slight darkening	+	orange thick	+++
6	no change	−	orangey-red thick	++++
7	no change	−	brick-red thick	+++++

1. Explain why each of the following protocols was important:

   (a) All samples of banana in the Benedict's reagent were heated for 2 minutes: _____

   _____

   (b) The contents of the banana sample and Benedict's reagent were stirred after heating: _____

   _____

2. Explain what is happening to the relative levels of starch and glucose as bananas ripen: _____

   _____

   _____

3. Fructose is a ketose sugar (not an aldose with an aldehyde functional group like glucose).

   (a) Explain why fructose also gives a positive result in a Benedict's test: _____

   _____

   (b) What could this suggest to you about the results of this banana test? _____

   _____

LINK
DATA
64

© 2015 **BIOZONE** International
ISBN: 978-1-927309-13-1
Photocopying Prohibited

Key Idea: Practical work carried out in a careful and methodical way makes analysis of the results much easier.

The next stage after planning an experiment is to collect the data. Practical work may be laboratory or field based. Typical laboratory based experiments involve investigating how a biological response is affected by manipulating a particular **variable**, e.g. temperature. The data collected for a quantitative practical task should be recorded systematically, with due attention to safe practical techniques, a suitable quantitative method, and accurate measurements to an appropriate degree of precision. If your quantitative practical task is executed well, and you have taken care throughout, your evaluation of the experimental results will be much more straightforward and less problematic.

Carrying out your practical work

Preparation
Familiarise yourself with the equipment and how to set it up. If necessary, calibrate equipment to give accurate measurements.

Read through the methodology and identify key stages and how long they will take.

Execution
Identify any **assumptions** you make about your set up. Assumptions are features of the system that you assume to be true but do not (or cannot) test. Know how you will take your measurements, how often, and to what degree of precision.

Recording
Record your results systematically, in a hand-written table or on a spreadsheet.

Record your results to the appropriate number of significant figures according to the precision of your measurement.

Identifying variables

A variable is any characteristic or property able to take any one of a range of values. Investigations often look at the effect of changing one variable on another. It is important to identify all variables in an investigation: independent, dependent, and controlled, although there may be nuisance factors of which you are unaware. In all fair tests, only one variable is changed by the investigator.

Dependent variable
- Measured during the investigation.
- Recorded on the y axis of the graph.

(graph: y-axis labelled "Dependent variable", x-axis labelled "Independent variable")

Controlled variables
- Factors that are kept the same or controlled.
- List these in the method, as appropriate to your own investigation.

Independent variable
- Set by the experimenter.
- Recorded on the graph's x axis.

Experimental controls

A control refers to standard or reference treatment or group in an experiment. It is the same as the experimental (test) group, except that it lacks the one variable being manipulated by the experimenter. Controls are used to demonstrate that the response in the test group is due a specific variable (e.g. temperature). The control undergoes the same preparation, experimental conditions, observations, measurements, and analysis as the test group. This helps to ensure that responses observed in the treatment groups can be reliably interpreted.

The experiment above tests the effect of a certain nutrient on microbial growth. All the agar plates are prepared in the same way, but the control plate does not have the test nutrient applied. Each plate is inoculated from the same stock solution, incubated under the same conditions, and examined at the same set periods. The control plate sets the baseline; any growth above that seen on the control plate is attributed to the presence of the nutrient.

Examples of investigations

Aim		Variables	
Investigating the effect of varying...	on the following...	Independent variable	Dependent variable
Temperature	Leaf width	Temperature	Leaf width
Light intensity	Activity of woodlice	Light intensity	Woodlice activity
Soil pH	Plant height at age 6 months	pH	Plant height

LINK **169**   LINK **92**   LINK **26**   KNOW

Investigation: catalase activity

Catalase is an enzyme that converts hydrogen peroxide (H_2O_2) to oxygen and water.

An experiment to investigate the effects of temperature on the rate of the catalase reaction is described below.

- 10 cm^3 test tubes were used for the reactions, each tube contained 0.5 cm^3 of catalase enzyme and 4 cm^3 of H_2O_2.

- Reaction rates were measured at four temperatures (10°C, 20°C, 30°C, 60°C).

- For each temperature, there were two reaction tubes (e.g. tubes 1 and 2 were both kept at 10°C).

- The height of oxygen bubbles present after one minute of reaction was used as a measure of the reaction rate. A faster reaction rate produced more bubbles than a slower reaction rate.

- The entire experiment was repeated on two separate days.

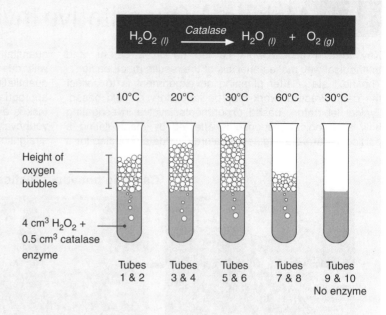

$$H_2O_2 \, {}_{(l)} \xrightarrow{\text{Catalase}} H_2O \, {}_{(l)} \quad + \quad O_2 \, {}_{(g)}$$

1. Write a suitable aim for this experiment: _____

_____

2. Write an hypothesis for this experiment: _____

_____

3. (a) What is the independent variable in this experiment? _____

   (b) What is the range of values for the independent variable? _____

   (c) Name the unit for the independent variable: _____

   (d) List the equipment needed to set the independent variable, and describe how it was used: _____

   _____

   _____

   _____

4. (a) What is the dependent variable in this experiment? _____

   (b) Name the unit for the dependent variable: _____

   (c) List the equipment needed to measure the dependent variable, and describe how it was used: _____

   _____

5. (a) Each temperature represents a treatment/sample/trial (circle one):

   (b) How many tubes are at each temperature? _____

   (c) What is the sample size for each treatment?_____

   (d) How many times was the whole investigation repeated? _____

6. Which tubes are the control for this experiment? _____

7. Identify three variables that might have been controlled in this experiment, and how they could have been monitored:

   (a) _____

   (b) _____

   (c) _____

© 2015 **BIOZONE** International
ISBN: 978-1-927309-13-1
Photocopying Prohibited

6 | Accuracy and Precision

Key Idea: Accuracy refers to the correctness of a measurement (how true it is to the real value). Precision refers to how close the measurements are to each other. Accuracy refers to how close a measured or derived value is to its true value. Simply put, it is the correctness of the measurement. Precision refers to the closeness of repeated measurements to each other, i.e. the ability to be exact. A balance with a fault in it could give very precise (repeatable) but inaccurate (untrue) results. Data can only be reported as accurately as the measurement of the apparatus allows and is often expressed as significant figures (the digits in a number that express meaning to a degree of accuracy).

The accuracy of a measurement refers to how close the measured (or derived) value is to the true value. The precision of a measurement relates to its repeatability. In most laboratory work, we usually have no reason to suspect a piece of equipment is giving inaccurate measurements (is biased), so making precise measures is usually the most important consideration. We can test the precision of our measurements by taking repeated measurements from individual samples.

Population studies present us with an additional problem. When a researcher makes measurements of some variable in a study (e.g. fish length), they are usually trying to obtain an estimate of the true value for a parameter of interest, e.g. the mean size (which is correlated with age) of fish. Populations are variable, so we can more accurately estimate a population parameter if we take a large number of random samples from the population.

Accurate but imprecise	**Inaccurate and imprecise**	**Precise but inaccurate**	**Accurate and precise**

The measurements are all close to the true value but quite spread apart.	The measurements are all far apart and not close to the true value.	The measurements are all clustered close together but not close to the true value.	The measurements are all close to the true value and also clustered close together.
Analogy: The arrows are all close to the bullseye.	**Analogy**: The arrows are spread around the target.	**Analogy**: The arrows are all clustered close together but not near the bullseye.	**Analogy**: The arrows are clustered close together near the bullseye.

Significant figures

Significant figures (sf) are the digits of a number that carry meaning contributing to its precision. They communicate how well you could actually measure the data.

For example, you might measure the height of 100 people to the nearest cm. When you calculate their mean height, the answer is 175.0215 cm. If you reported this number, it implies that your measurement technique was accurate to 4 decimal places. You would have to round the result to the number of significant figures you had accurately measured. In this instance the answer is 175 cm.

Non-zero numbers (1-9) are always **significant**.

All zeros between non-zero numbers are always **significant**.

$$0.005704510$$

Zeros to the left of the first non-zero digit after a decimal point are **not significant**.

Zeros at the end of number where there is a decimal place are **significant** (e.g. 4600.0 has five sf).
BUT
Zeros at the end of a number where there is no decimal point are **not significant** (e.g. 4600 has two sf).

1. Distinguish between accuracy and precision: _Accuracy - how close a measured value is to a true value_ _Precision - repeatability_

2. State the number of significant figures in the following examples:

   (a) 3.15985 ___6___

   (b) 0.0012 ___2___

   (c) 1000 ___1___

   (d) 1000.0 ___5___

   (e) 42.3006 ___6___

   (f) 120 ___2___

© 2015 **BIOZONE** International
ISBN: 978-1-927309-13-1
Photocopying Prohibited

LINK
7

DATA

7 Working with Numbers

Key Idea: Using correct mathematical notation and being able to carry out simple calculations and conversions are fundamental skills in biology.

Mathematics is used in biology to analyse, interpret, and compare data. It is important that you are familiar with mathematical notation (the language of mathematics) and can confidently apply some basic mathematical principles and calculations to your data.

Commonly used mathematical symbols

In mathematics, universal symbols are used to represent mathematical concepts. They save time and space when writing. Some commonly used symbols are shown below.

=   Equal to

<   The value on the left is **less than** the value on the right

<<   The value on the left is **much less than** the value on the right

>   The value on the left is **greater than** the value on the right

>>   The value on the left is **much greater than** the value on the right

∝   Proportional to. A ∝ B means that A = a constant X B

~   Approximately equal to

Conversion factors and expressing units

Measurements can be converted from one set of units to another by the use of a **conversion factor**.

A conversion factor is a numerical factor that multiplies or divides one unit to convert it into another. Conversion factors are commonly used to convert non-SI units to SI units (e.g. converting pounds to kilograms). Note that mL and cm^3 are equivalent, as are L and dm^3.

In the space below, convert 5.6 cm^3 to mm^3 (1 cm^3 = 1000 mm^3):

1.   5600

The value of a variable must be written with its units where possible. SI units or their derivations should be used in recording measurements: volume in cm^3 or dm^3, mass in kilograms (kg) or grams (g), length in metres (m), time in seconds (s).

For example the rate of oxygen consumption would be expressed:

Oxygen consumption$/cm^3 g^{-1} s^{-1}$

Estimates

When carrying out mathematical calculations, typing the wrong number into your calculator can put your answer out by several orders of magnitude. An **estimate** is a way of roughly calculating what answer you should get, and helps you decide if your final calculation is correct.

Numbers are often rounded to help make estimation easier. The rounding rule is, if the next digit is 5 or more, round up. If the next digit is 4 or less, it stays as it is.

For example, to estimate 6.8 x 704 you would round the numbers to 7 x 700 = 4900. The actual answer is 4787, so the estimate tells us the answer (4787) is probably right.

Use the following examples to practise estimating:

2.   43.2 x 1044:   ~~43100~~   44892

3.   3.4 x (72 ÷ 15):   ~~16~~   14.4

4.   658 ÷ 22:   32.9

Decimal and standard form

Decimal form (also called ordinary form) is the longhand way of writing a number (e.g. 15 000 000). Very large or very small numbers can take up too much space if written in decimal form and are often expressed in a condensed **standard form**. For example, 15 000 000 is written as 1.5 x 10^7 in standard form.

In standard form a number is always written as A x 10^n, where A is a number between 1 and 10, and n (the exponent) indicates how many places to move the decimal point. n can be positive or negative.

For the example above, A = 1.5 and n = 7 because the decimal point moved seven places (see below).

$$1.5\,000\,000 = 1.5 \times 10^7$$

Small numbers can also be written in standard form. The exponent (n) will be negative. For example, 0.00101 is written as 1.01 x 10^{-3}.

$$0.00101 = 1.01 \times 10^{-3}$$

Converting can make calculations easier. Work through the following example to solve 4.5 x 10^4 + 6.45 x 10^5.

5.   Convert 4.5 x 10^4 + 6.45 x 10^5 to decimal form:

   _____

6.   Add the two numbers together: _____

7.   Convert to standard form: _____

Rates

Rates are expressed as a measure per unit of time and show how a variable changes over time. Rates are used to provide meaningful comparisons of data that may have been recorded over different time periods.

Often rates are expressed as a mean rate over the duration of the measurement period, but it is also useful to calculate the rate at various times to understand how rate changes over time. The table below shows the reaction rates for a gas produced during a chemical reaction. A worked example for the rate at 4 minutes is provided below the table.

Time / Minute	Cumulative gas produced / cm^3	Rate of reaction / cm^3 min^{-1}
0	0	0
2	34	17
4	42	4*
6	48	3
8	50	1
10	50	0

* Gas produced between 2 – 4 min: 42 cm^3 – 34 cm^3 = 8 cm^3

   Rate of reaction between 2 – 4 mins: 8 ÷ 2 minutes = 4 cm^3 min^{-1}

© 2015 **BIOZONE** International
ISBN: 978-1-927309-13-1

DATA

8 Fractions, Percentages, and Ratios

Key Idea: Percentages and ratios are alternative ways to express fractions. All forms are commonly used in biology. The data collected in the field or laboratory are called raw data. Data are often expressed in ways that make them easy to understand, visualise, and work with. Fractions, ratios, and percentages are widely used in biology and are often used to provide a meaningful comparison of sample data where the sample sizes are different.

Fractions

- Fractions express how many parts of a whole are present.

- Fractions are expressed as two numbers separated by a solidus (/) (e.g. 1/2).

- The top number is the numerator. The bottom number is the denominator. The denominator can not be zero.

- Fractions are often written in their simplest form (the top and bottom numbers cannot be any smaller, while still being whole numbers). Simplifying makes working with fractions easier.

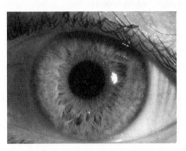

In a class of 20 students, five had blue eyes. This fraction is 5/20. To simplify this fraction, divide the numerator and denominator by a common factor (a number which both are divisible by). In this instance the lowest common factor is five (1/4). To add fractions with different denominators, obtain a common denominator, add numerators, then simplify.

Ratios

- Ratios give the relative amount of two or more quantities, and provide an easy way to identify patterns.

- Ratios do not require units.

- Ratios are usually expressed as a : b.

- Ratios are calculated by dividing all the values by the smallest number.

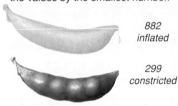

882 inflated

299 constricted

Pea pod shape:
Ratio = 2.95 : 1

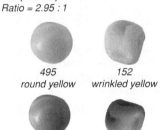

495 round yellow

152 wrinkled yellow

158 round green

55 wrinkled green

Pea seed shape and colour:
Ratio = 9 : 2.8 : 2.9 : 1

Example: Calculating phenotype ratios in Mendelian genetics

Percentages

- Percentages are expressed as a fraction of 100 (e.g. 20/100 = 20%).

- Percentages provide a clear expression of what proportion of data fall into any particular category, e.g. for pie graphs.

- Allows meaningful comparison between different samples.

- Useful to monitor change (e.g. % increase from one year to the next).

Volume of food colouring / cm³	Volume of water / cm³	Concentration of solution / %
10	0	100
8	2	80
6	4	60
4	6	40
2	8	20
0	10	0

Example: Producing standards for a calibration curve.

---

1. (a) A student prepared a slide of the cells of an onion root tip and counted the cells at various stages in the cell cycle. The results are presented in the table (right). Calculate the ratio of cells in each stage (show your working):

   _____

   _____

   (b) Assuming the same ratio applies in all the slides examined in the class, calculate the number of cells in each phase for a cell total count of 4800.

Cell cycle stage	No. of cells counted	No. of cells calculated
Interphase	140	
Prophase	70	
Telophase	15	
Metaphase	10	
Anaphase	5	
Total	240	4800

2. Simplify the following fractions:

   (a) 3/9 : _____ ¹/3 _____   (b) 84/90: _____ ¹⁴/15 _____   (c) 11/121: _____ ¹/11 _____

3. In the fraction example pictured above 5/20 students had blue eyes. In another class, 5/12 students had blue eyes. What fraction of students had blue eyes in both classes combined?

   _____

4. The total body mass and lean body mass for women with different body types is presented in the table (right). Complete the table by calculating the % lean body mass column.

Women	Body mass / kg	Lean body mass / kg	% lean body mass
Athlete	50	38	
Lean	56	41	
Normal weight	65	46	
Overweight	80	48	
Obese	95	52	

© 2015 **BIOZONE** International
ISBN: 978-1-927309-13-1
Photocopying Prohibited

DATA

9 Logs and Exponents

Key Idea: A function relates an input to an output. Functions are often defined through a formula that tells us how to compute the output for a given input. Logarithmic, power, and exponential functions are all common in biology.

A function is a rule that allows us to calculate an output for any given input. In biology, power functions are often observed in biological scaling, for example, heart beat slows with increasing size in mammals. Exponential growth is often seen in bacterial populations and also with the spread of viral diseases if intervention does not occur. The 2014 Ebola outbreak is one such example. The numbers associated with exponential growth can be very large and are often log transformed. Log transformations reduce skew in data and make data easier to analyse and interpret.

Power function

Power functions are a type of scaling function showing the relationship between two variables, one of which is usually size.

- In power functions, the base value is variable and the exponent (power number) is fixed (constant).

- The equation for an exponential function is $y = x^c$.

- Power functions are not linear, one variable changes more quickly relative to the other.

- Examples of power functions include metabolic rate versus body mass (below), or surface area to volume ratio.

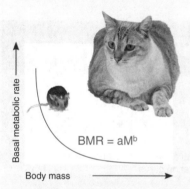

Example: Relationship between body mass and metabolic rate.
M = mass and a and b are constants.

$BMR = aM^b$ (axes: Basal metabolic rate vs Body mass)

Exponential function

Exponential growth occurs at an increasingly rapid rate in proportion to the growing total number or size.

- In an exponential function, the base number is fixed (constant) and the exponent is variable.

- The equation for an exponential function is $y = c^x$.

- Exponential growth is easy to identify because the curve has a J-shape appearance due to its increasing steepness over time. It grows more rapidly than a power function

- Examples of exponential growth include the growth of microorganisms in an unlimiting growth environment.

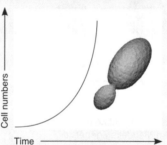

Example: Cell growth in a yeast culture in optimal growth conditions. (axes: Cell numbers vs Time)

Log transformations

A log transformation has the effect of normalising data and making very large numbers easier to work with. Biological data often have a positive skew so log transformations can be very useful.

- The log of a number is the exponent to which a fixed value (the base) is raised to get that number. So $\log_{10}(1000) = 3$ because $10^3 = 1000$.

- Both $\log_{10}$ and $\log_e$ (natural logs or *ln*) are commonly used.

- Log transformations are useful for data where there is an exponential increase in numbers (e.g. cell growth). In these cases the log transformed data will plot as a straight line.

- To find the $\log_{10}$ of a number, e.g. 32, using a calculator, key in $\log$ $\boxed{32}$ $=$. The answer should be 1.51.

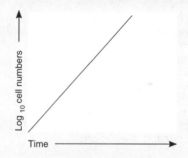

Example: Yeast cell growth plotted on logarithmic scale. (axes: $\log_{10}$ cell numbers vs Time)

1. Describe the relationship between body mass and metabolic rate: _____
_____

2. Describe the difference between a power function and exponential growth: _____
_____
_____
_____

3. (a) On what type of data would you carry out a log transformation? _____
_____

(b) What is the purpose of a log transformation? _____
_____
_____

10 Practising with Data

Key Idea: This activity allows you to practise working with data and applying the skills you have learned in previous activities.

1. Complete the transformations for each of the tables below. The first value is provided in each case.

(a) Photosynthetic rate at different light intensities

Light intensity / %	Average time for leaf disc to float / min	Reciprocal of time* / min^{-1}
100	15	0.067
50	25	
25	50	
11	93	
6	187	

* Reciprocal of time gives a crude measure of rate.

(b) Plant water loss using a bubble potometer

Time / min	Pipette arm reading / cm^3	Plant water loss / cm^3 min^{-1}
0	9.0	–
5	8.0	0.2
10	7.2	
15	6.2	
20	4.9	

(c) Incidence of cyanogenic clover in different areas

Clover plant type	Frost free area		Frost prone area		Totals
	Number	%	Number	%	
Cyanogenic	124	78	26		
Acyanogenic	35		115		
Total	159				

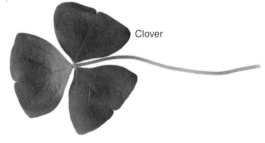

Clover

(d) Frequency of size classes in a sample of eels

Size class / mm	Frequency	Relative frequency / %
0-50	7	2.6
50-99	23	
100-149	59	
150-199	98	
200-249	50	
250-299	30	
300-349	3	
Total	270	

2. Convert the following decimal form numbers to standard form:

(a) 8970 8.97×10^3 (b) 0.046 4.6×10^{-2} (c) 1 467 851 _____

3. Convert the following standard form numbers to decimal form:

(a) 4.3×10^{-1} _____ (b) 0.0031×10^{-2} _____ (c) 6.2×10^4 _____

4. (a) The table on the right shows the nutritional label found on a can of chilli beans. Use the information provided to complete the table by calculating the percentage composition for each of the nutritional groups listed:

(b) How much of the total carbohydrates is made up of:

Dietary fibre? _____

Sugars? _____

(c) Manufacturers do not have to state the volume of water, which makes up the remainder of the serving size. What percentage of the can of beans is water?

_____

Chilli Beans Nutrition Facts Serving size 1 cup (253 g)		
Amount per serving		% Composition
Total Fat	8 g	
– Saturated Fat	3 g	
Total Carbohydrate	22 g	
– Dietary Fibre	9 g	
– Sugars	4 g	
Protein	25 g	

© 2015 **BIOZONE** International
ISBN: 978-1-927309-13-1
Photocopying Prohibited

LINK 8 LINK 7 DATA

Key Idea: The apparatus used in experimental work must be appropriate for the experiment or analysis and it must be used correctly to eliminate experimental errors.
Using scientific equipment can generate experimental errors.

These can be reduced by selecting the right equipment for what you want to measure and by using it correctly. Some error is inevitable, but evaluating experimental error helps to interpret and assess the validity of the results.

Selecting the correct equipment

When measuring physical properties it is vital that you choose equipment that is appropriate for the type of measurement you want to take. For example, if you wanted to accurately weigh out 5.65 g of sucrose, you need a balance that accurately weighs to two decimal places. A balance that weighs to only one decimal place would not allow you to make an accurate enough measurement.

Study the glassware (right). Which would you use if you wanted to measure 225 mL? The graduated cylinder has graduations every 10 mL whereas the beaker has graduations every 50 mL. It would be more accurate to measure 225 mL in a graduated cylinder.

Percentage errors

Percentage error is a way of mathematically expressing how far out your result is from the ideal result. The equation for measuring percentage error is:

$$\frac{\text{experimental value - ideal value}}{\text{ideal value}} \times 100$$

For example, you want to know how accurate a 5 mL pipette is. You dispense 5 mL of water from a pipette and weigh the dispensed volume on a balance. The volume is 4.98 mL.

$$\frac{\text{experimental value (\textbf{4.98}) - ideal value (\textbf{5.0})}}{\text{ideal value (\textbf{5.0})}} \times 100$$

The percentage error = –0.4% (the negative sign tells you the pipette is dispensing **less** than it should).

Recognising potential sources of error

It is important to know how to use equipment correctly to reduce errors. A spectrophotometer measures the amount of light absorbed by a solution at a certain wavelength. This information can be used to determine the concentration of the absorbing molecule (e.g. density of bacteria in a culture). The more concentrated the solution, the more light is absorbed. Incorrect use of the spectrophotometer can alter the results. Common mistakes include incorrect calibration, errors in sample preparation, and errors in sample measurement.

A cuvette (left) is a small clear tube designed to hold spectrophotometer samples. Inaccurate readings occur when:

- The cuvette is dirty or scratched (light is absorbed giving a falsely high reading).

- Some cuvettes have a frosted side to aid alignment. If the cuvette is aligned incorrectly, the frosted side absorbs light, giving a false reading.

- Not enough sample is in the cuvette and the beam passes over, rather than through the sample, giving a lower absorbance reading.

---

1. Assume that you have the following measuring devices available: 50 mL beaker, 50 mL graduated cylinder, 25 mL graduated cylinder, 10 mL pipette, 10 mL beaker. What would you use to accurately measure:

   (a) 21 mL: _____ (b) 48 mL: _____ (c) 9 mL: _____

2. Calculate the percentage error for the following situations (show your working):

   (a) A 1 mL pipette delivers a measured volume of 0.98 mL: _____

   _____

   (b) A 10 mL pipette delivers a measured volume of 9.98 mL: _____

   _____

   (c) The pipettes used in (a) and (b) above both under-delivered 0.02 mL, yet the percentage errors are quite different. Use this data to describe the effect of volume on percentage error:

   _____

   _____

12 Recording Results

Key Idea: Accurately recording results in a table makes it easier to understand and analyse your data later.

A table is a good way to record your results systematically, both during the course of your experiment and in presenting your results. A table can also be used to show calculated values, such as rates or means. An example of a table for recording results is shown below. It relates to an investigation of the net growth of plants at three pH levels, but it represents a relatively standardised layout. The labels on the columns and rows are chosen to represent the design features of the investigation. The first column shows the entire range of the independent variable. There are spaces for multiple sampling units, repeats (trials), and calculated mean values. A version of this table would be given in the write-up of the experiment.

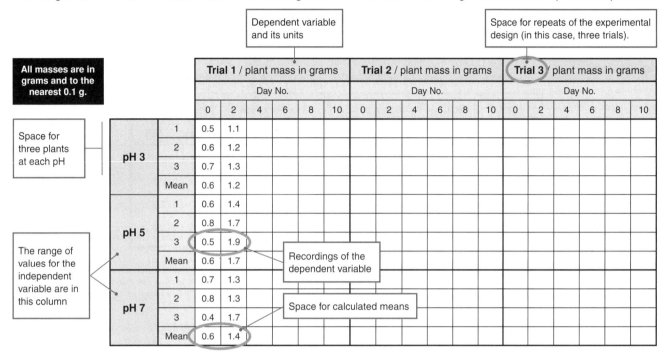

All masses are in grams and to the nearest 0.1 g.			Trial 1 / plant mass in grams						Trial 2 / plant mass in grams						Trial 3 / plant mass in grams					
			Day No.						Day No.						Day No.					
			0	2	4	6	8	10	0	2	4	6	8	10	0	2	4	6	8	10
pH 3	1		0.5	1.1																
	2		0.6	1.2																
	3		0.7	1.3																
	Mean		0.6	1.2																
pH 5	1		0.6	1.4																
	2		0.8	1.7																
	3		0.5	1.9																
	Mean		0.6	1.7																
pH 7	1		0.7	1.3																
	2		0.8	1.3																
	3		0.4	1.7																
	Mean		0.6	1.4																

Labels: *Dependent variable and its units* · *Space for repeats of the experimental design (in this case, three trials).* · *Space for three plants at each pH* · *The range of values for the independent variable are in this column* · *Recordings of the dependent variable* · *Space for calculated means*

1. In the box (below) design a table to collect data from the case study below. Include space for individual results and averages from the three set ups (use the table above as a guide).

CO₂ levels in a respiration chamber

A datalogger was used to monitor the concentrations of carbon dioxide (CO_2) in respiration chambers containing five green leaves from one plant species. The entire study was performed in conditions of full light (quantified) and involved three identical set-ups.

The CO_2 concentrations were measured every minute, over a period of 10 minutes, using a CO_2 sensor. A mean CO_2 concentration (for the three set-ups) was calculated. The study was carried out two more times, two days apart.

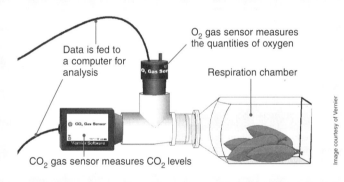

O₂ gas sensor measures the quantities of oxygen

Data is fed to a computer for analysis

Respiration chamber

CO₂ gas sensor measures CO₂ levels

Image courtesy of Vernier

2. Next, the effect of various light intensities (low light, half-light, and full light) on CO_2 concentration was investigated. How would the results table for this investigation differ from the one you have drawn above (for full light only):

_____

_____

© 2015 **BIOZONE** International
ISBN: 978-1-927309-13-1
Photocopying Prohibited

LINK 169 LINK 138 LINK 104 LINK 26 LINK 23 KNOW

Key Idea: Tables and graphs provide a way to organise and visualise data in a way that helps to identify trends.

Tables and graphs are ways to present data and they have different purposes. **Tables** provide an accurate record of numerical values and allow you to organise your data so that relationships and trends are apparent. **Graphs** provide a visual image of trends in the data in a minimum of space.

It is useful to plot your data as soon as possible, even during your experiment, as this will help you to evaluate your results as you proceed and make adjustments as necessary (e.g. to the sampling interval). The choice between graphing or tabulation in the final report depends on the type and complexity of the data and the information that you are wanting to convey. Usually, both are appropriate.

Presenting data in tables

An accurate, descriptive title.

Table 1: Length and growth of the third internode of bean plants receiving three different hormone treatments (data are given ± standard deviation).

Independent variable in left column.

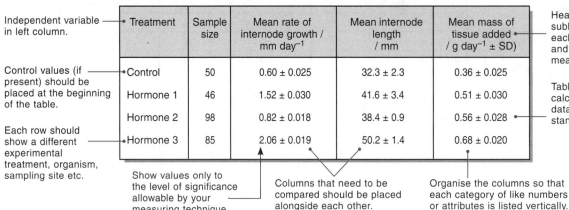

Treatment	Sample size	Mean rate of internode growth / mm day^{-1}	Mean internode length / mm	Mean mass of tissue added / g day^{-1} ± SD)
Control	50	0.60 ± 0.025	32.3 ± 2.3	0.36 ± 0.025
Hormone 1	46	1.52 ± 0.030	41.6 ± 3.4	0.51 ± 0.030
Hormone 2	98	0.82 ± 0.018	38.4 ± 0.9	0.56 ± 0.028
Hormone 3	85	2.06 ± 0.019	50.2 ± 1.4	0.68 ± 0.020

Heading and subheadings identify each set of data and show units of measurement.

Control values (if present) should be placed at the beginning of the table.

Tables can show a calculated measure of data variability (e.g. standard deviation).

Each row should show a different experimental treatment, organism, sampling site etc.

Show values only to the level of significance allowable by your measuring technique.

Columns that need to be compared should be placed alongside each other.

Organise the columns so that each category of like numbers or attributes is listed vertically.

Presenting data in graph format

Plot points accurately. Different responses can be distinguished using different symbols, lines or bar colours.

Fig. 1: Yield of two bacterial strains at different antibiotic levels (± 95% confidence intervals, n= 6)

Graphs (called figures) should have a concise, explanatory title. If several graphs appear in your report they should be numbered consecutively.

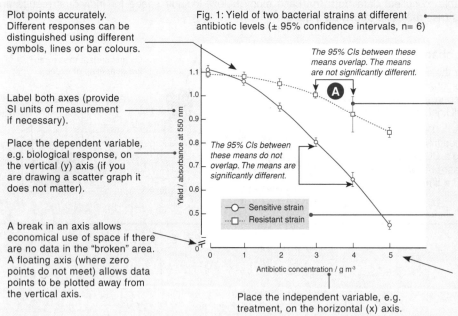

The 95% CIs between these means overlap. The means are not significantly different.

The 95% CIs between these means do not overlap. The means are significantly different.

Key:
- Sensitive strain
- Resistant strain

Label both axes (provide SI units of measurement if necessary).

Place the dependent variable, e.g. biological response, on the vertical (y) axis (if you are drawing a scatter graph it does not matter).

A break in an axis allows economical use of space if there are no data in the "broken" area. A floating axis (where zero points do not meet) allows data points to be plotted away from the vertical axis.

Measures of spread about the plotted mean value can be shown on the graph. Such measures include standard deviation and 95% confidence intervals (CI). The values are plotted as **error bars** and give an indication of the reliability of the mean value. If the 95% confidence intervals do not overlap between points, then these means will be significantly different.

A key identifies symbols. This information sometimes appears in the title or the legend.

Each axis should have an appropriate scale. Decide on the scale by finding the maximum and minimum values for each variable.

Place the independent variable, e.g. treatment, on the horizontal (x) axis.

1. What can you conclude about the difference (labelled A) between the two means plotted above? Explain your answer:

_____

2. Explain the reasons for including both graphs and tables in a final report: _____

_____

_____

_____

© 2015 **BIOZONE** International
ISBN: 978-1-927309-13-1
Photocopying Prohibited

14 Which Graph to Use?

Key Idea: The type of graph you choose to display your data depends on the type of data you have collected.

Before you graph your data, it is important to identify what type of data you have. Choosing the correct type of graph can highlight trends or reveal relationships between variables. Choosing the wrong type of graph can obscure information and make the data difficult to interpret. Examples of common types of graphs and when to use them are provided below.

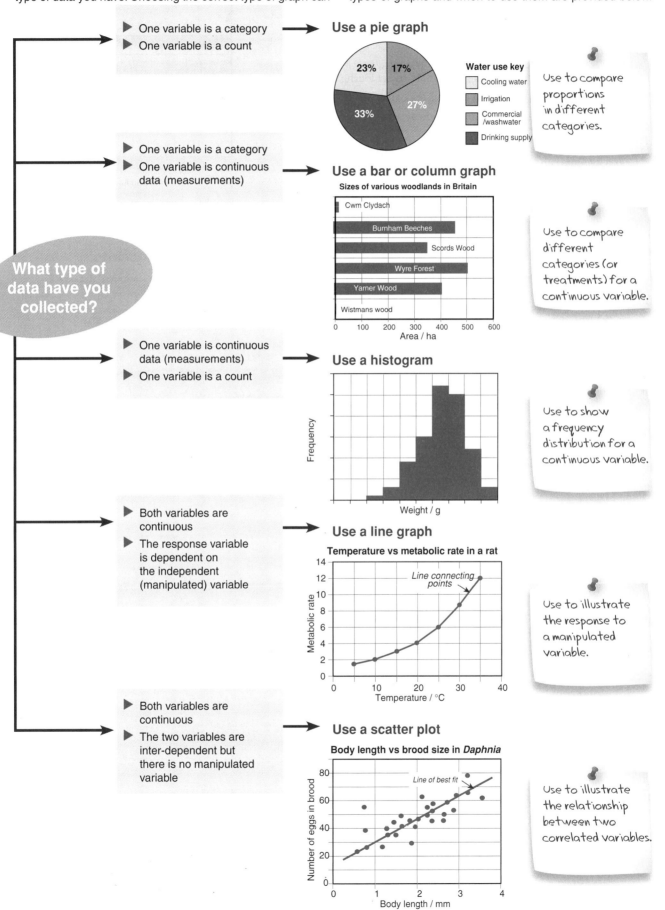

What type of data have you collected?

- One variable is a category
- One variable is a count

→ **Use a pie graph**

Water use key: Cooling water, Irrigation, Commercial /washwater, Drinking supply
23%, 17%, 27%, 33%

Use to compare proportions in different categories.

- One variable is a category
- One variable is continuous data (measurements)

→ **Use a bar or column graph**

Sizes of various woodlands in Britain
Cwm Clydach, Burnham Beeches, Scords Wood, Wyre Forest, Yarner Wood, Wistmans wood
Area / ha

Use to compare different categories (or treatments) for a continuous variable.

- One variable is continuous data (measurements)
- One variable is a count

→ **Use a histogram**

Frequency vs Weight / g

Use to show a frequency distribution for a continuous variable.

- Both variables are continuous
- The response variable is dependent on the independent (manipulated) variable

→ **Use a line graph**

Temperature vs metabolic rate in a rat
Line connecting points
Metabolic rate vs Temperature / °C

Use to illustrate the response to a manipulated variable.

- Both variables are continuous
- The two variables are inter-dependent but there is no manipulated variable

→ **Use a scatter plot**

Body length vs brood size in *Daphnia*
Line of best fit
Number of eggs in brood vs Body length / mm

Use to illustrate the relationship between two correlated variables.

LINK 18 LINK 17 LINK 16 LINK 15 REFER

15 Drawing Bar Graphs

Key Idea: Bar graphs are used to plot data that is non-numerical or discrete for at least one variable.

Guidelines for bar graphs

Bar graphs are appropriate for data that are non-numerical and **discrete** for at least one variable, i.e. they are grouped into categories. There are no dependent or independent variables. Important features of this type of graph include:

- Data are collected for discontinuous, non-numerical categories (e.g. colour, species), so the bars do not touch.

- Data values may be entered on or above the bars.

- Multiple sets of data can be displayed side by side for comparison (e.g. males and females).

- Axes may be reversed so that the categories are on the x axis, i.e. bars can be vertical or horizontal. When they are vertical, these graphs are called column graphs.

Size of various woodlands in Britain

Woodland	Area of woodland / Ha
Cwm Clydach	20
Burnham Beeches	450
Scords Wood	350
Wyre Forest	500
Yarner Wood	400
Wistmans Wood	4

1. Counts of eight mollusc species were made from a series of quadrat samples at two sites on a rocky shore. The summary data are presented here.

(a) Tabulate the mean (**average**) numbers per square metre at each site in Table 1 (below left).

(b) Plot a **bar graph** of the tabulated data on the grid below. For each species, plot the data from both sites side by side using different colours to distinguish the sites.

Mean abundance of 8 molluscan species from two sites along a rocky shore.

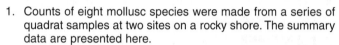

Species	Mean / no. m^{-2}	
	Site 1	Site 2

Field data notebook

Total counts at site 1 (11 quadrats) and site 2 (10 quadrats). Quadrats 1 sq m.

	Site 1		Site 2	
	No m^{-2}		No m^{-2}	
Species	Total	Mean	Total	Mean
Ornate limpet	232	21	299	30
Radiate limpet	68	6	344	34
Limpet sp. A	420	38	0	0
Cats-eye	68	6	16	2
Top shell	16	2	43	4
Limpet sp. B	628	57	389	39
Limpet sp. C	0	0	22	2
Chiton	12	1	30	3

© 2015 **BIOZONE** International
ISBN: 978-1-927309-13-1
Photocopying Prohibited

16 Drawing Histograms

Key Idea: Histograms graphically show the frequency distribution of continuous data.

Guidelines for histograms

Histograms are plots of **continuous** data and are often used to represent frequency distributions, where the y-axis shows the number of times a particular measurement or value was obtained. For this reason, they are often called frequency histograms. Important features of this type of graph include:

- The data are numerical and continuous (e.g. height or weight), so the bars touch.

- The x-axis usually records the class interval. The y-axis usually records the number of individuals in each class interval (frequency).

- A neatly constructed tally chart doubles as a simple histogram.

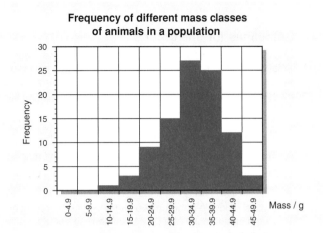

Frequency of different mass classes of animals in a population

1. The weight data provided below were recorded from 95 individuals (male and female), older than 17 years.

   (a) Create a tally chart (frequency table) in the frame provided, organising the weight data into a form suitable for plotting. An example of the tally for the weight grouping 55-59.9 kg has been completed for you as an example. Note that the raw data values are crossed off the data set in the notebook once they are recorded as counts on the tally chart. It is important to do this in order to prevent data entry errors.

   (b) Plot a **frequency histogram** of the tallied data on the grid provided below.

Weight / kg	Tally	Total
45 - 49.9		
50 - 54.9		
55 - 59.9	Ⅲℋ II	7
60 - 64.9		
65 - 69.9		
70 - 74.9		
75 - 79.9		
80 - 84.9		
85 - 89.9		
90 - 94.9		
95 - 99.9		
100 - 104.9		
105 - 109.9		

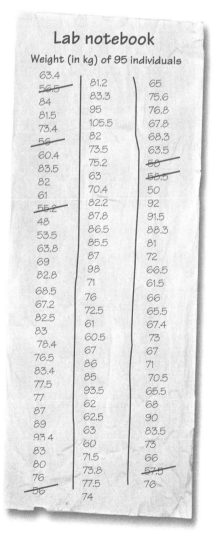

Lab notebook

Weight (in kg) of 95 individuals

63.4	81.2	65
56.5	83.3	75.6
84	95	76.8
81.5	105.5	67.8
73.4	82	68.3
56	73.5	63.5
60.4	75.2	58
83.5	63	58.5
82	70.4	50
61	82.2	92
55.2	87.8	91.5
48	86.5	88.3
53.5	85.5	81
63.8	87	72
69	98	66.5
82.8	71	61.5
68.5	76	66
67.2	72.5	65.5
82.5	61	67.4
83	60.5	73
78.4	67	67
76.5	86	71
83.4	85	70.5
77.5	93.5	65.5
77	62	68
87	62.5	90
89	63	83.5
93.4	60	73
83	71.5	66
80	73.8	57.5
76	77.5	76
56	74	

17 Drawing Line Graphs

Key Idea: Line graphs are used to plot continuous data in which one variable (the independent variable) directly affects the other (dependent) variable. They are appropriate for data in which the independent variable is manipulated.

Guidelines for line graphs

Line graphs are used when one variable (the independent variable) affects another, the dependent variable. Line graphs can be drawn without a measure of spread (top figure, right) or with some calculated measure of data variability (bottom figure, right). Important features of line graphs include:

- The data must be continuous for both variables.

- The dependent variable is usually the biological response.

- The independent variable is often time or experimental treatment.

- The relationship between two variables can be represented as a continuum and the data points are plotted accurately and connected directly (point to point).

- Line graphs may be drawn with measure of error. The data are presented as points (which are the calculated means), with bars above and below, indicating a measure of variability or spread in the data (e.g. standard error, standard deviation, or 95% confidence intervals).

- Where no error value has been calculated, the scatter can be shown by plotting the individual data points vertically above and below the mean. By convention, bars are not used to indicate the range of raw values in a data set.

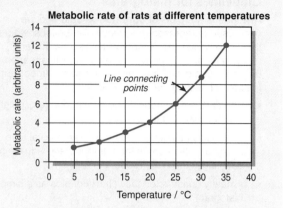

Metabolic rate of rats at different temperatures

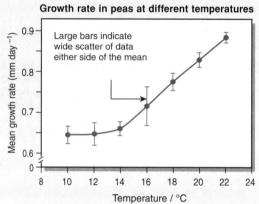

Growth rate in peas at different temperatures

1. The results (shown right) were collected in a study investigating the effect of temperature on the activity of an enzyme.

   (a) Using the results provided (right), plot a line graph on the grid below:

   (b) Estimate the rate of reaction at 15°C: _____

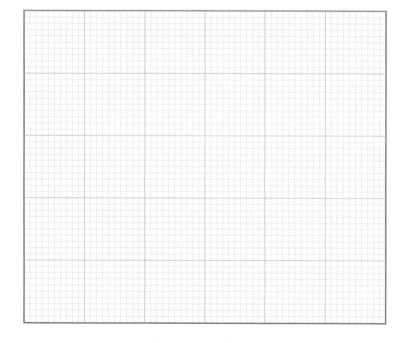

Lab Notebook

An enzyme's activity at different temperatures

Temperature / °C	Rate of reaction (mg of product formed per minute)
10	1.0
20	2.1
30	3.2
35	3.7
40	4.1
45	3.7
50	2.7
60	0

© 2015 **BIOZONE** International
ISBN: 978-1-927309-13-1
Photocopying Prohibited

Plotting multiple data sets

A single figure can be used to show two or more data sets, i.e. more than one curve can be plotted per set of axes. This type of presentation is useful when comparing the trends for two or more treatments, or the response of one species against the response of another. Important points regarding this format are:

- If the two data sets use the same measurement units and a similar range of values for the dependent variable, one scale on the y axis is used.

- If the two data sets use different units and/or have a very different range of values for the dependent variable, two scales for the y axis are used (see example right). The scales can be adjusted if necessary to avoid overlapping plots

- The two curves must be distinguished with a key.

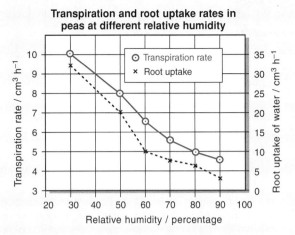

Transpiration and root uptake rates in peas at different relative humidity

2. The number of perch and trout in a hydro-electric reservoir were monitored over 19 years. A colony of black shag was also present. Shags feed on perch and (to a lesser extent) trout. In 1960-61, 424 shags were removed from the lake during the nesting season and nest counts were made every spring in subsequent years. In 1971, 60 shags were removed from the lake, and all existing nests dismantled. The results of the population survey are tabulated below.

(a) Plot a line graph (joining the data points) for the survey results. Use one scale (on the left) for numbers of perch and trout and another scale for the number of shag nests. Use different symbols to distinguish the lines and include a key.

(b) Use a vertical arrow to indicate the point at which shags and their nests were removed.

Year	Mean number of fish per haul		Shag nest numbers	Year (continued)	Mean number of fish per haul		Shag nest numbers
	Trout	Perch			Trout	Perch	
1960	–	–	16	1970	1.5	6	1.5
1961	–	–	4	1971	0.5	0.7	1.5
1962	1.5	11	5	1972	1	0.8	0
1963	0.8	9	10	1973	0.2	4	0
1964	0	5	22	1974	0.5	6.5	0
1965	1	1	25	1975	0.6	7.6	2
1966	1	2.9	35	1976	1	1.2	10
1967	2	5	40	1977	1.2	1.5	32
1968	1.5	4.6	26	1978	0.7	1.2	28
1969	1.5	6	32				

Source: Data adapted from 1987 Bursary Examination

18 Drawing Scatter Plots

Key Idea: Scatter graphs are used to plot continuous data where there is a relationship between two interdependent variables.

Guidelines for scatter graphs

A scatter graph is used to display continuous data where there is a relationship between two interdependent variables.

- The data must be continuous for both variables.

- There is no independent (manipulated) variable, but the variables are often correlated, i.e. they vary together in some predictable way.

- Scatter graphs are useful for determining the relationship (correlation) between two variables. A relationship does not imply that change in one variable causes change in the other variable.

- The points on the graph are not connected, but a line of best fit is often drawn through the points to show the relationship between the variables (this may be drawn by eye or computer generated).

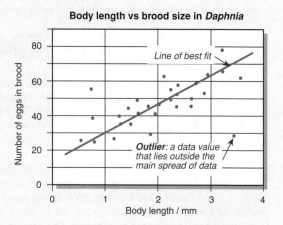

Body length vs brood size in *Daphnia*

1. In the example below, metabolic measurements were taken from seven Antarctic fish *Pagothenia borchgrevinski*. The fish are affected by a gill disease, which increases the thickness of the gas exchange surfaces and affects oxygen uptake. The results of oxygen consumption of fish with varying amounts of affected gill (at rest and swimming) are tabulated below.

(a) Using **one** scale only for oxygen consumption, plot the data on the grid below to show the relationship between oxygen consumption and the amount of gill affected by disease. Use different symbols or colours for each set of data (at rest and swimming).

(b) Draw a line of best fit through each set of points. NOTE: A line of best fit is drawn so that the points are evenly distributed on either side of the line.

2. Describe the relationship between the amount of gill affected and oxygen consumption in the fish:

(a) For the **at rest** data set: _____

_____

_____

_____

_____

_____

(b) For the **swimming** data set: _____

_____

_____

_____

_____

3. How does the gill disease affect oxygen uptake in resting fish?

_____

_____

_____

Oxygen consumption of fish with affected gills

Fish number	Percentage of gill affected	Oxygen consumption / cm³ g⁻¹ h⁻¹	
		At rest	**Swimming**
1	0	0.05	0.29
2	95	0.04	0.11
3	60	0.04	0.14
4	30	0.05	0.22
5	90	0.05	0.08
6	65	0.04	0.18
7	45	0.04	0.20

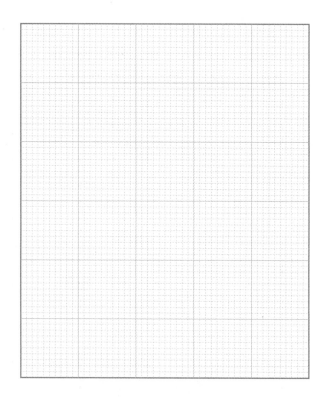

19 Interpreting Line Graphs

Key Idea: The equation for a straight line is y = mx + c. A line may have a positive, negative, or zero slope.
The equation for a linear (straight) line on a graph is y = mx + c. The equation can be used to calculate the gradient (slope) of a straight line and tells us about the relationship between x and y (how fast y is changing relative to x). For a straight line, the rate of change of y relative to x is always constant. A line may have a positive, negative, or zero slope.

Measuring gradients and intercepts

The equation for a straight line is written as:

y = mx + c

Where :

y = the y-axis value
m = the slope (or gradient)
x = the x-axis value
c = the y intercept (where the line cross the y-axis).

Determining "m" and "c"

To find "c" just find where the line crosses the y-axis.

To find m:

1. Choose any two points on the line.
2. Draw a right-angled triangle between the two points on the line.
3. Use the scale on each axis to find the triangle's vertical length and horizontal length.
4. Calculate the gradient of the line using the following equation:

$$\frac{\text{change in y}}{\text{change in x}}$$

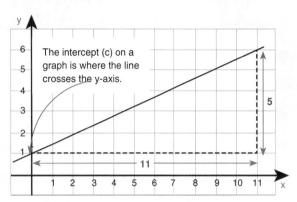

The intercept (c) on a graph is where the line crosses the y-axis.

For the example above:

c = 1

m = 0.45 (5 ÷11)

Once c and m have been determined you can choose any value for x and find the corresponding value for y.

For example, when x = 9, the equation would be:

y = 9 x 0.45 + 1

y = 5.05

Interpreting gradients

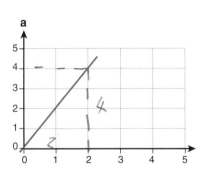

Positive gradients: the line slopes upward to the right (y is increasing as x increases).

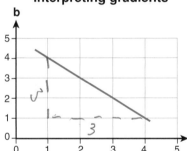

Negative gradients: the line slopes downward to the right (y is decreasing as x increases).

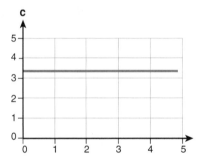

Zero gradients: the line is horizontal (y does not change as x increases).

1. State the gradient for graphs a, b, and c (above): (a) $\frac{4}{2} = 2$ (b) $\frac{3}{3} = 1$ (c) 0

2. For a straight line y = 3x + 2,

   (a) Identify the value of c: 2 (b) Determine y if x = 4: 14

3. For the graph (right):

   (a) Identify the value of c: 3

   (b) Calculate the value of m: 2

   (c) Determine y if x = 2: $y = 2x + 3$
   $y = 4 + 3 \quad y = 7$

   (d) Describe the slope of the line: positive

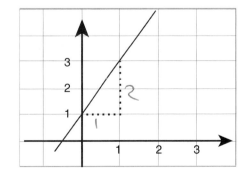

© 2015 **BIOZONE** International
ISBN: 978-1-927309-13-1
Photocopying Prohibited

LINK   LINK

169   **88**   DATA

20 Which Test to Use?

Key Idea: How your data is analysed depends on the type of data you have collected. Plotting your initial data can help you to decide what statistical analysis to carry out.

Data analysis provides information on the biological significance of your investigation. Never under-estimate the value of plotting your data, even at a very early stage. This will help you decide on the best type of data analysis. Sometimes, statistical analysis may not be required.

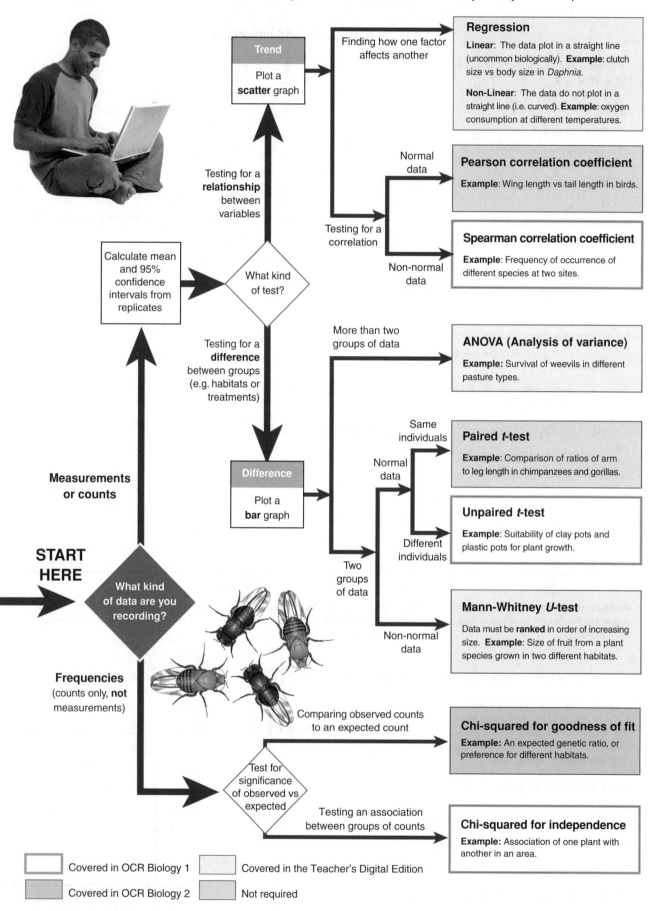

Trend

Plot a **scatter** graph

Finding how one factor affects another

Regression

Linear: The data plot in a straight line (uncommon biologically). **Example**: clutch size vs body size in *Daphnia*.

Non-Linear: The data do not plot in a straight line (i.e. curved). **Example**: oxygen consumption at different temperatures.

Testing for a relationship between variables

Normal data

Pearson correlation coefficient

Example: Wing length vs tail length in birds.

Testing for a correlation

Non-normal data

Spearman correlation coefficient

Example: Frequency of occurrence of different species at two sites.

Calculate mean and 95% confidence intervals from replicates

What kind of test?

Testing for a difference between groups (e.g. habitats or treatments)

More than two groups of data

ANOVA (Analysis of variance)

Example: Survival of weevils in different pasture types.

Difference

Plot a **bar** graph

Same individuals

Paired *t*-test

Example: Comparison of ratios of arm to leg length in chimpanzees and gorillas.

Normal data

Different individuals

Unpaired *t*-test

Example: Suitability of clay pots and plastic pots for plant growth.

Measurements or counts

Two groups of data

Non-normal data

Mann-Whitney *U*-test

Data must be **ranked** in order of increasing size. **Example**: Size of fruit from a plant species grown in two different habitats.

START HERE

What kind of data are you recording?

Frequencies (counts only, **not** measurements)

Comparing observed counts to an expected count

Chi-squared for goodness of fit

Example: An expected genetic ratio, or preference for different habitats.

Test for significance of observed vs expected

Testing an association between groups of counts

Chi-squared for independence

Example: Association of one plant with another in an area.

☐ Covered in OCR Biology 1		▨ Covered in the Teacher's Digital Edition	
▨ Covered in OCR Biology 2		☐ Not required	

LINK 198   LINK 199   LINK 229   LINK 230
REFER

© 2015 **BIOZONE** International
ISBN: 978-1-927309-13-1
Photocopying Prohibited

Key Idea: Mean, median, and mode are measures of the central tendency of data. The distribution of the data will determine which measurement of central tendency you use. Measures of a biological response are usually made from more than one sampling unit. In lab-based investigations, the sample size (the number of sampling units) may be as small as three or four (e.g. three test-tubes in each of four treatments). In field studies, each individual may be a sampling unit, and the sample size can be very large (e.g. 100 individuals). It is useful to summarise data using **descriptive statistics.** Descriptive statistics, such as mean, median, and mode, can identify the central tendency of a data set. Each of these statistics is appropriate to certain types of data or distribution (as indicated by a frequency distribution).

Variation in data

Whether they are obtained from observation or experiments, most biological data show variability. In a set of data values, it is useful to know the value about which most of the data are grouped, i.e. the centre value. This value can be the mean, median, or mode depending on the type of variable involved (see below). The main purpose of these statistics is to summarise important features of your data and to provide the basis for statistical analyses.

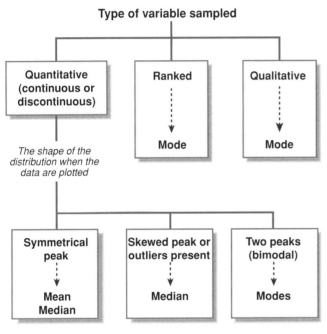

The shape of the distribution will determine which statistic (mean, median, or mode) best describes the central tendency of the sample data.

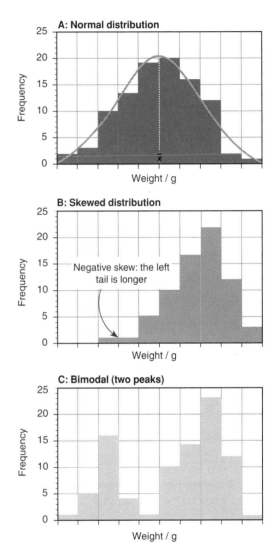

Statistic	Definition and use	Method of calculation
Mean	• The average of all data entries. • Measure of central tendency for normally distributed data.	• Add up all the data entries. • Divide by the total number of data entries.
Median	• The middle value when data entries are placed in rank order. • A good measure of central tendency for skewed distributions.	• Arrange the data in increasing rank order. • Identify the middle value. • For an even number of entries, find the mid point of the two middle values.
Mode	• The most common data value. • Suitable for bimodal distributions and qualitative data.	• Identify the category with the highest number of data entries using a tally chart or a bar graph.
Range	• The difference between the smallest and largest data values. • Provides a crude indication of data spread.	• Identify the smallest and largest values and find the difference between them.

When NOT to calculate a mean:

In some situations, calculation of a simple arithmetic mean is not appropriate.

Remember:

• *DO NOT* calculate a mean from values that are already means (averages) themselves.

• *DO NOT* calculate a mean of ratios (e.g. percentages) for several groups of different sizes. Go back to the raw values and recalculate.

• *DO NOT* calculate a mean when the measurement scale is not linear, e.g. pH units are not measured on a linear scale.

Total of data entries	=	5221	=	**180**	cm
Number of entries		29			

Mean

Case study: height of swimmers

Data (below) and descriptive statistics (left) from a survey of the height of 29 members of a male swim squad.

Height of swimmers (in rank order)		
174	177	185
175	177	185
175	178	185
175	178	186
176	178	186
176	178	186
176	180	188
176	180	188
176	180	189
177	181	

Mode

Median

Height (cm)	Tally	Total
174	✔	1
175	✔✔✔	3
176	✔✔✔✔✔	5
177	✔✔✔	3
178	✔✔✔✔	4
179		0
180	✔✔✔	3
181	✔	1
182		0
183		0
184		0
185	✔✔✔	3
186	✔✔✔	3
187		0
188	✔✔	2
189	✔	1

Raw data: Height / cm

178	177	188	176	186	175
180	181	178	178	176	175
180	185	185	175	189	174
178	186	176	185	177	176
176	188	180	186	177	

1. Give a reason for the difference between the mean, median, and mode for the swimmers' height data:

_____

_____

_____

Case study: fern reproduction

Raw data (below) and descriptive statistics (right) from a survey of the number of sori found on the fronds of a fern plant.

Fern spores

Raw data: Number of sori per frond

64	60	64	62	68	66	63
69	70	63	70	70	63	62
71	69	59	70	66	61	70
67	64	63	64			

Total of data entries	=	1641	=	**66**	sori
Number of entries		25			

Mean

Number of sori per frond (in rank order)	
59	66
60	66
61	67
62	68
62	69
63	69
63	70
63	70
63	70
64	70
64	70
64	71
64	

Median

Mode

Sori per frond	Tally	Total
59	✔	1
60	✔	1
61	✔	1
62	✔✔	2
63	✔✔✔✔	4
64	✔✔✔✔	4
65		0
66	✔✔	2
67	✔	1
68	✔	1
69	✔✔	2
70	✔✔✔✔✔	5
71	✔	1

2. Give a reason for the difference between the mean, median, and mode for the fern sori data:

_____

_____

_____

_____

3. Calculate the mean, median, and mode for the data on ladybird masses below. Draw up a tally chart and show all calculations:

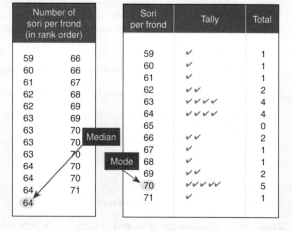

Ladybird mass / mg		
10.1	8.2	7.7
8.0	8.8	7.8
6.7	7.7	8.8
9.8	8.8	8.9
6.2	8.8	8.4

_____

_____

_____

_____

_____

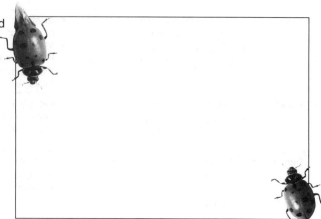

© 2015 **BIOZONE** International
ISBN: 978-1-927309-13-1
Photocopying Prohibited

22 Spread of Data

Key Idea: Standard deviation is used to quantify the variability around the central value and evaluate the reliability of estimates of the true mean.

While it is important to know the central tendency (e.g. mean) of a data set, it is also important to know how well the mean represents the data set. This is determined by measuring the spread of data around the central measure. The variance (s^2) or its square root, standard deviation (s) are often used to give a simple measure of the spread or dispersion in data. In general, if the spread of values in a data set around the mean is small, the mean will more accurately represent the data than if the spread of data is large.

Standard deviation

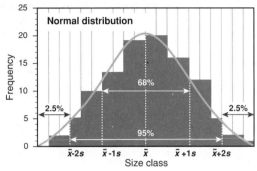

The **standard deviation** is a frequently used measure of the variability (spread) in a set of data. It is usually presented in the form $\bar{x} \pm s$. In a normally distributed set of data, 68% of all data values will lie within one standard deviation (s) of the mean ($\bar{x}$) and 95% of all data values will lie within two standard deviations of the mean (left).

Two different sets of data can have the same mean and range, yet the distribution of data within the range can be quite different. In both the data sets pictured in the histograms below, 68% of the values lie within the range $\bar{x} \pm 1s$ and 95% of the values lie within $\bar{x} \pm 2s$. However, in B, the data values are more tightly clustered around the mean.

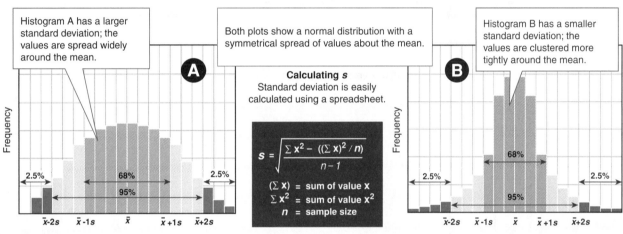

Histogram A has a larger standard deviation; the values are spread widely around the mean.

Both plots show a normal distribution with a symmetrical spread of values about the mean.

Histogram B has a smaller standard deviation; the values are clustered more tightly around the mean.

Calculating s
Standard deviation is easily calculated using a spreadsheet.

$$S = \sqrt{\frac{\sum x^2 - ((\sum x)^2 / n)}{n-1}}$$

$(\sum x)$ = sum of value x
$\sum x^2$ = sum of value x^2
n = sample size

NOTE: you may sometimes see the standard deviation equation written as:

$$S = \sqrt{\frac{\sum (x - \bar{x})^2}{n-1}}$$

This equation gives the same answer as the equation above. The denominator n-1 provides a unbiased sample standard deviation for small sample sizes (large samples can use n).

Birth weights / kg

3.740	3.810	3.220
3.830	2.640	3.135
3.530	2.980	3.090
3.095	3.350	3.830
1.560	3.780	3.840
3.910	3.260	4.710
4.180	3.800	4.050
3.570	4.170	4.560
3.150	4.400	3.380
3.400	3.770	3.690
3.380	3.825	1.495
2.660	3.130	3.260
3.840	3.400	
3.630	3.260	

1. Two data sets have the same mean. The standard deviation of the first data set is much larger than the standard deviation of the second data set. What does this tell you about the spread of data around the central measure for each set?

_____

_____

_____

2. The data on the left are the birth weights of 40 newborn babies.

(a) Calculate the mean for the data: _____

_____

(b) Calculate the standard deviation (s) for the data: _____

(c) State the mean ± 1s: _____

(d) What percentage of values are within 1s of the mean? _____

(e) What does this tell you about the spread of the data? _____

_____

LINK 26   LINK 21   WEB 22

DATA

23 Interpreting Sample Variability

Key Idea: The sampling method can affect the results of the study, especially if it has an unknown bias.

The **standard deviation** (s) gives a simple measure of the spread or **dispersion** in data. It is usually preferred over the **variance** (s^2) because it is expressed in the original units. Two data sets could have the same mean, but very different values of dispersion. If we simply used the mean to compare these data sets, the results would (incorrectly) suggest that they were alike. The assumptions we make about a population will be affected by what the sample data tell us. This is why it is important that sample data are unbiased (e.g. collected by **random sampling**) and that the sample set is as large as practicable. This exercise will help to illustrate this principle.

Random sampling, sample size, and dispersion in data

Sample size and sampling bias can both affect the information we obtain when we sample a population. In this exercise you will calculate some descriptive statistics for some sample data. The complete set of sample data we are working with comprises 689 length measurements of year zero (young of the year) perch (column left). Basic descriptive statistics for the data have been calculated for you below and the frequency histogram has also been plotted.

Look at this data set and then complete the exercise to calculate the same statistics from each of two smaller data sets (tabulated right) drawn from the same population. This exercise shows how random sampling, large sample size, and sampling bias affect our statistical assessment of variation in a population.

Complete sample set
n = 689 (random)

Length in mm	Freq
25	1
26	0
27	0
28	0
29	0
30	0
31	0
32	2
33	3
34	3
35	4
36	5
37	10
38	23
39	22
40	33
41	39
42	41
43	41
44	36
45	49
46	32
47	14
48	32
49	27
50	25
51	24
52	17
53	18
54	27
55	21
56	20
57	11
58	18
59	16
60	22
61	13
62	8
63	10
64	5
65	7
66	2
67	3
68	3
69	1
70	0
71	1
	689

Small sample set
n = 30 (random)

Length in mm	Freq
25	1
26	0
27	0
28	0
29	0
30	0
31	0
32	0
33	0
34	0
35	2
36	0
37	0
38	3
39	2
40	1
41	3
42	0
43	0
44	0
45	0
46	1
47	0
48	2
49	0
50	0
51	1
52	3
53	0
54	0
55	0
56	0
57	1
58	0
59	3
60	2
61	2
62	0
63	0
64	0
65	0
66	0
67	2
68	1
	30

Small sample set
n = 50 (bias)

Length in mm	Freq
46	1
47	0
48	0
49	1
50	0
51	0
52	1
53	1
54	1
55	1
56	0
57	2
58	2
59	4
60	1
61	0
62	8
63	10
64	13
65	2
66	0
67	2
	50

The person gathering this set of data was biased towards selecting larger fish because the mesh size on the net was too large to retain small fish

This population was sampled randomly to obtain this data set

This column records the number of fish of each size

Number of fish in the sample

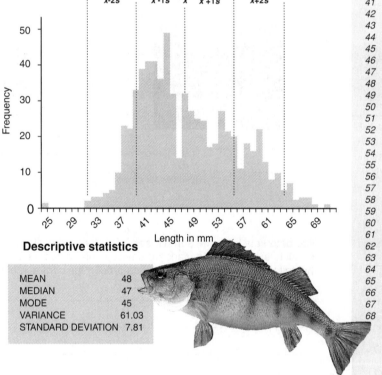

Length of year zero perch

Frequency vs Length in mm
(markers: $\bar{x}-2s$, $\bar{x}-1s$, $\bar{x}$, $\bar{x}+1s$, $\bar{x}+2s$)

Descriptive statistics

MEAN	48
MEDIAN	47
MODE	45
VARIANCE	61.03
STANDARD DEVIATION	7.81

1. For the complete data set ($n = 689$) calculate the percentage of data falling within:

   (a) ± one standard deviation of the mean: _____

   (b) ± two standard deviations of the mean: _____

   (c) Explain what this information tells you about the distribution of year zero perch from this site: _____

   _____

2. Give another reason why you might reach the same conclusion about the distribution: _____

   _____

LINK 21   LINK 22

DATA

© 2015 **BIOZONE** International
ISBN: 978-1-927309-13-1
Photocopying Prohibited

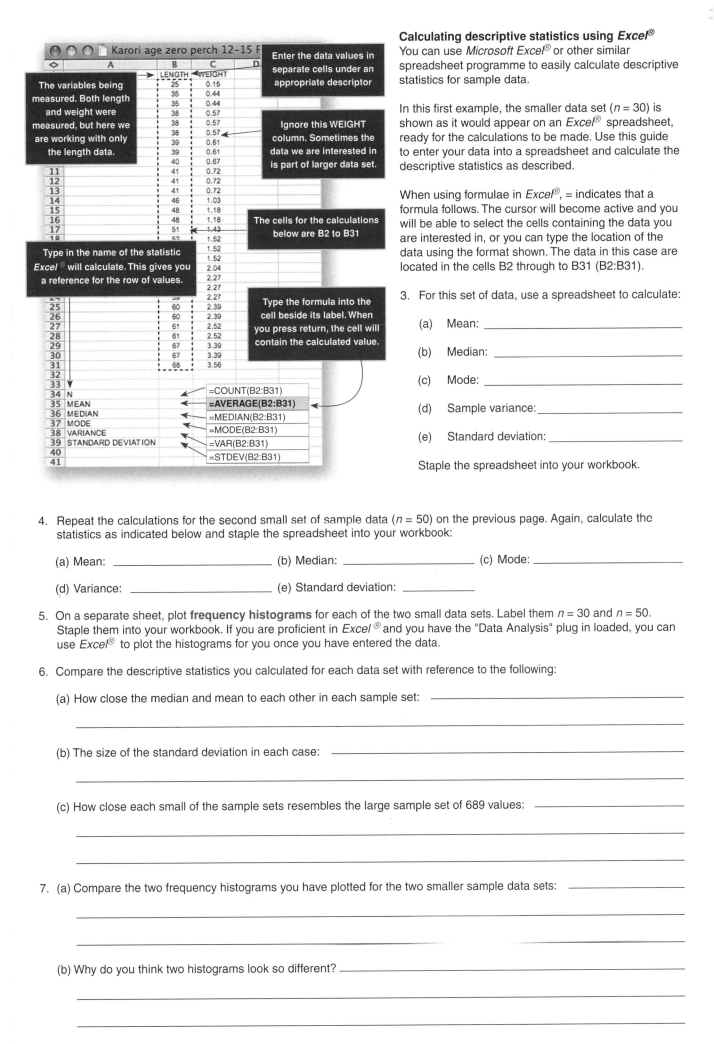

Calculating descriptive statistics using *Excel*®

You can use *Microsoft Excel*® or other similar spreadsheet programme to easily calculate descriptive statistics for sample data.

In this first example, the smaller data set (n = 30) is shown as it would appear on an *Excel*® spreadsheet, ready for the calculations to be made. Use this guide to enter your data into a spreadsheet and calculate the descriptive statistics as described.

When using formulae in *Excel*®, = indicates that a formula follows. The cursor will become active and you will be able to select the cells containing the data you are interested in, or you can type the location of the data using the format shown. The data in this case are located in the cells B2 through to B31 (B2:B31).

3. For this set of data, use a spreadsheet to calculate:

    (a) Mean: _____

    (b) Median: _____

    (c) Mode: _____

    (d) Sample variance: _____

    (e) Standard deviation: _____

    Staple the spreadsheet into your workbook.

4. Repeat the calculations for the second small set of sample data (n = 50) on the previous page. Again, calculate the statistics as indicated below and staple the spreadsheet into your workbook:

    (a) Mean: _____ (b) Median: _____ (c) Mode: _____

    (d) Variance: _____ (e) Standard deviation: _____

5. On a separate sheet, plot **frequency histograms** for each of the two small data sets. Label them n = 30 and n = 50. Staple them into your workbook. If you are proficient in *Excel*® and you have the "Data Analysis" plug in loaded, you can use *Excel*® to plot the histograms for you once you have entered the data.

6. Compare the descriptive statistics you calculated for each data set with reference to the following:

    (a) How close the median and mean to each other in each sample set: _____

    _____

    (b) The size of the standard deviation in each case: _____

    _____

    (c) How close each small of the sample sets resembles the large sample set of 689 values: _____

    _____

    _____

7. (a) Compare the two frequency histograms you have plotted for the two smaller sample data sets: _____

    _____

    _____

    (b) Why do you think two histograms look so different? _____

    _____

    _____

24 | Biological Drawings

Key Idea: Good biological drawings provide an accurate record of the specimen you are studying and enable you to make a record of its important features.

Drawing is a very important skill to have in biology. Drawings record what a specimen looks like and give you an opportunity to record its important features. Often drawing something will help you remember its features at a later date (e.g. in a test). Annotated drawings provide explanatory notes about the labelled structures, while plan diagrams label the main structures observed, but provide no additional detail.

▶ Biological drawings require you to pay attention to detail. It is very important that you draw what you actually see, and not what you think you should see.

▶ Biological drawings should include as much detail as you need to distinguish different structures and types of tissue, but avoid unnecessary detail which can make your drawing confusing.

▶ Attention should be given to the symmetry and proportions of your specimen. Accurate labeling, a statement of magnification or scale, the view (section type), and type of stain used (if applicable) should all be noted on your drawing.

▶ Some key points for making good biological drawing are described on the example below. The drawing of *Drosophila* (right) is well executed but lacks the information required to make it a good biological drawing.

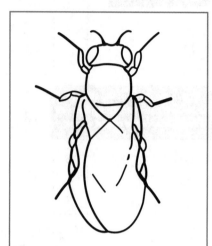

This drawing of *Drosophila* is a fair representation of the animal, but has no labels, title, or scale.

All drawings must include a title. Underline the title if it is a scientific name. ⟶ **Copepod**

Centre your drawing on the page, not in a corner. This will leave room to place labels around the drawing.

Single eye

Antenna

Trunk

If you need to represent depth, use stippling (dotting). Do not use shading as this can smudge and obscure detail.

Proportions should be accurate. If necessary, measure the lengths of various parts with a ruler.

Use simple, narrow lines to make your drawings.

Egg sac

Thorax

Caudal rami

Use a sharp pencil to draw with. Make your drawing on plain white paper.

Setae

All parts of your drawing must be labelled accurately.

Labeling lines should be drawn with a ruler and should not cross over other label lines. Try to use only vertical or horizontal lines.

Your drawing must include a scale or magnification to indicate the size of your subject.

Scale

0.2 mm

© 2015 **BIOZONE** International
ISBN: 978-1-927309-13-1
Photocopying Prohibited

Annotated diagrams

An annotated diagram is a diagram that includes a series of explanatory notes. These provide important or useful information about your subject.

Transverse section through collenchyma of *Helianthus* stem. Magnification x 450

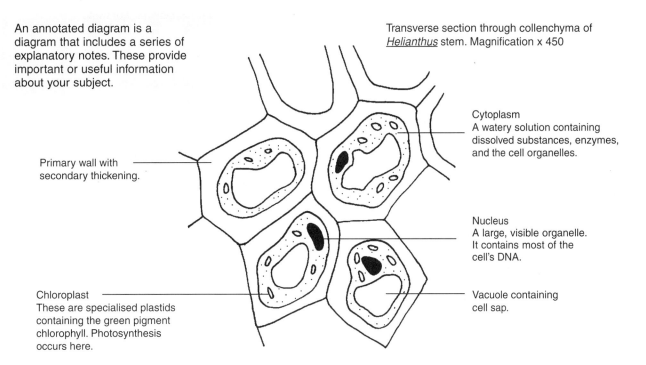

Primary wall with secondary thickening.

Cytoplasm
A watery solution containing dissolved substances, enzymes, and the cell organelles.

Nucleus
A large, visible organelle. It contains most of the cell's DNA.

Chloroplast
These are specialised plastids containing the green pigment chlorophyll. Photosynthesis occurs here.

Vacuole containing cell sap.

Plan diagrams

Plan diagrams are drawings made of samples viewed under a microscope at low or medium power. They are used to show the distribution of the different tissue types in a sample without any cellular detail. The tissues are identified, but no detail about the cells within them is included.

The example here shows a plan diagram produced after viewing a light micrograph of a transverse section through a dicot stem.

Light micrograph of a transverse section through a dicot stem.

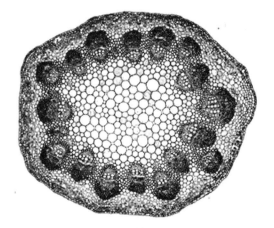

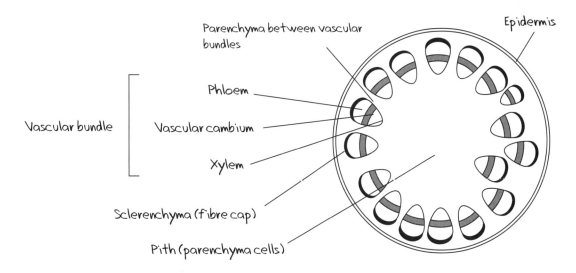

Parenchyma between vascular bundles

Epidermis

Phloem

Vascular cambium

Xylem

Vascular bundle

Sclerenchyma (fibre cap)

Pith (parenchyma cells)

25 Practising Biological Drawings

Key Idea: Attention to detail is vital when making accurate and useful biological drawings.

In this activity, you will practise the skills required to translate what is viewed into a good biological drawing.

Above: Use relaxed viewing when drawing at the microscope. Use one eye (the left for right handers) to view and the right eye to look at your drawing.

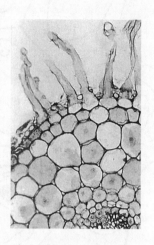

Above: Light micrograph Transverse section (TS) through a *Ranunculus* root.

Right: A biological drawing of the same section.

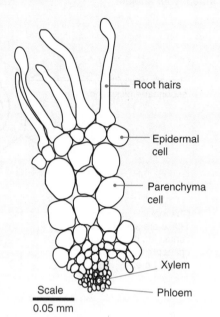

Root hairs

Epidermal cell

Parenchyma cell

Xylem

Phloem

Scale
0.05 mm

1. During your course of study, you will be required to identify and draw cells in a prepared blood smear viewed with a light microscope. It is often difficult to identify cell types in prepared smears under the magnification commonly used in school microscopes (X400). An example of what you are likely to see is shown below.

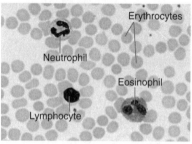

Erythrocytes

Neutrophil

Eosinophil

Lymphocyte

Looking at your slide, draw what you can see and try to identify as many cell types as you can. Use the picture (below, right) to help you. The drawn cells are organised from left to right in order of most common to least common. White blood cells are framed by the rectangle. Platelets are cell fragments and may not be visible. White blood cells are distinguished by the presence and staining of granules in the cytoplasm and the shape of the nucleus. Lymphocytes and monocytes do not have a granular cytoplasm.

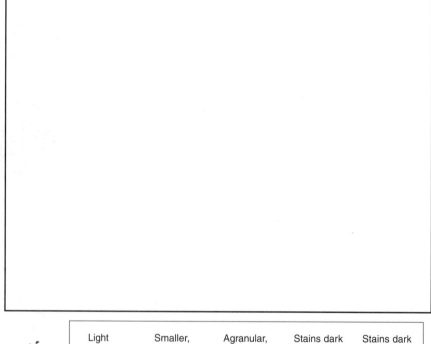

Platelets

Light staining granules

Smaller, rounder, agranular

Agranular, lobed nucleus

Stains dark pink

Stains dark purple

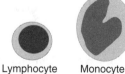

Erythrocyte | Neutrophil | Lymphocyte | Monocyte | Eosinophil | Basophil

Most common

Least common

LINK 24   LINK 29   LINK 31

© 2015 **BIOZONE** International
ISBN: 978-1-927309-13-1
Photocopying Prohibited

Key Idea: Systematic recording and analysis of results can help identify trends and draw conclusions about a biological response in an experiment.

Using the information below, analyse results and draw conclusions about the effect of a nitrogen fertiliser on the growth of radish plants.

Radishes

The Aim
To investigate the effect of a nitrogen fertiliser on the growth of radish plants.

Hypothesis
If plants need nitrogen to grow, radish growth will increase with increasing nitrogen concentration.

Background
Inorganic fertilisers revolutionised crop farming when they were introduced during the late 19th and early 20th century. Crop yields soared and today it is estimated around 50% of crop yield is attributable to the use of fertiliser. Nitrogen is a very important element for plant growth and several types of purely nitrogen fertiliser are manufactured to supply it, e.g. urea.

Experimental method
This experiment was designed to test the effect of nitrogen fertiliser on plant growth. Radish seeds were planted in separate identical pots (5 cm x 5 cm wide x 10 cm deep) and grown together in normal room temperature (22°C) conditions.

The radishes were watered every day at 10 am and 3 pm with 1.25 L per treatment. Water soluble fertiliser was mixed and added with the first watering on the 1st, 11th and 21st days. The fertiliser concentrations used were: 0.00, 0.06, 0.12, 0.18, 0.24, and 0.30 g dm^{-3} with each treatment receiving a different concentration. The plants were grown for 30 days before being removed, washed, and the root (radish) weighed. Results were tabulated below:

To investigate the effect of nitrogen on plant growth, a group of students set up an experiment using different concentrations of nitrogen fertiliser. Radish seeds were planted into a standard soil mixture and divided into six groups, each with five sample plants (30 plants in total).

Table 1: Mass (g) of radish plant roots under six different fertiliser concentrations (data given to 1 dp).

Fertiliser concentration / g dm^{-3}	Mass of radish root / g[†]					Total mass	Mean mass
	Sample / n						
	1	2	3	4	5		
0	80.1	83.2	82.0	79.1	84.1	408.5	81.7
0.06	109.2	110.3	108.2	107.9	110.7		
0.12	117.9	118.9	118.3	119.1	117.2		
0.18	128.3	127.3	127.7	126.8	DNG*		
0.24	23.6	140.3	139.6	137.9	141.1		
0.30	122.3	121.1	122.6	121.3	123.1		

† Based on data from M S Jilani, *et al* Journal Agricultural Research

* DNG: Did not germinate

1. Identify the independent variable for the experiment and its range: _____

_____

2. What is the sample size for each concentration of fertiliser? _____

3. One of the radishes recorded in Table 1 did not grow as expected and produced an extreme value. Record the **outlying value** here and decide whether or not you should include it in future calculations:

_____

_____

_____

4. Complete the table on the previous page by calculating the **total mass** and **mean mass** of the radish roots:

5. Use the grid below to draw a **line graph** of the experimental results. Use your calculated means and remember to include a title and correctly labelled axes.

6. The students recorded the wet mass of the root (the root still containing water) in their table. What mass should they have actually recorded to get a better representation of the effect of the fertiliser on root mass?

_____

_____

_____

7. Why would measuring just root mass not be a totally accurate way of measuring the effect of fertiliser on radish growth?

_____

_____

8. Describe some other measurements the students could have taken to make their experiment more complete:

_____

_____

© 2015 **BIOZONE** International
ISBN: 978-1-927309-13-1
Photocopying Prohibited

9. Complete Table 2 by calculating the mean, median and mode for each concentration of fertiliser:

The students decided to further their experiment by recording the number of leaves on each radish plant:

Table 2: Number of leaves on radish plant under six different fertiliser concentrations.

| Fertiliser concentration / g dm⁻³ | Number of leaves | | | | | Mean | Median | Mode |
| | Sample / n | | | | | | | |
	1	2	3	4	5			
0	9	9	10	8	7			
0.06	15	16	15	16	16			
0.12	16	17	17	17	16			
0.18	18	18	19	18	DNG*			
0.24	6	19	19	18	18			
0.30	18	17	18	19	19			

* DNG: Did not germinate

10. (a) Identify the outlier in the table above: _____

(b) Recalculate the mean if the outlier was included: _____

(c) Calculate the standard deviation for the fertiliser concentration affected by an outlier:

With the outlier included: _____

Without the outlier included: _____

(d) Compare the results in (c). What can you conclude about how accurately the mean reflects the data set when the outlier is included?

_____

_____

11. Which concentration of fertiliser appeared to produce the best growth results? _____

12. Describe some sources of error for the experiment: _____

_____

_____

_____

13. Write a conclusion for the experiment with reference to the aim, hypothesis, and results: _____

_____

_____

_____

_____

14. The students decided to replicate the experiment (carry it out again). How might this improve the experiment's results?

_____

_____

_____

© 2015 **BIOZONE** International
ISBN: 978-1-927309-13-1
Photocopying Prohibited

1. For the graph (right) use the equation $y = mx + c$ to answer the following questions:

   (a) What is the value of c?: _____ b _____

   (b) Using the two reference points marked on the graph, calculate m: _____ -3/4 _____

   (c) Describe the slope and the relationship between the variables: _____ Steep _____
   _____ negative slope. When x increase, y decreases _____

   (d) What is the value of y when x=5? _____ $y = m(5) + 6 = -3/4(5) + 6 = 2'1/4$ _____

2. A balance has a calibration error of +0.04 g. A student weighs out 11.71 g of sodium hydroxide. Calculate the percentage error (show your working):

   _____

   _____

3. The table (below right) shows the rate of sweat production in an athlete on a stationary cycle. Complete the table to:

   (a) Convert the cumulative sweat loss to cm^3:

   (b) Determine the rate of sweat loss $(cm^3 min^{-1})$:

   (c) Plot a double axis graph on the grid below to show cumulative sweat loss in cm^3 and rate of sweat loss against time.

   (d) Describe how the rate of sweat loss changes over time:

   _____

   _____

   _____

Time / minutes	Cumulative sweat loss / mm^3	Cumulative sweat loss / cm^3	Rate of sweat loss / cm^3 min^{-1}
0	0		
10	50 000		
20	130 000		
30	220 000		
60	560 000		

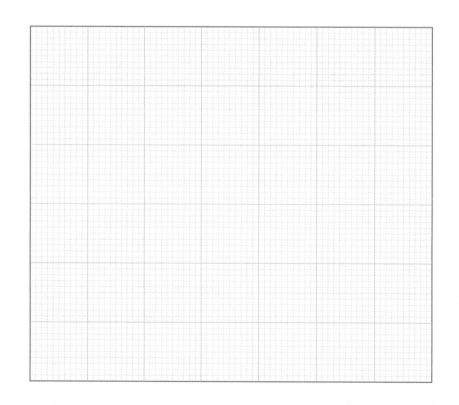

© 2015 **BIOZONE** International
ISBN: 978-1-927309-13-1
Photocopying Prohibited

Cell Structure

Key terms

cell wall

centrioles

chloroplast

cilia

cytoplasm

cytoskeleton

electron micrograph

endoplasmic reticulum (ER)

eukaryotic

eyepiece graticule

flagella

Golgi apparatus

laser scanning confocal microscope

light (=optical) microscope

lysosome

magnification

mitochondrion

nuclear envelope

nucleolus

nucleus

organelle

plasma membrane

prokaryotic

resolution

ribosome

rough ER (rER)

scanning electron microscope

smooth ER (sER)

stage micrometer

stain

transmission electron microscope

vacuole

Microscopy

Learning outcomes

Activity number

☐ 1 Appreciate that microscopy has a long history and was fundamental to the development of the cell theory. — 28 35

☐ 2 Describe how microscopes are used to observe and investigate the structure and range of cell types in a variety of eukaryotic organisms. Recognise and account for differences between the images produced by light microscopes, transmission electron microscopes, scanning electron microscopes, and laser scanning confocal microscopes. — 28 29 32

☐ 3 **PAG1** Prepare and examine microscope slides for viewing with a light microscope at high and low power. Demonstrate use of an eyepiece graticule and stage micrometer to calculate the size of specimens. — 31 33

☐ 4 Using examples, explain the purpose of stains in microscopy. — 31

☐ 5 **PAG1** Use simple staining techniques to show features of cells. — 31

☐ 6 **PAG1** Make drawings or annotated diagrams of cells to show cell structure. — 24 25

☐ 7 Distinguish between magnification and resolution. Compare the magnification and resolution achieved using different microscopes. — 29

☐ 8 Calculate the linear magnification of images viewed with a microscope by using and manipulating the formula: magnification = image size÷object size. — 34

The ultrastructure of cells

Learning outcomes

Activity number

☐ 9 Describe the ultrastructure of eukaryotic cells and the functions of the different cellular components, including the nucleus, nucleolus, nuclear envelope, plasma membrane, rough and smooth endoplasmic reticulum, Golgi apparatus, cell wall, ribosomes, mitochondria, lysosomes, chloroplasts, centrioles, flagella, and cilia. — 35 36 38 39 41 45

☐ 10 Identify cellular components in photomicrographs produced by light and electron microscopy (SEM and TEM). — 40 42 46

☐ 11 Describe the interrelationships between the organelles involved in the production and secretion of proteins (rough ER and Golgi). — 44

☐ 12 Describe the structure and role of the cell's cytoskeleton. — 43

☐ 13 **PAG1** Compare and contrast the structure and ultrastructure of prokaryotic and eukaryotic cells. Include reference to the presence or absence of a nucleus and membrane-bound organelles and cell size. — 35 36 37 38 39 41

28 History of Microscopy

Key Idea: Microscopes are used to view objects that cannot be viewed in detail with the naked eye. Microscopes have become increasingly sophisticated over time with improvements in both magnification and resolution.

Lenses of various descriptions have been used for around 4000 years to view objects, but it is only in the last few hundred years that techniques have developed to build sophisticated devices for viewing microscopic objects. Early microscopes suffered from image distortion such as chromatic aberration (the production of images with the light split into the different colours). The development of more sophisticated techniques in lens and microscope production reduced this problem. The development of electron microscopes has made it possible to image objects to the atomic level.

Milestones in microscopy

1500	Convex lenses with a magnification greater than x5 became available.
1595	**Zacharias Janssen** of Holland has been credited with the first compound microscope (more than one lens).
1662	**Robert Hooke** of England used the term 'cell' in describing the microscopic structure of cork.
1675	**Antoni van Leeuwenhoek** of Holland produced over 500 single lens microscopes that had a magnification of 270 times.
1800s	The discovery that lenses combining two types of glass reduced chromatic aberration (the production of images with the light split into the different colours) allows clear images to be viewed.
1830	**Joseph Jackson Lister** demonstrated that spherical aberration (the focussing of light rays at different points due to the curve of the lens) could be reduced by using different lenses at precise distances from each other.
1878	**Ernst Abbe** produced a formula for correlating resolution to the wavelength of light, and so describes the maximum resolution of a light microscope.
1903	**Richard Zsigmondy** developed the ultramicroscope allowing objects smaller than the wavelength of light to be viewed.
1932	**Frits Zernike** invented the phase-contrast microscope making transparent or colourless objects easier to view.
1938	**Ernst Ruska** developed the transmission electron microscope (TEM). Electrons pass through an object and are focused by magnets. The short wavelength of electrons allows study of incredibly small objects. **Manfred von Ardenne** developed the scanning electron microscope (SEM) around the same time allowing the surface of objects to be imaged.
1957-80	**Marvin Minsky** patented the principle of the confocal laser scanning microscope (CLSM) but it takes 30 years for development.
1981	**Gerd Binning** and **Heinrich Rohrer** invented the scanning tunneling electron microscope (STM), producing three dimensional images at the atomic level.

1595
The first compound microscope (the Janssen microscope, right) consisted of three draw tubes with lenses inserted into the tubes. The microscope was focussed by sliding the draw tube in or out.

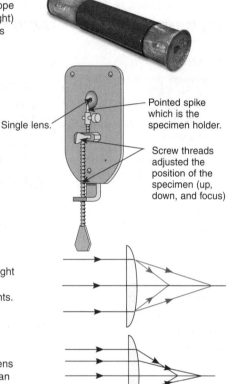

Single lens.

Pointed spike which is the specimen holder.

Screw threads adjusted the position of the specimen (up, down, and focus)

1675
A Leeuwenhoek microscope c. 1673 (right) was only a glorified magnifying glass by today's standards.

1800s
Chromatic aberration. Blue light refracts more than red light producing different focal points.

1830
Spherical aberration. Light entering at the edge of the lens focuses closer to the lens than light entering near the centre of the lens.

1932

Onion cells viewed by phase contrast.

1938

SEM of blood cells

TEM of mitochondrion

1957- 80

Image: Synapomorphy

CLSM image of proteins in the tobacco mosaic virus. Specimens for viewing with a CLSM are often treated with fluorescent dyes and it is possible to produce optical sections through thick samples of living tissue.

1981

Image: Erwinossen public domain

Gold atoms imaged with an STM

29 Optical Microscopes

Key Idea: Optical microscopes use light focussed through a series of lenses to magnify objects up to several 100 times. The light (or optical) microscope is an important tool in biology and using it correctly is an essential skill. High power compound light microscopes use visible light and a combination of lenses to magnify objects up to several 100 times. The resolution of light microscopes is limited by the wavelength of light and specimens must be thin and mostly transparent so that light can pass through. No detail will be seen in specimens that are thick or opaque.

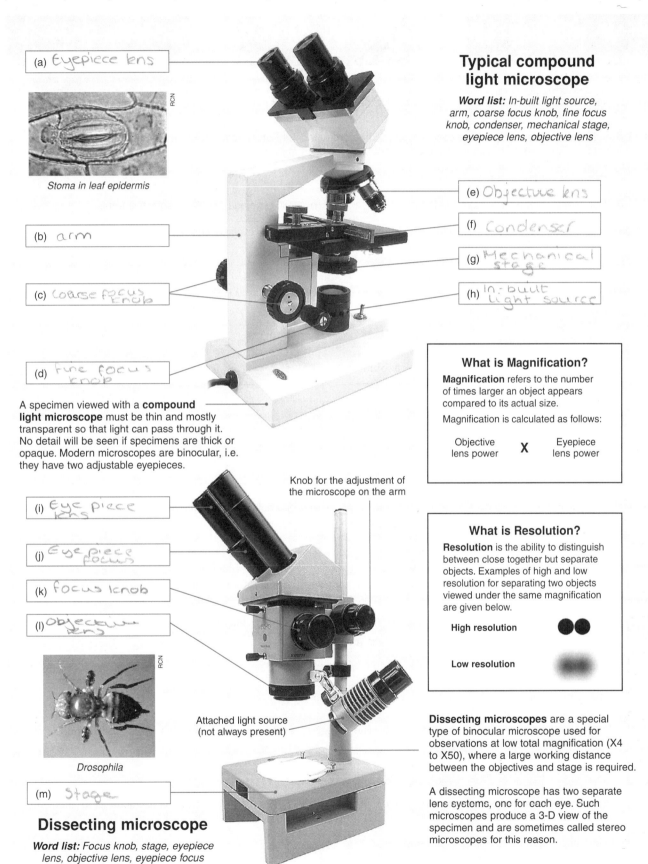

(a) Eyepiece lens

Stoma in leaf epidermis

(b) arm

(c) coarse focus knob

(d) fine focus knob

A specimen viewed with a **compound light microscope** must be thin and mostly transparent so that light can pass through it. No detail will be seen if specimens are thick or opaque. Modern microscopes are binocular, i.e. they have two adjustable eyepieces.

Typical compound light microscope

Word list: *In-built light source, arm, coarse focus knob, fine focus knob, condenser, mechanical stage, eyepiece lens, objective lens*

(e) Objective lens

(f) Condenser

(g) Mechanical stage

(h) In-built light source

What is Magnification?

Magnification refers to the number of times larger an object appears compared to its actual size.

Magnification is calculated as follows:

Objective lens power **X** Eyepiece lens power

(i) Eye piece lens

(j) Eye piece focus

(k) focus knob

(l) Objective lens

Knob for the adjustment of the microscope on the arm

What is Resolution?

Resolution is the ability to distinguish between close together but separate objects. Examples of high and low resolution for separating two objects viewed under the same magnification are given below.

High resolution

Low resolution

Drosophila

Attached light source (not always present)

(m) Stage

Dissecting microscope

Word list: *Focus knob, stage, eyepiece lens, objective lens, eyepiece focus*

Dissecting microscopes are a special type of binocular microscope used for observations at low total magnification (X4 to X50), where a large working distance between the objectives and stage is required.

A dissecting microscope has two separate lens systems, one for each eye. Such microscopes produce a 3-D view of the specimen and are sometimes called stereo microscopes for this reason.

© 2015 **BIOZONE** International
ISBN: 978-1-927309-13-1
Photocopying Prohibited

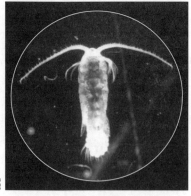

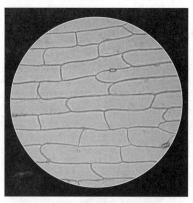

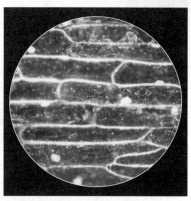

Dissecting microscopes are used for identifying and sorting organisms, observing microbial cultures, and dissections.

These onion epidermal cells are viewed with standard **bright field** lighting. Very little detail can be seen (only cell walls) and the cell nuclei are barely visible.

Dark field illumination is excellent for viewing specimens that are almost transparent. The nuclei of these onion epidermal cells are clearly visible.

1. Label the two photographs on the previous page, the compound light microscope (a) to (h) and the dissecting microscope (i) to (m). Use words from the lists supplied for each image.

2. Determine the magnification of a microscope using:

    (a) 15 X eyepiece and 40 X objective lens: _600_   (b) 10 X eyepiece and 60 X objective lens: _600_

3. Describe the main difference between a compound light microscope and a dissecting microscope: _____

    A dissecting microscope produces a 3D image but light only produces 2D images

4. What type of microscope would you use to:

    (a) Count stream invertebrates in a sample: _Dissecting_ (b) Observe cells in mitosis: _Light_

5. (a) Distinguish between **magnification** and **resolution**: _Magnification is the number of times bigger an image is made, resolution is the smallest measurable distance between two points_

    (b) Explain the benefits of a higher resolution: _____

    It allows greater detail to be seen under the microscope

6. Below is a list of ten key steps taken to set up a microscope and optimally view a sample. The steps have been mixed up. Put them in their **correct order** by numbering each step:

    [ ] Focus and centre the specimen using the high objective lens. Adjust focus using the fine focus knob only.

    [ ] Adjust the illumination to an appropriate level by adjusting the iris diaphragm and the condenser. The light should appear on the slide directly below the objective lens, and give an even amount of illumination.

    [1] Rotate the objective lenses until the shortest lens is in place (pointing down towards the stage).
    This is the lowest / ~~highest~~ power objective lens (delete one).

    [2] Place the slide on the microscope stage. Secure with the sample clips.

    [ ] Fine tune the illumination so you can view maximum detail on your sample.

    [ ] Focus and centre the specimen using the medium objective lens. Focus firstly with the coarse focus knob, then with the fine focus knob (if needed).

    [3] Turn on the light source.

    [ ] Focus and centre the specimen using the low objective lens. Focus firstly with the coarse focus knob, then with the fine focus knob.

    [ ] Focus the eyepieces to adjust your view.

    [ ] Adjust the distance between the eyepieces so that they are comfortable for your eyes.

30 Preparing a Slide

Key Idea: Correctly preparing and mounting a specimen on a slide is important if structures are to be seen clearly under a microscope. A wet mount is suitable for most slides.

Specimens are often prepared in some way before viewing in order to highlight features and reveal details. A wet mount is a temporary preparation in which a specimen and a drop of fluid are trapped under a thin coverslip. Wet mounts are used to view thin tissue sections, live microscopic organisms, and suspensions such as blood. A wet mount improves a sample's appearance and enhances visible detail. Sections must be made very thin for two main reasons. A thick section stops light shining through making it appear dark when viewed. It also ends up with too many layers of cells, making it difficult to make out detail.

Preparing a specimen

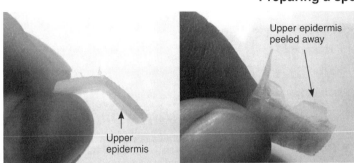

Upper epidermis

Upper epidermis peeled away

Onions make good subjects for preparing a simple wet mount. A square segment is cut from a thick leaf from the bulb. The segment is then bent towards the upper epidermis and snapped so that just the epidermis is left attached. The epidermis can then be peeled off to provide a thin layer of cells for viewing.

Sections through stems or other soft objects need to be made with a razor blade or scalpel, and must be very thin. Cutting at a slight angle to produce a wedge shape creates a thin edge. Ideally specimens should be set in wax first, to prevent crushing and make it easier to cut the specimen accurately.

Mounting a specimen

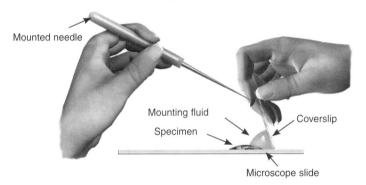

Mounted needle

Mounting fluid

Specimen

Coverslip

Microscope slide

Mounting: The thin layer is placed in the centre of a clean glass microscope slide and covered with a drop of mounting liquid (e.g. water, glycerol, or stain). A coverslip is placed on top using a mounted needle to support and lower it gently over the specimen. This avoids including air in the mount.

Viewing

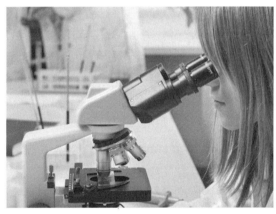

Locate the specimen or region of interest at the lowest magnification. Focus using the lowest magnification first, before switching to the higher magnifications.

1. Why must sections viewed under a microscope be very thin? _To ensure only one layer of cells is being viewed_

2. What is the purpose of the coverslip? _To keep the specimen in place_

3. Why would no chloroplasts be visible in an onion epidermis cell slide? _Photosynthesis does not occur in the onion epidermis so no chloroplasts will be there_

4. Why is it necessary to focus on the lowest magnification first, before switching to higher magnifications? _____
_____
_____

© 2015 **BIOZONE** International
ISBN: 978-1-927309-13-1
Photocopying Prohibited

LINK WEB
31 30 KN

31 Staining a Slide

Key Idea: Staining material to be viewed under a microscope can make it easier to distinguish particular cell structures.

Stains and dyes can be used to highlight specific components or structures. Most stains are **non-viable**, and are used on dead specimens, but harmless viable stains can be applied to living material. Stains contain chemicals that interact with molecules in the cell. Some stains bind to a particular molecule making it easier to see where those molecules are. Others cause a change in a target molecule, which changes their colour, making them more visible.

Some commonly used stains		
Stain	Final colour	Used for
Iodine solution	blue-black	Starch
Crystal violet	purple	Gram staining
Aniline sulfate	yellow	lignin
Methylene blue	blue	Nuclei
Hematoxylin and eosin (H&E)	H=dark blue/violet E=red/pink	H=Nuclei E=Proteins

Iodine stain

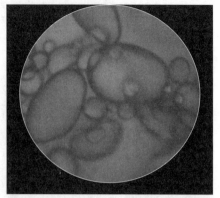
Iodine stains starch-containing organelles, such as **potato amyloplasts**, blue-black.

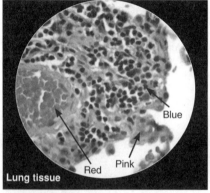
Blue
Red   Pink
Lung tissue

H&E stain is one of the most common histological stains. Nuclei stain dark blue, whereas proteins, extracellular material, and red blood cells stain pink or red.

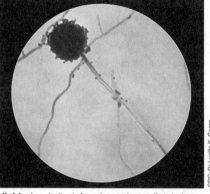

Viable (or vital) **stains** do not immediately harm living cells. **Trypan blue** is a vital stain that stains dead cells blue but is excluded by live cells. It is also used to study fungal hyphae.

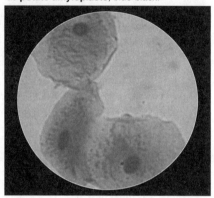
CDC: Dr Lucille K. Georg

Methylene blue is a common temporary stain for animal cells, such as these **cheek cells**. It stains DNA and so makes the **nuclei** more visible. It is distinct from methyl blue, a histological stain.

How to apply a simple stain

If a specimen is already mounted, a drop of stain can be placed at one end of the coverslip and drawn through using filter paper (below). Water can be drawn through in the same way to remove excess stain.

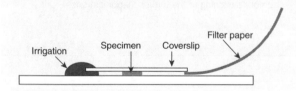
Irrigation   Specimen   Coverslip   Filter paper

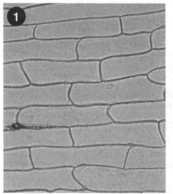
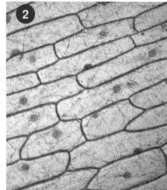

The light micrographs 1 and 2 (above) illustrate how the use of a stain can enhance certain structures. The left image (1) is unstained and only the cell wall is easily visible. Adding iodine (2) makes the cell wall and nuclei stand out.

1. What is the main purpose of using a stain? _To highlight specific structures_

2. What is the difference between a viable and non-viable stain? _Viable stains can be applied to alive specimens, non-viable cannot_

3. Identify a stain that would be appropriate for distinguishing each of the following:

   (a) Live vs dead cells: _Trypan blue_   (c) Lignin in a plant root section: _Aniline sulfate_

   (b) Red blood cells in a tissue preparation: _H & E_   (d) Nuclei in cheek cells: _Methylene blue_

© 2015 **BIOZONE** International
ISBN: 978-1-927309-13-1
Photocopying Prohibited

Key Idea: Electron microscopes use the short wavelengths of electrons to produce high resolution images of extremely small objects.

Electron microscopes (EMs) use a beam of electrons, instead of light, to produce an image. The higher resolution of EMs is due to the shorter wavelengths of electrons. There are two basic types of electron microscope: **scanning electron microscopes** (SEM) and **transmission electron microscopes** (TEM). In SEMs, the electrons are bounced off the surface of an object to produce detailed images of the external appearance. TEMs produce very clear images of specially prepared thin sections.

Transmission electron microscope (TEM)

The transmission electron microscope is used to view extremely thin sections of material. Electrons pass through the specimen and are scattered. Magnetic lenses focus the image onto a fluorescent screen or photographic plate. The sections are so thin that they have to be prepared with a special machine, called an ultramicrotome, which can cut wafers to just 30 thousandths of a millimetre thick. It can magnify several hundred thousand times.

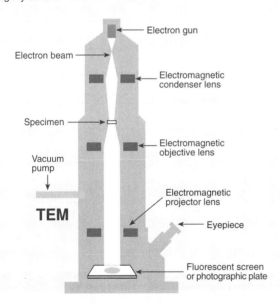

TEM — labels: Electron gun, Electron beam, Electromagnetic condenser lens, Specimen, Vacuum pump, Electromagnetic objective lens, Electromagnetic projector lens, Eyepiece, Fluorescent screen or photographic plate

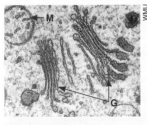

TEM photo showing the Golgi (**G**) and a mitochondrion (**M**).

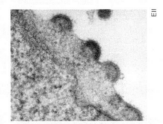

Three HIV viruses budding out of a human lymphocyte (TEM).

Scanning electron microscope (SEM)

The scanning electron microscope scans a sample with a beam of primary electrons, which knocks electrons from the sample's surface. These secondary electrons are picked up by a collector, amplified, and transmitted onto a viewing screen or photographic plate, producing a 3-D image. A microscope of this power easily obtains clear images of very small organisms such as bacteria, and small particles such as viruses. The image produced is of the outside surface only.

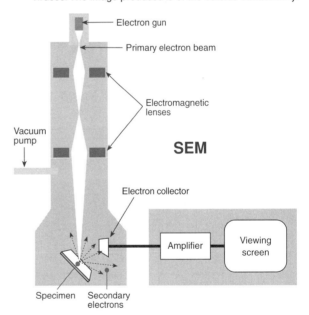

SEM — labels: Electron gun, Primary electron beam, Electromagnetic lenses, Vacuum pump, Electron collector, Amplifier, Viewing screen, Specimen, Secondary electrons

SEM photo of stoma and epidermal cells on the upper surface of a leaf.

Image of hair louse clinging to two hairs on a Hooker's sealion (SEM).

	Light microscope	Transmission electron microscope (TEM)	Scanning electron microscope (SEM)
Radiation source:	light	electrons	electrons
Wavelength:	400-700 nm	0.005 nm	0.005 nm
Lenses:	glass	electromagnetic	electromagnetic
Specimen:	living or non-living supported on glass slide	non-living supported on a small copper grid in a vacuum	non-living supported on a metal disc in a vacuum
Maximum resolution:	200 nm	1 nm	10 nm
Maximum magnification:	1500 x	250 000 x	100 000 x
Stains:	coloured dyes	impregnated with heavy metals	coated with carbon or gold
Type of image:	coloured, surface or section	monochrome, section	monochrome, surface only

1. Explain why electron microscopes are able to resolve much greater detail than a light microscope:

   Instead of light, electron microscopes use beams of electrons with shorter wavelengths

2. Which type of microscope [TEM, SEM, compound light microscope, or dissecting microscope] would you use for each of the following scenarios. Explain your choice in each case:

   (a) Distinguishing extinct plant species on the basis of pollen surface features: _____

   (b) Resolving the ultrastructure of a chloroplast: _____

   (c) Performing a count of white blood cells from the blood of a person with an infection: _____

   (d) Counting the heart rate and rate of limb beating in a water flea (*Daphnia*): _____

3. Identify which type of electron microscope (SEM or TEM) or optical microscope (compound light microscope or dissecting) was used to produce each of the images in the photos below (A-H):

Cardiac muscle

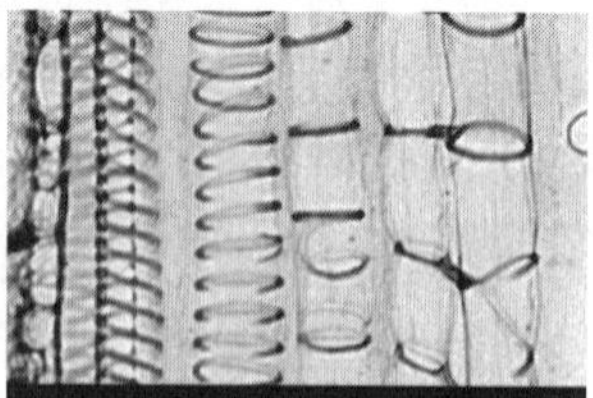

Plant vascular tissue

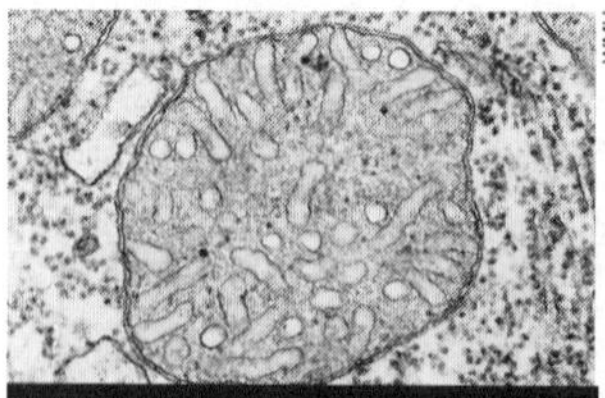

Mitochondrion

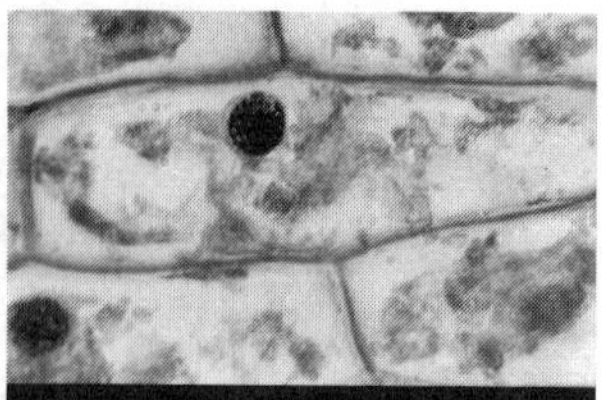

Plant epidermal cells

A _____ B _____ C _____ D _____

Head louse

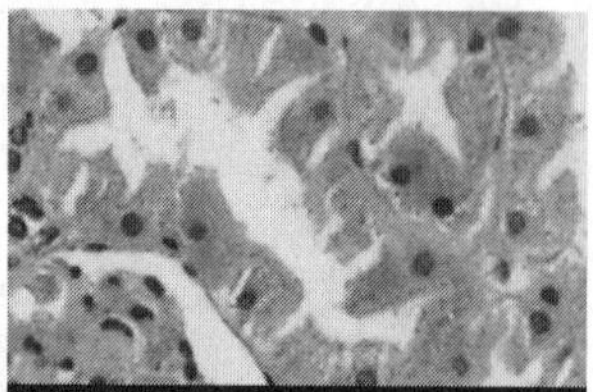

Kidney cells

Alderfly larva

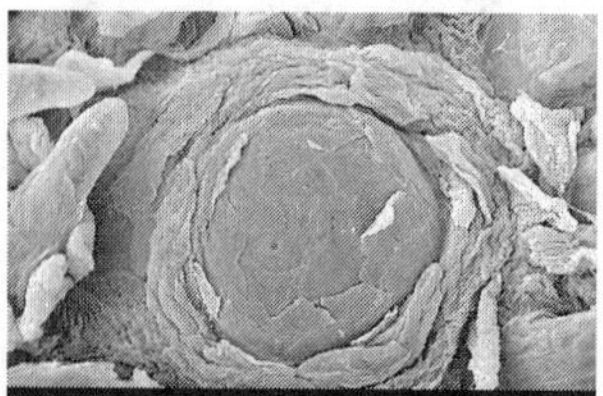

Tongue papilla

E _____ F _____ G _____ H _____

© 2015 BIOZONE International
ISBN: 978-1-927309-13-1
Photocopying Prohibited

33 Measuring and Counting Using a Microscope

Key Idea: Graticules make it possible to measure cell size. Haemocytometers are used to count the number of cells. Measuring and counting objects to be viewed under a microscope requires precisely marked measuring equipment.

Two common pieces of equipment are the graticule and the haemocytometer. A graticule can be used to measure the size of an object whereas a haemocytometer is used to count the number of cells in a set area or volume.

Measuring cell size

A graticule is a scale placed in the eyepiece of a microscope. It is usually about 1 mm long and divided into 100 equal units. A graticule is used in combination with a stage micrometer to work out the size of an object being viewed. The stage micrometer is a slide with a scale that is exactly 1 mm long and also divided into 100 divisions (so that each division is 0.01 mm) and is placed on the microscope stage. The stage micrometer allows the graticule to be calibrated so that a precise scale can be calculated at each magnification.

The scale on the graticule is lined up with the stage micrometer. The number of graticule divisions between the divisions of the stage micrometer can then be read off. In the example right, each division of the stage micrometer is equal to four large divisions of the graticule. Each large division of the graticule is therefore 2.5×10^{-3} mm at 400x magnification.

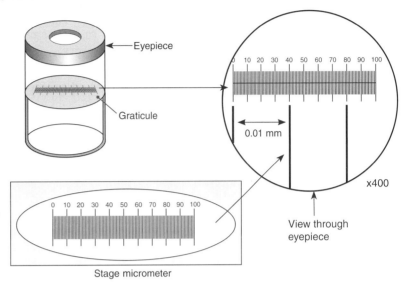

Stage micrometer

Counting cells

Microscopes can be used as a tool to count cells or other small objects (e.g pollen grains). By counting the number of cells in a known area, the total number of cells in a larger area can be calculated. A haemocytometer is commonly used to count cells viewed with a light microscope. It is a simple slide with precisely etched lines forming a grid and was developed for counting blood cells. There are a number of types of haemocytometer, including the Improved Neubauer, shown below. The slide holds a coverslip 0.1 mm above the surface of the grid, allowing volume to be calculated. The central counting grid is divided into 25 large squares, each of which is further divided into 16 squares.

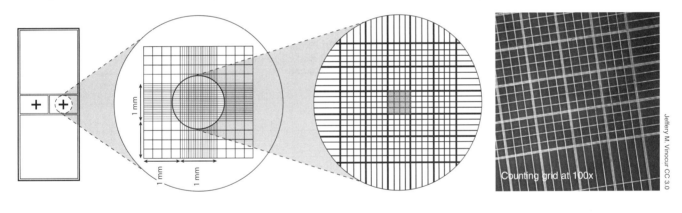

Counting grid at 100x

Jeffery M. Vinocur CC 3.0

1. A student using the graticule scale shown at the top of this page found a cell to be 56 divisions wide. Calculate the width of the cell in mm and in µm:

   _____

2. A second student grew yeast cells in 5 cm^3 of nutrient solution. The student used the haemocytometer shown above to count the number of yeast cells each day for 3 days.

   (a) Calculate the area and volume of the grid shown in blue: Area: _____ Volume: _____

   (b) The student counted yeast cells in the central blue grid. Complete the table below based on the counts obtained:

	Day 1	Day 2	Day 3
Number of cells counted	4	9	17
Cells in 5 cm^3			

3. A botanist wished to know the number of pollen grains produced per anther by a flower with eight anthers. She cut the anthers and placed them in 3 cm^3 of distilled water, shaking the mix vigorously. Using a haemocytometer she counted 6 grains in the large central counting grid (1 x 1 mm). Calculate the total number of pollen grains produced **per anther**:

   _____

LINK
34 DATA

34 Calculating Linear Magnification

Key Idea: Magnification is how much larger an object appears compared to its actual size. Magnification can be calculated from the ratio of image size to object size.

Microscopes produce an enlarged (magnified) image of an object allowing it to be observed in greater detail than is possible with the naked eye. **Magnification** refers to the number of times larger an object appears compared to its actual size. Linear magnification is calculated by taking a ratio of the image height to the object's actual height. If this ratio is greater than one, the image is enlarged. If it is less than one, it is reduced. To calculate magnification, all measurements are converted to the same units. Often, you will be asked to calculate an object's actual size, in which case you will be told the size of the object and the magnification.

Calculating linear magnification: a worked example

1.0 mm

1 Measure the body length of the bed bug image (right). Your measurement should be 40 mm (*not* including the body hairs and antennae).

2 Measure the length of the scale line marked 1.0 mm. You will find it is 10 mm long. The magnification of the scale line can be calculated using equation 1 (below right).

The magnification of the scale line is **10** (10 mm / 1 mm)

NB: The magnification of the bed bug image will also be 10x because the scale line and image are magnified to the same degree.

3 Calculate the actual (real) size of the bed bug using equation 2 (right):

The actual size of the bed bug is **4 mm** (40 mm / 10 x magnification)

Microscopy Equations

1. $\text{Magnification} = \dfrac{\text{measured size of the object}}{\text{actual size of the object}}$

2. $\text{Actual object size} = \dfrac{\text{size of the image}}{\text{magnification}}$

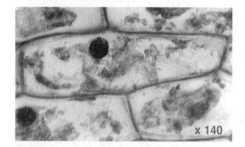

x 140

1. The bright field microscopy image on the left is of onion epidermal cells. The measured length of the onion cell in the centre of the photograph is 52 000 μm (52 mm). The image has been magnified 140 x. Calculate the actual size of the cell:

$140 = \dfrac{52000}{actual}$

$actual = \dfrac{52000}{140} = 371 \mu m$

2. The image of the flea (left) has been captured using light microscopy.

(a) Calculate the magnification using the scale line on the image:

Mag =

(b) The body length of the flea is indicated by a line. Measure along the line and calculate the actual length of the flea:

0.5 mm

3. The image size of the *E.coli* cell (left) is 43 mm, and its actual size is 2 μm. Using this information, calculate the magnification of the image:

© 2015 **BIOZONE** International
ISBN: 978-1-927309-13-1
Photocopying Prohibited

Key Idea: All living organisms are composed of cells. Cells are broadly classified as prokaryotic or eukaryotic.

The cell theory is a fundamental idea of biology. This idea, that all living things are composed of cells, developed over many years and is strongly linked to the invention and refinement of the microscope in the 1600s.

The cell theory

The idea that cells are fundamental units of life is part of the cell theory. The basic principles of the theory are:

► All living things are composed of cells and cell products.

► New cells are formed only by the division of pre-existing cells.

► The cell contains inherited information (genes) that are used as instructions for growth, functioning, and development.

► The cell is the functioning unit of life; all chemical reactions of life take place within cells.

All cells show the functions of life

Cells use food (e.g. glucose) to maintain a stable internal environment, grow, reproduce, and produce wastes. The sum total of all the chemical reactions that sustain life is called metabolism.

Movement
Respiration
Sensitivity
Growth
Reproduction
Excretion
Nutrition

Living things

Prokaryotic (bacterial) cells

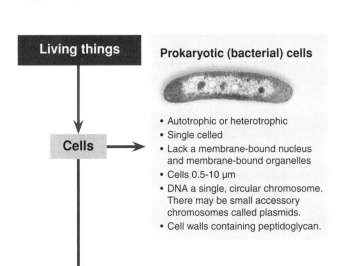

Cells

- Autotrophic or heterotrophic
- Single celled
- Lack a membrane-bound nucleus and membrane-bound organelles
- Cells 0.5-10 µm
- DNA a single, circular chromosome. There may be small accessory chromosomes called plasmids.
- Cell walls containing peptidoglycan.

Viruses are non-cellular

- Non-cellular.
- Typical size range: 20-300 nm.
- Contain no cytoplasm or organelles.
- No chromosome, just RNA or DNA strands.
- Enclosed in a protein coat.
- Depend on cells for metabolism and reproduction (replication).

Influenzavirus

Eukaryotic cells

- Cells 30-150 µm • Membrane-bound nucleus and membrane-bound organelles • Linear chromosomes

Plant cells
- Exist as part of multicellular organism with specialisation of cells into many types.
- Autotrophic (make their own food): photosynthetic cells with chloroplasts.
- Cell walls of cellulose.

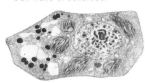

Generalised plant cell

Animal cells
- Exist as part of multicellular organism with specialisation of cells into many types.
- Lack cell walls.
- Heterotrophic (rely on other organisms for food).

White blood cell

Protoctist cells
- Mainly single-celled or exist as cell colonies.
- Some are autotrophic and carry out photosynthesis.
- Some are heterotrophic.

Amoeba cell

Fungal cells
- Rarely exist as discrete cells, except for some unicellular forms (e.g. yeasts)
- Plant-like, but lack chlorophyll.
- Rigid cell walls containing chitin.
- Heterotrophic.

Yeast cell

1. What are the characteristic features of a prokaryotic cell? _Single celled, no membrane bound organelles, single chromosomal DNA, peptidoglycan cell membran_

2. What are the characteristic features of a eukaryotic cell? _____

3. Why are viruses considered to be non-cellular (non-living)? _They have no chromosomes or organelles, only strands of DNA_

LINK
WEB

213 **35** KNOW

36 Cell Sizes

Key Idea: Cells vary in size (2-100 µm), with prokaryotic cells being approximately 10 times smaller than eukaryotic cells. Cells can only be seen properly when viewed through the magnifying lenses of a microscope. The images below show a variety of cell types, including a multicellular microscopic animal and a virus (non-cellular) for comparison. For each of these images, note the scale and relate this to the type of microscopy used.

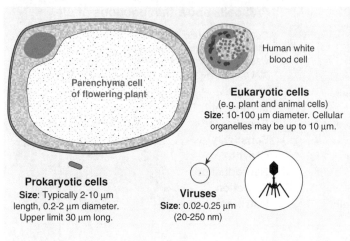

Parenchyma cell of flowering plant

Human white blood cell

Eukaryotic cells
(e.g. plant and animal cells)
Size: 10-100 µm diameter. Cellular organelles may be up to 10 µm.

Prokaryotic cells
Size: Typically 2-10 µm length, 0.2-2 µm diameter. Upper limit 30 µm long.

Viruses
Size: 0.02-0.25 µm (20-250 nm)

Unit of length (international system)

Unit	Metres	Equivalent
1 metre (m)	1 m	= 1000 millimetres
1 millimetre (mm)	10^{-3} m	= 1000 micrometres
1 micrometre (µm)	10^{-6} m	= 1000 nanometres
1 nanometre (nm)	10^{-9} m	= 1000 picometres

Micrometres are sometime referred to as microns. Smaller structures are usually measured in nanometres (nm) e.g. molecules (1 nm) and plasma membrane thickness (10 nm).

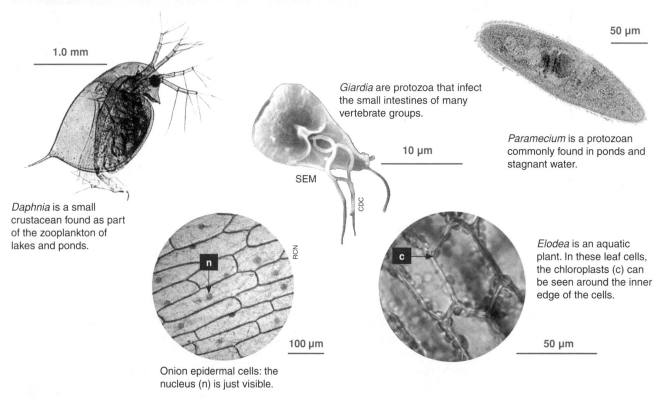

1.0 mm

50 µm

Giardia are protozoa that infect the small intestines of many vertebrate groups.

10 µm

SEM

Paramecium is a protozoan commonly found in ponds and stagnant water.

Daphnia is a small crustacean found as part of the zooplankton of lakes and ponds.

RCN

CDC

100 µm

Onion epidermal cells: the nucleus (n) is just visible.

Elodea is an aquatic plant. In these leaf cells, the chloroplasts (c) can be seen around the inner edge of the cells.

50 µm

1. Using the measurement scales provided on each of the photographs above, determine the longest dimension (length or diameter) of the cell/animal/organelle indicated in µm and mm. Attach your working:

   (a) *Daphnia*: _____ µm _____ mm   (d) *Elodea* leaf cell: _____ µm _____ mm

   (b) *Giardia*: _____ µm _____ mm   (e) Chloroplast: _____ µm _____ mm

   (c) Nucleus _____ µm _____ mm   (f) *Paramecium*: _____ µm _____ mm

2. (a) List a-f in question 1 in order of size, from the smallest to the largest:

   _____

   (b) Study your ruler. Which one of the above could you see with your unaided eye?_____

3. Calculate the equivalent length in millimetres (mm) of the following measurements:

   (a) 0.25 µm: _____   (b) 450 µm: _____   (c) 200 nm: _____

WEB 36   LINK 34

DATA

© 2015 **BIOZONE** International
ISBN: 978-1-927309-13-1
Photocopying Prohibited

37 Prokaryotic Cells

Key Idea: Prokaryotic cells lack many of the features of eukaryotic cells, including membrane-bound organelles. Bacterial (prokaryotic) cells are much smaller than eukaryotic cells and lack many eukaryotic features, such as a distinct nucleus and membrane-bound cellular organelles. The cell wall is an important feature. It is a complex, multi-layered structure and has a role in the organism's ability to cause disease. A generalised prokaryote, *E. coli*, is shown below.

E. coli structure

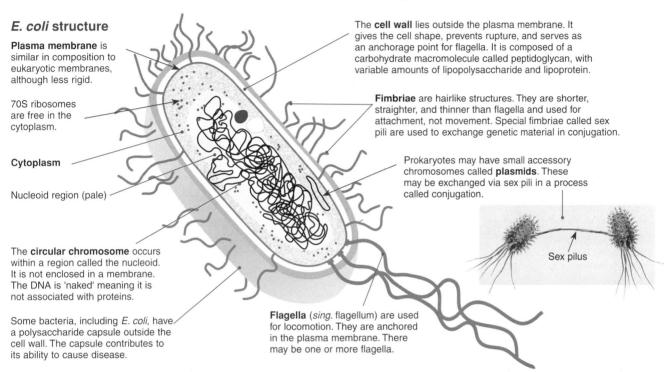

Plasma membrane is similar in composition to eukaryotic membranes, although less rigid.

70S ribosomes are free in the cytoplasm.

Cytoplasm

Nucleoid region (pale)

The **circular chromosome** occurs within a region called the nucleoid. It is not enclosed in a membrane. The DNA is 'naked' meaning it is not associated with proteins.

Some bacteria, including *E. coli*, have a polysaccharide capsule outside the cell wall. The capsule contributes to its ability to cause disease.

The **cell wall** lies outside the plasma membrane. It gives the cell shape, prevents rupture, and serves as an anchorage point for flagella. It is composed of a carbohydrate macromolecule called peptidoglycan, with variable amounts of lipopolysaccharide and lipoprotein.

Fimbriae are hairlike structures. They are shorter, straighter, and thinner than flagella and used for attachment, not movement. Special fimbriae called sex pili are used to exchange genetic material in conjugation.

Prokaryotes may have small accessory chromosomes called **plasmids**. These may be exchanged via sex pili in a process called conjugation.

Sex pilus

Flagella (*sing.* flagellum) are used for locomotion. They are anchored in the plasma membrane. There may be one or more flagella.

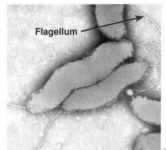

Flagellum

A spiral shape is one of four bacterial shapes (the others being rods, commas, and spheres). These *Campylobacter* cells also have flagella.

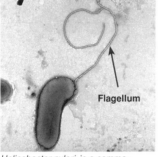

Flagellum

Helicobacter pylori, is a comma-shaped vibrio bacterium that causes stomach ulcers in humans. It moves by means of polar flagella.

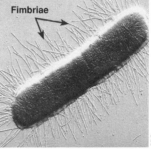

Fimbriae

Escherichia coli is a rod-shaped bacterium, common in the human gut. The fimbriae surrounding the cell are used to adhere to the intestinal wall.

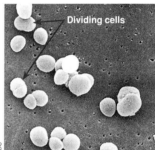

Dividing cells

Bacteria usually divide by binary fission. During this process, DNA is copied and the cell splits into two cells, as in these round (cocci) cells.

1. Describe three features distinguishing prokaryotic cells from eukaryotic cells:

   (a) *Prokaryotes do not have nuclei*

   (b) *Prokaryotes are much smaller*

   (c) *Mitochondria are bigger in eukaryotes*

2. (a) Describe the function of flagella in bacteria: *They help with movement*

   (b) Explain how fimbriae differ structurally and functionally from flagella: *They are shorter, straighter and thinner. They are used for attachment*

3. Describe the location and general composition of the bacterial cell wall: _____

   _____

   _____

© 2015 **BIOZONE** International
ISBN: 978-1-927309-13-1
Photocopying Prohibited

LINK 213   LINK 38   LINK 35   WEB 37

KN

38 Unicellular Eukaryotes

Key Idea: Most of the eukaryote kingdom Protoctista is made up of unicellular organisms. They show great variation in the ways in which they carry out the functions of life.

Unicellular (single-celled) **eukaryotes** make up most of the kingdom, Protoctista. They are found almost anywhere there is water, including within larger organisms (as parasites or symbionts). The protoctists are a diverse group, and are not a natural group in modern classifications. They show some features typical of generalised eukaryotic cells, as well as specialised features. Note that even within the genera below there is considerable variation in size and appearance. *Amoeba* and *Paramecium* are both **heterotrophic**, ingesting food, which accumulates inside a **vacuole**. *Chlamydomonas* is an autotrophic algae using light to produce sugars.

Amoeba

Size: up to 800 x 400 μm
Habitat: Most moist habitats, including soil

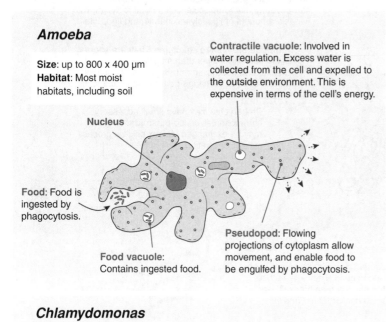

Nucleus

Contractile vacuole: Involved in water regulation. Excess water is collected from the cell and expelled to the outside environment. This is expensive in terms of the cell's energy.

Food: Food is ingested by phagocytosis.

Food vacuole: Contains ingested food.

Pseudopod: Flowing projections of cytoplasm allow movement, and enable food to be engulfed by phagocytosis.

Chlamydomonas

Size: 20 x 10 μm
Habitat: Freshwater

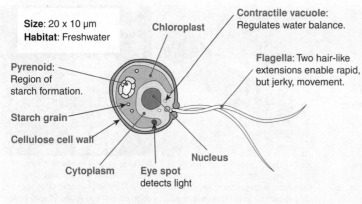

Chloroplast

Contractile vacuole: Regulates water balance.

Flagella: Two hair-like extensions enable rapid, but jerky, movement.

Pyrenoid: Region of starch formation.

Starch grain

Cellulose cell wall

Nucleus

Cytoplasm

Eye spot detects light

Paramecium

Size: 240 x 80 μm
Habitat: Freshwater, brackish, marine

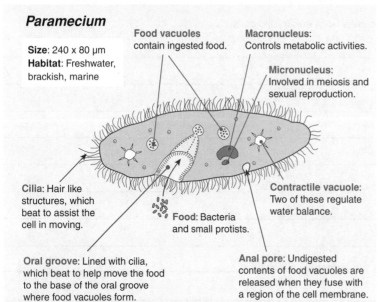

Food vacuoles contain ingested food.

Macronucleus: Controls metabolic activities.

Micronucleus: Involved in meiosis and sexual reproduction.

Cilia: Hair like structures, which beat to assist the cell in moving.

Food: Bacteria and small protists.

Contractile vacuole: Two of these regulate water balance.

Oral groove: Lined with cilia, which beat to help move the food to the base of the oral groove where food vacuoles form.

Anal pore: Undigested contents of food vacuoles are released when they fuse with a region of the cell membrane.

1. Summarise the features and life functions of each of the protoctistan genera shown left:

   (a) *Amoeba*

   Nutrition: _____

   Movement: _____

   Osmoregulation: _____

   Cell wall: present / absent (delete one)

   Eye spot: present / absent (delete one)

   (b) *Chlamydomonas*

   Nutrition: _____

   Movement: _____

   Osmoregulation: _____

   Cell wall: present / absent (delete one)

   Eye spot: present / absent (delete one)

   (c) *Paramecium*

   Nutrition: _____

   Movement: _____

   Osmoregulation: _____

   Cell wall: present / absent (delete one)

   Eye spot: present / absent (delete one)

2. List these three organisms in order of size (largest first):

   _____

   _____

3. Why would an autotroph have an eye spot?

   _____

   _____

   _____

4. Why would freshwater protoctists require a mechanism for constantly expelling water?

   _____

   _____

   _____

© 2015 **BIOZONE** International
ISBN: 978-1-927309-13-1
Photocopying Prohibited

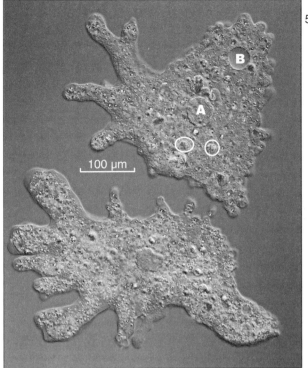

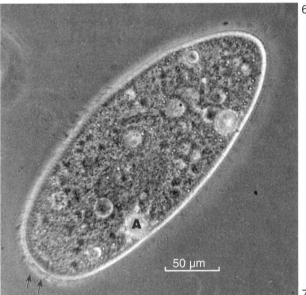

5. (a) Identify the structure labelled **A**:

_____

(b) Circle the same structure in the unlabelled specimen:

(c) What feature(s) helped you identify this organelle?

_____

(d) Identify the structure labelled **B**:_____

_____

(e) Describe the function of this structure: _____

_____

_____

(f) Identify the structures circled: _____

_____

(g) Describe the function of these structures: _____

_____

6. (a) Identify this organism:_____

(b) What feature(s) helped you make your identification?

_____

_____

(c) Identify the organelle labelled **A**:_____

_____

(d) Circle another organelle with the same function:

(e) Identify the structures indicated by the arrows and describe their purpose:

_____

_____

7. (a) Identify the organelle labelled **A**: _____

(b) Describe the function of this organelle: _____

_____

(c) Identify the organelle labelled **B**. What is the dark granular material you can see?

_____

(d) Identify the ribbon-like structures in this image, and explain how you came to your conclusion about what they are:

_____

_____

_____

_____

_____

Cell wall

Starch granule

Eye spot

Vacuole

Chlamydomonas

TEM

istock

Barfooz CC 3.0

Dartmouth College

39 Plant Cells

Key Idea: Plant cells are eukaryotic cells. They have features in common with animal cells, but also several unique features. Eukaryotic cells have a similar basic structure, although they may vary tremendously in size, shape, and function. Certain features are common to almost all eukaryotic cells, including their three main regions: a **nucleus**, surrounded by a watery **cytoplasm**, which is itself enclosed by the **plasma membrane**. Plant cells are enclosed in a cellulose cell wall, which gives them a regular, uniform appearance. The cell wall protects the cell, maintains its shape, and prevents excessive water uptake. It provides rigidity to plant structures but permits the free passage of materials into and out of the cell.

Generalised Plant Cell

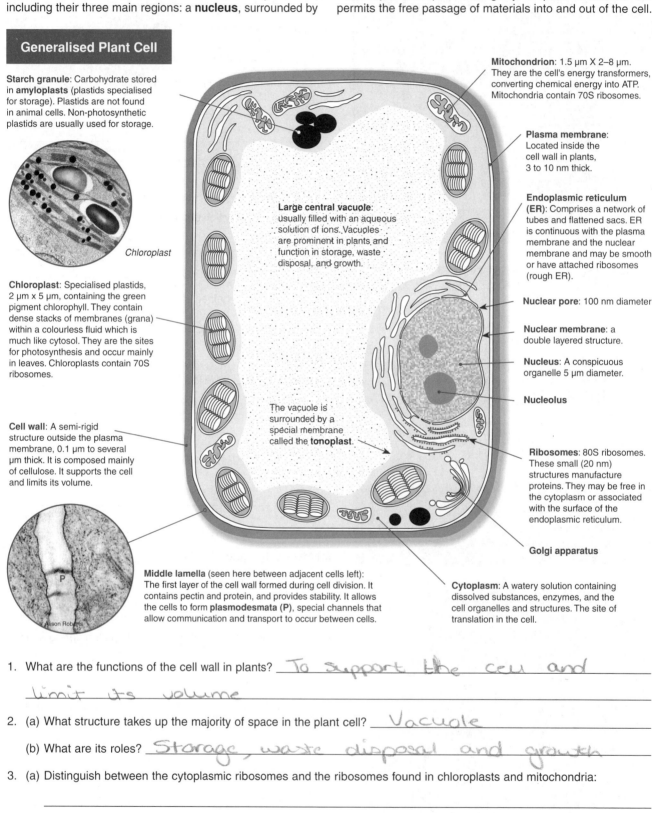

Starch granule: Carbohydrate stored in **amyloplasts** (plastids specialised for storage). Plastids are not found in animal cells. Non-photosynthetic plastids are usually used for storage.

Chloroplast

Chloroplast: Specialised plastids, 2 µm x 5 µm, containing the green pigment chlorophyll. They contain dense stacks of membranes (grana) within a colourless fluid which is much like cytosol. They are the sites for photosynthesis and occur mainly in leaves. Chloroplasts contain 70S ribosomes.

Cell wall: A semi-rigid structure outside the plasma membrane, 0.1 µm to several µm thick. It is composed mainly of cellulose. It supports the cell and limits its volume.

Mitochondrion: 1.5 µm X 2–8 µm. They are the cell's energy transformers, converting chemical energy into ATP. Mitochondria contain 70S ribosomes.

Plasma membrane: Located inside the cell wall in plants, 3 to 10 nm thick.

Large central vacuole: usually filled with an aqueous solution of ions. Vacuoles are prominent in plants and function in storage, waste disposal, and growth.

Endoplasmic reticulum (ER): Comprises a network of tubes and flattened sacs. ER is continuous with the plasma membrane and the nuclear membrane and may be smooth or have attached ribosomes (rough ER).

Nuclear pore: 100 nm diameter

Nuclear membrane: a double layered structure.

Nucleus: A conspicuous organelle 5 µm diameter.

Nucleolus

The vacuole is surrounded by a special membrane called the **tonoplast**.

Ribosomes: 80S ribosomes. These small (20 nm) structures manufacture proteins. They may be free in the cytoplasm or associated with the surface of the endoplasmic reticulum.

Golgi apparatus

Middle lamella (seen here between adjacent cells left): The first layer of the cell wall formed during cell division. It contains pectin and protein, and provides stability. It allows the cells to form **plasmodesmata (P)**, special channels that allow communication and transport to occur between cells.

Cytoplasm: A watery solution containing dissolved substances, enzymes, and the cell organelles and structures. The site of translation in the cell.

1. What are the functions of the cell wall in plants? _To support the cell and limit its volume_

2. (a) What structure takes up the majority of space in the plant cell? _Vacuole_

   (b) What are its roles? _Storage, waste disposal and growth_

3. (a) Distinguish between the cytoplasmic ribosomes and the ribosomes found in chloroplasts and mitochondria:

   _____

   (b) What might this suggest about the origins of these organelles? _____

   _____

4. Identify two structures in the diagram that are not found in animal cells: _Cell wall and vacuole_

WEB   LINK   LINK

KNOW 39 40 41

© 2015 **BIOZONE** International
ISBN: 978-1-927309-13-1
Photocopying Prohibited

40 Identifying Structures in a Plant Cell

Key Idea: The position and appearance of the organelles in an electron micrograph can be used to identify them.

1. Study the diagrams on the other pages in this chapter to familiarise yourself with the structures found in eukaryotic cells. Identify the 11 structures in the cell below using the following word list: *cytoplasm, smooth endoplasmic reticulum, mitochondrion, starch granule, chromosome, nucleus, vacuole, plasma membrane, cell wall, chloroplast, nuclear membrane*

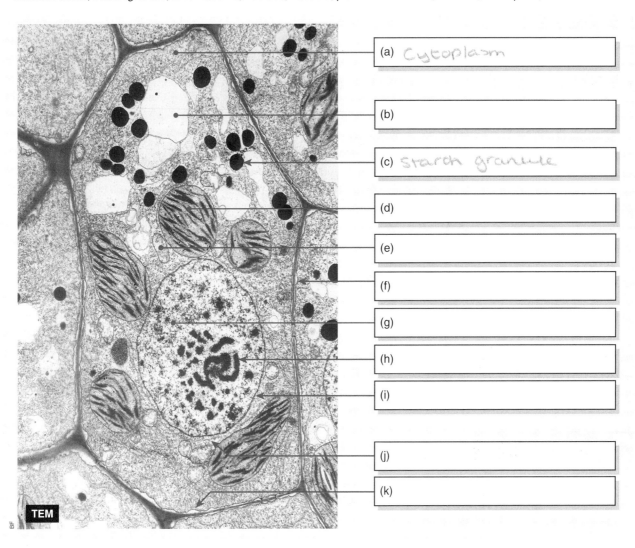

(a) Cytoplasm

(b)

(c) Starch granule

(d)

(e)

(f)

(g)

(h)

(i)

(j)

(k)

TEM

2. State how many cells, or parts of cells, are visible in the electron micrograph above: _____

3. Describe the features that identify this cell as a plant cell: ___Chloroplasts - Photosynthesis,___ ___Starch granules, vacuole, cell wall___ _____

4. (a) Explain where cytoplasm is found in the cell: _____

   (b) Describe what cytoplasm is made up of: _____

5. Describe two structures, pictured in the cell above, that are associated with storage:

   (a) ___Vacuole___ _____

   (b) _____

© 2015 **BIOZONE** International
ISBN: 978-1-927309-13-1
Photocopying Prohibited

LINK **46** LINK **39** WEB **40** KNOW

41 Animal Cells

Key Idea: Animal cells are eukaryotic cells. They have many features in common with plant cells, but also have a number of unique features.

Animal cells, unlike plant cells, do not have a regular shape. In fact, some animal cells (such as phagocytes) are able to alter their shape for various purposes (e.g. engulfing foreign material). The diagram below shows the structure and organelles of a liver cell. It contains organelles common to most relatively unspecialised human cells. Note the differences between this cell and the generalised plant cell. The plant cells activity provides further information on the organelles listed here but not described.

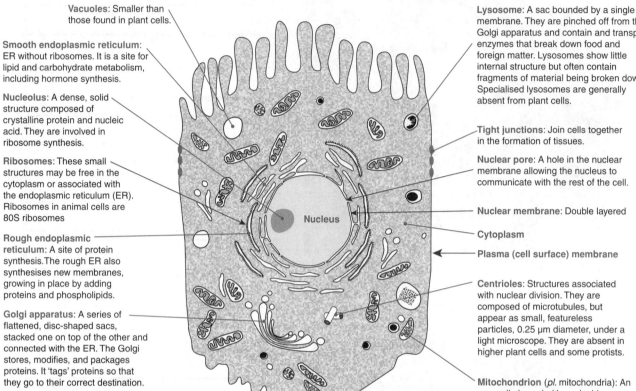

Vacuoles: Smaller than those found in plant cells.

Smooth endoplasmic reticulum: ER without ribosomes. It is a site for lipid and carbohydrate metabolism, including hormone synthesis.

Nucleolus: A dense, solid structure composed of crystalline protein and nucleic acid. They are involved in ribosome synthesis.

Ribosomes: These small structures may be free in the cytoplasm or associated with the endoplasmic reticulum (ER). Ribosomes in animal cells are 80S ribosomes

Rough endoplasmic reticulum: A site of protein synthesis. The rough ER also synthesises new membranes, growing in place by adding proteins and phospholipids.

Golgi apparatus: A series of flattened, disc-shaped sacs, stacked one on top of the other and connected with the ER. The Golgi stores, modifies, and packages proteins. It 'tags' proteins so that they go to their correct destination.

Lysosome: A sac bounded by a single membrane. They are pinched off from the Golgi apparatus and contain and transport enzymes that break down food and foreign matter. Lysosomes show little internal structure but often contain fragments of material being broken down. Specialised lysosomes are generally absent from plant cells.

Tight junctions: Join cells together in the formation of tissues.

Nuclear pore: A hole in the nuclear membrane allowing the nucleus to communicate with the rest of the cell.

Nuclear membrane: Double layered

Cytoplasm

Plasma (cell surface) membrane

Centrioles: Structures associated with nuclear division. They are composed of microtubules, but appear as small, featureless particles, 0.25 µm diameter, under a light microscope. They are absent in higher plant cells and some protists.

Mitochondrion (*pl*. mitochondria): An organelle bounded by a double membrane system. The number in a cell depends on its metabolic activity.

Nucleus

Generalised animal cell

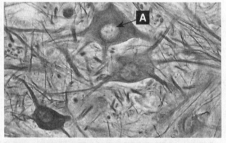

Neurones (nerve cells) in the spinal cord

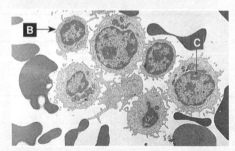

White blood cells and red blood cells (blood smear)

1. The two photomicrographs (left) show several types of animal cells. Identify the features indicated by the letters **A-C**:

   A: _____

   B: _____

   C: _____

2. White blood cells are mobile, phagocytic cells, whereas red blood cells are smaller than white blood cells and, in humans, lack a nucleus.

   (a) In the photomicrograph (lower, left), circle a white blood cell and a red blood cell:

   (b) With respect to the features that you can see, explain how you made your decision.

   _____

   _____

   _____

   _____

3. Name one structure or organelle present in generalised animal cells but absent from plant cells and describe its function:

_____

_____

Photos: EII

© 2015 **BIOZONE** International
ISBN: 978-1-927309-13-1
Photocopying Prohibited

42 Identifying Structures in an Animal Cell

Key Idea: The position of the organelles in an electron micrograph can result in variations in their appearance. Transmission electron microscopy (TEM) is the most frequently used technique for viewing cellular organelles.

When viewing TEMs, the cellular organelles may have quite different appearances depending on whether they are in transverse or longitudinal section.

1. Identify and label the structures in the animal cell below using the following list of terms: *cytoplasm, plasma membrane, rough endoplasmic reticulum, mitochondrion, nucleus, centriole, Golgi apparatus, lysosome*

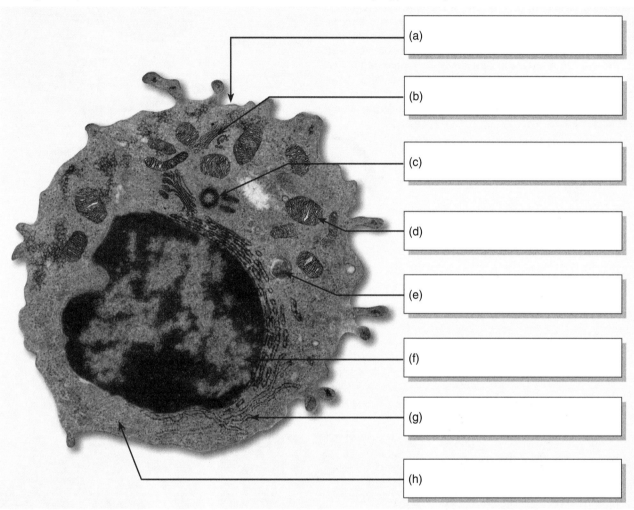

(a)

(b)

(c)

(d)

(e)

(f)

(g)

(h)

2. Which of the organelles in the EM above are obviously shown in both transverse and longitudinal section?

_____

3. Why do plants lack any of the mobile phagocytic cells typical of animal cells? _____

_____

_____

4. The animal cell pictured above is a lymphocyte. Describe the features that suggest to you that:

   (a) It has a role in producing and secreting proteins: _____

   _____

   (b) It is metabolically very active: _____

   _____

5. What features of the lymphocyte cell above identify it as eukaryotic? _____

_____

_____

© 2015 **BIOZONE** International
ISBN: 978-1-927309-13-1
Photocopying Prohibited

43 The Cell's Cytoskeleton

Key Idea: The cytoskeleton is a complex structure of tubules and fibres. It resists tension and so provides structural support to maintain the cell's shape.

The cell's cytoplasm is not a fluid filled space; it contains a complex network of fibres called the **cytoskeleton**. The cytoskeleton is made up of three proteinaceous elements: microfilaments, intermediate filaments, and microtubules. Each has a distinct size, structure, and protein composition, and a specific role in cytoskeletal function. Cilia and flagella are made up of microtubules and for this reason they are considered to be part of the cytoskeleton. The elements of the cytoskeleton are dynamic; they move and change to alter the cell's shape, move materials within the cell, and move the cell itself. This movement is achieved through the action of motor proteins, which transport material by 'walking' along cytoskeletal 'tracks', hydrolysing ATP at each step.

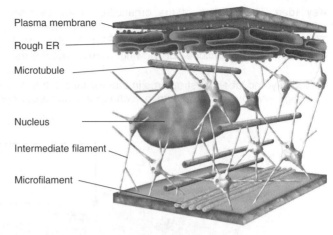

Plasma membrane
Rough ER
Microtubule
Nucleus
Intermediate filament
Microfilament

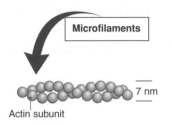

Microfilaments

7 nm

Actin subunit

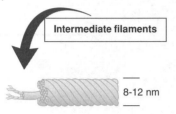

Intermediate filaments

8-12 nm

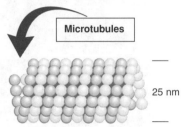

Microtubules

25 nm

	Microfilaments	Intermediate filaments	Microtubules
Protein subunits	Actin	Fibrous proteins, e.g. keratin	α and β tubulin dimers
Structure	Two intertwined strands	Fibres wound into thicker cables	Hollow tubes
Functions	• Maintain cell shape • Motility (pseudopodia) • Contraction (muscle) • Cytokinesis of cell division	• Maintain cell shape • Anchor nucleus and organelles	• Maintain cell shape • Motility (cilia and flagella) • Move chromosomes (spindle) • Move organelles

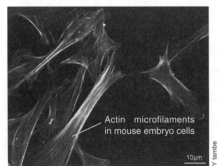

Actin microfilaments in mouse embryo cells

10µm

Y tambe

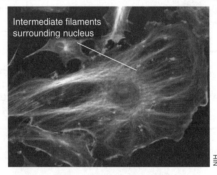

Intermediate filaments surrounding nucleus

NIH

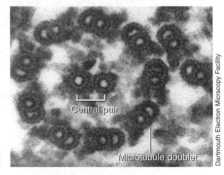

Central pair

Microtubule doublet

Dartmouth Electron Micrscopy Facility

Microfilaments are long polymers of the protein actin. Microfilaments can grow and shrink as actin subunits are added or taken away from either end. Networks of microfilaments form a matrix that helps to define the cell's shape. Actin microfilaments are also involved in cell division (during cytokinesis) and in muscle contraction.

Intermediate filaments can be composed of a number of different fibrous proteins and are defined by their size rather than composition. The protein subunits are wound into cables around 10 nm in diameter. Intermediate filaments form a dense network within and projecting from the nucleus, helping to anchor it in place.

Microtubules are the largest cytoskeletal components and grow or shrink in length as tubulin subunits are added or subtracted from one end. The are involved in movement of material within the cell and in moving the cell itself. This EM shows a cilia from *Chlamydomonas*, with the 9+2 arrangement of microtubular doublets.

1. Describe what all components of the cytoskeleton have in common: _____

2. Explain the importance of the cytoskeleton being a dynamic structure: _____

_____

3. Explain how the presence of a cytoskeleton could aid in directing the movement of materials within the cell:

_____

_____

© 2015 **BIOZONE** International
ISBN: 978-1-927309-13-1
Photocopying Prohibited

44 Packaging Proteins

Key Idea: Proteins destined for secretion are produced in the rough endoplasmic reticulum and transported in transport vesicles to the Golgi for processing. Vesicles containing mature proteins bud from the Golgi and may fuse with the plasma membrane to secrete the proteins or form lysosomes which help breakdown cells products.

The **Golgi** is made up of stacks of flattened membranes in the shape of curved sacs. At its *cis-* face, the Golgi receives transport vesicles from the ER. Transported substances are modified, stored and shipped from the *trans-* face to the surface of the cell or other destinations.

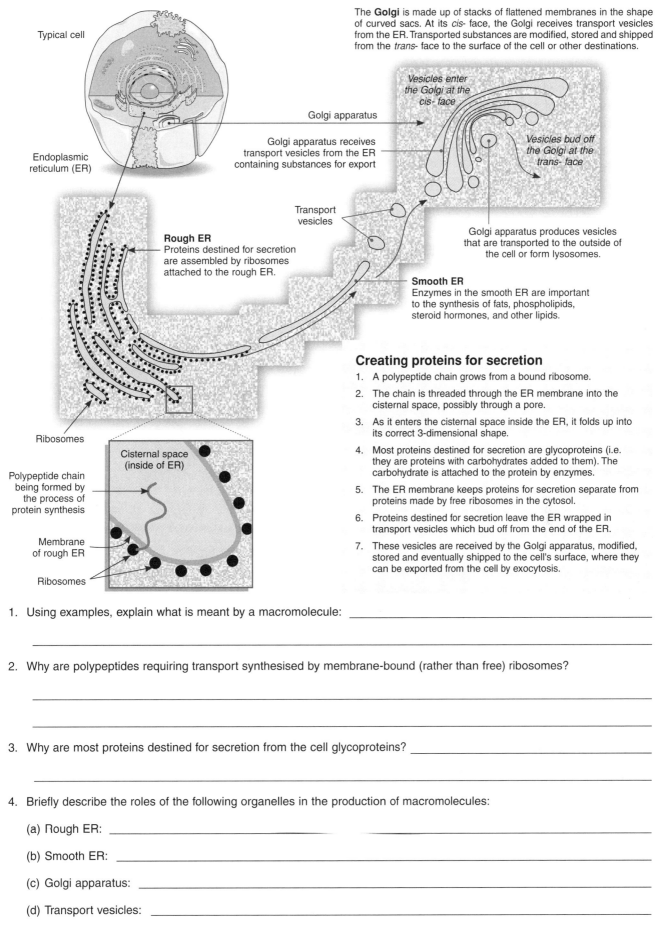

Typical cell

Endoplasmic reticulum (ER)

Golgi apparatus

Vesicles enter the Golgi at the *cis-* face

Golgi apparatus receives transport vesicles from the ER containing substances for export

Vesicles bud off the Golgi at the *trans-* face

Transport vesicles

Golgi apparatus produces vesicles that are transported to the outside of the cell or form lysosomes.

Rough ER
Proteins destined for secretion are assembled by ribosomes attached to the rough ER.

Smooth ER
Enzymes in the smooth ER are important to the synthesis of fats, phospholipids, steroid hormones, and other lipids.

Ribosomes

Polypeptide chain being formed by the process of protein synthesis

Membrane of rough ER

Ribosomes

Cisternal space (inside of ER)

Creating proteins for secretion

1. A polypeptide chain grows from a bound ribosome.
2. The chain is threaded through the ER membrane into the cisternal space, possibly through a pore.
3. As it enters the cisternal space inside the ER, it folds up into its correct 3-dimensional shape.
4. Most proteins destined for secretion are glycoproteins (i.e. they are proteins with carbohydrates added to them). The carbohydrate is attached to the protein by enzymes.
5. The ER membrane keeps proteins for secretion separate from proteins made by free ribosomes in the cytosol.
6. Proteins destined for secretion leave the ER wrapped in transport vesicles which bud off from the end of the ER.
7. These vesicles are received by the Golgi apparatus, modified, stored and eventually shipped to the cell's surface, where they can be exported from the cell by exocytosis.

1. Using examples, explain what is meant by a macromolecule: _____

_____

2. Why are polypeptides requiring transport synthesised by membrane-bound (rather than free) ribosomes?

_____

_____

3. Why are most proteins destined for secretion from the cell glycoproteins? _____

_____

4. Briefly describe the roles of the following organelles in the production of macromolecules:

   (a) Rough ER: _____   _____

   (b) Smooth ER: _____

   (c) Golgi apparatus: _____

   (d) Transport vesicles: _____

LINK 81   LINK 45   WEB 44   KNOW

45 Cell Structures and Organelles

Key Idea: Each type of organelle in a cell has a specific role. Not all cell types contain every type of organelle. The diagram below provides spaces for you to summarise

information about the organelles found in eukaryotic cells. The log scale of measurements (top of next page) illustrates the relative sizes of some cellular structures.

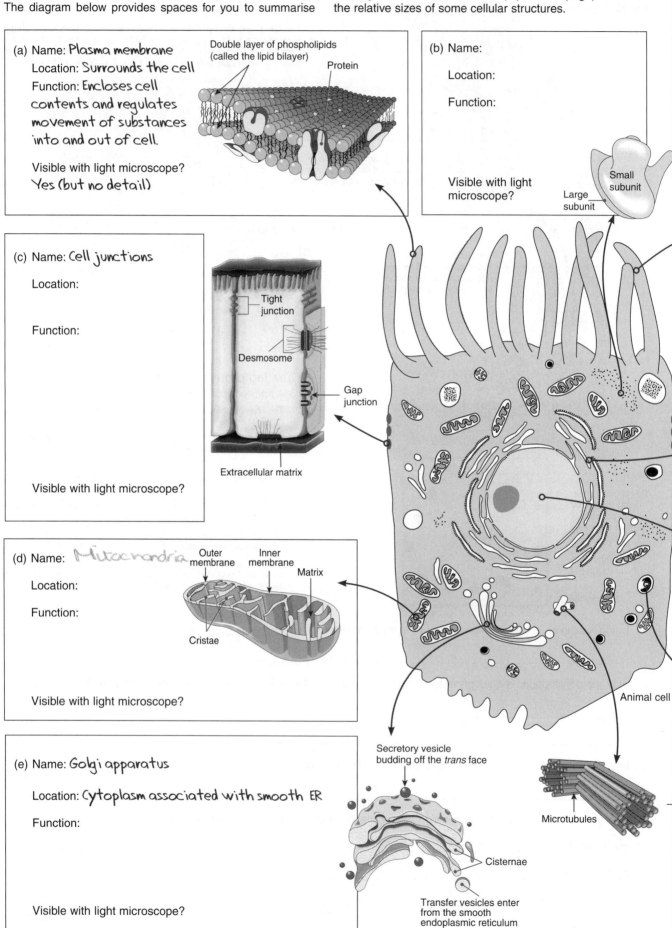

(a) Name: Plasma membrane

Location: Surrounds the cell

Function: Encloses cell contents and regulates movement of substances into and out of cell.

Visible with light microscope?
Yes (but no detail)

Double layer of phospholipids (called the lipid bilayer)
Protein

(b) Name:

Location:

Function:

Visible with light microscope?

Large subunit
Small subunit

(c) Name: Cell junctions

Location:

Function:

Visible with light microscope?

Tight junction
Desmosome
Gap junction
Extracellular matrix

(d) Name: Mitochondria

Location:

Function:

Visible with light microscope?

Outer membrane
Inner membrane
Matrix
Cristae

(e) Name: Golgi apparatus

Location: Cytoplasm associated with smooth ER

Function:

Visible with light microscope?

Secretory vesicle budding off the *trans* face
Cisternae
Transfer vesicles enter from the smooth endoplasmic reticulum

Microtubules

Animal cell

© 2015 **BIOZONE** International
ISBN: 978-1-927309-13-1
Photocopying Prohibited

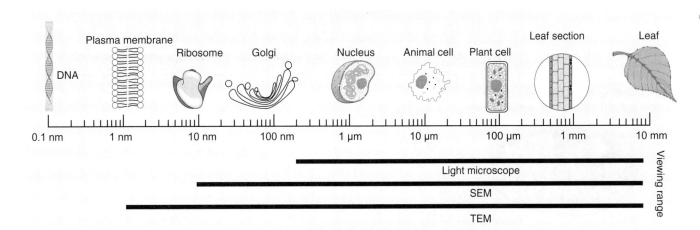

DNA | Plasma membrane | Ribosome | Golgi | Nucleus | Animal cell | Plant cell | Leaf section | Leaf

0.1 nm   1 nm   10 nm   100 nm   1 µm   10 µm   100 µm   1 mm   10 mm

Light microscope

SEM

TEM

Viewing range

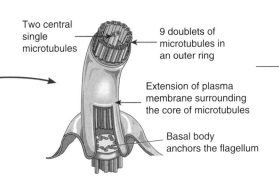

Two central single microtubules

9 doublets of microtubules in an outer ring

Extension of plasma membrane surrounding the core of microtubules

Basal body anchors the flagellum

(f) Name: Cilia and flagella (some eukaryotic cells).

Location:

Function:

Visible with light microscope?

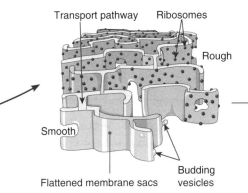

Transport pathway   Ribosomes

Rough

Smooth

Flattened membrane sacs

Budding vesicles

(g) Name: Smooth and rough endoplasmic reticulum

Location: Penetrates the whole cytoplasm

Function of smooth ER:

Function of rough ER:

Visible with light microscope?

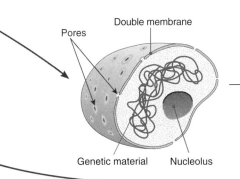

Double membrane

Pores

Genetic material   Nucleolus

(h) Name:

Location: Position is variable within a cell

Function:

Visible with light microscope?

(i) Name: Centrioles

Location: In cytoplasm next to nucleus

Function:

Visible with light microscope?

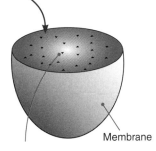

Membrane

Hydrolytic enzymes

(j) Name: Lysosome

Location:

Function:

Visible with light microscope?

© 2015 **BIOZONE** International
ISBN: 978-1-927309-13-1
Photocopying Prohibited

Plant cells share many organelles with animal cells, but they also have some structures and organelles that are unique.

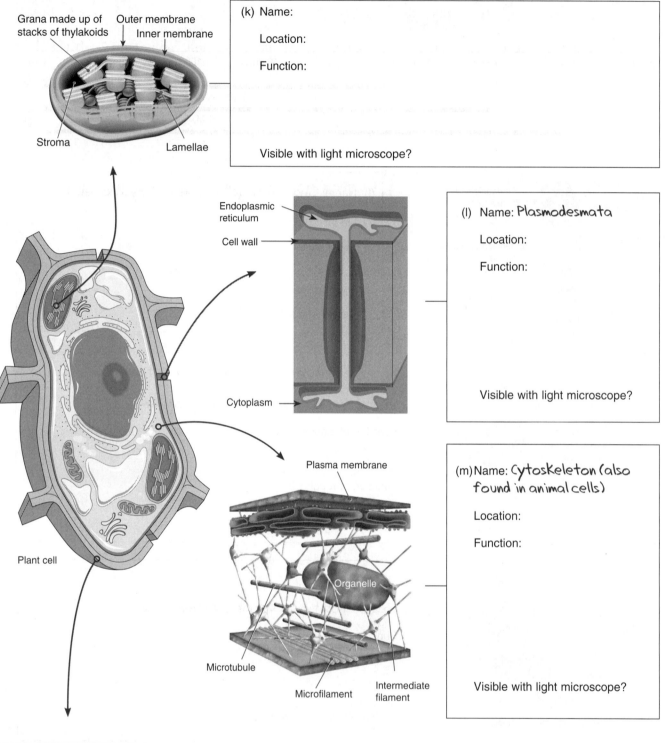

Grana made up of stacks of thylakoids
Outer membrane
Inner membrane
Stroma
Lamellae

(k) Name:

Location:

Function:

Visible with light microscope?

Endoplasmic reticulum
Cell wall
Cytoplasm

(l) Name: Plasmodesmata

Location:

Function:

Visible with light microscope?

Plasma membrane
Organelle
Microtubule
Microfilament
Intermediate filament

Plant cell

(m) Name: Cytoskeleton (also found in animal cells)

Location:

Function:

Visible with light microscope?

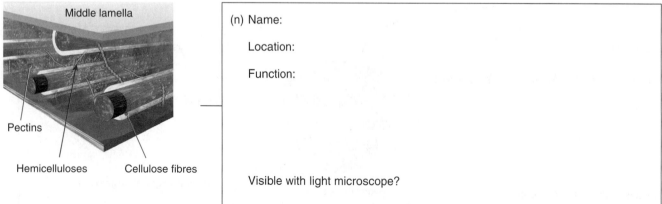

Middle lamella
Pectins
Hemicelluloses
Cellulose fibres

(n) Name:

Location:

Function:

Visible with light microscope?

46 Identifying Organelles

Key Idea: Cellular organelles can be identified in electron micrographs by their specific features.

Electron microscopes produce a magnified image at high resolution (distinguish between close together but separate objects). The transmission electron microscope (TEM) images below show the ultrastructure of some organelles.

1. (a) Name the circled organelle: _____

   (b) Which kind of cell(s) would this organelle be found in?

   _____

   (c) Describe the function of this organelle: _____

   _____

   _____

   _____

2. (a) Name this organelle (arrowed): _____

   (b) State which kind of cell(s) this organelle would be found in:

   _____

   (c) Describe the function of this organelle: _____

   _____

   _____

3. (a) Name the large, circular organelle: _____

   (b) State which kind of cell(s) this organelle would be found in:

   _____

   (c) Describe the function of this organelle: _____

   _____

   _____

   (d) Label **two** regions that can be seen **inside** this organelle.

4. (a) Name and label the ribbon-like organelle in this photograph (arrowed):

   _____

   (b) State which kind of cell(s) this organelle is found in:

   _____

   (c) Describe the function of this organelle: _____

   _____

   (d) Name the dark 'blobs' attached to the organelle you have labelled:

   _____

5. (a) Name this large circular organelle (arrowed): _____

   (b) State which kind of cell(s) this organelle would be found in: _____

   _____

   (c) Describe the function of this organelle: _____

   _____

   (d) Label three features relating to this organelle in the photograph.

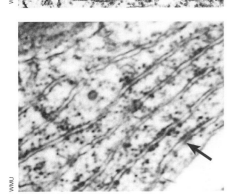

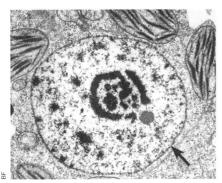

© 2015 **BIOZONE** International
ISBN: 978-1-927309-13-1
Photocopying Prohibited

TEST

Summarise what you know about this topic under the headings provided. You can draw diagrams or mind maps, or write short notes to organise your thoughts. Use the images and hints included to help you:

Microscopy

HINT: Describe developments in microscopy. Explain the use of microscopy to study cells.

Types of living things
HINT: Describe differences between prokaryotes and eukaryotes.

Cell structure
HINT: Identify the typical organelles of eukaryotic cells and describe their function.

48 KEY TERMS: Did You Get It?

1. Test your vocabulary by matching each term to its definition, as identified by its preceding letter code.

cell wall **K**

chloroplast **M**

cytoplasm **I**

eukaryotic **C**

magnification **E**

mitochondrion **A**

nucleus **I**

optical microscope **J**

organelle **G**

plasma membrane **H**

prokaryotic **B**

resolution **L**

stain **D**

A Organelle responsible for producing the cell's ATP. It appears oval in shape with an outer double membrane and a convoluted interior membrane. Contains its own circular DNA.

B With reference to cells, lacking a distinct nucleus and with no membrane-bound organelles DNA is present as a single, circular, naked chromosome.

C Cell types with a distinct membrane-bound nucleus and membrane-bound organelles.

D A chemical that binds to parts of the cell and allows those parts to be seen more easily under a microscope.

E How many times larger an image is than the original object.

F The watery contents of the cell within the plasma membrane, but excluding the contents of the nucleus.

G A structural and functional part of the cell usually bound within its own membrane. Examples include the mitochondria and chloroplasts.

H Lipid bilayer membrane surrounding the cell. Proteins are embedded in it and are responsible for the passage of material into and out of the cell.

I Membrane-bound region within a eukaryotic cell where the chromosomes are found.

J Microscope that uses lenses to focus visible light waves passing through an object into an image.

K A structure, present in plants and bacteria, which is found outside the plasma membrane and gives rigidity to the cell.

L The ability to distinguish between close together but separate objects.

M An organelle found in photosynthetic organisms such as plants, which contains chlorophyll and in which the reactions of photosynthesis take place.

2. (a) Identify organelle 1: _____

   (b) The organelle in (a) is found in a plant cell / animal cell / both plant and animal cells (circle the correct answer).

   (c) Identify organelle 2: _____

   (d) The organelle in (c) is found in a plant / animal cell / plant and animal cell (circle the correct answer).

3. Match the statements in the table below to form a complete paragraph. The left hand column is in the correct order, the right hand column is not.

Cells are the basic...	...such as photosynthesis or respiration.
A cell is enclosed by a plasma membrane...	...hydrophilic head and a hydrophobic tail.
A phospholipid is made up of a...	...units of life.
Proteins are embedded...	...in the plasma membrane.
Eukaryotic cells contain many different types of organelle...	...made of a phospholipid bilayer.
Each organelle carries out a specific function in the cell...	...some of which are composed of membranes.

4. What are the four groups that eukaryotes are commonly divided into? _Plants, animals, protoctist, fungi_

TEST

Module 2.1.2

Biological Molecules

Key terms

amino acid
biosensor
Benedict's test
biuret test
carbohydrate
cholesterol
chromatography
colorimetry
condensation
denaturation
dipeptide
disaccharide
emulsion test
fatty acid
fibrous protein
hydrolysis
globular protein
glycerol
hydrogen bond
hydrolysis
inorganic ion
iodine test
isomer
lipid
macromolecule
monomer
monosaccharide
nucleic acid
phospholipid
polymer
polypeptide
polysaccharide
primary structure
protein
quaternary structure
saturated fatty acid
secondary structure
tertiary structure
triglyceride
unsaturated fatty acid
water

The chemical nature of cells

Learning outcomes

		Activity number
☐	1 Describe the structure of water. Explain the physical and chemical properties of water that are important to its various roles in biological systems.	50 51
☐	2 Distinguish between monomers and polymers. Describe how condensation and hydrolysis are involved in the formation and breakdown of polymers.	54 57 59
☐	3 Identify the chemical elements that make up carbohydrates, lipids, proteins, and nucleic acids.	49 52
☐	4 Describe the ring structure and properties of glucose (hexose monosaccharide) and the structure of ribose (a pentose monosaccharide). Explain the biological significance of monosaccharide isomers.	53
☐	5 Describe how glycosidic bonds are formed and broken in the synthesis (by condensation) and hydrolysis of a disaccharide (e.g. sucrose, lactose, maltose) and a polysaccharide (e.g. amylose).	54
☐	6 Compare and contrast the structure of glucose polymers: starch, cellulose, and glycogen. Relate the structure to their biological function in each case.	55 56
☐	7 Describe the structure of a triglyceride (fat or oil) and a phospholipid. Explain how triglycerides are formed by condensation from fatty acids and glycerol.	57 58
☐	8 Explain how the properties of triglycerides, phospholipids, and cholesterol relate to their roles in living organisms.	58
☐	9 Describe the general structure of an amino acid. Explain how dipeptides and polypeptides are formed and broken apart by condensation and hydrolysis.	59
☐	10 Describe the levels of protein structure to include primary (1°), secondary (2°), tertiary (3°), and quaternary structure (4°) and relate these to function.	59 60 61
☐	11 Describe the structure and function of a globular proteins, including an enzyme (e.g. insulin) and a conjugated protein (e.g. haemoglobin).	60 61 62
☐	12 **PAG10** Use computer modelling to investigate levels of protein structure.	60 62
☐	13 Describe the properties and roles of fibrous proteins (collagen, keratin, elastin).	62
☐	14 Using the correct chemical symbols, identify the key inorganic ions involved in biological processes and their roles.	63

Testing for biological molecules

Learning outcomes

		Activity number
☐	15 **PAG9** Describe and use simple tests for sugars, starch, proteins, and lipids.	64
☐	16 **PAG5** Use quantitative methods (e.g. colorimetry and biosensors) to determine the concentration of a chemical substance in a solution.	65
☐	17 Explain how chromatography is used to separate biological molecules. Calculate Rf values for some common biological molecules, e.g. chlorophyll *a*.	66
☐	18 **PAG6** Analyse a biological solution using paper or thin layer chromatography.	66

49 The Biochemical Nature of Cells

Key Idea: The main components of a cell are water and compounds of carbon, hydrogen, nitrogen, and oxygen.
Water is the main component of organisms, and provides an equable environment in which metabolic reactions can occur. Apart from water, most other substances in cells are compounds of carbon, hydrogen, oxygen, and nitrogen. The combination of carbon with other elements provides a huge variety of molecular structures, called **organic molecules**. The organic molecules that make up living things can be grouped into four broad classes: carbohydrates, lipids, proteins, and nucleic acids. In addition, a small number of inorganic ions are also components of larger molecules.

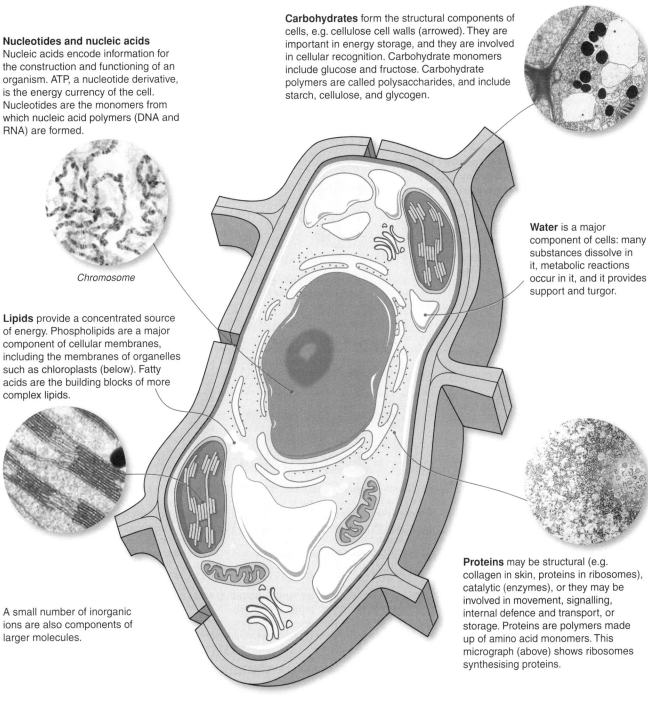

Nucleotides and nucleic acids
Nucleic acids encode information for the construction and functioning of an organism. ATP, a nucleotide derivative, is the energy currency of the cell. Nucleotides are the monomers from which nucleic acid polymers (DNA and RNA) are formed.

Chromosome

Carbohydrates form the structural components of cells, e.g. cellulose cell walls (arrowed). They are important in energy storage, and they are involved in cellular recognition. Carbohydrate monomers include glucose and fructose. Carbohydrate polymers are called polysaccharides, and include starch, cellulose, and glycogen.

Water is a major component of cells: many substances dissolve in it, metabolic reactions occur in it, and it provides support and turgor.

Lipids provide a concentrated source of energy. Phospholipids are a major component of cellular membranes, including the membranes of organelles such as chloroplasts (below). Fatty acids are the building blocks of more complex lipids.

A small number of inorganic ions are also components of larger molecules.

Proteins may be structural (e.g. collagen in skin, proteins in ribosomes), catalytic (enzymes), or they may be involved in movement, signalling, internal defence and transport, or storage. Proteins are polymers made up of amino acid monomers. This micrograph (above) shows ribosomes synthesising proteins.

1. Summarise the role of each of the following cell components:

    (a) Carbohydrates: _Help with energy storage_

    (b) Lipids: _Provide a concentrated energy source_

    (c) Proteins: _Movement, internal defence, transport or storage_

    (d) Nucleic acids: _Encode information of organisms functions_

    (e) Inorganic ions: _Make up larger molecules_

© 2015 **BIOZONE** International
ISBN: 978-1-927309-13-1
Photocopying Prohibited

LINK 52   LINK 50   **KNOW**

50 Water

Key Idea: Water forms bonds between other water molecules and also with ions allowing water to act as a medium for transporting molecules and the biological reactions of life.
Water (H_2O) is the main component of living things, and typically makes up about 70% of any organism. Water is important in cell chemistry as it takes part in, and is a common product of, many reactions. Water can form bonds with other water molecules, and also with other ions (charged molecules). Because of this chemical ability, water is regarded as the universal solvent.

Water forms hydrogen bonds

A water molecule is polar, meaning it has a positively and a negatively charged region. In water, oxygen has a slight negative charge and each of the hydrogens have a slight positive charge. Water molecules have a weak attraction for each other, forming large numbers of weak hydrogen bonds with other water molecules (far right).

Intermolecular bonds between water and other polar molecules or ions are important for biological systems. Inorganic ions may have a positive or negative charge (e.g sodium ion is positive, chloride ion is negative). The charged water molecule is attracted to the charged ion and surrounds it (right). This formation of intermolecular bonds between water and the ions is what keeps the ions dissolved in water. Polar molecules such as amino acids and carbohydrates also dissolve readily in water.

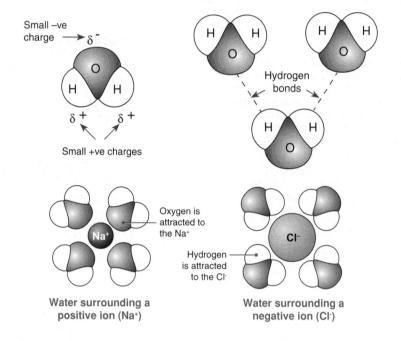

Small –ve charge → δ^-

Small +ve charges δ^+ δ^+

Hydrogen bonds

Oxygen is attracted to the Na$^+$

Hydrogen is attracted to the Cl$^-$

Water surrounding a positive ion (Na$^+$)

Water surrounding a negative ion (Cl$^-$)

The importance of water

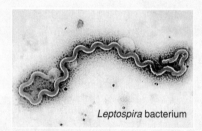

Leptospira bacterium

The metabolic reactions carried out by all organisms depend on dissolved reactants (solutes) coming into contact. Water provides the medium for metabolic reactions. Water can also act as an acid (donating H^+) or a base (receiving H^+) in chemical reactions.

Water provides an aquatic environment for organisms to live in. Ice is less dense than water and floats, insulating the underlying water and maintaining the aquatic habitat. A lot of energy is needed for water to change state, so water has a buffering effect on climate.

Water is colourless, with a high transmission of visible light. Light penetrates aquatic environments, allowing photosynthesis to continue at depth. Water also has a high heat capacity, absorbing and releasing energy slowly. This means large bodies of water are thermally stable.

1. The diagram at the top of the page shows a positive sodium ion and a negative chloride ion surrounded by water molecules. On the diagram, draw on the charge of the water molecules.

2. Explain the formation of hydrogen bonds between water and other polar molecules: _____

_____

_____

_____

3. Explain the central role of water in metabolic processes: _____

_____

_____

_____

© 2015 **BIOZONE** International
ISBN: 978-1-927309-13-1
Photocopying Prohibited

51 The Properties of Water

Key Idea: Water's chemical properties influence its physical properties and its ability to transport molecules in solution. Water's cohesive, adhesive, thermal, and solvent properties come about because of its polarity and ability to form hydrogen bonds with other polar molecules. These physical properties allow water, and water based substances (such as blood), to transport polar molecules in solution. The ability of substances to dissolve in water varies. **Hydrophilic** (water-loving) substances dissolve readily in water (e.g. salts, sugars). **Hydrophobic** (water-hating) substances (e.g. oil) do not dissolve in water. Blood must transport many different substances, including hydrophobic ones.

Cohesive properties

Water molecules are cohesive, they stick together because hydrogen bonds form between water molecules. Cohesion allows water to form drops and allows the development of surface tension.
Example: The cohesive and adhesive properties of water allow it to be transported as an unbroken column through the xylem of plants.

Adhesive properties

Water is attracted to other molecules because it forms hydrogen bonds with other polar molecules.
Example: The adhesion of water molecules to the sides of a capillary tube is responsible for a meniscus (the curved upper surface of a liquid in a tube).

Solvent properties

Other substances dissolve in water because water's dipolar nature allows it to surround other charged molecules and prevent them from clumping together.
Example: Mineral transport through a plant.

Thermal properties

▶ Water has the highest heat capacity of all liquids, so it takes a lot of energy before it will change temperature. As a result, water heats up and cools down slowly, so large bodies of water maintain a relatively stable temperature.

▶ Water is liquid at room temperature and has a high boiling point because a lot of energy is needed to break the hydrogen bonds. The liquid environment supports life and metabolic processes.

▶ Water has a high latent heat of vaporisation, meaning it takes a lot of energy to transform it from the liquid to the gas phase. In sweating, the energy is provided by the body, so sweat has a cooling effect.

Transporting substances in blood

Cholesterol — Protein
Phospholipid
Triglyceride

Sodium chloride	Glucose	Amino acids	Oxygen	Fats and cholesterol
Sodium chloride (NaCl) is highly soluble. NaCl dissolves in blood plasma into the ions Na⁺ and Cl⁻.	Glucose is a polar molecule so readily dissolves into blood plasma for transport around the body.	All amino acids have both a positive or negative charge, and are highly soluble in blood. However, their variable R-chain can alter the solubility of amino acids slightly.	Oxygen has low solubility in water. In blood, it is bound to the protein haemoglobin in red blood cells so it can be transported around the body.	Fats are non-polar substances and are insoluble in water. Cholesterol has a slight charge, but is also water insoluble. Both are transported in blood within lipoprotein complexes, spheres of phospholipids arranged with the hydrophilic heads and proteins facing out and hydrophobic tails facing inside.

1. (a) Describe the difference between a **hydrophilic** and **hydrophobic** molecule: _____

_____

_____

(b) Use an example to describe how a hydrophilic and a hydrophobic molecule are transported in blood: _____

_____

_____

_____

2. How does water act as a coolant during sweating? _____

_____

_____

LINK   WEB
50   51   KNOW

52 Organic Molecules

Key Idea: Organic molecules are those with carbon-hydrogen bonds. They make up most of the chemicals found in living organisms and can be portrayed as formulae or models.

Molecular biology is a branch of science that studies the molecular basis of biological activity. All life is based around carbon, which is able to combine with many other elements to form a large number of carbon-based (or organic) molecules.

Specific groups of atoms, called functional groups, attach to a C-H core and determine the specific chemical properties of the molecule. The organic macromolecules that make up living things can be grouped into four classes: carbohydrates, lipids, proteins, and nucleic acids. The diagram (bottom) illustrates some of the common ways in which organic molecules are portrayed.

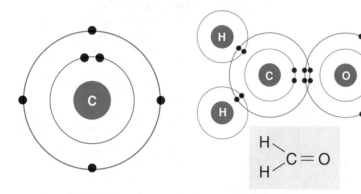

Organic macromolecule	Structural unit	Elements
Carbohydrates	Sugar monomer	C, H, O
Proteins	Amino acid	C, H, O, N, S
Lipids	Not applicable	C, H, O
Nucleic acids	Nucleotide	C, H, O, N, P

A carbon atom (above) has four electrons that are available to form up to four **covalent bonds** with other atoms. A covalent bond forms when two atoms share a pair of electrons. The number of covalent bonds formed between atoms in a molecule determines the shape and chemical properties of the molecule.

Methanal (molecular formula CH_2O) is a simple organic molecule. A carbon (C) atom bonds with two hydrogen (H) atoms and an oxygen (O) atom. In the structural formula (blue box), the bonds between atoms are represented by lines. Covalent bonds are very strong, so the molecules formed are very stable.

The most common elements found in organic molecules are carbon, hydrogen, and oxygen, but organic molecules may also contain other elements, such as nitrogen, phosphorus, and sulfur. Most organic macromolecules are built up of one type of repeating unit or 'building block', except lipids, which are quite diverse in structure.

Portraying organic molecules

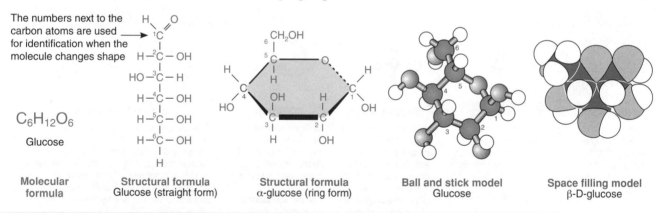

| Molecular formula | Structural formula Glucose (straight form) | Structural formula α-glucose (ring form) | Ball and stick model Glucose | Space filling model β-D-glucose |

The molecular formula expresses the number of atoms in a molecule, but does not convey its structure. This is indicated by the structural formula.

A ball and stick model shows the arrangement of bonds while a space filling model gives a more realistic appearance of a molecule.

---

1. Study the table above and state the three main elements that make up the structure of organic molecules: _____

_____

2. Name two other elements that are also frequently part of organic molecules: _____

3. (a) On the diagram of the carbon atom top left, mark with arrows the electrons that are available to form covalent bonds with other atoms.

   (b) State how many covalent bonds a carbon atom can form with neighbouring atoms: _____

4. Distinguish between molecular and structural formulae for a given molecule: _____

_____

_____

© 2015 **BIOZONE** International
ISBN: 978-1-927309-13-1
Photocopying Prohibited

53 Sugars

Key Idea: Monosaccharides are the building blocks for larger carbohydrates. They can exist as isomers.

Sugars (monosaccharides and disaccharides) play a central role in cells, providing energy and joining together to form carbohydrate macromolecules, such as starch and glycogen.

Monosaccharide polymers form the major component of most plants (as cellulose). Monosaccharides are important as a primary energy source for cellular metabolism. Carbohydrates have the general formula $C_x(H_2O)_y$, where x and y are variable numbers (often but not always the same).

Monosaccharides

Monosaccharides are single-sugar molecules and include glucose (grape sugar and blood sugar) and fructose (honey and fruit juices). They are used as a primary energy source for fuelling cell metabolism. They can be joined together to form disaccharides (two monomers) and polysaccharides (many monomers).

Monosaccharides can be classified by the number of carbon atoms they contain. Some important monosaccharides are the hexoses (6 carbons) and the pentoses (5 carbons). The most common arrangements found in sugars are hexose (6 sided) or pentose (5 sided) rings (below).

The commonly occurring monosaccharides contain between three and seven carbon atoms in their carbon chains and, of these, the 6C hexose sugars occur most frequently. All monosaccharides are reducing sugars (they can participate in reduction reactions).

Examples of monosaccharide structures

Triose	Pentose	Hexose
e.g. glyceraldehyde	e.g. ribose, deoxyribose	e.g. glucose, fructose, galactose

Ribose: a pentose monosaccharide

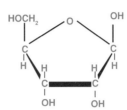

Ribose is a pentose (5 carbon) monosaccharide which can form a ring structure (left). Ribose is a component of the nucleic acid ribonucleic acid (RNA).

Glucose isomers

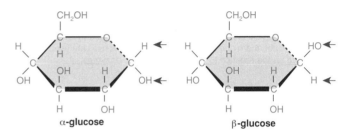

α-glucose   β-glucose

Isomers are compounds with the same chemical formula (same types and numbers of atoms) but different arrangements of atoms. The different arrangement of the atoms means that each isomer has different properties.

Molecules such as glucose can have many different isomers (e.g. α and β glucose, above) including straight and ring forms.

Glucose is a versatile molecule. It provides energy to power cellular reactions, can form energy storage molecules such as glycogen, or it can be used to build structural molecules.

Plants make their glucose via the process of photosynthesis. Animals and other heterotrophic organisms obtain their glucose by consuming plants or other organisms.

Fructose, often called fruit sugar, is a simple monosaccharide. It is often derived from sugar cane (above). Both fructose and glucose can be directly absorbed into the bloodstream.

1. Describe the two major functions of monosaccharides:

   (a) _____

   (b) _____

2. Describe the structural differences between the ring forms of glucose and ribose: _____

   _____

   _____

3. Using glucose as an example, define the term **isomer** and state its importance: _____

   _____

   _____

© 2015 **BIOZONE** International
ISBN: 978-1-927309-13-1
Photocopying Prohibited

54 Condensation and Hydrolysis of Sugars

Key Idea: Condensation reactions join monosaccharides together to form disaccharides and polysaccharides. Hydrolysis reactions split disaccharides and polysaccharides into smaller molecules.

Monosaccharide monomers can be linked together by **condensation reactions** to produce larger molecules

(disaccharides and polysaccharides). The reverse reaction, **hydrolysis**, breaks compound sugars down into their constituent monosaccharides. Disaccharides (double-sugars) are produced when two monosaccharides are joined together. Different disaccharides are formed by joining together different combinations of monosaccharides (below).

Condensation and hydrolysis reactions

Monosaccharides can combine to form compound sugars in what is called a condensation reaction. Compound sugars can be broken down by hydrolysis to simple monosaccharides.

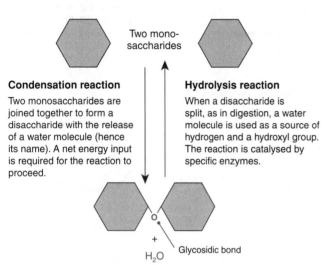

Two mono-saccharides

Condensation reaction

Two monosaccharides are joined together to form a disaccharide with the release of a water molecule (hence its name). A net energy input is required for the reaction to proceed.

Hydrolysis reaction

When a disaccharide is split, as in digestion, a water molecule is used as a source of hydrogen and a hydroxyl group. The reaction is catalysed by specific enzymes.

+ H₂O — Glycosidic bond

Disaccharide + water

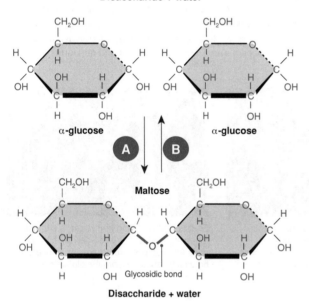

α-glucose   α-glucose

A   **B**

Maltose

Glycosidic bond

Disaccharide + water

Disaccharides

Disaccharides (below) are double-sugar molecules and are used as energy sources and as building blocks for larger molecules. They are important in human nutrition and are found in milk (lactose), table sugar (sucrose), and malt (maltose).

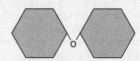

The type of disaccharide formed depends on the monomers involved and whether they are in their α- or β- form. Only a few disaccharides (e.g. lactose) are classified as reducing sugars. Some common disaccharides are described below.

Lactose, a milk sugar, is made up of β-glucose + β-galactose. Milk contains 2-8% lactose by weight. It is the primary carbohydrate source for suckling mammalian infants.

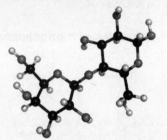

Maltose is composed of two α-glucose molecules. Germinating seeds contain maltose because the plant breaks down their starch stores to use it for food.

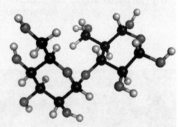

Sucrose (table sugar) is a simple sugar derived from plants such as sugar cane, sugar beet, or maple sap. It is composed of an α-glucose molecule and a β-fructose molecule.

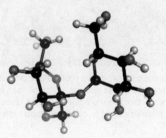

1. Explain briefly how disaccharide sugars are formed and broken down: _____

_____

_____

_____

2. On the diagram above, name the reaction occurring at points **A** and **B** and name the product that is formed:

_____

_____

3. On the lactose, maltose, and sucrose molecules (above right), circle the two monomers on each molecule.

55 Polysaccharides

Key Idea: Polysaccharides consist of many monosaccharides joined by condensation. Their functional properties depend on composition and monosaccharide isomer involved.

Polysaccharides are macromolecules consisting of straight or branched chains of many monosaccharides. They can consist of one or more types of monosaccharides. The most

common polysaccharides (cellulose, starch, and glycogen) contain only glucose, but their properties are very different. These differences are a function of the glucose isomer involved and the types of linkages joining the monomers. Different polysaccharides can thus be a source of readily available glucose or a structural material that resists digestion.

Cellulose

Cellulose is a structural material found in the cell walls of plants. It is made up of unbranched chains of β-glucose molecules held together by β-1,4 glycosidic links. As many as 10 000 glucose molecules may be linked together to form a straight chain. Parallel chains become cross-linked with hydrogen bonds and form bundles of 60-70 molecules called **microfibrils**. Cellulose microfibrils are very strong and are a major structural component of plants, e.g. as the cell wall. Few organisms can break the β-linkages so cellulose is an ideal structural material.

Starch

Starch is also a polymer of glucose, but it is made up of long chains of α-glucose molecules linked together. It contains a mixture of 25-30% amylose (unbranched chains linked by α-1,4 glycosidic bonds) and 70-75% amylopectin (branched chains with α-1, 6 glycosidic bonds every 24-30 glucose units). Starch is an energy storage molecule in plants and is found concentrated in insoluble starch granules within specialised plastids called amyloplasts in plant cells (see photo, right). Starch can be easily hydrolysed by enzymes to soluble sugars when required.

Glycogen

Glycogen, like starch, is a branched polysaccharide. It is chemically similar to amylopectin, being composed of α-glucose molecules, but there are more α-1,6 glycosidic links mixed with α-1,4 links. This makes it more highly branched and more water-soluble than starch. Glycogen is a storage compound in animal tissues and is found mainly in liver and muscle cells (photo, right). It is readily hydrolysed by enzymes to form glucose making it an ideal energy storage molecule for active animals.

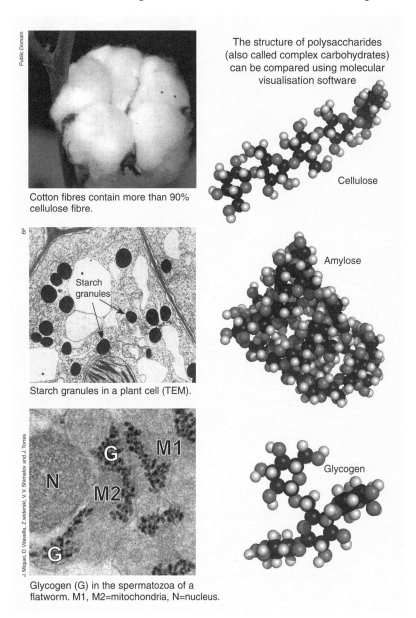

Cotton fibres contain more than 90% cellulose fibre.

Starch granules in a plant cell (TEM).

Glycogen (G) in the spermatozoa of a flatworm. M1, M2=mitochondria, N=nucleus.

The structure of polysaccharides (also called complex carbohydrates) can be compared using molecular visualisation software

Cellulose

Amylose

Glycogen

1. (a) Why are polysaccharides such a good source of energy?_____

   _____

   (b) How is the energy stored in polysaccharides mobilised?_____

   _____

2. Contrast the properties of the polysaccharides starch, cellulose, and glycogen and relate these to their roles in the cell:

   _____

   _____

   _____

   _____

© 2015 **BIOZONE** International
ISBN: 978-1-927309-13-1
Photocopying Prohibited

LINK

WEB

56 55

KNOW

56 Starch and Cellulose

Key Idea: Starch and cellulose are important polysaccharides in plants. Starch is a storage carbohydrate made up of two α-glucose polymers, amylose and amylopectin. Cellulose is a β-glucose polymer which forms the plant cell wall.

Glucose monomers can be linked in condensation reactions to form large structural and energy storage polysaccharides. The glucose isomer involved and the type of glycosidic linkage determines the properties of the molecule.

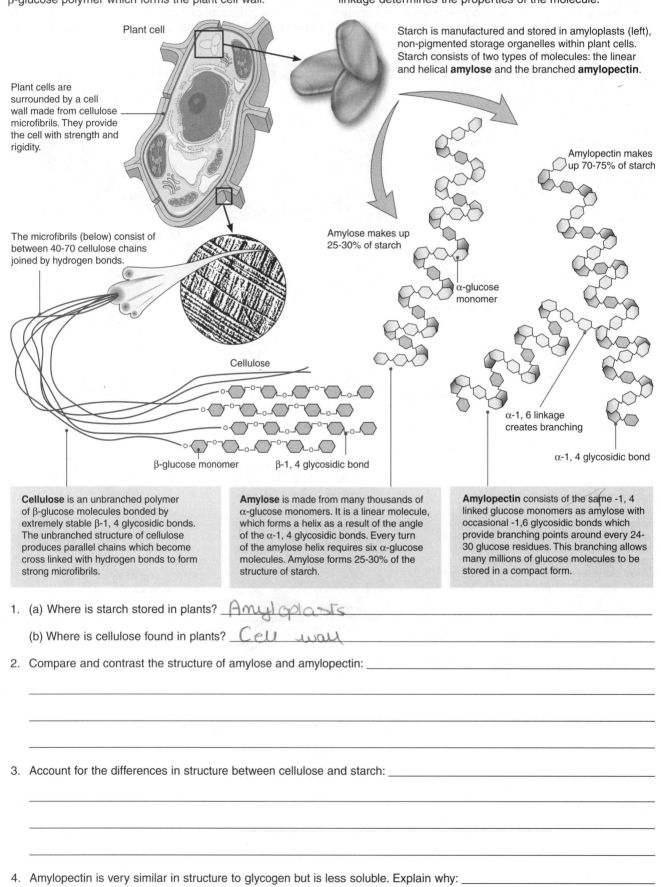

Plant cell

Plant cells are surrounded by a cell wall made from cellulose microfibrils. They provide the cell with strength and rigidity.

Starch is manufactured and stored in amyloplasts (left), non-pigmented storage organelles within plant cells. Starch consists of two types of molecules: the linear and helical **amylose** and the branched **amylopectin**.

Amylopectin makes up 70-75% of starch

The microfibrils (below) consist of between 40-70 cellulose chains joined by hydrogen bonds.

Amylose makes up 25-30% of starch

α-glucose monomer

Cellulose

β-glucose monomer   β-1, 4 glycosidic bond

α-1, 6 linkage creates branching

α-1, 4 glycosidic bond

Cellulose is an unbranched polymer of β-glucose molecules bonded by extremely stable β-1, 4 glycosidic bonds. The unbranched structure of cellulose produces parallel chains which become cross linked with hydrogen bonds to form strong microfibrils.

Amylose is made from many thousands of α-glucose monomers. It is a linear molecule, which forms a helix as a result of the angle of the α-1, 4 glycosidic bonds. Every turn of the amylose helix requires six α-glucose molecules. Amylose forms 25-30% of the structure of starch.

Amylopectin consists of the same -1, 4 linked glucose monomers as amylose with occasional -1,6 glycosidic bonds which provide branching points around every 24-30 glucose residues. This branching allows many millions of glucose molecules to be stored in a compact form.

1. (a) Where is starch stored in plants? _Amyloplasts_

   (b) Where is cellulose found in plants? _Cell wall_

2. Compare and contrast the structure of amylose and amylopectin: _____

   _____

   _____

   _____

3. Account for the differences in structure between cellulose and starch: _____

   _____

   _____

   _____

4. Amylopectin is very similar in structure to glycogen but is less soluble. Explain why: _____

   _____

© 2015 **BIOZONE** International
ISBN: 978-1-927309-13-1
Photocopying Prohibited

57 Lipids

Key Idea: Lipids are non-polar, hydrophobic organic molecules, which have many important biological functions. Fatty acids are the building blocks of more complex lipids.

Lipids are organic compounds which are mostly nonpolar (have no overall charge) and hydrophobic, so they do not readily dissolve in water. Lipids include fats, waxes, sterols, and phospholipids. Fatty acids are a major component of neutral fats and phospholipids. Most fatty acids consist of an even number of carbon atoms, with hydrogen bound along the length of the chain. The carboxyl group (–COOH) at one end makes them an acid. They are generally classified as saturated or unsaturated fatty acids (below).

Triglycerides

Glycerol   Ester bond   Fatty acids

Triglyceride: an example of a neutral fat

Neutral fats and oils are the most abundant lipids in living things. They make up the fats and oils found in plants and animals. They consist of a glycerol attached to one (mono-), two (di-) or three (tri-) fatty acids by **ester bonds**. Lipids have a high proportion of hydrogen present in the fatty acid chains. When the molecule is metabolised, the chemical energy is released. Being so reduced and anhydrous, they are an economical way to store fuel reserves, and provide more than twice as much energy as the same quantity of carbohydrate.

Lipids containing a high proportion of saturated fatty acids tend to be solids at room temperature (e.g. butter). Lipids with a high proportion of unsaturated fatty acids are oils and tend to be liquid at room temperature (e.g. olive oil). This is because the unsaturation causes kinks in the straight chains so that the fatty acid chains do not pack closely together.

Saturated and unsaturated fatty acids

Fatty acids are carboxylic acids with long hydrocarbon chains. They are classed as either saturated or unsaturated. **Saturated fatty acids** contain the maximum number of hydrogen atoms. **Unsaturated fatty acids** contain some double-bonds between carbon atoms and are not fully saturated with hydrogens. A chain with only one double bond is called monounsaturated, whereas a chain with two or more double bonds is called polyunsaturated.

Formula (above) and molecular model (below) for a saturated fatty acid (palmitic acid).

Formula (above) and molecular model (right) for an unsaturated fatty acid (linoleic acid). The arrows indicate double bonded carbon atoms that are not fully saturated with hydrogens.

---

1. Identify the main components (a-c) of the symbolic triglyceride below:

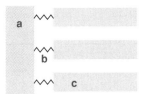

(a) _glycerol_

(b) _ester bond_

(c) _fatty acid_

2. Why do lipids have such a high energy content? _____

_____

_____

3. (a) Distinguish between saturated and unsaturated fatty acids: _____

_____

(b) Relate the properties of a neutral fat to the type of fatty acid present: _____

_____

_____

© 2015 **BIOZONE** International
ISBN: 978-1-927309-13-1
Photocopying Prohibited

LINK   LINK   WEB

64   **58**   **57**   KNOW

Triglycerides are formed by condensation reactions

Triglycerides form when glycerol bonds with three fatty acids. Glycerol is an alcohol containing three carbons. Each of these carbons is bonded to a hydroxyl (-OH) group.

When glycerol bonds with the fatty acid, an **ester bond** is formed and water is released. Three separate condensation reactions are involved in producing a triglyceride.

Esterification: A condensation reaction of an alcohol (e.g. glycerol) with an acid (e.g. fatty acid) to produce an ester and water. In the diagram right, the ester bonds are indicated by blue lines.

Lipolysis: The breakdown of lipids. It involves hydrolysis of triglycerides into glycerol molecules and free fatty acids.

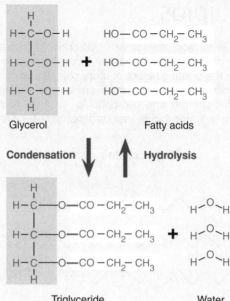

Glycerol   Fatty acids

Condensation ↓   ↑ **Hydrolysis**

Triglyceride   Water

Biological functions of lipids

Lipids are concentrated sources of energy and provide fuel for aerobic respiration.

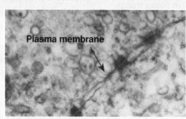

Phospholipids form the structure of cellular membranes in eukaryotes and prokaryotes.

Waxes and oils secreted onto surfaces provide waterproofing in plants and animals.

Fat absorbs shocks. Organs that are prone to bumps and shocks (e.g. kidneys) are cushioned with a relatively thick layer of fat.

Lipids are a source of metabolic water. During respiration stored lipids are metabolised for energy, producing water and carbon dioxide.

Stored lipids provide insulation. Increased body fat levels in winter reduce heat losses to the environment.

---

4. (a) Describe what happens during the esterification (condensation) process to produce a triglyceride:

_____

_____

(b) Describe what happens when a triglyceride is hydrolysed: _____

_____

_____

5. Discuss the biological role of lipids: _____

_____

_____

_____

_____

_____

© 2015 **BIOZONE** International
ISBN: 978-1-927309-13-1
Photocopying Prohibited

58 Phospholipids and Cholesterol

Key idea: Phospholipids and cholesterol are examples of lipids. Both are important components of cellular membranes. **Phospholipids** are similar in structure to a triglyceride except that a phosphate group replaces one of the fatty acids attached to the glycerol. Phospholipids naturally form bilayers and are the main component of all cellular membranes. Steroids are complex lipids and include the sterol lipid **cholesterol**. Cholesterol has important roles in membrane fluidity and also acts as a precursor for the production of many other steroids.

Phospholipids

Phospholipids consist of a glycerol attached to two fatty acid chains and a phosphate (PO_4^{3-}) group. The phosphate end of the molecule is attracted to water (it is hydrophilic) while the fatty acid end is repelled (hydrophobic). The hydrophobic ends turn inwards in the membrane to form a **phospholipid bilayer**.

Steroids and cholesterol

Although steroids are classified as lipids, their structure is quite different to that of other lipids. Steroids have a basic structure of three rings made of 6 carbon atoms each and a fourth ring containing 5 carbon atoms. Examples of steroids include the male and female sex hormones (testosterone and oestrogen), and the hormones cortisol and aldosterone.

Cholesterol, while not a steroid itself, is a sterol lipid and is a precursor to several steroid hormones. It is present in the plasma membrane, where it regulates membrane fluidity by preventing the phospholipids packing too closely together.

Like phospholipids, cholesterol is **amphipathic**. The hydroxyl (-OH) group on cholesterol interacts with the polar head groups of the membrane phospholipids, while the steroid ring and hydrocarbon chain tuck into the hydrophobic portion of the membrane. This helps to stabilise the outer surface of the membrane and reduce its permeability to small water-soluble molecules.

Cholesterol: structural formula

Cholesterol: space filling molecule

1. (a) Relate the structure of phospholipids to their chemical properties and their functional role in cellular membranes:

_____

_____

_____

(b) Suggest how the cell membrane structure of an Arctic fish might differ from that of tropical fish species: _____

_____

_____

2. How does the structure of cholesterol enable it to perform structural and functional roles within membranes? _____

_____

_____

_____

© 2015 **BIOZONE** International
ISBN: 978-1-927309-13-1
Photocopying Prohibited

KNOW

59 Amino Acids

Key Idea: Amino acids join together in a linear chain by condensation reactions to form polypeptides. The sequence of amino acids in a protein is defined by a gene and encoded in the genetic code. In the presence of water, they can be broken apart by hydrolysis into their constituent amino acids.

Amino acids are the basic units from which proteins are made. Twenty amino acids commonly occur in proteins and they can be linked in many different ways by peptide bonds to form a huge variety of polypeptides. Proteins are made up of one or more polypeptide molecules.

The structure and properties of amino acids

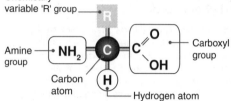

Chemically variable 'R' group

Amine group — NH₂

Carboxyl group

Carbon atom

Hydrogen atom

All amino acids have a common structure (above), but the R group is different in each kind of amino acid (right). The property of the R group determines how it will interact with other amino acids and ultimately determines how the amino acid chain folds up into a functional protein. For example, the hydrophobic R groups of soluble proteins are folded into the protein's interior, while the hydrophilic groups are arranged on the outside.

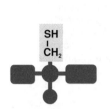

Cysteine

This 'R' group can form **disulfide bridges** with other cysteines to create cross linkages in a polypeptide chain.

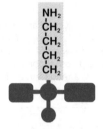

Lysine

This 'R' group gives the amino acid an **alkaline** property.

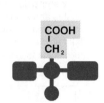

Aspartic acid

This 'R' group gives the amino acid an **acidic** property.

Condensation and hydrolysis reactions

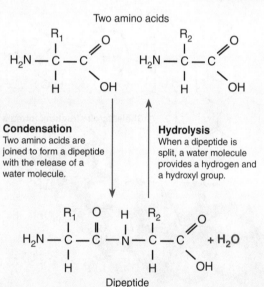

Two amino acids

Condensation
Two amino acids are joined to form a dipeptide with the release of a water molecule.

Hydrolysis
When a dipeptide is split, a water molecule provides a hydrogen and a hydroxyl group.

Dipeptide

Amino acids are linked by **peptide bonds** to form long **polypeptide chains** of up to several thousand amino acids. Peptide bonds form between the carboxyl group of one amino acid and the amine group of another (left). Water is formed as a result of this bond formation.

The sequence of amino acids in a polypeptide is called the **primary structure** and is determined by the order of nucleotides in DNA and mRNA. The linking of amino acids to form a polypeptide occurs on ribosomes. Once released from the ribosome, a polypeptide will fold into a secondary structure determined by the composition and position of the amino acids making up the chain.

A polypeptide chain

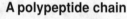
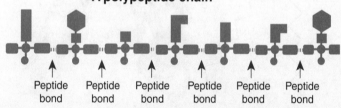

Peptide bond Peptide bond Peptide bond Peptide bond Peptide bond Peptide bond

1. (a) What makes each of the amino acids in proteins unique? _The order of codons_

   (b) What is the primary structure of a protein? _The sequence of amino acid_

   (c) What determines the primary structure? _The order of bases in the sequence_

   (d) How do the sequence and composition of amino acids in a protein influence how a protein folds up? _____

   _____

2. (a) What type of bond joins neighbouring amino acids together? _dipeptide bond_

   (b) How is this bond formed? _by the release of a water molecule_

   (c) Circle this bond in the dipeptide above:

   (d) How are di- and polypeptides broken down? _water provides a hydrogen and hydroxyl group_

© 2015 **BIOZONE** International
ISBN: 978-1-927309-13-1
Photocopying Prohibited

60 Protein Shape is Related to Function

Key idea: Interactions between amino acid R groups direct a polypeptide chain to fold into a specific shape that reflects its role. When a protein is denatured, it loses its functionality. A protein may consist of one polypeptide chain, or several polypeptide chains linked together. Hydrogen bonds between amino acids cause it to form its **secondary structure**, either an α-helix or a β-pleated sheet. The interaction between R groups causes a polypeptide to fold into its **tertiary structure**, a three dimensional shape held by ionic bonds and disulfide bridges (bonds formed between sulfur containing amino acids). If bonds are broken (through denaturation), the protein loses its tertiary structure, and its functionality.

The shape of a protein reflects its biological role

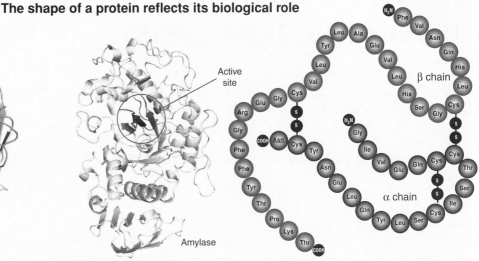

Active site

Amylase

β chain

α chain

Channel proteins
Proteins that fold to form channels in the plasma membrane present non-polar R groups to the membrane and polar R groups to the inside of the channel. Hydrophilic molecules and ions are then able to pass through these channels into the interior of the cell. Ion channels are found in nearly all cells and many organelles.

Enzymes
Enzymes are globular proteins that catalyse specific reactions. Enzymes that are folded to present polar R groups at the active site will be specific for polar substances. Non-polar active sites will be specific for non-polar substances. Alteration of the active site by extremes of temperature or pH cause a loss of function.

Sub-unit proteins
Many proteins, e.g. insulin and haemoglobin, consist of two or more sub-units in a complex quaternary structure, often in association with a metal ion. Active insulin is formed by two polypeptide chains stabilised by disulfide bridges between neighbouring cysteines. Insulin stimulates glucose uptake by cells.

Protein denaturation

When the chemical bonds holding a protein together become broken the protein can no longer hold its three dimensional shape. This process is called **denaturation**, and the protein usually loses its ability to carry out its biological function.

There are many causes of denaturation including exposure to heat or pH outside of the protein's optimum range. The main protein in egg white is albumin. It has a clear, thick fluid appearance in a raw egg (right). Heat (cooking) denatures the albumin protein and it becomes insoluble, clumping together to form a thick white substance (far right).

Raw (native) egg white

Cooked (denatured) egg white

1. Explain the importance of the amino acid sequence in protein folding: _____

_____

_____

2. Why do channel proteins often fold with non-polar R groups to the channel's exterior and polar R groups to its interior?

_____

_____

3. Why does **denaturation** often result in the loss of protein functionality? _____

_____

_____

_____

© 2015 **BIOZONE** International
ISBN: 978-1-927309-13-1
Photocopying Prohibited

LINK 62   LINK 61   WEB 60   **KNOW**

61 Protein Structure

Key Idea: The sequence and type of amino acids in a protein determine its three-dimensional shape and function.

Proteins are large, complex **macromolecules**, built up from a linear sequence of repeating units called **amino acids**. Proteins account for more than 50% of the dry weight of most cells and are important in virtually every cellular process. The various properties of the amino acids, which are conferred by the different R groups, determine how the polypeptide chain folds up. This three dimensional **tertiary structure** gives a protein its specific chemical properties. If a protein loses this precise structure (through **denaturation**), it is usually unable to carry out its biological function.

Primary (1°) structure (amino acid sequence)

Peptide bond   Amino acid

Hundreds of amino acids are linked by peptide bonds to form polypeptide chains. The attractive and repulsive charges on the amino acids determines the higher levels of organisation in the protein and its biological function.

Secondary (2°) structure (α-helix or β pleated sheet)

Secondary (2°) structure is maintained by hydrogen bonds between neighbouring CO and NH groups. The hydrogen bonds are individually weak but collectively strong.

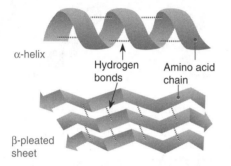

α-helix

Hydrogen bonds

Amino acid chain

β-pleated sheet

Polypeptide chains fold into a secondary (2°) structure based on H bonding. The coiled α-helix and β-pleated sheet are common 2° structures. Most globular proteins contain regions of both 2° configurations.

Tertiary (3°) structure (folding of the 2° structure)

Tertiary (3°) structure is maintained by more distant interactions such as **disulfide bridges** between cysteine amino acids, ionic bonds, and hydrophobic interactions.

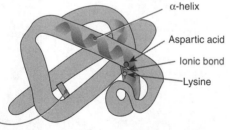

α-helix

Aspartic acid

Ionic bond

Lysine

Disulfide bond

A protein's 3° structure is the three-dimensional shape formed when the 2° structure folds up and more distant parts of the polypeptide chains interact.

Quaternary (4°) structure

Some complex proteins are only functional when as a group of polypeptide chains. Haemoglobin has a 4° structure made up of two alpha and two beta polypeptide chains, each enclosing a complex iron-containing prosthetic (or haem) group.

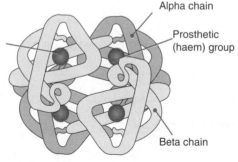

Alpha chain

Prosthetic (haem) group

Beta chain

A protein's 4° structure describes the arrangement and position of each of the subunits in a multiunit protein. The shape is maintained by the same sorts of interactions as those involved in 3° structure.

1. Describe the main features in the formation of each part of a protein's structure:

   (a) Primary structure: _____

   _____

   _____

   _____

   _____

   (b) Secondary structure: _____

   _____

   _____

   _____

   _____

   (c) Tertiary structure: _____

   _____

   _____

   _____

   _____

   _____

   (d) Quaternary structure: _____

   _____

   _____

   _____

   _____

   _____

2. How are proteins built up into a functional structure?

   _____

   _____

   _____

   _____

   _____

   _____

   _____

© 2015 **BIOZONE** International
ISBN: 978-1-927309-13-1
Photocopying Prohibited

62 Comparing Globular and Fibrous Proteins

Key Idea: The very different structure and properties of globular and fibrous proteins reflect their contrasting roles. Proteins can be classified according to structure or function. **Globular proteins** are spherical and soluble in water (e.g. enzymes). **Fibrous proteins** have an elongated structure and are not water soluble. They provide stiffness and rigidity to the more fluid components of cells and tissues and have important structural and contractile roles.

Globular proteins

Properties
- Easily water soluble
- Tertiary structure critical to function
- Polypeptide chains folded into a spherical shape

Function
- Catalytic, *e.g. enzymes*
- Regulatory, *e.g. hormones (insulin)*
- Transport, *e.g. haemoglobin*
- Protective, *e.g. immunoglobulins (antibodies)*

Fibrous proteins

Properties
- Water insoluble
- Very tough physically; may be supple or stretchy
- Parallel polypeptide chains in long fibres or sheets

Function
- Structural role in cells and organisms e.g. *collagen in connective tissues, skin, and blood vessel walls.*
- Contractile e.g. *myosin, actin*

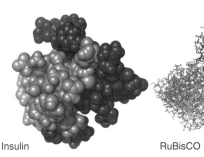

Insulin

RuBisCO

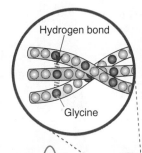

Hydrogen bond

Glycine

The collagen molecule consists of three polypeptides wound around each other to form a helical 'rope'. Every third amino acid in each polypeptide is a glycine (Gly) where hydrogen bonding holds the three strands together. The collagen molecules self assemble into **fibrils** of many molecules held together by covalent cross linkages (below). Bundles of fibrils form fibres.

Insulin is a peptide hormone involved in the regulation of blood glucose. Insulin is composed of two peptide chains (the A chain and the B chain) linked together by two disulfide bonds.

RuBisCo is a large multi-unit enzyme found in green plants and catalyses the first step of carbon fixation in the Calvin cycle. It consists of 8 large (L) and 8 small (S) subunits arranged as 4 dimers. RuBisCO is the most abundant protein on Earth.

Many collagen molecules form fibrils and the fibrils group together to form larger fibres.

Covalent cross links between the collagen molecules

Haemoglobin is an oxygen-transporting protein found in vertebrate red blood cells. One haemoglobin molecule consists of four polypeptide chains (two identical alpha chains and two identical beta chains). Each polypeptide subunit contains a non-protein prosthetic group, an iron-containing haem group, which binds oxygen.

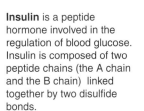

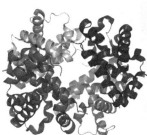

Haemoglobin

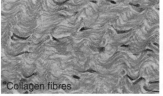

*Collagen fibres

Rhinoceros horn is keratin

Collagen is the main component of connective tissue, and is mostly found in fibrous tissues (e.g. tendons, ligaments, and skin). The elastic properties of **elastin** allows tissues to resume their shape after stretching. Skin, arteries, lungs, and bladder all contain elastin. **Keratin** is found in hair, nails, horn, hooves, wool, feathers, and the outer layers of the skin. The polypeptide chains of keratin are arranged in parallel sheets held together by hydrogen bonding.

1. How are proteins involved in the following roles? Give examples to help illustrate your answer:

   (a) Structural tissues of the body: _____

   _____

   _____

   (b) Catalysing metabolic reactions in cells: _____

   _____

   _____

2. How does the shape of a fibrous protein relate to its functional role? _____

   _____

3. How does the shape of a catalytic protein (enzyme) relate to its functional role? _____

   _____

© 2015 **BIOZONE** International
ISBN: 978-1-927309-13-1
Photocopying Prohibited

LINK 61   LINK 60   WEB 62

KNOW

63 Inorganic Ions

Key Idea: Inorganic ions are charged molecules that do not contain carbon-hydrogen bonds. They are central to many biological structures and processes.

Inorganic compounds do not contain C-H bonds. An **inorganic ion** is an atom (or group of atoms) that has gained or lost one or more electrons and therefore has a positive or negative charge. Inorganic ions are central to the structure and metabolism of all living organisms, participating in metabolic reactions and combining with organic molecules to form complex molecules (e.g. iron and haemoglobin).

Cation: A positive ion; an atom or group of atoms that has lost one or more electrons.

Anion: A negative ion; an atom or group of atoms that has gained one or more electrons.

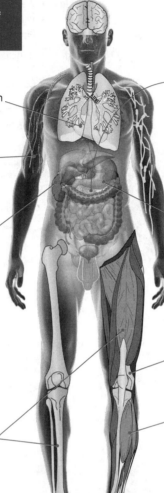

Potassium (K^+)
Roles: The main intracellular cation in all cell types. Involved in heart function and transmission of the nerve impulses. In plants, K^+ is involved in controlling stomatal opening via the guard cells.

Sodium (Na^+)
Roles: The major extracellular cation in animal cells, involved in transmission of nerve impulses and in fluid and electrolyte balance. In plants, Na^+ is involved in maintaining cell turgor and in opening and closing stomata.

Ammonium (NH_4^+)
Roles: An important source of nitrogen for many plant species. Generated in the mammalian kidney as part of acid-base regulation.

Hydrogen (H^+)
Roles: Important in acid-base chemistry. Establish trans-membrane electrochemical gradients which can be used to generate ATP.

Calcium (Ca^{2+})
Roles: In vertebrates, Ca^{2+} is a component of teeth and bone (as calcium phosphate) and is involved in muscle contraction, blood clotting, activation of some enzymes, and cell signalling. In plants, it is a component of the cell wall.

Hydrogen carbonate (HCO_3^-)
Also called bicarbonate ion.
Roles: Bicarbonate is alkaline and acts as a pH buffer in the human body to maintain acid-base homeostasis. A buffer is a molecule that can bind or release hydrogen ions in order to maintain a particular pH. Bicarbonate is released from the pancreas to neutralise the acidic chyme entering the small intestine from the stomach.

Chloride (Cl^-)
Roles: Essential electrolyte present in all body fluids. Involved in fluid balance, acid-base balance, and to form hydrochloric acid in gastric juice

Nitrate (NO_3^-)
An important source of nitrogen for plants (unlike animals, which obtain their nitrogen by eating other organisms). Nitrogen is a component of amino acids and nucleotides.

Phosphate (PO_4^{3-})
Roles: Component of phospholipids, nucleotides and ATP. Combines with calcium as calcium phosphate in bones and teeth

Hydroxide (OH^-)
Roles: Important in acid-base chemistry. Central to many biological reactions.

1. (a) Define a cation: _+ve ion. Atom that has lost 1 or more electrons_

   (b) Define an anion: _-ve ion. Atom that has gained one or more electrons_

2. (a) Describe the role of Ca^{2+} in organisms: _In vertebrates, involved in muscle contraction, blood clotting, activation of some enzymes. Component of cell walls in plants_

   (b) Predict the biological consequences of inadequate levels of calcium in the diet: _____

   _____

3. (a) Why is NO_3^- so important for plants? _____

   (b) Why is it not directly important to animals? _____

   _____

4. (a) Which inorganic ions are involved in acid-base regulation: _____

   (b) What feature of their structure enables this role: _____

   _____

© 2015 **BIOZONE** International
ISBN: 978-1-927309-13-1
Photocopying Prohibited

64 Biochemical Tests

Key Idea: Qualitative biochemical tests detect the presence of a specific molecule in food.

Qualitative biochemical tests can be used to detect the presence of molecules such as lipids, proteins, or carbohydrates (sugars and starch). However, they cannot be used directly to determine absolute concentrations or distinguish between different molecules of the same type (e.g. different sugars in a mixed solution).

Simple food tests

Proteins: The Biuret Test

Reagent:	Biuret solution.
Procedure:	A sample is added to biuret solution and gently heated.
Positive result:	Solution turns from blue to lilac.

Starch: The Iodine Test

Reagent:	Iodine.
Procedure:	Iodine solution is added to the sample.
Positive result:	Blue-black staining occurs.

Lipids: The Emulsion Test

Reagent:	Ethanol.
Procedure:	The sample is shaken with ethanol. After settling, the liquid portion is distilled and mixed with water.
Positive result:	The solution turns into a cloudy-white emulsion of suspended lipid molecules.

Sugars: The Benedict's Test

Reagent:	Benedict's solution.
Procedure:	Non reducing sugars: The sample is boiled with dilute hydrochloric acid (acid hydrolysis), then cooled and neutralised. A test for reducing sugars is then performed.
	Reducing sugar: Benedict's solution is added, and the sample is placed in a water bath.
Positive result:	Solution turns from blue to orange to red-brown.

A Qualitative test for reducing sugar

To determine whether this muffin contains any reducing sugars (e.g. glucose), the Benedict's test for reducing sugar is carried out.

The muffin is placed in a blender with some water and mixed until it forms an homogenous (uniform) mixture.

2 -3 mL of the muffin mixture is placed into a test tube with 1 mL of Benedict's solution. The tubes are heated for 4 -10 minutes.

The intensity of the colour depends on the concentration of glucose present in the sample. The darker the colour, the more glucose is present. A **colorimetric analysis** enables the amount of glucose present to be quantified (see the following activity).

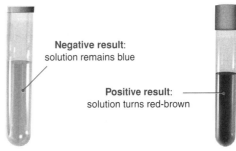

Negative result: solution remains blue

Positive result: solution turns red-brown

1. Explain why lipids must be mixed in ethanol before they will form an emulsion in water: _____

_____

_____

2. Explain why the emulsion of lipids, ethanol, and water appears cloudy: _____

_____

_____

3. What is the purpose of the acid hydrolysis step when testing for non-reducing sugars with Benedict's reagent?

_____

_____

4. What are the limitations of qualitative tests such as those described above? _____

_____

_____

LINK 66　LINK 65　WEB 64　KNOW

65 Determining the Concentration of a Substance

Key Idea: Colorimetric analysis and simple biosensors can be used to quantify the concentration of a substance.
Colorimetry is a technique for determining the concentration of a substance in solution. A reagent is added to the solution where it reacts with the substance of interest to produce a colour. Samples are placed in a colorimeter, which measures the solution's absorbance at a specific wavelength. A dilution series can be used to produce a calibration curve, which can then be used to quantify that substance in samples of unknown concentration. Another technique is to use a biosensor in which the product of an enzyme-catalysed reaction is used to quantify the concentration of reactant.

Colorimetric analysis of glucose

Prepare glucose standards

Solutions containing a range of known glucose concentrations are prepared in test tubes. Benedict's reagent is added and the test tubes are heated in a boiling waterbath for 4-10 minutes. Samples containing glucose will change colour. The samples are cooled, then filtered or centrifuged to remove suspended particles.

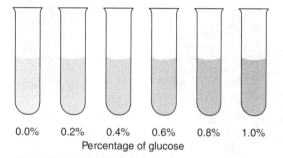

| 0.0% | 0.2% | 0.4% | 0.6% | 0.8% | 1.0% |

Percentage of glucose

> Benedict's reagent in boiling water bath 4-10 minutes

Produce a calibration curve

The absorbance of each standard is measured in a colorimeter (or sometimes a spectrophotometer) at 735 nm. These values are used to produce a calibration curve for glucose. The calibration curve can then be used to determine the glucose concentration of any 'unknown' based on its absorbance.

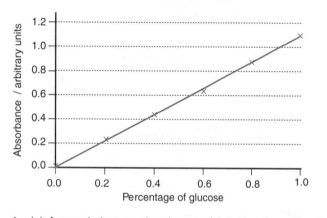

Biosensors

Biosensors are electronic monitoring devices that use biological material to detect the presence or concentration of a particular substance. Enzymes are ideally suited for use in biosensors because of their specificity and sensitivity. This example illustrates how glucose oxidase from the fungus *Aspergillus niger* is used in a biosensor to measure blood glucose level in diabetics.

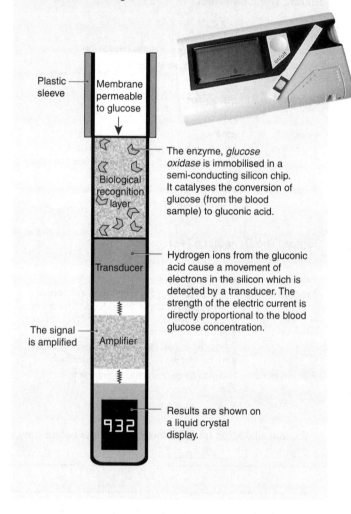

Plastic sleeve — Membrane permeable to glucose

Biological recognition layer — The enzyme, *glucose oxidase* is immobilised in a semi-conducting silicon chip. It catalyses the conversion of glucose (from the blood sample) to gluconic acid.

Transducer — Hydrogen ions from the gluconic acid cause a movement of electrons in the silicon which is detected by a transducer. The strength of the electric current is directly proportional to the blood glucose concentration.

The signal is amplified — Amplifier

932 — Results are shown on a liquid crystal display.

1. (a) A sample has an absorbance of 0.5. Use the calibration curve above to estimate how much glucose it contains.

_____

(b) What would you do if the absorbance values you obtained for most of your 'unknowns' were outside the range of your calibration curve?

_____

_____

2. Outline the basic principle of enzyme-based biosensors: _____

_____

_____

LINK 17   LINK 86

© 2015 **BIOZONE** International
ISBN: 978-1-927309-13-1
Photocopying Prohibited

66 Chromatography Techniques

Key Idea: Paper chromatography is used to separate a mix of substances within a sample.

Chromatography is a technique used to separate a mixture of molecules. Chromatography involves passing a mixture dissolved in a mobile phase (a solvent) through a stationary phase, which separates the molecules according to their specific characteristics (e.g. size or charge). Paper chromatography is a simple technique in which porous paper serves as the stationary phase and a solvent, either water or ethanol, serves as the mobile phase.

Paper chromatography

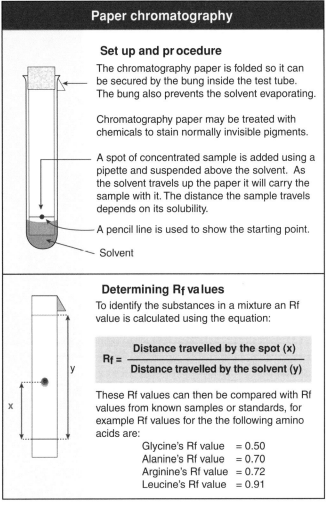

Set up and procedure

The chromatography paper is folded so it can be secured by the bung inside the test tube. The bung also prevents the solvent evaporating.

Chromatography paper may be treated with chemicals to stain normally invisible pigments.

A spot of concentrated sample is added using a pipette and suspended above the solvent. As the solvent travels up the paper it will carry the sample with it. The distance the sample travels depends on its solubility.

A pencil line is used to show the starting point.

Solvent

Determining R$_f$ values

To identify the substances in a mixture an Rf value is calculated using the equation:

$$R_f = \frac{\text{Distance travelled by the spot (x)}}{\text{Distance travelled by the solvent (y)}}$$

These Rf values can then be compared with Rf values from known samples or standards, for example Rf values for the the following amino acids are:

Glycine's Rf value = 0.50
Alanine's Rf value = 0.70
Arginine's Rf value = 0.72
Leucine's Rf value = 0.91

Using chromatography to separate sugars

Mixtures of sugars can be separated by paper chromatography. The R$_f$ values for sugars separated using aniline diphenylamine reagent as the solvent are given below:

Glucose: 0.64
Fructose: 0.68
Lactose: 0.46
Maltose: 0.50
Sucrose: 0.62

A student was given a solution containing two unknown sugars. They separated them by paper chromatography using aniline diphenylamine reagent as the solvent and obtained the results below.

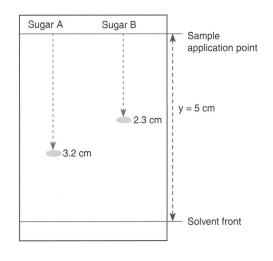

1. Calculate the R$_f$ value for **spot X** in the example given above left (show your working): _____

_____

2. Why is the R$_f$ value of a substance always less than 1? _____

_____

3. When is it appropriate to use chromatography instead of a simple food test? _____

_____

_____

4. Predict what would happen if a sample was immersed in the chromatography solvent, instead of suspended above it:

_____

_____

5. (a) Calculate the R$_f$ values for the two unknown sugar samples above: _____

_____

(b) Based on the R$_f$ values calculated in (a), identify the two sugars:

Sugar A: _____   Sugar B: _____

67 Chapter Review

Summarise what you know about this topic under the headings provided. You can draw diagrams or mind maps, or write short notes to organise your thoughts. Use the images and hints included to help you:

Water
HINT. Describe how water can form bonds with other molecules, and why this is important.

Analytical tests:
HINT. Describe how analytical tests can be used to identify and quantify biological molecules.

Carbohydrates:
HINT. Relate carbohydrate structure to function.

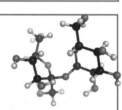

Proteins:
HINT. Describe the structure and function of proteins.

Lipids:
HINT. Compare the structure and biological role of different lipids.

68 KEY TERMS: Did You Get It?

1. Test your vocabulary by matching each term to its correct definition, as identified by its preceding letter code.

amino acids	**A** The loss of a protein's three dimensional functional structure is called this.
carbohydrates	**B** A class of organic compounds with an oily, greasy, or waxy consistency. Important as energy storage molecules and as components of cellular membranes.
condensation	**C** The sequence of amino acids in a polypeptide.
denaturation	**D** The building blocks of proteins.
fibrous proteins	**E** An atom (or group of atoms) with no C-H bonds and a positive or negative charge.
globular proteins	**F** Long carbohydrate molecules made up of monosaccharide units joined together by glycosidic bonds.
hydrogen bond	**G** The splitting of a molecule into smaller components by addition of a water molecule.
hydrolysis	**H** A general term for a reaction in which water is released.
inorganic ion	**I** Carbohydrate monomers. Examples include fructose and glucose.
lipids _I_	**J** Fatty acids containing less than the maximum number of possible hydrogen atoms because of the presence of double bonded carbon atoms.
monosaccharides	**K** Water soluble proteins with a spherical tertiary structure. They are involved in many cellular functions including as catalysts and in transport and regulation.
polypeptides	**L** Organic compounds, usually linear polymers, made of amino acids linked together by peptide bonds.
polysaccharides	**M** Weak attractive interaction between polar molecules.
primary structure _C_	**N** The structure of a protein maintained by disulfide bonds and hydrophilic and hydrophobic interactions.
saturated fatty acids	**O** Organic molecules consisting only of carbon, hydrogen and oxygen that serve as structural components in cells and as energy sources.
tertiary structure	**P** Fatty acids containing the maximum number of hydrogen bonds.
unsaturated fatty acids	**Q** Proteins with a rod or wire-like structure that are important in structure or storage.

2. The diagram (right) symbolically represents a phospholipid.

   (a) Label the hydrophobic and hydrophilic regions of the phospholipid.

   (b) Explain how the properties of the phospholipid molecule result in the bilayer structure of membranes:

   _____

   _____

3. (a) What general reaction combines two molecules to form a larger molecule? _____

   (b) What general reaction cleaves a larger molecule by the addition of water? _____

4. (a) Which class of biological molecules contains carbon, hydrogen, and oxygen only: _____

   (b) In addition to carbon, hydrogen, and oxygen, name the other element that all proteins contain: _____

   (c) Some proteins also contain sulfur. What is the effect of sulfur on a protein's structure: _____

   _____

© 2015 **BIOZONE** International
ISBN: 978-1-927309-13-1

TEST

Nucleotides and Nucleic Acids

Key terms

anticodon

ATP

base-pairing rule

coding strand

codon (on mRNA)

DNA

double-helix

exons

gene

gene expression

genetic code

hydrogen bonding

introns

mutation

nucleic acids

nucleotides

phosphodiester bond

polynucleotide

protein

purine

pyrimidine

ribosome

RNA (mRNA, rRNA, tRNA)

template strand

transcription

translation

triplet (on DNA)

Nucleotides and nucleic acids

Learning outcomes

		Activity number
☐	1 Use an annotated diagram to describe the structure of a nucleotide.	69
☐	2 Describe the basic structure of nucleic acids (DNA and RNA), identifying differences between them.	70
☐	3 *PAG10* Use computer modelling to investigate nucleic acid structure.	70
☐	4 Describe the formation and breakdown of polynucleotides.	70
☐	5 Describe the structure of the nucleotide derivatives ADP and ATP.	69
☐	6 Describe the Watson-Crick double-helix model of DNA. Include reference to the base-pairing rule, the anti-parallel strands, and the role of hydrogen bonding between purines and pyrimidines.	71 72
☐	7 Understand the evidence for the structure of DNA. In what way did the structure of DNA provide a mechanism for its self-replication? (HSW)	71
☐	8 *PAG9* Purify DNA by precipitation.	71
☐	9 Describe the semi-conservative replication of DNA, including the role of helicase and DNA polymerase. Explain the role of proofreading in DNA replication and the importance of this.	73 74
☐	10 Analyse the results of Meselson and Stahl's experiments on DNA replication and use modelling to reproduce these for yourself. (HSW)	75 76

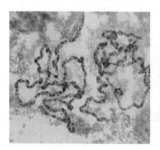 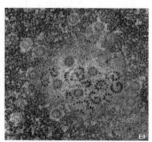 

The genetic code

Learning outcomes

		Activity number
☐	11 Explain the features of the genetic code, including: • The 4-letter alphabet and the 3-letter triplet code (codon) of base sequences. • The non-overlapping, linear nature of the code, which is read from start to finish in one direction. The specific punctuation codons and their significance. • The universal nature and degeneracy of the code.	77 78
☐	12 Explain what is meant by a gene and explain how a gene determines the sequence of amino acids in a polypeptide (the primary structure of a protein).	79
☐	13 Recognise transcription and translation as the two stages of gene expression. Describe the simple one gene-one polypeptide model for gene expression, understanding that this model has been modified in light of current understanding.	79
☐	14 Recall the structure of RNA and describe the range of RNA molecules and their roles in cellular activities.	70
☐	15 Describe the formation of mRNA in transcription, including the role of RNA polymerase and the significance of the coding (sense) strand and template (antisense) strand. Determine the DNA base sequence for a mRNA strand.	80 82
☐	16 Describe translation (protein synthesis), including the role of tRNA, anticodons, and the general structure and role of ribosomes. Use the genetic code to determine the amino acids encoded by different codons.	81 82

69 Nucleotides

Key Idea: Nucleotides make up nucleic acids. A nucleotide is made up of a base, a sugar, and a phosphate group.

Nucleotides are the building blocks of the nucleic acids DNA and RNA, which are involved in the transmission of inherited information. Nucleotide derivatives, such as ATP and GTP, are involved in energy transfers in cells. A nucleotide has

three components: a base, a sugar, and a phosphate group. Nucleotides may contain one of five bases. The combination of bases in the nucleotides making up DNA or RNA stores the information controlling the cell's activity. The bases in DNA are the same as RNA except that thymine (T) in DNA is replaced with uracil (U) in RNA.

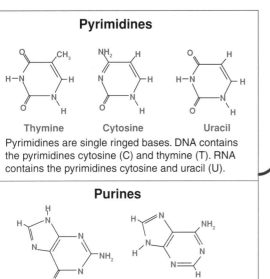

Pyrimidines

Thymine   Cytosine   Uracil

Pyrimidines are single ringed bases. DNA contains the pyrimidines cytosine (C) and thymine (T). RNA contains the pyrimidines cytosine and uracil (U).

Purines

Guanine   Adenine

Purines are double ringed bases. Both DNA and RNA contain the purines adenine (A) and guanine (G).

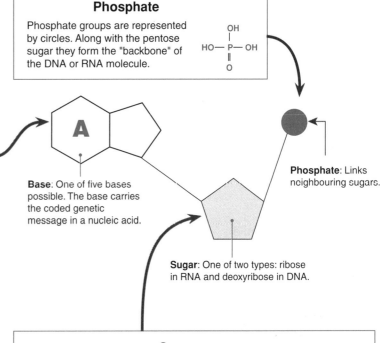

Phosphate

Phosphate groups are represented by circles. Along with the pentose sugar they form the "backbone" of the DNA or RNA molecule.

Base: One of five bases possible. The base carries the coded genetic message in a nucleic acid.

Phosphate: Links neighbouring sugars.

Sugar: One of two types: ribose in RNA and deoxyribose in DNA.

Nucleotide derivatives

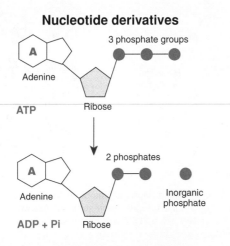

3 phosphate groups

Adenine

ATP   Ribose

2 phosphates

Adenine   Inorganic phosphate

ADP + Pi   Ribose

ATP is a nucleotide derivative used to provide chemical energy for metabolism. It consists of an adenine linked to a ribose sugar and 3 phosphate groups. Energy is made available when a phosphate group is transferred to a target molecule. Other nucleoside triphosphates (NTPs) have similar roles.

Sugars

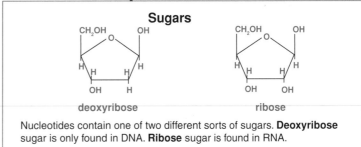

deoxyribose   ribose

Nucleotides contain one of two different sorts of sugars. **Deoxyribose** sugar is only found in DNA. **Ribose** sugar is found in RNA.

Nucleotide formation

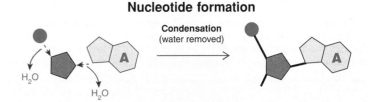

Condensation (water removed)

Phosphoric acid and a base are chemically bonded to a sugar molecule by a **condensation** reaction in which water is given off. The reverse reaction is **hydrolysis**.

1. List the nucleotide bases present:

   (a) In DNA: _Adenine, guanine, thymine, cytosine_

   (b) In RNA: _Adenine, guanine, cytosine, uracil_

2. Name the sugar present: (a) In DNA: _Deoxyribose_   (b) In RNA: _Ribose_

3. How can simple nucleotide units combine to store genetic information? _____

   _____

   _____

LINK 72   LINK 70   WEB 69   KNOW

70 Nucleic Acids

Key Idea: Nucleic acids are macromolecules made up of long chains of nucleotides, which store and transmit genetic information. DNA and RNA are nucleic acids.

DNA and RNA are nucleic acids involved in the transmission of inherited information. Nucleic acids have the capacity to store the information that controls cellular activity. The central nucleic acid is called **deoxyribonucleic acid** (DNA). **Ribonucleic acids** (RNA) are involved in the 'reading' of the DNA information. All nucleic acids are made up of nucleotides linked together to form chains or strands. The strands vary in the sequence of the bases found on each nucleotide. It is this sequence which provides the 'genetic instructions' for the cell.

Joining nucleotides

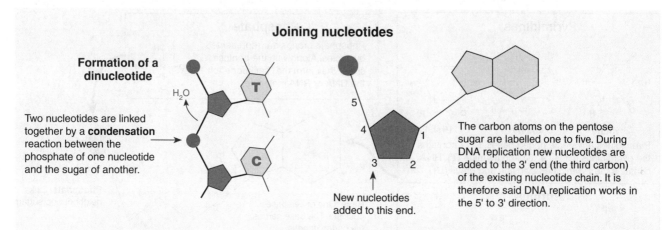

Formation of a dinucleotide

Two nucleotides are linked together by a **condensation** reaction between the phosphate of one nucleotide and the sugar of another.

New nucleotides added to this end.

The carbon atoms on the pentose sugar are labelled one to five. During DNA replication new nucleotides are added to the 3' end (the third carbon) of the existing nucleotide chain. It is therefore said DNA replication works in the 5' to 3' direction.

RNA molecule

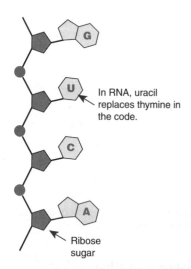

In RNA, uracil replaces thymine in the code.

Ribose sugar

Ribonucleic acid (RNA) comprises a single strand of nucleotides linked together. Although it is single stranded, it is often found folded back on itself, with complementary bases joined by hydrogen bonds.

DNA molecule

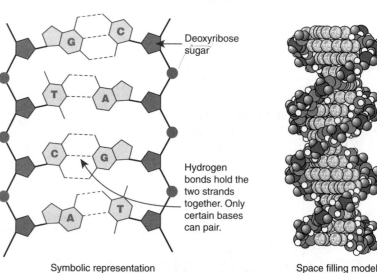

Deoxyribose sugar

Hydrogen bonds hold the two strands together. Only certain bases can pair.

Symbolic representation

Space filling model

Deoxyribonucleic acid (DNA) comprises a double strand of nucleotides linked together. It is shown unwound in the symbolic representation (above left). The DNA molecule takes on a twisted, double helix shape as shown in the space filling model above right.

Double-stranded DNA

The double-helix structure of DNA is like a ladder twisted into a corkscrew shape around its longitudinal axis. It is 'unwound' here to show the relationships between the bases.

▸ The DNA backbone is made up of alternating phosphate and sugar molecules, giving the DNA molecule an asymmetrical structure.

▸ The asymmetrical structure gives a DNA strand **direction**. Each strand runs in the opposite direction to the other.

▸ The ends of a DNA strand are labelled the 5' (five prime) and 3' (three prime) ends. The **5'** end has a terminal phosphate group (off carbon 5), the **3'** end has a terminal hydroxyl group (off carbon 3).

▸ The way the pairs of bases come together to form hydrogen bonds is determined by the number of bonds they can form and the configuration of the bases.

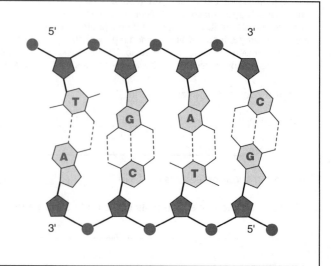

© 2015 **BIOZONE** International
ISBN: 978-1-927309-13-1
Photocopying Prohibited

RNAs are involved in decoding the genetic information in DNA, as messenger RNA (mRNA), transfer RNA (tRNA), and ribosomal RNA (rRNA). RNA is also involved in modifying mRNA after transcription and in regulating translation.

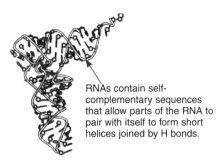

RNAs contain self-complementary sequences that allow parts of the RNA to pair with itself to form short helices joined by H bonds.

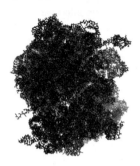

Messenger RNA (above) is transcribed (written) from DNA. It carries a copy of the genetic instructions from the DNA to ribosomes in the cytoplasm, where it is translated into a polypeptide chain.

Transfer RNA (above) carries amino acids to the growing polypeptide chain. One end of the tRNA carries the genetic code in a three-nucleotide sequence called the **anticodon**. The amino acid links to the 3' end of the tRNA.

Ribosomal RNA (above) forms ribosomes from two separate ribosomal components (the large and small subunits) and assembles amino acids into a polypeptide chain.

1. Label the following parts on the diagram of the double-stranded DNA molecule at the bottom of page 92:
   (a) Deoxyrlbose   (b) Phosphate   (c) Hydrogen bonds   (d) Purine bases   (e) Pyrimidine bases

2. (a) Explain the **base-pairing rule** that applies in double-stranded DNA: _____

   _____

   _____

   (b) How is the base-pairing rule for mRNA different? _____

   (c) What is the purpose of the hydrogen bonds in double-stranded DNA? _____

   _____

3. Briefly describe the roles of RNA: _____

   _____

4. (a) If you wanted to use a radioactive or fluorescent tag to label only the RNA in a cell and not the DNA, what molecule(s) would you label?

   _____

   (b) If you wanted to use a radioactive or fluorescent tag to label only the DNA in a cell and not the RNA, what molecule(s) would you label?

   _____

5. (a) Why do the DNA strands have an asymmetrical structure? _____

   _____

   (b) What are the differences between the 5' and 3' ends of a DNA strand? _____

   _____

6. Complete the following table summarising the differences between DNA and RNA molecules:

	DNA	RNA
Sugar present		
Bases present		
Number of strands		
Relative length		

71 Determining the Structure of DNA

Key Idea: Once the structure of DNA was known, it immediately suggested a mechanism for its replication. DNA is easily extracted and isolated from cells (see below). This was first done in 1869, but it took the work of many scientists working in different areas many years to determine DNA's structure. The final pieces of evidence came from a photographic technique called X-ray crystallography in which X-rays are shone through crystallised molecules to produce a pattern on a film. The pattern can be used to understand the structure of the molecule. The focus of much subsequent research on DNA has been on DNA products, i.e. proteins and non-protein regulatory molecules (regulatory RNAs).

Discovering the structure of DNA

Although James Watson and Francis Crick are often credited with the discovery of the structure of DNA, at least two other scientists were instrumental in acquiring the images on which Watson and Crick based their discovery.

Maurice Wilkins and Rosalind Franklin produced X-ray diffraction patterns of the DNA molecule. The patterns provided measurements of different parts of the molecule and the position of different groups of atoms. Wilkins showed Franklin's X-ray image (photo 51) to Watson and Crick who then correctly interpreted the image and produced a model of the DNA molecule.

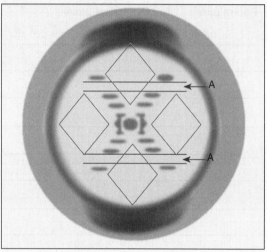

Diagram representing the image produced by Rosalind Franklin

Numerous distinct parts of the X-ray image indicate specific qualities of the DNA. The distinct X pattern indicates a helix structure, but Watson and Crick realised that the apparent gaps in the X (labelled **A**) were due to the repeating pattern of a *double* helix. The diamond shapes (in blue) indicate the helix is continuous and of constant dimensions and that the sugar-phosphate backbone is on the outside of the helix. The distance between the dark horizontal bands allows the calculation of the length of one full turn of the helix.

Structure and replication

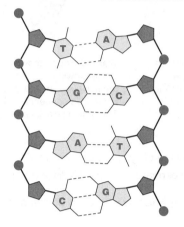

The realisation that DNA was a double helix consisting of antiparallel strands made of bases that followed a strict base pairing rule suggested a mechanism for its replication.

Watson and Crick hypothesised that each strand served as a template and that DNA replication was semi-conservative, producing two daughter strands consisting of half new and half parent material. This was confirmed by Meselson and Stahl.

DNA extraction by ethanol precipitation

DNA is easily extracted and precipitated out of solution using ice cold ethanol. Tissue is macerated in an extraction buffer and then cold ethanol is added so that the DNA precipitates out of the filtered suspension as visible whitish, glue-like strands (below left). The DNA can then be centrifuged with ethanol to form a pellet. Full methodologies are readily available through texts and online.

DNA extraction buffer contains water, detergent, and salt. The **detergent** helps to dissolve the cellular membranes of the tissue and deactivate DNases, which would chop up the DNA. The **salt** helps to remove the proteins bound to the DNA and keeps them in solution. Cations in the salt also neutralises the negative charge of the DNA. **Ethanol** causes the DNA to precipitate out by removing the water from around the molecule. Low temperatures speed up the precipitation and limit DNase activity.

Strawberries are good candidates for DNA because they are octaploid (8 sets of chromosomes) and their colour makes it easy to see the precipitating DNA.

1. What made Watson and Crick realise that DNA was a double helix? _____

2. In the extraction and isolation of DNA:

   (a) Why is it necessary to dissolve the cellular membranes? _____

   (b) Why does the DNA precipitate out in ethanol? _____

   (c) For a DNA extraction, why is it helpful that strawberries are octaploid? _____

3. In a DNA extraction, student A obtained DNA in long threads, whereas student B obtained DNA that appeared fluffy. Account for the differences in these two results and suggest what student B might have done incorrectly?

© 2015 **BIOZONE** International ISBN: 978-1-927309-13-1 Photocopying Prohibited

72 Constructing a DNA Model

Key Idea: Nucleotides pair together in a specific way called the base pairing rule. In DNA, adenine always pairs with thymine, and cytosine always pairs with guanine.
DNA molecules are double stranded. Each strand is made up of nucleotides. The chemical properties of each nucleotide mean it can only bind with one other type of nucleotide. This is called the **base pairing rule** and is explained in the table below. This exercise will help you to learn this rule.

DNA base pairing rule			
Adenine	is always attracted to	**Thymine**	A ←→ T
Thymine	is always attracted to	**Adenine**	T ←→ A
Cytosine	is always attracted to	**Guanine**	C ←→ G
Guanine	is always attracted to	**Cytosine**	G ←→ C

1. Cut around the nucleotides on page 97 and separate each of the 24 nucleotides by cutting along the columns and rows (see arrows indicating two such cutting points). Although drawn as geometric shapes, these symbols represent chemical structures.

2. Place one of each of the four kinds of nucleotide on their correct spaces below:

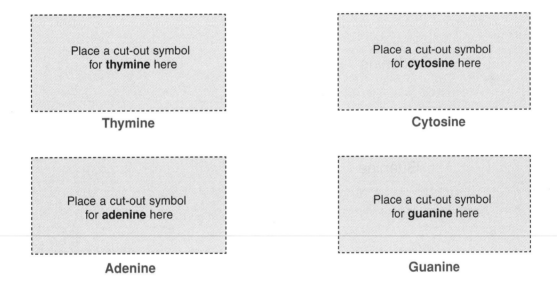

Place a cut-out symbol for **thymine** here

Thymine

Place a cut-out symbol for **cytosine** here

Cytosine

Place a cut-out symbol for **adenine** here

Adenine

Place a cut-out symbol for **guanine** here

Guanine

3. Identify and **label** each of the following features on the adenine nucleotide immediately above:
    phosphate, sugar, base, hydrogen bonds

4. Create one strand of the DNA molecule by placing the 9 correct 'cut out' nucleotides in the labelled spaces on the following page (DNA molecule). Make sure these are the right way up (with the **P** on the left) and are aligned with the left hand edge of each box. Begin with thymine and end with guanine.

5. Create the complementary strand of DNA by using the base pairing rule above. Note that the nucleotides have to be arranged upside down.

6. Under normal circumstances, it is not possible for adenine to pair up with guanine or cytosine, nor for any other mismatches to occur. Describe the **two factors** that prevent a mismatch from occurring:

    Factor 1: _____

    _____

    Factor 2: _____

    _____

7. Once you have checked that the arrangement is correct, you may glue, paste or tape these nucleotides in place.

> **NOTE:** There may be some value in keeping these pieces loose in order to practise the base pairing rule. For this purpose, *removable tape* would be best.

PRAC

DNA molecule

Put the named nucleotides on the left hand side to create the template strand

Put the matching **complementary** nucleotides opposite the template strand

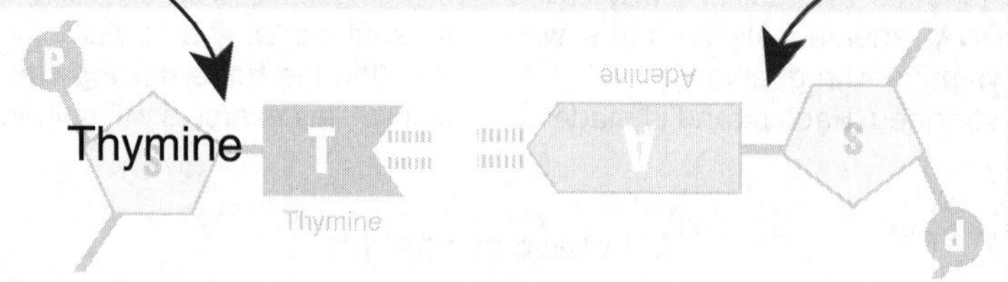

P

S

Thymine

T

Thymine

Adenine

A

S

P

Cytosine

Adenine

Adenine

Guanine

Thymine

Thymine

Cytosine

Guanine

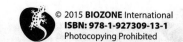

Nucleotides

Tear out this page and separate each of the 24 nucleotides
by cutting along the columns and rows (see arrows indicating the cutting points).

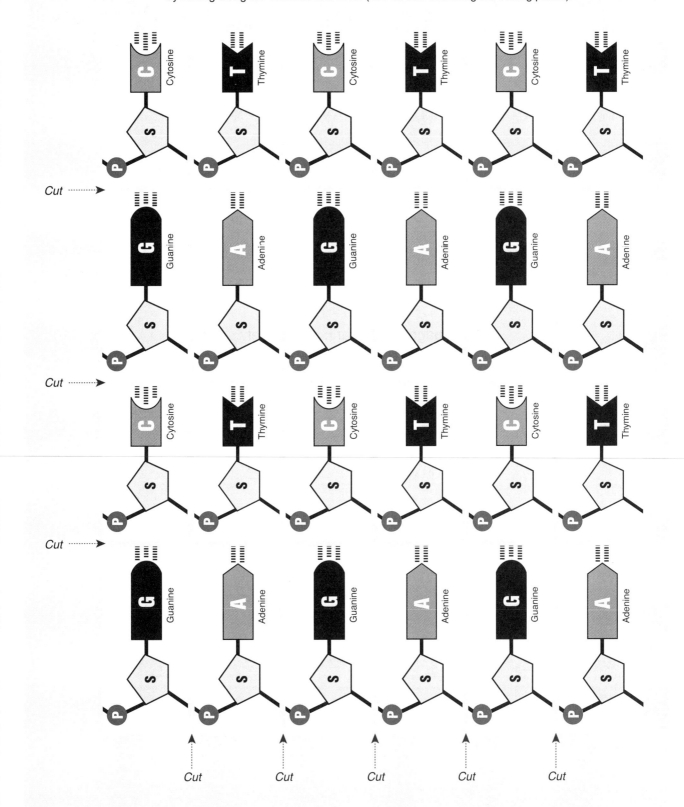

This page is left blank deliberately

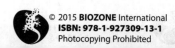

73 DNA Replication

Key Idea: Semi conservative DNA replication produces two identical copies of DNA, each containing half original material and half new material.

Before a cell can divide, it must double its DNA. It does this by a process called DNA replication. This process ensures that each resulting cell receives a complete set of genes from the original cell. After the DNA has replicated, each chromosome is made up of two chromatids, joined at the centromere. The two chromatids will become separated during cell division to form two separate chromosomes. During DNA replication, nucleotides are added at the replication fork. Enzymes are responsible for all of the key events.

Step 1
Unwinding the DNA molecule

A normal chromosome consists of an unreplicated DNA molecule. Before cell division, this long molecule of double stranded DNA must be replicated.

For this to happen, it is first untwisted and separated (unzipped) at high speed at its replication fork by an enzyme called helicase. Another enzyme relieves the strain that this generates by cutting, winding and rejoining the DNA strands.

Step 2
Making new DNA strands

The formation of new DNA is carried out mostly by an enzyme complex called DNA polymerase.

DNA polymerase catalyses the condensation reaction that joins adjacent nucleotides. The strand is synthesised in a 5' to 3' direction, with the polymerase moving 3' to 5' along the strand it is reading. Thus the nucleotides are assembled in a continuous fashion on one strand but in short fragments on the other strand. These fragments are later joined by an enzyme to form one continuous length.

Step 3
Rewinding the DNA molecule

Each of the two new double-helix DNA molecules has one strand of the original DNA (dark grey and white) and one strand that is newly synthesised (blue). The two DNA molecules rewind into their double-helix shape again.

DNA replication is semi-conservative, with each new double helix containing one old (parent) strand and one newly synthesised (daughter) strand. The new chromosome has twice as much DNA as a non-replicated chromosome. The two chromatids will become separated in the cell division process to form two separate chromosomes.

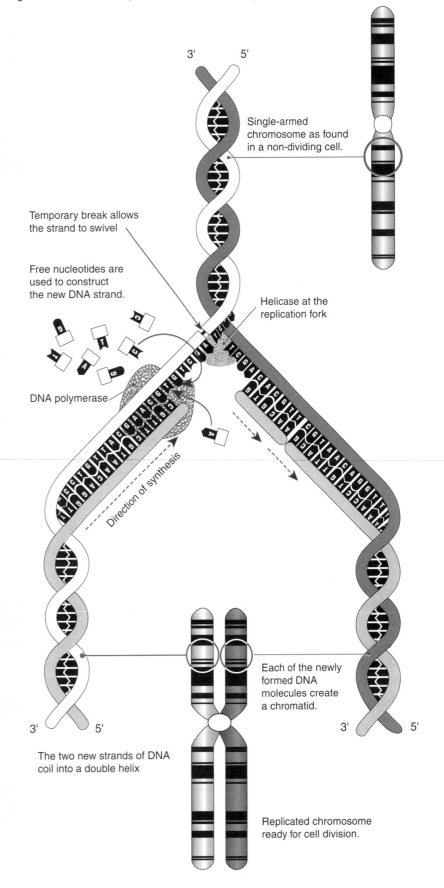

Single-armed chromosome as found in a non-dividing cell.

Temporary break allows the strand to swivel

Free nucleotides are used to construct the new DNA strand.

Helicase at the replication fork

DNA polymerase

Direction of synthesis

The two new strands of DNA coil into a double helix

Each of the newly formed DNA molecules create a chromatid.

Replicated chromosome ready for cell division.

LINK 75   LINK 74   WEB 73 KNOW

1. What is the purpose of DNA replication? _____

_____

2. Summarise the three main steps involved in DNA replication:

(a) _____

_____

(b) _____

_____

(c) _____

_____

3. For a cell with 22 chromosomes, state how many chromatids would exist following DNA replication: _____

4. State the percentage of DNA in each daughter cell that is new and the percentage that is original: _____

_____

5. What does it mean when we say DNA replication is semi-conservative? _____

_____

6. How are the new strands of DNA lengthened during replication: _____

_____

_____

7. What rule ensures that the two new DNA strands are identical to the original strand? _____

_____

_____

8. Why does one strand of DNA need to be copied in short fragments? _____

_____

_____

_____

9. Match the statements in the table below to form complete sentences, then put the sentences in order to make a coherent paragraph about DNA replication and its role:

The enzymes also proofread the DNA during replication...	...is required before mitosis or meiosis can occur.
DNA replication is the process by which the DNA molecule...	...by enzymes.
Replication is tightly controlled...	...to correct any mistakes.
After replication, the chromosome...	...and half new DNA.
DNA replication...	...during mitosis.
The chromatids separate...	...is copied to produce two identical DNA strands.
A chromatid contains half original ...	...is made up of two chromatids.

Write the complete paragraph here: _____

_____

_____

_____

_____

_____

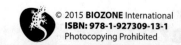

© 2015 **BIOZONE** International
ISBN: 978-1-927309-13-1
Photocopying Prohibited

74 Enzyme Control of DNA Replication

Key Idea: DNA replication is a directional process controlled by several different enzymes.

DNA replication involves many enzyme-controlled steps. They are shown below as separate, but many of the enzymes are clustered together as enzyme complexes. As the DNA is replicated, enzymes 'proof-read' it and correct mistakes. The polymerase enzyme can only work in one direction, so that one new strand is constructed as a continuous length (the leading strand) while the other new strand (the lagging strand) is made in short segments to be later joined together.

DNA replication occurs during interphase of the cell cycle at an astounding rate. As many as 4000 nucleotides per second are replicated. This explains how bacterial cells, with as many as 4 million nucleotides, can complete a cell cycle in about 20 minutes. Note that the nucleotides are present as deoxynucleoside triphosphates. When hydrolysed, these provide the energy for incorporating the nucleotide into the strand.

During the replication of the DNA, a mistake is made about once every 100 000 nucleotides replicated. These mistakes are corrected in two ways. A process called proof-reading occurs during replication. A second process called mismatch repair occurs after replication.

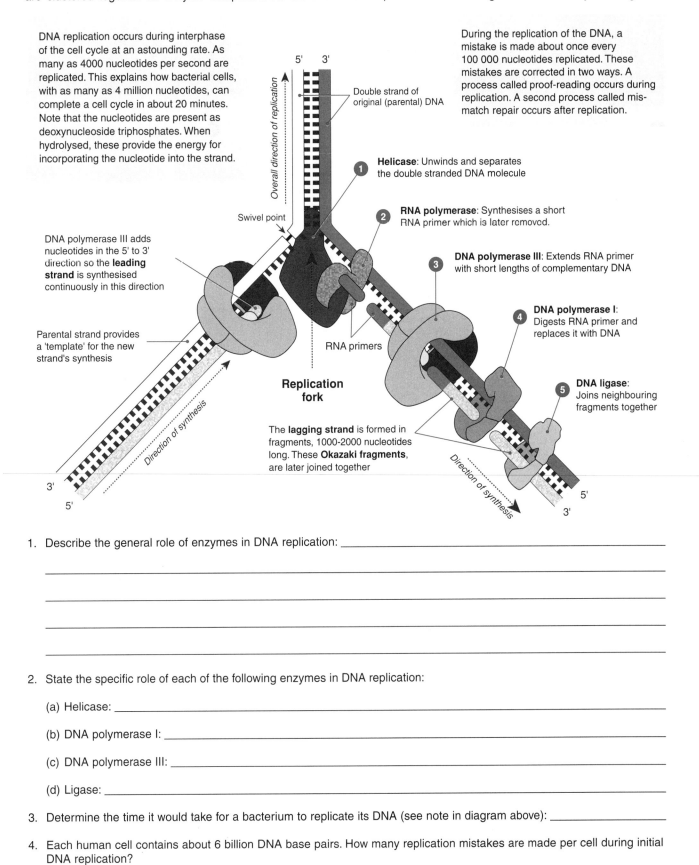

Overall direction of replication

5'   3'

Double strand of original (parental) DNA

Swivel point

DNA polymerase III adds nucleotides in the 5' to 3' direction so the **leading strand** is synthesised continuously in this direction

Parental strand provides a 'template' for the new strand's synthesis

1 **Helicase**: Unwinds and separates the double stranded DNA molecule

2 **RNA polymerase**: Synthesises a short RNA primer which is later removed.

3 **DNA polymerase III**: Extends RNA primer with short lengths of complementary DNA

4 **DNA polymerase I**: Digests RNA primer and replaces it with DNA

5 **DNA ligase**: Joins neighbouring fragments together

RNA primers

Replication fork

The **lagging strand** is formed in fragments, 1000-2000 nucleotides long. These **Okazaki fragments**, are later joined together

Direction of synthesis

3'

5'

Direction of synthesis

5'

3'

1. Describe the general role of enzymes in DNA replication: _____

_____

_____

_____

_____

2. State the specific role of each of the following enzymes in DNA replication:

(a) Helicase: _____

(b) DNA polymerase I: _____

(c) DNA polymerase III: _____

(d) Ligase: _____

3. Determine the time it would take for a bacterium to replicate its DNA (see note in diagram above): _____

4. Each human cell contains about 6 billion DNA base pairs. How many replication mistakes are made per cell during initial DNA replication?

_____

LINK   WEB

75 **74**   KNOW

75 | Meselson and Stahl's Experiment

Key Idea: Meselson and Stahl devised an experiment that showed DNA replication is semi-conservative. The anti-parallel, complementary structure of DNA suggested three possible mechanisms for its replication. The **semi-conservative model** proposed that each strand served as a template, forming new DNA molecules that were half old and half new DNA. The **conservative model** proposed that the original DNA served as a complete template so that the new DNA comprised two new strands. The **dispersive model** proposed that the two new DNA molecules had new and old DNA mixed throughout them. **Meselson and Stahl** devised a simple experiment to determine which model was correct.

Meselson and Stahl's experiment

E. coli were grown for several generations in a medium containing a **heavy nitrogen isotope** (^{15}N). Once all the bacterial DNA contained ^{15}N, they were transferred to a medium containing a **light nitrogen isotope** (^{14}N). After the transfer, newly synthesised DNA would contain ^{14}N and old DNA would contain ^{15}N.

1
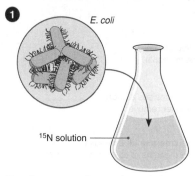

E. coli were grown in a nutrient solution containing ^{15}N. After 14 generations, all the bacterial DNA contained ^{15}N. A sample is removed. This is **generation 0**.

2
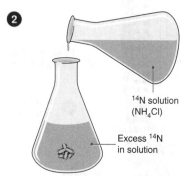

Generation 0 is added to a solution containing excess ^{14}N (as NH_4Cl). During replication, new DNA will incorporate ^{14}N and be 'lighter' than the original DNA (which contains only ^{15}N).

3
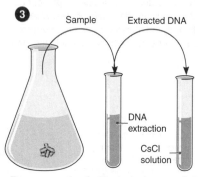

Every generation (~ 20 minutes), a sample is taken and treated to release the DNA. The DNA is placed in a CsCl solution which provides a density gradient for separation of the DNA.

4
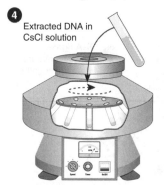

Samples are spun in a high speed ultracentrifuge at 140,000 *g* for 20 hours. Heavier ^{15}N DNA moves closer to the bottom of the test tube than light ^{14}N DNA or intermediate $^{14}N/^{15}N$ DNA.

5
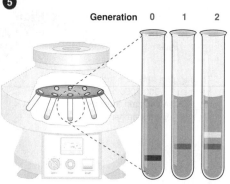
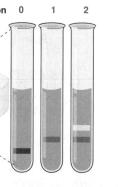

All the DNA in the generation 0 sample moved to the bottom of the test tube. All the DNA in the generation 1 sample moved to an intermediate position. At generation 2 half the DNA was at the intermediate position and half was near the top of the test tube. In subsequent generations, more DNA was near the top and less was in the intermediate position.

Models for DNA replication

Conservative   Semi-conservative   Dispersive

1. Describe each of the DNA replication models:

   (a) Conservative: _____

   _____

   (b) Semi-conservative: _____

   _____

   (c) Dispersive: _____

   _____

2. Explain why the *E. coli* were grown in an ^{15}N solution before being transferred to an ^{14}N solution: _____

   _____

   _____

© 2015 **BIOZONE** International
ISBN: 978-1-927309-13-1
Photocopying Prohibited

1C

76 Modelling DNA Replication

Key Idea: Meselson and Stahl's experiment to determine the nature of DNA replication can be modelled.

There were three possible models proposed to explain how DNA replicated. Meselson and Stahl's experiment was able to determine which method was used by starting with parent DNA that was heavier than would normally be expected. They were then able to analyse the relative weight of the replicated DNA to work out the correct replication method.

Instructions:

1. Cut out the DNA shapes provided on this page.

2. Intertwine the first pair (labelled 0) of heavy ^{15}N (black) DNA. This forms Generation 0 (parental DNA).

3. Use the descriptions of the three possible models for DNA replication on the previous page to model DNA replication in semi-conservative, conservative, and dispersive DNA replication.

4. For each replication method, record in the spaces provided on page 105 the percentage of **heavy** ^{15}N-^{15}N (black-black), **intermediate** ^{15}N-^{14}N (black-grey), **light** ^{14}N-^{14}N (grey-grey), or other DNA molecules formed.

5. For the dispersive model you will need to cut the DNA along the dotted lines and then stick them back together in the dispersed sequence with tape. **Construct the dispersive model LAST.**

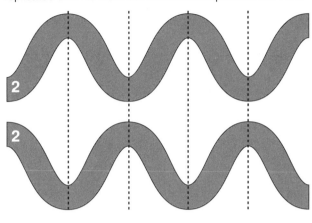

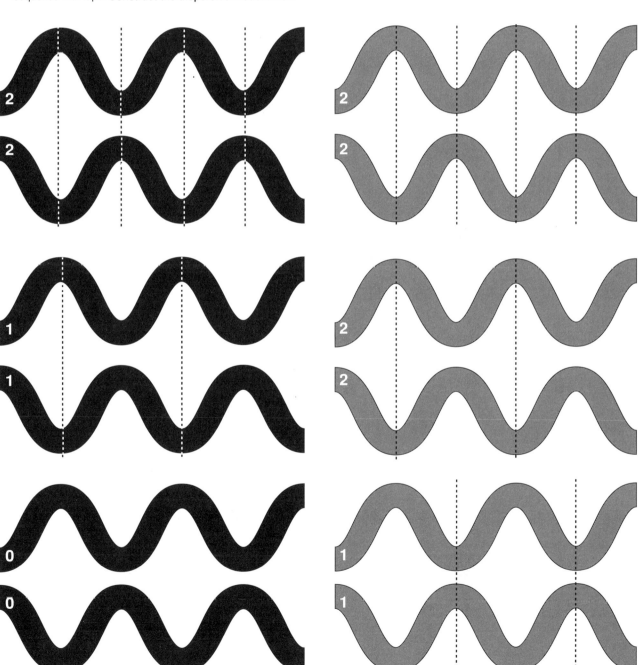

© 2015 **BIOZONE** International
ISBN: 978-1-927309-13-1
Photocopying Prohibited

LINK
75 PRAC

This page is left blank deliberately

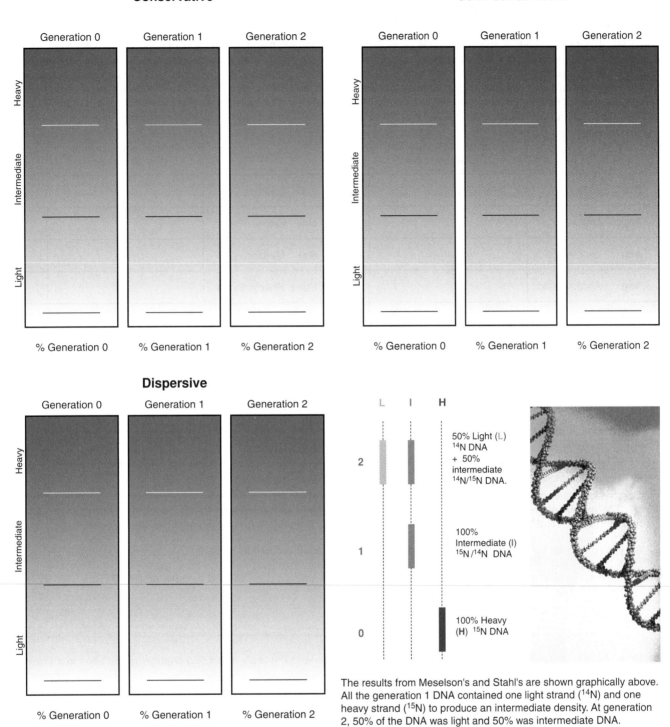

Conservative

Generation 0 | **Generation 1** | **Generation 2**

Heavy — Intermediate — Light

% Generation 0 | % Generation 1 | % Generation 2

Semi-conservative

Generation 0 | **Generation 1** | **Generation 2**

Heavy — Intermediate — Light

% Generation 0 | % Generation 1 | % Generation 2

Dispersive

Generation 0 | **Generation 1** | **Generation 2**

Heavy — Intermediate — Light

% Generation 0 | % Generation 1 | % Generation 2

L I H

2 — 50% Light (L) ^{14}N DNA + 50% intermediate ^{14}N/^{15}N DNA.

1 — 100% Intermediate (I) ^{15}N/^{14}N DNA

0 — 100% Heavy (H) ^{15}N DNA

The results from Meselson's and Stahl's are shown graphically above. All the generation 1 DNA contained one light strand (^{14}N) and one heavy strand (^{15}N) to produce an intermediate density. At generation 2, 50% of the DNA was light and 50% was intermediate DNA.

1. (a) Compare your modelling results to the results gained by Meselson and Stahl to decide which of the three DNA replication models is supported by the data:

_____

_____

(b) Was Watson and Crick's proposal correct? _____

2. Identify the replication model that fits the following data:

(a) 100% of generation 0 is "heavy DNA", 50% of generation 1 is "heavy" and 50% is "light", and 25% of generation 2 is "heavy" and 75% is "light":

_____

(b) 100% of generation 0 is "heavy DNA", 100% of generation 1 is "intermediate DNA", and 100% generation 2 lies between the "intermediate" and "light" DNA regions:

_____

77 The Genetic Code

Key Idea: The genetic code is the set of rules by which the genetic information in DNA or mRNA is translated into proteins. The genetic information for the assembly of amino acids is stored as three-base sequence. These three letter codes on mRNA are called **codons**. Each codon represents one of 20 amino acids used to make proteins. The code is effectively universal, being the same in all living things (with a few minor exceptions). The genetic code is summarised in a mRNA-amino acid table, which identifies the amino acid encoded by each mRNA codon. The code is degenerate, meaning there may be more than one codon for each amino acid. Most of this degeneracy is in the third nucleotide of a codon.

Amino acid		Codons that code for this amino acid	No.	Amino acid		Codons that code for this amino acid	No.
Ala	Alanine	GCU, GCC, GCA, GCG	4	**Leu**	Leucine		
Arg	Arginine			**Lys**	Lysine		
Asn	Asparagine			**Met**	Methionine		
Asp	Aspartic acid			**Phe**	Phenylalanine		
Cys	Cysteine			**Pro**	Proline		
Gln	Glutamine			**Ser**	Serine		
Glu	Glutamic acid			**Thr**	Threonine		
Gly	Glycine			**Trp**	Tryptophan		
His	Histidine			**Tyr**	Tyrosine		
Ile	Isoleucine			**Val**	Valine		

1. Use the **mRNA-amino acid table** (below) to list in the table above all the **codons** that code for each of the amino acids and the number of different codons that can code for each amino acid (the first amino acid has been done for you).

2. (a) How many amino acids could be coded for if a codon consisted of just two bases?_____

   (b) Why is this number of bases inadequate to code for the 20 amino acids required to make proteins?

   _____

   _____

3. Describe the consequence of the degeneracy of the genetic code to the likely effect of a change to one base in a triplet:

   _____

   _____

mRNA-amino acid table

How to read the table: The table on the right is used to 'decode' the genetic code as a sequence of amino acids in a polypeptide chain, from a given mRNA sequence. To work out which amino acid is coded for by a codon (triplet of bases) look for the first letter of the codon in the row label on the left hand side. Then look for the column that intersects the same row from above that matches the second base. Finally, locate the third base in the codon by looking along the row from the right hand end that matches your codon.

Example: Determine **CAG**

C on the left row,
A on the top column,
G on the right row
CAG is Gln (**glutamine**)

Read second letter here
Read first letter here →
Read third letter here

Second letter					
First letter	**U**	**C**	**A**	**G**	Third letter
U	UUU Phe UUC Phe UUA Leu UUG Leu	UCU Ser UCC Ser UCA Ser UCG Ser	UAU Tyr UAC Tyr UAA STOP UAG STOP	UGU Cys UGC Cys UGA STOP UGG Trp	U C A G
C	CUU Leu CUC Leu CUA Leu CUG Leu	CCU Pro CCC Pro CCA Pro CCG Pro	CAU His CAC His CAA Gln CAG Gln	CGU Arg CGC Arg CGA Arg CGG Arg	U C A G
A	AUU Ile AUC Ile AUA Ile AUG Met	ACU Thr ACC Thr ACA Thr ACG Thr	AAU Asn AAC Asn AAA Lys AAG Lys	AGU Ser AGC Ser AGA Arg AGG Arg	U C A G
G	GUU Val GUC Val GUA Val GUG Val	GCU Ala GCC Ala GCA Ala GCG Ala	GAU Asp GAC Asp GAA Glu GAG Glu	GGU Gly GGC Gly GGA Gly GGG Gly	U C A G

© 2015 **BIOZONE** International
ISBN: 978-1-927309-13-1
Photocopying Prohibited

78 Cracking the Genetic Code

Key Idea: Scientists used mathematics and experiments to unlock the genetic code. A series of three nucleotides, called a triplet, codes for a single amino acid.

In the 1960s, two scientists, Marshall Nirenberg and Heinrich

Matthaei, developed an experiment to crack the genetic code. Their experiment, which is sometimes called the poly-U experiment because it used a synthetic mRNA containing only uracil, is shown below.

The genetic code

Once it was discovered that DNA carries the genetic code needed to produce proteins, the race was on to "crack the code" and find out how it worked.

The first step was to find out how many nucleotide bases code for an amino acid. Scientists knew that there were four nucleotide bases in mRNA, and that there are 20 amino acids. Simple mathematics (below) showed that a one or two base code did not produce enough amino acids, but a triplet code produced more amino acids than existed.

The triplet code was accepted once scientists confirmed that some amino acids have multiple codes.

Number of bases in the code	Working	Number of amino acids produced
Single (4^1)	4	4 amino acids
Double (4^2)	4 x 4	16 amino acids
Triple (4^3)	4 x 4 x 4	64 amino acids

A triplet (three nucleotide bases) codes for a single amino acid. The triplet code on mRNA is called a codon.

How was the genetic code cracked?

Once the triplet code was discovered, the next step was to find out which amino acid each codon produced. Two scientists, Marshall Nirenberg and Heinrich Matthaei, developed an experiment (below) to crack the code.

A cell free *E. coli* extract was produced for their experiment by rupturing the bacterial cells to release the cytoplasm. The extract had all the components needed to make proteins (except mRNA).

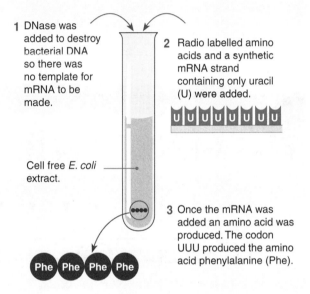

1 DNase was added to destroy bacterial DNA so there was no template for mRNA to be made.

2 Radio labelled amino acids and a synthetic mRNA strand containing only uracil (U) were added.

Cell free *E. coli* extract.

3 Once the mRNA was added an amino acid was produced. The codon UUU produced the amino acid phenylalanine (Phe).

4 Over the next few years, similar experiments were carried out using different combinations of nucleotides until all of the codes were known.

---

1. (a) How many types of nucleotide bases are there in mRNA? _____

   (b) How many types of amino acids are there? _____

   (c) Why did scientists reject a one or two base code when trying to work out the genetic code? _____

   _____

   _____

2. A triplet code could potentially produce 64 amino acids. Why are only 20 amino acids produced? _____

   _____

3. (a) Why was DNase added to the cell free *E. coli* extract? _____

   _____

   _____

   (b) What would it have been difficult to crack the code if no DNase was added?_____

   _____

   _____

79 Genes to Proteins

Key Idea: Genes are sections of DNA that code for proteins. Genes are expressed when they are transcribed into messenger RNA (mRNA) and then translated into a protein. **Gene expression** is the process of rewriting a gene into a protein. It involves **transcription** of the DNA into mRNA and **translation** of the mRNA into protein. A gene is bounded by a start (promoter) region, upstream of the gene, and a terminator region, downstream of the gene. These regions control transcription by telling RNA polymerase where to start and stop transcription of the gene. The information flow for gene to protein is shown below. Nucleotides are read in groups of three called triplets. The equivalent on the mRNA molecule is the codon. Some codons have special control functions (start and stop) in the making of a protein.

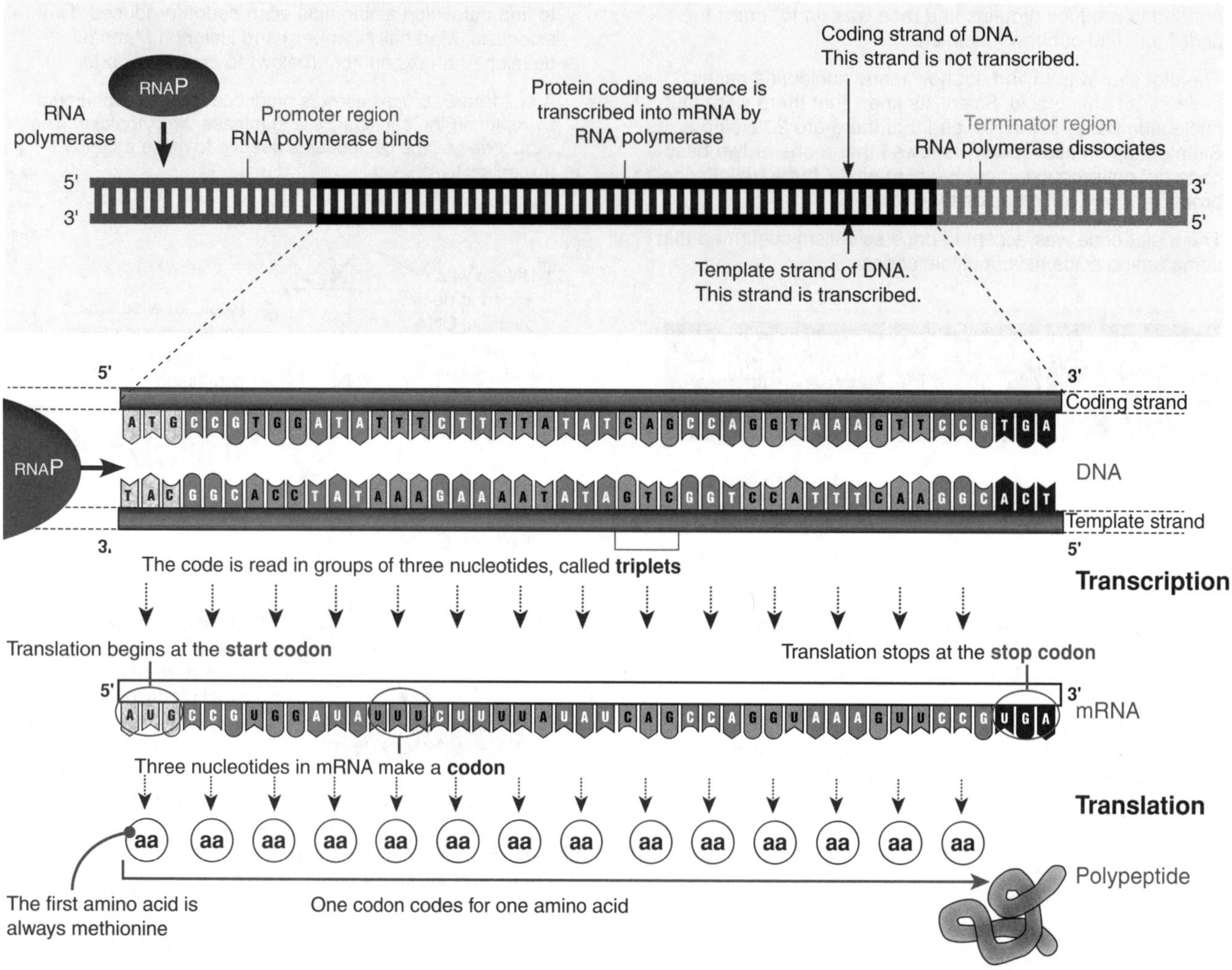

Coding strand of DNA. This strand is not transcribed.

RNA polymerase

RNAP

Promoter region RNA polymerase binds

Protein coding sequence is transcribed into mRNA by RNA polymerase

Terminator region RNA polymerase dissociates

5'
3'
3'
5'

Template strand of DNA. This strand is transcribed.

5'
3'
Coding strand

RNAP

DNA

Template strand
5'

3. The code is read in groups of three nucleotides, called **triplets**

Transcription

Translation begins at the **start codon**

Translation stops at the **stop codon**

5'
3'
mRNA

Three nucleotides in mRNA make a **codon**

Translation

aa aa aa aa aa aa aa aa aa aa aa aa aa aa

Polypeptide

The first amino acid is always methionine

One codon codes for one amino acid

1. (a) The three base code on DNA is called: _____

   (b) The three base code on mRNA is called: _____

2. (a) What is a **gene**? _____

   _____

   (b) What molecule transcribes the gene? _____

   (c) What is the role of the promoter and terminator regions? _____

   _____

3. What does the term **gene expression** mean? _____

   _____

4. Recall the anti-parallel nature of DNA, with the strands orientated in opposite directions. Explain its significance:

   _____

   _____

© 2015 **BIOZONE** International
ISBN: 978-1-927309-13-1
Photocopying Prohibited

80 Transcription in Eukaryotes

Key Idea: Transcription is the first step of gene expression. A segment of DNA is transcribed (rewritten) into mRNA. In eukaryotes, transcription takes place in the nucleus.

The enzyme that directly controls transcription is RNA polymerase, which makes a strand of mRNA using the single strand of DNA (the **template strand**) as a template. The enzyme transcribes a gene length of DNA at a time and recognises start and stop signals (codes) at the beginning and end of the gene. Only RNA polymerase is involved in mRNA synthesis as it unwinds the DNA as well. It is common to find several RNA polymerase enzyme molecules on the same gene at any one time, allowing a high rate of mRNA synthesis to occur. In eukaryotes, non-coding sections called **introns** must first be removed and the remaining **exons** spliced together to form mature mRNA before the mRNA can be translated into a protein.

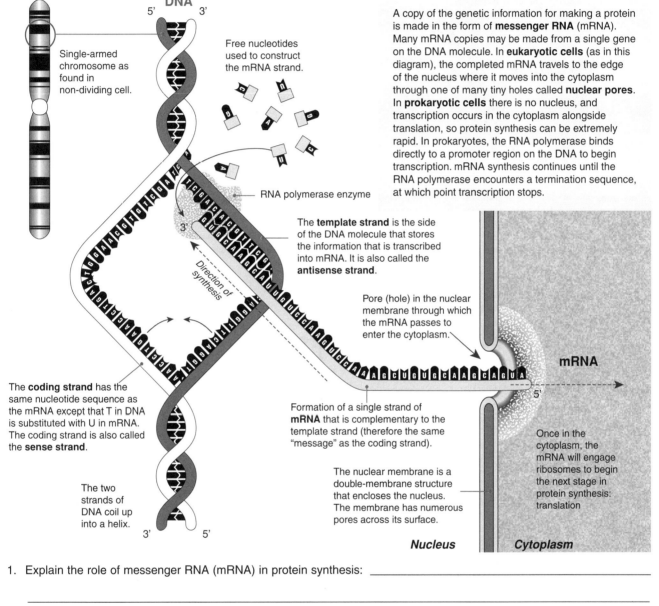

A copy of the genetic information for making a protein is made in the form of **messenger RNA** (mRNA). Many mRNA copies may be made from a single gene on the DNA molecule. In **eukaryotic cells** (as in this diagram), the completed mRNA travels to the edge of the nucleus where it moves into the cytoplasm through one of many tiny holes called **nuclear pores**. In **prokaryotic cells** there is no nucleus, and transcription occurs in the cytoplasm alongside translation, so protein synthesis can be extremely rapid. In prokaryotes, the RNA polymerase binds directly to a promoter region on the DNA to begin transcription. mRNA synthesis continues until the RNA polymerase encounters a termination sequence, at which point transcription stops.

Single-armed chromosome as found in non-dividing cell.

Free nucleotides used to construct the mRNA strand.

RNA polymerase enzyme

The **template strand** is the side of the DNA molecule that stores the information that is transcribed into mRNA. It is also called the **antisense strand**.

Pore (hole) in the nuclear membrane through which the mRNA passes to enter the cytoplasm.

mRNA

The **coding strand** has the same nucleotide sequence as the mRNA except that T in DNA is substituted with U in mRNA. The coding strand is also called the **sense strand**.

Formation of a single strand of **mRNA** that is complementary to the template strand (therefore the same "message" as the coding strand).

Once in the cytoplasm, the mRNA will engage ribosomes to begin the next stage in protein synthesis: translation

The nuclear membrane is a double-membrane structure that encloses the nucleus. The membrane has numerous pores across its surface.

The two strands of DNA coil up into a helix.

Nucleus   ***Cytoplasm***

1. Explain the role of messenger RNA (mRNA) in protein synthesis: _____

_____

_____

2. The genetic code contains punctuation codons to mark the starting and finishing points of the code for synthesis of polypeptide chains and proteins. Consult the mRNA–amino acid table earlier in this workbook and state the codes for:

   (a) Start codon: _____ (b) Stop (termination) codons: _____

3. For the following triplets on the DNA, determine the **codon** sequence for the mRNA that would be synthesised:

   (a) Triplets on the DNA: T A C   T A G   C C G   C G A   T T T

   Codons on the mRNA: _____

   (b) Triplets on the DNA: T A C   A A G   C C T   A T A   A A A

   Codons on the mRNA: _____

LINK   LINK   WEB
82   81   80

KNOW

81 Translation

Key Idea: Translation is the second step of gene expression. It occurs in the cytoplasm, where ribosomes read the mRNA code and decode it to synthesise protein.

In eukaryotes, translation occurs in the cytoplasm associated with free ribosomes or ribosomes on the rough endoplasmic reticulum. The diagram below shows how a mRNA molecule can be 'serviced' by many ribosomes at the same time. The role of the tRNA molecules is to bring in the individual amino acids. The anticodon of each tRNA must make a perfect complementary match with the mRNA codon before the amino acid is released. Once released, the amino acid is added to the growing polypeptide chain by enzymes.

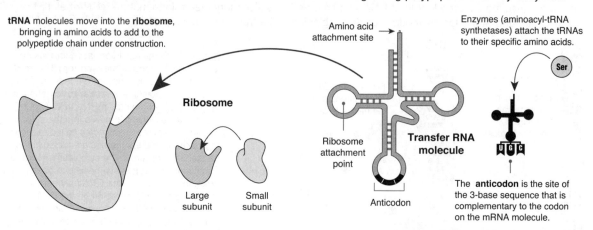

tRNA molecules move into the **ribosome**, bringing in amino acids to add to the polypeptide chain under construction.

Ribosome

Large subunit   Small subunit

Amino acid attachment site

Enzymes (aminoacyl-tRNA synthetases) attach the tRNAs to their specific amino acids.

Ser

Ribosome attachment point

Transfer RNA molecule

Anticodon

UGG

The **anticodon** is the site of the 3-base sequence that is complementary to the codon on the mRNA molecule.

Ribosomes are made up of a complex of ribosomal RNA (rRNA) and proteins. They exist as two separate sub-units (above) until they are attracted to a binding site on the mRNA molecule, when they join together. Ribosomes have binding sites that attract transfer RNA (**tRNA**) molecules loaded with amino acids. The tRNA molecules are about 80 nucleotides in length and are made under the direction of genes in the chromosomes. There is a different tRNA molecule for each of the different possible anticodons (see the diagram below) and, because of the degeneracy of the genetic code, there may be up to six different tRNAs carrying the same amino acid.

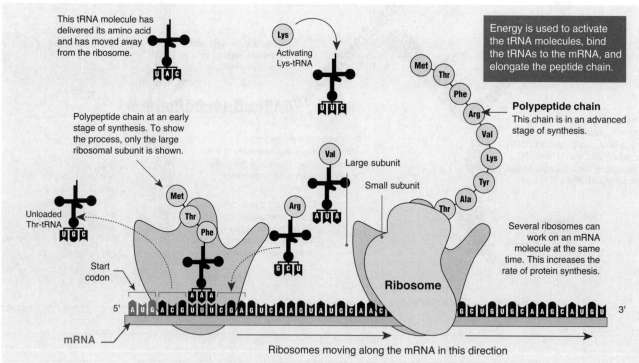

This tRNA molecule has delivered its amino acid and has moved away from the ribosome.

UAC

Polypeptide chain at an early stage of synthesis. To show the process, only the large ribosomal subunit is shown.

Unloaded Thr-tRNA

UGC

Start codon

Met
Thr
Phe

AAA

Lys

Activating Lys-tRNA

UUC

Val

Arg

AUA

Large subunit

Small subunit

GCU

Met
Thr
Phe
Arg
Val
Lys
Tyr
Ala
Thr

Energy is used to activate the tRNA molecules, bind the tRNAs to the mRNA, and elongate the peptide chain.

Polypeptide chain
This chain is in an advanced stage of synthesis.

Several ribosomes can work on an mRNA molecule at the same time. This increases the rate of protein synthesis.

Ribosome

5' AUGACGUUUCGAGUCAAGUAUGCAAC   GCUGUGCAAGCAUGU 3'

mRNA

Ribosomes moving along the mRNA in this direction

1. For the following codons on the mRNA, determine the **anticodons** for each tRNA that would deliver the amino acids:

   Codons on the mRNA: U A C   U A G   C C G   C G A   U U U

   Anticodons on the tRNAs: _____

2. There are many different types of tRNA molecules, each with a different anticodon (HINT: see the mRNA table).

   (a) How many different tRNA types are there, each with a unique anticodon? _____

   (b) Explain your answer: _____

   _____

© 2015 **BIOZONE** International
ISBN: 978-1-927309-13-1
Photocopying Prohibited

82 Protein Synthesis Summary

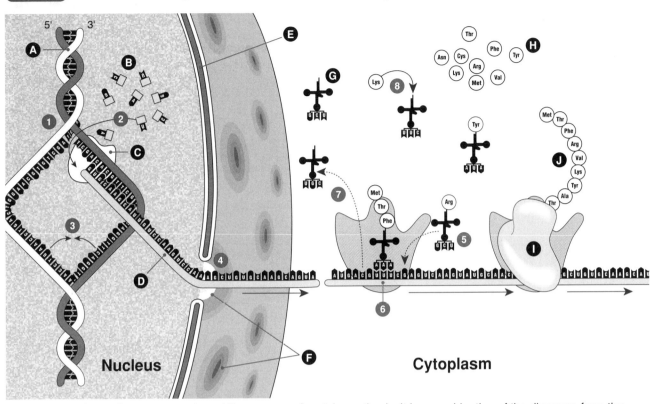

Nucleus

Cytoplasm

The diagram above shows an overview of the process of protein synthesis. It is a combination of the diagrams from the previous two pages. Each of the major steps in the process are numbered, while structures are labelled with letters.

1. Briefly describe each of the numbered processes in the diagram above:

(a) Process 1: _____

(b) Process 2: _____

(c) Process 3: _____

(d) Process 4: _____

(e) Process 5: _____

(f) Process 6: _____

(g) Process 7: _____

(h) Process 8: _____

2. Identify each of the structures marked with a letter and write their names below in the spaces provided:

(a) Structure A: _____   (f) Structure F: _____

(b) Structure B: _____   (g) Structure G: _____

(c) Structure C: _____   (h) Structure H: _____

(d) Structure D: _____   (i) Structure I: _____

(e) Structure E: _____   (j) Structure J: _____

3. Describe two factors that would determine whether or not a particular protein is produced in the cell:

(a) _____

_____

(b) _____

_____

© 2015 **BIOZONE** International
ISBN: 978-1-927309-13-1
Photocopying Prohibited

LINK
81

LINK
80

WEB
82

REVISE

83 Chapter Review

Summarise what you know about this topic under the headings provided. You can draw diagrams or mind maps, or write short notes to organise your thoughts. Use the images and hints included to help you:

Nucleotides and nucleic acids

HINT: Structure and function of nucleotides and nucleic acids.

DNA
HINT: How does the structure of DNA relate to its replication.

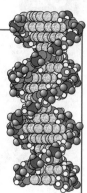

Genes to proteins
HINT: DNA to mRNA, mRNA to polypeptides. The genetic code.

1. Test your vocabulary by matching each term to its correct definition, as identified by its preceding letter code.

base-pairing rule

A Single stranded nucleic acid that consists of nucleotides containing ribose sugar.

coding strand

B A set of rules by which information encoded in DNA or mRNA is translated into proteins.

DNA

C The rule governing the pairing of complementary bases in DNA.

D A two-ringed organic base that forms adenine and guanine in nucleic acids.

genetic code

E Form of intermolecular bonding between hydrogen and an electronegative atom such as oxygen.

hydrogen bonding

F The sequence of DNA that is read during the synthesis of mRNA.

nucleic acids

G Universally found macromolecules composed of chains of nucleotides. These molecules carry genetic information within cells.

nucleotides

H The DNA strand with the same base sequence as the RNA transcript produced (although with thymine replaced by uracil in mRNA).

purine

I Macromolecule consisting of many millions of units containing a phosphate group, sugar and a base (A,T, C or G). Stores the genetic information of the cell.

pyrimidine

J The structural units of nucleic acids, DNA and RNA.

RNA

K A single-ringed organic base that forms uracil, cytosine, or thymine in nucleic acids.

template strand

2. (a) On the diagram shown right, highlight the structure that indicates a DNA helix.

   (b) Circle the region that indicates there is a double helix.

   (c) What do the blank diamond shaped areas in the diagram indicate?

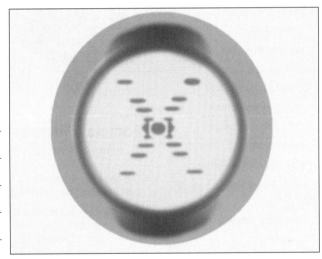

_____

_____

_____

_____

_____

3. For the following DNA sequence, give the mRNA sequence and then Identify the amino acids that are encoded. For this question you may consult the mRNA-amino acid table earlier in the chapter.

   DNA: G A A C C C T T A C A T A T C G T G C T

   mRNA: _____

   Amino acids: _____

4. Complete the following paragraph by **deleting** one of the words in the **bracketed () pairs** below:

   In eukaryotes, gene expression begins with (transcription/translation) which occurs in the (cytoplasm/nucleus).

   (Transcription/Translation) is the copying of the DNA code into (mRNA/tRNA). The (mRNA/tRNA) is then transported to

   the (cytoplasm/nucleus) where (transcription/translation) occurs. Ribosomes attach to the (mRNA/tRNA) and help match

   the codons on (mRNA/tRNA) with the anticodons on (mRNA/tRNA). The (mRNA/tRNA) transports the animo acids to the

   ribosome where they are added to the growing (polypeptide/carbohydrate) chain.

© 2015 **BIOZONE** International
ISBN: 978-1-927309-13-1
Photocopying Prohibited

Enzymes

Enzymes as catalysts

Learning outcomes

Activity number

☐ 1 Explain the role of enzymes in catalysing reactions that regulate metabolism at both the cellular level and at the level of the whole organism. Distinguish between anabolic and catabolic reactions.

85 86

☐ 2 Using examples, describe the role of enzymes in catalysing both intracellular and extracellular reactions, including reference to catalase (intracellular) and amylase and trypsin (extracellular).

85 86

☐ 3 Describe the mechanism of enzyme action, including reference to the enzyme's tertiary structure and the role of the active site, specificity, and lowering of activation energy.

85 86

☐ 4 Explain the lock-and-key and induced fit models for enzyme function, with reference to the enzyme-substrate complex, enzyme-product complex, and product formation.

87

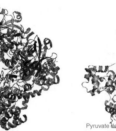 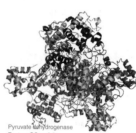 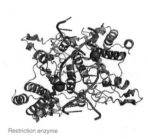

Catalase   Pyruvate dehydrogenase   Restriction enzyme
FontanaCG cc 3.0

Factors affecting enzyme activity

Learning outcomes

Activity number

☐ 5 Describe the effect of pH, temperature, substrate concentration, and enzyme concentration on enzyme activity. Recognise that enzymes can be denatured.

85 88

☐ 6 **PAG4** Investigate the effects of pH, temperature, substrate concentration, or enzyme concentration on enzyme activity. If appropriate, prepare enzyme and substrate dilutions using serial dilution technique.

89 92

☐ 7 Using examples, explain the role of cofactors (e.g. Cl^- for amylase), coenzymes (e.g. vitamins), and prosthetic groups (e.g. Zn^{2+} for carbonic anhydrase) in enzyme-controlled reactions.

90

☐ 8 Using examples, describe the effects of inhibitors on the rate of enzyme-controlled reactions. Include reference to competitive and non-competitive inhibition and identify these on graphs of reaction rate vs substrate concentration.

91

☐ 9 Distinguish between reversible and non-reversible inhibitors with reference to the action of metabolic poisons and some medicinal drugs. Explain the role of end-product inhibition in regulating metabolic pathways.

91

☐ 10 Explain the role of enzymes in activating inactive precursors in metabolic pathways, e.g. activation of pepsinogen by acid in the stomach to form the active enzyme pepsin, and the fibrinogen-fibrin blood clotting pathway (A level only).

93

85 Enzymes

Key Idea: Enzymes are biological catalysts. The active site is critical to this functional role.

Most enzymes are proteins. Enzymes are called biological catalysts because they speed up biochemical reactions, but the enzyme itself remains unchanged. The substrate in a reaction binds to a region of the enzyme called the active site, which is formed by the precise folding of the enzyme's amino acid chain. Enzymes control metabolic pathways. One enzyme will act on a substance to produce the next reactant in a pathway, which will be acted on by a different enzyme.

The active site

Enzymes have an **active site** to which specific substrates bind. The shape and chemistry of the active site is specific to an enzyme, and is a function of the polypeptide's complex tertiary structure.

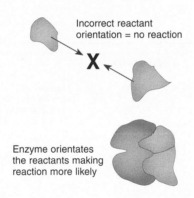

The chemical that an enzyme acts on is the **substrate**. An enzyme acts on a specific substrate.

Extremes of temperature or pH can alter the enzyme's active site and lead to loss of function. This is called **denaturation**.

Substrates collide with an enzyme's active site

For a reaction to occur reactants must collide with sufficient speed and with the correct orientation. Enzymes enhance reaction rates by providing a site for reactants to come together in such a way that a reaction will occur. They do this by orientating the reactants so that the reactive regions are brought together. They may also destabilise the bonds within the reactants making it easier for a reaction to occur.

Incorrect reactant orientation = no reaction

X

Enzyme orientates the reactants making reaction more likely

Enzymes can be intracellular or extracellular

Enzymes can be defined based on where they are produced relative to where they are active.

An **intracellular enzyme** is an enzyme that performs its function within the cell that produces it. Most enzymes are intracellular enzymes, e.g. respiratory enzymes. **Example**: Catalase.

Many metabolic processes produce hydrogen peroxide, which is harmful to cells. Catalase converts hydrogen peroxide into water and oxygen (below) to prevent damage to cells and tissues.

$2H_2O_2$ 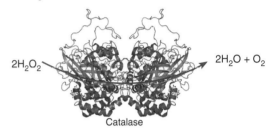 $2H_2O + O_2$

Catalase

An **extracellular enzyme** is an enzyme that functions outside the cell from which it originates (i.e. it is produced in one location but active in another). **Examples**: Amylase and trypsin.
Amylase is a digestive enzyme produced in the salivary glands and pancreas in humans. However, it acts in the mouth and small intestine respectively to hydrolyse starch into sugars.

Trypsin is a protein-digesting enzyme and hydrolyses the peptide bond immediately after a basic residue (e.g. arginine). It is produced in an inactive form (called trypsinogen) and secreted into the small intestine by the pancreas. It is activated in the intestine by the enzyme enteropeptidase to form trypsin. Active trypsin can convert more trypsinogen to trypsin.

1. (a) What is meant by the **active site** of an enzyme and relate it to the enzyme's tertiary structure: _____

_____

_____

_____

   (b) Why are enzymes specific to one substrate (or group of closely related substrates)? _____

_____

_____

2. How do substrate molecules come into contact with an enzyme's active site? _____

_____

3. (a) Suggest why digestion (the breakdown of large macromolecules) is largely performed by extracellular enzymes:

_____

   (b) Why would an extracellular enzyme be produced and secreted in an inactive form? _____

_____

© 2015 **BIOZONE** International
ISBN: 978-1-927309-13-1
Photocopying Prohibited

LINK **88** LINK **86** WEB **85** KNOW

86 How Enzymes Work

Key Idea: Enzymes increase the rate of biological reactions by lowering the reaction's activation energy.

Chemical reactions in cells are accompanied by energy changes. The amount of energy released or taken up is directly related to the tendency of a reaction to run to completion (for all the reactants to form products). Any reaction needs to raise the energy of the substrate to an unstable transition state before the reaction will proceed (below). The amount of energy needed to do this is the **activation energy** (*Ea*). Enzymes lower the *Ea* by destabilising bonds in the substrate so that it is more reactive. Enzyme reactions can break down a single substrate molecule into simpler substances (catabolic reactions), or join two or more substrate molecules together (anabolic reactions).

Lowering the activation energy

The presence of an enzyme simply makes it easier for a reaction to take place. All catalysts speed up reactions by influencing the stability of bonds in the reactants. They may also provide an alternative reaction pathway, thus lowering the activation energy (Ea) needed for a reaction to take place (see the graph below).

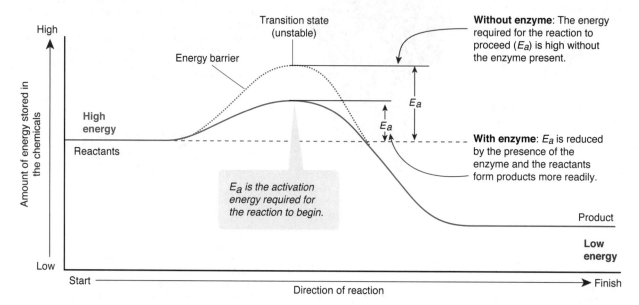

Without enzyme: The energy required for the reaction to proceed (*Ea*) is high without the enzyme present.

With enzyme: *Ea* is reduced by the presence of the enzyme and the reactants form products more readily.

Ea is the activation energy required for the reaction to begin.

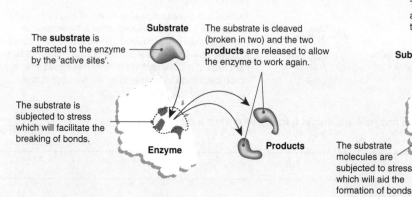

Catabolic reactions

Some enzymes can cause a single substrate molecule to be drawn into the active site. Chemical bonds are broken, causing the substrate molecule to break apart to become two separate molecules. Catabolic reactions break down complex molecules into simpler ones and involve a net release of energy, so they are called exergonic.
Examples: *hydrolysis, cellular respiration*.

Anabolic reactions

Some enzymes can cause two substrate molecules to be drawn into the active site. Chemical bonds are formed, causing the two substrate molecules to form bonds and become a single molecule. Anabolic reactions involve a net use of energy (they are endergonic) and build more complex molecules and structures from simpler ones.
Examples: *protein synthesis, photosynthesis*.

1. How do enzymes lower the activation energy for a reaction? _____

_____

_____

2. Describe the difference between a catabolic and anabolic reaction: _____

_____

© 2015 **BIOZONE** International
ISBN: 978-1-927309-13-1
Photocopying Prohibited

87 Models of Enzyme Activity

Key Idea: Enzymes catalyse reactions by providing a reaction site for a substrate. The model that describes the behaviour of enzymes the best is the induced fit model.

The initial model of enzyme activity was the lock and key model proposed by Emil Fischer in the 1890s. Fischer proposed enzymes were rigid structures, similar to a lock, and the substrate was the key. While some aspects of

Fischer's model were correct, for example, substrates align with enzymes in a way that is likely to make a reaction more likely, the model has been adapted as techniques to study molecular structures have developed. The current 'induced-fit' model of enzyme function is supported by studies of enzyme inhibitors, which show that enzymes are flexible and change shape when interacting with the substrate.

The lock and key model of enzyme function

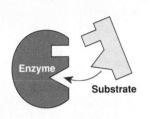

1 The substrate molecule is drawn into site of the enzyme. The enzyme's active site does not change shape.

2 The enzyme-substrate (ES) complex is formed.

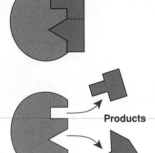

3 The enzyme reaction takes place to form the enzyme-product (EP) complex.

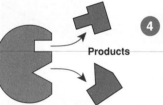

4 The products are released from the enzyme. Note there has been no change in the shape of the active site throughout the reaction.

The **lock and key model** first proposed in 1894 suggested that the (perfectly fitting) substrate was simply drawn into a matching site on the enzyme molecule. If the substrate did not perfectly fit the active site, the reaction did not proceed. This model was supported by early X-ray crystallography studies but has since been modified to recognise the flexibility of enzymes (the induced fit model).

The current induced fit model

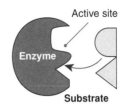

1 A substrate molecule is drawn into the enzyme's active site, which is like a cleft into which the substrate molecule(s) fit.

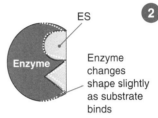

2 The enzyme changes shape as the substrate binds, forming an enzyme-substrate (ES) complex. The shape change makes the substrate more amenable to alteration. In this way, the enzyme's interaction with its substrate is best regarded as an induced fit.

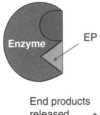

3 The ES interaction results in an intermediate enzyme-product (EP) complex. The substrate becomes bound to the enzyme by weak chemical bonds, straining bonds in the substrate and allowing the reaction to proceed more readily.

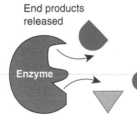

4 The end products are released and the enzyme returns to its previous shape.

Once the substrate enters the active site, the shape of the active site changes to form an active complex. The formation of an ES complex strains substrate bonds and lowers the energy required to reach the transition state. The induced-fit model is supported by X-ray crystallography, chemical analysis, and studies of enzyme inhibitors, which show that enzymes are flexible and change shape when interacting with the substrate.

1. Describe the key features of the '**lock and key**' model of enzyme action and explain its deficiencies as a working model:

_____

_____

_____

2. How does the current '**induced fit**' model of enzyme action differ from the lock and key model?

_____

_____

_____

88 Enzyme Kinetics

Key Idea: Enzymes operate most effectively within a narrow range of conditions. The rate of enzyme-catalysed reactions is influenced by both enzyme and substrate concentration. Enzymes usually have an optimum set of conditions (e.g. of pH and temperature) under which their activity is greatest. Many plant and animal enzymes show little activity at low temperatures. Enzyme activity increases with increasing temperature, but falls off after the optimum temperature is exceeded and the enzyme is denatured. Extremes in pH can also cause denaturation. Within their normal operating conditions, enzyme reaction rates are influenced by enzyme and substrate concentration in a predictable way.

Graph 1

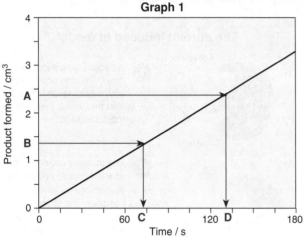

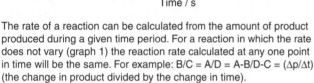

Graph 2

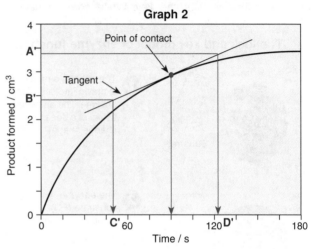

The rate of a reaction can be calculated from the amount of product produced during a given time period. For a reaction in which the rate does not vary (graph 1) the reaction rate calculated at any one point in time will be the same. For example: $B/C = A/D = A-B/D-C = (\Delta p/\Delta t)$ (the change in product divided by the change in time).

In a reaction in which the rate varies (graph 2) a reaction rate can be calculated for any instantaneous moment in time by using a tangent. The tangent must touch the curve at only one point. The gradient of the tangent can then be used to calculate the rate of reaction at that point in time (A'-B'/D'-C').

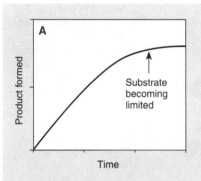

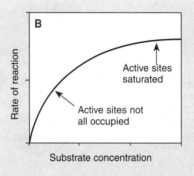

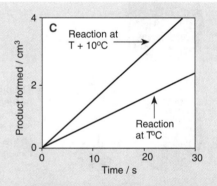

In a reaction where there is a limited amount of substrate, the reaction rate will slow down over time as the substrate is used up (graph A).

If there is unlimited substrate but the enzyme is limited, the reaction rate will increase until the enzyme is saturated, at which point the rate will remain static (graph B).

The effect of temperature on a reaction rate is expressed as the temperature coefficient, usually given as the Q_{10}. Q_{10} expresses the increase in the rate of reaction for every rise of 10°C. **Q_{10} = rate of reaction at (T + 10°C)/ rate of reaction at T**, where T is the temperature in °C (graph C).

1. Calculate the reaction rate in graph 1: _____

2. For graph 2, A Level students calculate:

   (a) The reaction rate at 90 seconds: _____

   (b) The reaction rate at 30 seconds: _____

3. (a) What would need to be happening to the reaction mix in graph 1 to produce a straight line (constant reaction rate)?

   _____

   _____

   (b) Explain why the reaction rate in graph 2 changes over time: _____

   _____

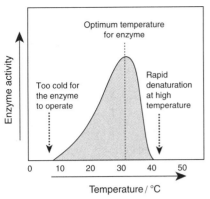

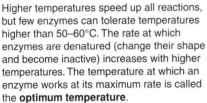

Temperature / °C

Antarctic icefish

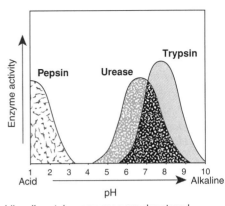

Higher temperatures speed up all reactions, but few enzymes can tolerate temperatures higher than 50–60°C. The rate at which enzymes are denatured (change their shape and become inactive) increases with higher temperatures. The temperature at which an enzyme works at its maximum rate is called the **optimum temperature**.

Enzymes performing the same function in species in different environments are very slightly different in order to maintain optimum performance. For example, the enzyme acetylcholinesterase has an optimum temperature of -2°C in the nervous system of an Antarctic icefish but an optimum temperature of 25°C in grey mullet found in the Mediterranean.

Like all proteins, enzymes are denatured by extremes of pH (very acid or alkaline). Within these extremes, most enzymes have a specific pH range for optimum activity. For example, digestive enzymes are specific to the region of the gut where they act: pepsin in the acid of the stomach and trypsin in the alkaline small intestine. Urease catalyses the hydrolysis of urea at a pH near neutral.

4. (a) Describe the change in reaction rate when the enzyme concentration is increased and the substrate is not limiting:

_____

_____

(b) Suggest how a cell may vary the amount of enzyme present: _____

_____

_____

5. Describe the change in reaction rate when the substrate concentration is increased (with a fixed amount of enzyme):

_____

_____

6. (a) Describe what is meant by an **optimum temperature** for enzyme activity: _____

_____

_____

(b) Explain why most enzymes perform poorly at low temperatures: _____

_____

_____

(c) For graph C opposite, calculate the Q_{10} for the reaction: _____

_____

_____

_____

7. (a) State the optimum pH for each of the enzymes:

Pepsin: _____   Trypsin: _____   Urease: _____

(b) Explain how the pH optima of each of these enzymes is suited to its working environment: _____

_____

_____

_____

89 Investigating Enzyme Reaction Rates

Key Idea: The rate of a reaction can be measured indirectly by measuring the volume of reaction products.

A group of students decided to use cubes of potato, which naturally contain the enzyme catalase, placed in hydrogen peroxide to test the effect of enzyme concentration on reaction rate. The reaction rate could be measured by the volume of oxygen produced as the hydrogen peroxide was decomposed into oxygen and water.

Aim
To investigate the effect of potato mass (and therefore enzyme concentration) on the rate of H_2O_2 decomposition.

Hypothesis
A greater mass of potato will have more enzyme present and will produce a greater reaction rate.

Method
The students cut raw potato into cubes with a mass of one gram. These were placed a conical flask with excess hydrogen peroxide (right). The reaction was left for five minutes and the volume of oxygen produced recorded. The students recorded the results for three replicates each of 1, 2, 3, 4, and 5 cubes of potato below:

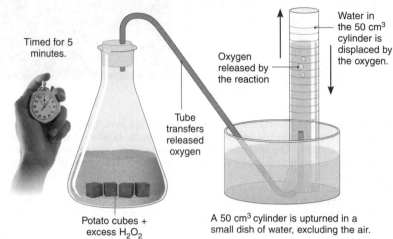

Timed for 5 minutes.

Water in the 50 cm^3 cylinder is displaced by the oxygen.

Oxygen released by the reaction

Tube transfers released oxygen

Potato cubes + excess H_2O_2

A 50 cm^3 cylinder is upturned in a small dish of water, excluding the air.

Mass of potato / g	Volume oxygen / cm^3 (5 minutes)			Mean	Mean rate of O$_2$ production / cm^3 min^{-1}
	Test 1	Test 2	Test 3		
1	6	5	6		
2	10	9	9		
3	14	15	15		
4	21	20	20		
5	24	23	25		

1. Complete the table by filling in the mean volume of oxygen produced and the rate of oxygen production.

2. Plot the mass of the potato vs the rate of production on the grid (right):

3. Relate the rate of the reaction to the amount of enzyme present.

_____

_____

_____

4. Why did the students add excess H_2O_2 to the reaction? _____

_____

5. State one extra reaction that should have been carried out by the students: _____

_____

6. (a) The students decide to cook some potato and carry out the test again with two grams of potato. Predict the result:

_____

_____

(b) Explain this result: _____

_____

© 2015 **BIOZONE** International
ISBN: 978-1-927309-13-1
Photocopying Prohibited

90 | Enzyme Cofactors

Key Idea: Some enzymes can act as catalysts on their own, but others need the addition of another molecule to function. Nearly all enzymes are made of protein. Some enzymes are functional protein-only molecules, but others require additional non-protein components, called **cofactors**, to have catalytic activity. Cofactors may be inorganic ions (e.g. Ca^{2+}, Zn^{2+}) or organic molecules (**coenzymes**) such as vitamins.

They also may be tightly or loosely bound to the enzyme. Permanently bound cofactors are called **prosthetic groups**. Many enzymes require several cofactors, often both organic coenzymes and inorganic ions, to function. Examples include the haem prosthetic groups, which consist of an iron atom in the centre of a porphyrin ring. The haem prosthetic group is a cofactor in catalase and some respiratory enzymes.

Protein-only enzymes	Conjugated protein enzymes

Where extra non-protein components are required for enzyme function, the enzyme is called the **apoenzyme** and the additional chemical component is called a **cofactor**. Neither the apoenzyme nor the cofactor has catalytic activity on its own.

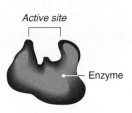

Active site — Enzyme

A cofactor completes the active site or makes the active site more reactive.

Active site

Prosthetic group is tightly bound or permanently attached.

Apoenzyme

Active site

Coenzyme loosely attached to the enzyme, detaching after the reaction to take part in other reactions.

Apoenzyme

Enzyme with no cofactor
Functional enzyme consists of only protein.
Examples: lysozyme, pepsin

Enzyme with prosthetic group
Contains apoenzyme (protein) plus a prosthetic group which is a tightly or permanently bound cofactor.
Example: flavoproteins + FAD

Enzyme with coenzyme loosely attached
Contains apoenzyme (protein) plus a coenzyme (non-protein).
Example: dehydrogenases + NAD. NAD is the coenzyme form of the vitamin niacin (B_3). Many coenzymes are vitamin derivatives.

The enzyme α amylase is present in saliva where it starts the hydrolysis of starch into the simple sugars maltose and glucose. To work correctly, it needs the ions Ca^{2+} and Cl^-. Cl^- increases the binding of Ca^{2+} by 100 times. It also shifts the optimum pH for amylase from 6 to 6.8.

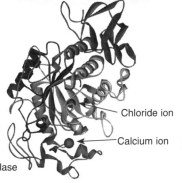

Chloride ion

Calcium ion

α-amylase

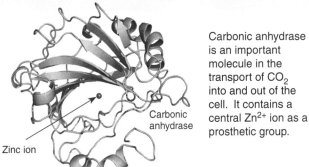

Zinc ion

Carbonic anhydrase

Carbonic anhydrase is an important molecule in the transport of CO_2 into and out of the cell. It contains a central Zn^{2+} ion as a prosthetic group.

1. What are enzyme **cofactors**? _____

_____

2. How do cofactors enable an enzyme's catalytic activity? _____

_____

_____

3. Distinguish between the apoenzyme and the cofactor: _____

_____

_____

4. Identify the two broad categories of cofactors and describe an example of each: _____

_____

5. With reference to enzyme activity, describe the importance of adequate vitamin and mineral intake in the diet:

_____

_____

91 Enzyme Inhibitors

Key Idea: Enzymes activity can be reduced or stopped by inhibitors. These may be competitive or non-competitive. Enzyme activity can be stopped, temporarily or permanently, by chemicals called enzyme inhibitors. **Irreversible inhibitors** bind tightly to the enzyme and are not easily displaced. **Reversible inhibitors** can be displaced from the enzyme and have a role as enzyme regulators in metabolic pathways.

Competitive inhibitors compete directly with the substrate for the active site and their effect can be overcome by increasing the concentration of available substrate. A **non-competitive inhibitor** does not occupy the active site, but distorts it so that the substrate and enzyme can no longer interact. Both competitive and non-competitive inhibition may be irreversible, in which case the inhibitors act as poisons.

Allosteric enzyme regulation

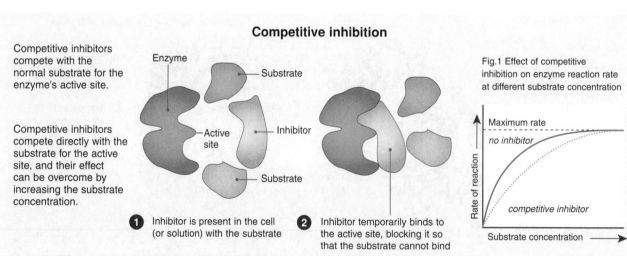

Allosteric site: The place on an enzyme where a molecule that is not a substrate may bind

Active site

1 Active form of the enzyme — Substrate molecules

Enzyme catalyses the reaction between the substrates producing a new molecule.

2 Enzyme-substrate complex

The new molecule attaches to the allosteric site of the enzyme, inhibiting the enzyme's activity.

3 Inactive form of the enzyme

Metabolic pathways can be regulated by the products they produce. The action is usually by **feedback inhibition** (negative feedback) (shown above). This can be achieved by **allosteric regulation**. When concentrations of the end product are high it will bind to the allosteric site of the first enzyme in the pathway, inhibiting the enzyme and shutting down the pathway. When the concentration of the end product is reduced it is released from the allosteric site and the pathway is activated again.

Competitive inhibition

Competitive inhibitors compete with the normal substrate for the enzyme's active site.

Competitive inhibitors compete directly with the substrate for the active site, and their effect can be overcome by increasing the substrate concentration.

Enzyme — Substrate

Active site — Inhibitor

Substrate

1 Inhibitor is present in the cell (or solution) with the substrate

2 Inhibitor temporarily binds to the active site, blocking it so that the substrate cannot bind

Fig.1 Effect of competitive inhibition on enzyme reaction rate at different substrate concentration

Maximum rate
no inhibitor

Rate of reaction

competitive inhibitor

Substrate concentration ⟶

Non-competitive inhibition

Non-competitive inhibitors bind with the enzyme at a site other than the active site.

They inactivate the enzyme by altering its shape so that the substrate and enzyme can no longer interact.

Non-competitive inhibition cannot be overcome by increasing the substrate concentration.

Substrate

Inhibitor

Enzyme   Substrate

1 Without the inhibitor bound, the enzyme can bind the substrate

Active site cannot bind the substrates

2 When the inhibitor binds, the enzyme changes shape.

Fig.2 Effect of non-competitive inhibition on enzyme reaction rate at different substrate concentration

Maximum rate
no inhibitor

Rate of reaction

non-competitive inhibitor

Substrate concentration ⟶

© 2015 **BIOZONE** International
ISBN: 978-1-927309-13-1
Photocopying Prohibited

Poisons are irreversible inhibitors

Some enzyme inhibitors are poisons because the enzyme-inhibitor binding is irreversible. Irreversible inhibitors form strong covalent bonds with an enzyme. These inhibitors may act at, near, or remotely from the active site and modify the enzyme's structure to such an extent that it ceases to work. For example, the poison **cyanide** is an irreversible enzyme inhibitor that combines with the copper and iron in the active site of **cytochrome c oxidase** and blocks cellular respiration.

Since many enzymes contain sulfhydryl (-SH), alcohol, or acidic groups as part of their active sites, any chemical that can react with them may act as an irreversible inhibitor. Heavy metals, Ag^+, Hg^{2+}, or Pb^{2+}, have strong affinities for -SH groups and destroy catalytic activity. Most heavy metals are non-competitive inhibitors.

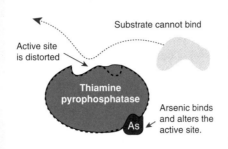

Active site is distorted

Substrate cannot bind

Thiamine pyrophosphatase

Arsenic binds and alters the active site.

As

Arsenic and phosphorus share some structural similarities so arsenic will often substitute for phosphorus in biological systems. It therefore targets a wide variety of enzyme reactions. Arsenic can act as either a competitive or a non-competitive inhibitor (as above) depending on the enzyme.

Drugs

Many drugs work by irreversible inhibition of a pathogen's enzymes. Penicillin (below) and related antibiotics inhibit transpeptidase, a bacterial enzyme which forms some of the linkages in the bacterial cell wall. Susceptible bacteria cannot complete cell wall synthesis and cannot divide. Human cells are unaffected by the drug.

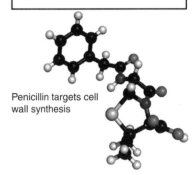

Penicillin targets cell wall synthesis

1. Distinguish between **competitive** and **non-competitive** inhibition: _____

_____

_____

_____

2. (a) Compare and contrast the effect of competitive and non-competitive inhibition on the relationship between the substrate concentration and the rate of an enzyme controlled reaction (figures 1 and 2 on the previous page):

_____

_____

_____

_____

(b) Suggest how you could distinguish between competitive and non-competitive inhibition in an isolated system:

_____

_____

3. Describe how an **allosteric regulator** can regulate enzyme activity: _____

_____

_____

4. Explain why heavy metals, such as lead and arsenic, are poisonous: _____

_____

_____

5. (a) In the context of enzymes, explain how penicillin is exploited to control human diseases: _____

_____

_____

(b) Explain why the drug is poisonous to the target organism, but not to humans: _____

_____

92 Investigating Catalase Activity

Key Idea: Catalase activity can be measured in germinating seeds. Activity changes with stage of germination.
Enzyme activity can be measured easily in simple experiments. This activity describes an experiment in which germinating seeds of different ages were tested for their level of **catalase** activity using hydrogen peroxide solution as the substrate and a simple apparatus to measure oxygen production (see background). Completing this activity, which involves a critical evaluation of the second-hand data provided, will help to prepare you for making your own similar investigations.

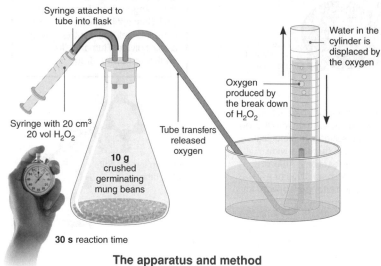

Syringe attached to tube into flask

Syringe with 20 cm³ 20 vol H₂O₂

Tube transfers released oxygen

10 g crushed germinating mung beans

Oxygen produced by the break down of H₂O₂

Water in the cylinder is displaced by the oxygen

30 s reaction time

The aim and hypothesis

To investigate the effect of germination age on the level of catalase activity in mung beans. The students hypothesised that if metabolic activity increased with germination age, catalase activity would also increase with germination age.

Background

Germinating seeds are metabolically very active and this metabolism inevitably produces reactive oxygen species, including hydrogen peroxide (H_2O_2). H_2O_2 helps germination by breaking dormancy, but it is also toxic. To counter the toxic effects of H_2O_2 and prevent cellular damage, germinating seeds also produce **catalase**, an enzyme that catalyses the breakdown of H_2O_2 to water and oxygen.

A class was divided into six groups with each group testing the seedlings of each age. Each group's set of results (for 0.5, 2, 4, 6, and 10 days) therefore represents one trial.

The apparatus and method

In this experiment, 10 g germinating mung bean seeds (0.5, 2, 4, 6, or 10 days old) were ground by hand with a mortar and pestle and placed in a conical flask as above. There were six trials at each of the five seedling ages. With each trial, 20 cm³ of 20 vol H_2O_2 was added to the flask at time 0 and the reaction was allowed to run for 30 seconds. The oxygen released by the decomposition of the H_2O_2 by catalase in the seedlings was collected via a tube into an inverted measuring cylinder. The volume of oxygen produced is measured by the amount of water displaced from the cylinder. The results from all trials are tabulated below:

Stage of germination / days	Group (trial) #								Mean rate / cm³ s⁻¹ g⁻¹
	Volume of oxygen collected after 30 s / cm³						Mean	Standard deviation	
	1	2	3	4	5	6			
0.5	9.5	10	10.7	9.5	10.2	10.5			
2	36.2	30	31.5	37.5	34	40			
4	59	66	69	60.5	66.5	72			
6	39	31.5	32.5	41	40.3	36			
10	20	18.6	24.3	23.2	23.5	25.5			

1. Write the equation for the catalase reaction with hydrogen peroxide: _____

2. Complete the table above to summarise the data from the six trials:

   (a) Calculate the mean volume of oxygen for each stage of germination and enter the values in the table.

   (b) Calculate the standard deviation for each mean and enter the values in the table (you may use a spreadsheet).

   (c) Calculate the mean rate of oxygen production in cm³ per second per gram. For the purposes of this exercise, assume that the weight of germinating seed in every case was 10.0 g.

3. In another scenario, group (trial) #2 obtained the following measurements for volume of oxygen produced: 0.5 d: 4.8 cm³, 2 d: 29.0 cm³, 4 d: 70 cm³, 6 d: 30.0 cm³, 10 d: 8.8 cm³ (pencil these values in beside the other group 2 data set).

   (a) Describe how group 2's new data compares with the measurements obtained from the other group: _____

   _____

   (b) Describe how you would approach a reanalysis of the data set incorporating group 2's new data: _____

   _____

   _____

© 2015 **BIOZONE** International
ISBN: 978-1-927309-13-1
Photocopying Prohibited

(c) Explain the rationale for your approach _____

_____

4. Use the tabulated data to plot an appropriate graph of the results on the grid provided below:

5. (a) Describe the trend in the data: _____

_____

_____

(b) Explain the relationship between stage of germination and catalase activity shown in the data: _____

_____

_____

(c) Do the results support the students' hypothesis? _____

_____

6. Describe any potential sources of errors in the apparatus or the procedure: _____

_____

_____

_____

7. Describe two things that might affect the validity of findings in this experimental design: _____

_____

_____

_____

© 2015 **BIOZONE** International
ISBN: 978-1-927309-13-1

93 Enzyme Control of Metabolic Pathways

Key Idea: Metabolic pathways can be regulated with inactive precursors or end product inhibition.

Metabolism refers to all the chemical activities (metabolic reactions) of life. These metabolic reactions form a tremendously complex network of reactions, which is necessary to 'maintain' the organism. Often the products of

a **metabolic pathway** regulate the pathway itself, e.g. the end product of a pathway might inhibit earlier reactions in the pathway so that no more product is produced (negative feedback). Many pathways include inactive precursors which are activated in steps and produce a cascade effect that produces a rapid response to a stimulus.

Blood clotting

Many of the chemicals needed for metabolic reactions are present in an inactive form. They require a signal molecule or interaction with an enzyme to become active and carry out their role. The pathway that leads to blood clotting is an example. It is also an example of how a single signal can be amplified in the cell to produce a large response. The pathway is triggered by the tearing of a blood vessel. Clotting factors are released from damaged cells. A cascade is produced in which a single molecule can activate many hundreds of molecules, which in turn each activate many hundreds more molecules in the next step of the pathway. The pathway ultimately leads to the production of fibrin molecules which help to bind and close the wound, producing a blood clot.

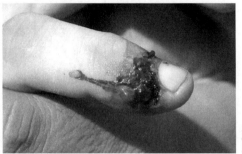
Dan Butler

Clotting factors catalyse the conversion of prothrombin (a plasma protein) to thrombin (an active enzyme). → **Clotting factors** ← Thrombin also activates more clotting factors, amplifying the original clotting signal. This is an example of positive feedback.

(+)

Prothrombin → **Thrombin** ← The formation of fibrin inhibits the activity of thrombin. This is an example of negative feedback regulation of the pathway and it prevents too much clotting, which could block the blood flow.

(−)

Fibrinogen → **Fibrin** → **Blood clot**

Hydrolysis

1. Explain the importance of regulating metabolic pathways in a cell: _____

_____

_____

2. What might happen if one of the enzyme in the metabolic pathway failed to work correctly? _____

_____

_____

3. (a) What is the effect of thrombin on the clotting factors?: _____

_____

_____

   (b) What is the name of this method of signal amplification? _____

4. (a) How is the clotting process brought under control? _____

_____

_____

   (b) Why is this process important? _____

_____

   (c) What is the name give to this method of pathway inhibition? _____

KNOW

94 Chapter Review

Summarise what you know about this topic under the headings provided. You can draw diagrams or mind maps, or write short notes to organise your thoughts. Use the images and hints included to help you:

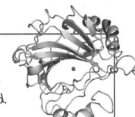

Enzyme cofactors and inhibitors

HINT: Explain the importance of enzyme cofactors. Describe how enzyme activity can be inhibited.

Enzyme activity

HINT: Describe how enzymes catalyse a reaction. Explain enzyme kinetics.

95 KEY TERMS: Did You Get It?

1. Complete the crossword below, which will test your understanding of key terms in this chapter and their meanings

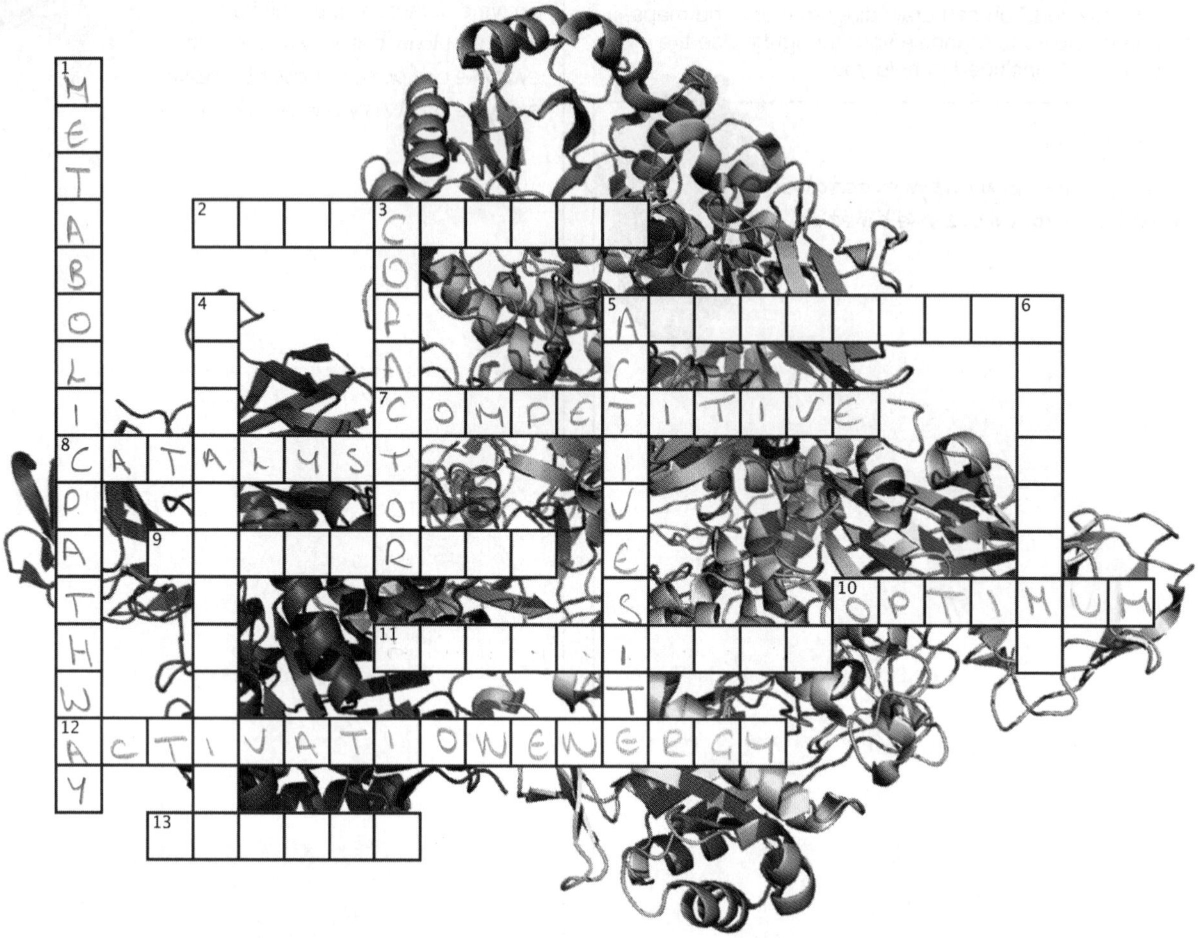

Clues across

2. Modern theory of enzyme action, in which the enzyme changes shape as the substrate binds.
5. The type of enzyme regulation that occurs when a substance binds to a site on an enzyme other than the active site is called _______________ regulation.
7. A type of enzyme inhibition where the substance and inhibitor compete to bind in the active site.
8. A chemical that lowers the activation energy of a reaction but is not itself used up during the reaction.
9. The chemical the enzyme acts upon.
10. The term that describes the conditions at which an enzyme is most active.
11. A process whereby an enzyme activity is stopped, either permanently or temporarily.
12. Energy required to initiate a chemical reaction (2 words; 10, 6)
13. A globular protein that acts as catalyst to speed up a specific biological reaction.

Clues down

1. A chain of enzyme catalysed biochemical reactions in living cells (2 words: 9, 7).
3. An additional non-protein substance essential for the operation of some enzymes.
4. The loss of the three-dimensional structure of proteins, often caused by pH or heat.
5. The region of an enzyme responsible for substrate binding and reaction catalysis (2 words; 6, 4)
6. An organic molecule that acts as a cofactor in an enzyme reaction but is only loosely bound to the enzyme.

2. (a) Label the graph, right, with appropriate axes and the following labels: Reactants, products, activation energy, transition state.

   (b) Assume the reaction has had no enzyme added. Draw the shape of the graph if an enzyme was added to the reaction mix.

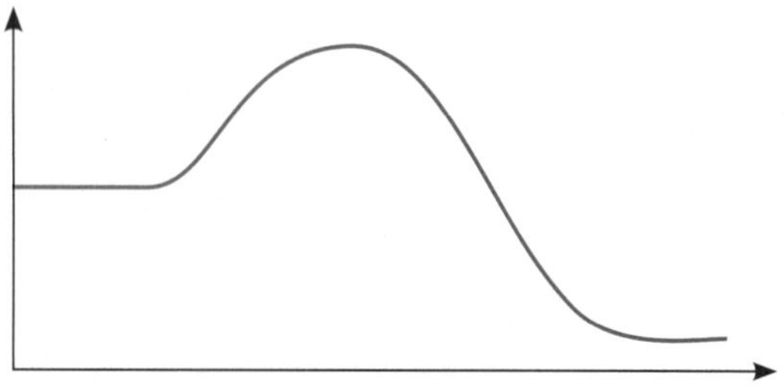

ISBN: 978-1-927309-13-1

Module 2.1.5

Biological Membranes

Key terms

active transport

carrier protein

channel protein

cholesterol

concentration gradient

diffusion

endocytosis

exocytosis

facilitated diffusion

fluid mosaic model

glycolipid

glycoprotein

hypertonic

hypotonic

ion pump

isotonic

osmolarity

osmosis

partially permeable

passive transport

phagocytosis

phospholipid

pinocytosis

plasma membrane

plasmolysis

solute potential

surface area: volume ratio

turgor

water potential

Cellular membranes

Learning outcomes

Activity number

☐ 1 Describe the various roles of membranes in cells, including the role of the plasma membrane as a partially permeable barrier to the movement of substances into and out of the cell. — 96

☐ 2 Describe the fluid mosaic model of membrane structure. Include reference to the significance of phospholipid orientation and the role of transmembrane proteins in the integral structure of the membrane. — 97

☐ 3 Describe the roles of the phospholipids, cholesterol, glycolipids, proteins, and glycoproteins in the plasma membrane. Include reference to membrane stability, fluidity, cellular communication, and cellular transport. — 97

☐ 4 Describe and explain factors affecting membrane structure and permeability, including reference to the effects of temperature and solvents. — 98

☐ 5 **PAG8** Investigate factors affecting membrane structure and permeability. — 98

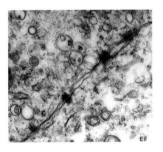
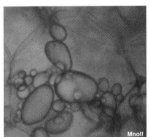
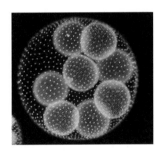

Cellular transport processes

Learning outcomes

Activity number

☐ 6 Describe the movement of molecules across membranes by diffusion and facilitated diffusion, identifying them as passive transport processes. Explain factors affecting diffusion rates across membranes: membrane thickness, surface area, and concentration gradient. — 99-101

☐ 7 **PAG8** Investigate factors affecting diffusion rates in model cells. — 100 101

☐ 8 Explain the movement of water across membranes by osmosis with reference to gradients in water potential. Explain the effects that solutions of different water potential can have on plant and animal cells. — 102 103

☐ 9 Explain turgor and plasmolysis in plant cells. Understand the role of the cell wall in turgor pressure and the role of turgor pressure in plant support. — 103

☐ 10 **PAG8** Investigate the effects of solutions of different water potential on plant or animal cells. — 104 110

☐ 11 Understand the terms hypotonic, isotonic, and hypertonic with respect to solutions of differing solute concentration. — 102

☐ 12 Explain why cell size is limited by the rate of diffusion. Explain the significance of surface area to volume ratio to cells and relate this to organism size. — 100 101

☐ 13 Distinguish between passive transport and active transport, identifying the involvement of membrane proteins and energy in active transport processes. — 105 108

☐ 14 Using examples, describe and explain active transport processes in cells, including ion pumps, endocytosis, and exocytosis. — 106-108

96 The Role of Membranes in Cells

Key Idea: Membranes create compartments, control entry and exit of substances from the cell and organelles, and enable cell communication.

Many cell organelles are composed of membranes.

Membranes within eukaryotic cells share the same basic structure as the plasma membrane that encloses the entire cell. Membranes have many functions (below) and create compartments within the cell where reactions can be localised.

Isolating enzymes
Membrane-bound lysosomes contain enzymes to destroy wastes and foreign material.

Lipid synthesis
Lipids and steroids are manufactured in the smooth endoplasmic reticulum.

Containing DNA
The nucleus is surrounded by a nuclear envelope of two membranes, forming a separate compartment for the cell's genetic material. The nuclear envelope is continuous with the ER.

Protein synthesis
Some protein synthesis occurs on free ribosomes, but much occurs on membrane-bound ribosomes on the rough endoplasmic reticulum. The protein is synthesised directly into the space within the ER membranes.

Entry and export of substances
The plasma membrane may take up material and form membrane-bound vesicles (or larger vacuoles) within the cell. Transport vesicles move substances to the inner surface of the cell where they can be exported from the cell by exocytosis.

Cell communication and recognition
Proteins in the membrane act as receptors for signal molecules like hormones. Glycoproteins and glycolipids act as cell identity markers, helping cells to organise themselves into tissues.

Transport
Channel and carrier proteins are involved in selective transport across the plasma membrane.

Packaging and secretion
The Golgi apparatus is a specialised membrane-bound organelle, producing lysosomes and modifying, packaging, and secreting substances such as proteins and hormones.

Energy transfer
The reactions of cellular respiration take place in the membrane-bound mitochondria. In plant cells, the reactions of photosynthesis are located in specialised membranous organelles called chloroplasts.

Animal cell

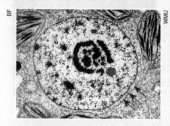

The **nuclear membrane** around the nucleus helps to control the passage of genetic information to the cytoplasm. It may also serve to protect the DNA.

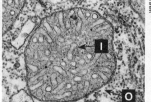

Mitochondria have an outer membrane (**O**) which controls the movement of materials involved in respiration. Inner membranes (**I**) provide attachment sites for enzyme activity.

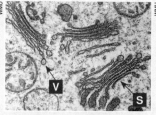

The **Golgi apparatus** comprises stacks of membrane-bound sacs (**S**). It is involved in packaging materials for transport or export from the cell as secretory vesicles (**V**).

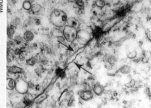

The cell's **plasma membrane** controls the movement of most substances into and out of the cell. This photo shows the plasma membranes of two neighbouring cells (arrows).

1. Explain the crucial role of membrane systems and organelles in the following:

    (a) Providing compartments within the cell: _____

    _____

    _____

    (b) Increasing the total membrane surface area within the cell: _____

    _____

    _____

2. (a) Name a membrane-bound cellular organelle: _____

    (b) What is the function of the organelle?_____

    (c) What is the membrane's role in this organelle?_____

    _____

    _____

© 2015 **BIOZONE** International
ISBN: 978-1-927309-13-1
Photocopying Prohibited

97 The Structure of Membranes

Key Idea: The plasma membrane is composed of a lipid bilayer with proteins moving freely within it.

All cells have a plasma membrane, which forms the outer limit of the cell and regulates the passage of materials into and out of the cell. A cell wall, if present, lies outside this, and it is quite distinct from it. Membranes are also found inside eukaryotic cells as part of membranous organelles. The original model of membrane structure was as a lipid bilayer coated with protein. This model was modified after the discovery that the protein molecules were embedded within the bilayer rather than coating the outside. The now-accepted **fluid-mosaic model** of membrane structure (below) satisfies the observed properties of membranes. The self-orientating properties of the phospholipids allows cellular membranes to reseal themselves when disrupted. The double layer of lipids is also quite fluid, and proteins move quite freely within it.

The fluid mosaic model of membrane structure

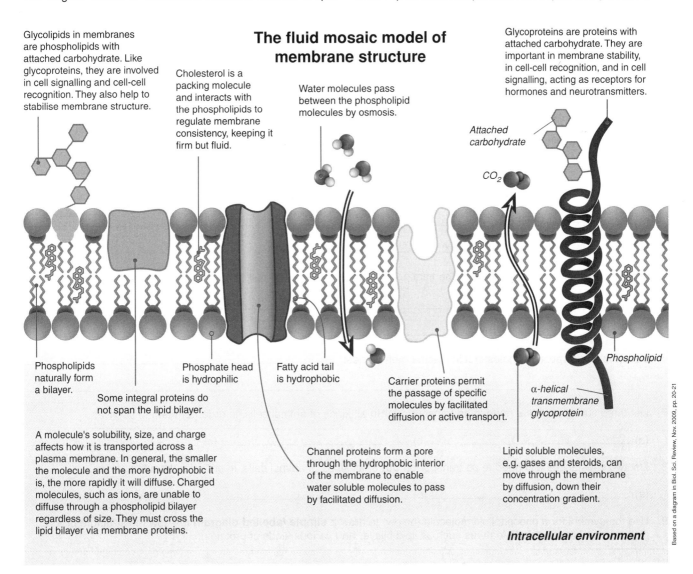

Glycolipids in membranes are phospholipids with attached carbohydrate. Like glycoproteins, they are involved in cell signalling and cell-cell recognition. They also help to stabilise membrane structure.

Cholesterol is a packing molecule and interacts with the phospholipids to regulate membrane consistency, keeping it firm but fluid.

Water molecules pass between the phospholipid molecules by osmosis.

Glycoproteins are proteins with attached carbohydrate. They are important in membrane stability, in cell-cell recognition, and in cell signalling, acting as receptors for hormones and neurotransmitters.

Attached carbohydrate

CO_2

Phospholipids naturally form a bilayer.

Some integral proteins do not span the lipid bilayer.

Phosphate head is hydrophilic

Fatty acid tail is hydrophobic

Carrier proteins permit the passage of specific molecules by facilitated diffusion or active transport.

α-helical transmembrane glycoprotein

Phospholipid

A molecule's solubility, size, and charge affects how it is transported across a plasma membrane. In general, the smaller the molecule and the more hydrophobic it is, the more rapidly it will diffuse. Charged molecules, such as ions, are unable to diffuse through a phospholipid bilayer regardless of size. They must cross the lipid bilayer via membrane proteins.

Channel proteins form a pore through the hydrophobic interior of the membrane to enable water soluble molecules to pass by facilitated diffusion.

Lipid soluble molecules, e.g. gases and steroids, can move through the membrane by diffusion, down their concentration gradient.

Intracellular environment

Based on a diagram in Biol. Sci. Review, Nov. 2009, pp. 20-21

1. Identify the component(s) of the plasma membrane involved in:

   (a) Facilitated diffusion: _____

   (b) Active transport: _____

   (c) Cell signalling: _____

   (d) Regulating membrane fluidity: _____

2. How do the properties of phospholipids contribute to their role in forming the structural framework of membranes?

   _____

   _____

3. (a) Describe the modern fluid mosaic model of membrane structure: _____

   _____

   _____

   _____

LINK   WEB

98 **97**   KNOW

(b) Explain how the fluid mosaic model accounts for the observed properties of cellular membranes:

_____

_____

_____

_____

_____

_____

4. Explain the importance of each of the following to cellular function:

(a) Carrier proteins in the plasma membrane: _____

_____

(b) Channel proteins in the plasma membrane: _____

_____

5. Non-polar (lipid-soluble) molecules diffuse more rapidly through membranes than polar (lipid-insoluble) molecules:

(a) Explain the reason for this: _____

_____

(b) Discuss the implications of this to the transport of substances into the cell through the plasma membrane:

_____

_____

6. Describe the purpose of cholesterol in plasma membranes: _____

_____

7. List three substances that need to be transported **into** all kinds of animal cells, in order for them to survive:

(a) _____ (b) _____ (c) _____

8. List two substances that need to be transported **out** of all kinds of animal cells, in order for them to survive:

(a) _____ (b) _____

9. Use the symbol for a phospholipid molecule (below) to draw a **simple labelled diagram** to show the structure of a plasma membrane (include features such as lipid bilayer and various kinds of proteins):

Symbol for phospholipid

98 Factors Altering Membrane Permeability

Key Idea: Temperature and solvents can disrupt the structure of cellular membranes and alter their permeability.

Membrane permeability can be disrupted if membranes are subjected to high temperatures or solvents. At temperatures above the optimum, the membrane proteins become denatured. Alcohols, e.g. ethanol, can also denature proteins. In both instances, the denatured proteins no longer function properly and the membrane loses its selective permeability and becomes leaky. In addition, the combination of alcohol and high temperature can also dissolve lipids.

Beetroot cubes

Experimental method

Raw beetroot was cut into uniform cubes using a cork borer with a 4 mm internal diameter. The cubes were trimmed to 20 mm lengths and placed in a beaker of distilled water for 30 minutes.

Five cm³ of distilled water was added to 15 clean test tubes. Three were placed into a beaker containing ice. These were the 0°C samples. Three test tubes were placed into water baths at 20, 40, 60, or 90°C and equilibrated for 30 minutes. Once the tubes were at temperature, the beetroot cubes were removed from the distilled water and blotted dry on a paper towel. One beetroot cube was added to each of the test tubes. After 30 minutes, they were removed. The colour of the solution in each test tube was observed by eye and then the absorbance of each sample was measured at 530 nm. Results are given in the table below.

The aim and hypothesis

To investigate the effect of temperature on membrane permeability. The students hypothesised that the amount of pigment leaking from the beetroot cubes would increase with increasing temperature.

Background

Plant cells often contain a large central vacuole surrounded by a membrane called a **tonoplast**. In beetroot plants, the vacuole contains a water-soluble red pigment called betacyanin, which gives beetroot its colour. If the tonoplast is damaged, the red pigment leaks out into the surrounding environment. The amount of leaked pigment relates to the amount of damage to the tonoplast.

Absorbance of beetroot samples at varying temperatures					
Temperature / °C		**Absorbance at 530 nm**			**Mean**
	Observation	**Sample 1**	**Sample 2**	**Sample 3**	
0	No colour,	0	0.007	0.004	
20	Very pale pink	0.027	0.022	0.018	
40	Very pale pink	0.096	0.114	0.114	
60	Pink	0.580	0.524	0.509	
90	Red	3	3	3	

1. Why is it important to wash the beetroot cubes in distilled water prior to carrying out the experiment? _____

_____

2. (a) Complete the table above by calculating the mean absorbance for each temperature:

    (b) Based on the results in the table above, describe the effect of temperature on membrane permeability: _____

_____

_____

_____

    (c) Explain why this effect occurs: _____

_____

_____

_____

Method for determining effect of ethanol concentration on membrane permeability

Beetroot cubes were prepared the same way as described on the previous page. The following ethanol concentrations were prepared using serial dilution: 0, 6.25, 12.5, 25, 50, and 100%. Eighteen clean test tubes were divided into six groups of three and labelled with one of the six ethanol concentrations. Three cm³ of the appropriate ethanol solution was placed into each test tube. A dried beetroot cube was added to each test tube. The test tubes were covered with parafilm (plastic paraffin film with a paper backing) and left at room temperature. After one hour the beetroot cubes were removed and the absorbance measured at 477 nm.
Results are given in the table, right.

Ethanol concentration / %	Absorbance of beetroot samples at varying ethanol concentrations			Mean
	Absorbance at 477 nm			
	Sample 1	Sample 2	Sample 3	
0	0.014	0.038	0.038	
6.25	0.009	0.015	0.023	
12.5	0.010	0.041	0.018	
25	0.067	0.064	0.116	
50	0.945	1.100	0.731	
100	1.269	1.376	0.907	

3. What was the purpose of the 0% ethanol solution in the experiment described above?

_____

_____

_____

4. (a) Why do you think the tubes were covered in parafilm?

_____

_____

_____

_____

(b) How could the results have been affected if the test tubes were not covered with parafilm?

_____

_____

_____

_____

5. (a) Complete the table above by calculating the mean absorbance for each ethanol concentration:

(b) Plot a line graph of ethanol concentration against mean absorbance on the grid (above):

(c) Describe the effect of ethanol concentration on the membrane permeability of beetroot: _____

_____

_____

_____

_____

6. How does ethanol affect membrane permeability? _____

_____

© 2015 **BIOZONE** International
ISBN: 978-1-927309-13-1
Photocopying Prohibited

99 Diffusion

Key Idea: Diffusion is the movement of molecules from higher concentration to a lower concentration (i.e. down a concentration gradient).

The molecules that make up substances are constantly moving about in a random way. This random motion causes molecules to disperse from areas of high to low concentration. This dispersal is called **diffusion** and it requires no energy. Each type of molecule moves down its own concentration gradient. Diffusion is important in allowing exchanges with the environment and in the regulation of cell water content.

What is diffusion?

Diffusion is the movement of particles from regions of high concentration to regions of low concentration (down a concentration gradient). Diffusion is a **passive process**, meaning it needs no input of energy to occur. During diffusion, molecules move randomly about, becoming evenly dispersed.

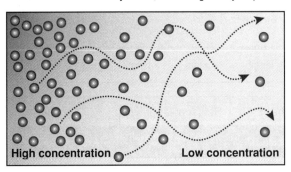

Concentration gradient

If molecules can move freely, they move from high to low concentration (down a concentration gradient) until evenly dispersed.

Factors affecting the rate of diffusion

Concentration gradient	The rate of diffusion is higher when there is a greater difference between the concentrations of two regions.
The distance moved	Diffusion over shorter distance occurs at a greater rate than over a larger distance.
The surface area involved	The larger the area across which diffusion occurs, the greater the rate of diffusion.
Barriers to diffusion	Thick barriers have a slower rate of diffusion than thin barriers.
Temperature	Particles at a high temperature diffuse at a greater rate than at a low temperature.

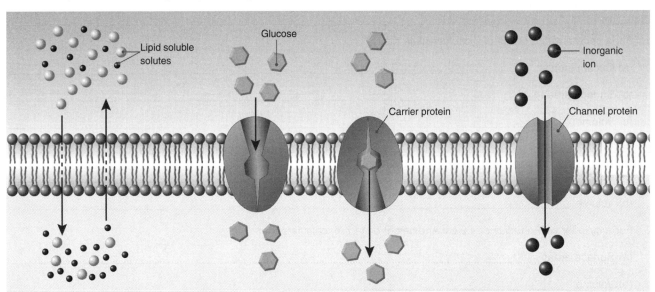

Simple diffusion
Molecules move directly through the membrane without assistance.
<u>Example</u>: O_2 diffuses into the blood and CO_2 diffuses out.

Carrier-mediated facilitated diffusion
Carrier proteins allow large lipid-insoluble molecules that cannot cross the membrane by simple diffusion to be transported into the cell.
<u>Example</u>: the transport of glucose into red blood cells.

Channel-mediated facilitated diffusion
Channels (hydrophilic pores) in the membrane allow inorganic ions to pass through the membrane.
<u>Example</u>: K^+ ions exiting nerve cells to restore resting potential.

1. What is diffusion? _____

_____

2. What do the three types of diffusion described above all have in common? _____

_____

3. How does facilitated diffusion differ from simple diffusion? _____

_____

© 2015 **BIOZONE** International
ISBN: 978-1-927309-13-1
Photocopying Prohibited

LINK | WEB
101 **99** **KNOW**

100 Properties of Geometric Shapes

Key Idea: Circumference, surface area, and volume are useful calculations that can be applied in biological situations. Biology often requires you to evaluate the effect of a physical property, such as cell volume, on function. For example, how does surface area to volume ratio influence the transport of materials into a cell? The cells of organisms, and sometimes the organisms themselves, are often rather regular shapes, so their physical properties (e.g. cell volume or surface area) can be calculated (or approximated) using the simple formulae applicable to standard geometric shapes.

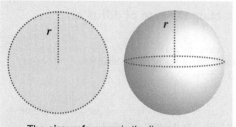

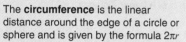

The **circumference** is the linear distance around the edge of a circle or sphere and is given by the formula $2\pi r$

r = radius	l = length	w = width	h = height	$\pi = 3.14$

	Sphere	Cube	Rectangular prism	Cylinder
Biological example	*Staphylococcus* bacterial cell	Kidney tubule cell	Intestinal epithelial cell	Axon of neuron
Surface area: The sum of all areas of all shapes covering an object's surface.	$4\pi r^2$	$6w^2$	$2(lh + lw + hw)$	$(2\pi r^2) + (2\pi rh)$
Volume: The amount that a 3-dimensional shape can hold.	$\frac{4}{3}\pi r^3$	w^3	lwh	$\pi r^2 h$

1. For a sphere with a radius of 2 cm, calculate the:

   (a) Circumference: _____

   (b) Surface area: _____

   (c) Volume: _____

2. For a rectangular prism with the dimensions l = 3 mm, w = 0.3 mm, and h = 2 mm calculate the:

   (a) Surface area: _____

   (b) Volume: _____

3. For a cylinder with a radius of 4.9 cm and height of 11 cm, calculate the:

   (a) Surface area: _____

   (b) Volume: _____

4. Find the height of a rectangular prism with a volume of 48 cm³, a length of 4 cm, and a width of 2.5 cm: _____

_____

5. Find the radius of a cylinder with a volume of 27 cm³ and a height of 3 cm: _____

_____

6. A spherical bacterium with a radius of 0.2 μm divides in two. Each new cell has a radius that is 80% of the original cell.

   (a) Calculate the surface area of the 'parent' bacterial cell: _____

   (b) Calculate the volume of the 'parent' bacterial cell: _____

   (c) Calculate the surface area of each new cell: _____

   (d) Calculate the volume of each new cell: _____

   (e) Which cell has the greatest surface area to volume ratio: _____

LINK

DATA 101

101 Diffusion and Cell Size

Key Idea: Diffusion is less efficient in cells with a small surface area relative to their volume than in cells with a large surface area relative to their volume.

When an object (e.g. a cell) is small it has a large surface area in comparison to its volume. Diffusion is an effective way to transport materials (e.g. gases) into the cell. As an object becomes larger, its surface area compared to its volume is smaller. Diffusion is no longer an effective way to transport materials to the inside. This places a physical limit on the size a cell can grow, with the effectiveness of diffusion being the controlling factor. Larger organisms overcome this constraint by becoming multicellular.

Single-celled organisms

Single-celled organisms (e.g. *Amoeba*), are small and have a large surface area relative to the cell's volume. The cell's requirements can be met by the diffusion or active transport of materials into and out of the cell (below).

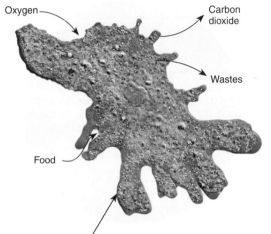

Oxygen

Carbon dioxide

Wastes

Food

The **plasma membrane**, which surrounds every cell, regulates movements of substances into and out of the cell. For each square micrometre of membrane, only so much of a particular substance can cross per second.

Multicellular organisms

Multicellular organisms (e.g. plants and animals) are often quite large and large organisms have a small surface area compared to their volume. They require specialised systems to transport the materials they need to and from the cells and tissues in their body.

In a multicellular organism, such as an elephant, the body's need for respiratory gases cannot be met by diffusion through the skin.

A specialised gas exchange surface (lungs) and circulatory (blood) system are required to transport substances to the body's cells.

The diagram below shows four hypothetical cells of different sizes. They range from a small 2 cm cube to a 5 cm cube. This exercise investigates the effect of cell size on the efficiency of diffusion.

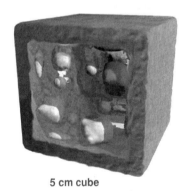

2 cm cube   3 cm cube   4 cm cube   5 cm cube

1. Calculate the volume, surface area and the ratio of surface area to volume for each of the four cubes above (the first has been done for you). When completing the table below, show your calculations.

Cube size	Surface area	Volume	Surface area to volume ratio
2 cm cube	$2 \times 2 \times 6 = 24\ cm^2$ (2 cm x 2 cm x 6 sides)	$2 \times 2 \times 2 = 8\ cm^3$ (height x width x depth)	24 to 8 = 3:1
3 cm cube			
4 cm cube			
5 cm cube			

© 2015 **BIOZONE** International
ISBN: 978-1-927309-13-1
Photocopying Prohibited

LINK   WEB

100 101 DATA

2. Create a graph, plotting the surface area against the volume of each cube, on the grid on the right. Draw a line connecting the points and label axes and units.

3. Which increases the fastest with increasing size: the **volume** or the **surface area**?

_____

4. Explain what happens to the ratio of surface area to volume with increasing size.

_____

_____

_____

_____

_____

5. The diffusion of molecules into a cell can be modelled by using agar cubes infused with phenolphthalein indicator and soaked in sodium hydroxide (NaOH). Phenolphthalein turns a pink colour when in the presence of a base. As the NaOH diffuses into the agar, the phenolphthalein changes to pink and thus indicates how far the NaOH has diffused into the agar. By cutting an agar block into cubes of various sizes, it is possible to show the effect of cell size on diffusion.

(a) Use the information below to fill in the table on the right:

Cube 1

2 cm

Cube 2

1 cm

NaOH solution

4 cm

Cube 3

Region of no colour change

Region of colour change

Agar cubes infused with phenolphthalein

Cubes shown to same scale

Cube	1	2	3
1. Total volume / cm^3			
2. Volume not pink / cm^3			
3. Diffused volume / cm^3 (subtract value 2 from value 1)			
4. Percentage diffusion			

(b) Diffusion of substances into and out of a cell occurs across the plasma membrane. For a cuboid cell, explain how increasing cell size affects the effective ability of diffusion to provide the materials required by the cell:

_____

_____

_____

_____

6. Explain why a single large cell of 2 cm x 2 cm x 2 cm is less efficient in terms of passively acquiring nutrients than eight cells of 1 cm x 1 cm x 1 cm:

_____

_____

_____

_____

102 Osmosis

Key Idea: Osmosis is the term describing the diffusion of water molecules down their concentration gradient across a partially permeable membrane.

The diffusion of water down its concentration gradient across a partially permeable membrane is called **osmosis** and it is the principal mechanism by which water moves in and out of living cells. A partially permeable membrane, such as the plasma membrane, allows some molecules, but not others, to pass through. Water molecules can diffuse directly through the lipid bilayer, but movement is aided by specific protein channels called aquaporins. There is a net movement of water molecules until an equilibrium is reached and net movement is then zero. Osmosis is a passive process and does not require any energy input.

Demonstrating Osmosis

Osmosis can be demonstrated using dialysis tubing in a simple experiment (described below). Dialysis tubing, like all cellular membranes, is a partially permeable membrane.

A sucrose solution (high solute concentration) is placed into dialysis tubing, and the tubing is placed into a beaker of water (low solute concentration). The difference in concentration of sucrose (solute) between the two solutions creates an osmotic gradient. Water moves by osmosis into the sucrose solution and the volume of the sucrose solution inside the dialysis tubing increases.

The dialysis tubing acts as a partially permeable membrane, allowing water to pass freely, while keeping the sucrose inside the dialysis tubing.

Osmotic potential

Osmotic potential is a term often used when studying animal cells. The presence of solutes (dissolved substances) in a solution increases the tendency of water to move into that solution. This tendency is called the osmotic potential or osmotic pressure. The greater a solution's concentration (i.e. the more total dissolved solutes it contains) the greater the osmotic potential.

Describing solutions

Water movements in cells, particularly plant cells, are often explained in terms of water potential (see next activity). But you will often see other terms used to compare solutions of different solute concentration, especially in animal biology:

Isotonic solution: Having the same solute concentration relative to another solution (e.g. the cell's contents).

Hypotonic solution: Having a lower solute concentration relative to another solution.

Hypertonic solution: Having a higher solute concentration relative to another solution.

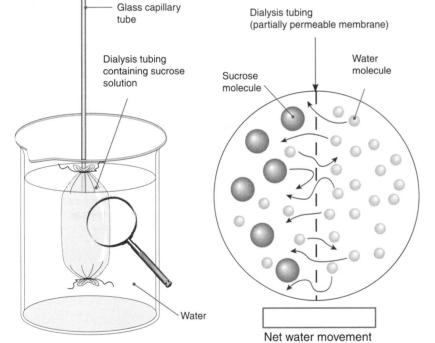

Glass capillary tube

Dialysis tubing (partially permeable membrane)

Dialysis tubing containing sucrose solution

Sucrose molecule

Water molecule

Water

Net water movement

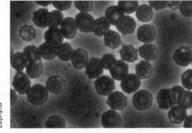

The red blood cells above were placed into a hypertonic solution. As a result, the cells have lost water and have begun to shrink, losing their usual discoid shape.

1. What is osmosis? _____

_____

_____

2. (a) In the blue box on the diagram above, draw an arrow to show the direction of net water movement.

(b) Why did water move in this direction? _____

_____

_____

3. What would happen to the height of the water in the capillary tube if the sucrose concentration was increased?

_____

LINK   LINK   WEB
103 101 102 KNOW

103 Water Movement in Plant Cells

Key Idea: Water potential explains the tendency of water to move from one region to another by osmosis. Water molecules moves to regions of lower water potential.

The water potential of a solution (denoted by ψ) is the term given to the tendency for water molecules to enter or leave a solution by osmosis. The tendency for water to move in any particular direction can be calculated on the basis of the water potential of the cell sap relative to its surrounding environment. The use of water potential to express the water relations of plant cells is used in preference to osmotic potential and osmotic pressure although these terms are still frequently used in areas of animal physiology and medicine.

Water potential and water movement

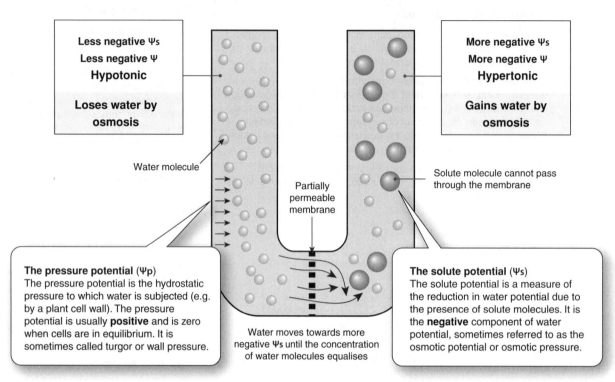

Less negative Ψs
Less negative Ψ
Hypotonic

Loses water by osmosis

More negative Ψs
More negative Ψ
Hypertonic

Gains water by osmosis

Water molecule

Solute molecule cannot pass through the membrane

Partially permeable membrane

The pressure potential (Ψp)
The pressure potential is the hydrostatic pressure to which water is subjected (e.g. by a plant cell wall). The pressure potential is usually **positive** and is zero when cells are in equilibrium. It is sometimes called turgor or wall pressure.

Water moves towards more negative Ψs until the concentration of water molecules equalises

The solute potential (Ψs)
The solute potential is a measure of the reduction in water potential due to the presence of solute molecules. It is the **negative** component of water potential, sometimes referred to as the osmotic potential or osmotic pressure.

As water molecules move around some collide with the plasma membrane and create pressure on the membrane called **water potential** (ψ). The greater the movement of water molecules, the higher their water potential. The presence of solutes (e.g. sucrose) lowers water potential because the solutes restrict the movement of water molecules. Pure water has the highest water potential (zero). Dissolving any solute in water lowers the water potential (makes it more negative).

Water always diffuses from regions of less negative to more negative water potential. Water potential is determined by two components: the **solute potential**, ψs (of the cell sap) and the **pressure potential**, ψp, expressed by:

$$\psi cell = \psi s + \psi p$$

The closer a value is to zero, the higher its water potential.

1. What is the water potential of pure water? _____

2. The diagrams below show three hypothetical situations where adjacent cells have different water potentials. Draw arrows on each pair of cells (a)-(c) to indicate the net direction of water movement and calculate ψ for each side:

(a)

A	B
ψs = –400 kPa	ψs = –500 kPa
ψp = 300 kPa	ψp = 300 kPa

(b)

A	B
ψs = –500 kPa	ψs = –600 kPa
ψp = 100 kPa	ψp = 100 kPa

(c)

A	B
ψs = –600 kPa	ψs = –500 kPa
ψp = 200 kPa	ψp = 300 kPa

ψ for side A: _____ _____ _____

ψ for side B: _____ _____ _____

© 2015 **BIOZONE** International
ISBN: 978-1-927309-13-1
Photocopying Prohibited

When the contents of a plant cell push against the cell wall they create **turgor** (tightness) which provides support for the plant body. When cells lose water, there is a loss of turgor and the plant wilts. Complete loss of turgor from a cell is called plasmolysis and is irreversible. The diagram below shows two situations: when the external water potential is less negative than the cell and when it is more negative than the cell. When the external water potential is the same as that of the cell, there is no net movement of water.

Plasmolysis in a plant cell

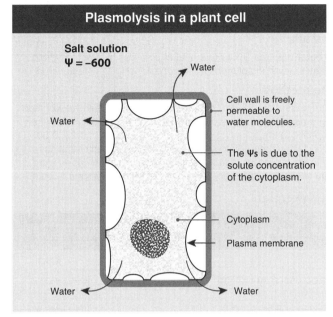

Salt solution
$\Psi = -600$

Water

Water

- Cell wall is freely permeable to water molecules.
- The Ψs is due to the solute concentration of the cytoplasm.
- Cytoplasm
- Plasma membrane

Water

Water

Turgor in a plant cell

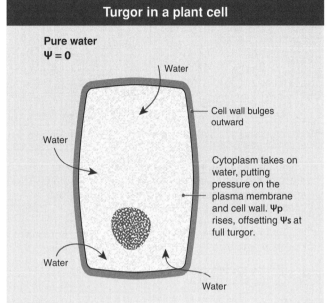

Pure water
$\Psi = 0$

Water

Water

- Cell wall bulges outward
- Cytoplasm takes on water, putting pressure on the plasma membrane and cell wall. **Ψp** rises, offsetting **Ψs** at full turgor.

Water

Water

When external water potential is more negative than the water potential of the cell ($\Psi cell = \Psi s + \Psi p$), water leaves the cell and, because the cell wall is rigid, the plasma membrane shrinks away from the cell wall. This process is termed **plasmolysis** and the cell becomes flaccid ($\Psi p = 0$). Full plasmolysis is irreversible; the cell cannot recover by taking up water.

When the external water potential is less negative than the $\Psi cell$, water enters the cell. A pressure potential is generated when sufficient water has been taken up to cause the cell contents to press against the cell wall. Ψp rises progressively until it offsets Ψs. Water uptake stops when the $\Psi cell = 0$. The rigid cell wall prevents cell rupture. Cells in this state are **turgid**.

3. What is the effect of dissolved solutes on water potential? _____

_____

_____

4. Why don't plant cells burst when water enters them? _____

_____

_____

5. (a) Distinguish between plasmolysis and turgor: _____

_____

_____

(b) Describe the state of the plant in the photo on the right and explain your reasoning:

_____

_____

6. (a) Explain the role of pressure potential in generating cell turgor in plants: _____

_____

_____

(b) Explain the purpose of cell turgor to plants: _____

_____

_____

104 Estimating Osmolarity

Key Idea: A cell placed in a hypotonic solution will gain water while a cell placed in a hypertonic solution will lose water.
The osmolarity (which is directly proportional to the solute potential) of a cell or tissue can be estimated by placing the tissue into a series of solutions of known concentration and observing if the tissue loses or gains water. The solution in which the tissue remains unchanged indicates the osmolarity of the tissue. You can then use an equation to estimate solute potential (ψs). At equilibrium, ψp equals zero and the ψ of the cell will therefore equal the ψs ($\psi = \psi s + \psi p$).

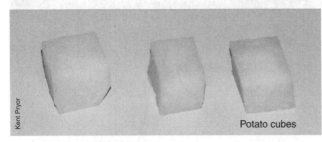

Kent Pryor

Potato cubes

The aim
To determine the solute potential of potatoes by placing potato cubes in varying solutions of sucrose, $C_{12}H_{22}O_{11}$ (table sugar).

The method
Fifteen identical 1.5 cm³ cubes of potato where cut and weighed in grams to two decimal places. Five solutions of sucrose were prepared in the following range (in mol dm^{-3}): 0.00, 0.25, 0.50, 0.75, 1.00. Three potato cubes were placed in each solution, at 22°C, for two hours, stirring every 15 minutes. The cubes were then retrieved, patted dry on blotting paper and weighed again.

1. Complete the table (right) by calculating the total mass of the potato cubes, the total change in mass, and the total % change in mass for all the sucrose concentrations:

2. Use the grid below to draw a line graph of the sucrose concentration vs total percentage change in mass:

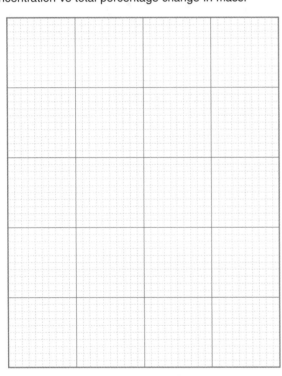

3. (a) Use the graph to estimate the osmolarity of the potato (the point where there is no change in mass):

_____

(b) Calculate the solute potential (ψs) of your potato (in kPa) using the equation below and write it in the space provided. You may use the spreadsheet from weblinks to help you.

The solute potential of a solution is calculated using:

$$\psi_s = -iCRT$$

i = ionisation constant (for sucrose, this is 1)
C = molar concentration (from your graph)
R = pressure constant = 8.31 dm³ kPa K^{-1}mol^{-1}
T = temperature (°K) = 273 + °C of solution.

The results

	Potato sample	Initial mass (I) / g	Final mass (F) / g
[Sucrose] 0.00 mol dm⁻³	1	5.11	6.00
	2	5.15	6.07
	3	5.20	5.15
Total			
Change (C) (F-I) / g			
% Change (C/I x 100)			
[Sucrose] 0.25 mol dm⁻³	1	6.01	4.98
	2	6.07	5.95
	3	7.10	7.00
Total			
Change (C) (F-I) / g			
% Change (C/I x 100)			
[Sucrose] 0.50 mol dm⁻³	1	6.12	5.10
	2	7.03	6.01
	3	5.11	5.03
Total			
Change (C) (F-I) / g			
% Change (C/I x 100)			
[Sucrose] 0.75 mol dm⁻³	1	5.03	3.96
	2	7.10	4.90
	3	7.03	5.13
Total			
Change (C) (F-I) / g			
% Change (C/I x 100)			
[Sucrose] 1.00 mol dm⁻³	1	5.00	4.03
	2	5.04	3.95
	3	6.10	5.02
Total			
Change (C) (F-I) / g			
% Change (C/I x 100)			

Solute potential (show your working): _____

_____

105 Active Transport

Key Idea: Active transport uses energy to transport molecules against their concentration gradient across a partially permeable membrane.

Active transport is the movement of molecules (or ions) from regions of low concentration to regions of high concentration across a cellular membrane by a transport protein. Active transport needs energy to proceed because molecules are being moved against their concentration gradient.

▶ The energy for active transport comes from **ATP** (adenosine triphosphate). Energy is released when ATP is hydrolysed (water is added) forming ADP (adenosine diphosphate) and inorganic phosphate (Pi).

▶ Transport (carrier) proteins in the membrane are used to actively transport molecules from one side of the membrane to the other (below).

▶ Active transport can be used to move molecules into and out of a cell.

▶ Active transport can be either primary or secondary. Primary active transport directly uses ATP for the energy to transport molecules. In secondary active transport, energy is stored in a concentration gradient. The transport of one molecule is coupled to the movement of another down its concentration gradient, ATP is not directly involved in the transport process.

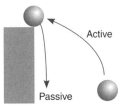

A ball falling is a passive process (it requires no energy input). Replacing the ball requires active energy input.

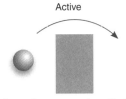

It requires energy to actively move an object across a physical barrier.

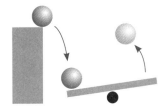

Sometimes the energy of a passively moving object can be used to actively move another. For example, a falling ball can be used to catapult another (left).

Active transport

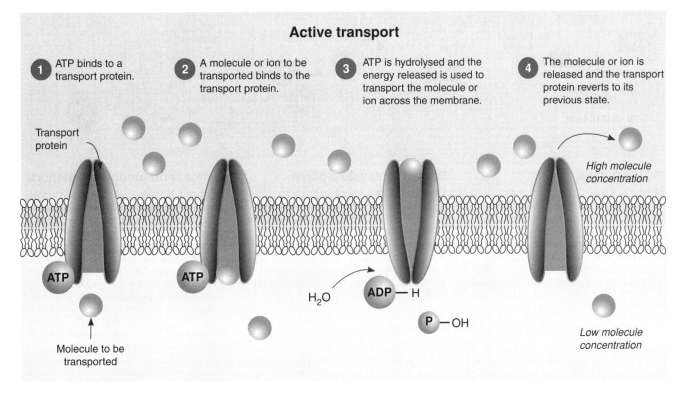

1 ATP binds to a transport protein.

2 A molecule or ion to be transported binds to the transport protein.

3 ATP is hydrolysed and the energy released is used to transport the molecule or ion across the membrane.

4 The molecule or ion is released and the transport protein reverts to its previous state.

Transport protein

ATP

ATP

H_2O

ADP — H

P — OH

High molecule concentration

Low molecule concentration

Molecule to be transported

1. What is **active transport**? _____

_____

_____

_____

2. Where does the energy for active transport come from? _____

3. What is the difference between primary active transport and secondary active transport? _____

_____

_____

_____

© 2015 **BIOZONE** International
ISBN: 978-1-927309-13-1
Photocopying Prohibited

LINK 107 LINK 106 WEB 105

KNOW

106 Ion Pumps

Key Idea: Ion pumps are transmembrane proteins that use energy to move ions and molecules across a membrane against their concentration gradient.

Sometimes molecules or ions are needed in concentrations that diffusion alone cannot supply to the cell, or they cannot diffuse through the plasma membrane. In this case ion pumps move ions (and some molecules) across the plasma membrane. The sodium-potassium pump (below) is found in almost all animal cells and is common in plant cells also. The concentration gradient created by ion pumps is often coupled to the transport of other molecules such as glucose across the membrane.

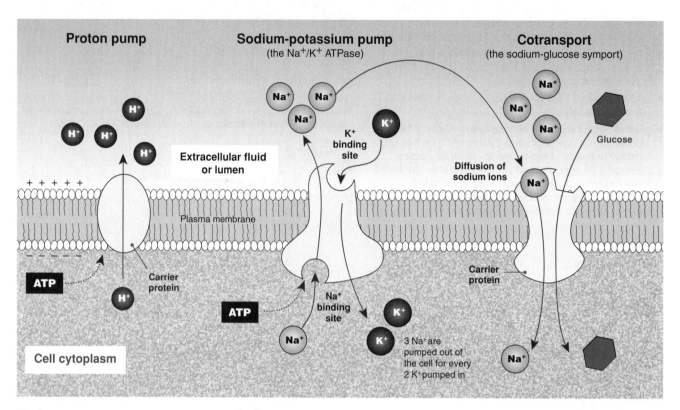

Proton pump

Sodium-potassium pump (the Na⁺/K⁺ ATPase)

Cotransport (the sodium-glucose symport)

Proton pumps

ATP driven proton pumps use energy to remove hydrogen ions (H⁺) from inside the cell to the outside. This creates a large difference in the proton concentration either side of the membrane, with the inside of the plasma membrane being negatively charged. This potential difference can be coupled to the transport of other molecules.

Sodium-potassium pump

The sodium-potassium pump is a specific protein in the membrane that uses energy in the form of ATP to exchange sodium ions (Na⁺) for potassium ions (K⁺) across the membrane. The unequal balance of Na⁺ and K⁺ across the membrane creates large concentration gradients that can be used to drive transport of other substances (e.g. cotransport of glucose).

Cotransport (coupled transport)

A gradient in sodium ions drives the active transport of **glucose** in intestinal epithelial cells. The specific transport protein couples the return of Na⁺ down its concentration gradient to the transport of glucose into the intestinal epithelial cell. A low intracellular concentration of Na⁺ (and therefore the concentration gradient) is maintained by a sodium-potassium pump.

1. Why is ATP required for membrane pump systems to operate? _____

_____

2. (a) Explain what is meant by cotransport: _____

_____

(b) How is cotransport used to move glucose into the intestinal epithelial cells? _____

_____

_____

(c) What happens to the glucose that is transported into the intestinal epithelial cells? _____

_____

3. Describe two consequences of the extracellular accumulation of sodium ions: _____

_____

_____

© 2015 **BIOZONE** International
ISBN: 978-1-927309-13-1
Photocopying Prohibited

107 Exocytosis and Endocytosis

Key Idea: Endocytosis and exocytosis are active transport processes. Endocytosis involves the cell engulfing material. Exocytosis involves the cell expelling material.

Most cells carry out **cytosis**, a type of active transport in which the plasma membrane folds around a substance to transport it across the plasma membrane. The ability of cells to do this is a function of the flexibility of the plasma membrane. Cytosis results in bulk transport of substances into or out of the cell and is achieved through the localised activity of the cell's cytoskeleton. **Endocytosis** involves material being engulfed and taken into the cell. It typically occurs in protozoans and some white blood cells of the mammalian defence system (phagocytes). **Exocytosis** is the reverse of endocytosis and involves expelling material from the cell in vesicles that fuse with the plasma membrane. Exocytosis is common in cells that export material (secretory cells).

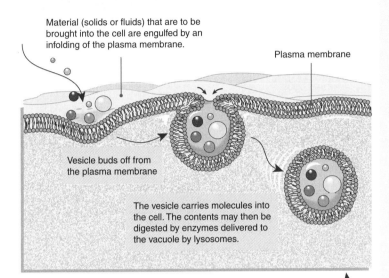

Material (solids or fluids) that are to be brought into the cell are engulfed by an infolding of the plasma membrane.

Plasma membrane

Vesicle buds off from the plasma membrane

The vesicle carries molecules into the cell. The contents may then be digested by enzymes delivered to the vacuole by lysosomes.

Both endocytosis and exocytosis require energy in the form of ATP.

The contents of the vesicle are expelled into the intercellular space.

Vesicle fuses with the plasma membrane.

Vesicle carrying molecules for export moves to the perimeter of the cell.

Areas of enlargement

Endocytosis

Endocytosis (left) occurs by invagination (infolding) of the plasma membrane, which then forms vesicles or vacuoles that become detached and enter the cytoplasm. There are two main types of endocytosis:

Phagocytosis: 'cell-eating'
Phagocytosis involves the cell engulfing **solid material** to form large vesicles or vacuoles (e.g. food vacuoles). Examples: Feeding in *Amoeba*, phagocytosis of foreign material and cell debris by neutrophils and macrophages. Some endocytosis is **receptor mediated** and is triggered when receptor proteins on the extracellular surface of the plasma membrane bind to specific substances. Examples include the uptake of lipoproteins by mammalian cells.

Pinocytosis: 'cell-drinking'
Pinocytosis involves the non-specific uptake of **liquids** or fine suspensions into the cell to form small pinocytic vesicles. Pinocytosis is used primarily for absorbing extracellular fluid. Examples: Uptake in many protozoa, some cells of the liver, and some plant cells.

Exocytosis

Exocytosis (left) is the reverse process to endocytosis. In multicellular organisms, various types of cells are specialised to manufacture and export products, such as proteins, from the cell to elsewhere in the body or outside it. Exocytosis occurs by fusion of the vesicle membrane and the plasma membrane, followed by release of the vesicle contents to the outside of the cell.

1. Distinguish between **phagocytosis** and **pinocytosis**: _____

_____

_____

2. Describe an example of phagocytosis and identify the cell type involved: _____

_____

3. Describe an example of exocytosis and identify the cell type involved: _____

_____

4. How does each of the following substances enter a living macrophage:

(a) Oxygen: _____ (c) Water: _____

(b) Cellular debris: _____ (d) Glucose: _____

108 Active and Passive Transport Summary

Key Idea: Cells move materials into and out of the cell by either passive transport, which does not require energy, or by active transport which requires energy, often as ATP.

Cells need to move materials into and out of the cell. Molecules needed for metabolism must be accumulated from outside the cell, where they may be in low concentration. Waste products and molecules for use in other parts of the organism must be 'exported' out of the cell. Some materials (e.g. gases and water) move into and out of the cell by passive transport processes, without energy expenditure. Other molecules (e.g. sucrose) are moved into and out of the cell using active transport. Active transport processes involve the expenditure of energy in the form of ATP, and therefore use oxygen.

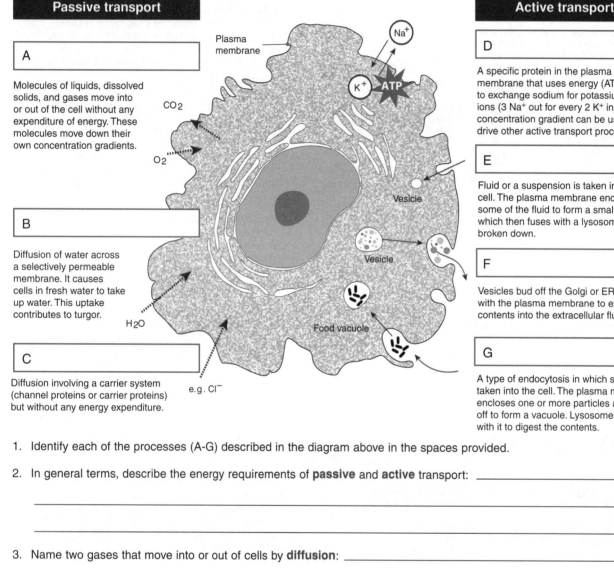

Passive transport

A

Molecules of liquids, dissolved solids, and gases move into or out of the cell without any expenditure of energy. These molecules move down their own concentration gradients.

B

Diffusion of water across a selectively permeable membrane. It causes cells in fresh water to take up water. This uptake contributes to turgor.

C

Diffusion involving a carrier system (channel proteins or carrier proteins) but without any energy expenditure.

Active transport

D

A specific protein in the plasma membrane that uses energy (ATP) to exchange sodium for potassium ions (3 Na^+ out for every 2 K^+ in). The concentration gradient can be used to drive other active transport processes.

E

Fluid or a suspension is taken into the cell. The plasma membrane encloses some of the fluid to form a small vesicle, which then fuses with a lysosome and is broken down.

F

Vesicles bud off the Golgi or ER and fuse with the plasma membrane to expel their contents into the extracellular fluid.

G

A type of endocytosis in which solids are taken into the cell. The plasma membrane encloses one or more particles and buds off to form a vacuole. Lysosomes fuse with it to digest the contents.

1. Identify each of the processes (A-G) described in the diagram above in the spaces provided.

2. In general terms, describe the energy requirements of **passive** and **active** transport: _____

_____

_____

3. Name two gases that move into or out of cells by **diffusion**: _____

4. Identify the transport mechanism involved in each of the following processes in cells:

   (a) Uptake of extracellular fluid by liver cells: _____

   (b) Capture and destruction of a bacterial cell by a white blood cell: _____

   (c) Movement of water into the cell: _____

   (d) Secretion of digestive enzymes from cells of the pancreas: _____

   (e) Uptake of lipoproteins in the blood by mammalian cells: _____

   (f) Ingestion of a food particle by a protozoan: _____

   (g) Transport of chloride ions into a cell: _____

   (h) Uptake of glucose into red blood cells: _____

   (i) Establishment of a potential difference across the membrane of a nerve cell: _____

TEST

109 Chapter Review

Summarise what you know about this topic under the headings provided. You can draw diagrams or mind maps, or write short notes to organise your thoughts. Use the images and hints included to help you:

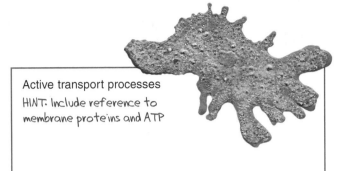

Active transport processes

HINT: Include reference to membrane proteins and ATP

Passive transport processes

HINT: Include reference to the concentration gradient

Membrane structure

HINT: Define the fluid mosaic model and draw a plasma membrane. What factors alter membrane permeability?

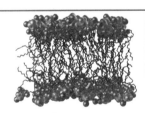

REVISE

110 KEY TERMS: Did You Get It?

1. Match each term to its definition, as identified by its preceding letter code.

active transport **F**

carrier protein

concentration gradient

diffusion **C**

endocytosis

facilitated diffusion

fluid mosaic model

ion pump

osmosis

passive transport

plasma membrane **A**

surface area: volume ratio **L**

water potential

A   A partially-permeable phospholipid bilayer forming the boundary of all cells.

B   The movement of substances across a biological membrane without energy expenditure.

C   The passive movement of molecules from high to low concentration.

D   A measure of the tendency of water to move from one area to another by osmosis. Its components are solute potential and pressure potential.

E   A membrane-bound protein involved in the transport of a specific molecule across the membrane either by active transport or facilitated diffusion.

F   The energy-requiring movement of substances across a biological membrane against a concentration gradient.

G   Active transport in which molecules are engulfed by the plasma membrane, forming a phagosome or food vacuole within the cell.

H   Passive movement of water molecules across a partially permeable membrane down a concentration gradient.

I   A transmembrane protein that moves ions across a plasma membrane against their concentration gradient.

J   Gradual change in the concentration of solutes as a function of distance through the solution. In biology, this usually results from unequal distribution of ions across a membrane.

K   The model for membrane structure which proposes a double phospholipid bilayer in which proteins and cholesterol are embedded.

L   This relationship determines capacity for effective diffusion in a cell.

M   A type of passive transport, facilitated by transport proteins.

2. Match the statements in the table below to form a complete paragraph. The left hand column is in the correct order, the right hand column is not.

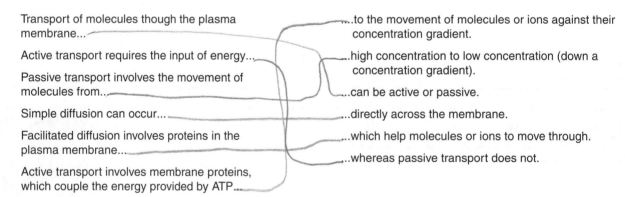

Transport of molecules though the plasma membrane...

Active transport requires the input of energy...

Passive transport involves the movement of molecules from...

Simple diffusion can occur...

Facilitated diffusion involves proteins in the plasma membrane...

Active transport involves membrane proteins, which couple the energy provided by ATP...

...to the movement of molecules or ions against their concentration gradient.

...high concentration to low concentration (down a concentration gradient).

...can be active or passive.

...directly across the membrane.

...which help molecules or ions to move through.

...whereas passive transport does not.

3. The diagrams below depict what happens when a red blood cell is placed into three solutions with differing water potentials. Describe the water potential of the solution (in relation to the cell) and describe what is happening:

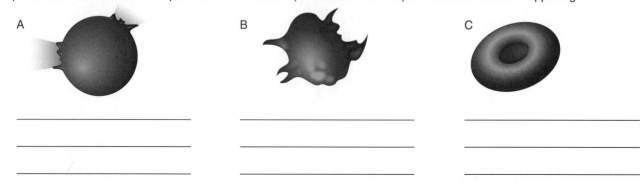

A

B

C

TEST

Module 2.1.6 — Cellular Division, Diversity, and Organisation

The cell cycle and mitosis

Learning outcomes

		Activity number

☐ 1 Describe stages in the eukaryotic cell cycle: interphase, mitosis, cytokinesis. Describe the events occurring during interphase stages: G1, S, and G2. — 112

☐ 2 Describe the outcome of mitotic division and explain the significance and roles of mitosis in eukaryotic life cycles. — 111

☐ 3 Explain the regulation of the cell cycle, including the role of checkpoints. — 114

☐ 4 Describe mitosis as a continuous process, with distinct stages. Describe the events in the main stages in mitosis: prophase, metaphase, anaphase, telophase. Include reference to changes in the nuclear envelope, chromosomes, chromatids, centromere, centrioles (animal cells) spindle fibres, and plasma membrane. — 112

☐ 5 **PAG1** Draw labelled diagrams of mitotic stages from stained sections and squashes of plant tissue viewed with a light microscope. — 113

 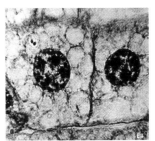 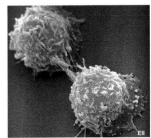

Meiosis

Learning outcomes

		Activity number

☐ 6 Describe the purpose and genetic outcome of meiosis. Explain the contribution of independent assortment and crossing over in meiosis to genetic variation. — 111 115 116 117

☐ 7 Outline events in the main stages in meiosis and their significance. Stages to include prophase 1, metaphase 1, anaphase 1, telophase 1, prophase 2, metaphase 2, anaphase 2, and telophase 2. — 115 117

☐ 8 Distinguish between mitosis and meiosis in terms of their cellular outcomes and role in the life cycle of organisms. — 118

Cell specialisation and organisation

Learning outcomes

		Activity number

☐ 9 Using examples, describe how the cells of multicellular organisms are specialised for particular functions. — 119 120 121

☐ 10 **PAG1** Identify specialised cells in stained sections of plant and animal tissues viewed with a light microscope. — 123 124

☐ 11 Using examples, describe the organisation of cells into tissues, organs, and organ systems. Comment on the benefits of this organisation. — 122

☐ 12 Describe the properties and differentiation of stem cells. Explain the role of stem cells in embryonic development and in the adult organism. — 125 126

☐ 13 Describe how erythrocytes and neutrophils are produced by differentiation from stem cells in bone marrow. — 125

☐ 14 Describe how xylem vessels and phloem sieve tubes are produced by differentiation in meristems (meristematic tissue). — 128 129

☐ 15 Describe the potential uses of stem cells in research and medicine, including in repairing tissue, treating neurological conditions, and in developmental biology. — 126 127

111 Cell Division

Key Idea: New cells arise from the division of existing cells. There are two types of cell division, mitosis and meiosis.

New cells are formed when existing cells divide. In eukaryotes, cell division begins with the replication of a cell's DNA followed by division of the nucleus. There are two forms of cell division. **Mitosis** produces two identical daughter cells from each parent cell. Mitosis is responsible for growth and repair processes in multicellular organisms, and asexual reproduction in some eukaryotes, e.g. yeasts. **Meiosis** is a special type of cell division concerned with producing sex cells (gametes or haploid spores) for sexual reproduction. It occurs in the sex organs of plants and animals.

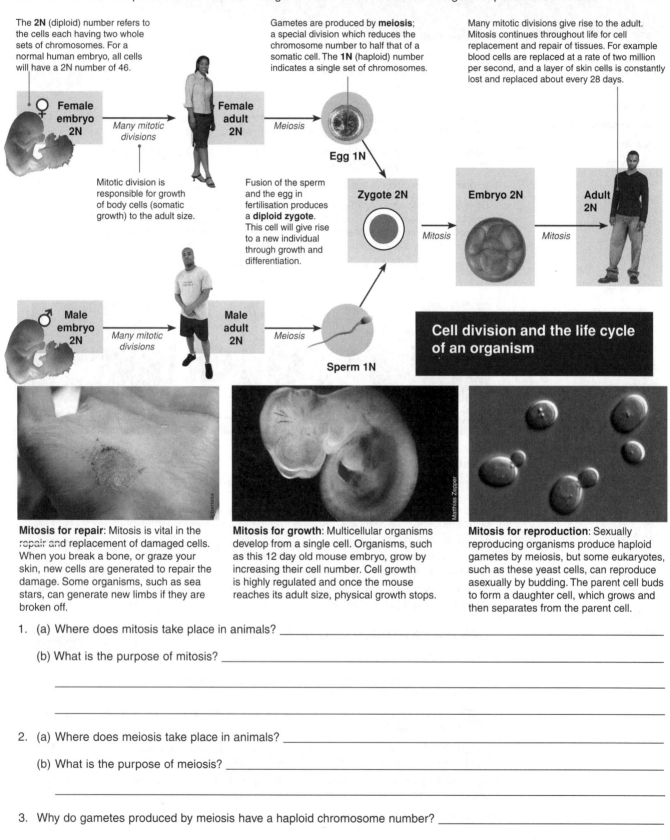

The **2N** (diploid) number refers to the cells each having two whole sets of chromosomes. For a normal human embryo, all cells will have a 2N number of 46.

Gametes are produced by **meiosis**; a special division which reduces the chromosome number to half that of a somatic cell. The **1N** (haploid) number indicates a single set of chromosomes.

Many mitotic divisions give rise to the adult. Mitosis continues throughout life for cell replacement and repair of tissues. For example blood cells are replaced at a rate of two million per second, and a layer of skin cells is constantly lost and replaced about every 28 days.

Female embryo 2N — *Many mitotic divisions* → Female adult 2N — *Meiosis* → Egg 1N

Mitotic division is responsible for growth of body cells (somatic growth) to the adult size.

Fusion of the sperm and the egg in fertilisation produces a **diploid zygote**. This cell will give rise to a new individual through growth and differentiation.

Zygote 2N — *Mitosis* → Embryo 2N — *Mitosis* → Adult 2N

Male embryo 2N — *Many mitotic divisions* → Male adult 2N — *Meiosis* → Sperm 1N

Cell division and the life cycle of an organism

Mitosis for repair: Mitosis is vital in the repair and replacement of damaged cells. When you break a bone, or graze your skin, new cells are generated to repair the damage. Some organisms, such as sea stars, can generate new limbs if they are broken off.

Mitosis for growth: Multicellular organisms develop from a single cell. Organisms, such as this 12 day old mouse embryo, grow by increasing their cell number. Cell growth is highly regulated and once the mouse reaches its adult size, physical growth stops.

Mitosis for reproduction: Sexually reproducing organisms produce haploid gametes by meiosis, but some eukaryotes, such as these yeast cells, can reproduce asexually by budding. The parent cell buds to form a daughter cell, which grows and then separates from the parent cell.

1. (a) Where does mitosis take place in animals? _____

   (b) What is the purpose of mitosis? _____

   _____

   _____

2. (a) Where does meiosis take place in animals? _____

   (b) What is the purpose of meiosis? _____

   _____

3. Why do gametes produced by meiosis have a haploid chromosome number? _____

   _____

   _____

© 2015 **BIOZONE** International
ISBN: 978-1-927309-13-1
Photocopying Prohibited

112 Mitosis and the Cell Cycle

Key Idea: Mitosis is an important part of the cell cycle in which the replicated chromosomes are separated and the cell divides, producing two new identical cells.

Mitosis (or M-phase) is part of the **cell cycle** in which an existing cell (the parent cell) divides into two daughter cells. Unlike meiosis, mitosis does not result in a change of chromosome numbers and the daughter cells are identical to the parent cell. Although mitosis is part of a continuous cell cycle, it is often divided into stages to help differentiate the processes occurring. Mitosis is one of the shortest stages of the cell cycle. When a cell is not undergoing mitosis, it is said to be in interphase. Interphase accounts for 90% of the cell cycle. Cytokinesis (the division of the newly formed cells) is distinct from nuclear division.

The cell cycle

Interphase

Cells spend most of their time in interphase. Interphase is divided into three stages (right):

▶ The first gap phase (G1).
▶ The S-phase.
▶ The second gap phase (G2).

During interphase the cell grows, carries out its normal activities, and replicates its DNA in preparation for cell division.
Interphase is not a stage in mitosis.

Mitosis and cytokinesis (M-phase)

Mitosis and cytokinesis occur during M-phase. During mitosis, the cell nucleus (containing the replicated DNA) divides in two equal parts. Cytokinesis occurs at the end of M-phase. During cytokinesis the cell cytoplasm divides, and two new daughter cells are produced.

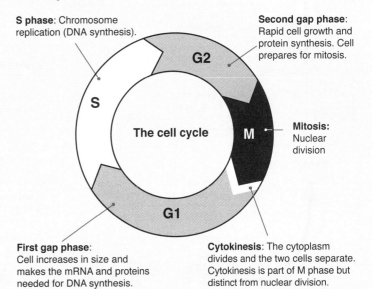

S phase: Chromosome replication (DNA synthesis).

Second gap phase: Rapid cell growth and protein synthesis. Cell prepares for mitosis.

Mitosis: Nuclear division

First gap phase: Cell increases in size and makes the mRNA and proteins needed for DNA synthesis.

Cytokinesis: The cytoplasm divides and the two cells separate. Cytokinesis is part of M phase but distinct from nuclear division.

Mitosis produces identical daughter cells

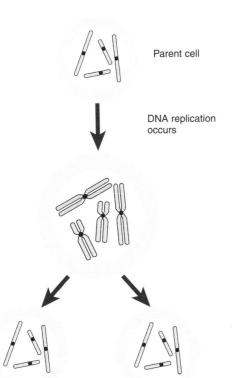

Parent cell

DNA replication occurs

The cell divides forming two identical daughter cells. The chromosome number remains the same as the parent cell.

Cytokinesis

In plant cells (below top), cytokinesis (division of the cytoplasm) involves construction of a cell plate (a precursor the new cell wall) in the middle of the cell. The cell wall materials are delivered by vesicles derived from the Golgi. The vesicles coalesce to become the plasma membranes of the new cell surfaces.

Animal cell cytokinesis (below bottom) begins shortly after the sister chromatids have separated in anaphase of mitosis. A contractile ring of microtubular elements assembles in the middle of the cell, next to the plasma membrane, constricting it to form a cleavage furrow. In an energy-using process, the cleavage furrow moves inwards, forming a region of abscission (separation) where the two cells will separate.

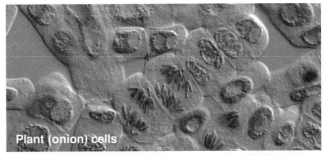

Plant (onion) cells

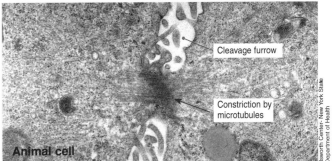

Cleavage furrow

Constriction by microtubules

Animal cell

LINK 114 LINK 113 WEB 112 KNOW

The cell cycle and stages of mitosis in a plant cell

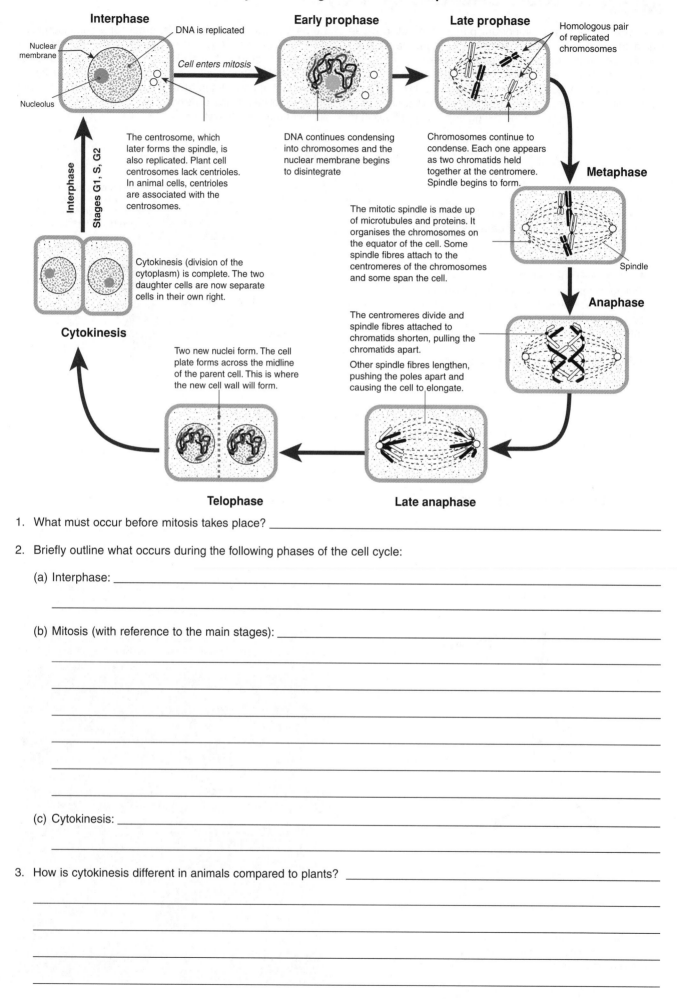

Interphase

Nuclear membrane

DNA is replicated

Nucleolus

Cell enters mitosis

Interphase Stages G1, S, G2

The centrosome, which later forms the spindle, is also replicated. Plant cell centrosomes lack centrioles. In animal cells, centrioles are associated with the centrosomes.

Cytokinesis (division of the cytoplasm) is complete. The two daughter cells are now separate cells in their own right.

Cytokinesis

Two new nuclei form. The cell plate forms across the midline of the parent cell. This is where the new cell wall will form.

Telophase

Early prophase

DNA continues condensing into chromosomes and the nuclear membrane begins to disintegrate

Late prophase

Homologous pair of replicated chromosomes

Chromosomes continue to condense. Each one appears as two chromatids held together at the centromere. Spindle begins to form.

Metaphase

The mitotic spindle is made up of microtubules and proteins. It organises the chromosomes on the equator of the cell. Some spindle fibres attach to the centromeres of the chromosomes and some span the cell.

Spindle

Anaphase

The centromeres divide and spindle fibres attached to chromatids shorten, pulling the chromatids apart.

Other spindle fibres lengthen, pushing the poles apart and causing the cell to elongate.

Late anaphase

1. What must occur before mitosis takes place? _____

2. Briefly outline what occurs during the following phases of the cell cycle:

   (a) Interphase: _____

   _____

   (b) Mitosis (with reference to the main stages): _____

   _____

   _____

   _____

   _____

   _____

   _____

   _____

   (c) Cytokinesis: _____

   _____

3. How is cytokinesis different in animals compared to plants? _____

   _____

   _____

   _____

© 2015 **BIOZONE** International
ISBN: 978-1-927309-13-1
Photocopying Prohibited

113 Recognising Stages in Mitosis

Key Idea: The stages of mitosis can be recognised by the organisation of the cell and chromosomes.
Although mitosis is a continuous process, it is divided into four stages (prophase, anaphase, metaphase, and telophase) to more easily describe the processes occurring during its progression.

The mitotic index

The mitotic index measures the ratio of cells in mitosis to the number of cells counted. It is a measure of cell proliferation and can be used to diagnose cancer. In areas of high cell growth the mitotic index is high such as in plant apical meristems or the growing tips of plant roots. The mitotic index can be calculated using the formula:

$$\text{Mitotic index} = \frac{\text{Number of cells in mitosis}}{\text{Total number of cells}}$$

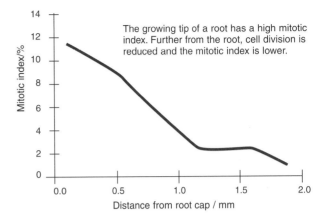

The growing tip of a root has a high mitotic index. Further from the root, cell division is reduced and the mitotic index is lower.

1. Use the information on the previous page to identify which stage of mitosis is shown in each of the photographs below:

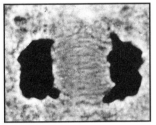 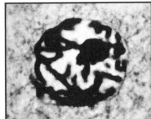  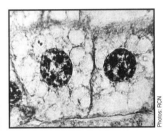

(a) _____   (b) _____   (c) _____   (d) _____

2. (a) The light micrograph (right) shows a section of cells in an onion root tip. These cells have a cell cycle of approximately 24 hours. The cells can be seen to be in various stages of the cell cycle. By counting the number of cells in the various stages it is possible to calculate how long the cell spends in each stage of the cycle. Count and record the number of cells in the image that are in mitosis and those that are in interphase. Cells in cytokinesis can be recorded as in interphase. Estimate the amount of time a cell spends in each phase.

Stage	No. of cells	% of total cells	Estimated time in stage
Interphase			
Mitosis			
Total		100	

(b) Use your counts from 2(a) to calculate the mitotic index for this section of cells.

_____

_____

Onion root tip cells

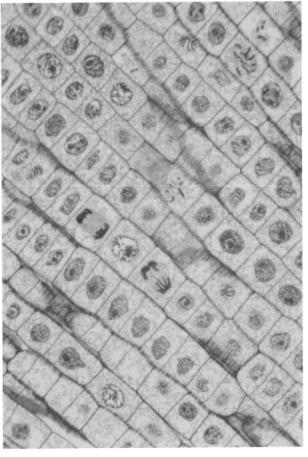

3. What would you expect to happen to the mitotic index of a population of cells that loses the ability to divide as they mature?

_____

_____

LINK
112 DATA

114 Regulation of the Cell Cycle

Key Idea: The cell cycle is regulated by checkpoints, which ensure the cell has met certain conditions before it continues to the next phase of the cell cycle.

The cell cycle is an orderly sequence of events, but its duration varies enormously between cells of different species and between cell types in one organism. For example, human intestinal cells normally divide around twice a day, whereas cells in the liver typically divide once a year. However, if these tissues are damaged, cell division increases rapidly to repair the damage. Progression through the cell cycle is controlled by regulatory checkpoints, which ensure the cell has met the conditions required to successfully complete the next phase.

Checkpoints during the cell cycle

There are three **checkpoints** during the cell cycle. A checkpoint is a critical regulatory point in the cell cycle. At each checkpoint, a set of conditions determines whether or not the cell will continue into the next phase. For example, cell size is important in regulating whether or not the cell can pass through the G_1 checkpoint.

G_1 checkpoint
Pass this checkpoint if:
▶ Cell size is large enough.
▶ Sufficient nutrients are available.
▶ Signals from other cells have been received.

G_2 checkpoint:
Pass this checkpoint if:
▶ Cell size is large enough.
▶ Replication of chromosomes has been successfully completed.
▶ Proteins required for mitosis have been synthesised.

Metaphase checkpoint
Pass this checkpoint if:
▶ All chromosomes are attached to the mitotic spindle.

The cell cycle — S, G2, M, G1

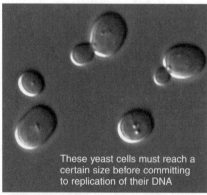

These yeast cells must reach a certain size before committing to replication of their DNA

The G_1 checkpoint is the critical regulatory point in cells. At this checkpoint, the cell decides whether to commit to the cell cycle or to enter an arrested phase called G_0. Once sufficient nutrients or cell size is reached and the checkpoint is passed the cell is committed to replication of the nuclear material. Most cells that pass G_1 complete the cell cycle.

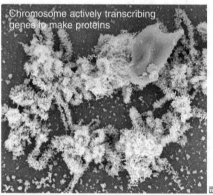

Chromosome actively transcribing genes to make proteins

The G_2 checkpoint determines if DNA synthesis was completed correctly, that the necessary proteins for mitosis have been synthesised, and that the cell has reached a size suitable for cell division. Damage to the DNA prevents entry to M phase. The entry into M phase is controlled by a protein called cyclin B, which reaches a concentration peak at the G_2-M phase boundary.

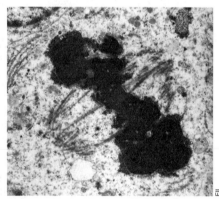

The metaphase checkpoint, or spindle checkpoint, checks that all the chromatids are attached to the spindle fibres and under the correct tension. At this point, cyclin B is degraded, ultimately resulting in the sister chromatids separating and the cell entering anaphase, pulling the chromatids apart. The cell then begins cytokinesis and produces two new daughter cells.

1. What is the general purpose of cell cycle checkpoints? _____

_____

_____

2. (a) What is the purpose of the metaphase checkpoint? _____

_____

(b) Why is this checkpoint important? _____

_____

3. What would happen if the cell cycle was not regulated? _____

_____

© 2015 **BIOZONE** International
ISBN: 978-1-927309-13-1
Photocopying Prohibited

115 Meiosis

Key Idea: Meiosis is a special type of cell division. It produces sex cells (gametes) for the purpose of sexual reproduction. Meiosis involves a single chromosomal duplication followed by two successive nuclear divisions, and results in a halving of the diploid chromosome number. Meiosis occurs in the sex organs of plants and animals. If genetic mistakes (**gene** and **chromosome mutations**) occur here, they will be passed on to the offspring (they will be inherited).

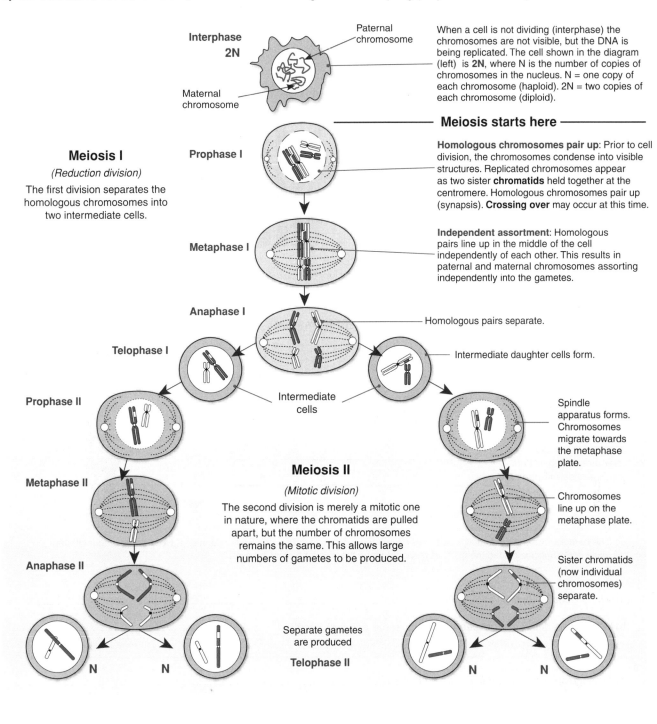

Interphase 2N

Paternal chromosome

Maternal chromosome

When a cell is not dividing (interphase) the chromosomes are not visible, but the DNA is being replicated. The cell shown in the diagram (left) is **2N**, where N is the number of copies of chromosomes in the nucleus. N = one copy of each chromosome (haploid). 2N = two copies of each chromosome (diploid).

——————— **Meiosis starts here** ———————

Meiosis I

(Reduction division)

The first division separates the homologous chromosomes into two intermediate cells.

Prophase I

Homologous chromosomes pair up: Prior to cell division, the chromosomes condense into visible structures. Replicated chromosomes appear as two sister **chromatids** held together at the centromere. Homologous chromosomes pair up (synapsis). **Crossing over** may occur at this time.

Metaphase I

Independent assortment: Homologous pairs line up in the middle of the cell independently of each other. This results in paternal and maternal chromosomes assorting independently into the gametes.

Anaphase I

Homologous pairs separate.

Telophase I

Intermediate daughter cells form.

Prophase II

Intermediate cells

Spindle apparatus forms. Chromosomes migrate towards the metaphase plate.

Meiosis II

(Mitotic division)

The second division is merely a mitotic one in nature, where the chromatids are pulled apart, but the number of chromosomes remains the same. This allows large numbers of gametes to be produced.

Metaphase II

Chromosomes line up on the metaphase plate.

Anaphase II

Sister chromatids (now individual chromosomes) separate.

Separate gametes are produced

Telophase II

N   **N**

N   **N**

1. Describe the behaviour of the chromosomes in the first division of meiosis: _____

_____

_____

_____

2. Describe the behaviour of the chromosomes in the second division of meiosis: _____

_____

_____

LINK   LINK   WEB

117 116 115 KNOW

Crossing over and recombination

Prophase I of meiosis

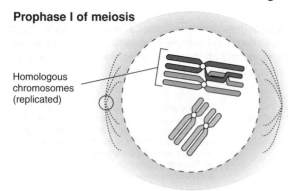

Homologous
chromosomes
(replicated)

Crossing over refers to the mutual exchange of pieces of chromosome (and their genes) **between the homologous chromosomes**. It can occur only during prophase in the first division of meiosis. **Recombination** as a result of crossing over is an important mechanism to increase genetic variability in the offspring and has the general effect of allowing genes to move independently of each other through the generations in a way that allows concentration of beneficial alleles.

In prophase I homologous chromosomes pair up to form **bivalents**. This process is called **synapsis**. While they are paired, the non-sister chromatids of homologous pairs may become tangled and segments may be exchanged in a process called **crossing over**. The crossing over occurs at points called chiasmata.

Crossing over results in the **recombination** of alleles, producing greater variation in the offspring than would otherwise occur.

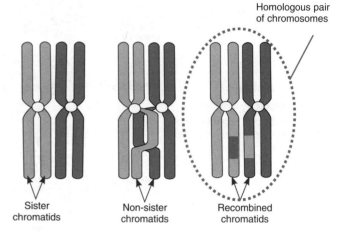

Homologous pair of chromosomes

Sister chromatids

Non-sister chromatids

Recombined chromatids

Gamete formation

Blue = paternal chromosome

Grey = maternal chromosome

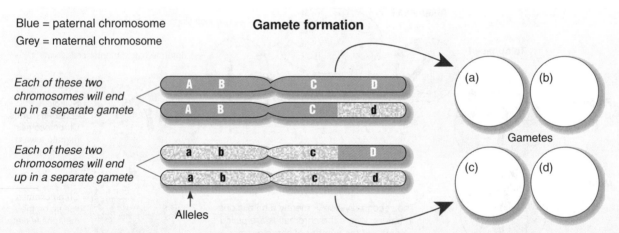

Each of these two chromosomes will end up in a separate gamete

Each of these two chromosomes will end up in a separate gamete

Alleles

Gametes

(a) (b)

(c) (d)

The homologous chromosomes above have completed a crossing over event. Recombination have resulted in four different allele combinations instead the two that would appear if there was no crossing over.

3. (a) When does DNA replication occur? _____

   (b) What is the difference between a chromosome and a chromatid: _____

   _____

4. (a) Distinguish between a haploid and a diploid cell: _____

   _____

   _____

   (b) Circle the **haploid** cells in the diagram on the previous page

5. Complete the diagram above (a) - (d) by drawing the gametes formed:

6. (a) How does crossing over alter the genotype of the gametes produced by meiosis? _____

   _____

   (b) What is the consequence of this? _____

   _____

© 2015 **BIOZONE** International
ISBN: 978-1-927309-13-1
Photocopying Prohibited

116 Crossing Over Problems

Key Idea: Crossing over can occur in multiple places in chromosomes, producing a huge amount of genetic variation. The diagram below shows a pair of homologous chromosomes about to undergo chiasma formation during the first cell division in the process of meiosis. There are known crossover points along the length of the chromatids (same on all four chromatids shown in the diagram). In the prepared spaces below, draw the gene sequences after crossing over has occurred on three unrelated and separate occasions (it would be useful to use different coloured pens to represent the genes from the two different chromosomes). See the diagrams on the previous page as a guide.

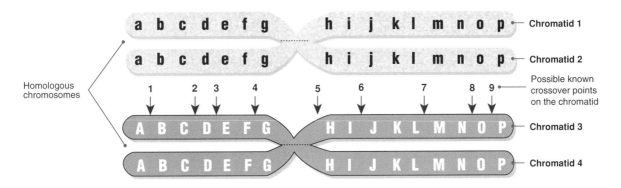

1. Crossing over occurs at a **single** point between the chromosomes above.

   (a) Draw the gene sequences for the four chromatids (on the right), after crossing over has occurred at crossover point: **2**

   (b) Which genes have been exchanged with those on its homologue (neighbour chromosome)?

   _____

2. Crossing over occurs at **two** points between the chromosomes above.

   (a) Draw the gene sequences for the four chromatids (on the right), after crossing over has occurred between crossover points: **6** and **7**.

   (b) Which genes have been exchanged with those on its homologue (neighbour chromosome)?

   _____

3. Crossing over occurs at **four** points between the chromosomes above.

   (a) Draw the gene sequences for the four chromatids (on the right), after crossing over has occurred between crossover points: **1** and **3**, and **5** and **7**.

   (b) Which genes have been exchanged with those on its homologue (neighbour chromosome)?

   _____

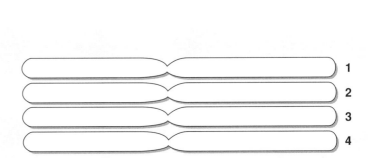

4. What would be the genetic consequences if there was no crossing over between chromatids during meiosis?

   _____

   _____

   _____

KNOW

117 Modelling Meiosis

Key Idea: We can simulate crossing over, gamete production, and the inheritance of alleles during meiosis using ice-block sticks to represent chromosomes.

This practical activity simulates the production of gametes (sperm and eggs) by meiosis and shows you how crossing over increases genetic variability. This is demonstrated by studying how two of your own alleles are inherited by the child produced at the completion of the activity. Completing this activity will help you to visualise and understand meiosis. It will take 25-45 minutes.

Background

Each of your somatic cells contain 46 chromosomes. You received 23 chromosomes from your mother (**maternal chromosomes**), and 23 chromosomes from your father (**paternal chromosomes**). Therefore, you have 23 homologous (same) pairs. For simplicity, the number of chromosomes studied in this exercise has been reduced to four (two homologous pairs). To study the effect of crossing over on genetic variability, you will look at the inheritance of two of your own traits: the ability to **tongue roll** and **handedness**.

Chromosome #	Phenotype	Genotype
10	Tongue roller	TT, Tt
10	Non-tongue roller	tt
2	Right handed	RR, Rr
2	Left handed	rr

Record your phenotype and genotype for each trait in the table (right). **NOTE:** If you have a dominant trait, you will not know if you are heterozygous or homozygous for that trait, so you can choose either genotype for this activity.

BEFORE YOU START THE SIMULATION: Partner up with a classmate. Your gametes will combine with theirs (fertilisation) at the end of the activity to produce a child. Decide who will be the female, and who will be the male. You will need to work with this person again at step 6.

1. Collect four ice-blocks sticks. These represent four chromosomes. Colour two sticks blue or mark them with a P. These are the paternal chromosomes. The plain sticks are the maternal chromosomes. Write your initial on each of the four sticks. Label each chromosome with their chromosome number (right).

   Label four sticky dots with the alleles for each of your phenotypic traits, and stick it onto the appropriate chromosome. For example, if you are heterozygous for tongue rolling, the sticky dots with have the alleles **T** and **t**, and they will be placed on chromosome 10. If you are left handed, the alleles will be **r** and **r** and be placed on chromosome 2 (right).

2. Randomly drop the chromosomes onto a table. This represents a cell in either the testes or ovaries. **Duplicate** your chromosomes (to simulate DNA replication) by adding four more identical ice-block sticks to the table (below). This represents **interphase**.

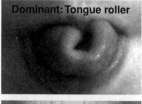

Dominant: Tongue roller

Dominant: Right hand

Recessive: Non-roller

Recessive: Left hand

Trait	Phenotype	Genotype
Handedness		
Tongue rolling		

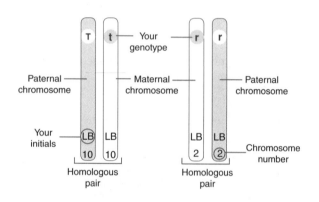

3. Simulate **prophase I** by lining the duplicated chromosome pair with their homologous pair (below). For each chromosome number, you will have four sticks touching side-by-side (A). At this stage **crossing over** occurs. Simulate this by swapping sticky dots from adjoining homologs (B).

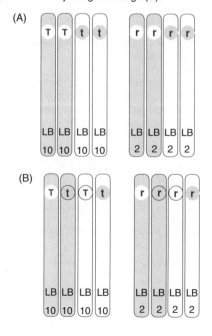

© 2015 **BIOZONE** International
ISBN: 978-1-927309-13-1
Photocopying Prohibited

4. Randomly align the homologous chromosome pairs to simulate alignment on the metaphase plate (as occurs in **metaphase I**). Simulate **anaphase I** by separating chromosome pairs. For each group of four sticks, two are pulled to each pole.

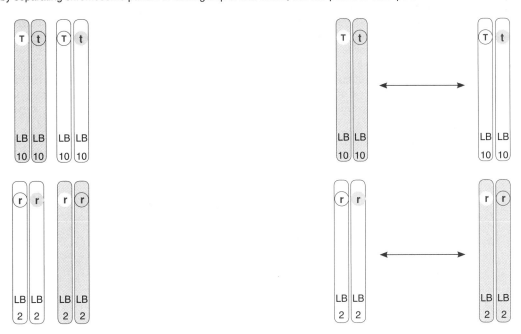

5. **Telophase I:** Two intermediate cells are formed. If you have been random in the previous step, each intermediate cell will contain a mixture of maternal and paternal chromosomes. This is the end of **meiosis 1**.

   Now that meiosis 1 is completed, your cells need to undergo **meiosis 2**. Carry out prophase II, metaphase II, anaphase II, and telophase II. Remember, there is no crossing over in meiosis II. At the end of the process each intermediate cell will have produced two haploid gametes (below).

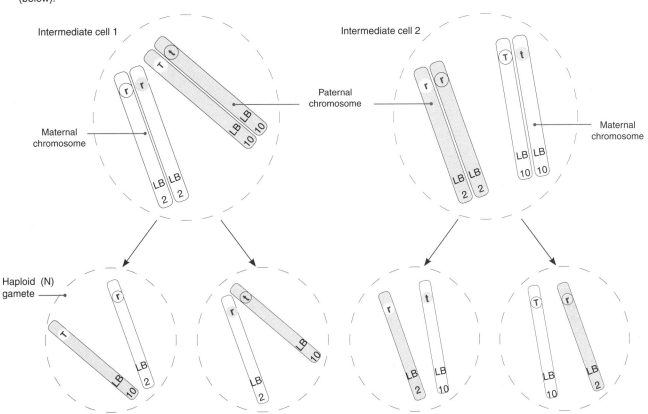

6. Pair up with the partner you chose at the beginning of the exercise to carry out **fertilisation**. Randomly select one sperm and one egg cell. The unsuccessful gametes can be removed from the table. Combine the chromosomes of the successful gametes. You have created a child! Fill in the following chart to describe your child's genotype and phenotype for tongue rolling and handedness.

Trait	Phenotype	Genotype
Handedness		
Tongue rolling		

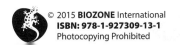

118 Mitosis vs Meiosis

Key Idea: Mitosis produces two daughter cells genetically identical to the parent cell. Meiosis produces four daughter cells that contain half the genetic information of the parent cell. Cell division is fundamental to all life, as cells arise only by the division of existing cells. All types of cell division begin with replication of the cell's DNA. In eukaryotes, this is followed by division of the nucleus. There are two forms of nuclear division: **mitosis** and **meiosis**, and they have quite different purposes and outcomes. Mitosis is the simpler of the two and produces two identical daughter cells from each parent cell. Mitosis is responsible for growth and repair processes in multicellular organisms and reproduction in single-celled and asexual eukaryotes. Meiosis involves a **reduction division** in which haploid gametes are produced for the purposes of sexual reproduction. Fusion of haploid gametes in fertilisation restores the diploid cell number in the **zygote**.

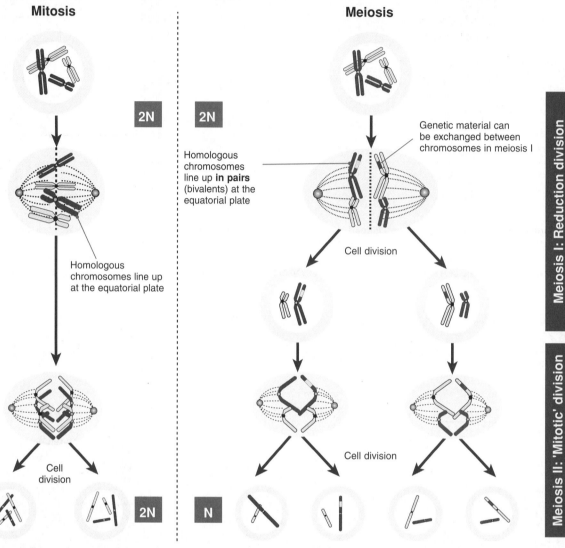

1. Explain how mitosis conserves chromosome number while meiosis reduces the number from diploid to haploid:

_____

_____

_____

2. Describe a fundamental difference between the first and second divisions of meiosis: _____

_____

_____

3. How does meiosis introduce genetic variability into gametes and offspring (following gamete fusion in fertilisation)?

_____

_____

_____

© 2015 **BIOZONE** International
ISBN: 978-1-927309-13-1
Photocopying Prohibited

119 Cellular Differentiation

Key Idea: Many different cell types arise during development of the embryo. Activation of specific genes determines what type of cell will develop.

Mitosis produces genetically identical cells, yet a multicellular organism is made up of many different types of cells, each specialised to carry out a particular role. The variety of cell types arise through **cellular differentiation**, a process by which cells become specialised. Although each cell has the same genetic material (genes) different genes are turned on (activated) or off in different patterns during development in particular types of cells. The differences in gene activation controls what type of cell forms. Once the developmental pathway of a cell is determined, it cannot alter its path and change into another cell type.

A zygote begins development by dividing into a small ball of a few dozen identical cells called **embryonic stem cells**. These can give rise to any type of cell. During embryonic development, the cells specialise to take on the roles of 230 different cell types. Some cells stop dividing once the body has reached a given size, while others (**adult stem cells**) keep on dividing for the rest of the individual's life. Adult stem cells include undifferentiated epithelial cells and bone marrow cells.

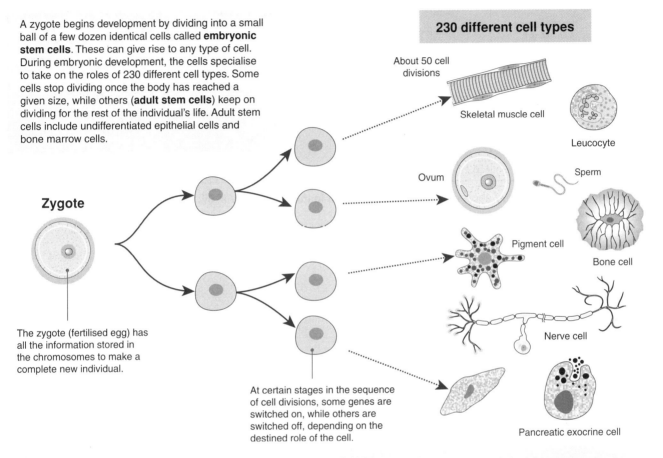

230 different cell types

About 50 cell divisions

Skeletal muscle cell

Leucocyte

Ovum

Sperm

Pigment cell

Bone cell

Nerve cell

Zygote

The zygote (fertilised egg) has all the information stored in the chromosomes to make a complete new individual.

At certain stages in the sequence of cell divisions, some genes are switched on, while others are switched off, depending on the destined role of the cell.

Pancreatic exocrine cell

Development

Development is the process of progressive change through the lifetime of an organism. It involves growth (increase in size), cell division (to generate the multicellular body), **cellular differentiation** (to produce specialised cells) and **morphogenesis** (creating the shape and form of the body).

Selective cell proliferation combined with programmed cell death sculpts the tissues in all vertebrates. In a human embryo, mesoderm forms between the fingers and toes giving the appearance of a webbed, paddle like structure (right). As the embryo develops, this webbing is selectively destroyed. At 14 weeks, each of the individual digits are visible (far right).

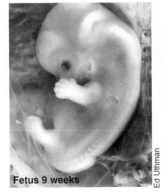

Fetus 9 weeks

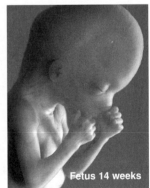

Fetus 14 weeks

Ed Uthman

1. How can so many different types of cell arise from one unspecialised cell (the zygote)? _____

_____

_____

_____

2. Why can't a differentiated cell change into another cell type? _____

_____

_____

120 Specialisation in Human Cells

Key Idea: Specialised cells carry out specific roles in animals. Humans have at least 230 specialised cell types, each with features that enable it to perform its designated role. The eight cell types below are a representative sample of these.

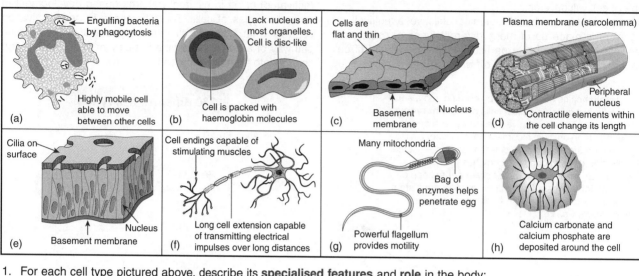

(a) Engulfing bacteria by phagocytosis. Highly mobile cell able to move between other cells

(b) Lack nucleus and most organelles. Cell is disc-like. Cell is packed with haemoglobin molecules

(c) Cells are flat and thin. Basement membrane. Nucleus

(d) Plasma membrane (sarcolemma). Peripheral nucleus. Contractile elements within the cell change its length

(e) Cilia on surface. Nucleus. Basement membrane

(f) Cell endings capable of stimulating muscles. Long cell extension capable of transmitting electrical impulses over long distances

(g) Many mitochondria. Bag of enzymes helps penetrate egg. Powerful flagellum provides motility

(h) Calcium carbonate and calcium phosphate are deposited around the cell

1. For each cell type pictured above, describe its **specialised features** and **role** in the body:

(a) **Phagocytic white blood cell (neutrophil)**. Specialised features: _____

_____

Role of cell within body: _____

(b) **Red blood cell (erythrocyte)**. Specialised features: _____

_____

Role of cell within body: _____

(c) **Squamous epithelial cell**. Specialised features: _____

_____

Role of cell within body: _____

(d) **Skeletal muscle cell**. Specialised features: _____

_____

Role of cell within body: _____

(e) **Ciliated epithelial cell**. Specialised features: _____

_____

Role of cell within body: _____

(f) **Motor neurone**. Specialised features: _____

_____

Role of cell within body: _____

(g) **Sperm cell**. Specialised features: _____

_____

Role of cell within body: _____

(h) **Bone cell (osteocyte)**. Specialised features: _____

_____

Role of cell within body: _____

© 2015 **BIOZONE** International
ISBN: 978-1-927309-13-1
Photocopying Prohibited

121 Specialisation in Plant Cells

Key Idea: The specialised cells in a plant have specific features associated with their particular roles.
The differentiation of cells gives rise to specialised cell types that fulfil specific roles in the plant, e.g. support, transport, or photosynthesis. Each of the cell types illustrated below has features that set it apart from other cell types.

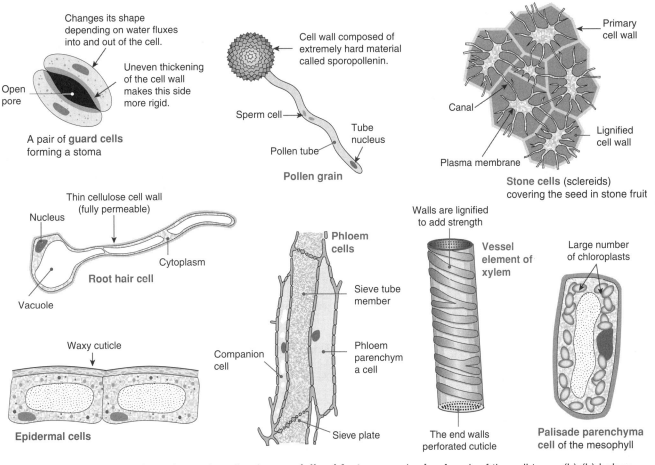

Pollen grain

Stone cells (sclereids) covering the seed in stone fruit

Root hair cell

Phloem cells

Epidermal cells

Palisade parenchyma cell of the mesophyll

1. Using the information given above, describe the **specialised features** and **role** of each of the cell types (b)-(h) below:

(a) **Guard cell**: Features: Curved, sausage shaped cell, unevenly thickened.

Role in plant: Turgor changes alter the cell shape to open or close the stoma.

(b) **Pollen grain**: Features: _____

Role in plant: _____

(c) **Palisade parenchyma cell**: Features: _____

Role in plant: _____

(d) **Epidermal cell**: Features: _____

Role in plant: _____

(e) **Vessel element**: Features: _____

Role in plant: _____

(f) **Stone cell**: Features: _____

Role in plant: _____

(g) **Sieve tube member** (of phloem): Features: _____

Role in plant: _____

(h) **Root hair cell**: Features: _____

Role in plant: _____

© 2015 **BIOZONE** International
ISBN: 978-1-927309-13-1
Photocopying Prohibited

LINK 128   LINK 124   LINK 120   WEB 121   KNOW

122 Levels of Organisation

Key Idea: Structural organisation in multicellular organisms is hierarchical, with new properties arising at each level. Organisation and the emergence of novel properties in complex systems are two of the defining features of living organisms. Organisms are organised according to a hierarchy of structural levels, each level building on the one before it. At each level, new properties arise that were absent at the simpler level. Hierarchical organisation allows specialised cells to group together into tissues and organs to perform a specific function. This improves efficiency in the organism.

All multicellular organisms are organised in a hierarchy of structural levels, where each level builds on the one below it. It is traditional to start with the simplest components (parts) and build from there. Higher levels of organisation are more complex than lower levels.

Hierarchical organisation enables **specialisation** so that individual components perform a specific function or set of related functions. Specialisation enables organisms to function more efficiently.

The diagram below explains this hierarchical organisation for a human.

1. Assign each of the following emergent properties to the level at which it first appears:

   (a) Metabolism: _____

   (b) Behaviour: _____

   (c) Replication: _____

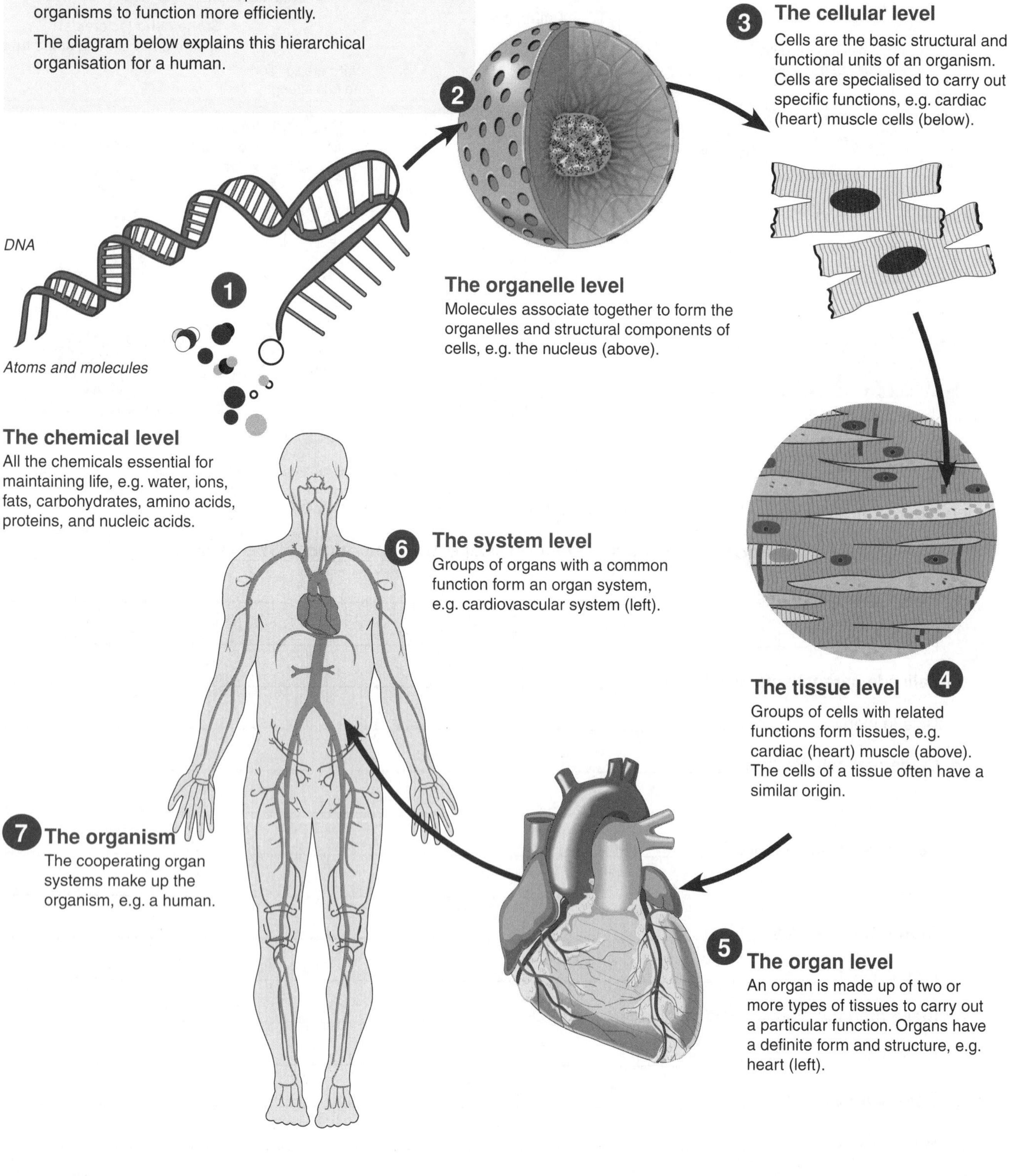

DNA

Atoms and molecules

1

The chemical level
All the chemicals essential for maintaining life, e.g. water, ions, fats, carbohydrates, amino acids, proteins, and nucleic acids.

2

The organelle level
Molecules associate together to form the organelles and structural components of cells, e.g. the nucleus (above).

3 **The cellular level**
Cells are the basic structural and functional units of an organism. Cells are specialised to carry out specific functions, e.g. cardiac (heart) muscle cells (below).

4 **The tissue level**
Groups of cells with related functions form tissues, e.g. cardiac (heart) muscle (above). The cells of a tissue often have a similar origin.

6 **The system level**
Groups of organs with a common function form an organ system, e.g. cardiovascular system (left).

7 **The organism**
The cooperating organ systems make up the organism, e.g. a human.

5 **The organ level**
An organ is made up of two or more types of tissues to carry out a particular function. Organs have a definite form and structure, e.g. heart (left).

123 Animal Tissues

Key Idea: A tissue is a collection of related cell types that work together to carry out a specific function. Four main tissue types make up the animal body.

Tissues are formed from related cell types that carry out a specific function. They improve functional efficiency because tasks can be shared amongst specialised cells. Animal tissues fall into four broad groups: epithelial, connective, muscle, and nervous tissues. Different tissues come together to form organs. For example, the heart consists of cardiac muscle tissue, but also has epithelial tissue, which lines the heart chambers, connective tissue for strength and elasticity, and nervous tissue, which directs muscle contraction.

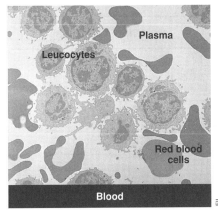

Blood

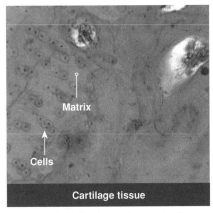

Cartilage tissue

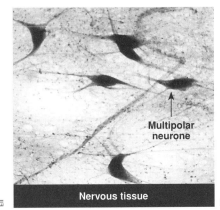

Nervous tissue

Connective tissues form the major supporting tissue of the body made up of cells within a semi-fluid matrix. Connective tissues bind structures together and provide support and protection. They include dentine (teeth), adipose (fat) tissue, bone, and cartilage (above centre), and the tissues around the organs and blood vessels. Blood is a specialised liquid tissue, made up of cells floating in a liquid matrix.

Nervous tissue contains densely packed nerve cells (neurones) which transmit information in the form of nerve impulses. There may also be supporting connective tissue and blood vessels.

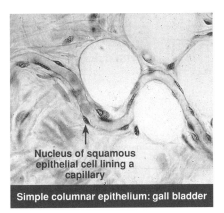

Simple columnar epithelium: gall bladder

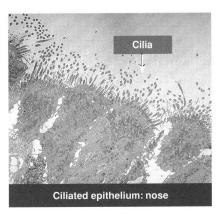

Ciliated epithelium: nose

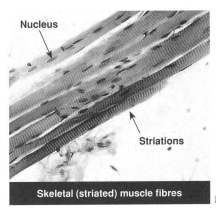

Skeletal (striated) muscle fibres

Epithelial tissue is organised into single or layered sheets. It lines internal and external surfaces (e.g. blood vessels, ducts, gut lining) and protects the structures underneath from wear, infection, or pressure. The cells may be specialised for absorption, secretion, or excretion. Examples: stratified epithelium of vagina, ciliated epithelium of respiratory tract, cuboidal epithelium of kidney ducts, columnar epithelium of the intestine, and the squamous epithelium found in capillaries, alveoli, and the glomeruli of the kidney.

Muscle tissue consists of specialised cells called fibres, held together by connective tissue. The three muscle types are cardiac, skeletal, and smooth muscle. Muscles bring about movement of body parts by contracting.

1. Explain how the development of tissues improves functional efficiency: _____

_____

_____

2. Describe the general function of each of the following broad tissue types:

(a) Epithelial tissue: _____   (c) Muscle tissue: _____

(b) Nervous tissue: _____   (d) Connective tissue: _____

3. Identify the particular features that contribute to the particular functional role of each of the following tissue types:

(a) Muscle tissue: _____

_____

(b) Nervous tissue: _____

_____

© 2015 **BIOZONE** International
ISBN: 978-1-927309-13-1
Photocopying Prohibited

LINK   WEB
120 123   **KNOW**

124 Plant Tissues

Key Idea: Plant tissues are either simple or complex tissues. Plant tissues are divided into simple and complex tissues. **Simple tissues** contain only one cell type and form packing and support tissues. **Complex tissues** contain more than one cell type and form the conducting and support tissues of plants. Tissues are grouped into tissue systems which make up the plant body. Vascular plants have dermal, vascular, and ground tissue systems. The dermal system covers the plant providing protection and reducing water loss. Vascular tissue provides the water and nutrient transport system of the plant. The ground tissue system carries out a variety of roles within the plant (e.g. photosynthesis, storage, and support).

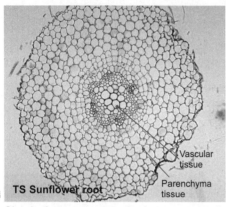

TS Sunflower root

Labels: Vascular tissue, Parenchyma tissue

Simple tissues consists of only one or two cell types. **Parenchyma tissue** is the most common and involved in storage, photosynthesis, and secretion. **Collenchyma tissue** comprises thick-walled collenchyma cells alternating with layers of intracellular substances to provide flexible support. The fibres and sclereids of **sclerenchyma** tissue have rigid cell walls which provide support.

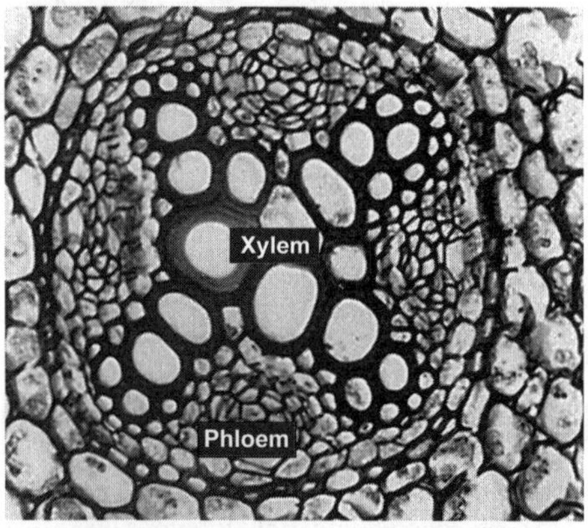

Labels: Xylem, Phloem

Complex tissues comprise more than two cell types. **Xylem** and **phloem**, which make up the plant **vascular tissue** system, are complex tissues. Each is made up of several cell types: tracheids, vessels, parenchyma, and fibres in xylem, and sieve tube members, companion cells, parenchyma and sclerenchyma in phloem.

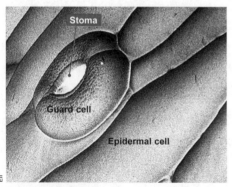

Labels: Stoma, Guard cell, Epidermal cell

Dermal tissue covers the outside of the plant. Its composition varies depending on its location. The leaf epidermis has a waxy cuticle to reduce water loss and guard cells to regulate water loss and gas exchange via pores in the leaf (stomata).

Simple tissue	Cell type(s)	Role within the plant
Parenchyma	Parenchyma cells	Photosynthesis, storage and secretion.
Collenchyma		
Sclerenchyma		
Root endodermis	Endodermal cells	
Pericycle		

Complex tissue	Cell type(s)	Role within the plant
Leaf mesophyll	Spongy mesophyll cells, palisade mesophyll cells	
Xylem		
Phloem		
Epidermis		

1. Identify the three tissue systems of plants:_____

_____

2. The tables above list the major types of simple and complex plant tissues. Complete the tables by filling in the cell types that make up the tissue and the role that each tissue has within the plant. The first example has been completed for you. Use the weblinks sites to help you.

125 Stem Cells and Differentiation

Key Idea: Stem cells are undifferentiated cells found in multicellular organisms. They are characterised by the properties of self renewal and potency.

A zygote can differentiate into many different types of cells because early on it divides into stem cells. Stem cells are unspecialised and can give rise to the many cell types that make up the tissues and organs of a multicellular organism. The differentiation of multipotent stem cells in bone marrow gives rise to all the cell types that make up blood, a fluid connective tissue. Multipotent (or adult) stem cells are found in most body organs, where they replace old or damaged cells and replenish the body's cells throughout life.

Stem cells and blood cell production

New blood cells are produced in the red bone marrow, which becomes the main site of blood production after birth, taking over from the fetal liver. All types of blood cells develop from a single cell type: called a **multipotent stem cell**. These cells are capable of mitosis and of differentiation into 'committed' precursors of each of the main types of blood cell. Each of the different cell lines is controlled by a specific **growth factor**. When a stem cell divides, one of its daughters remains a stem cell, while the other becomes a precursor cell, either a **lymphoid cell** or **myeloid cell**. These cells continue to mature into the various specialised cell types.

Properties of stem cells

Self renewal: The ability to divide many times while maintaining an unspecialised state.

Potency: The ability to differentiate into specialised cells.

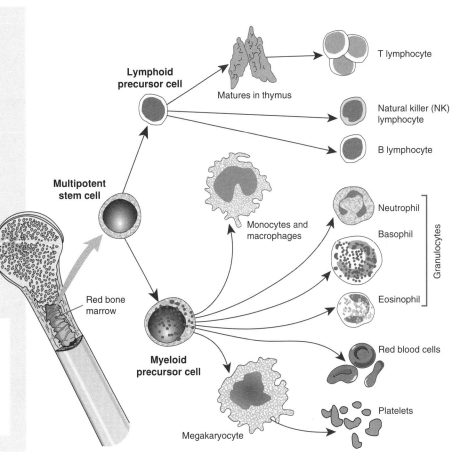

Categories of stem cells

Totipotent stem cells

These stem cells can differentiate into all the cells in an organism.
Example: In humans, the zygote and its first few divisions. The meristematic tissue of plants is also totipotent.

Pluripotent stem cells

These stem cells can give rise to any cells of the body, except extra-embryonic cells (e.g. placenta and chorion).
Example: Embryonic stem cells.

Multipotent stem cells

These adult stem cells can give rise a limited number of cell types, related to their tissue of origin.
Example: Bone marrow stem cells, skin stem cells, bone stem cells (osteoblasts).

---

1. Describe the two defining features of stem cells:

   (a) _____

   (b) _____

2. Explain the role of stem cells in the development of specialised tissues in multicellular organisms: _____

   _____

   _____

   _____

   _____

LINK   WEB
126 125
KNOW

126 Types of Stem Cells

Key Idea: The potency of stem cells depends on their origin. Both embryonic and adult stem cells can be used to replace diseased and damaged tissue.

The properties of self renewal and potency make stem cells suitable for a wide range of applications. Stem cells from early stage embryos (embryonic stem cells) are pluripotent and can potentially be cultured to provide a renewable source of cells for studies of human development and gene regulation, for tests of new drugs and vaccines, for monoclonal antibody production, and for treating any type of diseased or damaged tissue. Adult stem cells from bone marrow or umbilical cord blood can give rise to a more limited number of cell types. Although their potential use is more restricted, there are fewer ethical issues associated with their use.

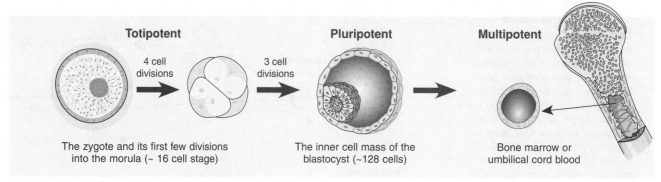

Totipotent

4 cell divisions → 3 cell divisions →

The zygote and its first few divisions into the morula (~ 16 cell stage)

Pluripotent

The inner cell mass of the blastocyst (~128 cells)

Multipotent

Bone marrow or umbilical cord blood

Embryonic stem cells

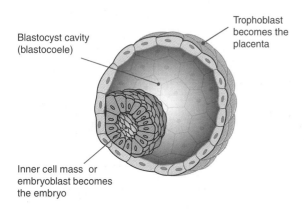

Trophoblast becomes the placenta

Blastocyst cavity (blastocoele)

Inner cell mass or embryoblast becomes the embryo

Embryonic stem cells (**ESC**) are derived from the inner cell mass of blastocysts (above). Blastocysts are embryos that are about five days old and consist of a hollow ball of 50-150 cells. Cells derived from the inner cell mass are **pluripotent**. They can become any cells of the body, with the exception of placental cells. When cultured without any stimulation to differentiate, ESC retain their potency through multiple cell divisions. This means they have great potential for therapeutic use in regenerative medicine and tissue replacement. However, the use of ESC involves the deliberate creation and destruction of embryos and is therefore is ethically unacceptable to many people.

Adult stem cells

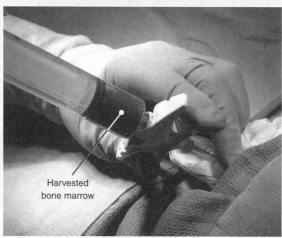

Harvested bone marrow

Adult stem cells (ASC) are undifferentiated cells found in several types of tissues (e.g. brain, bone marrow, fat, and liver) in adults, children, and umbilical cord blood. Unlike ESCs, they are **multipotent** and can only differentiate into a limited number of cell types, usually related to the tissue of origin. There are fewer ethical issues associated with using ASC for therapeutic purposes, because no embryos are destroyed. For this reason, ASC are already widely used to treat a number of diseases including leukemia and other blood disorders.

1. (a) Distinguish between embryonic stem cells and adult stem cells with respect to their **potency**:

_____

_____

_____

(b) What is the significance of this difference to their use in the treatment of disease: _____

_____

_____

_____

_____

_____

© 2015 **BIOZONE** International
ISBN: 978-1-927309-13-1
Photocopying Prohibited

Embryonic stem cell (ESC) cloning

ESC can come from embryos that have been fertilised *in vitro* and then donated for research. These cell lines will not be patient-matched because each new embryo is unique. However, ESC can also come from cloned embryos created using somatic cell nuclear transfer using a donor nucleus from the patient, as shown below. These ESC lines will patient-matched.

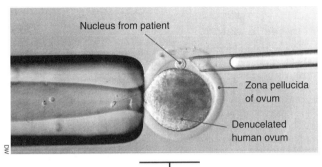

Nucleus from patient

Zona pellucida of ovum

Denucelated human ovum

A mild electric shock induces the development of a pre-embryo cell containing the patient's DNA.

After 5 days development, the inner cell mass of about 30 stem cells is removed.

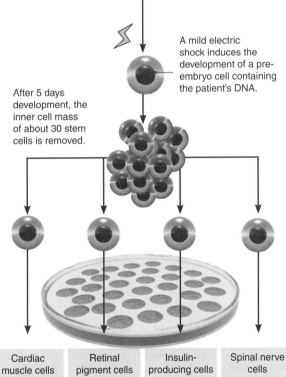

Cardiac muscle cells	Retinal pigment cells	Insulin-producing cells	Spinal nerve cells

When ESCs are provided with appropriate growth factors and conditions, they will differentiate into specific specialised cell types.

Issues in ESC cloning

For all tissue transplants, e.g. blood transfusions and bone marrow transplants, tissues must be matched for histocompatibility between different individuals. If donor material is poorly matched to the recipient, the recipient's immune system rejects the donor cells. Stem cell cloning (**therapeutic cloning**) provides a way around this problem. Stem cell cloning produces genetically matched stem cells that can be turned into any cell type in the human body.

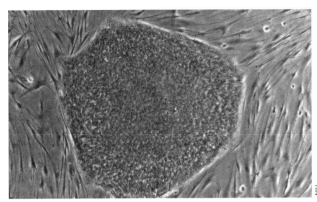

Human embryonic stem cells (hESC) growing on mouse embryonic fibroblasts. The mouse fibroblasts act as feeder cells for the culture, releasing nutrients and providing a surface for the ESCs to grow on.

ESC therapy has enormous potential to make life changing improvements to the health of people with diseased or damaged organs. Organs or tissues derived from a patient's ESC could be transplanted back into that patient without fear of tissue rejection or the need for ongoing immunosuppressive drug therapies. Despite this, many groups oppose the use of therapeutic cloning for many reasons including:

▶ The technology used to create the embryo could be used for reproductive cloning, i.e. creating a clone of the original human.

▶ The creation of stem cell line requires the destruction of a human embryo and thus human life.

▶ Human embryos have the potential to develop into an individual and thus have the same rights of the individual.

▶ Saving or enhancing the quality of life of an individual does not justify the destruction of the life of another (i.e. the embryo).

▶ ESC research has not produced any viable long term treatment, while other techniques (e.g. adult stem cells) have.

▶ There are other stem cell techniques that do not require the creation of an embryo but achieve similar results (e.g. cell lines grown from adult stem cells or umbilical cord blood).

2. (a) In your opinion, what is the one most important ethical issue associated with the use of ESC in medicine?

_____

_____

(b) What advantage does therapeutic cloning offer over conventional therapeutic use of embryonic stem cells?

_____

_____

_____

3. Umbilical cord blood is promoted as a rich source of multipotent stem cells for autologous (self) transplants. Can you see a problem with the use of a baby's cord blood to treat a disease in that child at a later date?

_____

_____

_____

127 Using Stem Cells to Treat Disease

Key Idea: Embryonic stem cells have been used to treat Stargardt's disease with apparent success. New techniques make it possible to produce pluripotent cells for widespread therapeutic use in an ethically acceptable way.

The therapeutic use of embryonic stem cells (ESC) to replace lost retinal cells in patients with Stargardt's disease (an eye disease) has shown that such therapies are able to restore function to diseased organs. Both Parkinson's disease and Alzheimer's disease are subjects of considerable research involving the possible use of stem cells in treatments.

Stem cells for Stargardt's disease

Stargardt's disease is an inherited form of juvenile macular degeneration (a loss of the central visual field of the eye). The disease is associated with a number of mutations and results in dysfunction of the retinal pigment epithelium (RPE) cells, which nourish the retinal photoreceptor cells and protect the retina from excess light. Dysfunction of the RPE causes deterioration of the photoreceptor cells in the central portion of the retina and progressive loss of central vision. This often begins between ages 6 and 12 and continues until a person is legally blind. Trials using stem cells have obtained promising results in treating the disease.

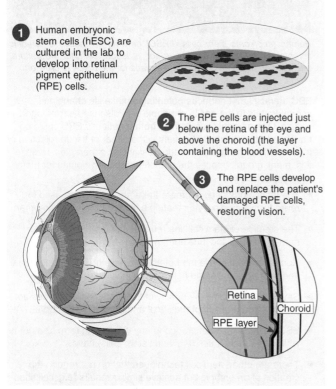

1 Human embryonic stem cells (hESC) are cultured in the lab to develop into retinal pigment epithelium (RPE) cells.

2 The RPE cells are injected just below the retina of the eye and above the choroid (the layer containing the blood vessels).

3 The RPE cells develop and replace the patient's damaged RPE cells, restoring vision.

Retina
Choroid
RPE layer

Stem cell research

Patients with **Parkinson's disease** show reduced dopamine production in the substantia nigra region of the brain. This is usually the result of the death of nerve cells. The symptoms (slow physical movement and spasmodic tremors) often don't begin to appear until a person has lost 70% of their dopamine-producing cells.

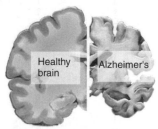

Normal

Parkinson's
PET scans showing difference in activity of dopamine neurons in people with and without Parkinson's.

Image: NASA

Parkinson's is not curable but it can be treated by using drugs that increase dopamine levels in the brain. Researchers have spent many years researching treatments involving stem cells. In a 2014 study, rats were induced to have Parkinson's by destroying the dopamine cells of the brain. Human stem cells treated to form dopamine-producing nerve cells were injected into the rats' brains. The rats showed some recovery from symptoms.

Alzheimer's disease is also the subject of stem cell research. Alzheimer's is caused by the accumulation of plaques in the brain and it results in loss of memory and dementia. One area of stem cell research aims to produce cells that over-express the enzymes that remove these plaques.

Healthy brain | Alzheimer's

In the field of **developmental biology**, stem cells play a role in helping us to understand the role of genes in development. By switching different genes on or off in stem cells, the effect of the gene on a cell's development can be studied. This gives insight as to the cause and treatment of various genetic diseases.

1. (a) Explain the basis for correcting Stargardt's disease using stem cell technology: _____

_____

_____

(b) Suggest why researchers derived the RPE cells from embryos rather than by reprogramming a patient's own cells:

_____

_____

(c) What advantage is there in reprogramming a patient's own cells and when would this be a preferable option?

_____

_____

2. How can stem cell research help us understand how cells develop? _____

_____

_____

© 2015 **BIOZONE** International
ISBN: 978-1-927309-13-1
Photocopying Prohibited

128 Plant Meristems

Key Idea: The differentiation of plant cells occurs at specific regions called meristems, where the cells are totipotent.

Two types of growth can contribute to an increase in the size of a plant. **Primary growth**, which occurs in the **apical meristem** of the buds and root tips, increases the length (height) of a plant. Meristematic cells are totipotent (can give rise to all the cells of the adult plant). **Secondary growth** increases plant girth and occurs in the lateral meristem in the stem. All plants show primary growth but only some show secondary growth (the growth that produces woody tissues).

Primary growth

Three types of **primary meristem** (procambium, protoderm, and ground meristem) are produced from the apical meristem. In dicots, the **procambium** forms vascular bundles, which are found in a ring near the epidermis, surrounded by cortex. Cells in the procambium divide to become primary **xylem** to the inside and primary **phloem** to the outside.

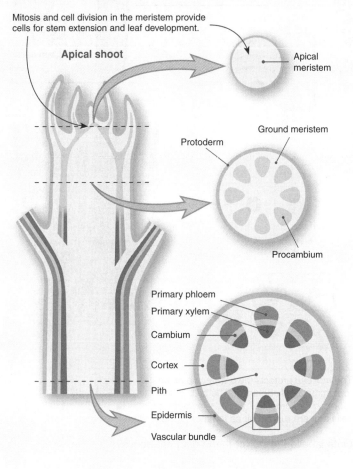

Mitosis and cell division in the meristem provide cells for stem extension and leaf development.

Apical shoot

Apical meristem

Protoderm

Ground meristem

Procambium

Primary phloem
Primary xylem
Cambium
Cortex
Pith
Epidermis
Vascular bundle

Primary tissues generated by the meristem

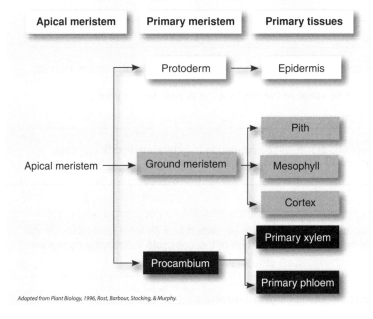

Apical meristem	Primary meristem	Primary tissues

Apical meristem → Protoderm → Epidermis

Apical meristem → Ground meristem → Pith / Mesophyll / Cortex

Procambium → Primary xylem / Primary phloem

Adapted from Plant Biology, 1996, Rost, Barbour, Stocking, & Murphy.

1. Describe the role of the meristems in plants:

_____

_____

2. Describe the location of the meristems and relate this to how plants grow:

_____

_____

_____

_____

_____

3. Describe a distinguishing feature of meristematic tissue:

_____

_____

_____

_____

_____

_____

4. Discuss the structure and formation of the primary tissues in dicot plants:

_____

_____

_____

_____

_____

_____

_____

_____

_____

_____

_____

LINK   WEB
129 128   KNOW

129 Root Cell Development

Key Idea: In plants, mitosis occurs in the zone of meristematic tissue at the root and shoot tips. Beyond this zone cells elongate and then become specialised.

In plants, mitosis occurs only in the meristems. Primary growth (increase in length) occurs in the apical meristems

(growing tips) of every stem and root. Plants that show lateral growth also have lateral meristems (cambium) where growth in diameter occurs. The zones of cell division, expansion, and specialisation in a root are shown below. Similar zones occur in stem tips, which produce all above-ground plant organs.

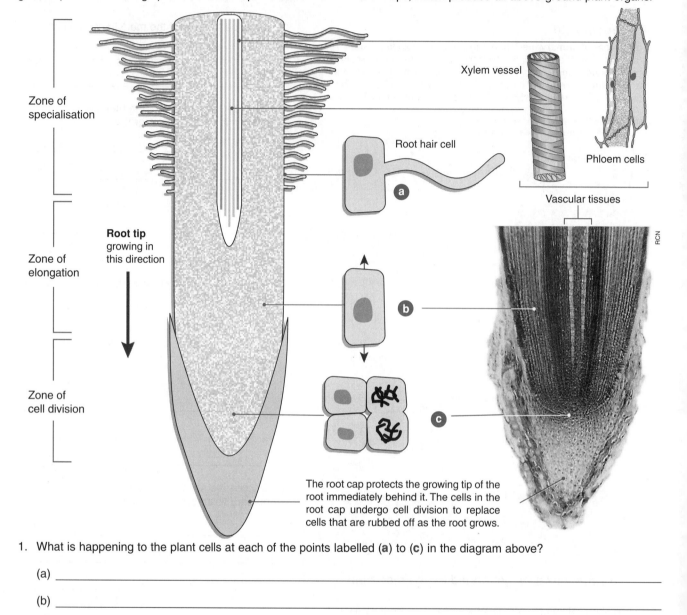

Zone of specialisation

Xylem vessel

Root hair cell

Phloem cells

Vascular tissues

Root tip growing in this direction

Zone of elongation

Zone of cell division

The root cap protects the growing tip of the root immediately behind it. The cells in the root cap undergo cell division to replace cells that are rubbed off as the root grows.

1. What is happening to the plant cells at each of the points labelled (**a**) to (**c**) in the diagram above?

    (a) _____

    (b) _____

    (c) _____

2. The light micrograph (below) shows a section of the cells of an onion root tip, stained to show up the chromosomes.

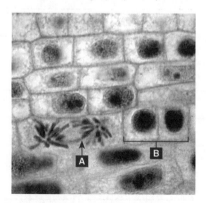

    (a) State the mitotic stage of the cell labelled **A** and explain your answer:

    _____

    (b) State the mitotic stage just completed in the cells labelled **B** and explain:

    _____

    _____

    (c) If, in this example, 250 cells were examined and 25 were found to be in the process of mitosis, what proportion of the cell cycle is occupied by mitosis:

    _____

3. Identify the cells that divide and specialise when a tree increases its girth (diameter): _____

© 2015 **BIOZONE** International
ISBN: 978-1-927309-13-1
Photocopying Prohibited

130 Chapter Review

Summarise what you know about this topic under the headings provided. You can draw diagrams or mind maps, or write short notes to organise your thoughts. Use the images and hints included to help you:

Cell Division
HINT: Describe differences between mitosis and meiosis. Describe the cell cycle.

Cells and tissues
HINT: Identify different cell types and their function.

Stem cells
HINT: Describe different types of stem cell and their medical applications.

131 KEY TERMS: Did You Get It?

1. (a) Label the cell cycle right with the following labels: G_1, G_2, M, S, cytokinesis, G_1 checkpoint, G_2 checkpoint, metaphase checkpoint.

   (b) Briefly describe what happens in each of the following phases:

   G_1: _____

   _____

   _____

   G_2: _____

   _____

   _____

   M phase: _____

   _____

   _____

   S phase: _____

   _____

   _____

2. (a) Identify the process occurring in the circled chromosomes right:

   _____

   (b) Does this occur during mitosis or meiosis? _____

   (c) At what stage of your answer in (b) does this occur? _____

3. Test your vocabulary by matching each term to its definition, as identified by its preceding letter code.

cell cycle	A	The stage in the cell cycle between divisions.
cellular differentiation	B	The phase of a cell cycle involving nuclear division in which the replicated chromosomes in a cell nucleus are separated into two identical sets.
cell division	C	Process by which a parent cell divides into two or more daughter cells.
interphase	D	Name given to a group of related cells organised together to perform a specific function.
meiosis	E	The changes that take place in a cell in the period between its formation as a product of cell division and its own subsequent division.
mitosis	F	The process by which a less specialised cell becomes a more specialised cell type.
stem cell	G	An undifferentiated cell, with the properties of self renewal and potency.
tissue	H	The process of double nuclear division (reduction division) to produce four nuclei, each containing half the original number of chromosomes (haploid).

4. (a) Match the following stem cell types with their potency: Zygote, Adult stem cell, Embryonic stem cell

   Potency: Pluripotent: _____ Totipotent: _____ Multipotent: _____

   (b) Describe each of the potency types:

   Pluripotency: _____

   Totipotency: _____

   Multipotency: _____

 © 2015 **BIOZONE** International
ISBN: 978-1-927309-13-1
Photocopying Prohibited

Module 3.1.1

Exchange Surfaces

Key terms

alveoli

breathing

bronchi

bronchioles

carbon dioxide

cellular respiration

countercurrent flow

diaphragm

expiration (exhalation)

extraction rate

gas exchange

gills

inspiration (inhalation)

lungs

oxygen

respiratory gas

root hairs

spiracles

spirometry

surfactant

trachea

tracheae (tracheal tubes)

tracheoles

ventilation

Principles of gas exchange

Learning outcomes

Activity number

☐ 1 Distinguish between cellular respiration and gas exchange and explain why organisms must exchange respiratory gases with their environment. — 132

☐ 2 With reference to metabolic rate and surface area and volume ratios, explain why organisms need specialised gas exchange surfaces. — 132

☐ 3 Using examples, describe the features of gas exchange surfaces and their significance in terms of gas exchange rates. Illustrative examples include root hair cells (higher plants), alveoli (mammalian lungs), and gills (fish). — 132 133

☐ 4 **PAG1** Identify features of gas exchange surfaces in histological preparations. — 133 135

☐ 5 Describe how gases are exchanged across gas exchange surfaces. Explain the constraints the environment (water/air) places on animal gas exchange systems. — 99 132

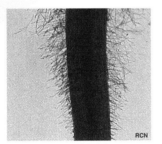 RCN  Angela Simpson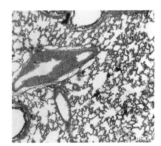

The mammalian gas exchange system

Learning outcomes

Activity number

☐ 6 Describe the structure and functions of the components of the mammalian gas exchange system to include the distribution and roles of the specialised cells and tissues in the trachea, bronchi, bronchioles, and alveoli. Describe how the structure of an alveolus facilitates gas exchange. Include reference to alveolar cells (pneumocytes), surfactant, and the gas exchange membrane. — 134 135

☐ 7 Describe the role of ventilation (breathing) in gas exchange in mammals. Explain breathing with reference to the pressure and volume changes in the thorax as a result of the muscular activity of the intercostal muscles and diaphragm. — 136

☐ 8 Describe the use of spirometry to measure changes in lung volume. Describe the relationship between vital capacity, tidal volume, breathing rate, and oxygen uptake in humans. — 137

☐ 9 **PAG10** Analyse and interpret primary and secondary data from a spirometer or data logger. To collect primary data, determine and compare vital capacity for males and females in your class using simple apparatus. — 138

Gas exchange in insects and bony fish

Learning outcomes

Activity number

☐ 10 Describe the structure and function of tracheae (tracheal tubes) in insects, including the role of the spiracles. Describe how the tracheal system is ventilated. — 134 139

☐ 11 Describe the structure and function of gills in bony fish. Describe how the gills are ventilated in bony fish and explain how countercurrent exchange achieves high oxygen extraction rates. — 134 140

☐ 12 **PAG2** Dissect and draw the gas exchange system of a bony fish or an insect. — 142

132 Exchange Surfaces

Key Idea: Gas exchange is the process by which respiratory gases are exchanged between the cells of an organism and the environment. Large, complex organisms require special adaptations to ensure adequate gas exchange.

Energy is released in cells by the breakdown of sugars and other substances in cellular respiration. As a consequence of this process, respiratory gases (carbon dioxide and oxygen) need to be exchanged by diffusion. Gas are exchanged in opposite directions across a gas exchange surface between the lungs (or gills) and the external environment. Diffusion gradients are maintained by transport of gases away from the gas exchange surface. Gas exchange surfaces must be in close proximity to the blood for this to occur effectively.

The need for gas exchange

Gas exchange is the process by which respiratory gases (oxygen and carbon dioxide) enter and leave the body by diffusion across **gas exchange surfaces**. To achieve effective gas exchange rates, gas exchange surfaces must be thin, they must have a high surface area, and there must be a concentration gradient for diffusion. The concentration gradients for diffusion are maintained by transport of gases away from the gas exchange surface. Because gases must be in solution to cross the membrane, gas exchange surfaces are also moist.

Gas exchange surfaces provide a means for gases to enter and leave the body. Some organisms use the body surface as the sole gas exchange surface, but many have specialised gas exchange structures (e.g. lungs, gills, or stomata). Amphibians use the body surface and simple lungs to provide for their gas exchange requirements.

Carbon dioxide gas

Oxygen gas

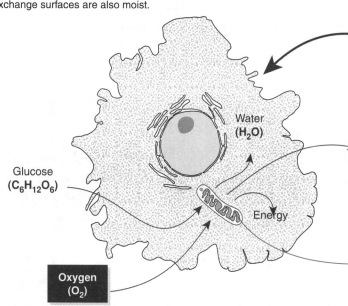

Cellular respiration takes place in every cell of an organism's body. Cellular respiration creates a constant demand for oxygen (O_2) and a need to eliminate carbon dioxide gas (CO_2).

Water (H_2O)

Carbon dioxide (CO_2)

Glucose ($C_6H_{12}O_6$)

Energy

Oxygen (O_2)

Living cells require energy for the activities of life. **Mitochondria** are the main sites where glucose is broken down to release energy. In the process, oxygen is used to make water, and carbon dioxide is released as a waste product.

Features of gas exchange surfaces

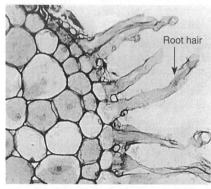

Root hair

Root hair cells are thin-walled extensions of the root epidermis that greatly increase the surface area over which the plant can absorb minerals and dissolved gases. A study of the roots of a four-month old rye plant (*Secale cereale*) found the root system covered 639 m^2 (of which the root hair cells made up 401 m^2), 130 times the area of the shoot system. It was estimated there were 14 billion root hair cells. The volume of space occupied by the root system was just 6 dm^3.

Alveolar walls

Nephron

In mammalian lungs, the surface area for gas exchange is greatly increased by alveoli, the microscopic air sacs at the terminal ends of the airways. The walls of the alveoli are only one cell thick and are enveloped by capillaries. Oxygen diffuses across the alveolar walls into the blood in the capillaries and is transported away to the body's cells. Carbon dioxide is brought from the body's cells to the alveoli, where it diffuses into the alveolar space and is breathed out.

Blood cells within a capillary. The blood cells carry O_2 and CO_2

Effective gas exchange relies on maintaining a concentration gradient for the diffusion of gases. Oxygen is transported from the alveoli or gills by the blood, reducing its concentration relative to the environmental side of the gas exchange surface (respiratory membrane). Carbon dioxide is transported to the alveoli or gills, increasing its concentration relative to the environmental side of the membrane. It then diffuses out of the blood, across the membrane, and into the external environment.

WEB 132   LINK 133   LINK 134

© 2015 **BIOZONE** International
ISBN: 978-1-927309-13-1
Photocopying Prohibited

Gas exchange in unicellular and multicellular organisms

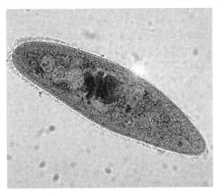

Gills

Spiracle

Single celled organisms are small enough that gases can diffuse into their interior without the need for gas exchange or transport systems. Oxygen and carbon dioxide diffuse into and out of the cell over the cell's entire surface.

Larger animals require specialised systems to obtain and transport oxygen to the cells of the body and remove carbon dioxide. Aquatic animals have gills, thin feathery structures, which remain moist and functional in water.

Terrestrial animals protect their respiratory membranes internally. Insects exchange gases by way of tubes called tracheae, which open to the outside through spiracles. Terrestrial vertebrates have lungs, which are ventilated to maintain gas exchange rates.

Fick's law of diffusion expresses the rate of diffusion of a given molecule across a membrane at a given temperature. At a given temperature the rate is affected by three main factors:

▶ **Concentration gradient**: The greater the concentration gradient, the greater the diffusion rate.
▶ **Surface area**: The larger the area across which diffusion occurs, the greater the rate of diffusion.
▶ **Barriers to diffusion**: Thicker barriers slow diffusion rate. Pores in a barrier enhance diffusion.

Fick's law

The diffusion rate across gas exchange surfaces is described by Fick's law:

$$\frac{\text{Surface area of membrane} \times \text{Difference in concentration across the membrane}}{\text{Thickness of the membrane}}$$

1. Distinguish between cellular respiration and gas exchange: _____

2. (a) What gases are involved in cellular respiration? _____

   (b) How do these gases move across the gas exchange surface? _____

3. What is the main function of a gas exchange surface? _____

4. Describe the three properties that all gas exchange surfaces have in common and state the significance of each:

   (a) _____

   (b) _____

   (c) _____

5. Explain the function of root hairs: _____

6. State the effect on diffusion rate in the following situations:

   (a) The surface area for diffusion is increased: _____

   (b) The thickness of the membrane is decreased: _____

   (c) The difference in concentration on either side of the membrane is decreased: _____

7. Explain how mammals maintain a gradient for oxygen uptake across the gas exchange surface: _____

133 Gas Exchange in Plants

Key Idea: Plants require a constant supply of carbon dioxide for photosynthesis. Some of the oxygen released is used for respiration but the rest is released to the environment. The leaf epidermis of angiosperms is covered with tiny pores, called **stomata**. Angiosperms have many air spaces between the cells of the stems, leaves, and roots. These air spaces are continuous and gases are able to move freely through them and into the plant's cells via the stomata. Each stoma has a special **guard cell** on each side which regulate the stomata's size to control the passage of gases and water vapour. Stomata allow gas exchange between the air and the photosynthetic cells inside the leaf, but they are also the major routes for water loss through transpiration. About 90% of water loss occurs via stomata. About 10% occurs directly through the waxy cuticle, but this figure can be higher if the cuticle is thin (as in ferns), or lower in plants with thick, waxy leaves.

Gas exchanges and the function of stomata

Gases enter and leave the leaf by way of stomata. Inside the leaf (as illustrated by a dicot, right), the large air spaces and loose arrangement of the spongy mesophyll facilitate the diffusion of gases and provide a large surface area for gas exchanges. For example, in a tree with a leaf surface area of 200 m², the surface area of the spongy mesophyll will be ~ 6000 m².

Respiring plant cells use oxygen (O_2) and produce carbon dioxide (CO_2). These gases move in and out of the plant and through the air spaces by diffusion.

When the plant is photosynthesising, the situation is more complex. Overall there is a net consumption of CO_2 and a net production of oxygen. The fixation of CO_2 maintains a gradient in CO_2 concentration between the inside of the leaf and the atmosphere. Oxygen is produced in excess of respiratory needs and diffuses out of the leaf. These **net** exchanges are indicated by the arrows on the diagram.

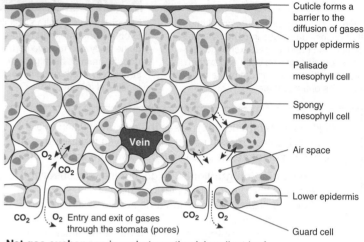

Cuticle forms a barrier to the diffusion of gases
Upper epidermis
Palisade mesophyll cell
Spongy mesophyll cell
Air space
Lower epidermis
Guard cell

CO_2 / O_2 Entry and exit of gases through the stomata (pores)

Net gas exchanges in a photosynthesising dicot leaf

Adaptations for gas exchange in plants

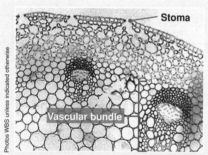

Stoma
Vascular bundle

The stems of some plants (e.g. buttercup above) are photosynthetic and gas exchange must occur between the stem tissue and the environment. The epidermis has stomata and there are large air spaces in the cortex.

Lenticel

In woody plants, the wood prevents gas exchange. A lenticel is a small area in the bark where the loosely arranged cells allow the entry and exit of gases into the stem tissue underneath.

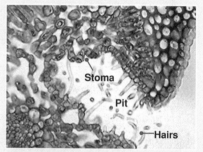

Stoma
Pit
Hairs

Water loss is a problem to plants. Plants have many solutions to this including placing stomata at the bottom of pits on the underside of the leaf. The pits restrict water loss to a greater extent than they reduce CO_2 uptake, e.g. oleander (above).

1. Name the gas produced by cellular respiration that is also a raw material for photosynthesis: _____

2. Describe the role of lenticels in plant gas exchange: _____
_____

3. Identify two ways in which the continuous air spaces through the plant facilitate gas exchange:

   (a) _____

   (b) _____

4. (a) Briefly outline the role of stomata in gas exchange in an angiosperm: _____
   _____

   (b) Why are stomata usually on the lower surface of a dicot leaf? _____
   _____
   _____

KNOW **133** **168**

© 2015 **BIOZONE** International
ISBN: 978-1-927309-13-1
Photocopying Prohibited

134 Gas Exchange in Animals

Key Idea: Animal gas exchange systems are suited to the animal's environment, body form, and metabolic needs.

The way an animal exchanges gases with its environment is influenced by the animal's body form and by the environment in which the animal lives. Small or flat organisms in moist or aquatic environments, such as sponges and flatworms, require no specialised structures for gas exchange. Larger or more complex animals have specialised systems to supply the oxygen to support their metabolic activities. The type and complexity of the exchange system reflects the demands of metabolism for gas exchange (oxygen delivery and carbon dioxide removal) and the environment (aquatic or terrestrial).

1. Describe two reasons for the development of gas exchange structures and systems in animals:

(a) _____

_____

(b) _____

_____

2. Describe two ways in which air breathers manage to keep their gas exchange surfaces moist:

(a) _____

_____

(b) _____

_____

3. Explain why gills would not work in a terrestrial environment:

_____

_____

_____

_____

_____

_____

4. Explain why mammals must ventilate their lungs (breathe in and out):

_____

_____

_____

_____

_____

_____

Representative gas exchange systems

Small, simple organisms
The high surface area to volume ratio of very flat or very small organisms, such as this nematode, enables them to use the body surface as the gas exchange surface.

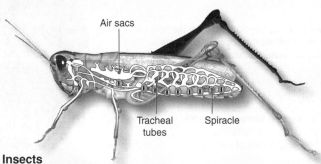

Insects
Insects transport gases via a system of branching tubes called **tracheae** (or tracheal tubes). The tracheae deliver oxygen directly to the tissues. Larger insects can increase the air moving in and out of these tubes by contracting and expanding the abdomen.

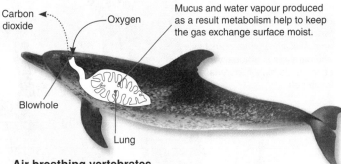

Mucus and water vapour produced as a result metabolism help to keep the gas exchange surface moist.

Air breathing vertebrates
The gas exchange surface in mammals and other air breathing vertebrates is located in internal **lungs**. Their internal location within the body keeps the exchange surfaces moist and prevents them from drying out. The many alveoli of the lungs provide a large surface area for maximising gas exchange. For example, human lungs have 600 million alveoli with a total surface area of 100 m^2.

Gills under gill cover (operculum).

Bony fish, sharks, and rays
Fish extract oxygen dissolved in water using **gills**. Gills achieve high extraction rates of oxygen from the water which is important because there is less oxygen in water than air. Bony fish ventilate the gill surfaces by movements of the gill cover. The water supports the gills, and the gill lamellae (the gas exchange surface) can be exposed directly to the environment without drying out.

© 2015 **BIOZONE** International
ISBN: 978-1-927309-13-1
Photocopying Prohibited

135 The Human Gas Exchange System

Key idea: Lungs are internal sac-like organs connected to the outside by a system of airways. The smallest airways end in thin-walled alveoli, where gas exchange occurs.

The gas exchange (or respiratory system) includes all the structures associated with exchanging respiratory gases with the environment. In humans, this system consists of paired lungs connected to the outside air by way of a system of tubular passageways: the trachea, bronchi, and bronchioles. The details of exchanges across the gas exchange membrane are described on the next page.

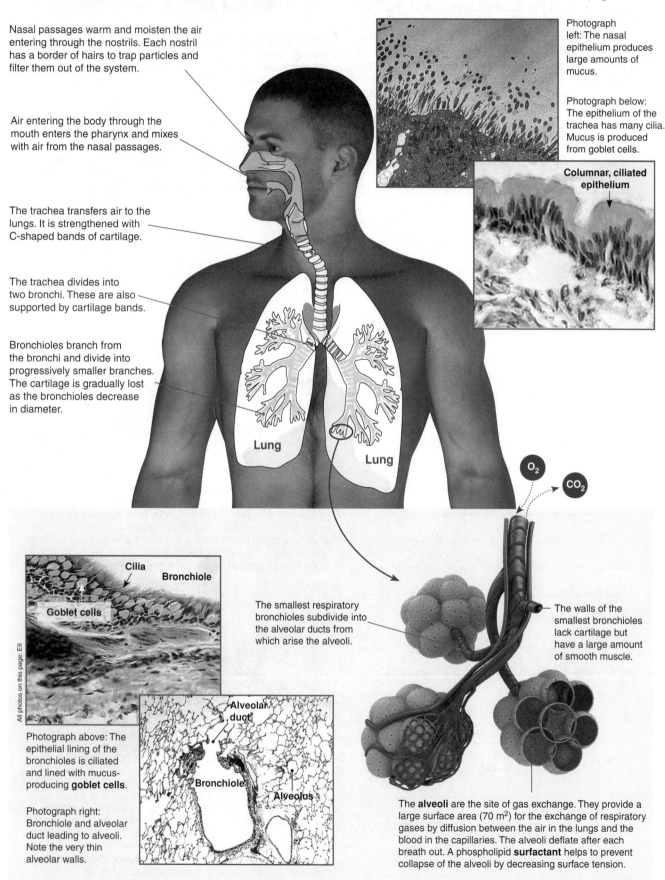

Nasal passages warm and moisten the air entering through the nostrils. Each nostril has a border of hairs to trap particles and filter them out of the system.

Air entering the body through the mouth enters the pharynx and mixes with air from the nasal passages.

The trachea transfers air to the lungs. It is strengthened with C-shaped bands of cartilage.

The trachea divides into two bronchi. These are also supported by cartilage bands.

Bronchioles branch from the bronchi and divide into progressively smaller branches. The cartilage is gradually lost as the bronchioles decrease in diameter.

Photograph left: The nasal epithelium produces large amounts of mucus.

Photograph below: The epithelium of the trachea has many cilia. Mucus is produced from goblet cells.

Columnar, ciliated epithelium

Lung

Lung

O_2

CO_2

Cilia

Bronchiole

Goblet cells

All photos on this page: Eli

Photograph above: The epithelial lining of the bronchioles is ciliated and lined with mucus-producing **goblet cells**.

Photograph right: Bronchiole and alveolar duct leading to alveoli. Note the very thin alveolar walls.

Alveolar duct

Bronchiole

Alveolus

The smallest respiratory bronchioles subdivide into the alveolar ducts from which arise the alveoli.

The walls of the smallest bronchioles lack cartilage but have a large amount of smooth muscle.

The **alveoli** are the site of gas exchange. They provide a large surface area (70 m^2) for the exchange of respiratory gases by diffusion between the air in the lungs and the blood in the capillaries. The alveoli deflate after each breath out. A phospholipid **surfactant** helps to prevent collapse of the alveoli by decreasing surface tension.

WEB LINK

KNOW 135 136

Cross section through an alveolus

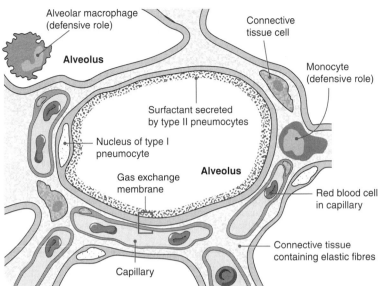

Alveolar macrophage (defensive role)

Connective tissue cell

Alveolus

Monocyte (defensive role)

Surfactant secreted by type II pneumocytes

Nucleus of type I pneumocyte

Alveolus

Gas exchange membrane

Red blood cell in capillary

Connective tissue containing elastic fibres

Capillary

The gas exchange membrane

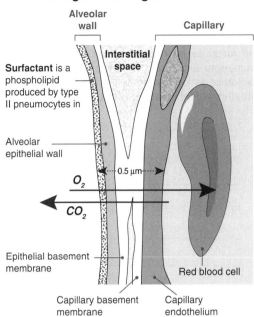

Alveolar wall

Capillary

Interstitial space

Surfactant is a phospholipid produced by type II pneumocytes in

Alveolar epithelial wall

0.5 μm

O_2

CO_2

Epithelial basement membrane

Red blood cell

Capillary basement membrane

Capillary endothelium

The alveoli are very close to the blood-filled capillaries. The alveolus is lined with alveolar epithelial cells or **pneumocytes**. Type I pneumocytes (90-95% of aveolar cells) contribute to the gas exchange membrane (right). Type II pneumocytes secrete a **surfactant**, which decreases surface tension within the alveoli and prevents them from collapsing and sticking to each other. Macrophages and monocytes defend the lung tissue against pathogens. Elastic connective tissue gives the alveoli their ability to expand and recoil.

The **gas exchange membrane** is the term for the layered junction between the alveolar epithelial cells (pneumocytes), the endothelial cells of the capillary, and their associated basement membranes (thin, collagenous layers that underlie the epithelial tissues). Gases move freely across this membrane.

1. (a) Explain how the basic structure of the human gas exchange system provides such a large area for gas exchange:

_____

_____

(b) Identify the general region of the lung where exchange of gases takes place: _____

2. Describe the structure and purpose of the alveolar-capillary membrane: _____

_____

_____

3. Describe the role of the surfactant in the alveoli: _____

_____

4. Using the information above and opposite, complete the table below summarising the **histology of the gas exchange pathway**. Name each numbered region and use a tick or cross to indicate the presence or absence of particular tissues.

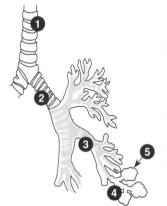

	Region	Cartilage	Ciliated epithelium	Goblet cells (mucus)	Smooth muscle	Connective tissue
1						✓
2						
3		gradually lost				
4	Alveolar duct		✗	✗		
5					very little	

5. Babies born prematurely are often deficient in surfactant. This causes respiratory distress syndrome; a condition where breathing is very difficult. From what you know about the role of surfactant, explain the symptoms of this syndrome:

_____

_____

136 Breathing in Humans

Key Idea: Breathing provides a continual supply of air to the lungs to maintain the concentration gradients for gas exchange. Different muscles are used in inspiration and expiration to force air in and out of the lungs.

Breathing (ventilation) provides a continual supply of oxygen-rich air to the lungs and expels air high in carbon dioxide. Together with the cardiovascular system, which transports respiratory gases between the alveolar and the cells of the body, breathing maintains concentration gradients for gas exchange. Breathing is achieved by the action of muscles.

1. Explain the purpose of breathing: _____

_____

_____

2. In general terms, how is breathing achieved?

_____

_____

_____

_____

3. (a) Describe the sequence of events involved in quiet breathing:

_____

_____

_____

_____

_____

(b) What is the essential difference between this and the situation during forced breathing:

_____

_____

_____

4. During inspiration, which muscles are:

(a) Contracting: _____

_____

(b) Relaxed: _____

_____

5. During forced expiration, which muscles are:

(a) Contracting: _____

_____

(b) Relaxed: _____

_____

6. Explain the role of antagonistic muscles in breathing:

_____

_____

_____

Breathing and muscle action

Muscles can only do work by contracting, so they can only perform movement in one direction. To achieve motion in two directions, muscles work as antagonistic pairs. Antagonistic pairs of muscles have opposing actions and create movement when one contracts and the other relaxes. Breathing in humans involves two sets of antagonistic muscles. The external and internal intercostal muscles of the ribcage, and the diaphragm and abdominal muscles.

Inspiration (inhalation or breathing in)

During quiet breathing, inspiration is achieved by increasing the thoracic volume (therefore decreasing the pressure inside the lungs). Air then flows into the lungs in response to the decreased pressure inside the lung. Inspiration is always an active process involving muscle contraction.

1 External intercostal muscles contract causing the ribcage to expand and move up. Diaphragm contracts and moves down.

Intercostal muscles

2 Thoracic volume increases, lungs expand, and the pressure inside the lungs decreases.

3 Air flows into the lungs in response to the pressure gradient.

Diaphragm contracts and moves down

Expiration (exhalation or breathing out)

In quiet breathing, expiration is a passive process, achieved when the external intercostals and diaphragm relax and thoracic volume decreases. Air flows passively out of the lungs to equalise with the air pressure. In active breathing, muscle contraction is involved in bringing about both inspiration and expiration.

1 In **quiet breathing**, external intercostals and diaphragm relax. The elasticity of the lung tissue causes recoil.

In **forced breathing**, the internal intercostals and abdominal muscles contract to compress the thoracic cavity and increase the force of the expiration.

2 Thoracic volume decreases and the pressure inside the lungs increases.

3 Air flows passively out of the lungs in response to the pressure gradient.

Diaphragm relaxes and moves up

© 2015 **BIOZONE** International
ISBN: 978-1-927309-13-1
Photocopying Prohibited

137 Measuring Lung Function

Key Idea: A lung function test, called spirometry, measures changes in lung volume and can be used diagnostically.

The volume of gases exchanged during breathing varies according to the physiological demands placed on the body (e.g. by exercise) and an individual's lung function. **Spirometry** measures changes in lung volume by measuring how much air a person can breathe in and out and how fast the air can be expelled. Spirometry can measure changes in ventilation rates during exercise and can be used to assess impairments in lung function, as might occur as a result of disease. In humans, the total adult lung capacity varies between 4 and 6 dm^3 and is greater in males.

Determining changes in lung volume using spirometry

The apparatus used to measure the amount of air exchanged during breathing and the rate of breathing is a **spirometer** (also called a respirometer). A simple spirometer consists of a weighted drum, containing oxygen or air, inverted over a chamber of water. A tube connects the air-filled chamber with the subject's mouth, and soda lime in the system absorbs the carbon dioxide breathed out. Breathing results in a trace called a spirogram, from which lung volumes can be measured directly.

During inspiration
Air is removed from the chamber, the drum sinks, and an upward deflection is recorded on the paper on the rotating drum.

During expiration
Air is added to the chamber, the drum rises, and a downward deflection is recorded.

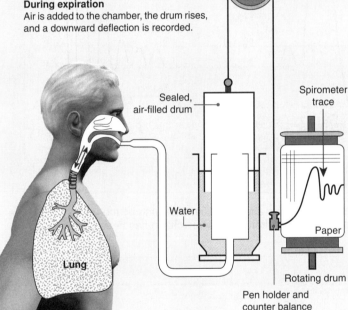

Labels: Pulley, Sealed, air-filled drum, Spirometer trace, Lung, Water, Paper, Rotating drum, Pen holder and counter balance

Lung volumes and capacities

The air in the lungs can be divided into volumes. Lung capacities are combinations of volumes.

DESCRIPTION OF VOLUME	Vol (dm^3)
Tidal volume (TV) Volume of air breathed in and out in a single breath	0.5
Inspiratory reserve volume (IRV) Volume breathed in by a maximum inspiration at the end of a normal inspiration	3.3
Expiratory reserve volume (ERV) Volume breathed out by a maximum effort at the end of a normal expiration	1.0
Residual volume (RV) Volume of air remaining in the lungs at the end of a maximum expiration	1.2

DESCRIPTION OF CAPACITY	
Inspiratory capacity (IC) = TV + IRV Volume breathed in by a maximum inspiration at the end of a normal expiration	3.8
Vital capacity (VC) = IRV + TV + ERV Volume that can be exhaled after a maximum inspiration.	4.8
Total lung capacity (TLC) = VC + RV The total volume of the lungs. Only a fraction of TLC is used in normal breathing	6.0

PRIMARY INDICATORS OF LUNG FUNCTION

Forced expiratory volume in 1 second (FEV_1)
The volume of air that is maximally exhaled in the first second of exhalation.

Forced vital capacity (FVC)
The total volume of air that can be forcibly exhaled after a maximum inspiration.

---

1. Describe how each of the following might be expected to influence values for lung volumes and capacities obtained using spirometry:

    (a) Height: _____

    (b) Gender: _____

    (c) Age: _____

2. A percentage decline in FEV_1 and FVC (to <80% of normal) are indicators of impaired lung function, e.g in asthma:

    (a) Explain why a forced volume is a more useful indicator of lung function than tidal volume:

    _____

    (b) Asthma is treated with drugs to relax the airways. Suggest how spirometry could be used during asthma treatment:

    _____

LINK   WEB
138 **137**   DATA

Respiratory gas	Approximate percentages of O_2 and CO_2		
	Inhaled air	Air in lungs	Exhaled air
O_2	21.0	13.8	16.4
CO_2	0.04	5.5	3.6

Above: The percentages of respiratory gases in air (by volume) during normal breathing. The percentage volume of oxygen in the alveolar air (in the lung) is lower than that in the exhaled air because of the influence of the **dead air volume** (the air in the spaces of the nose, throat, larynx, trachea and bronchi). This air (about 30% of the air inhaled) is unavailable for gas exchange.

Left: During exercise, the breathing rate, tidal volume, and **pulmonary ventilation rate** or **PV** (the amount of air exchanged with the environment per minute) increase up to a maximum (as indicated below).

Spirogram for a male during quiet and forced breathing, and during exercise

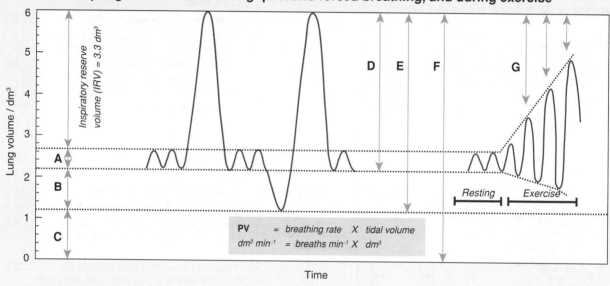

PV = breathing rate X tidal volume
dm^3 min^{-1} = breaths min^{-1} X dm^3

3. Using the definitions given on the previous page, identify the volumes and capacities indicated by the letters **A-F** on the spirogram above. For each, indicate the volume (vol) in dm^3. The inspiratory reserve volume has been identified:

(a) **A:** _____ Vol: _____ (d) **D:** _____ Vol: _____

(b) **B:** _____ Vol: _____ (e) **E:** _____ Vol: _____

(c) **C:** _____ Vol: _____ (f) **F:** _____ Vol: _____

4. Explain what is happening in the sequence indicated by the letter **G:** _____

_____

5. Calculate PV when breathing rate is 15 breaths per minute and tidal volume is 0.4 dm^3: _____

6. (a) Describe what would happen to PV during strenuous exercise: _____

(b) Explain how this is achieved: _____

7. The table above gives approximate percentages for respiratory gases during breathing. Study the data and then:

(a) Calculate the difference in CO_2 between inhaled and exhaled air: _____

(b) Explain where this 'extra' CO_2 comes from: _____

(c) Explain why the dead air volume raises the oxygen content of exhaled air above that in the lungs: _____

_____

_____

© 2015 **BIOZONE** International
ISBN: 978-1-927309-13-1
Photocopying Prohibited

138 Investigating Ventilation in Humans

Key Idea: Vital capacity can be affected by several factors including age, gender, height, ethnicity, and disease.

Vital capacity is the greatest volume of air that can be expelled from the lungs after taking the deepest possible breath. It is easily measured using a spirometer or a bell jar system (as described below). In healthy adults, vital capacity ranges between 4-6 dm³, but is influenced by several factors including gender, age, height, ethnicity, and fitness.

Measuring vital capacity

Vital capacity can be measured using a 6 dm³ calibrated glass bell jar, supported in a sink of water (right). The jar is calibrated by inverting it, pouring in known volumes of water, and marking the level on the bell jar with a marker pen.

To measure vital capacity, a person breathes in as far as possible (maximal inhalation), and then exhales as far as possible (maximal exhalation) into a mouth piece connected to tubing. The drop in volume within the bell jar is measured (this is the vital capacity in dm³).

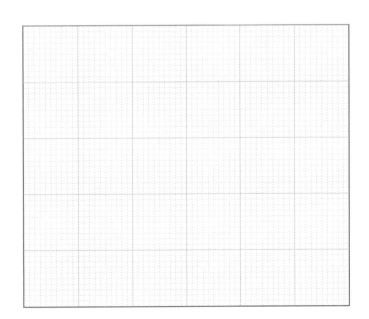

Bell jar

Tubing. Disposable mouthpiece attached for each subject.

Wedge: allows water to circulate

Investigating vital capacity

A class of high school biology students investigated the vital capacity of the whole class using the bell jar method described above.

The students recorded their heights as well as their vital capacity. The results are presented on the table (right).

1. Calculate the mean vital capacity for:

   (a) Females: _____

   (b) Males: _____

   (c) Explain if these results are what you would expect?

   _____

   _____

   _____

   _____

Females		Males	
Height / cm	Vital capacity / dm³	Height / cm	Vital capacity / dm³
156	2.75	181	4.00
145	2.50	163	2.50
155	3.25	167	4.00
170	4.00	174	4.00
162	2.75	177	4.00
164	2.75	177	3.75
163	3.40	176	3.75
158	2.75	177	3.25
167	4.00	178	4.00
165	3.00	178	3.75

2. (a) Plot height versus vital capacity as a scatter graph on the grid provided (right). Use different symbols or colours for each set of data (female and male).

   (b) Draw a line of best fit through each set of points. For a line of best fit, the points should fall equally either side of the line.

   (c) Describe the relationship between height and vital capacity:

   _____

   _____

   _____

   _____

   _____

LINK
18
DATA

139 Gas Exchange in Insects

Key Idea: Insects transport air throughout their bodies via a system of tracheal tubes. Spiracles allow air to enter and leave the body.

Terrestrial air breathers lose water from their gas exchange surfaces to the environment. Most terrestrial insects have a large surface area to volume ratio and so are at risk of drying out. They minimise water losses with a waxy outer layer to their exoskeleton and a system of **tracheal tubes** for gas exchange that loses very little water to the environment.

Tracheal systems, which open to the air via paired openings (**spiracles**) in the body wall, are the most common gas exchange organs of insects. Filtering devices stop the system clogging and valves control the degree to which the spiracles are open. In small insects, diffusion is the only mechanism needed to exchange gases, because it occurs so rapidly through the air-filled tubules. Larger, active insects, such as locusts, have air sacs, which can be compressed and expanded to assist in moving air through the tubules.

Insect tracheal tubes

Insects, and some spiders, transport gases via a system of branching tubes called tracheae or tracheal tubes. Respiratory gases move by diffusion across the moist lining directly to and from the tissues. The end of each tube contains a small amount of fluid in which the respiratory gases are dissolved. The fluid is drawn into the muscle tissues during their contraction, and is released back into the tracheole when the muscle rests. Insects ventilate their tracheal system by making rhythmic body movements to help move the air in and out of the tracheae.

Spiracle openings on the abdomen

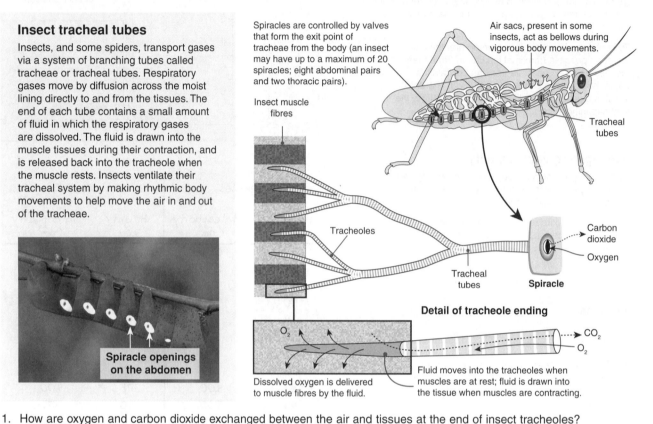

Spiracles are controlled by valves that form the exit point of tracheae from the body (an insect may have up to a maximum of 20 spiracles; eight abdominal pairs and two thoracic pairs).

Insect muscle fibres

Air sacs, present in some insects, act as bellows during vigorous body movements.

Tracheal tubes

Tracheoles

Tracheal tubes

Carbon dioxide

Oxygen

Spiracle

Detail of tracheole ending

CO_2

O_2

O_2

Dissolved oxygen is delivered to muscle fibres by the fluid.

Fluid moves into the tracheoles when muscles are at rest; fluid is drawn into the tissue when muscles are contracting.

1. How are oxygen and carbon dioxide exchanged between the air and tissues at the end of insect tracheoles?

_____

_____

_____

_____

2. Valves in the spiracles can regulate the amount of air entering the tracheal system. Suggest a reason for this adaptation:

_____

_____

3. How is ventilation achieved in a terrestrial insect? _____

_____

_____

4. Even though most insects are small, they have evolved an efficient and highly developed gas exchange system that is independent of diffusion across the body surface. Why do you think this is the case?

_____

_____

_____

© 2015 **BIOZONE** International
ISBN: 978-1-927309-13-1
Photocopying Prohibited

140 Gas Exchange in Fish

Key Idea: The gills of fish exchange gases between the blood and the environment. Gills are thin filamentous, vascular structures located just behind the head.

Fish obtain the oxygen they need from the water using gills, which are membranous structures supported by cartilaginous or bony struts. Gill surfaces are very large and as water flows over the gill surface, respiratory gases are exchanged between the blood and the water. The percentage of dissolved oxygen in a volume of water is much less than in the same volume of air. Air is 21% oxygen, whereas in water, dissolved oxygen is about 1% by volume. Active organisms with gills must therefore be able to extract oxygen efficiently from the water. In fish, high oxygen extraction rates are achieved using countercurrent mechanisms and by pumping water across the gill surface (bony fish) or swimming continuously with the mouth open (sharks and rays).

Fish gills

The gills of fish have a great many folds, which are supported and kept apart from each other by the water. This gives them a high surface area for gas exchange. The outer surface of the gill is in contact with the water, and blood flows in vessels inside the gill. Gas exchange occurs by diffusion between the water and blood across the gill membrane and capillaries. The operculum (gill cover) permits exit of water and acts as a pump, drawing water past the gill filaments. The gills of fish are very efficient and achieve an 80% extraction rate of oxygen from water; over three times the rate of human lungs from air.

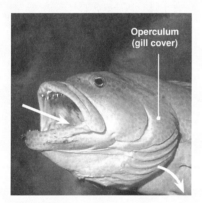

Operculum (gill cover)

Ventilation of the gills

Bony fish ventilate the gills by opening and closing the mouth in concert with opening and closing the operculum. The mouth opens, increasing the volume of the buccal (mouth) cavity and causing water to enter. The operculum bulges slightly, moving water into the opercular cavity. The mouth closes and the operculum opens and water flows out over the gills. These continual pumping movements keep oxygenated water flowing over the gills, maintaining the concentration gradient for diffusion.

Breathing in bony fish

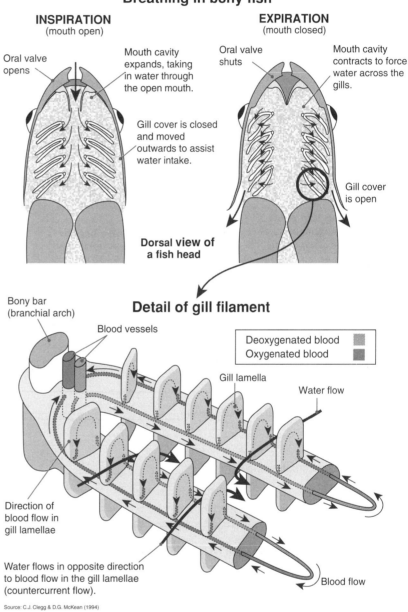

INSPIRATION (mouth open)

Oral valve opens

Mouth cavity expands, taking in water through the open mouth.

Gill cover is closed and moved outwards to assist water intake.

EXPIRATION (mouth closed)

Oral valve shuts

Mouth cavity contracts to force water across the gills.

Gill cover is open

Dorsal view of a fish head

Detail of gill filament

Bony bar (branchial arch)

Blood vessels

Gill lamella

Water flow

Deoxygenated blood
Oxygenated blood

Direction of blood flow in gill lamellae

Water flows in opposite direction to blood flow in the gill lamellae (countercurrent flow).

Blood flow

Source: C.J. Clegg & D.G. McKean (1994)

1. Describe three features of a fish gas exchange system (gills and related structures) that facilitate gas exchange:

(a) _____

(b) _____

(c) _____

2. Why do fish need to ventilate their gills? _____

_____

_____

Countercurrent flow

▶ The structure of fish gills and their physical arrangement in relation to the blood flow maximises gas exchange rates. A constant stream of oxygen-rich water flows over the gill filaments in the opposite direction to the blood flowing through the gill filaments.

▶ This is called countercurrent flow (below left) and it is an adaptation for maximising the amount of O_2 removed from the water. Blood flowing through the gill capillaries encounters water of increasing oxygen content.

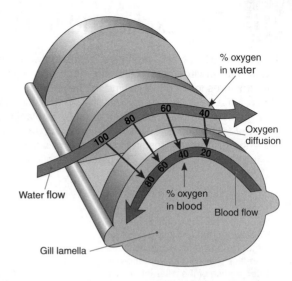

The concentration gradient (for oxygen uptake) across the gill is maintained across the entire distance of the gill lamella and oxygen continues to diffuse into the blood (CO_2 diffuses out at the same time).

A parallel current flow would not achieve the same oxygen extraction rates because the concentrations across the gill would quickly equalise (far right).

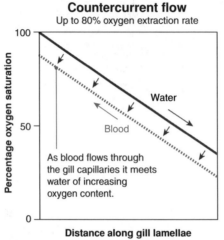

Countercurrent flow
Up to 80% oxygen extraction rate

As blood flows through the gill capillaries it meets water of increasing oxygen content.

Parallel current flow
Up to 50% oxygen extraction rate

At this point, blood and water have the same O_2 concentration and no more O_2 exchange takes place.

3. Describe how bony fish achieve adequate ventilation of the gills through:

(a) Pumping (mouth and operculum): _____

_____

(b) Continuous swimming (mouth open): _____

_____

4. Describe countercurrent flow: _____

_____

_____

5. (a) How does the countercurrent system in a fish gill increase the efficiency of oxygen extraction from the water?

_____

_____

_____

(b) Explain why parallel flow would not achieve the same rates of oxygen extraction: _____

_____

_____

6. In terms of the amount of oxygen available in the water, explain why fish are very sensitive to increases in water temperature or suspended organic material in the water:

_____

_____

141 Chapter Review

Summarise what you know about this topic under the headings provided. You can draw diagrams or mind maps, or write short notes to organise your thoughts. Use the images and hints included to help you:

Gas exchange
HINT: Describe the features of an efficient gas exchange surface.

Mammalian gas exchange
HINT: Describe the mammalian gas exchange system, ventilation, and use of spirometry.

Gas exchange in insects
HINT: Describe how the tracheal system functions.

Gas exchange in fish
HINT: Gill structure and the role of countercurrent flow.

142 KEY TERMS: Did You Get It?

1. (a) On the photo of the dissection of a fish's gills, label the following: *gills, operculum, branchial arch*.

    (b) Draw arrows on the photo to show the direction of water flow when the fish was in the water.

    (c) Explain how these gills are ventilated by the fish:

    _____

    _____

    _____

    _____

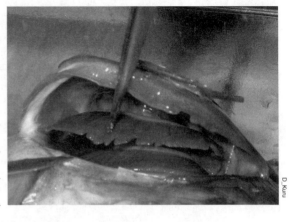

2. The image below shows a cross section through a jasmine leaf. On the image label the following: *Palisade mesophyll cell, spongy mesophyll cell, upper epidermis, stomata, guard cell, vascular bundle (leaf vein), lower epidermis, air spaces.*

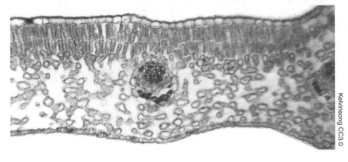

3. On the diagram below, label the components of the gas exchange system (a-f) and the components and processes involved in breathing (i - vi).

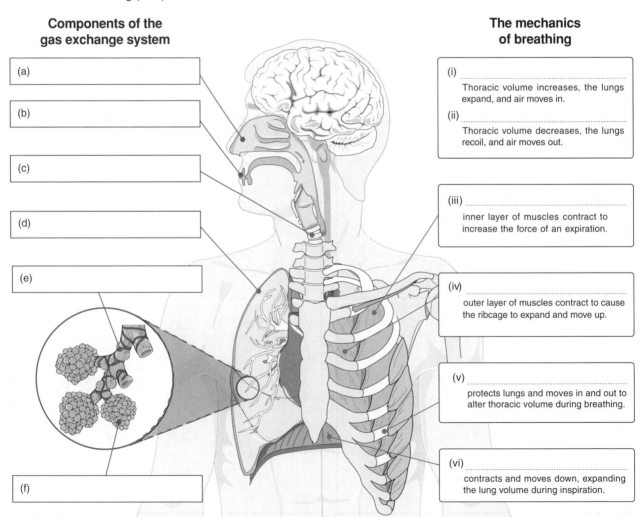

Components of the gas exchange system

(a) _____

(b) _____

(c) _____

(d) _____

(e) _____

(f) _____

The mechanics of breathing

(i) _____
Thoracic volume increases, the lungs expand, and air moves in.

(ii) _____
Thoracic volume decreases, the lungs recoil, and air moves out.

(iii) _____
inner layer of muscles contract to increase the force of an expiration.

(iv) _____
outer layer of muscles contract to cause the ribcage to expand and move up.

(v) _____
protects lungs and moves in and out to alter thoracic volume during breathing.

(vi) _____
contracts and moves down, expanding the lung volume during inspiration.

© 2015 **BIOZONE** International
ISBN: 978-1-927309-13-1
Photocopying Prohibited

TEST

Module 3.1.2

Transport in Animals

Key terms

artery (pl. arteries)

atrium (pl. atria)

blood

bradycardia

capillary (pl. capillaries)

cardiac cycle

circulatory fluid

closed circulatory system

double circulatory system

ectopic heartbeat

fibrillation

haemolymph

heart

lymph

open circulatory system

single circulatory system

tachycardia

tissue fluid

vein

ventricle

Transport systems in multicellular animals

Learning outcomes

	Activity number
☐ 1 With reference to size, metabolic rate, and surface area and volume ratios, explain why multicellular animals require an internal transport system. Describe the components and functions of a typical animal transport system.	143
☐ 2 Explain the role of the circulatory fluid (e.g. blood or haemolymph) in the transport systems of vertebrates and invertebrates respectively.	144

☐ 3 Describe the structure and function of circulatory systems in animals, including:

	Activity number
(a) Open circulatory systems (arthropods, e.g. insects, and most molluscs).	145
(b) Closed circulatory systems (vertebrates and some invertebrates).	146 147
☐ 4 Explain how the type of circulatory system and the efficiency of transport are related to metabolic needs and environment.	145 146
☐ 5 Describe and explain differences in the structure and function of blood vessels in mammals, including arteries, arterioles, capillaries, venules, and veins.	148-151
☐ 6 **PAG2** Identify and describe different types of blood vessels in tissue sections.	148-150
☐ 7 Distinguish between blood, tissue fluid, and lymph. Explain how tissue fluid is formed from plasma with reference to differences in hydrostatic pressure and oncotic pressure at either end of a capillary bed.	152

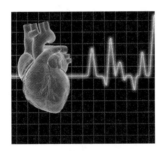 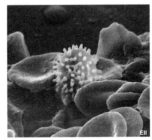 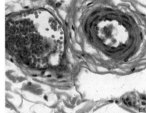

The mammalian heart

Learning outcomes

	Activity number
☐ 8 Describe the structure and function of the mammalian heart. Identify pulmonary and systemic circuits and the vessels entering and leaving the heart.	153 159
☐ 9 **PAG2** Dissect, examine, and draw a mammalian heart to show its external and internal structure.	154
☐ 10 Describe the cardiac cycle, including the role of the heart valves and the pressure changes occurring in the heart and associated vessels.	155
☐ 11 Explain how the heartbeat is initiated and regulated, including reference to the myogenic nature of the beat, and the role of the sinoatrial node or pacemaker, atrioventricular node, and Purkyne tissue.	156 159
☐ 12 Relate the events in the cardiac cycle to the electrical activity on an electro-cardiograph (ECG). Interpret ECG traces of normal and abnormal heart activity.	155 157

Gas transport

Learning outcomes

	Activity number
☐ 13 Describe the role of haemoglobin in transporting oxygen and carbon dioxide.	158
☐ 14 Describe and explain the oxygen dissociation curve for fetal and adult haemoglobin, including reference to the significance of different affinities for oxygen and the significance of the Bohr effect.	158

143 Transport and Exchange in Animals

Key Idea: Internal transport systems in animals move materials between exchange surfaces by mass transport. Living cells require a constant supply of nutrients and oxygen, and continuous removal of wastes. Simple, small organisms achieve this through diffusion. Larger, more complex organisms require specialised systems to facilitate

exchanges as their surface area to volume ratio decreases. **Mass transport** (also known as mass flow or bulk flow) describes the movement of materials at equal rates or as a single mass. Mass transport accounts for the long distance transport of fluids in living organisms. It includes the movement of blood in the circulatory systems of animals.

Exchanges across a body surface

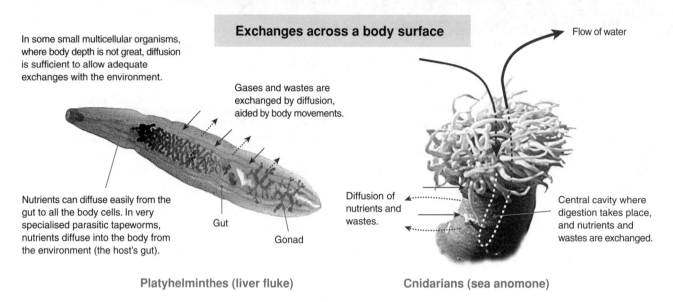

In some small multicellular organisms, where body depth is not great, diffusion is sufficient to allow adequate exchanges with the environment.

Gases and wastes are exchanged by diffusion, aided by body movements.

Flow of water

Nutrients can diffuse easily from the gut to all the body cells. In very specialised parasitic tapeworms, nutrients diffuse into the body from the environment (the host's gut).

Gut

Gonad

Diffusion of nutrients and wastes.

Central cavity where digestion takes place, and nutrients and wastes are exchanged.

Platyhelminthes (liver fluke)

Cnidarians (sea anomone)

Systems for exchange and transport

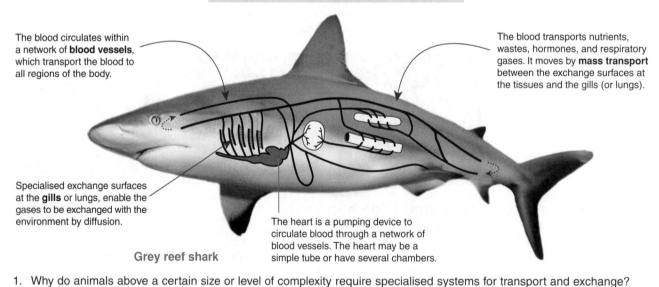

The blood circulates within a network of **blood vessels**, which transport the blood to all regions of the body.

The blood transports nutrients, wastes, hormones, and respiratory gases. It moves by **mass transport** between the exchange surfaces at the tissues and the gills (or lungs).

Specialised exchange surfaces at the **gills** or lungs, enable the gases to be exchanged with the environment by diffusion.

The heart is a pumping device to circulate blood through a network of blood vessels. The heart may be a simple tube or have several chambers.

Grey reef shark

1. Why do animals above a certain size or level of complexity require specialised systems for transport and exchange?

_____

_____

_____

2. (a) How do materials move within the circulatory system of a vertebrate? _____

_____

(b) Contrast this with how materials are transported in a flatworm or single celled eukaryote: _____

_____

_____

(c) Identify two exchange sites in a vertebrate: _____

© 2015 **BIOZONE** International
ISBN: 978-1-927309-13-1
Photocopying Prohibited

144 Circulatory Fluids

Key Idea: Circulatory fluid transports nutrients, wastes, hormones, and often respiratory gases around the body. The internal transport system of most animals includes a circulating fluid. In animals with closed systems, the fluid in the blood vessels is distinct from the tissue fluid outside the vessels and is called **blood**. Blood can have many different appearances, depending on the animal group, but it usually consists of cells and cell fragments suspended in a watery fluid. It serves many functions, including transporting dissolved gases, nutrients, wastes, and hormones. In animals with open systems, there is no difference between the fluid in the vessels and that in the sinuses (haemocoel) so the circulating fluid is called **haemolymph**. In insects, the haemolymph carries nutrients but not respiratory gases.

Insect haemolymph

Moulted exoskeleton

Emerged cricket

Fluid pressure is used to facilitate moulting in insects. Overwintering insects even have antifreezes, such as glycerol, in the plasma so they don't freeze during winter.

Haemolymph may make up between 11% and 40% of the total body mass of an insect

Haemolymph is a blood-like substance found in all invertebrates with open circulatory systems. The haemolymph fills the **haemocoel** and surrounds all cells.

About 90% of **insect haemolymph** is plasma, a watery fluid, which is usually clear. Compared to vertebrate blood, it contains relatively high concentrations of amino acids, proteins, sugars, and inorganic ions.

The remaining 10% of haemolymph volume is made up of various cell types (**haemocytes**). These are involved in clotting and internal defence. Unlike vertebrate blood, insect haemolymph lacks red blood cells and (with a few exceptions) lacks respiratory pigment, because oxygen is delivered directly to tissues by the tracheal system.

Mammalian blood

NON-CELLULAR COMPONENTS

The non-cellular part of the blood is the plasma, a watery matrix making up 50-60% of blood volume.

Most of the blood is water. It transports dissolved substances, provides cells with water, distributes heat, and maintains blood volume. The plasma also contains ions (e.g. Ca^{2+}) and proteins.

CELLULAR COMPONENTS

The formed elements of blood float in the plasma and make up 40-50% of the total blood volume

White blood cells and platelets
2-3% of the total blood volume. White blood cells are involved in internal defence. Platelets are involved in blood clotting.

Lymphocytes: 24% of the white cell count. Lymphocytes are responsible for immunity.

Granulocytes: White blood cells with a role in phagocytosis, inflammation, and allergic responses.

Platelets: Small, membrane-bound cell fragments with a role in blood clotting.

2 µm

Red blood cells (RBCs)
38-48% of total blood volume. RBCs transport oxygen (carried bound to haemoglobin) and a small amount of carbon dioxide.

7-8 µm

1. Describe two common functions of mammalian blood and insect haemolymph:

   (a) _____

   (b) _____

2. Describe one function of mammalian blood not performed by insect haemolymph: _____

3. Describe one function of insect haemolymph not performed by mammalian blood: _____

4. Describe one feature distinguishing red and white blood cells in mammalian blood: _____

5. Contrast the proportions of cellular and non-cellular components in blood and haemolymph: _____

© 2015 **BIOZONE** International
ISBN: 978-1-927309-13-1
Photocopying Prohibited

145 Open Circulatory Systems

Key Idea: In open circulatory systems, the haemolymph circulates in the body cavity, not enclosed in vessels.

The circulatory systems of animals may be open or closed. **Open circulatory systems**, in which the body fluid (haemolymph) circulates freely in the body cavity, are typical of most invertebrates. Insects, unlike most other arthropods, do not use the haemolymph to transport oxygen, which is delivered directly to the tissues via a system of tracheal tubes. In addition to its usual transport functions, the circulatory system may also be important in hydraulic movements of the body (e.g. many molluscs) or its parts (e.g. butterflies expand the wings after moulting).

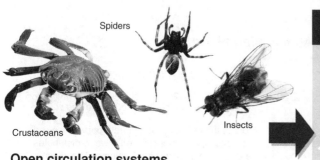

Spiders

Crustaceans

Insects

Open circulation systems

Arthropods and molluscs (except cephalopods) have open circulatory systems in which the haemolymph is pumped by a tubular, or sac-like, heart through short vessels into large spaces (sinuses) in the body cavity. The haemolymph bathes the cells before reentering the heart through holes (**ostia**). Muscle action may assist in circulating the fluid.

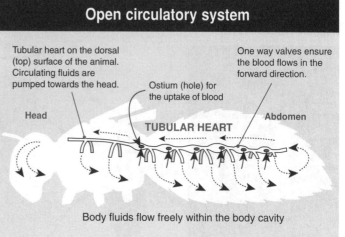

Open circulatory system

Tubular heart on the dorsal (top) surface of the animal. Circulating fluids are pumped towards the head.

One way valves ensure the blood flows in the forward direction.

Ostium (hole) for the uptake of blood

Head

TUBULAR HEART

Abdomen

Body fluids flow freely within the body cavity

The haemolymph occupies up to 40% of the body mass of an insect and is usually under low pressure due its lack of confinement in vessels. The circulation of the haemolymph is aided by body movements such as the ventilating movements of the abdomen.

In spiders, arteries from the dorsal heart empty the haemolymph into tissue spaces and then into a large ventral sinus that bathes the book lungs where gas exchange takes place. Venous channels conduct the haemolymph back to the heart.

Although the circulatory system of crabs is open by definition, much of the haemolymph is actually enclosed within vessels. The thoracic heart has three pairs of ostia and a number of arteries, which leave the heart and branch extensively to supply various organs before draining into channel-like sinuses.

1. How does an open circulatory system move fluid (haemolymph) about the body? _____

_____

_____

2. Describe one disadvantage of an open circulatory system: _____

_____

3. Compare insects and decapod crustaceans (e.g. crabs) in the degree to which the circulatory system is closed:

_____

_____

4. (a) Why is the crab's circulatory system usually described as an open system? _____

_____

(b) In what way is this description not entirely accurate? _____

_____

© 2015 **BIOZONE** International
ISBN: **978-1-927309-13-1**
Photocopying Prohibited

146 Closed Circulatory Systems

Key Idea: In closed circulatory systems, the blood is contained within blood vessels.

In closed circulatory systems, the blood is contained within vessels and pumped around the body by a heart. Oxygen is transported by the blood and diffuses through capillary walls into the body cells. In large, active animals closed systems efficiently distribute oxygen and nutrients to the body's cells. Closed systems allow the animal to control the distribution of blood flow to different organs and parts of the body by contracting or dilating blood vessels. Vertebrate systems have a pulmonary circuit taking up oxygen and a systemic circuit delivering oxygenated blood to the body.

INVERTEBRATE CLOSED SYSTEMS

Polychaete worm

Earthworm

Wiki: Hans Hillewaert

The closed systems of many annelids (e.g. earthworms) circulate blood through a series of vessels before returning it to the heart. In annelids, the dorsal (upper) and ventral (lower) blood vessels are connected by lateral vessels in every segment (right). The dorsal vessel receives blood from the lateral vessels and carries it towards the head. The ventral vessel carries blood posteriorly and distributes it to the segmental vessels. The dorsal vessel is contractile and is the main method of propelling the blood, but there are also several contractile aortic arches ('hearts') which act as accessory organs for blood propulsion.

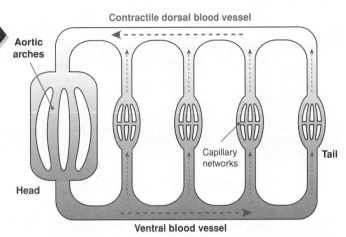

Contractile dorsal blood vessel

Aortic arches

Capillary networks

Tail

Head

Ventral blood vessel

VERTEBRATE CLOSED SYSTEMS

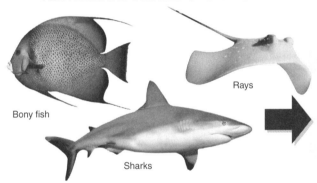

Rays

Bony fish

Sharks

Closed, single circuit systems

In closed circulation systems, the blood is contained within vessels and is returned to the heart after every circulation of the body. Exchanges between the blood and the fluids bathing the cells occurs by diffusion across capillaries. In single circuit systems, typical of fish, the blood goes directly from the gills to the body. The blood loses pressure at the gills and flows at low pressure around the body.

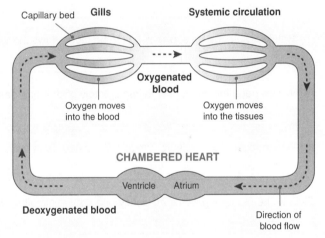

Capillary bed   **Gills**   **Systemic circulation**

Oxygenated blood

Oxygen moves into the blood

Oxygen moves into the tissues

CHAMBERED HEART

Ventricle   Atrium

Deoxygenated blood

Direction of blood flow

Reptiles

Amphibians

Birds

Mammals

Closed, double circuit systems

Double circulation systems occur in all vertebrates other than fish. The blood is pumped through a pulmonary circuit to the lungs, where it is oxygenated. The blood returns to the heart, which pumps the oxygenated blood, through a systemic circuit, to the body. In amphibians and most reptiles, the heart is not completely divided and there is some mixing of oxygenated and deoxygenated blood. In birds and mammals, the heart is fully divided and there is no mixing.

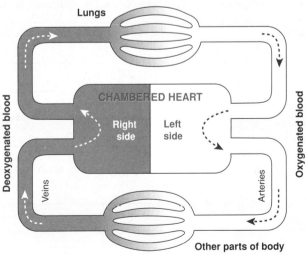

Lungs

CHAMBERED HEART

Deoxygenated blood

Right side

Left side

Oxygenated blood

Veins

Arteries

Other parts of body

LINK   WEB
147 **146**   KNOW

Fish heart

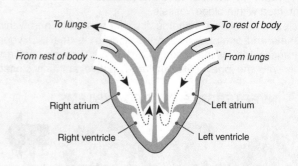

The fish heart is linear, with a sequence of chambers in series. There are two main chambers (atrium and ventricle) as well as an entry (the sinus venosus) and sometimes a smaller exit chamber (the conus). Blood from the body first enters the heart through the sinus venosus, then passes into the atrium and the ventricle. A series of one-way valves between the chambers prevents reverse blood flow. Blood leaving the heart travels to the gills.

Mammalian heart

In birds and mammals, the heart is fully partitioned into two halves, resulting in four chambers. Blood circulates through two circuits, with no mixing of the two. Oxygenated blood from the lungs is kept separated from the deoxygenated blood returning from the rest of the body.

1. What is the main difference between closed and open systems of circulation? _____

_____

_____

2. (a) Where does the blood flow to immediately after it has passed through the gills in a fish? _____

_____

   (b) Relate this to the pressure at which the blood flows in the systemic circulation: _____

_____

3. (a) Where does the blood flow to immediately after it has passed through the lungs in a mammal? _____

_____

   (b) Relate this to the pressure at which the blood flows in the systemic circulation: _____

_____

4. Explain the higher functional efficiency of a double circuit system, relative to a single circuit system: _____

_____

_____

5. Hearts range from being simple contractile structures to complex chambered organs. Describe basic heart structure in:

   (a) Fish: _____

_____

   (b) Mammals: _____

_____

_____

6. How does a closed circulatory system give an animal finer control over the distribution of blood to tissues and organs?

_____

_____

_____

_____

© 2015 **BIOZONE** International
ISBN: 978-1-927309-13-1
Photocopying Prohibited

147 The Mammalian Transport System

Key Idea: The mammalian circulatory system is a double circuit made up of a pulmonary circuit and a systemic circuit. The blood vessels of the circulatory system form a network of tubes that carry blood away from the heart, transport it to the tissues of the body, and then return it to the heart. The figure below shows a number of the basic circulatory routes. Mammals have a double circulatory system: a **pulmonary** **system**, which carries blood between the heart and lungs, and a **systemic system**, which carries blood between the heart and the rest of the body. The systemic circulation has many subdivisions. Two important subdivisions are the coronary (cardiac) circulation, which supplies the heart muscle, and the hepatic portal circulation, which runs from the gut to the liver.

Schematic overview of the human circulatory system

Deoxygenated blood (coloured blue below) travels to the right side of the heart via the vena cavae. The heart pumps the deoxygenated blood to the lungs where it releases carbon dioxide and receives oxygen. The oxygenated blood (coloured white below) travels via the pulmonary vein back to the heart from where it is pumped to all parts of the body. The **venous system** (figure, left) returns blood from the capillaries to the heart. The **arterial system** (figure right) carries blood from the heart to the capillaries. **Portal systems** carry blood between two capillary beds.

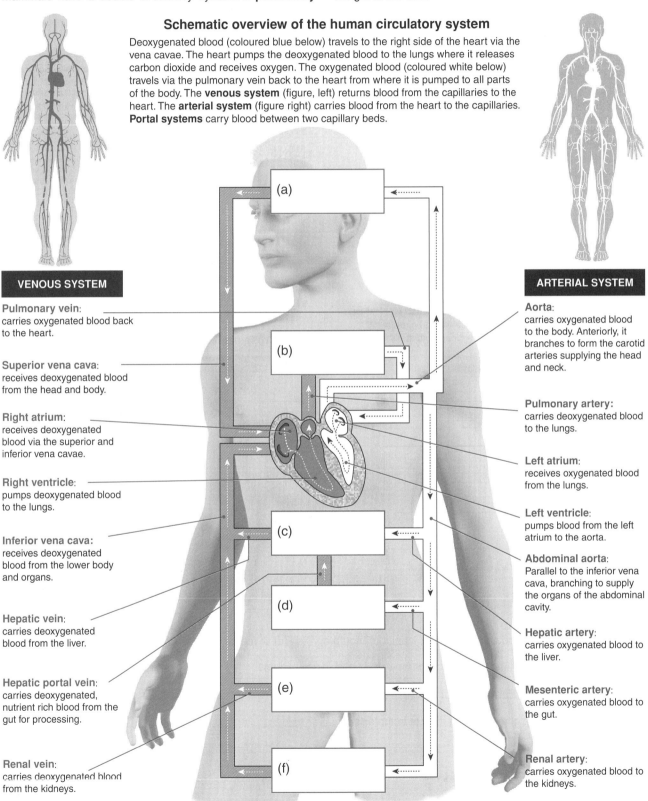

VENOUS SYSTEM

Pulmonary vein: carries oxygenated blood back to the heart.

Superior vena cava: receives deoxygenated blood from the head and body.

Right atrium: receives deoxygenated blood via the superior and inferior vena cavae.

Right ventricle: pumps deoxygenated blood to the lungs.

Inferior vena cava: receives deoxygenated blood from the lower body and organs.

Hepatic vein: carries deoxygenated blood from the liver.

Hepatic portal vein: carries deoxygenated, nutrient rich blood from the gut for processing.

Renal vein: carries deoxygenated blood from the kidneys.

ARTERIAL SYSTEM

Aorta: carries oxygenated blood to the body. Anteriorly, it branches to form the carotid arteries supplying the head and neck.

Pulmonary artery: carries deoxygenated blood to the lungs.

Left atrium: receives oxygenated blood from the lungs.

Left ventricle: pumps blood from the left atrium to the aorta.

Abdominal aorta: Parallel to the inferior vena cava, branching to supply the organs of the abdominal cavity.

Hepatic artery: carries oxygenated blood to the liver.

Mesenteric artery: carries oxygenated blood to the gut.

Renal artery: carries oxygenated blood to the kidneys.

1. Complete the diagram above by labelling the boxes with the correct organs: *lungs, liver, head, intestines, genitals/lower body, kidneys.*

2. Circle the two blood vessels involved in the pulmonary circuit.

LINK 153   LINK 150   LINK 149   LINK 148   WEB 147   KNOW

148 Arteries

Key Idea: Arteries are thick-walled blood vessels that carry blood away from the heart to the capillaries within the tissues. In vertebrates, **arteries** are the blood vessels that carry blood away from the heart to the capillaries within the tissues. The large arteries that leave the heart divide into medium-sized (distributing) arteries. Within the tissues and organs, these distributing arteries branch to form **arterioles**, which deliver blood to capillaries. Arterioles lack the thick layers of arteries and consist only of an endothelial layer wrapped by a few smooth muscle fibres at intervals along their length. Blood flow to the tissues is altered by contraction (**vasoconstriction**) or relaxation (**vasodilation**) of the blood vessel walls. Vasoconstriction increases blood pressure whereas vasodilation has the opposite effect.

Arteries

Arteries, regardless of size, can be recognised by their well-defined rounded **lumen** (internal space) and the muscularity of the vessel wall. Arteries have an elastic, stretchy structure that gives them the ability to withstand the high pressure of blood being pumped from the heart. At the same time, they help to maintain pressure by having some contractile ability themselves (a feature of the central muscle layer). Arteries nearer the heart have more elastic tissue, giving greater resistance to the higher blood pressures of the blood leaving the left ventricle. Arteries further from the heart have more muscle to help them maintain blood pressure. Between heartbeats, the arteries undergo elastic recoil and contract. This tends to smooth out the flow of blood through the vessel.

Arteries comprise three main regions (right):

1. A thin inner layer of epithelial cells called the **tunica intima** (endothelium) lines the artery.

2. A thick central layer (the **tunica media**) of elastic tissue and smooth muscle that can both stretch and contract.

3. An outer connective tissue layer (the **tunica externa**) has a lot of elastic tissue.

Structure of an artery

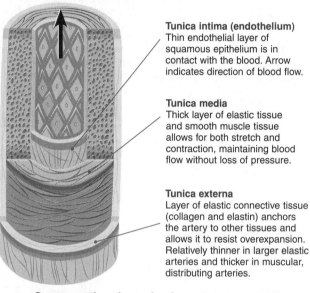

Tunica intima (endothelium)
Thin endothelial layer of squamous epithelium is in contact with the blood. Arrow indicates direction of blood flow.

Tunica media
Thick layer of elastic tissue and smooth muscle tissue allows for both stretch and contraction, maintaining blood flow without loss of pressure.

Tunica externa
Layer of elastic connective tissue (collagen and elastin) anchors the artery to other tissues and allows it to resist overexpansion. Relatively thinner in larger elastic arteries and thicker in muscular, distributing arteries.

Cross section through a large artery

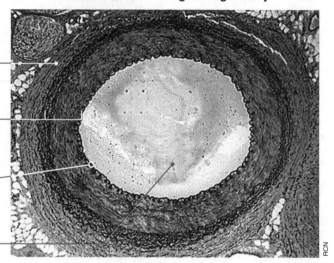

(a)

(b)

(c)

(d)

1. Using the information above to help you, label the photograph (a)-(d) of the cross section through an artery (above).

2. Why do the walls of arteries need to be thick with a lot of elastic tissue? _____

_____

3. What is the purpose of the smooth muscle in the artery walls? _____

_____

4. How to arteries contribute to the regulation of blood pressure? _____

_____

_____

_____

© 2015 **BIOZONE** International
ISBN: 978-1-927309-13-1
Photocopying Prohibited

149 Veins

Key Idea: Veins are blood vessels that return the blood from the tissues to the heart. Veins have a large lumen.

Veins are the blood vessels that return blood to the heart from the tissues. The smallest veins (**venules**) return blood from the capillaries to the veins. Veins and their branches contain about 59% of the blood in the body. The structural differences between veins and arteries are mainly associated with differences in the relative thickness of the vessel layers and the diameter of the lumen (space within the vessel). These, in turn, are related to the vessel's functional role.

Veins

When several capillaries unite, they form small veins called **venules**. The venules collect the blood from capillaries and drain it into **veins**. Veins are made up of the same three layers as arteries but they have less elastic and muscle tissue, a relatively thicker tunica externa, and a larger, less defined **lumen**. The venules closest to the capillaries consist of an **endothelium** and a tunica externa of connective tissue. As the venules approach the veins, they also contain the tunica media characteristic of veins (right). Although veins are less elastic than arteries, they can still expand enough to adapt to changes in the pressure and volume of the blood passing through them. Blood flowing in the veins has lost a lot of pressure because it has passed through the narrow capillary vessels. The low pressure in veins means that many veins, especially those in the limbs, need to have valves to prevent backflow of the blood as it returns to the heart.

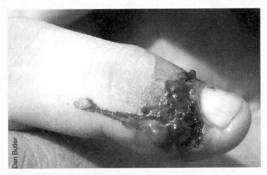

If a vein is cut, as is shown in this severed finger wound, the blood oozes out slowly in an even flow, and usually clots quickly as it leaves. In contrast, arterial blood spurts rapidly and requires pressure to staunch the flow.

Structure of a vein

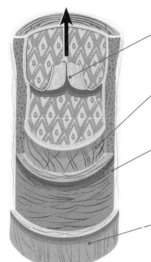

One-way valves
Valves located along the length of veins keep the blood moving towards the heart (prevent back-flow). Arrow indicates direction of blood flow.

Tunica intima (endothelium)
Thin endothelial layer of squamous epithelium lines the vein.

Tunica media
Layer of smooth muscle tissue with collagen fibres (connective tissue). The tunica media is much thinner relative to that of an artery and the smaller venules may lack this layer.

Tunica externa
Layer of connective tissue (mostly collagen) is relatively thicker than in arteries and thicker than the tunica media.

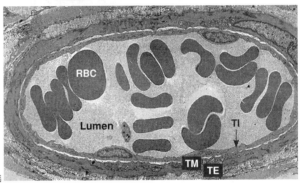

Above: TEM of a vein showing red blood cells (RBC) in the lumen, and the tunica intima (TI), tunica media (TM), and tunica externa (TE).

1. Contrast the structure of veins and arteries for each of the following properties:

   (a) Thickness of muscle and elastic tissue: _____

   _____

   (b) Size of the lumen (inside of the vessel): _____

   _____

2. With respect to their functional roles, explain the differences you have described above: _____

   _____

   _____

3. What is the role of the valves in assisting the veins to return blood back to the heart? _____

   _____

4. Why does blood ooze from a venous wound, rather than spurting as it does from an arterial wound?

   _____

   _____

150 Capillaries

Key Idea: Capillaries are small, thin-walled vessels that allow the exchange of material between the blood and the tissues. In vertebrates, **capillaries** are very small vessels that connect arterial and venous circulation and allow efficient exchange of nutrients and wastes between the blood and tissues. Capillaries form networks or beds and are abundant where metabolic rates are high. Fluid that leaks out of the capillaries has an essential role in bathing the tissues.

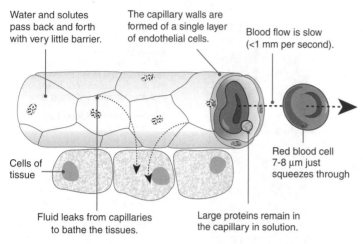

Water and solutes pass back and forth with very little barrier.

The capillary walls are formed of a single layer of endothelial cells.

Blood flow is slow (<1 mm per second).

Cells of tissue

Red blood cell 7-8 μm just squeezes through

Fluid leaks from capillaries to bathe the tissues.

Large proteins remain in the capillary in solution.

Exchanges in capillaries

Blood passes from the arterioles into the capillaries where the exchange of materials between the body cells and the blood takes place. Capillaries are small blood vessels with a diameter of just 4-10 μm. The only tissue present is an **endothelium** of squamous epithelial cells. Capillaries are so numerous that no cell is more than 25 μm from any capillary.

Blood pressure causes fluid to leak from capillaries through small gaps where the endothelial cells join. This fluid bathes the tissues, supplying nutrients and oxygen, and removing wastes (left). The density of capillaries in a tissue is an indication of that tissue's metabolic activity. For example, cardiac muscle relies heavily on oxidative metabolism. It has a high demand for blood flow and is well supplied with capillaries. Smooth muscle is far less active than cardiac muscle, relies more on anaerobic metabolism, and does not require such an extensive blood supply.

Blood, tissue fluid, and lymph

	Blood	Tissue fluid	Lymph
Cells	Erythrocytes, leucocytes, platelets	Some leucocytes	Lymphocytes
Proteins	Hormones and plasma proteins	Some hormones and proteins	Few
Glucose	High	None	Low
Amino acids	High	Used by body cells	Low
Oxygen	High	Used by body cells	Low
Carbon dioxide	Low	Produced by body cells	High

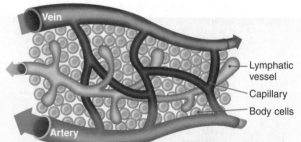

Vein

Lymphatic vessel

Capillary

Body cells

Artery

The pressure at the arterial end of the capillaries forces fluid through gaps between the capillary endothelial cells. The fluid contains nutrients and oxygen and is called tissue fluid. Some of this fluid returns to the blood at the venous end of the capillary bed, but some is drained by lymph vessels to form lymph. Blood transports nutrients, wastes, and respiratory gases to and from the tissues. Tissue fluid facilitates the transport of these between the blood and the tissues. Lymph drains excess tissue fluid and returns it to the general circulation, and it has a role in the immune system.

1. What is the role of capillaries? _____

_____

2. Describe the structure of a capillary, contrasting it with the structure of a vein and an artery:

_____

_____

_____

_____

_____

3. Distinguish between blood, tissue fluid, and lymph: _____

_____

_____

_____

_____

151 Capillary Networks

Key Idea: Capillaries form branching networks where exchanges between the blood and tissues take place.

The flow of blood through a capillary bed is called microcirculation. In most parts of the body, there are two types of vessels in a capillary bed: the true capillaries, where exchanges take place, and a vessel called a vascular shunt, which connects the arteriole and venule at either end of the bed. The shunt diverts blood past the true capillaries when the metabolic demands of the tissue are low. When tissue activity increases, the entire network fills with blood.

1. Describe the structure of a capillary network:

_____

_____

_____

_____

_____

_____

2. Explain the role of the smooth muscle sphincters and the vascular shunt in a capillary network:

_____

_____

_____

_____

_____

_____

3. (a) Describe a situation where the capillary bed would be in the condition labelled **A**:

_____

_____

_____

_____

(b) Describe a situation where the capillary bed would be in the condition labelled **B**:

_____

_____

_____

_____

4. How does a portal venous system differ from other capillary systems?

_____

_____

_____

_____

_____

_____

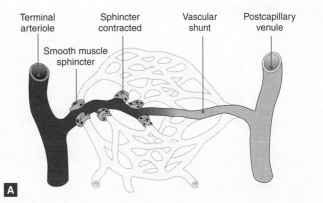

A

When the sphincters contract (close), blood is diverted via the vascular shunt to the postcapillary venule, bypassing the exchange capillaries.

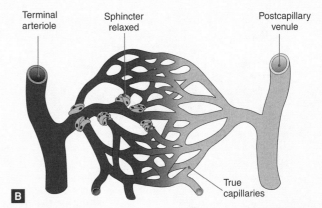

B

When the sphincters are relaxed (open), blood flows through the entire capillary bed allowing exchanges with the cells of the surrounding tissue.

Connecting capillary beds
The role of portal venous systems

Arterial blood   **Gut capillaries**   **Liver sinusoids**   Venous blood

Absorption

Nutrient rich portal blood has high osmolarity

Liver cells

Nutrients (e.g. glucose, amino acids) and toxins are absorbed from the gut lumen into the capillaries

Portal blood passes through the liver lobules where nutrients and toxins are absorbed, excreted, or converted.

A portal venous system occurs when a capillary bed drains into another capillary bed through veins, without first going through the heart. Portal systems are relatively uncommon. Most capillary beds drain into veins which then drain into the heart, not into another capillary bed. The diagram above depicts the hepatic portal system, which includes both capillary beds and the blood vessels connecting them.

152 The Formation of Tissue Fluid

Key Idea: Tissue fluid is formed by leakage from capillaries. It provides oxygen and nutrients to tissues and removes wastes. The network of capillaries supplying the body's tissues ensures that no cell is far from a supply of nutrients and oxygen. Substances reach the cells through the tissue fluid, moving into and out of the capillaries by diffusion, by cytosis, and through gaps where the membranes are not tightly joined. Specialised capillaries, such as those in the intestine and kidney, where absorption or filtration is important, are relatively more leaky. Fluid moves across the leaky capillary membranes in a direction that depends on the balance between the blood pressure and the oncotic pressure at each end of a capillary bed. Oncotic pressure (also called colloid osmotic pressure) tends to pull water into the capillaries.

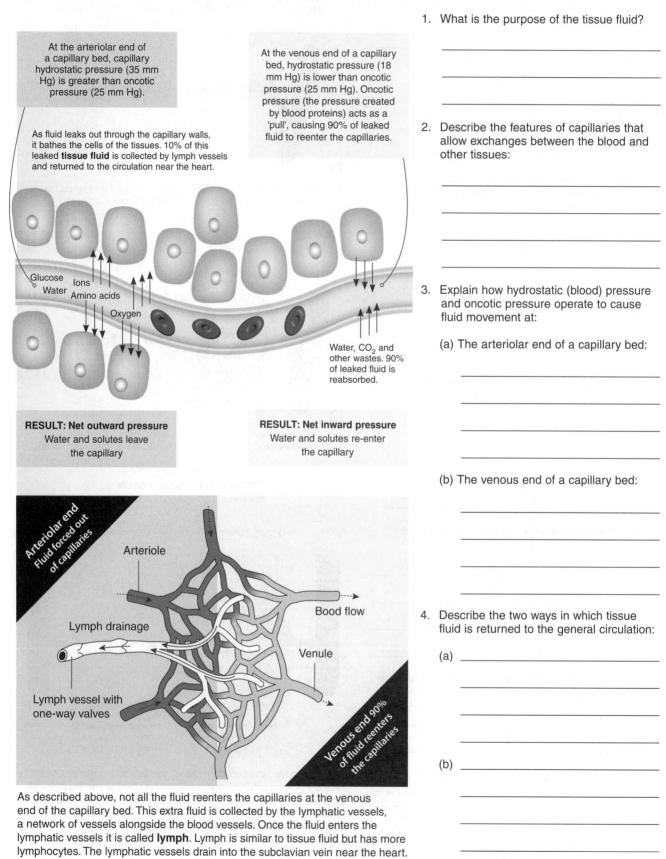

At the arteriolar end of a capillary bed, capillary hydrostatic pressure (35 mm Hg) is greater than oncotic pressure (25 mm Hg).

At the venous end of a capillary bed, hydrostatic pressure (18 mm Hg) is lower than oncotic pressure (25 mm Hg). Oncotic pressure (the pressure created by blood proteins) acts as a 'pull', causing 90% of leaked fluid to reenter the capillaries.

As fluid leaks out through the capillary walls, it bathes the cells of the tissues. 10% of this leaked **tissue fluid** is collected by lymph vessels and returned to the circulation near the heart.

Glucose
Water
Ions
Amino acids
Oxygen

Water, CO$_2$ and other wastes. 90% of leaked fluid is reabsorbed.

RESULT: Net outward pressure
Water and solutes leave the capillary

RESULT: Net inward pressure
Water and solutes re-enter the capillary

Arteriolar end
Fluid forced out of capillaries

Arteriole

Lymph drainage

Blood flow

Venule

Lymph vessel with one-way valves

Venous end 90% of fluid reenters the capillaries

As described above, not all the fluid reenters the capillaries at the venous end of the capillary bed. This extra fluid is collected by the lymphatic vessels, a network of vessels alongside the blood vessels. Once the fluid enters the lymphatic vessels it is called **lymph**. Lymph is similar to tissue fluid but has more lymphocytes. The lymphatic vessels drain into the subclavian vein near the heart.

1. What is the purpose of the tissue fluid?

_____

_____

_____

2. Describe the features of capillaries that allow exchanges between the blood and other tissues:

_____

_____

_____

_____

3. Explain how hydrostatic (blood) pressure and oncotic pressure operate to cause fluid movement at:

(a) The arteriolar end of a capillary bed:

_____

_____

_____

_____

(b) The venous end of a capillary bed:

_____

_____

_____

_____

4. Describe the two ways in which tissue fluid is returned to the general circulation:

(a) _____

_____

_____

_____

(b) _____

_____

_____

_____

© 2015 **BIOZONE** International
ISBN: 978-1-927309-13-1
Photocopying Prohibited

153 The Human Heart

Key Idea: Humans have a four chambered heart divided into left and right halves. It acts as a double pump.

The heart is the centre of the human cardiovascular system. It is a hollow, muscular organ made up of four chambers (two **atria** and two **ventricles**) that alternately fill and empty of blood, acting as a double pump. The left side (systemic circuit) pumps blood to the body tissues and the right side (pulmonary circuit) pumps blood to the lungs. The heart lies between the lungs, to the left of the midline, and is surrounded by a double layered pericardium of connective tissue, which prevents over distension of the heart and anchors it within the central compartment of the thoracic cavity.

Human heart structure

(sectioned, anterior view)

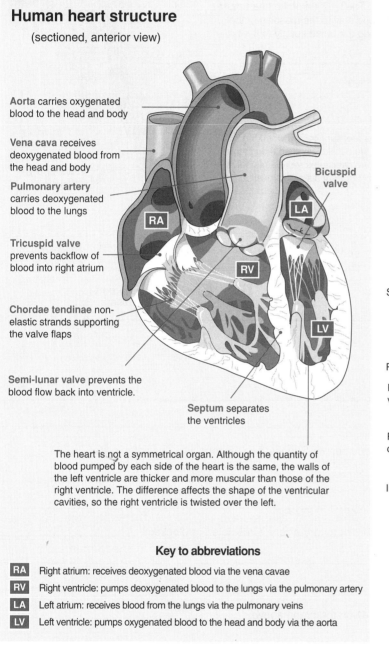

Aorta carries oxygenated blood to the head and body

Vena cava receives deoxygenated blood from the head and body

Pulmonary artery carries deoxygenated blood to the lungs

Tricuspid valve prevents backflow of blood into right atrium

Chordae tendinae non-elastic strands supporting the valve flaps

Semi-lunar valve prevents the blood flow back into ventricle.

Bicuspid valve

Septum separates the ventricles

The heart is not a symmetrical organ. Although the quantity of blood pumped by each side of the heart is the same, the walls of the left ventricle are thicker and more muscular than those of the right ventricle. The difference affects the shape of the ventricular cavities, so the right ventricle is twisted over the left.

Key to abbreviations

RA Right atrium: receives deoxygenated blood via the vena cavae
RV Right ventricle: pumps deoxygenated blood to the lungs via the pulmonary artery
LA Left atrium: receives blood from the lungs via the pulmonary veins
LV Left ventricle: pumps oxygenated blood to the head and body via the aorta

Top view of a heart in section to show valves

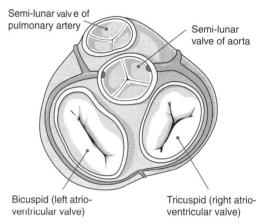

Semi-lunar valve of pulmonary artery

Semi-lunar valve of aorta

Bicuspid (left atrio-ventricular valve)

Tricuspid (right atrio-ventricular valve)

Anterior view of heart to show coronary arteries

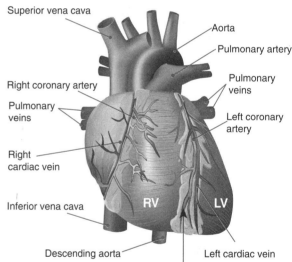

Superior vena cava

Aorta

Pulmonary artery

Right coronary artery

Pulmonary veins

Pulmonary veins

Left coronary artery

Right cardiac vein

Inferior vena cava

Descending aorta

Left cardiac vein

The high oxygen demands of the heart muscle are met by a dense capillary network branching from the coronary arteries. The coronary arteries (left and right) arise from the aorta and spread over the surface of the heart supplying the cardiac muscle with oxygenated blood. The left carries 70% of the coronary blood supply and the right the remaining 30%. Deoxygenated blood is collected by the cardiac veins and returned to the right atrium via a large coronary sinus.

1. In the schematic diagram of the heart, below, label the four chambers and the main vessels entering and leaving them. The arrows indicate the direction of blood flow. Use large coloured circles to mark the position of each of the four valves.

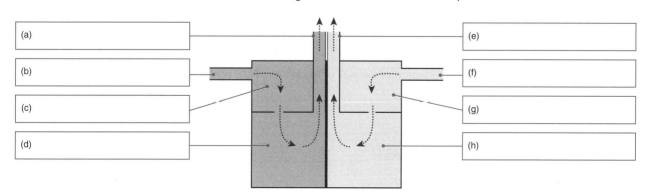

(a) (b) (c) (d) (e) (f) (g) (h)

Pressure changes and the asymmetry of the heart

The heart is not a symmetrical organ. The left ventricle and its associated arteries are thicker and more muscular than the corresponding structures on the right side. This asymmetry is related to the necessary pressure differences between the pulmonary (lung) and systemic (body) circulations (not to the distance over which the blood is pumped *per se*). The graph below shows changes in blood pressure in each of the major blood vessel types in the systemic and pulmonary circuits (the horizontal distance not to scale). The pulmonary circuit must operate at a much lower pressure than the systemic circuit to prevent fluid from accumulating in the alveoli of the lungs. The left side of the heart must develop enough "spare" pressure to enable increased blood flow to the muscles of the body and maintain kidney filtration rates without decreasing the blood supply to the brain.

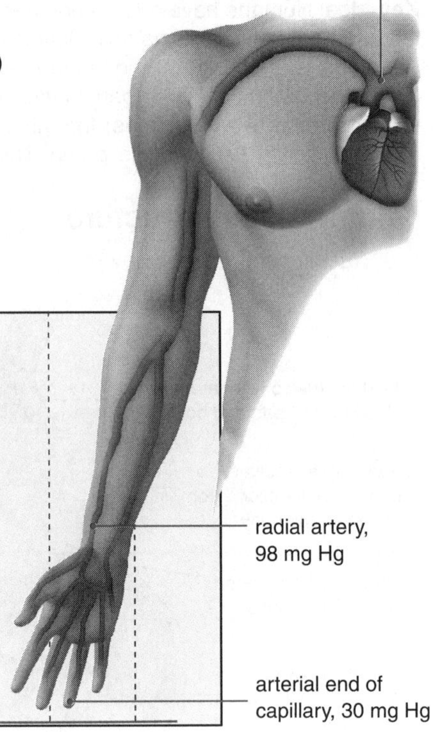
aorta, 100 mg Hg
radial artery, 98 mg Hg
arterial end of capillary, 30 mg Hg

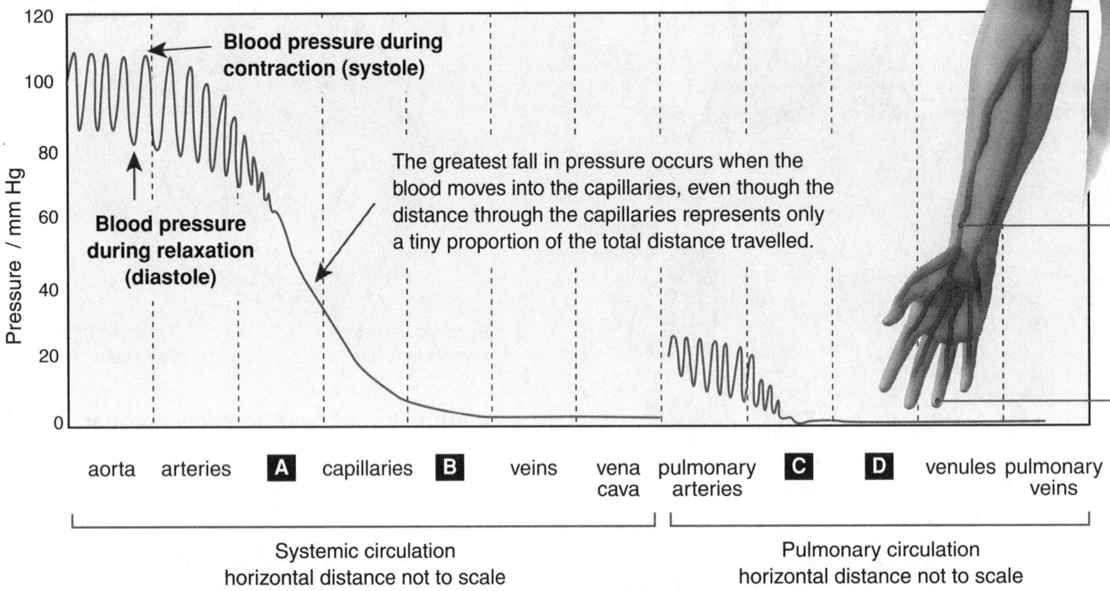
120
100
80
60
40
20
0
Pressure / mm Hg
Blood pressure during contraction (systole)
Blood pressure during relaxation (diastole)
The greatest fall in pressure occurs when the blood moves into the capillaries, even though the distance through the capillaries represents only a tiny proportion of the total distance travelled.
aorta
arteries
A
capillaries
B
veins
vena cava
pulmonary arteries
C
D
venules
pulmonary veins
Systemic circulation horizontal distance not to scale
Pulmonary circulation horizontal distance not to scale

2. What is the purpose of the valves in the heart? To prevent the backflow of blood.

3. The heart is full of blood, yet it requires its own blood supply. Suggest two reasons why this is the case:

   (a) __________

   (b) __________

4. Predict the effect on the heart if blood flow through a coronary artery is restricted or blocked: __________

5. Identify the vessels corresponding to the letters **A-D** on the graph above:

   A: ________ B: ________ C: ________ D: ________

6. (a) Why must the pulmonary circuit operate at a lower pressure than the systemic system? __________

   (b) Relate this to differences in the thickness of the wall of the left and right ventricles of the heart: __________

7. What are you recording when you take a pulse? __________

ISBN: 978-1-927309-13-1

154 Dissecting a Mammalian Heart

Key Idea: Dissecting a sheep's heart allows hands-on exploration of a mammalian heart.

The dissection of a sheep's heart is a common practical activity and allows hands-on exploration of the appearance and structure of a mammalian heart. A diagram of a heart is an idealised representation of an organ that may look quite different in reality. You must learn to transfer what you know from a diagram to the interpretation of the real organ.

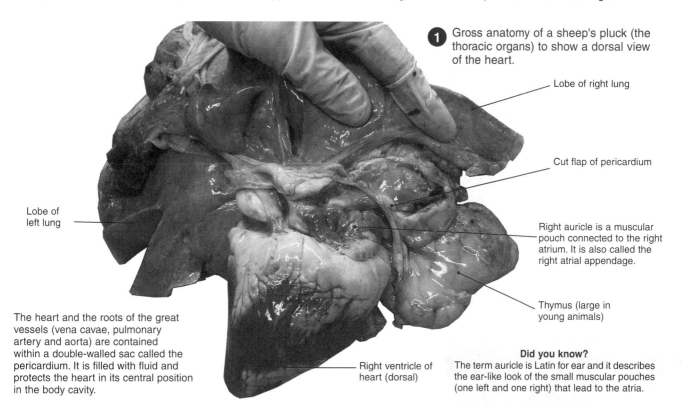

1 Gross anatomy of a sheep's pluck (the thoracic organs) to show a dorsal view of the heart.

Lobe of right lung

Cut flap of pericardium

Lobe of left lung

Right auricle is a muscular pouch connected to the right atrium. It is also called the right atrial appendage.

Thymus (large in young animals)

The heart and the roots of the great vessels (vena cavae, pulmonary artery and aorta) are contained within a double-walled sac called the pericardium. It is filled with fluid and protects the heart in its central position in the body cavity.

Right ventricle of heart (dorsal)

Did you know?
The term auricle is Latin for ear and it describes the ear-like look of the small muscular pouches (one left and one right) that lead to the atria.

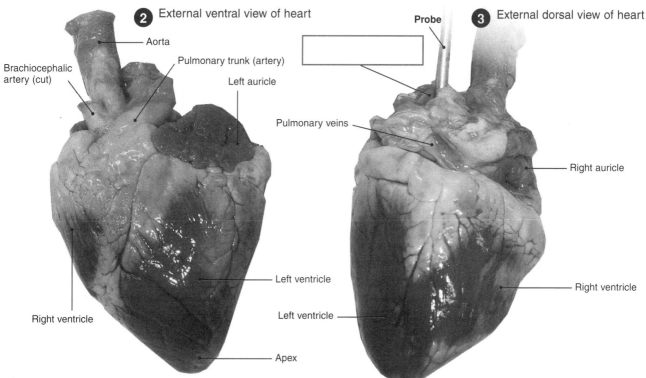

2 External ventral view of heart

Aorta

Pulmonary trunk (artery)

Brachiocephalic artery (cut)

Left auricle

Probe

3 External dorsal view of heart

Pulmonary veins

Right auricle

Left ventricle

Right ventricle

Right ventricle

Left ventricle

Apex

Note the main surface features of an isolated heart. The narrow pointed end forms the **apex** of the heart, while the wider end, where the blood vessels enter is the **base**. The ventral surface of the heart (above) is identified by a groove, the **interventricular sulcus**, which marks the division between the left and right ventricles.

1. Use coloured lines to indicate the interventricular sulcus and the base of the heart. Label the coronary arteries.

On the dorsal surface of the heart, above, locate the large thin-walled **vena cavae** and **pulmonary veins**. You may be able to distinguish between the anterior and posterior vessels. On the right side of the dorsal surface (as you look at the heart) at the base of the heart is the **right atrium**, with the **right ventricle** below it.

2. On this photograph, label the vessel indicated by the probe.

4 Dorsal view of heart

5 Shallow section, ventral view of heart

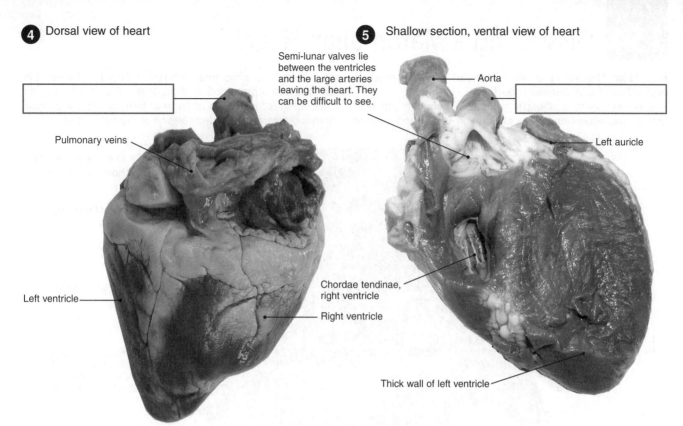

Semi-lunar valves lie between the ventricles and the large arteries leaving the heart. They can be difficult to see.

Pulmonary veins

Left ventricle

Aorta

Left auricle

Chordae tendinae, right ventricle

Right ventricle

Thick wall of left ventricle

3. On this **dorsal view**, label the vessel indicated. Palpate the heart and feel the difference in the thickness of the left and right ventricle walls.

4. This photograph shows a shallow section to expose the right ventricle. Label the vessel in the box indicated.

6 Frontal sections of heart to show chambers

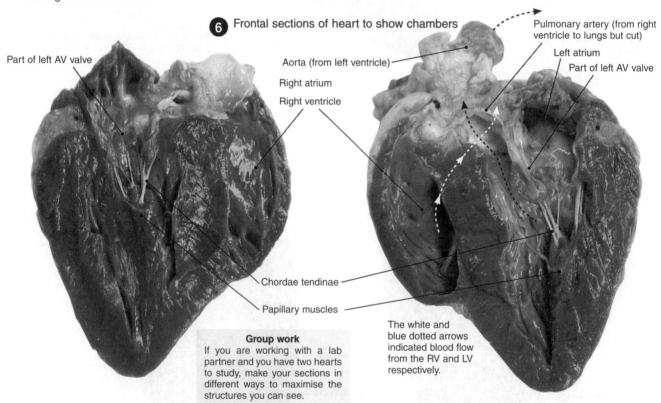

Part of left AV valve

Aorta (from left ventricle)

Right atrium

Right ventricle

Pulmonary artery (from right ventricle to lungs but cut)

Left atrium

Part of left AV valve

Chordae tendinae

Papillary muscles

The white and blue dotted arrows indicated blood flow from the RV and LV respectively.

Group work

If you are working with a lab partner and you have two hearts to study, make your sections in different ways to maximise the structures you can see.

If the heart is sectioned and the two halves opened, the valves of the heart can be seen. Each side of the heart has a one-way valve between the atrium and the ventricle known as the **atrioventricular valve**. They close during ventricular contraction to prevent back flow of the blood into the lower pressure atria.

5. Judging by their position and structure, what do you suppose is the function of the chordae tendinae?

_____

_____

The atrioventricular (AV) valves of the two sides of the heart are similar in structure except that the right AV valve has three cusps (tricuspid) while the left atrioventricular valve has two cusps (bicuspid or mitral valve). Connective tissue (**chordae tendineae**) run from the cusps to **papillary muscles** on the ventricular wall.

6. What feature shown here most clearly distinguishes the left and right ventricles?.

_____

_____

155 The Cardiac Cycle

Key Idea: The cardiac cycle refers to the sequence of events of a heartbeat and involves three main stages: atrial systole, ventricular systole, and complete cardiac diastole.
The heart pumps with alternate contractions (**systole**) and relaxations (**diastole**). Heartbeat occurs in a cycle involving three stages: atrial systole, ventricular systole, and complete cardiac diastole. Pressure changes in the heart's chambers generated by the cycle of contraction and relaxation are responsible for blood movement and cause the heart valves to open and close, preventing backflow of blood. The heartbeat occurs in response to electrical impulses, which can be recorded as a trace called an electrocardiogram.

The cardiac cycle

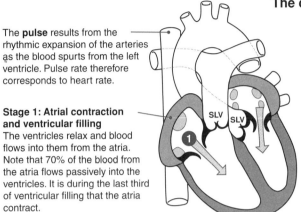

The **pulse** results from the rhythmic expansion of the arteries as the blood spurts from the left ventricle. Pulse rate therefore corresponds to heart rate.

Stage 1: Atrial contraction and ventricular filling
The ventricles relax and blood flows into them from the atria. Note that 70% of the blood from the atria flows passively into the ventricles. It is during the last third of ventricular filling that the atria contract.

Heart during ventricular filling

Stage 2: Ventricular contraction
The atria relax, the ventricles contract, and blood is pumped from the ventricles into the aorta and the pulmonary artery. The start of ventricular contraction coincides with the first heart sound.

Stage 3: (not shown) There is a short period of atrial and ventricular relaxation. Semilunar valves (**SLV**) close to prevent backflow into the ventricles (see diagram, left). The cycle begins again. For a heart beating at 75 beats per minute, one cardiac cycle lasts about 0.8 seconds.

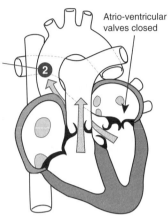

Atrio-ventricular valves closed

Heart during ventricular contraction

Cardiac cycle events and the electrocardiogram (ECG)

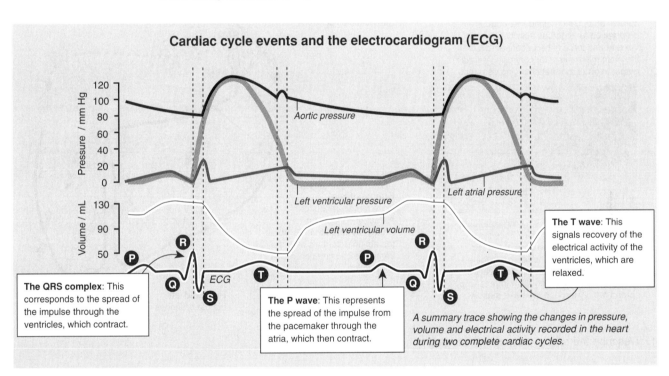

The QRS complex: This corresponds to the spread of the impulse through the ventricles, which contract.

The P wave: This represents the spread of the impulse from the pacemaker through the atria, which then contract.

The T wave: This signals recovery of the electrical activity of the ventricles, which are relaxed.

A summary trace showing the changes in pressure, volume and electrical activity recorded in the heart during two complete cardiac cycles.

1. On the ECG trace above:

   (a) When is the aortic pressure highest? _____

   (b) Which electrical event immediately precedes the increase in ventricular pressure? _____

   (c) What is happening when the pressure of the left ventricle is lowest? _____

2. Suggest the physiological reason for the period of electrical recovery experienced each cycle (the T wave):

   _____

3. Using the letters indicated, mark the points on trace above corresponding to each of the following:

   (a) E: Ejection of blood from the ventricle   (c) FV: Filling of the ventricle

   (b) BVC: Closing of the bicuspid valve   (d) BVO: Opening of the bicuspid valve

© 2015 **BIOZONE** International
ISBN: 978-1-927309-13-1
Photocopying Prohibited

156 Control of Heart Activity

Key Idea: Heartbeat is initiated by the sinoatrial node which acts as a pacemaker by setting the basic heart rhythm.
The heartbeat is myogenic, meaning it originates within the cardiac muscle itself. The heartbeat is regulated by a conduction system consisting of the pacemaker (**sinoatrial node**) and a specialised conduction system of Purkyne tissue. The pacemaker sets the basic heart rhythm, but this rate can be influenced by hormones and by the cardiovascular control centre. Changing the rate and force of heart contraction is the main mechanism for controlling cardiac output.

Generation of the heartbeat

The basic rhythmic heartbeat is **myogenic**. The nodal cells (SAN and atrioventricular node) spontaneously generate rhythmic action potentials without neural stimulation. The normal resting rate of self-excitation of the SAN is about 50 beats per minute.

The amount of blood ejected from the left ventricle per minute is called the **cardiac output**. It is determined by the **stroke volume** (the volume of blood ejected with each contraction) and the **heart rate** (number of heart beats per minute). Cardiac muscle responds to stretching by contracting more strongly. The greater the blood volume entering the ventricle, the greater the force of contraction. This relationship is important in regulating stroke volume in response to demand.

The hormone **epinephrine** also influences cardiac output, increasing heart rate in preparation for vigorous activity. Changing the rate and force of heart contraction is the main mechanism for controlling cardiac output in order to meet changing demands.

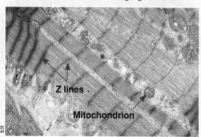

TEM of cardiac muscle showing striations in a fibre (muscle cell). The Z lines that delineate the contractile units of the rod-like units of the fibre. The fibres are joined by specialised electrical junctions called Intercalated discs, which allow impulses to spread rapidly through the heart muscle.

Sinoatrial node (SAN) is also called the **pacemaker**. It is a small mass of specialised muscle cells on the wall of the right atrium, near the entry point of the superior vena cava. The pacemaker initiates the cardiac cycle, spontaneously generating **action potentials** that cause the atria to contract. The SAN sets the basic heart rate, but this rate is influenced by hormones, such as adrenaline (epinephrine) and impulses from the autonomic nervous system.

Atrioventricular node (AVN) at the base of the atrium briefly delays the impulse to allow time for the atrial contraction to finish before the ventricles contract.

Bundle of His (atrioventricular bundle) A tract of conducting (Purkyne) fibres that distribute the action potentials over the ventricles causing ventricular contraction.

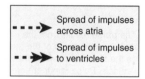

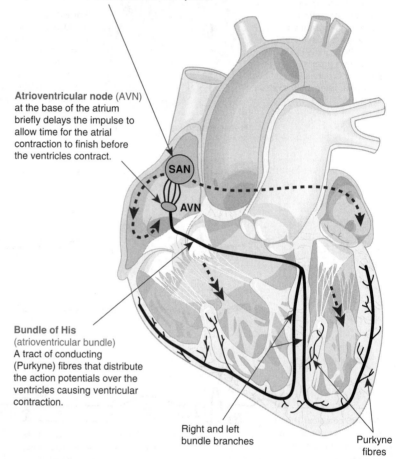

Right and left bundle branches

Purkyne fibres

1. Describe the role of each of the following in heart activity:

   (a) The sinoatrial node: _____

   (b) The atrioventricular node: _____

   (c) The bundle of His: _____

   (d) Intercalated discs: _____

2. What is the significance of delaying the impulse at the AVN? _____

3. What is the advantage of the physiological response of cardiac muscle to stretching? _____

4. The heart-beat is intrinsic. Why is it important to be able to influence the basic rhythm via the central nervous system?

_____

© 2015 **BIOZONE** International
ISBN: 978-1-927309-13-1
Photocopying Prohibited

Key Idea: ECGs can be used to test for and identify abnormalities in the rhythm of the heartbeat and therefore to diagnose heart disease.

An electrocardiogram (ECG) can be used to diagnose heart conditions by analysis of the size or the timing of the waves of electrical activity. For example a larger than normal P wave may indicate enlargement of an atrium, while a long QT interval may suggest an incorrect pumping rhythm. Sometimes diagnosis requires the heart to be under stress, e.g. during exercise, and is called a **stress test**. This is because narrowed arteries may perform adequately at rest, but not adjust to increased blood flows during exercise.

Applications of ECG diagnosis

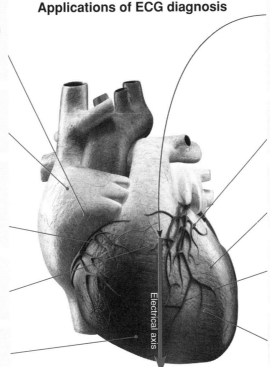

Pacemaker

Origin of the natural pacemaker (SAN) may vary (wandering pacemaker) causing changes in the P wave and PQ interval. The rhythm of an artificial pacemaker can also be tracked.

Arrhythmias (irregular rhythms)

Many arrhythmias originate from the SA node and are relatively common, especially in young children.

Heart rate

The ECG trace can indicate an abnormal increase (tachycardia) or decrease (bradycardia) in the contraction rate. A ventricular tachycardia is a result of a myocardial infarction (heart attack).

Activation sequence disorders

The pattern of the ECG can indicate problems with the passage of nerve signals through the heart.

Drug effects

Drugs affect the rhythm of the heart in different ways.

Electrical axis of the heart

Deviation to the right indicates an enlargement (hypertrophy) of the right ventricle which can be caused by obstructive lung disease. A left deviation indicates enlargement in the left ventricle which can be caused by hypertension.

Coronary circulation

Blockages in the coronary artery alter the shape of the T wave.

Hypertrophy

Enlargement of the atria or ventricles, as indicated by the electrical axis of the heart can indicate an "overloaded" heart.

Carditis

Inflammation of the heart can be suspected based on the T wave and ST segment.

Electrical imbalance

Imbalances in calcium and potassium can affect the intervals between waves on the ECG.

Abnormalities, even if similar, show different ECG traces in different parts of the heart. For example a sinus bradycardia produces a different trace to an atrial bradycardia or a ventricular bradycardia. The traces shown below are sinus bradycardia and sinus tachycardia.

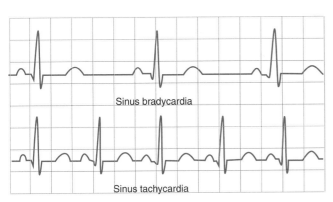

Sinus bradycardia

Sinus tachycardia

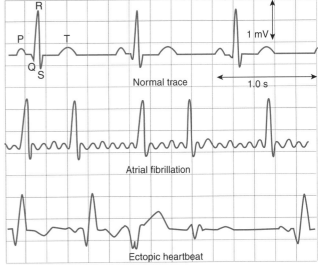

Normal trace   1.0 s

Atrial fibrillation

Ectopic heartbeat

1. Explain how the electrical axis of the heart can be used to diagnose hypertrophy in a ventricle:

_____

_____

2. (a) Ectopic heartbeats are generally normal but contain irregular abnormalities. Circle the **main** abnormality in the ectopic heartbeat trace shown above and describe its appearance:

_____

_____

(b) What is the result of this abnormality? _____

LINK
155 KNOW

158 Gas Transport in Mammals

Key Idea: Haemoglobin is a respiratory pigment in red blood cells, which binds oxygen and increases the efficiency of its transport and delivery to tissues throughout the body.

The transport of respiratory gases around the body is the role of the blood and its respiratory pigment. In vertebrates, e.g humans, oxygen is transported throughout the body chemically bound to the respiratory pigment **haemoglobin**

inside the red blood cells. In the muscles, oxygen from haemoglobin is transferred to and retained by **myoglobin**, a molecule that is chemically similar to haemoglobin except that it consists of only one haem-globin unit. Myoglobin has a greater affinity for oxygen than haemoglobin and acts as an oxygen store within muscles, releasing the oxygen during periods of prolonged or extreme muscular activity.

Gas exchange and transport

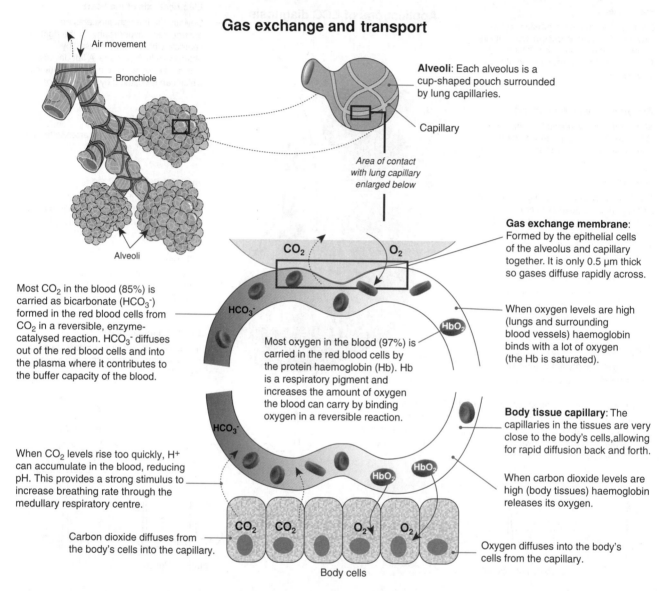

Alveoli: Each alveolus is a cup-shaped pouch surrounded by lung capillaries.

Air movement

Bronchiole

Capillary

Alveoli

Area of contact with lung capillary enlarged below

Gas exchange membrane: Formed by the epithelial cells of the alveolus and capillary together. It is only 0.5 μm thick so gases diffuse rapidly across.

Most CO_2 in the blood (85%) is carried as bicarbonate (HCO_3^-) formed in the red blood cells from CO_2 in a reversible, enzyme-catalysed reaction. HCO_3^- diffuses out of the red blood cells and into the plasma where it contributes to the buffer capacity of the blood.

Most oxygen in the blood (97%) is carried in the red blood cells by the protein haemoglobin (Hb). Hb is a respiratory pigment and increases the amount of oxygen the blood can carry by binding oxygen in a reversible reaction.

When oxygen levels are high (lungs and surrounding blood vessels) haemoglobin binds with a lot of oxygen (the Hb is saturated).

Body tissue capillary: The capillaries in the tissues are very close to the body's cells, allowing for rapid diffusion back and forth.

When carbon dioxide levels are high (body tissues) haemoglobin releases its oxygen.

When CO_2 levels rise too quickly, H+ can accumulate in the blood, reducing pH. This provides a strong stimulus to increase breathing rate through the medullary respiratory centre.

Carbon dioxide diffuses from the body's cells into the capillary.

Body cells

Oxygen diffuses into the body's cells from the capillary.

Transport of carbon dioxide in the blood

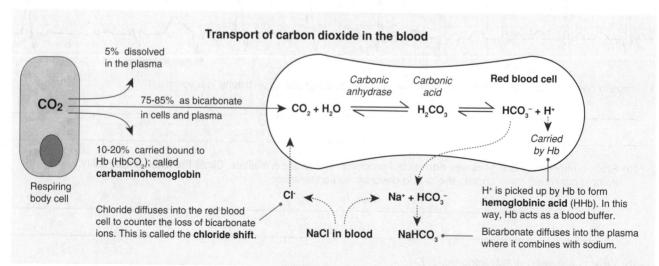

5% dissolved in the plasma

75-85% as bicarbonate in cells and plasma

10-20% carried bound to Hb ($HbCO_2$); called **carbaminohemoglobin**

Respiring body cell

CO_2

Chloride diffuses into the red blood cell to counter the loss of bicarbonate ions. This is called the **chloride shift**.

Carbonic anhydrase   *Carbonic acid*   **Red blood cell**

$$CO_2 + H_2O \rightleftharpoons H_2CO_3 \rightleftharpoons HCO_3^- + H^+$$

Carried by Hb

Cl^- ← → $Na^+ + HCO_3^-$

NaCl in blood $NaHCO_3$

H+ is picked up by Hb to form **hemoglobinic acid** (HHb). In this way, Hb acts as a blood buffer.

Bicarbonate diffuses into the plasma where it combines with sodium.

© 2015 **BIOZONE** International
ISBN: 978-1-927309-13-1
Photocopying Prohibited

Oxygen does not easily dissolve in blood, but is carried in chemical combination with haemoglobin (Hb) in red blood cells. The most important factor determining how much oxygen is carried by Hb is the level of oxygen in the blood. The greater the oxygen tension, the more oxygen will combine with Hb. This relationship can be illustrated with an oxygen-haemoglobin dissociation curve as shown below (Fig. 1). In the lung capillaries, (high O_2), a lot of oxygen is picked up and bound by Hb. In the tissues, (low O_2), oxygen is released. In skeletal muscle, myoglobin picks up oxygen from haemoglobin and therefore serves as an oxygen store when oxygen tensions begin to fall. The release of oxygen is enhanced by the **Bohr effect** (Fig. 2).

Respiratory pigments and the transport of oxygen

Fig. 1: Dissociation curves for haemoglobin and myoglobin at normal body temperature for fetal and adult human blood.

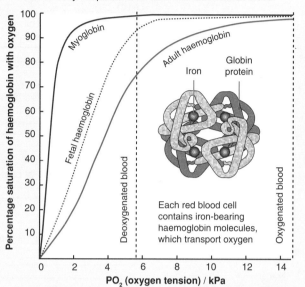

Fig. 2: Oxyhaemoglobin dissociation curves for human blood at normal body temperature at different blood pH.

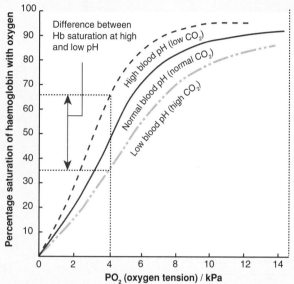

As oxygen level increases, more oxygen combines with haemoglobin (Hb). Hb saturation remains high, even at low oxygen tensions. Fetal Hb has a high affinity for oxygen and carries 20-30% more than maternal Hb. Myoglobin in skeletal muscle has a very high affinity for oxygen and will take up oxygen from haemoglobin in the blood.

As pH increases (lower CO_2), more oxygen combines with Hb. As the blood pH decreases (higher CO_2), Hb binds less oxygen and releases more to the tissues (the **Bohr effect**). The difference between Hb saturation at high and low pH represents the amount of oxygen released to the tissues.

1. (a) Identify two regions in the body where oxygen levels are very high: *Lungs, heart*

   (b) Identify two regions where carbon dioxide levels are very high: _____

2. Explain the significance of the **reversible binding** reaction of haemoglobin (Hb) to oxygen: _____

   _____

3. (a) Haemoglobin saturation is affected by the oxygen level in the blood. Describe the nature of this relationship:

   _____

   (b) Comment on the significance of this relationship to oxygen delivery to the tissues: _____

   _____

4. (a) Describe how fetal Hb is different to adult Hb: _____

   (b) Explain the significance of this difference to oxygen delivery to the fetus: _____

   _____

5. At low blood pH, less oxygen is bound by haemoglobin and more is released to the tissues:

   (a) Name this effect: _____

   (b) Comment on its significance to oxygen delivery to respiring tissue: _____

   _____

6. Explain the significance of the very high affinity of myoglobin for oxygen: _____

   _____

7. Identify the two main contributors to the buffer capacity of the blood: _____

159 Review of the Human Heart

Key Idea: The human heart comprises four chambers, which act as a double pump. Its contraction is myogenic, but can be influenced by other factors.

This activity summarises features of heart structure and function. Use it as a self-test, but see the earlier activities in this chapter if you need help.

1. On the diagram below, label the identified components of heart structure and intrinsic control (**a-n**).

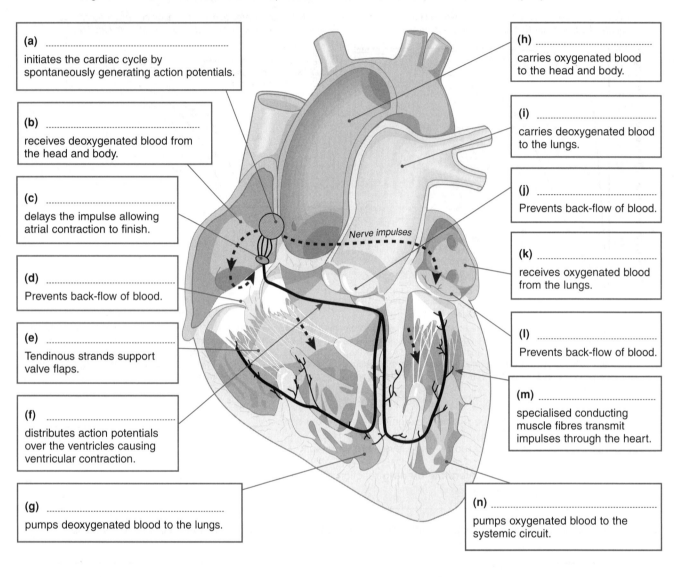

(a) ....
initiates the cardiac cycle by spontaneously generating action potentials.

(b) ....
receives deoxygenated blood from the head and body.

(c) ....
delays the impulse allowing atrial contraction to finish.

(d) ....
Prevents back-flow of blood.

(e) ....
Tendinous strands support valve flaps.

(f) ....
distributes action potentials over the ventricles causing ventricular contraction.

(g) ....
pumps deoxygenated blood to the lungs.

(h) ....
carries oxygenated blood to the head and body.

(i) ....
carries deoxygenated blood to the lungs.

(j) ....
Prevents back-flow of blood.

(k) ....
receives oxygenated blood from the lungs.

(l) ....
Prevents back-flow of blood.

(m) ....
specialised conducting muscle fibres transmit impulses through the heart.

(n) ....
pumps oxygenated blood to the systemic circuit.

Nerve impulses

2. An **ECG** is the result of different impulses produced at each phase of the **cardiac cycle** (the sequence of events in a heartbeat). For each electrical event indicated in the ECG below, describe the corresponding event in the cardiac cycle:

A --
The spread of the impulse from the pacemaker (sinoatrial node) through the atria.

B --
The spread of the impulse through the ventricles.

C --
Recovery of the electrical activity of the ventricles.

Electrical activity in the heart

3. (a) On the trace above, mark the region where the ventricular pressure is highest.

   (b) What is happening to the ventricular volume at this time? _____

   _____

© 2015 **BIOZONE** International
ISBN: 978-1-927309-13-1
Photocopying Prohibited

160 Chapter Review

Summarise what you know about this topic under the headings provided. You can draw diagrams or mind maps, or write short notes to organise your thoughts. Use the images and hints included to help you:

Blood vessels
HINT: Describe differences between various blood vessels and relate these differences to function.

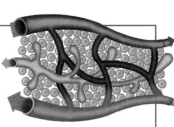

Circulatory fluids and circulatory systems
HINT: Summarise composition and role of circulatory fluids and features of open and closed, and single and double circulatory systems.

The heart
HINT: Describe the structure of the heart and the intrinsic control of heart activity.

REVISE

161 KEY TERMS: Did You Get It?

1. (a) What type of blood vessel transports blood away from the heart? _artery_

   (b) What type of blood vessel transports blood to the heart? _vein_

   (c) What type of blood vessel enables exchanges between the blood and tissues? _____

2. (a) What is the circulatory fluid in vertebrates called? _____

   (b) Which cell type in this fluid transports oxygen? _____

   (c) Which cell type in this fluid fights disease? _____

   (d) Which components of this fluid are involved in clotting? _____

3. (a) What is the general pattern of the mammalian circulatory system? _____

   (b) What is the general pattern of a fish circulatory system? _____

   (c) What is the general pattern of an insect circulatory system? _____

4. (a) What is the name given to the contraction phase of the cardiac cycle? _____

   (b) What is the name given to the relaxation phase of the cardiac cycle? _____

5.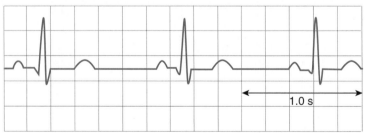

   (a) What does the image (left) show: _____

   (b) Circle the QRS complex.

   (c) Circle the region corresponding to lowest ventricular pressure.

   (d) Ventricular volume at this time is increasing/decreasing (delete one)

6. Match the following words with their definitions:

atrium _____

blood _____

closed circulatory system _____

double circulatory system _____

haemolymph _____

heart _____

tissue fluid _____

ventricle _____

A Circulatory system in which the blood is fully contained within vessels.

B A chamber of the mammalian heart that pumps blood into arteries.

C Circulatory fluid comprising numerous cell types, which transports respiratory gases, nutrients, and wastes.

D The circulatory fluid of invertebrates with an open circulatory system.

E A chamber of the mammalian heart that receives blood directly from the body or lungs.

F Muscular chambered organ of the vertebrate circulatory system.

G Circulatory system in which blood travels from the heart to lungs and back (via the pulmonary circuit) before being pumped to the rest of the body.

H A fluid derived from the blood plasma by leakage through capillaries. It bathes the tissues and is also called interstitial fluid.

7. The normal sinus rhythm of the heart is between 60 and 100 beats per minute at rest. A sinus rhythm of less than 60 BPM is called sinus bradycardia while a rhythm of over 100 BPM is called sinus tachycardia. Determine if the trace below is normal, sinus bradycardia, or sinus tachycardia and give a reason for your choice:

1.0 s

The ECG trace shows:

_____

_____

_____

_____

TEST

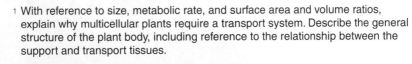

Module 3.1.3

Transport in Plants

Key terms

apoplast

cohesion-tension hypothesis

hydrophyte

phloem

potometer

pressure-flow hypothesis

root

sink

solute

source

stem

symplast

translocation

transpiration

transpiration rate

transpiration stream

vascular tissue

water potential

xerophyte

xylem

Transport tissues in plants

Learning outcomes

Activity number

☐ 1 With reference to size, metabolic rate, and surface area and volume ratios, explain why multicellular plants require a transport system. Describe the general structure of the plant body, including reference to the relationship between the support and transport tissues.

162

☐ 2 Describe the structure and function of the vascular system in the roots, stems, and leaves of herbaceous dicotyledonous plants. Describe the composition, arrangement, and role of phloem and xylem tissue.

163

☐ 3 **PAG1** Examine and draw stained sections of plant tissue to show the distribution of xylem and phloem.

164 165
166

☐ 4 **PAG2** Dissect stems longitudinally and transversely to show the position and structure of the xylem vessels.

164

  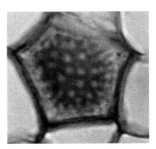

Transport processes in plants

Learning outcomes

Activity number

☐ 5 Describe the movement of water through the plant from the roots to the air. Include reference to the pathways for water movement (apoplast, symplast, vacuoles) and their relative importance.

167

☐ 6 Describe transpiration in plants as a consequence of gas exchange. Identify the environmental factors affecting the rate of transpiration and explain their effect.

168

☐ 7 Explain the transpiration stream in terms of osmosis, gradients in water potential, and the cohesion-tension hypothesis.

168

☐ 8 **PAG5** Use a potometer to estimate transpiration rates in different plants or different conditions. Interpret data from investigations of transpiration.

169

☐ 9 Describe the adaptations of plants to the availability of water in their environment, including reference to xerophytes and hydrophytes.

170 171

☐ 10 Describe translocation in plants as an energy requiring process. Explain how sucrose is transported in the phloem, including reference to the pressure-flow hypothesis and the active loading of sucrose at sources and unloading at sinks.

172

162 Plant Systems

Key Idea: The plant body is made up of two main connected systems: the root system and the shoot system.

The body of a flowering plant is composed of two distinct, but connected systems. Below the ground, the **root system** anchors the plant and absorbs water and nutrients from the soil. Above ground, the **shoot system** comprises the leaves and stems. The leaves produce sugars by photosynthesis, and the stems provide support for the leaves and reproductive structures and link the roots to the leaves. All plants rely to some extent on turgor pressure to support the tissues. For primitive plants, such as mosses and liverworts, which are small and low-growing, this turgor is sufficient to support the plant body. In vascular plants, which grow to a larger size, the vascular tissues (xylem and phloem) of the shoot and root systems have an important role in supporting the plant and moving materials around the plant body.

Shoot system

The above-ground parts of the plant: including the **leaves** (including buds, flowers, and fruit (or cones) if present) and **stems**.

Leaves

▶ Manufacture food via photosynthesis.

▶ Exchange gases with the environment.

▶ Store food and water.

Stems

▶ Transport water and nutrients between roots and leaves.

▶ Support and hold up the leaves, flowers and fruit.

▶ Produce new tissue for photosynthesis and support.

▶ Store food and water.

The shoot and root systems of plants are connected by **transport tissues** (**xylem** and **phloem**) that are continuous throughout the plant.

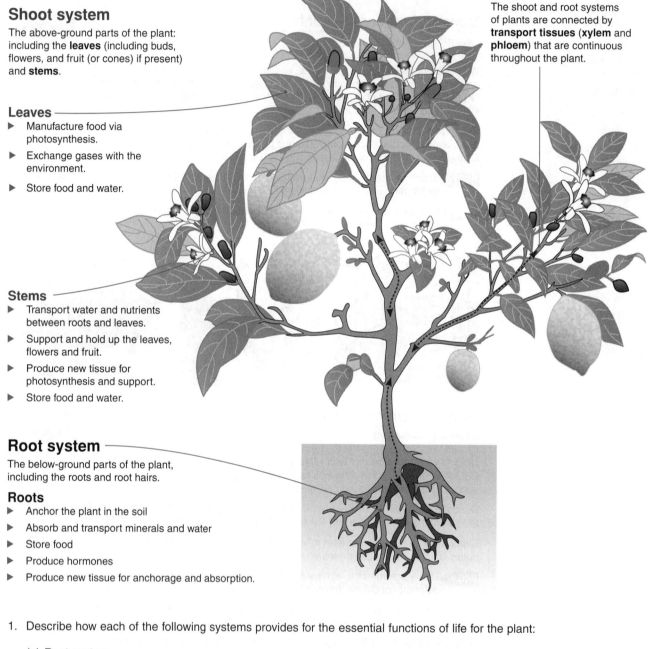

Root system

The below-ground parts of the plant, including the roots and root hairs.

Roots

▶ Anchor the plant in the soil

▶ Absorb and transport minerals and water

▶ Store food

▶ Produce hormones

▶ Produce new tissue for anchorage and absorption.

---

1. Describe how each of the following systems provides for the essential functions of life for the plant:

   (a) Root system: _____

   _____

   (b) Shoot system: _____

   _____

2. In the following list of plant functions, circle in blue the functions that are shared by the root and shoot system, circle in red those unique to the shoot system, and circle in black those unique to the root system:

   Photosynthesis, transport, absorption, anchorage, storage, sexual reproduction, growth

163 Vascular Tissue in Plants

Key Idea: The xylem and phloem form the vascular tissue that moves fluids and minerals about the plant.

The vascular tissues (**xylem** and **phloem**) link all parts of the plant so that water, minerals, and manufactured food can be transported between different regions of the plant. The xylem and phloem are found together in vascular bundles. In dicotyledonous plants (below) the vascular bundles are located in a ring towards the outer edge of the stem. In monocotyledonous plants, the bundles are scattered randomly throughout the stem. The xylem transports water and minerals from the roots to the leaves, while the phloem transports sugars through the plant to where they are needed.

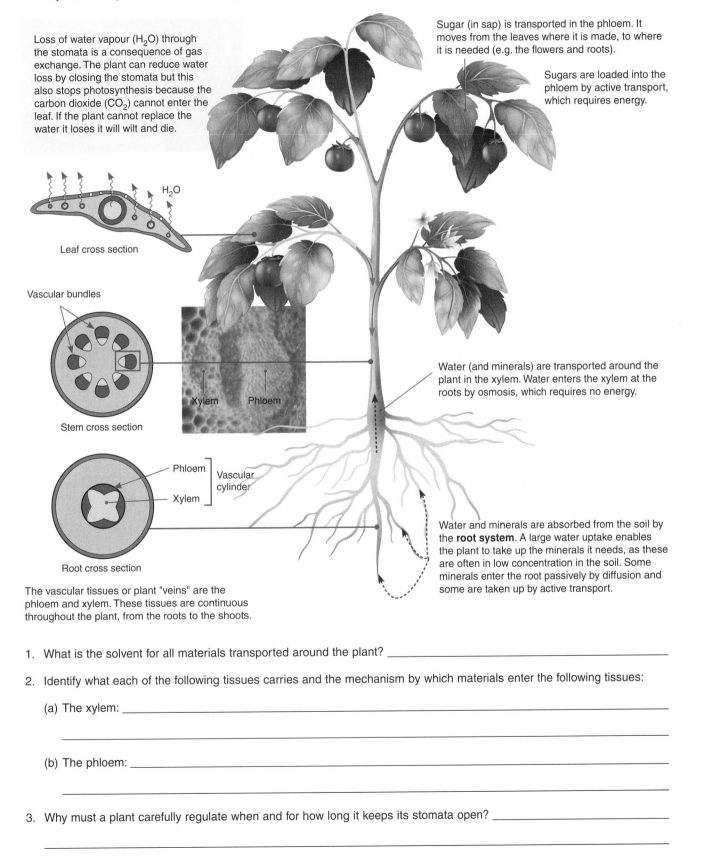

Loss of water vapour (H_2O) through the stomata is a consequence of gas exchange. The plant can reduce water loss by closing the stomata but this also stops photosynthesis because the carbon dioxide (CO_2) cannot enter the leaf. If the plant cannot replace the water it loses it will wilt and die.

Sugar (in sap) is transported in the phloem. It moves from the leaves where it is made, to where it is needed (e.g. the flowers and roots).

Sugars are loaded into the phloem by active transport, which requires energy.

H_2O

Leaf cross section

Vascular bundles

Xylem   Phloem

Stem cross section

Water (and minerals) are transported around the plant in the xylem. Water enters the xylem at the roots by osmosis, which requires no energy.

Phloem ⎤ Vascular
        ⎥ cylinder
Xylem ⎦

Root cross section

Water and minerals are absorbed from the soil by the **root system**. A large water uptake enables the plant to take up the minerals it needs, as these are often in low concentration in the soil. Some minerals enter the root passively by diffusion and some are taken up by active transport.

The vascular tissues or plant "veins" are the phloem and xylem. These tissues are continuous throughout the plant, from the roots to the shoots.

1. What is the solvent for all materials transported around the plant? _____

2. Identify what each of the following tissues carries and the mechanism by which materials enter the following tissues:

    (a) The xylem: _____

    _____

    (b) The phloem: _____

    _____

3. Why must a plant carefully regulate when and for how long it keeps its stomata open? _____

    _____

    _____

© 2015 **BIOZONE** International
ISBN: 978-1-927309-13-1
Photocopying Prohibited

LINK   LINK   WEB
165 164 163 KNOW

164 Xylem

Key Idea: The xylem is involved in water and mineral transport in vascular plants.

Xylem is the principal water conducting tissue in vascular plants. It is also involved in conducting dissolved minerals, in food storage, and in supporting the plant body. As in animals, tissues in plants are groupings of different cell types that work together for a common function. In angiosperms,

it is composed of five cell types: tracheids, vessels, xylem parenchyma, sclereids (short sclerenchyma cells), and fibres. The tracheids and vessel elements form the bulk of the tissue. They are heavily strengthened and are the conducting cells of the xylem. Parenchyma cells are involved in storage, while fibres and sclereids provide support. When mature, xylem is dead.

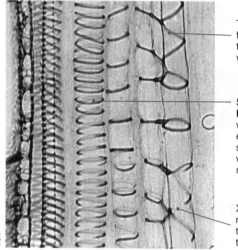

RCN

The cells of the xylem form a continuous tube through which water is conducted.

Spiral thickening of **lignin** around the walls of the vessel elements give extra strength allowing the vessels to remain rigid and upright.

Xylem is dead when mature. Note how the cells have lost their cytoplasm.

Vessel element　　　　**Tip of tracheid**

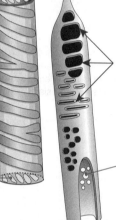

Secondary walls of cellulose are laid down after the cell has elongated or enlarged and lignin is deposited to add strength. This thickening is a feature of tracheids and vessels.

Vessels connect end to end. The end walls of the vessels are perforated to allow rapid water transport.

Pits and bordered pits allow transfer of water between cells but there are no end wall perforations.

No cytoplasm or nucleus in mature cell.

Tracheids are longer and thinner than vessels.

Vessel elements and tracheids are the two conducting cell types in xylem. Tracheids are long, tapering hollow cells. Water passes from one tracheid to another through thin regions in the wall called **pits**. Vessel elements have pits, but the end walls are also perforated and water flows unimpeded through the stacked elements.

The structure of xylem tissue

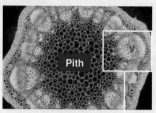

Pith

V

This cross section through a young stem of *Helianthus* (sunflower) shows the central pith, surrounded by a peripheral ring of vascular bundles (V). Note the xylem vessels with their thick walls.

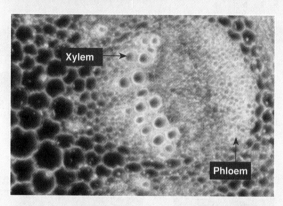

Xylem

Phloem

Mature xylem is dead

Mature xylem is dead. Its primary function is to conduct water from the roots to the leaves. This is a passive process, so there is no need for plasma membranes or transport proteins. Xylem that no longer transports water accumulates compounds such as gum and resin and is known as heartwood. In this form it is an important structural part of a mature tree.

Sapwood (transport)

Heartwood (structural)

1. (a) What is the function of **xylem**? _____

_____

(b) How can xylem be dead when mature and still carry out its function? _____

_____

2. Identify four main cell types in xylem and explain their role in the tissue:

(a) _____

(b) _____

(c) _____

(d) _____

3. Draw the structure of primary xylem from the larger image of a stem section above. Staple it to this page:

© 2015 **BIOZONE** International
ISBN: 978-1-927309-13-1
Photocopying Prohibited

165 Phloem

Key Idea: Phloem is the principal food (sugar) conducting tissue in vascular plants, transporting dissolved sugars around the plant.

Like xylem, **phloem** is a complex tissue, comprising a variable number of cell types. The bulk of phloem tissue comprises the **sieve tubes** (sieve tube members and sieve cells) and their companion cells. The sieve tubes are the principal

conducting cells in phloem and are closely associated with the **companion cells** (modified parenchyma cells) with which they share a mutually dependent relationship. Other parenchyma cells, concerned with storage, occur in phloem, and strengthening fibres and sclereids (short sclerenchyma cells) may also be present. Unlike xylem, phloem is alive when mature.

LS through a sieve tube end plate

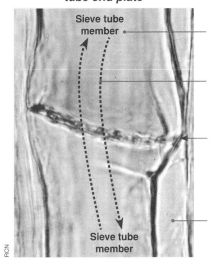

Sieve tube member

Sieve tube member

The sieve tube members lose most of their organelles but are still alive when mature

Sugar solution flows in both directions

Sieve tube end plate
Tiny holes (arrowed in the photograph below) perforate the sieve tube elements allowing the sugar solution to pass through.

Companion cell: a cell adjacent to the sieve tube member, responsible for keeping it alive

TS through a sieve tube end plate

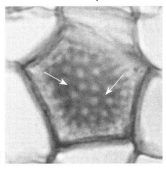

Adjacent sieve tube members are connected through **sieve plates** through which phloem sap flows.

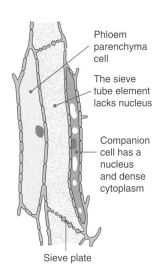

Phloem parenchyma cell

The sieve tube element lacks nucleus

Companion cell has a nucleus and dense cytoplasm

Sieve plate

The structure of phloem tissue

Phloem is alive at maturity and functions in the transport of sugars and minerals around the plant. Like xylem, it forms part of the structural vascular tissue of plants.

Fibres are associated with phloem as they are in xylem. Here they are seen in cross section where you can see the extremely thick cell walls and the way the fibres are clustered in groups. See the previous page for a view of fibres in longitudinal section.

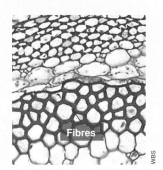

Fibres

In this cross section through a buttercup root, the smaller companion cells can be seen lying alongside the sieve tube members. It is the sieve tube members that, end on end, produce the **sieve tubes**. They are the conducting tissue of phloem.

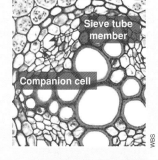

Sieve tube member

Companion cell

In this longitudinal section of a buttercup root, each sieve tube member has a thin **companion cell** associated with it. Companion cells retain their nucleus and control the metabolism of the sieve tube member next to them. They also have a role in the loading and unloading of sugar into the phloem.

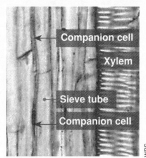

Companion cell

Xylem

Sieve tube

Companion cell

1. Describe the function of **phloem**: _____

2. Mature phloem is a live tissue, whereas xylem (the water transporting tissue) is dead when mature. Why is it necessary for phloem to be alive to be functional, whereas xylem can function as a dead tissue?

3. Describe two roles of the companion cell in phloem: _____

166 Identifying Xylem and Phloem

Key Idea: The vascular tissue in dicots can be identified by its appearance in sections viewed with a light microscope. The structure of the vascular tissue in dicotyledons (dicots) has a very regular arrangement with the xylem and phloem found close together. In the stem, the vascular tissue is distributed in a regular fashion near the outer edge of the stem. In the roots, the vascular tissue is found near the centre of the root.

Dicot stem structure

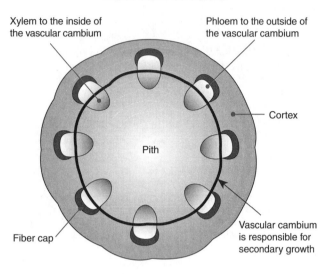

Xylem to the inside of the vascular cambium

Phloem to the outside of the vascular cambium

Cortex

Pith

Fiber cap

Vascular cambium is responsible for secondary growth

In dicots, the vascular bundles (xylem and phloem) are arranged in an orderly fashion around the stem. Each vascular bundle contains **xylem** (to the inside) and **phloem** (to the outside). Between the phloem and the xylem is the **vascular cambium**. This is a layer of cells that divide to produce the thickening of the stem.

Dicot root structure

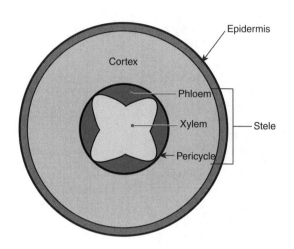

Epidermis

Cortex

Phloem

Xylem

Stele

Pericycle

In a dicot root, the vascular tissue, (xylem and phloem) forms a central cylinder through the root called the stele. The large cortex is made up of parenchyma (packing) cells, which store starch and other substances. Air spaces between the cells are essential for aeration of the root tissue, which is non-photosynthetic.

1. In the micrograph below of a dicot stem identify the phloem (P) and xylem (X) tissue:

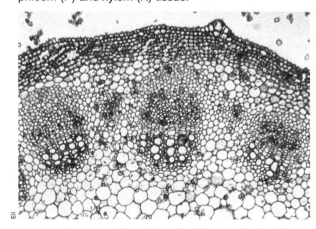

2. In the micrograph below of a dicot root identify the phloem (P) and xylem (X) tissue:

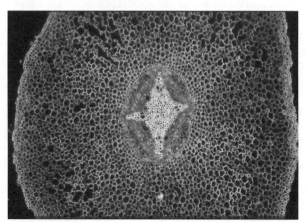

3. In the diagram below identify the labels A - F

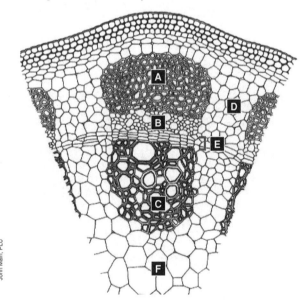

John Main, PLU

Cross section through a typical dicot stem

A. _____

B. _____

C. _____

D. _____

E. _____

F. _____

167 Uptake at the Root

Key Idea: Water uptake by the root is a passive process. Mineral uptake can be passive or active.

Plants need to take up water and minerals constantly. They must compensate for the continuous loss of water from the leaves and provide the materials the plant needs to make food. The uptake of water and minerals is mostly restricted to the younger, most recently formed cells of the roots and the root hairs. Water uptake occurs by osmosis, whereas mineral ions enter the root by diffusion and active transport. Pathways for water movements through the plant are outlined below.

Water and mineral uptake by roots

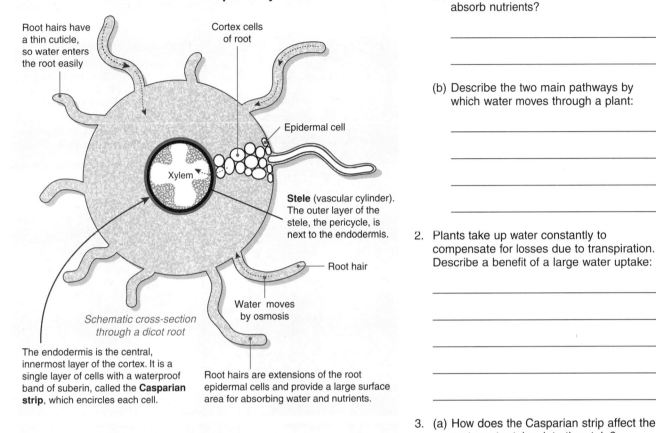

Root hairs have a thin cuticle, so water enters the root easily

Cortex cells of root

Epidermal cell

Xylem

Stele (vascular cylinder). The outer layer of the stele, the pericycle, is next to the endodermis.

Root hair

Water moves by osmosis

Schematic cross-section through a dicot root

The endodermis is the central, innermost layer of the cortex. It is a single layer of cells with a waterproof band of suberin, called the **Casparian strip**, which encircles each cell.

Root hairs are extensions of the root epidermal cells and provide a large surface area for absorbing water and nutrients.

1. (a) What two mechanisms do plants use to absorb nutrients?

_____

_____

(b) Describe the two main pathways by which water moves through a plant:

_____

_____

_____

_____

2. Plants take up water constantly to compensate for losses due to transpiration. Describe a benefit of a large water uptake:

_____

_____

_____

_____

_____

3. (a) How does the Casparian strip affect the route water takes into the stele?

_____

_____

_____

_____

(b) Why might this feature be an advantage in terms of selective mineral uptake?

_____

_____

_____

_____

_____

_____

_____

_____

_____

_____

_____

Paths for water movement through the plant

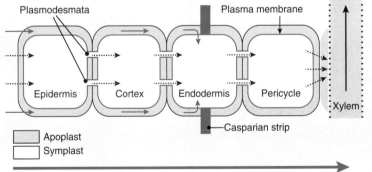

Plasmodesmata

Plasma membrane

Epidermis Cortex Endodermis Pericycle

Xylem

Casparian strip

Apoplast
Symplast

Higher water potential
May be due to fully turgid cells, higher wall pressure, or lower concentration of dissolved substances

Lower water potential
May be due to less turgid cells, lower wall pressure, or higher concentration of dissolved substances

The uptake of water through the roots occurs by osmosis, i.e. the diffusion of water from a higher (less negative) to a lower (more negative) water potential. Most water travels through the **apoplast**, i.e. the spaces within the cellulose cell walls, the water-filled spaces of dead cells, and the hollow tubes of xylem vessels. A smaller amount moves through the **symplast** (the cytoplasm of cells). A very small amount travels through the plant vacuoles.

Some dissolved mineral ions enter the root passively with water. Minerals that are in very low concentration in the soil are taken up by active transport. At the waterproof Casparian strip, water and dissolved minerals must pass into the symplast, so the flow of materials into the stele can be regulated.

168 Transpiration

Key Idea: Water moves through the xylem primarily as a result of evaporation from the leaves and the cohesive and adhesive properties of water molecules.

Plants lose water all the time through their stomata as a consequence of gas exchange. Approximately 99% of the water a plant absorbs from the soil is lost by evaporation from the leaves and stem. This loss is called **transpiration** and the flow of water through the plant is called the **transpiration**

stream. Plants rely on a gradient in water potential (ψ) from the roots to the air to move water through their cells. Water flows passively from soil to air along a gradient of decreasing water potential. The gradient is the driving force for the movement of water up a plant. Transpiration has benefits to the plant because evaporative water loss is cooling and the transpiration stream helps the plant to take up minerals. Factors contributing to water movement are described below.

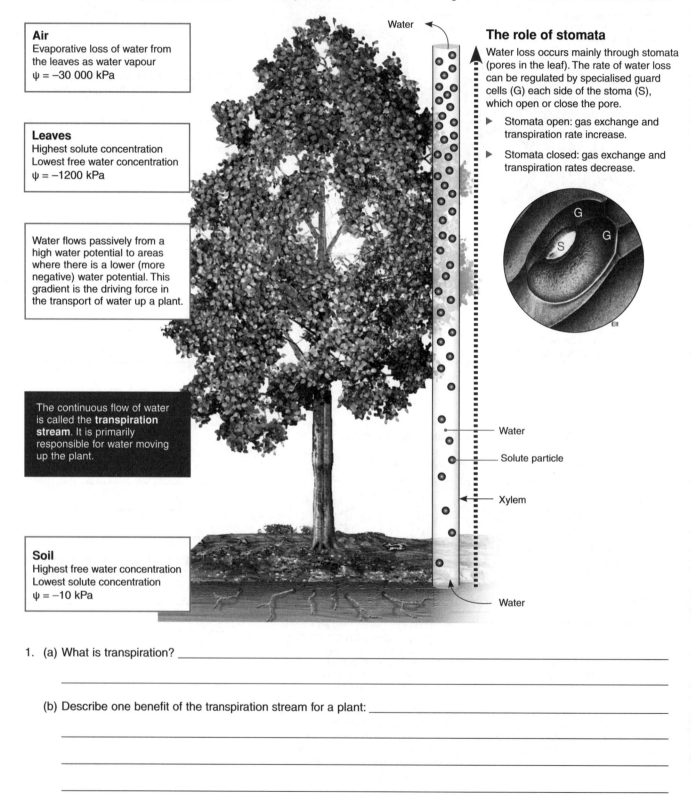

Air
Evaporative loss of water from the leaves as water vapour
ψ = −30 000 kPa

Leaves
Highest solute concentration
Lowest free water concentration
ψ = −1200 kPa

Water flows passively from a high water potential to areas where there is a lower (more negative) water potential. This gradient is the driving force in the transport of water up a plant.

The continuous flow of water is called the **transpiration stream**. It is primarily responsible for water moving up the plant.

Soil
Highest free water concentration
Lowest solute concentration
ψ = −10 kPa

Water
Solute particle
Xylem
Water
Water

The role of stomata

Water loss occurs mainly through stomata (pores in the leaf). The rate of water loss can be regulated by specialised guard cells (G) each side of the stoma (S), which open or close the pore.

▶ Stomata open: gas exchange and transpiration rate increase.

▶ Stomata closed: gas exchange and transpiration rates decrease.

1. (a) What is transpiration? _____

(b) Describe one benefit of the transpiration stream for a plant: _____

2. Why is transpiration an inevitable consequence of gas exchange? _____

Processes involved in moving water through the xylem

1 **Transpiration pull**
Water is lost from the air spaces by evaporation through stomata and is replaced by water from the mesophyll cells. The constant loss of water to the air (and production of sugars) creates a lower (more negative) water potential in the leaves than in the cells further from the evaporation site. Water is pulled through the plant down a **decreasing gradient in water potential**.

2 **Cohesion-tension**
The transpiration pull is assisted by the special **cohesive** properties of water. Water molecules cling together as they are pulled through the plant. They also **adhere** to the walls of the xylem (**adhesion**). This creates one **unbroken column of water** through the plant. The upward pull on the cohesive sap creates a tension (a negative pressure). This helps water uptake and movement up the plant.

3 **Root pressure**
Water entering the stele from the soil creates a **root pressure**; a weak 'push' effect for the water's upward movement through the plant. Root pressure can force water droplets from some small plants under certain conditions (**guttation**), but generally it plays a minor part in the ascent of water.

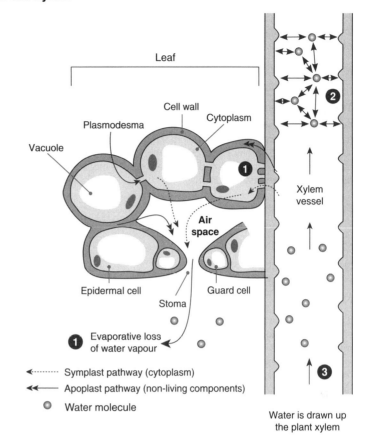

Leaf

Cell wall
Cytoplasm
Plasmodesma
Vacuole
Xylem vessel
Air space
Epidermal cell
Guard cell
Stoma

1 Evaporative loss of water vapour

⟵········· Symplast pathway (cytoplasm)
⟵⟵──── Apoplast pathway (non-living components)
◯ Water molecule

Water is drawn up the plant xylem

3. How does the plant regulate the amount of water lost from the leaves? _____

_____

4. (a) What would happen if too much water was lost from the leaves? _____

_____

(b) When might this happen? _____

5. Describe the three processes that assist the transport of water from the roots of the plant upward:

(a) _____

_____

_____

(b) _____

_____

_____

(c) _____

_____

_____

6. The maximum height water can move up the xylem by cohesion-tension alone is about 10 m. How then does water move up the height of a 40 m tall tree?

_____

_____

_____

© 2015 **BIOZONE** International
ISBN: 978-1-927309-13-1
Photocopying Prohibited

169 Investigating Plant Transpiration

Key Idea: The relationship between the rate of transpiration and the environment can be investigated using a potometer. This activity describes a typical experiment to investigate the effect of different environmental conditions on transpiration rate using a potometer. You will present and analyse the results provided.

The potometer

A potometer is a simple instrument for investigating transpiration rate (water loss per unit time). The equipment is simple to use and easy to obtain. A basic potometer, such as the one shown right, can easily be moved around so that transpiration rate can be measured under different environmental conditions.

Some physical conditions investigated are:

- Humidity or vapour pressure (high or low)
- Temperature (high or low)
- Air movement (still or windy)
- Light level (high or low)
- Water supply

It is also possible to compare the transpiration rates of plants with different adaptations e.g. comparing transpiration rates in plants with rolled leaves vs rates in plants with broad leaves. If possible, experiments like these should be conducted simultaneously using replicate equipment. If conducted sequentially, care should be taken to keep the environmental conditions the same for all plants used.

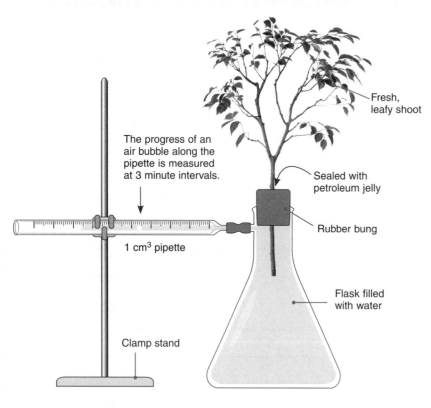

Fresh, leafy shoot

The progress of an air bubble along the pipette is measured at 3 minute intervals.

Sealed with petroleum jelly

Rubber bung

1 cm³ pipette

Flask filled with water

Clamp stand

The apparatus

This experiment investigated the influence of environmental conditions on plant transpiration rate. The experiment examined four conditions: room conditions (ambient), wind, bright light, and high humidity. After setting up the potometer, the apparatus was equilibrated for 10 minutes, and then the position of the air bubble in the pipette was recorded. This is the time 0 reading. The plant was then exposed to one of the environmental conditions. Students recorded the location of the air bubble every three minutes over a 30 minute period. The potometer readings for each environmental condition are presented in Table 1 (next page).

The aim

To investigate the effect of environmental conditions on the transpiration rate of plants.

Background

Plants lose water all the time by evaporation from the leaves and stem. This loss, mostly through pores in the leaf surfaces, is called **transpiration**. Despite the adaptations of plants to reduce water loss (e.g. waxy leaf cuticle), 99% of the water a plant absorbs from the soil is lost by evaporation. Environmental conditions affect transpiration rate by increasing or decreasing the gradient for diffusion of water molecules between the plant and its external environment.

Hypothesis

All the plants will lose water, but the greatest losses will be in hot or windy conditions.

A class was divided into four groups to study how four different environmental conditions (ambient, wind, bright light, and high humidity) affected transpiration rate. A **potometer** was used to measure transpiration rate (water loss per unit time). A basic potometer, such as the one shown left, can easily be moved around so that transpiration rate can be measured under different environmental conditions.

© 2015 **BIOZONE** International
ISBN: 978-1-927309-13-1
Photocopying Prohibited

Table 1. Potometer readings in cm³ water loss

Treatment \ Time / min	0	3	6	9	12	15	18	21	24	27	30
Ambient	0	0.002	0.005	0.008	0.012	0.017	0.022	0.028	0.032	0.036	0.042
Wind	0	0.025	0.054	0.088	0.112	0.142	0.175	0.208	0.246	0.283	0.325
High humidity	0	0.002	0.004	0.006	0.008	0.011	0.014	0.018	0.019	0.021	0.024
Bright light	0	0.021	0.042	0.070	0.091	0.112	0.141	0.158	0.183	0.218	0.239

1. (a) Plot the potometer data from Table 1 on the grid provided:

   (b) Identify the independent variable: _____

2. (a) Identify the control: _____

   (b) Explain the purpose of including an experimental control in an experiment: _____

   _____

   _____

   (c) Which factors increased water loss? _____

   (d) How does each environmental factor influence water loss? _____

   _____

   _____

   (e) Explain why the plant lost less water in humid conditions: _____

   _____

   _____

   _____

170 Adaptations of Xerophytes

Key Idea: Xerophytes are plants adapted for conserving water in dry (arid) conditions.

Plants adapted to dry conditions are called **xerophytes** and they show structural (xeromorphic) and physiological adaptations for water conservation. These include small,

hard leaves, an epidermis with a thick cuticle, sunken stomata, succulence (ability to store water), and absence of leaves. Salt tolerant plants (halophytes) and alpine plants may also show xeromorphic features due to the lack of free water and high evaporative losses in these environments.

Adaptations in cacti

Desert plants, such as cacti (below), must cope with low or sporadic rainfall and high transpiration rates.

Leaves modified into spines or hairs to reduce water loss. Light coloured spines reflect solar radiation.

Rounded shape reduces surface area.

Stem becomes the major photosynthetic organ, plus a reservoir for water storage.

The surface tissues of many cacti are tolerant of temperatures in excess of 50°C.

Cacti have a shallow, but extensive fibrous root system. When in the ground the roots are spread out around the plant.

Leaf adaptations

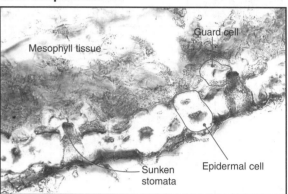

Above is a section through the edge of a pine needle at 400X magnification. Pines show xeromorphic characteristics in their leaves including sunken stomata. The stomata are often found in grooves along the needle which helps to reduce water loss.

1. Redraw the image from a slide (top) in the box above. Include labels and draw the mesophyll tissue in plan view. Use the magnification to produce a scale.

Other xeromorphic plants reduce water loss by covering their surface with fine hairs, reducing air movement, and trapping moisture near the leaf. Some, such as acacias (above left), have deep root systems that enable them to access water from lower water tables. Adaptations such as waxy leaves also reduce water loss and, in many desert plants, germination is triggered only by a certain quantity of rainfall.

Methods of water conservation

Adaptation for water conservation	Effect of adaptation	Example
Thick, waxy cuticle to stems and leaves	Reduces water loss through the cuticle.	*Pinus* sp. ivy (*Hedera*), sea holly (*Eryngium*), prickly pear (*Opuntia*).
Reduced number of stomata	Fewer pores through which water is lost.	Prickly pear (*Opuntia*), *Nerium* sp.
Stomata sunken in pits, grooves, or depressions. Leaf surface covered with fine hairs. Massing of leaves into a rosette at ground level.	Moist air is trapped close to the area of water loss, reducing the diffusion gradient and therefore the rate of water loss.	**Sunken stomata**: *Pinus* sp., *Hakea* sp. **Hairy leaves**: lamb's ear. **Leaf rosettes**: dandelion (*Taraxacum*), daisy.
Stomata closed during the light, open at night	CAM metabolism: CO_2 is fixed during the night, water loss in the day is minimised.	**CAM plants**, e.g. American aloe, pineapple, *Kalanchoe, Yucca*.
Leaves reduced to scales, stem photosynthetic Leaves curled, rolled, or folded when flaccid	Reduction in surface area from which transpiration can occur.	**Leaf scales**: broom (*Cytisus*). **Rolled leaf**: marram (*Ammophila*), *Erica* sp.
Fleshy or succulent stems Fleshy or succulent leaves	When readily available, water is stored in the tissues for times of low availability.	**Fleshy stems**: *Opuntia*, candle plant (*Kleinia*). **Fleshy leaves**: *Bryophyllum*.
Deep root system below the water table	Roots tap into the lower water table.	Acacias, oleander.
Shallow root system absorbing surface moisture	Roots absorb overnight condensation.	Most cacti.

© 2015 **BIOZONE** International ISBN: 978-1-927309-13-1 Photocopying Prohibited

Adaptations in halophytes and drought tolerant plants

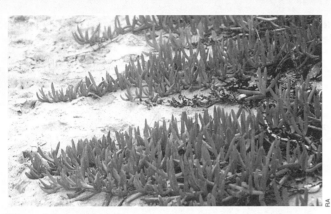

Ice plant (*Carpobrotus*): The leaves of many desert and beach dwelling plants are fleshy or succulent. The leaves are triangular in cross section and crammed with water storage cells. The water is stored after rain for use in dry periods. The shallow root system is able to take up water from the soil surface, taking advantage of any overnight condensation.

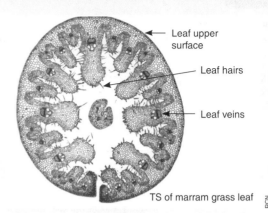

TS of marram grass leaf

Leaf upper surface
Leaf hairs
Leaf veins

Marram grass (*Ammophila*): The long, wiry leaf blades of this beach grass are curled downwards with the stomata on the inside. This protects them against drying out by providing a moist microclimate around the stomata. Plants adapted to high altitude often have similar adaptations.

Ball cactus (*Echinocactus grusonii*): In many cacti, the leaves are modified into long, thin spines which project outward from the thick fleshy stem. This reduces the surface area over which water loss can occur. The stem stores water and takes over as the photosynthetic organ. As in succulents, a shallow root system enables rapid uptake of surface water.

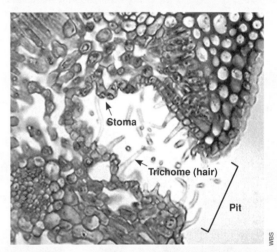

Stoma
Trichome (hair)
Pit

Oleander is a xerophyte from the Mediterranean region with many water conserving features. It has a thick multi-layered epidermis and the stomata are sunken in trichome-filled pits on the leaf underside. The pits restrict water loss to a greater extent than they reduce uptake of carbon dioxide.

2. Explain the purpose of **xeromorphic** adaptations: _____

_____

3. Describe three xeromorphic adaptations of plants:

(a) _____

(b) _____

(c) _____

4. Describe a physiological mechanism by which plants can reduce water loss during the daylight hours: _____

_____

_____

5. Explain why creating a moist microenvironment around the areas of water loss reduces transpiration rate: _____

_____

6. Explain why seashore plants (halophytes) exhibit many desert-dwelling adaptations: _____

_____

_____

171 Adaptations of Hydrophytes

Key Idea: Hydrophytes are adapted to living in water. They require little structural support tissue and have few adaptations to reduce water loss, although they have some special adaptations to facilitate gas exchange.

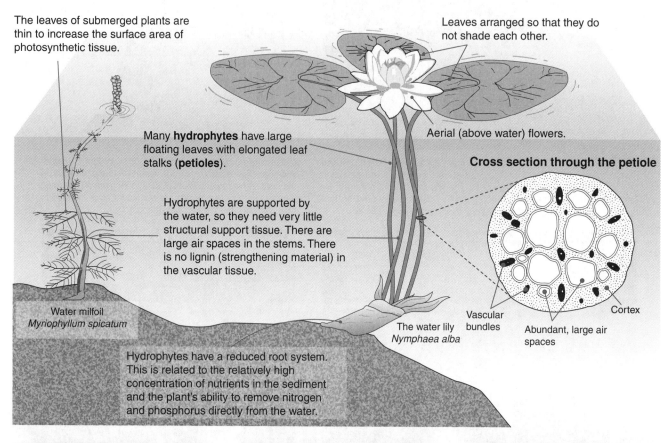

The leaves of submerged plants are thin to increase the surface area of photosynthetic tissue.

Leaves arranged so that they do not shade each other.

Many **hydrophytes** have large floating leaves with elongated leaf stalks (**petioles**).

Aerial (above water) flowers.

Cross section through the petiole

Hydrophytes are supported by the water, so they need very little structural support tissue. There are large air spaces in the stems. There is no lignin (strengthening material) in the vascular tissue.

Water milfoil
Myriophyllum spicatum

The water lily
Nymphaea alba

Vascular bundles

Cortex

Abundant, large air spaces

Hydrophytes have a reduced root system. This is related to the relatively high concentration of nutrients in the sediment and the plant's ability to remove nitrogen and phosphorus directly from the water.

Stephen Moore

Myriophyllum's submerged leaves are well spaced and taper to the surface to help with gas exchange and distribution of sunlight.

The floating leaves of water lilies (*Nymphaea*) have a high density of stomata on the upper leaf surface so they are not blocked by water.

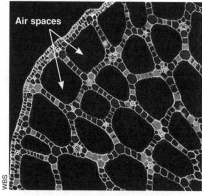

Air spaces

WBS

Cross section through *Potamogeton*, showing large air spaces which assist with flotation and gas exchange.

1. Explain how the following adaptations assist hydrophytes to survive in an aquatic environment:

    (a) Large air spaces within the plants tissues: _____

    _____

    (b) Thin cuticle: _____

    _____

    (c) High stomatal densities on the upper leaf surface: _____

    _____

2. Why do hydrophytic plants retain an aerial (above water) flowering system? _____

    _____

© 2015 **BIOZONE** International
ISBN: 978-1-927309-13-1
Photocopying Prohibited

172 Translocation

Key Idea: Phloem transports the organic products of photosynthesis (sugars) through the plant in an active, energy-requiring process called translocation.

In angiosperms, the sugar moves through the sieve-tube members, which are arranged end-to-end and perforated with sieve plates. Apart from water, phloem sap comprises mainly sucrose. It may also contain minerals, hormones, and amino acids, in transit around the plant. Movement of sap in the phloem is from a **source** (a plant organ where sugar is made or mobilised) to a **sink** (a plant organ where sugar is stored or used). Loading sucrose into the phloem at a source involves energy expenditure; it is slowed or stopped by high temperatures or respiratory inhibitors. In some plants, unloading the sucrose at the sinks also requires energy, although in others, diffusion alone is sufficient to move sucrose from the phloem into the cells of the sink organ.

Phloem transport

Phloem sap moves from source to sink at rates as great as 100 m h^{-1}, which is too fast to be accounted for by cytoplasmic streaming. The most acceptable model for phloem movement is the **pressure-flow** (bulk flow) hypothesis. Phloem sap moves by bulk flow, which creates a pressure (hence the term "pressure-flow"). The key elements in this model are outlined below and right. Note that, for simplicity, the cells that lie between the source (and sink) cells and the phloem sieve-tube have been omitted.

1 Loading sugar into the phloem from a source (e.g. leaf cell) increases the solute concentration (decreases the water potential, ψ) inside the sieve-tube cells. This causes the sieve-tubes to take up water from the surrounding tissues by osmosis.

2 The water uptake creates a hydrostatic pressure that forces the sap to move along the tube, just as pressure pushes water through a hose.

3 The pressure gradient in the sieve tube is reinforced by the active unloading of sugar and consequent loss of water by osmosis at the sink (e.g. root cell).

4 Xylem recycles the water from sink to source.

Measuring phloem flow

Experiments investigating flow of phloem often use aphids. Aphids feed on phloem sap (left) and act as natural **phloem probes**. When the mouthparts (stylet) of an aphid penetrate a sieve-tube cell, the pressure in the sieve-tube force-feeds the aphid. While the aphid feeds, it can be severed from its stylet, which remains in place in the phloem. The stylet serves as a tiny tap that exudes sap. Using different aphids, the rate of flow of this sap can be measured at different locations on the plant.

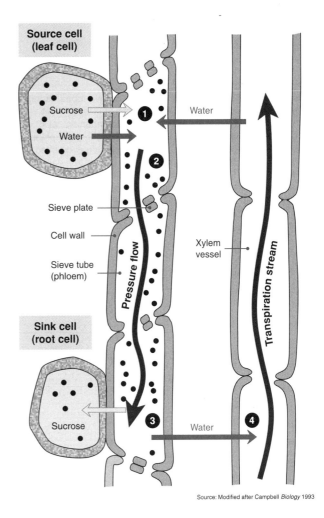

Source: Modified after Campbell *Biology* 1993

1. (a) From what you know about osmosis, explain why water follows the sugar as it moves through the phloem:

_____

_____

_____

_____

(b) What is meant by '**source to sink**' flow in phloem transport?_____

_____

_____

2. Why does a plant need to move food around, particularly from the leaves to other regions? _____

_____

_____

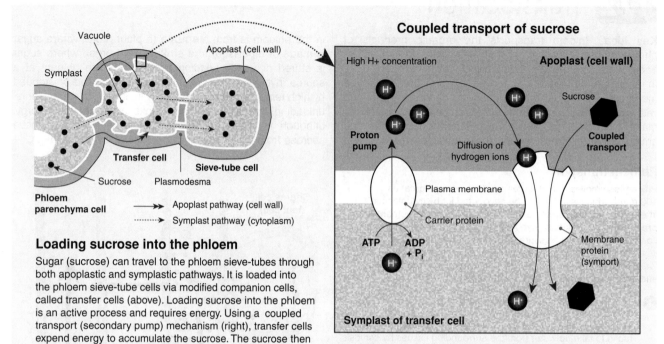

Loading sucrose into the phloem

Sugar (sucrose) can travel to the phloem sieve-tubes through both apoplastic and symplastic pathways. It is loaded into the phloem sieve-tube cells via modified companion cells, called transfer cells (above). Loading sucrose into the phloem is an active process and requires energy. Using a coupled transport (secondary pump) mechanism (right), transfer cells expend energy to accumulate the sucrose. The sucrose then passes into the sieve tube through plasmodesmata. The transfer cells have wall ingrowths that increase surface area for the transport of solutes. Using this mechanism, some plants can accumulate sucrose in the phloem to 2-3 times the concentration in the mesophyll.

Above: Proton pumps generate a hydrogen ion gradient across the membrane of the transfer cell. This process requires expenditure of energy. The gradient is then used to drive the transport of sucrose, by coupling the sucrose transport to the diffusion of hydrogen ions back into the cell.

3. In your own words, describe what is meant by the following:

(a) Translocation: _____

_____

(b) Pressure-flow movement of phloem: _____

_____

(c) Coupled transport of sucrose: _____

_____

4. Briefly explain how sucrose is transported into the phloem: _____

_____

_____

5. Explain the role of the companion (transfer) cell in the loading of sucrose into the phloem: _____

_____

_____

_____

_____

6. The sieve plate represents a significant barrier to effective mass flow of phloem sap. Suggest why the presence of the sieve plate is often cited as evidence against the pressure-flow model for phloem transport:

_____

_____

_____

_____

_____

173 Chapter Review

Summarise what you know about this topic under the headings provided. You can draw diagrams or mind maps, or write short notes to organise your thoughts. Use the images and hints included to help you:

Transport in the plant
HINT: Describe how water moves through the xylem and how sugars are transported in the phloem.

Vascular tissue
HINT: Describe the structure of vascular bundles and the structure of the phloem and xylem.

Plant adaptations
HINT: Describe the adaptations of xerophytes and hydrophytes.

REVISE

174 KEY TERMS: Did You Get It?

1. (a) What is the name given to the loss of water vapour from plant leaves and stems? _Transpiration_

   (b) What plant tissue is involved in this process? _____

   (c) Is this tissue alive or dead? _____

   (d) Does this process require energy? _____

2.

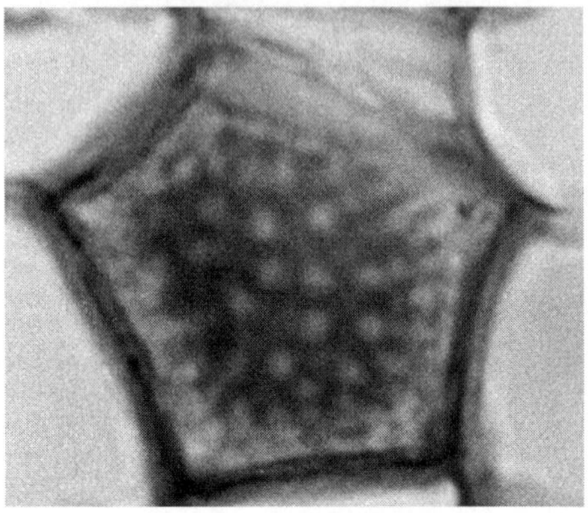

   (a) What does the image (left) show: _____

   (b) In what tissue would you find it? _____

   (c) Is this tissue alive or dead? _____

   (d) What transport process is it associated with? _____

   _____

   (e) What is being moved in this process? _____

   _____

3. The graph below right shows the transpiration rate for the plant *Opuntia ficus-indica*.

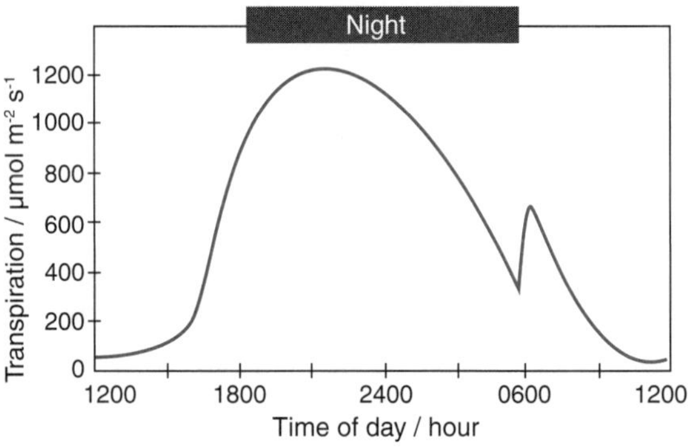

   (a) Which time of the day/night does the plant transpire the most?

   _____

   (b) Which time of the day/night does the plant transpire the least?

   _____

   (c) What kind of environment does this plant live in? Justify your answer:

   _____

   _____

   _____

   (d) Use your answer to (c) to explain why the plant transpires most when it does: _____

   _____

   _____

   _____

   (e) Explain why transpiration rate increases slightly at 0600 hours: _____

   _____

   _____

4. Match each term to its definition, as identified by its preceding letter code.

   phloem _____

   potometer ____C____

   stomata _____

   transpiration _____

   xylem _____

   A The loss of water vapour by plants, mainly from leaves via the stomata.

   B Tissue that conducts dissolved sugars in vascular plants. Comprises mostly sieve tubes and companion cells.

   C Device used for investigating the rate of transpiration.

   D Vascular tissue that conducts water and mineral salts from the roots to the rest of the plant. Dead in its functional state.

   E Pores in the leaf surface through which gases (including water vapour) can pass.

© 2015 **BIOZONE** International
ISBN: 978-1-927309-13-1
Photocopying Prohibited

TEST

Disease and the Immune System

Key terms

active immunity

antibody (=immunoglobulin)

antigen

autoimmune disease

B cell (=B lymphocyte)

bacteria

cell-mediated immunity

clonal selection

cytokines

fungi

humoral immunity

immunity

immunological memory

infection

inflammation

leucocyte

lymphocyte

macrophage

MHC

monoclonal antibody

non-specific defences (=innate immunity)

opsonins

passive immunity

pathogen

phagocyte

primary response

protoctistans

resistance

secondary response

specific (=adaptive) immune response

T cell (=T lymphocyte)

vaccination

viruses

Types and transmission of pathogens

Learning outcomes

☐ 1 Describe the range of pathogens in plants and animals and give examples of the communicable diseases that they cause. Include reference to bacteria, viruses, protoctistans, and fungi.

Activity number: 175-177

☐ 2 Explain how plant and animal pathogens are transmitted between hosts, including by direct and indirect transmission. Using examples, explain the role of vectors, spores, climate, and social factors (e.g. living conditions) in the transmission of some communicable diseases.

Activity number: 175-177

 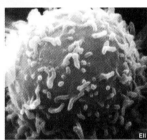 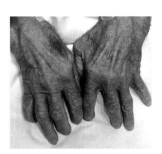

Defence mechanisms in plants

Learning outcomes

☐ 3 Describe the defence mechanisms of plants, including active and passive defences (e.g. physical and chemical barriers, cellular defences, and responses that limit the spread of the pathogen, such as the deposition of callose).

Activity number: 178

Defence mechanisms in animals

Learning outcomes

☐ 4 Describe non-specific (innate) defences against pathogens in animals. Describe the nature and role of the first (a) and second (b) lines of defence:
(a) Skin, mucous membranes, body secretions, expulsive reflexes.
(b) Inflammation, blood clotting and wound repair, the action of phagocytes, and the role of natural anti-microbial proteins (cytokines and opsonins).

Activity number: 179-183

☐ 5 **PAG1** Examine and draw cells observed in blood smears.

Activity number: 25 182

☐ 6 Describe the structure and roles of B and T lymphocytes in the specific immune response. Describe clonal selection and the basis of immunological memory.

Activity number: 183 184

☐ 7 Describe the structure and role of antibodies, outlining the action of opsonins, agglutinins, and anti-toxins in the antibody action.

Activity number: 185

☐ 8 Using examples, distinguish between naturally acquired and artificially acquired immunity and between active and passive immunity. Distinguish the primary and secondary immune responses.

Activity number: 186

☐ 9 Describe the basis of autoimmune diseases, e.g. lupus and rheumatoid arthritis.

Activity number: 187

☐ 10 Explain the basis of vaccination and the role of vaccination in public health programmes and the prevention of epidemics.

Activity number: 188

Controlling disease

Learning outcomes

☐ 11 Describe sources and potential applications of new medicines, including personalised medicines and synthetic drugs.

Activity number: 189

☐ 12 Describe the benefits and risks of antibiotic use. Include reference to the early discovery and use of antibiotics and the current rise in antibiotic resistance.

Activity number: 190

175 Infection and Disease

Key Idea: Pathogens are infectious agents that spread between hosts and cause disease.

Pathogens are disease-causing organisms. The goal of a pathogen is to multiply and spread between hosts before it is detected and disabled by the host's immune system.

Many pathogens have highly effective modes of transmission and so are highly infectious. Transmission and spread of a pathogen depends on its rate of growth, the density of the host population, the mobility of the host population, and the mode of transmission.

Types of pathogen

Bacterial pathogens

All **bacteria** are prokaryotes but only some cause disease. Pathogenic bacteria cause disease by their **invasiveness** and their ability to produce **toxins**, either during growth or released when the cell ruptures. Bacteria attach to mucous membranes with threadlike extensions called **fimbriae** allowing direct contact with the host's tissues, producing chemicals (**invasins**) to break down connective tissue and promote bacterial invasion. The capsules and cell walls of bacteria increase virulence. For example, the lipopolysaccharide (LPS) component of gram negative cells, such as *Neisseria*, acts as an endotoxin, causing symptoms of the disease but also alerting the host to invasion.

Protozoan pathogens

Protozoans are single celled eukaryotes that show animal-like behaviours. Those that are pathogens are specialised obligate parasites and usually alternate between proliferative stages (e.g. trophozoites) and dormant cysts, which enable survival outside the host. Serious diseases caused by protozoan infections include **malaria** (caused by the parasitic protozoan *Plasmodium*) and amoebic dysentery. The life cycle may be very complex, involving more than one host, with infection transmitted between hosts by a vector (e.g. a mosquito) or ingestion of contaminated food or water. For example, *Plasmodium* parasitises cause changes in red blood cells, evading the host's immune system for many cycles of multiplication.

Fungal pathogens

Very few **fungi** are pathogenic to animals. They spread by **spores** and the infections they cause are generally chronic (long-lasting) infections because fungi grow relatively slowly. Infection by fungi can occur when fungi or spores come in contact with damaged host material (e.g. a cut) or when the fungi is able to incubate in a warm moist environment without removal (e.g. failure to dry between toes before putting on socks and shoes).

Viral pathogens

Viruses are obligate intracellular parasites and need living host cells in order to multiply. Viruses gain entry to cells by matching proteins on their surface with receptors on the surface of specific host cells. The virus then commands the host's cellular machinery (for replication and protein synthesis) to replicate more viral particles. Retroviruses, such as HIV (right) replicate in the host cell through reverse transcription and are also able to integrate into the host's genome, remaining as latent infections and spreading as cells divide. HIV infects the host's own defensive T-lymphocytes, so is highly successful at weakening and destroying the host's defence capability.

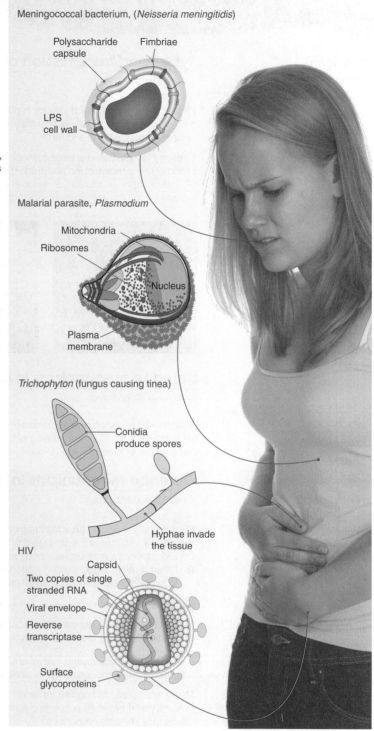

Meningococcal bacterium, (*Neisseria meningitidis*)
- Polysaccharide capsule
- Fimbriae
- LPS cell wall

Malarial parasite, *Plasmodium*
- Mitochondria
- Ribosomes
- Nucleus
- Plasma membrane

Trichophyton (fungus causing tinea)
- Conidia produce spores
- Hyphae invade the tissue

HIV
- Capsid
- Two copies of single stranded RNA
- Viral envelope
- Reverse transcriptase
- Surface glycoproteins

1. Describe one feature of each of the following pathogens that contributes to its ability to infect a host:

   (a) Bacterium: _They can produce toxins_

   (b) Protozoan parasite: _Cause changes in red blood cells_

   (c) Virus: _They infect the host's own defensive T-lymphocytes_

   (d) Fungus: _Spores grow and infect the host_

© 2015 **BIOZONE** International
ISBN: 978-1-927309-13-1
Photocopying Prohibited

Transmission and spread

Once inside the body, most pathogens multiply rapidly, producing symptoms and making the host infectious within a few days. Others take longer to present symptoms. The infectious period can last from a few days to weeks, but in some cases the host may be infectious for long periods of time.

Human cities can contain millions of people, often living very closely together. In these congested conditions, infectious diseases can spread rapidly, especially if sanitation or personal hygiene is poor, or if seasonal weather produces conditions favourable to spread of the pathogen. High speed transport can help spread a pathogen around a region very quickly.

The mode of transmission affects how quickly a pathogen spreads. Direct person to person contact (i.e. touching) is a slower method of spreading, whereas spreading via mucus droplets coughed into the air or by animal vectors can help a pathogen spread quickly and widely.

Portals of entry

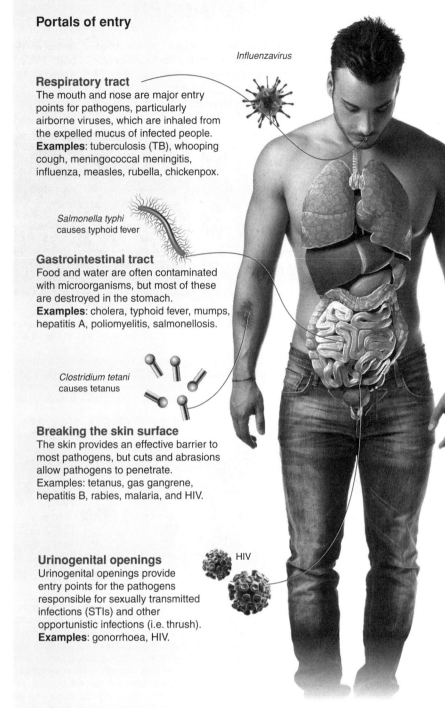

Influenzavirus

Respiratory tract
The mouth and nose are major entry points for pathogens, particularly airborne viruses, which are inhaled from the expelled mucus of infected people.
Examples: tuberculosis (TB), whooping cough, meningococcal meningitis, influenza, measles, rubella, chickenpox.

Salmonella typhi causes typhoid fever

Gastrointestinal tract
Food and water are often contaminated with microorganisms, but most of these are destroyed in the stomach.
Examples: cholera, typhoid fever, mumps, hepatitis A, poliomyelitis, salmonellosis.

Clostridium tetani causes tetanus

Breaking the skin surface
The skin provides an effective barrier to most pathogens, but cuts and abrasions allow pathogens to penetrate.
Examples: tetanus, gas gangrene, hepatitis B, rabies, malaria, and HIV.

HIV

Urinogenital openings
Urinogenital openings provide entry points for the pathogens responsible for sexually transmitted infections (STIs) and other opportunistic infections (i.e. thrush).
Examples: gonorrhoea, HIV.

---

2. Why can disease spread quickly in congested human cities? _Disease is spread by droplets (coughing, sneezing) and when people are in close proximity the droplets can be spread easily_

3. Why would transmission by direct touch be slower than transmission by coughing or sneezing? _____

_____

4. Identify a hygiene practise that would minimise the risk of transmitting a pathogen that invades via the respiratory tract:
Sneeze into a tissue and wash hands

176 Animal Pathogens

Key Idea: Pathogens are specialised to infect specific types of animals and have numerous strategies to infect their hosts. All animals can be infected by pathogens, although different species are susceptible to different pathogens. A number of pathogens can be transmitted between species. Humans have around 1500 known pathogens, of which almost two thirds spread from other animals (zoonoses). For instance, both rabies and Lyme disease can be transmitted from animals to humans. Of course pathogens also spread between humans, e.g. influenza and meningitis. Diseases caused by pathogens that can be passed on are called **infectious diseases** or **communicable diseases**.

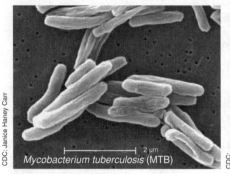
Mycobacterium tuberculosis (MTB) 2 µm

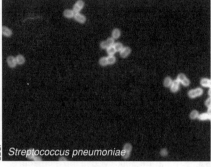
Streptococcus pneumoniae

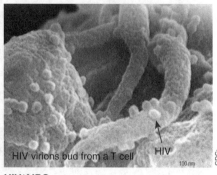
HIV virions bud from a T cell HIV 100 nm

Pulmonary tuberculosis
TB is an infectious bacterial disease caused by *Mycobacterium tuberculosis* (MTB). The pathogen is spread through the air when infectious people cough, sneeze, talk, or spit. MTB can enter a dormant phase in infected people, evading immune detection as a latent infection before becoming active again.

Bacterial meningitis
Bacterial meningitis is most commonly caused by the bacterial pathogens *Neisseria meningitidis* and *Streptococcus pneumoniae* (above). The bacteria infect the membranes (meninges) around the brain causing headaches, fever, rashes and sometimes death. The fatality rate is between 10%-20%.

HIV/AIDS
HIV (Human Immunodeficiency Virus) is a retrovirus that infects lymphocytes called T helper cells. Over time, the immune system loses its ability to fight infections as more T helper cells are destroyed. The disease that develops is called AIDS and is the result of complete immune system failure.

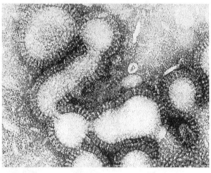

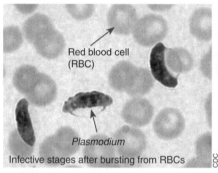
Red blood cell (RBC)
Plasmodium
Infective stages after bursting from RBCs

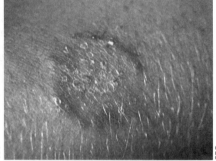

Influenza (the flu)
Influenzavirus, which causes the flu, occurs in seasonal epidemics, infecting around five million people globally and causing the death of up to 500 000 people annually. High mutation rates in the virus produce continual changes to the viral surface proteins. Each season, hosts will encounter new strains so the virus evades immediate immune system detection. New vaccines must be produced each year to counter the new strains.

Malaria
Malaria is a disease caused by protozoan parasites called plasmodia. Plasmodia have a life cycle involving two hosts, *Anopheles* mosquitoes and humans. Humans (the secondary host) become infected when bitten by infected mosquitoes (the vector for the disease). Infection has two phases, the first involving sexual reproduction in the liver cells and the second involving cycles of asexual reproduction within the red blood cells.

Ringworm
A common fungal pathogen of the skin in animals, including humans, is the genera *Trichophyton* which causes ringworm and athlete's foot. The ringworm fungus is spread by skin to skin contact, whereas athlete's foot is spread by spores produced by asexual reproduction and released from conidia. Fungal infections are slow-growing chronic infections making them relatively mild in most cases, but often difficult to treat.

1. (a) How does the *Plasmodium* parasite enter the body? _from Anopheles mosquitoes_

   (b) What is the significance of the cycle occurring in the host's RBCs: _____

   _____

2. HIV infection begins a long disease process with latent (non-symptomatic) periods and a slow destruction of the host's immune system. What features of HIV's biology make it such a successful pathogen?

   _____

   _____

3. (a) How is the *influenzavirus* able to evade the host's immune system? _____

   _____

   (b) What is the consequence of this to public health programmes? _____

   _____

© 2015 **BIOZONE** International
ISBN: 978-1-927309-13-1
Photocopying Prohibited

177 Plant Pathogens

Key Idea: Plants pathogens include fungi, bacteria, protozoa and some multicellular organisms such as nematodes.

Plants, like animals, suffer from disease. As well as being susceptible to single pathogens, plants also suffer from **disease complexes**. These occur when several microbial species act at one infection site at the same time. Sometimes two or more bacterial species, bacteria and insects, or bacteria and fungi, combine to produce a more damaging disease than would be produced by one agent alone. Arthropods may also act as vectors for the transmission of pathogens between plants. After a plant has been damaged by bacterial or fungal infection, saprophytic (decomposer) organisms usually follow closely and contribute to the decomposition of the dead or damaged tissue.

Viruses

A number of infectious plant diseases are the result of viral infection. Economically important plants that are affected include tobacco, potato, sugar beet, peach, elm, and orange. Symptoms include: stunted growth, colour change, malformations of leaves, or tissue death (wilt and necrosis). Viral infections are spread by direct contact of diseased with healthy plants (e.g. during cropping) or via vectors such as sap-sucking leafhoppers. Example: TMV (below) is spread by contact.

Tobacco Mosaic Virus - TMV

Bacteria

Over 150 bacterial species cause diseases in plants. These diseases are categorised broadly as galls, wilts, lesions, and soft rots. Examples include: *Clavibacter michiganensis* which causes ring rot in potatoes and *Agrobacterium tumefaciens* which causes crown gall disease in a variety of dicot plants. Bacterial pathogens generally invade plant tissues though damaged tissue.

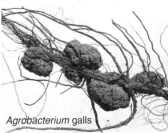
Agrobacterium galls

Fungi

All economically important plants are affected by fungal diseases, with many affected by a dozen or more, e.g. black sigatoka or black streak disease (caused by *Mycosphaerella fijiensis*) produces black streaks and death of leaf tissue on banana plant leaves. It can eventually reduce crop yield by 50%. Fungal diseases are spread by spores, which germinate in warm, humid conditions.

Black sigatoka on banana

Fred Brooks, University of Hawaii cc 3.0

Protoctista

Potato blight (late blight) is caused by the oomycete (water mould) parasite *Phytophthora infestans*. The motile spores of *Phytophthora* spread by wind or water in wet, warm, or humid conditions. Short-lived asexual spores can spread rapidly from host plants, whereas the sexual spores are long-lived and can remain viable for years. Potato blight causes damage to both the leaves and tubers of potatoes and can also infect tomato plants.

Potato blight

1. What is the difference between a disease and a disease complex: _____

_____

2. Fungi cause many plant diseases. What is the economic importance of controlling these diseases?

_____

_____

3. Describe briefly how each of the following plant diseases or pathogens is transmitted between plants:

    (a) Tobacco Mosaic Virus: _____

    (b) *Phytopthera* late blight: _____

    (c) Crown gall disease: _____

    (d) Black sigatoka: _____

LINK WEB
178 177 KNOW

178 Plant Defences

Key Idea: Plants possess biochemical and structural defence mechanisms, which protect them from infection and the activities of herbivorous animals that feed off them.

Some defence mechanisms are always present as part of the plant's basic make-up, while others are activated in response to an attack. **Passive defences** take the form of physical and chemical barriers. **Active defences** are produced in direct response to an infection or physical attack and act more specifically against the threat. Some plants produce chemicals that inhibit the growth others nearby (**allelopathy**).

Passive defences

Passive defences are always present and are not the result of contact with pathogens (e.g. fungi) or grazers (e.g. herbivorous mammals or insects). Passive defences may be **physical** or **chemical**. Various physical barriers help to prevent pathogens from penetrating the plant tissues. Despite these barriers, some pathogens may still gain entry into the host. If this occurs, chemical defences or more active cellular defence mechanisms (right) are used to protect the plant against further damage.

Examples of physical barriers

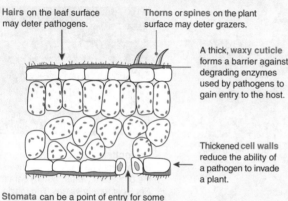

Hairs on the leaf surface may deter pathogens.

Thorns or spines on the plant surface may deter grazers.

A thick, waxy cuticle forms a barrier against degrading enzymes used by pathogens to gain entry to the host.

Thickened cell walls reduce the ability of a pathogen to invade a plant.

Stomata can be a point of entry for some pathogens. Plants may use hairs to guard these openings, or the stomata may be small enough to exclude some larger pathogens.

Examples of chemical barriers

Plants can cover their surfaces with compounds that inhibit the development of pathogens.

Many plants have developed distasteful chemicals as a defence to deter insects and other grazers.

Bracken (*Pteridium aquilinum*) contains hormones that disrupt the development of insect predators.

Bracken also contains a powerful carcinogen that is toxic to livestock when eaten.

Active defences

Once infected, a plant needs to respond actively to prevent any further damage. **Active defences** are invoked only after the **pathogen** has been recognised, or after wounding or attack by a herbivore. Many plant defences contribute to slowing pathogen growth without necessarily stopping it.

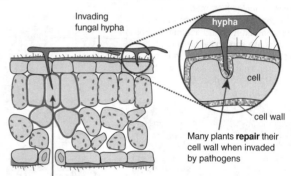

Invading fungal hypha

hypha

cell

cell wall

Many plants **repair** their cell wall when invaded by pathogens

Many plants produce an enzyme-activated **hypersensitive response** when invaded by pathogens. This leads to the production of reactive nitric oxide and cell death. Cell death in the infected region limits the spread of the pathogen.

Other cellular active defences

Phytoalexins	Antimicrobial substances that destroy a range of pathogens, e.g. by puncturing the cell wall or disrupting metabolism.
Reactive oxygen levels	An increase in reactive oxygen species (e.g. H_2O_2) in cells kills pathogens.
Wound repair	Infected areas are sealed off by layers of thickened cells called **cork cells**.

Sealing off infected areas gives rise to abnormal swellings called galls (oak gall, above left; bulls-eye galls on a maple leaf, above right). These galls limit the spread of the parasite or the infection in the plant.

1. Distinguish between **passive** and **active** defence mechanisms: _____

_____

_____

2. How are **galls** effective in reducing the spread of infection in some plants? _____

_____

3. What similarities are there between the active defence mechanisms of plants and the immune responses of animals?

_____

_____

179 The Body's Defences

Key Idea: The human body has a tiered system of defences against disease-causing organisms.

The body has several lines of defence against disease causing organisms (**pathogens**). The first line of defence consists of an external barrier to stop pathogens entering the body. If this fails, a second line of defence targets any foreign bodies (including pathogens) that enter. Lastly, the immune system provides specific or targeted defence against the pathogen. The ability to ward off disease through the various defence mechanisms is called **resistance**. **Non-specific** (or innate) **resistance** protects against a broad range of pathogens and is provided by the first and second lines of defence. **Specific resistance** (the immune response) is the third tier of defence and is specific to a particular pathogen. Part of the immune response involves the production of **antibodies** (proteins that identify and neutralise foreign material). Antibodies recognise and respond to **antigens**, foreign or harmful substances that cause an immune response.

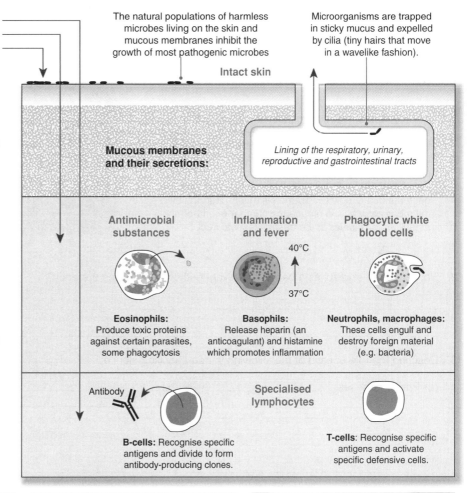

Most microorganisms find it difficult to get inside the body. If they succeed, they face a range of other defences.

The natural populations of harmless microbes living on the skin and mucous membranes inhibit the growth of most pathogenic microbes

Microorganisms are trapped in sticky mucus and expelled by cilia (tiny hairs that move in a wavelike fashion).

Intact skin

Mucous membranes and their secretions:

Lining of the respiratory, urinary, reproductive and gastrointestinal tracts

Antimicrobial substances

Inflammation and fever
40°C
37°C

Phagocytic white blood cells

Eosinophils:
Produce toxic proteins against certain parasites, some phagocytosis

Basophils:
Release heparin (an anticoagulant) and histamine which promotes inflammation

Neutrophils, macrophages:
These cells engulf and destroy foreign material (e.g. bacteria)

Antibody

Specialised lymphocytes

B-cells: Recognise specific antigens and divide to form antibody-producing clones.

T-cells: Recognise specific antigens and activate specific defensive cells.

1st Line of defence

The skin provides a physical barrier to the entry of pathogens. Healthy skin is rarely penetrated by microorganisms. Its low pH is unfavourable to the growth of many bacteria and its chemical secretions (e.g. sebum, antimicrobial peptides) inhibit growth of bacteria and fungi. Tears, mucus, and saliva also help to wash bacteria away.

2nd Line of defence

A range of defence mechanisms operate inside the body to inhibit or destroy pathogens. These responses react to the presence of any pathogen, regardless of which species it is. White blood cells are involved in most of these responses.

It includes the **complement system** whereby plasma proteins work together to bind pathogens and induce an inflammatory responses to help fight infection.

3rd Line of defence

Once the pathogen has been identified by the immune system, **lymphocytes** launch a range of specific responses to the pathogen, including the production of **antibodies**. Each type of antibody is produced by a B cell clone and is specific against a particular antigen.

Tears contain antimicrobial substances as well as washing contaminants from the eyes.

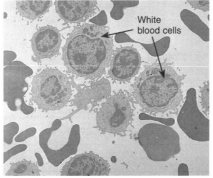

White blood cells

A range of white blood cells (arrowed above) form the second line of defence.

Coughing

Expulsive reflexes such as coughing and vomiting help remove pathogens from the body.

1. Distinguish between specific and non-specific resistance: _____

_____

_____

_____

_____

The importance of the first line of defence

The skin is the largest organ of the body. It forms an important physical barrier against the entry of pathogens into the body. A natural population of harmless microbes live on the skin, but most other microbes find the skin inhospitable. The continual shedding of old skin cells (arrow, right) physically removes bacteria from the surface of the skin. Sebaceous glands in the skin (top right) produce sebum, which has antimicrobial properties, and the slightly acidic secretions of sweat inhibit microbial growth.

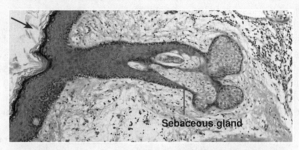

Sebaceous gland

Cilia line the epithelium of the **nasal passage** (below right). Their wave-like movement sweeps foreign material out and keeps the passage free of microorganisms, preventing them from colonising the body.

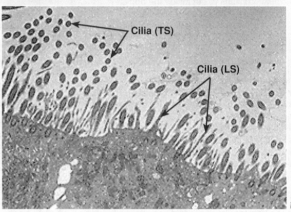

Cilia (TS)

Cilia (LS)

Antimicrobial chemicals are present in many bodily secretions. Tears, saliva, nasal secretions, and human breast milk all contain **lysozymes** and **phospholipases**. Lysozymes kill bacterial cells by catalysing the hydrolysis of cell wall linkages, whereas phospholipases hydrolyse the phospholipids in bacterial cell membranes, causing bacterial death. Low pH gastric secretions also inhibit microbial growth, and reduce the number of pathogens establishing colonies in the gastrointestinal tract.

2. How does the skin act as a barrier to prevent pathogens entering the body? _____

_____

_____

3. Describe the role of each of the following in non-specific defence:

(a) Phospholipases: _____

_____

(b) Cilia: _____

_____

(c) Sebum: _____

_____

4. Describe the functional role of each of the following defence mechanisms:

(a) Phagocytosis by white blood cells: _____

_____

(b) Antimicrobial substances: _____

_____

(c) Antibody production: _____

_____

5. Explain the value of a three tiered system of defence against microbial invasion: _____

_____

_____

_____

© 2015 **BIOZONE** International
ISBN: 978-1-927309-13-1
Photocopying Prohibited

180 Blood Clotting and Defence

Key Idea: Blood clotting restricts blood loss from a torn blood vessel, and prevents pathogens entering the wound.

Blood has a role in the body's defence against infection. Tearing or puncturing of a blood vessel initiates **blood clotting** through a cascade effect involving platelets, clotting factors, and plasma proteins (below). Clotting quickly seals off the tear, preventing blood loss and the invasion of bacteria into the site. Clot formation is triggered by the release of clotting factors from the damaged cells at the site of the damage. A hardened clot forms a scab, which acts to prevent further blood loss and acts as a mechanical barrier to the entry of pathogens.

Blood clotting

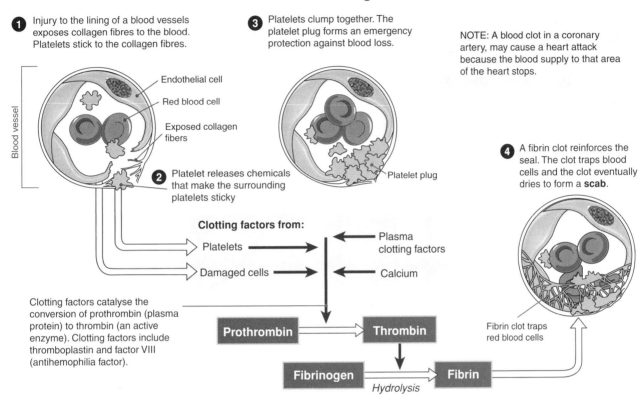

1 Injury to the lining of a blood vessels exposes collagen fibres to the blood. Platelets stick to the collagen fibres.

- Endothelial cell
- Red blood cell
- Exposed collagen fibers

Blood vessel

2 Platelet releases chemicals that make the surrounding platelets sticky

3 Platelets clump together. The platelet plug forms an emergency protection against blood loss.

- Platelet plug

NOTE: A blood clot in a coronary artery, may cause a heart attack because the blood supply to that area of the heart stops.

4 A fibrin clot reinforces the seal. The clot traps blood cells and the clot eventually dries to form a **scab**.

Fibrin clot traps red blood cells

Clotting factors from:

Platelets ⟶ ⟵ Plasma clotting factors

Damaged cells ⟶ ⟵ Calcium

Clotting factors catalyse the conversion of prothrombin (plasma protein) to thrombin (an active enzyme). Clotting factors include thromboplastin and factor VIII (antihemophilia factor).

Prothrombin ⟹ **Thrombin**

Fibrinogen ⟹ **Fibrin**

Hydrolysis

---

1. What role does blood clotting have in internal defence? _____

_____

2. Explain the role of each of the following in the sequence of events leading to a blood clot:

   (a) Injury: _____

   _____

   (b) Release of chemicals from platelets: _____

   _____

   (c) Clumping of platelets at the wound site: _____

   _____

   (d) Formation of a fibrin clot: _____

   _____

3. (a) What is the role of clotting factors in the blood in formation of the clot? _____

   _____

   (b) Why are these clotting factors not normally present in the plasma? _____

   _____

LINK   LINK   WEB
144 **93** **180**   KNOW

181 Inflammation

Key Idea: Inflammation is a type of non-specific resistance in response to harmful stimuli, such as pathogens.

Damage to the body's tissues (e.g. by sharp objects, heat, or microbial infection) triggers a defensive response called **inflammation**. It is usually characterised by four symptoms: pain, redness, heat, and swelling. The inflammatory response is beneficial and has the following functions: (1) to destroy the cause of the infection and remove it and its products from the body; (2) if this fails, to limit the effects on the body by confining the infection to a small area; (3) replacing or repairing tissue damaged by the infection. Inflammation can be divided into three distinct phases, shown below.

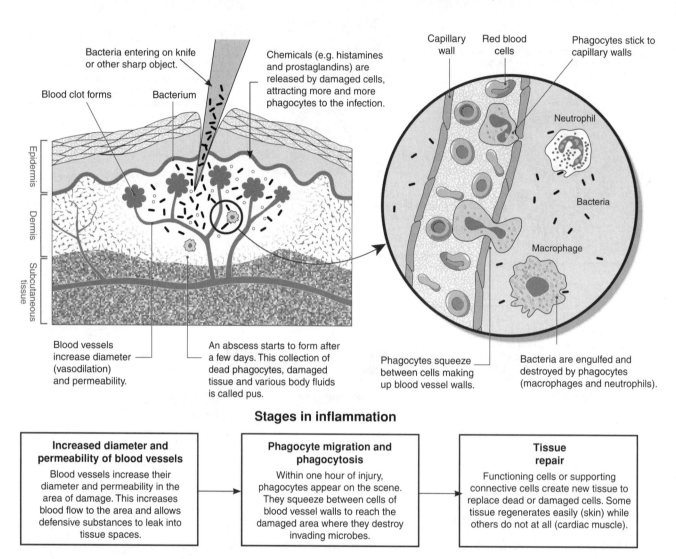

Bacteria entering on knife or other sharp object.

Blood clot forms

Bacterium

Chemicals (e.g. histamines and prostaglandins) are released by damaged cells, attracting more and more phagocytes to the infection.

Capillary wall

Red blood cells

Phagocytes stick to capillary walls

Neutrophil

Bacteria

Macrophage

Epidermis

Dermis

Subcutaneous tissue

Blood vessels increase diameter (vasodilation) and permeability.

An abscess starts to form after a few days. This collection of dead phagocytes, damaged tissue and various body fluids is called pus.

Phagocytes squeeze between cells making up blood vessel walls.

Bacteria are engulfed and destroyed by phagocytes (macrophages and neutrophils).

Stages in inflammation

Increased diameter and permeability of blood vessels	**Phagocyte migration and phagocytosis**	**Tissue repair**
Blood vessels increase their diameter and permeability in the area of damage. This increases blood flow to the area and allows defensive substances to leak into tissue spaces.	Within one hour of injury, phagocytes appear on the scene. They squeeze between cells of blood vessel walls to reach the damaged area where they destroy invading microbes.	Functioning cells or supporting connective cells create new tissue to replace dead or damaged cells. Some tissue regenerates easily (skin) while others do not at all (cardiac muscle).

1. Outline the three stages of inflammation and identify the beneficial role of each stage:

   (a) _____

   _____

   (b) _____

   _____

   (c) _____

   _____

2. Identify two features of phagocytes important in the response to microbial invasion: _____

   _____

3. What is the role of histamines and prostaglandins in inflammation? _____

4. Why does pus form at the site of infection? _____

   _____

© 2015 **BIOZONE** International
ISBN: 978-1-927309-13-1
Photocopying Prohibited

182 The Action of Phagocytes

Key Idea: Phagocytes are types of mobile white blood cells that ingest microbes and digest them by phagocytosis.
All types of **phagocytes** (e.g. neutrophils and macrophages) are white blood cells. These specialised cells have receptors on their surfaces that can detect foreign or antigenic material, such as microbes. They then ingest the microbes and digest them by **phagocytosis.** During many kinds of infections, the total number of white blood cells increases by two to four times the normal number. The ratio of various white blood cell types changes during the course of an infection.

How a phagocyte destroys microbes

1 Detection and interaction
Microbe coated in opsonins is detected by the phagocyte and attaches to it. Opsonins are molecules in the blood and coat foreign material (e.g. a bacterial cell), marking it as a target for phagocytosis.

2 Engulfment
The opsonin markers trigger engulfment of the microbe by the phagocyte. The microbe is taken in by endocytosis.

3 Phagosome forms
A phagosome forms, enclosing the microbe in a membrane.

4 Fusion with lysosome
Phagosome fuses with a lysosome containing powerful antimicrobial proteins. The fusion forms a phagolysosome.

5 Digestion
The microbe is broken down into its chemical constituents.

6 Discharge
Indigestible material is discharged from the phagocyte.

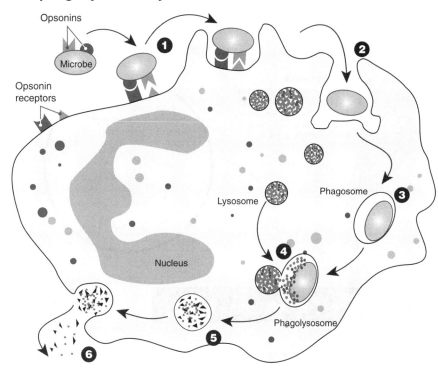

Neutrophils

Neutrophils, named for their neutral staining cytoplasm, are the most abundant type of white blood cell, constituting up to three-quarters of all white blood cells. Neutrophils are one of four types of granulocytes, distinguished by the granular appearance of the cytoplasm and their lobed nucleus.

When activated, neutrophils become highly mobile and amoeboid-like. They are some of the first immune cells to arrive at an infection site, attracted by microbial chemicals and by **cytokines** (proteins involved in cell signalling) expressed by macrophages and damaged endothelial cells. This movement to a site based on a gradient in chemical signals is called **chemotaxis**.

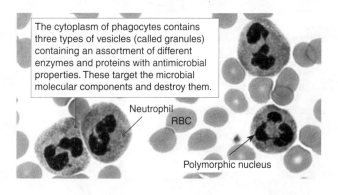

The cytoplasm of phagocytes contains three types of vesicles (called granules) containing an assortment of different enzymes and proteins with antimicrobial properties. These target the microbial molecular components and destroy them.

1. Identify the most common type of phagocytic white blood cell: _Neutrophils_

2. What is the role of chemotaxis in the body's response to infection? _____

3. How can a blood sample be used to diagnose a microbial infection (without looking for the microbes themselves)?

4. Explain the role of opsonins and phagocyte receptors in enhancing phagocytosis: _____

183 The Immune System

Key Idea: Antigens, such as the cell walls of microbial cells, presented on the surface of macrophages help activate cells of the immune system against specific foreign bodies.

There are two main components of the immune system: the humoral and the cell-mediated responses. They work separately and together to protect against disease. The **humoral immune response** is associated with the serum (the non-cellular part of the blood) and involves the action of antibodies secreted by B cell lymphocytes. Antibodies are

found in extracellular fluids including lymph, plasma, and mucus secretions and protect against viruses, and bacteria and their toxins. The **cell-mediated immune response** is associated with the production of specialised lymphocytes called **T cells**. Antigens are recognised by T cells only after antigen processing. The antigen is first engulfed by a macrophage, which processes the antigen and presents it on its surface. T helper cells can then recognise the antigen and activate other cells of the immune system.

Lymphocytes and their functions

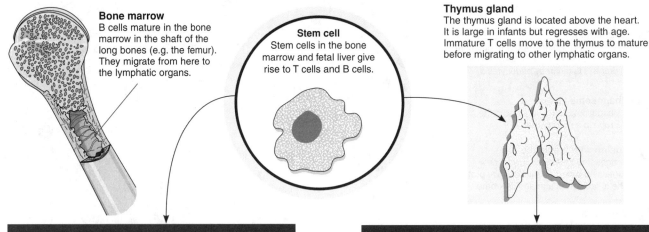

Bone marrow
B cells mature in the bone marrow in the shaft of the long bones (e.g. the femur). They migrate from here to the lymphatic organs.

Stem cell
Stem cells in the bone marrow and fetal liver give rise to T cells and B cells.

Thymus gland
The thymus gland is located above the heart. It is large in infants but regresses with age. Immature T cells move to the thymus to mature before migrating to other lymphatic organs.

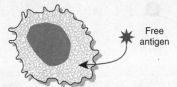

B cell

Free antigen

B cells recognise and bind antigens. Each B cell recognises one specific antigen. Helper T cells recognise specific antigens on B cell surfaces and induce their maturation and proliferation. A mature B cell may carry as many as 100 000 antigenic receptors embedded in its surface membrane. B cells defend against bacteria and viruses outside the cell and toxins produced by bacteria (free antigens).

Differentiate into two kinds of cells

Antibody

Memory cells

Some B cells differentiate into long-lived memory cells (see Clonal Selection, over page). When these cells encounter the same antigen again (even years or decades later), they rapidly differentiate into antibody-producing plasma cells.

Plasma cells

When stimulated by an antigen (see Clonal Selection Theory, over page), some B cells differentiate into plasma cells, which secrete antibodies into the blood system. The antibodies then inactivate the circulating antigens.

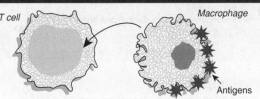

T cell

T cell   Macrophage

Antigens

T cells respond only to antigen fragments that have been processed and presented by infected cells or macrophages (phagocytic cells) (see opposite). They defend against:
- Intracellular bacteria and viruses
- Protozoa, fungi, flatworms, and roundworms
- Cancerous cells and transplanted foreign tissue

Differentiate into various kinds of cells:

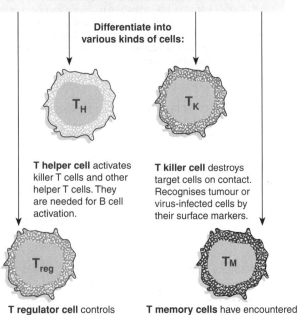

T_H

T_K

T helper cell activates killer T cells and other helper T cells. They are needed for B cell activation.

T killer cell destroys target cells on contact. Recognises tumour or virus-infected cells by their surface markers.

T_{reg}

T_M

T regulator cell controls immune response by turning it off when no more antigen is present.

T memory cells have encountered specific antigens before and can respond quickly and strongly when the antigen is encountered again.

© 2015 **BIOZONE** International
ISBN: 978-1-927309-13-1
Photocopying Prohibited

B cell and T cell activation

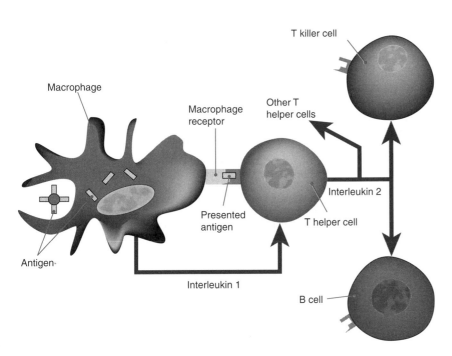

T killer cell

Macrophage

Macrophage receptor

Other T helper cells

Presented antigen

Interleukin 2

T helper cell

Antigen

Interleukin 1

B cell

T helper cells are activated by direct cell-to-cell signalling and by signalling to nearby cells using **cytokines** (including interleukins) from macrophages.

Macrophages ingest antigens, process them, and present them on the cell surface where they are recognised by T helper cells. The T helper cell binds to the antigen and to the macrophage receptor, which leads to activation of the T helper cell.

The macrophage also produces and releases interleukin 1, which enhances T cell activation. The activated T cell then releases interleukin 2 which causes the proliferation of other helper T cells (positive feedback) and helps to activate T killer cells and antibody-producing B cells.

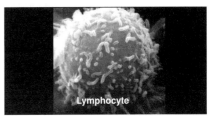

Lymphocyte

1. Where do B cells and T cells originate (before maturing)?_____

2. (a) Where do B cells mature?_____ (b) Where do T cells mature?_____

3. Describe the nature and general action of the two major divisions in the immune system:

   (a) Humoral immune system:_____

   _____

   _____

   (b) Cell-mediated immune system: _____

   _____

   _____

4. Explain how an antigen causes the activation and proliferation of T cells and B cells: _____

   _____

   _____

   _____

   _____

5. Describe the function of each of the following cells in the immune system response:

   (a) T helper cells: _____

   _____

   (b) T killer cells: _____

   _____

   (c) T regulator cells: _____

   _____

   (d) T memory cells: _____

   _____

184 Clonal Selection

Key Idea: Clonal selection theory explains how lymphocytes can respond to a large and unpredictable range of antigens. The **clonal selection theory** explains how the immune system can respond to the large and unpredictable range of potential antigens in the environment. The diagram below describes clonal selection after antigen exposure for B cells. In the same way, a T cell stimulated by a specific antigen will multiply and develop into different types of T cells. Clonal selection and differentiation of lymphocytes provide the basis for **immunological memory.**

Five (a-e) of the many B cells generated during development. Each one can recognise only one specific antigen.

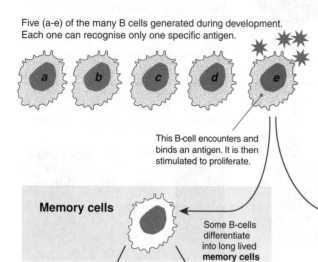

This B-cell encounters and binds an antigen. It is then stimulated to proliferate.

Clonal selection theory

Millions of B cells form during development. Antigen recognition is randomly generated, so collectively they can recognise many antigens, including those that have never been encountered. Each B cell has receptors on its surface for specific antigens and produces antibodies that correspond to these receptors. When a B cell encounters its antigen, it responds by proliferating and producing many clones that produce the same kind of antibody. This is called clonal selection because the antigen selects the B cells that will proliferate.

Memory cells

Some B-cells differentiate into long lived **memory cells**

Some B-cells differentiate into **plasma cells**

Plasma cells

The antibody produced corresponds to the antigenic receptors on the cell surface.

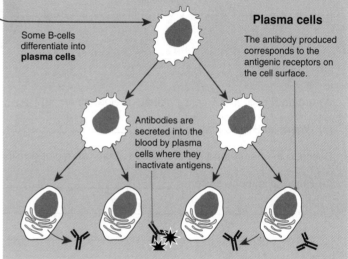

Antibodies are secreted into the blood by plasma cells where they inactivate antigens.

Some B cells differentiate into long lived **memory cells**. These are retained in the lymph nodes to provide future immunity (**immunological memory**). In the event of a second infection, memory B cells react more quickly and vigorously than the initial B cell reaction to the first infection.

Plasma cells secrete antibodies specific to the antigen that stimulated their development. Each plasma cell lives for only a few days, but can produce about 2000 antibody molecules per second. Note that during development, any B cells that react to the body's own antigens are selectively destroyed in a process that leads to **self tolerance** (acceptance of the body's own tissues).

1. Describe how clonal selection results in the proliferation of one particular B cell:

_____

_____

_____

2. (a) What is the function of the plasma cells in the immune system response? _____

_____

(b) What is the significance of B cells producing antibodies that correspond to (match) their antigenic receptors?

_____

_____

3. (a) Explain the basis of **immunological memory**: _____

_____

_____

(b) Why are memory B cells able to respond so rapidly to an encounter with an antigen long after an initial infection?

_____

© 2015 **BIOZONE** International
ISBN: 978-1-927309-13-1
Photocopying Prohibited

185 Antibodies

Key Idea: Antibodies are large, Y-shaped proteins, made by plasma cells, which destroy specific antigens.

Antibodies and antigens play key roles in the response of the immune system. **Antigens** are foreign molecules which promote a specific immune response. Antigens include pathogenic microbes and their toxins, as well as substances such as pollen grains, blood cell surface molecules, and the surface proteins on transplanted tissues. **Antibodies** (or immunoglobulins) are proteins made in response to antigens. They are secreted from B cells into the plasma where they can recognise, bind to, and help destroy antigens. There are five classes of antibodies, each plays a different role in the immune response. Each type of antibody is specific to only one particular antigen.

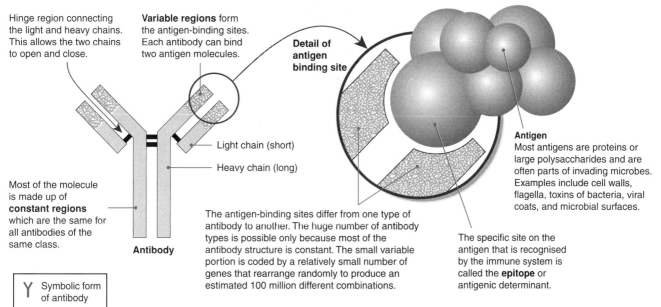

Hinge region connecting the light and heavy chains. This allows the two chains to open and close.

Variable regions form the antigen-binding sites. Each antibody can bind two antigen molecules.

Detail of antigen binding site

Light chain (short)

Heavy chain (long)

Most of the molecule is made up of **constant regions** which are the same for all antibodies of the same class.

Antibody

Y Symbolic form of antibody

The antigen-binding sites differ from one type of antibody to another. The huge number of antibody types is possible only because most of the antibody structure is constant. The small variable portion is coded by a relatively small number of genes that rearrange randomly to produce an estimated 100 million different combinations.

Antigen
Most antigens are proteins or large polysaccharides and are often parts of invading microbes. Examples include cell walls, flagella, toxins of bacteria, viral coats, and microbial surfaces.

The specific site on the antigen that is recognised by the immune system is called the **epitope** or antigenic determinant.

How antibodies inactivate antigens

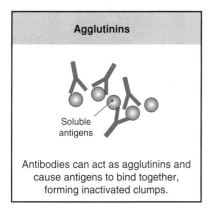

Agglutinins

Soluble antigens

Antibodies can act as agglutinins and cause antigens to bind together, forming inactivated clumps.

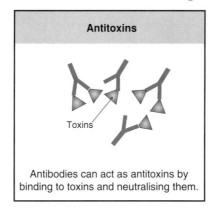

Antitoxins

Toxins

Antibodies can act as antitoxins by binding to toxins and neutralising them.

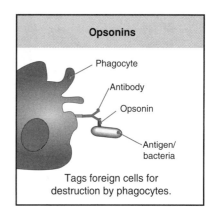

Opsonins

Phagocyte

Antibody

Opsonin

Antigen/ bacteria

Tags foreign cells for destruction by phagocytes.

1. Describe the structure of an antibody, identifying the specific features of its structure that contribute to its function:

_____

_____

_____

2. Explain how the following actions by antibodies enhance the immune systems ability to stop infections:

(a) Acting as agglutinins: _____

_____

(b) Acting as antitoxins: _____

_____

(c) Working with opsonins: _____

_____

186 Acquired Immunity

Key Idea: Acquired immunity is a resistance to specific pathogens acquired over the life-time of an organism.
We are born with natural or **innate resistance** which provides non-specific immunity to certain illnesses. In contrast, **acquired immunity** is protection developed over time to specific antigens. **Active immunity** develops after the immune system responds to being exposed to microbes or foreign substances. **Passive immunity** is acquired when antibodies are transferred from one person to another. Immunity may also be naturally acquired, through natural exposure to microbes, or artificially acquired as a result of medical treatment (below).

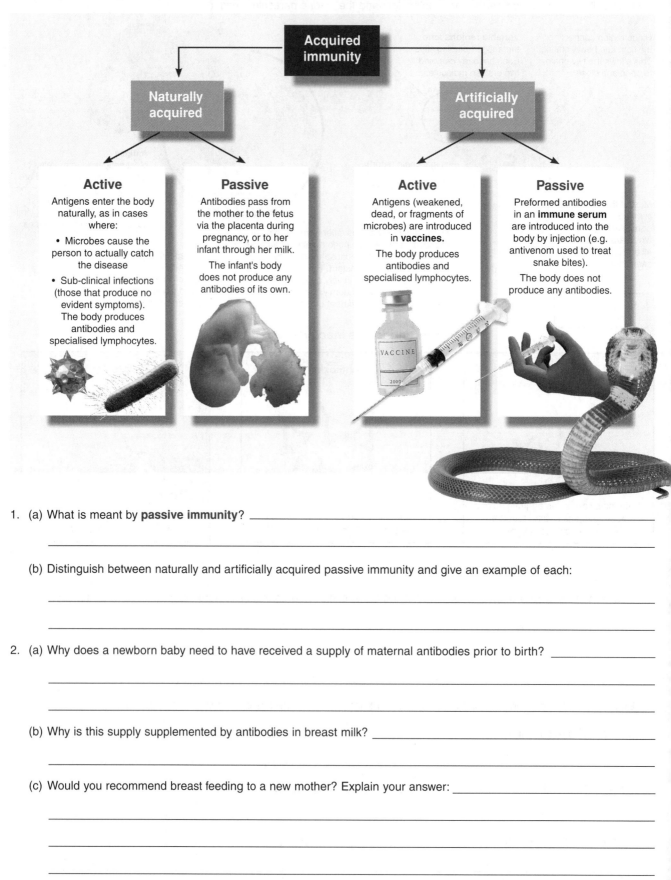

Acquired immunity

Naturally acquired

Artificially acquired

Active

Antigens enter the body naturally, as in cases where:

• Microbes cause the person to actually catch the disease

• Sub-clinical infections (those that produce no evident symptoms). The body produces antibodies and specialised lymphocytes.

Passive

Antibodies pass from the mother to the fetus via the placenta during pregnancy, or to her infant through her milk.

The infant's body does not produce any antibodies of its own.

Active

Antigens (weakened, dead, or fragments of microbes) are introduced in **vaccines.**

The body produces antibodies and specialised lymphocytes.

Passive

Preformed antibodies in an **immune serum** are introduced into the body by injection (e.g. antivenom used to treat snake bites).

The body does not produce any antibodies.

1. (a) What is meant by **passive immunity**? _____

_____

(b) Distinguish between naturally and artificially acquired passive immunity and give an example of each:

_____

_____

2. (a) Why does a newborn baby need to have received a supply of maternal antibodies prior to birth? _____

_____

_____

(b) Why is this supply supplemented by antibodies in breast milk? _____

_____

(c) Would you recommend breast feeding to a new mother? Explain your answer: _____

_____

_____

_____

© 2015 **BIOZONE** International
ISBN: 978-1-927309-13-1
Photocopying Prohibited

Primary and secondary responses to antigens

When the B cells encounter antigens and produce antibodies, the body develops **active immunity** against that antigen.

The initial response to antigenic stimulation, caused by the sudden increase in B cell clones, is called the **primary response**. Antibody levels as a result of the primary response peak a few weeks after the response begins and then decline. However, because the immune system develops an immunological memory of that antigen, it responds much more quickly and strongly when presented with the same antigen subsequently (the **secondary response**).

This forms the basis of immunisation programmes where one or more booster shots are provided following the initial vaccination.

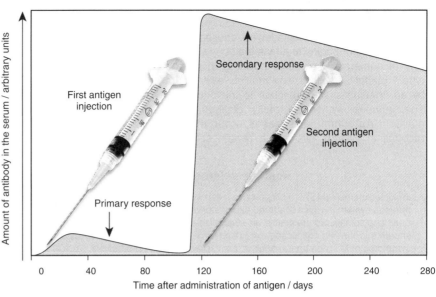

Amount of antibody in the serum / arbitrary units

First antigen injection

Secondary response

Second antigen injection

Primary response

Time after administration of antigen / days

0   40   80   120   160   200   240   280

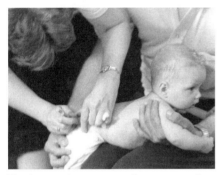

Vaccines against common diseases are given at various stages during childhood according to an immunisation schedule. Vaccination has been behind the decline of some once-common childhood diseases, such as mumps.

Many childhood diseases for which vaccination programmes exist are kept at a low level because of **herd immunity**. If most of the population is immune, those that are not immunised may be protected because the disease is uncommon.

Most vaccinations are given in childhood, but adults may be vaccinated against a disease (e.g. TB, influenza) if they are in a high risk group (e.g. the elderly) or if they are travelling to a region in the world where a disease is prevalent.

3. (a) What is **active immunity**? _____

_____

(b) Distinguish between naturally and artificially acquired active immunity and give an example of each: _____

_____

_____

4. (a) Describe two differences between the primary and secondary responses to presentation of an antigen: _____

_____

_____

(b) Why is the secondary response so different from the primary response? _____

_____

_____

5. (a) Explain the principle of **herd immunity**: _____

_____

_____

(b) Why are health authorities concerned when the vaccination rates for an infectious disease fall? _____

_____

_____

187 Autoimmune Diseases

Key Idea: Autoimmune diseases are caused when the body's immune system begins to attack the body's own tissues.

Any of numerous disorders, including rheumatoid arthritis, type 1 diabetes mellitus, and multiple sclerosis, are caused by an immune system reaction to the body's own tissues. The immune system normally distinguishes self from non-self. **Autoimmune diseases** occur when this normal recognition system fails and a certain cell or tissue type is no longer recognised as self. The exact mechanisms behind autoimmune malfunctions are not fully understood, but pathogens or drugs may play a role in triggering an autoimmune response in someone who already has a genetic predisposition. The reactions are similar to those that occur in allergies, except that in autoimmune disorders, the hypersensitivity response is to the body itself, rather than to an outside substance.

Multiple sclerosis

Multiple sclerosis (MS) is a progressive inflammatory disease of the central nervous system in which scattered patches of myelin (white matter) in the brain and spinal cord are destroyed. Myelin is the fatty connective tissue sheath surrounding conducting axons and its destruction results in the symptoms of MS: numbness, tingling, muscle weakness and paralysis.

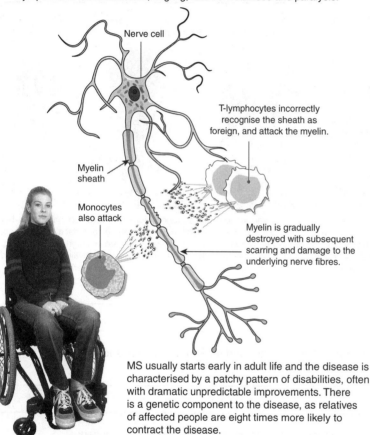

Nerve cell

T-lymphocytes incorrectly recognise the sheath as foreign, and attack the myelin.

Myelin sheath

Monocytes also attack

Myelin is gradually destroyed with subsequent scarring and damage to the underlying nerve fibres.

MS usually starts early in adult life and the disease is characterised by a patchy pattern of disabilities, often with dramatic unpredictable improvements. There is a genetic component to the disease, as relatives of affected people are eight times more likely to contract the disease.

Other immune system disorders

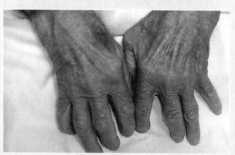

Rheumatoid arthritis is an autoimmune disease that causes joint inflammation, usually in the hands and feet, and results in destruction of cartilage and painful, swollen joints. The disease often begins in adulthood, but can also occur in children or the elderly. Rheumatoid arthritis affects more women than men and is treated with anti-inflammatory and immunosuppressant drugs, and physiotherapy.

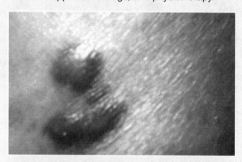

Lacking a sufficient immune response is called immune deficiency, and may be either congenital (present at birth) or acquired as a result of drugs, cancer, or infectious agents (e.g. HIV infection). HIV causes AIDS, which results in a steady destruction of the immune system. Sufferers then succumb to opportunistic infections and rare cancers such as Kaposi's sarcoma (above).

1. Explain the basis of the following autoimmune diseases:

   (a) Multiple sclerosis: _____

   _____

   (b) Rheumatoid arthritis: _____

   _____

2. Why are autoimmune diseases difficult to treat effectively? _____

   _____

   _____

3. Why do sufferers of immune deficiencies, such as AIDS, develop a range of debilitating infections? _____

   _____

   _____

© 2015 **BIOZONE** International
ISBN: 978-1-927309-13-1
Photocopying Prohibited

188 Vaccines and Vaccination

Key Idea: A vaccine is a suspension of microorganisms (or pieces of them) that is deliberately introduced into the body to protect against disease. It induces immunity by stimulating the production of antibodies.

A **vaccine** is a preparation of a harmless foreign antigen that is deliberately introduced into the body to produce an immune response. The antigen in the vaccine triggers the immune system to produce antibodies against the antigen, but it does not cause the disease. The immune system remembers its response and will produce the same antibodies if it encounters the antigen again. There are two basic types of vaccine, subunit vaccines and whole-agent vaccines (below). Vaccines are routinely given to prevent common childhood diseases, to prevent seasonal diseases (e.g. the flu), or given to people travelling to parts of the world where certain diseases are common. Vaccines are developed in response to a new disease. For example, the H1N1 "swine flu" pandemic of 2009 resulted in a new vaccine.

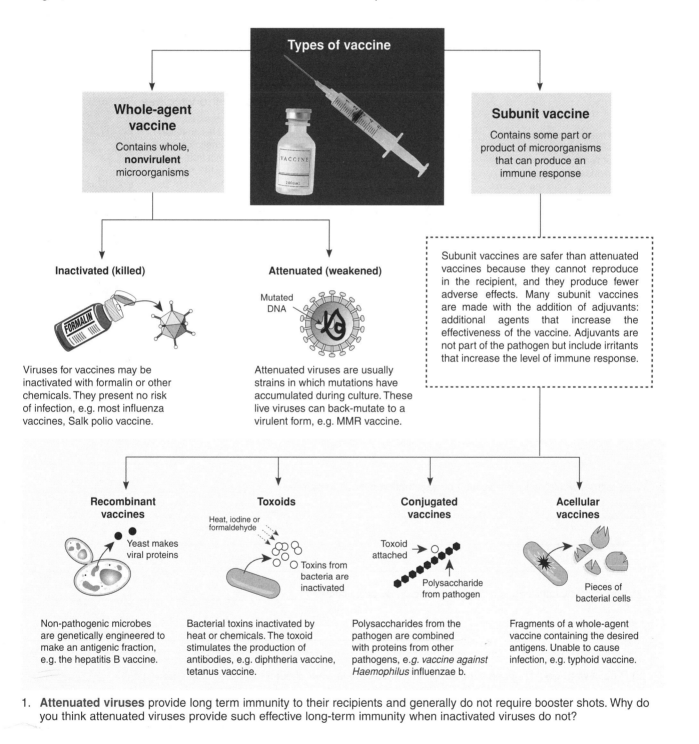

Types of vaccine

Whole-agent vaccine

Contains whole, **nonvirulent** microorganisms

Subunit vaccine

Contains some part or product of microorganisms that can produce an immune response

Inactivated (killed)

Viruses for vaccines may be inactivated with formalin or other chemicals. They present no risk of infection, e.g. most influenza vaccines, Salk polio vaccine.

Attenuated (weakened)

Mutated DNA

Attenuated viruses are usually strains in which mutations have accumulated during culture. These live viruses can back-mutate to a virulent form, e.g. MMR vaccine.

Subunit vaccines are safer than attenuated vaccines because they cannot reproduce in the recipient, and they produce fewer adverse effects. Many subunit vaccines are made with the addition of adjuvants: additional agents that increase the effectiveness of the vaccine. Adjuvants are not part of the pathogen but include irritants that increase the level of immune response.

Recombinant vaccines

Yeast makes viral proteins

Non-pathogenic microbes are genetically engineered to make an antigenic fraction, e.g. the hepatitis B vaccine.

Toxoids

Heat, iodine or formaldehyde

Toxins from bacteria are inactivated

Bacterial toxins inactivated by heat or chemicals. The toxoid stimulates the production of antibodies, e.g. diphtheria vaccine, tetanus vaccine.

Conjugated vaccines

Toxoid attached

Polysaccharide from pathogen

Polysaccharides from the pathogen are combined with proteins from other pathogens, e.g. *vaccine against Haemophilus* influenzae b.

Acellular vaccines

Pieces of bacterial cells

Fragments of a whole-agent vaccine containing the desired antigens. Unable to cause infection, e.g. typhoid vaccine.

1. **Attenuated viruses** provide long term immunity to their recipients and generally do not require booster shots. Why do you think attenuated viruses provide such effective long-term immunity when inactivated viruses do not?

_____

_____

_____

_____

LINK 189 WEB 188 KNOW

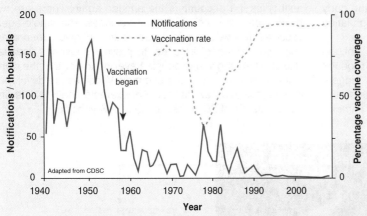

Whooping cough notifications and vaccine coverage (England and Wales) 1940-2008

Adapted from CDSC

Changes in vaccination programmes

National vaccination programmes can have new vaccines added and others removed depending on the prevalence of certain diseases at any one time. For example, in 2013, influenza and rotavirus vaccines were added to the NHS childhood vaccination schedule to lower transmission of these diseases in the community and reduce the burden on the health system.

Changes may also be made to the frequency of a vaccination to give better protection to those most at risk from a particular disease. In the UK, children under the age of one, and youth aged from 15-19 years old are most at risk from the bacterial disease meningitis C. The UK vaccination schedule was changed recently to offer better protection to these particular groups.

Changes to vaccines

Influenzavirus causes the 'flu' and is constantly undergo genetic changes that prevent it from being detected by the immune system. The ability of the virus to recombine its RNA enables it to change each year, so that different strains occur each 'flu' season. The 'flu' vaccination is updated annually to be effective against the current flu strains. Three strains are chosen for each year's vaccination. Selection is based on estimates of which strains will be predominant in the following year.

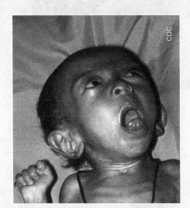

Whooping cough is caused by the bacterium *Bordetella pertussis*, and may last for two to three months. It is characterised by a whooping cough and painful coughing spasms, which may be followed by periods of vomiting. Infants under six months of age are most at risk of developing complications or dying because they are too young to be fully protected by the vaccine. Inclusion of the whooping cough vaccine into the UK immunisation schedule has greatly reduced the incidence rates of the disease (above).

2. How can vaccination help lead to the eradication of an infectious disease? _____

_____

_____

_____

3. What factors would make eradication by vaccination difficult to achieve? _____

_____

_____

_____

4. (a) Suggest why influenza is difficult to eradicate by vaccination? _____

_____

_____

(b) Predict what would happen if the wrong influenza strains were chosen for the seasonal flu vaccine: _____

_____

_____

5. In 1975, the UK vaccination rate for whooping cough decreased to 30% because of concerns about the vaccine's safety. Use the data in the graph above to describe what effect this had on rates of whooping cough reported:

_____

_____

© 2015 **BIOZONE** International
ISBN: 978-1-927309-13-1
Photocopying Prohibited

189 New Medicines

Key Idea: Plants and microbes are being investigated as potential sources of new medicines.

The discovery of new medicines has become increasingly important as microbial resistance to traditional antibiotics becomes more widespread. Many medicines prescribed today are derived from, or designed to mimic, natural compounds from plants, animals, and microbes. It is not surprising then that researchers look at natural biological resources as sources of new medicines. Around half of the pharmaceuticals in use today are of plant origin. Although many plants have antimicrobial properties, the pharmaceuticals of plant origin have been obtained from relatively few species. This is generally because antibiotic production and extraction from fungi and bacteria is more straightforward.

Medicines from plants

Opium poppy codeine, morphine

Periwinkle plant- anti-cancer

White willow bark yields the active ingredient of aspirin, used to treat pain fever, and inflammation.

Approximately 120 pure chemical substances extracted from higher plants are used in medicine throughout the world. Some, including **aspirin** (salicylic acid from willow bark) and **digitalin** (from foxglove) have been in medical use since antiquity. Others, including plant alkaloids such as **taxol** (an anticancer drug), are more recent discoveries. Most of the plant-derived medicines are now synthesised in the laboratory, but only about six are produced entirely by synthetic procedures. The rest are still extracted commercially from plants.

The bark and needles of the Pacific yew (left) provide the anti-cancer drug **taxol**.

In recent decades, the search for new medicines has focussed on tropical plants (e.g. periwinkle and opium). However, the increased sensitivity of the new chemical screening technologies has revealed potential new drugs from plants that were not detected by previous methods. Moreover, plants can be engineered as biofactories to manufacture medicines such as vaccines and antibodies.

Digitalin, containing cardiac glycosides derived from foxglove, is used in drugs to treat congestive heart disease.

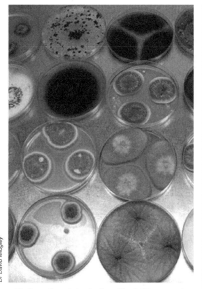

Various fungi, including Penicillium and Aspergillus, grown in sterile (axenic) culture

The use of drugs isolated from microorganisms is a relatively recent phenomenon, which started with the discovery of the antibiotic penicillin in 1928. Now the use of microbes to produce antimicrobial drugs is a huge industry.

Some medicines come from unlikely sources. The drug **botox**, derived from the toxin of *Clostridium botulinum*, is used to treat facial neuralgia as well as for cosmetic purposes.

New approaches to microbial medicines include using **bacteriophages** (viruses that infect bacteria) to control bacterial infections in different tissues. A better understanding of microbial diversity may also provide the means to produce more effective drugs against microbial pathogens.

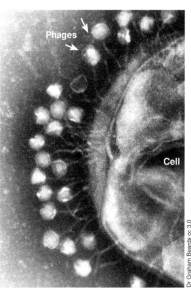

Bacteriophages attacking a bacterial cell.

LINK   WEB
190 189   KNOW

Isolating and testing antimicrobial compounds from plants

1

A plant is chosen for testing. Plants produce a wide range of compounds, but those with aromatic rings often have medicinal properties.

2

Pulping

Solvent extraction

Extraction: Plant material is pulped, then soaked in a solvent (water, alcohol), or boiled to release and crudely fractionate the compounds.

3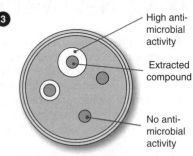

High anti-microbial activity

Extracted compound

No anti-microbial activity

Screening: Microbes are plated onto agar. Paper discs soaked with plant extract are placed on agar, or the plant extract is pipetted into wells cut into the agar. The plates are then incubated. The effectiveness of the extract can be determined by measuring the clear zone around the plant extract after incubation.

4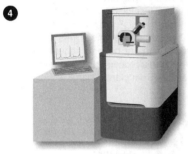

Separation and analysis: Mass spectroscopy is used to further separate and isolate compounds from the extracts that show antimicrobial activity.

5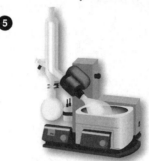

Concentration: The compounds may be further separated, (e.g. by chromatography), before they are concentrated using freeze drying or rotary evaporation (above).

6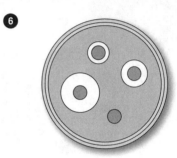

Testing: The isolated and concentrated compounds are tested for antimicrobial activity. This identifies which component of the initial extract is the antimicrobial.

The antimicrobial compound in chili peppers, is capsaicin, an antibacterial agent of relatively high potency.

The essential oil produced from the herb rosemary, acts as an effective general antimicrobial agent.

Phloretin is a polyphenol extracted from the leaves of apple trees. It acts as a highly potent antimicrobial.

Saponins (compounds that foam in water) extracted from ginseng are effective against a range of bacteria.

1. Describe the present and potential value of plants to modern medicine: _____

_____

_____

_____

2. Why could a loss of tropical biodiversity reduce the options for discovering new drugs? _____

_____

_____

3. How is the effectiveness of a new antimicrobial compound tested? _____

_____

_____

4. Why is research into antimicrobial plant extracts increasing? _____

_____

_____

© 2015 **BIOZONE** International
ISBN: 978-1-927309-13-1
Photocopying Prohibited

190 Antibiotics

Key Idea: Antibiotics are chemicals that kill bacteria or inhibit their growth by interfering with specific metabolic pathways. Some microbes have developed antibiotic resistance.

Antibiotics are chemical substances that act against bacterial infections by either killing the bacteria (**bactericidal**) or preventing them from growing (**bacteriostatic**). They are produced naturally by bacteria and fungi, but many are now produced synthetically. Since the discovery of the first antibiotic, penicillin, antibiotics have been widely used to treat bacterial infections. However antibiotic resistance is becoming increasingly more common (below). The cells of eukaryotes are not affected by antibiotics because they have different structures and metabolic pathways to bacterial (prokaryotic) cells. Antibiotics are ineffective against viruses.

How antimicrobial drugs work

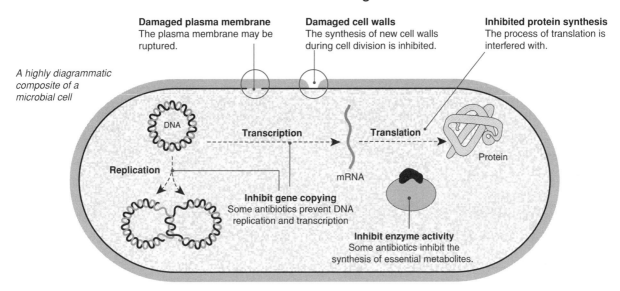

Damaged plasma membrane
The plasma membrane may be ruptured.

Damaged cell walls
The synthesis of new cell walls during cell division is inhibited.

Inhibited protein synthesis
The process of translation is interfered with.

A highly diagrammatic composite of a microbial cell

DNA

Transcription

Translation

Protein

Replication

mRNA

Inhibit gene copying
Some antibiotics prevent DNA replication and transcription

Inhibit enzyme activity
Some antibiotics inhibit the synthesis of essential metabolites.

Florey and Chain's penicillin experiments

The antibiotic properties of penicillins, a group of antibiotics produced by the fungus *Penicillium*, were discovered by Alexander Fleming in 1928. However, it wasn't until the 1940s that it was, grown, purified, and tested in significant quantities by a team of scientists including **Howard Florey** and **Ernst Chain**.

Florey and Chain experimented on mice (below) to treat streptococcal infections with penicillin. Its success quickly lead to human trials, and penicillin was eventually used with great success to treat World War II soldiers suffering from infected wounds. It saved millions of lives and is documented at the first successful antibiotic treatment.

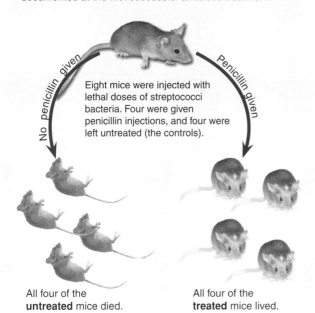

No penicillin given

Penicillin given

Eight mice were injected with lethal doses of streptococci bacteria. Four were given penicillin injections, and four were left untreated (the controls).

All four of the **untreated** mice died.

All four of the **treated** mice lived.

Bacteria can become resistant to antibiotics

Antibiotic resistance arises when a genetic change allows bacteria to tolerate levels of an antibiotic that would normally adversely affect it. Some bacteria have resistance to multiple antibiotics. Such bacteria are called superbugs. For example, methicillin resistant strains of *Staphylococcus aureus* (**MRSA**) have acquired genes for resistance to all penicillins. The infections they cause are very difficult to treat, and are more easily spread through the population. While once only a concern only for people in the hospital, MRSA is now causing infections in healthy people in the community.

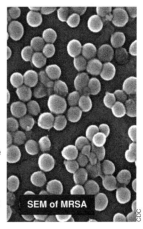

SEM of MRSA

Clostridium difficile is a bacterium that causes an infection which can cause life-threatening diarrhoea and intestinal damage. *C. difficile* is easily spread because it is naturally resistant to many drugs used to treat other infections. *C. difficile* infections often occur when a person has been on a medical regime or antibiotic treatment which reduces the numbers of their normal gut microbes. The normal intestinal bacteria keeps *C. difficile* numbers in check but, in their absence, *C. difficile* multiplies rapidly and produces toxins which cause illness. Most *C. difficile* infections occur in hospitals or aged-care facilities, but in recent years more cases are occurring in the general population which is concerning.

A hypervirulent *C. difficile* strain is becoming more common throughout the UK, Europe, and the US. The new strain is causing concern amongst the medical community because it is showing resistance to some antibiotics commonly used to treat *C. difficile* infections and is presenting in people who haven't been in the hospital or taken antibiotics.

1. Why are eukaryotic cells (such as human cells) not affected by antibiotics? _____

_____

_____

2. The graph right shows the effects of two antibiotics. Identify the antibiotic with a bacteriostatic action and the antibiotic with a bactericidal action. Explain your choice:

Bacteriostatic: _____

_____

_____

Bactericidal: _____

_____

_____

Control (no antibiotics)

10 µg mL^{-1} chloramphenicol

2.5 µg mL^{-1} ampicillin

Mean cfu mL^{-1} *Streptococcus pneumoniae*

Incubation time / hours

3. (a) What is **antibiotic resistance**? _____

_____

_____

(b) What are the implications to humans of bacteria acquiring resistance to several different antibiotics? _____

_____

_____

_____

4. Why were Florey and Chain's penicillin experiments such an important medical breakthrough? _____

_____

_____

5. Two students carried out an experiment to determine the effect of antibiotics on bacteria. They placed discs saturated with antibiotic on petri dishes evenly coated with bacterial colonies. Dish 1 contained four different antibiotics labelled A to D and a control labelled CL. Dish 2 contained four different concentrations of a single antibiotic and a control labelled CL.

Bacterial colonies

Zone of inhibition (no bacterial growth)

Paper discs saturated with antibiotic

5.5 µg mL^{-1}

7 µg mL^{-1}

4 µg mL^{-1}

2.5 µg mL^{-1}

Dish 1

Dish 2

(a) Which was the most effective antibiotic on Dish 1? _____

(b) Which was the most effective concentration on Dish 2? _____

(c) Explain your choice in question 5(b): _____

_____

191 Chapter Review

Summarise what you know about this topic under the headings provided. You can draw diagrams or mind maps, or write short notes to organise your thoughts. Use the images and hints included to help you:

Pathogens
HINT: Features of pathogens that make them infectious.

The immune system
HINT: Summarise the structure and role of phagocytes and the specific immune response.

Vaccinations and antimicrobials
HINT: Describe the principles and applications of vaccination. Describe how antibiotics work and the significance of bacterial resistance to them.

REVISE

192 KEY TERMS: Mix and Match

INSTRUCTIONS: *Test your vocabulary by matching each term to its correct definition, as identified by its preceding letter code.*

active immunity

antibodies (*sing.* antibody)

antigen

autoimmune disease

B cells

cell mediated immunity

clonal selection

humoral immunity

immunity   *C*

immunological memory

infection

inflammation

leucocytes

lymphocytes

macrophage

non-specific
defences (innate immunity)

passive immunity

pathogen   *U*

phagocytes   *K*

primary response

secondary response

specific (=adaptive) immune
response

T cells

vaccination

A A pathogen and antigen-specific immune response with both cell-mediated and humoral components. Characterised by immunological memory.

B The initial response of the immune system to exposure to an antigen.

C Resistance of an organism to infection or disease.

D Immune response involving the activation of macrophages, specific T cells, and cytokines against antigens.

E Lymphocytes that are responsible for the cell mediated immune response.

F The more rapid and stronger response of the immune system to an antigen that it has encountered before.

G The delivery of antigenic material (the vaccine) to produce immunity to a disease.

H White blood cells, including lymphocytes, and macrophages and other phagocytes.

I Lymphocytes that make antibodies against specific antigens.

J A model for how B and T cells are selected to target specific antigens invading the body.

K Specific white blood cells involved in the adaptive immune response.

L Immunoglobulin proteins in the blood or other bodily fluids, which identify and neutralise foreign material, such as bacteria and viruses.

M Large white blood cells within tissues, produced by the differentiation of monocytes.

N A disease resulting from an overactive immune response against substances and tissues normally present in the body.

O Long-lasting immunity that is induced in the host itself by the antigen.

P The invasion of a host organism by a pathogen to the detriment of the host.

Q The ability of the immune system to respond rapidly in the future to antigens encountered in the past

R Generalised defence mechanisms against pathogens, e.g. physical barriers, secretions, inflammation, and phagocytosis.

S Immunity gained by the receipt of ready-made antibodies.

T Immune response that is mediated by secreted antibodies.

U A disease-causing organism.

V White blood cells that destroy foreign material, e.g. bacteria, by ingesting them.

W A molecule that is recognised by the immune system as foreign.

X The protective response of vascular tissues to harmful stimuli, such as irritants, pathogens, or damaged cells.

Biodiversity

Measures of biodiversity

Learning outcomes

 Activity number

☐ 1 Distinguish between different levels of biodiversity: habitat (ecological) diversity, species diversity, and genetic diversity. — 193

☐ 2 Distinguish between species richness and species evenness in a habitat and explain how these are measured. — 193

☐ 3 Describe how sampling is used to measure biodiversity and identify important considerations when sampling natural habitats. Include reference to random and non-random sampling methods, and the importance of sample size so that samples are representative of the diversity of the community. — 193 194 195

☐ 4 Use and interpret the Simpson's Index of Diversity to calculate and describe the biodiversity of a habitat. — 196

☐ 5 **PAG3** Investigate biodiversity in a named habitat using random and non-random sampling techniques. Interpret data from such investigations. — 197

☐ 6 Use a statistical test, e.g. the chi-squared test for independence, to evaluate some aspect of species diversity, such as species associations. — 198 199

☐ 7 Explain how genetic diversity can be assessed. Show how genetic diversity can be calculated in isolated populations, e.g. by recording the percentage of alleles in the population. Particular examples where assessment is appropriate and useful include captive bred populations, rare breeds, and pedigree animals. — 200

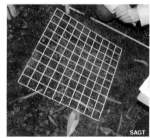

Factors affecting biodiversity

Learning outcomes

Activity number

☐ 8 Describe the factors affecting biodiversity to include human population growth (and the pressures this creates on ecosystems), intensive agricultural systems (such as monocultures), and climate change. — 201 202 203 204

☐ 9 Explain the ecological, economic, and aesthetic reasons for maintaining biodiversity, including reference to the ecosystem services provided by high diversity systems. — 205 206

▶ Ecological reasons include the protection of keystone species with critical roles in ecosystem function and maintenance of genetic resources (known or unknown).

▶ Economic reasons include reduction in soil depletion.

▶ Aesthetic reasons include protection of landscapes and pristine habitats.

☐ 10 Describe *in-situ* and *ex-situ* methods of maintaining biodiversity. *In-situ* conservation methods include marine protected areas and wildlife reserves. *Ex-situ* conservation methods include seed banks, botanic gardens and zoos. — 207 208

☐ 11 Describe the role of legislation in international and local conservation efforts. Examples include historic and current agreements such as CITES, the Rio Convention on Biological Diversity (CBD, and the new Countryside Stewardship Scheme (CSS). — 209

193 Biodiversity

Key Idea: Biodiversity is the sum of all biotic variation from the level of genes to ecosystems. All organisms within an ecosystem contribute to its functioning, but keystone species have a disproportionate effect on ecosystem functioning.

Biodiversity is defined as the sum of all biotic variation from the level of genes to ecosystems. Species diversity describes species richness (the number of species), genetic diversity is the diversity of genes within a species, and ecosystem diversity (of which habitat diversity is a part) refers to the diversity at the ecosystem level. Total biodiversity is threatened by the loss of just one of these components. While every species plays a role in ecosystem function, **keystone species** have a disproportionate effect on ecosystem stability because of their pivotal role in some aspect of ecosystem functioning, e.g. as predators or in nutrient cycling. The loss of a keystone species can result in rapid ecosystem change.

Habitat diversity

Habitat diversity (the presence of many different types of habitat) is important for maintaining biodiversity. Specific habitats are occupied by different organisms and, in general, the greater the number of habitats, the greater the species diversity. Within habitats, microhabitats (smaller areas with specific characteristics) further increase biodiversity. For example, in a stream habitat, microhabitats exist under the rocks, in riffles, in pools, and in vegetation at the stream edges. Some common English habitats are shown (right).

Habitat protection is important to maintain species biodiversity. Habitat loss is one of the biggest threats to biodiversity and is the most common cause of extinction. Examples of habitat destruction include clear cutting forests for logging and agriculture, ploughing natural meadows to make way for agriculture, draining wetland and peatlands, and creating dams that alter river flows.

Coastal sand dunes, Wales

Stream, Peak district

Bluebell woodland

Meadow, Yorkshire

Measuring biodiversity

Biodiversity is quantified for a variety of reasons, e.g. to assess the success of conservation work or to measure the impact of human activity.

One measure of biodiversity is to simply count all the species present (the **species richness**). Species richness (S) is directly related to the number of species in a sampled area. It is a crude measure of the homogeneity of a community but it does not give any information about the relative abundance of particular species and so is relatively meaningless by itself. Thus a sample area with 500 daisies and 3 dandelions has the same species richness as a sample area with 200 daisies and 300 dandelions.

Species evenness measures the proportion of individuals of each species in an area (the relative abundance). Species evenness is highest when the proportions of all species are the same and decreases as the proportions of species become less similar.

Sample of freshwater invertebrates in a stream			
Common name	Site 1 / $n\,m^{-2}$	Site 2 / $n\,m^{-2}$	Site 3 / $n\,m^{-2}$
Freshwater shrimp	67	20	5
Freshwater mite	4	15	1
Flat mayfly	23	21	0
Bighead stonefly	12	18	2
Blackfly	78	40	100
Bloodworm	21	22	43

Data for species richness and species evenness can be obtained by sampling, e.g. using quadrats. In the example above, three sites in a stream were sampled using quadrats and the species and number of individuals per m² recorded for each site. Using Site 1 as an example, species richness is 6, since $S = n$. Measures of species evenness are an integral component of biodiversity indices, such as Simpson's Index of biodiversity, but can also be estimated from the numbers of individuals of each species. In terms of species evenness, site 2 > site 1 > site 3.

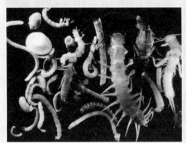
High species richness

Low species richness

1. Distinguish between species diversity and genetic diversity and explain the importance of both of these to our definition of total biological diversity:

_____

_____

_____

_____

© 2015 **BIOZONE** International
ISBN: 978-1-927309-13-1
Photocopying Prohibited

Keystone species in Europe and the UK

Grey wolf

European beaver

Scots pine

Grey or timber wolves (*Canis lupus*) are a keystone predator and were once widespread through North America, Europe, and Eurasia. Historically they have been eliminated because of their perceived threat to humans and livestock, and now occupy only a fraction of their former range. As a top predator, the wolf is a keystone species. When they are absent, populations of their prey (e.g. red deer) increase to the point that they adversely affect other flora and fauna.

The European beaver (*Caster fiber*) was originally distributed throughout most of Europe and northern Asia but populations have been decimated as a result of hunting and habitat loss. Where they occur, beavers are critical to ecosystem function and a number of species depend partly or entirely on beaver ponds for survival. Their tree-felling activity is akin to a natural coppicing process and promotes vigorous regrowth, while historically they helped the spread of alder (a water-loving species) in Britain.

Scots pine (*Pinus sylvestris*) is the most widely distributed conifer in the world. In the Scots pine forests in Scotland, this species occupies a unique position, both because of the absence of other native conifers and because it directly or indirectly supports so many other species. Among those dependent on Scots pine for survival are blaeberries, wood ants, pine martens, and a number of bird species including the capercaillie (wood grouse) and the UK's only endemic bird, the Scottish crossbill.

2. Why is habitat diversity important to maintaining species biodiversity? _____

_____

_____

3. (a) Distinguish between the two measures of biodiversity: species richness and species evenness: _____

_____

_____

_____

(b) Why is it is important to incorporate both these measures when considering species conservation? _____

_____

_____

4. Why are keystone species are so important to ecosystem function? _____

_____

_____

_____

5. On a separate sheet of paper, discuss the biological features of the grey wolf, European beaver, and Scots pine that contribute to their position as a keystone species. Attach the sheet to this workbook.

194 Sampling Populations

Key Idea: A population's characteristics may be inferred from data collected by sampling. Random sampling methods are preferred as they provide unbiased data.

In most ecological studies, it is not possible to measure or count all the members of a population. Instead, information is obtained through sampling in a manner that provides a fair (unbiased) representation of the organisms present and their distribution. This is usually achieved through **random**

sampling, a technique in which each individual has the same probability of being selected at any stage during the sampling process. Sometimes researchers collect information by **non-random sampling**, a process that does not give all the individuals in the population an equal chance of being selected. While faster and cheaper to carry out than random sampling, non-random sampling may not give a true representation of the population.

Sampling strategies

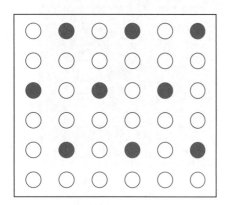

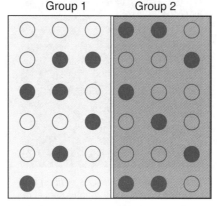

Group 1   Group 2

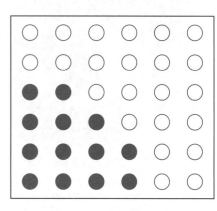

Systematic sampling

Samples from a larger population are selected according to a random starting point and a fixed, periodic sampling interval. For the example above, the sampling period is every fourth individual. Systematic sampling is a random sampling method, provided the periodic interval is determined beforehand and the starting point is random.

Example: Selecting individuals from a patient list.

Stratified sampling

Stratified sampling divides the population into subgroups before sampling. The strata should be mutually exclusive, and individuals must be assigned to only one stratum. Stratified sampling is used to highlight a specific subgroup within the population. Individuals are then randomly sampled from the strata to study.

Example: Dividing the population into males and females.

Opportunistic sampling

A non-random sampling technique in which subjects are selected because of they are easily accessible to the researcher. Opportunistic sampling excludes a large proportion of the population and is usually not representative of the population. It is sometimes used in pilot studies to gather data quickly and with little cost.

Example: Selecting 13 people at a cafe where you are having lunch.

1. Why do we sample populations? _____

_____

_____

2. Why is random sampling preferable to non-random sampling? _____

_____

3. (a) Why can stratified sampling be considered a random sampling method?_____

_____

(b) Describe a situation where its use might be appropriate? _____

_____

4. A student wants to investigate the incidence of asthma in their school. Describe how they might select samples from the school population using:

(a) Systematic sampling: _____

_____

(b) Stratified sampling: _____

_____

(c) Opportunistic sampling: _____

_____

© 2015 **BIOZONE** International
ISBN: 978-1-927309-13-1
Photocopying Prohibited

195 Interpreting Samples

Key Idea: If sample data are collected without bias and in sufficient quantity, even a simple analysis can provide useful information about the composition of a community and the possible physical factors influencing this.

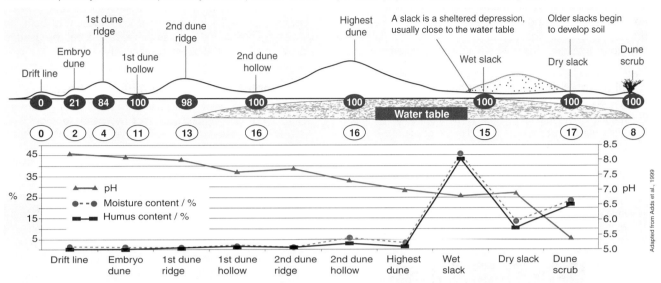

1. The beach dune profile (top) shows transect sampling points at fixed morphological features (e.g. dune ridges). The blue ovals on the dune profile represent the percentage vegetation cover at each sampling point. The white ovals record the number of plant species. Some physical data for each sampling site are presented in the graph below the profile.

   (a) What is the trend in pH from drift line to dune scrub? _____

   (b) Suggest why moisture and humus content increase along the transect? _____

   _____

   _____

   _____

2. The figure below shows changes in vegetation cover along a 2 m vertical transect up the trunk of an oak tree. Changes in the physical factors light, humidity, and temperature along the same transect were also recorded.

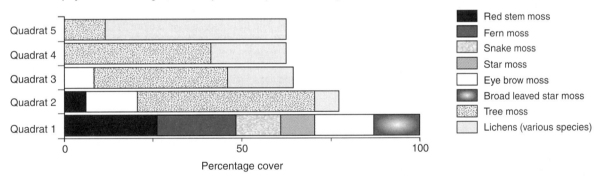

Legend:
- Red stem moss
- Fern moss
- Snake moss
- Star moss
- Eye brow moss
- Broad leaved star moss
- Tree moss
- Lichens (various species)

QUADRAT	1	2	3	4	5
Height / m	0.4	0.8	1.2	1.6	2.0
Light / arbitrary units	40	56	68	72	72
Humidity / percent	99	88	80	76	78
Temperature / °C	12.1	12.2	13	14.3	14.2

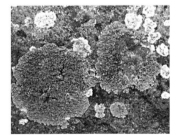

   (a) At which height were mosses most diverse and abundant? _____

   (b) What plant type predominates at 2.0 m height? _____

   (c) What can you deduce about the habitat preferences of most mosses and lichens from this study? _____

   _____

LINK
197

DATA

196 Diversity Indices

Key Idea: Diversity indices quantify the biodiversity in an area and can be used to measure ecosystem health.

The health of an ecosystem can be assessed by measuring both the number and relative abundances of organisms present. A change in species composition over time can therefore indicate changes in that ecosystem's status.

Certain **indicator species** are also useful in this respect as they are associated with habitats of a particular status, e.g. unpolluted water. Scientists quantify biodiversity using a diversity index. Diversity indices take account of both the species evenness and species richness and can be used to assess environmental stress (or recovery).

Simpson's index of diversity

Simpson's Index of Diversity (below) produces values ranging between 0 and almost 1. There are other variants of this index, but the more limited range of values provided by this calculation makes it more easily interpreted. No single index offers the "best" measure of diversity; each is chosen on the basis of suitability to different situations.

Simpson's Index of Diversity (D) is easily calculated using the following simple formula. Communities with a wide range of species produce a higher score than communities dominated by larger numbers of only a few species.

$$D = 1-(\Sigma(n/N)^2)$$

D = Diversity index
N = Total number of individuals (of all species) in the sample
n = Number of individuals of each species in the sample

Example of species diversity in a stream

The example below describes the results from a survey of stream invertebrates. It is not necessary to know the species to calculate a diversity index as long as the different species can be distinguished.

For the example below, Simpson's Index of Diversity using $D = 1 - (\Sigma(n/N)^2)$ is:

Species	n	n/N	$(n/N)^2$
A (backswimmer)	12	0.300	0.090
B (stonefly larva)	7	0.175	0.031
C (silver water beetle)	2	0.050	0.003
D (caddisfly larva)	6	0.150	0.023
E (water spider)	5	0.125	0.016
F (mayfly larva)	8	0.20	0.040
	$\Sigma n = 40$		$\Sigma(n/N)^2 = 0.201$

$$D = 1-0.201 = 0.799$$

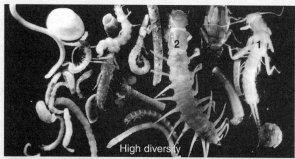
High diversity

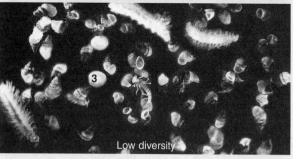
Low diversity

Photos: Stephen Moore

Using diversity indices and the role of indicator species

To be properly interpreted, indices are usually evaluated with reference to earlier measurement or a standard ecosystem measure. The photographs left show samples from two stream communities, a high diversity community with a large number of macroinverterbate species (top) and a low diversity community (lower photograph) with fewer species in large numbers. These photographs also show indicator species. The top image shows a stonefly (1) and an alderfly larva (2). These species (together with mayfly larvae) are typical of clean, well oxygenated water. The lower image is dominated by snails (3), which are tolerant of a wide range of conditions, included degraded environments.

The aptly named rat-tail maggot is the larva of the drone fly. This species is an indicator of gross pollution. Its prominent feature is a long snorkel-like breathing siphon.

Photo: C Johnson-Walker, c 3.0

1. Why might it be useful to have baseline data (prior knowledge of a system) before interpreting a diversity index?

2. (a) How might you monitor the recovery of a stream ecosystem following an ecological restoration project?

   (b) What role could indicator species play in the monitoring programme?

LINK 197

© 2015 BIOZONE International
ISBN: 978-1-927309-13-1
Photocopying Prohibited

197 Investigating Biodiversity

Key Idea: Sampling must be carefully planned in order to obtain meaningful results.

Careful planning is needed before sampling to ensure sound, unbiased data are obtained. If your sampling technique, assumptions, sample size, or sample unit are inadequate, your results will not provide a true representation of the community under study. The Simpson's index of diversity can be used to compare species diversity at two different sites.

Observation

Walking through a conifer plantation, a student observed that there seemed to be only a few different invertebrate species in the forest leaf litter. She wondered if more invertebrate species would be found in a nearby oak woodland.

Hypothesis

The oak woodland has a more varied leaf litter composition than the conifer plantation, so will support a wider variety of invertebrate species.

The **null hypothesis** is that there is no difference between the diversity of invertebrate species in oak woodland and coniferous plantation litter.

Oak woodland

Conifer plantation

Sampling programme

The student designed a sampling programme to test the prediction that there would be a greater diversity of invertebrates in the leaf litter of oak woodlands than in coniferous plantation.

Equipment and procedure

Sites: For each of the two forest types, an area 20 x 8 m was chosen and marked out in 2 x 2 m grids. Eight sampling sites were selected, evenly spaced along the grid as shown (right).

- The two general sampling areas for the study (oak and conifer) were **randomly selected**.
- Eight sites were chosen as the largest number feasible to collect and analyse in the time available.
- The two areas were sampled on sequential days.

Capture of invertebrates: At each site, a 0.4 x 0.4 m quadrat was placed on the forest floor and the leaf litter within the quadrat was collected. Leaf litter invertebrates were captured using a simple gauze lined funnel containing the leaf litter from within the quadrat. A lamp was positioned over each funnel for two hours and the invertebrates in the litter moved down and were trapped in the collecting jar.

- After two hours, each jar was labelled with the site number and returned to the lab for analysis.
- The litter in each funnel was bagged, labeled with the site number and returned to the lab for weighing.
- The number of each invertebrate species at each site was recorded.
- After counting and analysis of the samples, all the collected invertebrates were returned to the sites.

Assumptions

- The areas chosen in each forest were representative in terms of invertebrate abundance.
- Eight sites were sufficient to adequately sample the invertebrate populations in each forest.
- A quadrat size of 0.4 x 0.4 m contained enough leaf litter to adequately sample the invertebrates at each sample site.
- The invertebrates did not prey on each other once captured in the collecting jar.
- All the invertebrates within the quadrat were captured.
- Invertebrates moving away from the light are effectively captured by the funnel apparatus and cannot escape.
- Two hours was long enough for the invertebrates to move down through the litter and fall into the trap.

Note that these last two assumptions could be tested by examining the bagged leaf litter for invertebrates after returning to the lab.

Oak woodland or coniferous plantation

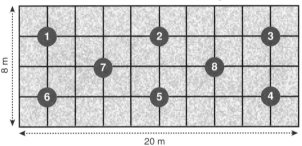

1 Sampling sites numbered 1-8 at evenly spaced intervals on a 2 x 2 m grid within an area of 20 m x 8 m.

Sampling equipment: leaf litter light trap

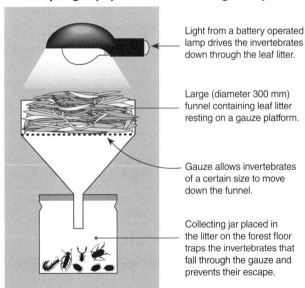

Light from a battery operated lamp drives the invertebrates down through the leaf litter.

Large (diameter 300 mm) funnel containing leaf litter resting on a gauze platform.

Gauze allows invertebrates of a certain size to move down the funnel.

Collecting jar placed in the litter on the forest floor traps the invertebrates that fall through the gauze and prevents their escape.

The importance of sample size

In any field study, two of the most important considerations are the **sample size** (the number of samples you will take) and the size of the **sampling unit** (e.g. quadrat size). An appropriate choice will enable you to collect sufficient, unbiased data to confidently test your hypothesis. The number of samples you take will be determined largely by the resources and time that you have available to collect and analyse your data (your **sampling effort**).

LINK
196
DATA

Results

The results from the student's study are presented in the tables and images below. The invertebrates are not drawn to scale.

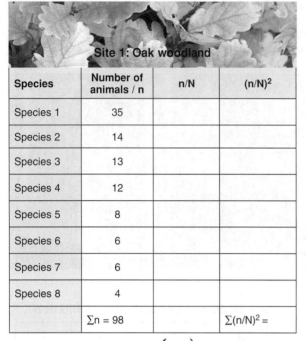

Site 1: Oak woodland

Species	Number of animals / n	n/N	(n/N)²
Species 1	35		
Species 2	14		
Species 3	13		
Species 4	12		
Species 5	8		
Species 6	6		
Species 7	6		
Species 8	4		
	$\Sigma n = 98$		$\Sigma (n/N)^2 =$

Site 2: Conifer plantation

Species	Number of animals / n	n/N	(n/N)²
Species 1	74		
Species 2	20		
Species 3	3		
Species 4	3		
Species 5	1		
Species 6	0		
Species 7	0		
Species 8	0		
	$\Sigma n = 101$		$\Sigma (n/N)^2 =$

Species 1	Species 2	Species 3	Species 4	Species 5	Species 6	Species 7	Species 8
Mite	Ant	Earwig	Woodlice	Centipede	Longhorn beetle	Small beetle	Pseudoscorpion

1. What type of sampling design is used in this study?_____

2. Explain the importance of each of the following in field studies:

   (a) Appropriately sized sampling unit: _____

   _____

   (b) Recognising any assumptions that you are making: _____

   _____

   (c) Appropriate consideration of the environment: _____

   _____

   (d) Return of organisms to the same place after removal: _____

   _____

   (e) Appropriate size of total sampling area within which the sites are located: _____

   _____

3. (a) Complete the two tables above by calculating the values for n/N and (n/N)² for the student's two sampling sites:

   (b) Calculate the Simpson's Index of Diversity for site 1: _____

   (c) Calculate the Simpson's Index of Diversity for site 2: _____

   (d) Compare the diversity of the two sites and suggest any reasons for it: _____

   _____

   _____

   _____

© 2015 **BIOZONE** International
ISBN: 978-1-927309-13-1
Photocopying Prohibited

198 Testing Species Associations

Key idea: The chi-squared test is used to compare sets of categorical data and evaluate if differences between them are statistically significant or due to chance.

The chi-squared test (χ^2) is used to determine differences between categorical data sets when working with frequencies (counts). For the test to be valid, the data recorded for each categorical variable (e.g. species) must be raw counts (not measurements or derived data). The chi-squared test is used for two types of comparison: test for goodness of fit and tests of independence (i.e. association or not). A test for goodness of fit is used to compare an experimental result with an expected theoretical outcome. You will perform this test later to compare the outcome of genetic crosses to an expected theoretical ratio. A test for independence evaluates whether two variables are associated. The chi-squared test is not valid when sample sizes are small (<20). Like all statistical tests, it aims to test the null hypothesis; the hypothesis of no difference (or no association) between groups of data. The worked example below uses the chi-squared test for independence in a study of habitat preference in mudfish.

Using the Chi-squared test for independence

The black mudfish is a small fish species native to New Zealand and found in wetlands and swampy streams. Researchers were interested in finding environmental indicators of favourable mudfish habitat. They sampled 80 wetland sites for the presence or absence of mudfish and recorded if there was emergent vegetation present or absent. Emergent vegetation, defined as vegetation rooted in water but emerging above the water surface, is an indicator of a relatively undisturbed environment. A chi-squared for independence was used to test if mudfish were found more often at sites with emergent vegetation than by chance alone. The null hypothesis was that there is no association (distribution is independent of vegetation). The worked example is below. The table of observed values records the number of sites with or without mudfish and with or without emergent vegetation.

Photo and data: Rhys Barrier, University of Waikato

Black mudfish (*Neochanna diversus*) can air-breathe and so can survive seasonal drying of their wetland habitat.

Step 1: Enter the observed values (O) in a contingency table
A χ^2 test for independence requires that the data (counts or frequencies) are entered in a **contingency table** (a matrix format to analyse and record the relationship between two or more categorical variables). Marginal totals are calculated for each row and column and a grand total is recorded in the bottom right hand corner (right).

	Mudfish absent (0)	Mudfish present (1)	Total
Emergent vegetation absent (0)	15	0	15
Emergent vegetation present (1)	26	39	65
Total	41	39	80

Step 2: Calculate the expected values (E)
Calculating the expected values for a contingency table is simple. For each category, divide the row total by the grand total and multiply by the column total. You can enter these in a separate table or as separate columns next to the observed values (right).

	Mudfish absent (0)	Mudfish present (1)	Total
Emergent vegetation absent (0)	7.69	7.31	15
Emergent vegetation present (1)	33.31	31.69	65
Total	41	39	80

Step 3: Calculate the value of chi-squared (χ^2) of (O - E)^2 ÷ (E)
The difference between the observed (O) and expected (E) values is calculated as a measure of the deviation from a predicted result. Since some deviations are negative, they are all squared to give positive values. This step is best done as a tabulation to obtain a value for (O - E)^2 ÷ (E) for each category. The sum of all these values is the value of chi squared (blue table right).

$$\chi^2 = \sum \frac{(O - E)^2}{E}$$

Where: O = the observed result
E = the expected result
Σ = sum of

Category	O	E	O–E	(O–E)^2	$\dfrac{(O–E)^2}{E}$
Mudfish 0/EmVeg 0	15	7.69	7.31	53.44	6.95
Mudfish 1/EmVeg 0	0	7.31	-7.31	53.44	7.31
Mudfish 0/EmVeg 1	26	33.31	-7.31	53.44	1.60
Mudfish 1/EmVeg 1	39	31.69	7.31	53.44	1.69

Total = 80 $\chi^2 \longrightarrow \Sigma = 17.55$

Step 4: Calculate the degrees of freedom (df)
The degrees of freedom for a contingency table is given by the formula: (rows-1) x (columns-1). For this example, degrees of freedom (df) is therefore (2-1) x (2-1) = 1.

Critical values of χ^2 at different levels of probability. By convention, the critical probability for rejecting the null hypothesis (H$_0$) is 5%. If the test statistic is greater than the tabulated value for P = 0.05 we reject H$_0$ in favour of the alternative hypothesis.

Step 5: Using the chi squared table

On the χ^2 table (relevant part reproduced in the table right) with 1 degree of freedom, the calculated value for χ^2 of 17.55 corresponds to a probability of less than 0.001 (see arrow). *This means that by chance alone a χ^2 value of 17.55 could be expected less than 0.1% of the time.* This probability is much lower than the 0.05 value which is generally regarded as significant. The null hypothesis can be rejected and we have reason to believe that black mudfish are associated with sites with emergent vegetation more than expected by chance alone.

	Level of Probability (P)				
df	0.05	0.025	0.01	0.005	0.001
1	3.84	5.02	6.63	7.88	10.83
2	5.99	7.38	9.21	10.60	13.82
3	7.81	9.35	11.34	12.84	16.27

LINK
199

199 Using the Chi-Squared Test for Independence

Key idea: Chi-squared can be used to determine if an association between two species is statistically significant.
In ecological studies, it is often found that two or more species are found in association. This is usually because of similar environmental requirements or because one species depends on the other. The following hypothetical example outlines a study in which the presence or absence of two plant species was recorded in a marked area. The two species are sometimes, but not always, found together. The chi squared test is used to test the significance of the association.

Using chi square to test species associations in a successional marsh-meadow community

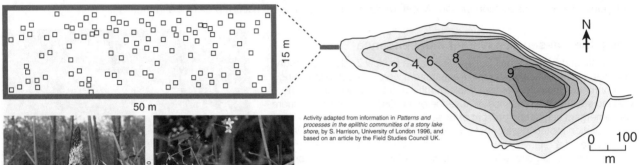

Activity adapted from information in *Patterns and processes in the epilithic communities of a stony lake shore*, by S. Harrison, University of London 1996, and based on an article by the Field Studies Council UK.

Lesser pond sedge (*Carex acutiformis*) is a swamp plant

Marsh bedstraw (*Galium palustre*) grows in ditches and wet meadows

Lake Crosemere (above) is a one of a series of kettle hole lakes in England, formed by glacial retreat at the end of the last glacial period. In a natural process of succession, the lake is gradually infilling from its western edge, and wet meadow and marsh species are replacing the species of the open water. Students investigated the association between two plants previously recorded in studies of the area: the lesser pond sedge (LPS) and marsh bedstraw (MBS). They recorded species presence or absence in 100 quadrats (0.5 m^2) placed in an area 15 X 50 m using coordinates generated using a random number function on a spreadsheet. The results are summarised in table 1 below. Follow the steps to complete the analysis.

1. State the null hypothesis (H$_0$) for this investigation:

_____

_____

2. In words, summarise the observed results in table 1:

_____

_____

_____

_____

	LPS present (1)	LPS absent (0)	Total
MBS present (1)	11	3	14
MBS absent (0)	31	55	86
Total	42	58	100

Table 1: Observed results for presence/absence of lesser pond-sedge (LPS) and marsh bedstraw (MBS).

3. Calculate the expected values for presence/absence of LPS and MBS. Enter the figures in table 2:

4. Complete the table to calculate the χ^2 value: _____

5. Calculate the degrees of freedom: _____

6. Using the χ^2, state the *P* value corresponding to your calculated χ^2 value (use the χ^2 table opposite):

_____

7. State whether or not you reject your null hypothesis:

reject H$_0$ / do not reject H$_0$ (*circle one*)

8. What could you conclude about this plant community:

_____

_____

_____

	LPS present (1)	LPS absent (0)	Total
MBS present (1)			
MBS absent (0)			
Total			

Table 2: Expected results for presence/absence of lesser pond-sedge (LPS) and marsh bedstraw (MBS).

Category	O	E	O–E	(O–E)^2	$\frac{(O-E)^2}{E}$
LPS 1/MBS 1					
LPS 0/MBS 1					
LPS 1/MBS 0					
LPS 0/MBS 0					
Total = 100					Σ =

LINK
DATA 198

© 2015 **BIOZONE** International
ISBN: 978-1-927309-13-1
Photocopying Prohibited

200 Measuring Genetic Diversity

Key Idea: Genetic diversity can be measured by calculating the allele diversity in a population. Species with low genetic diversity may be at risk of extinction.

Genetic diversity refers to the variety of alleles and genotypes present in a population. Genetic diversity is important to the survival and adaptability of a species.

Populations with low genetic diversity may not be able to respond to environmental change and are at greater risk of extinction. In contrast, species with greater genetic diversity are more likely to have the genetic resources to adapt and respond to environmental change. This increases their chance of species survival.

Measuring genetic diversity

Measuring genetic diversity can help identify at-risk populations and prioritise conservation efforts for rare breeds or animals in captive breeding programmes. Pedigree animals may be tested for genetic diversity to assist in planning breeding programmes so that loss of genetic diversity is minimised. Eukaryotic chromosomes contain many genes and, in any one population, each gene may have a number of versions called alleles. The presence of more than one allele at a specific gene location (locus) is called polymorphism. When only one allele is present the locus is said to be monomorphic. One of the simplest measures of genetic diversity involves calculating the proportions polymorphic loci across a genome or a species. The following equation can be used:

$$\text{Proportion of polymorphic gene loci} = \frac{\text{number of polymorphic gene loci}}{\text{total number of loci}}$$

Measuring genetic diversity in African lions

Allele variation at 26 enzyme loci in an African lion population was studied (below). Twenty loci showed no variation (they were monomorphic) and six loci showed variation (they were polymorphic).

Enzyme locus	Allele 1	Allele 2	Allele 3
ADA	0.56	0.33	0.11
DIAB	0.61	0.39	
ESI	0.88	0.12	
GPI	0.85	0.15	
GPT	0.89	0.11	
MPI	0.92	0.08	
20 Monomorphic loci	1.00		

Data: Newman et al. 1985

The effects of low genetic diversity

Until 1992, the Illinois prairie chicken was destined for extinction. The population had fallen from millions before European arrival to 25,000 in 1933 and then to 50 in 1992. The dramatic decline in the population in such a short time resulted in a huge loss of genetic diversity, which led to inbreeding and in turn resulted in a decrease in fertility and an ever-decreasing number of eggs hatching successfully. In 1992, a translocation programme began, bringing in 271 birds from Kansas and Nebraska. There was a rapid population response, as fertility and egg viability increased. The population is now recovering.

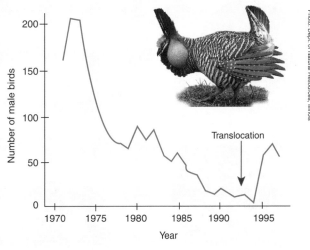

Photo: Dept. of Natural Resources, Illinois

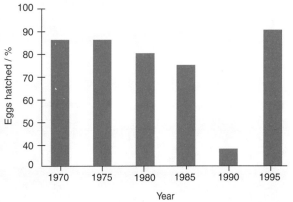

1. What is genetic diversity? _____

_____

_____

_____

_____

2. (a) For the lion data, identify the enzyme locus with the highest genetic diversity: _____

(b) Calculate the genetic diversity for the 26 loci studied above: _____

3. (a) Describe the factors contributing to the loss of diversity in the Illinois prairie chicken: _____

_____

(b) Why did the translocation of 271 birds from outside Illinois into the Illinois population halt the population decline?

_____

201 Global Biodiversity

Key Idea: Some regions are biodiversity hotspots; they have higher biodiversity than other regions but are under threat. Biodiversity is not distributed evenly on Earth, it tends to be clustered in certain parts of the world, called hotspots. **Hotspots** are biologically diverse and ecologically distinct regions under the greatest threat of destruction. They are identified on the basis of the number of species present, the amount of endemism (species unique to a specific geographic location), and the extent to which the species are threatened. Tropical forests and coral reefs are some of the most diverse ecosystems on Earth. Twenty five biodiversity hotspots are recognised (below).

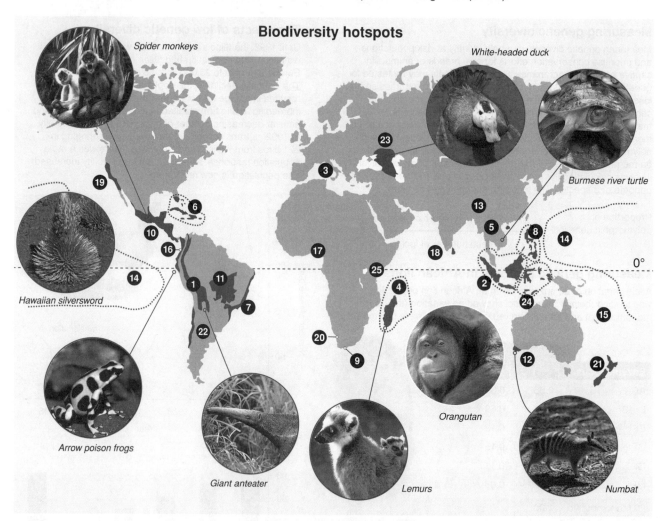

Biodiversity hotspots

Spider monkeys

White-headed duck

Burmese river turtle

Hawaiian silversword

Arrow poison frogs

Giant anteater

Lemurs

Orangutan

Numbat

0°

The Succulent Karoo in South Africa

Biodiversity hotspots make up less than 2% of Earth's land surface but support nearly 60% of the world's plant and vertebrate species. Conservation of hotspots is considered to be central to securing global biodiversity.

Deforestation (pale areas) in the Amazon

Habitat destruction (e.g. deforestation, above) and human-induced climate change are a major threat to biodiversity hotspots. The introduction of invasive or predatory species can also place hotspot biodiversity in danger.

Amazon forest, Brazil

According to Conservation International, to qualify as a hotspot a region must meet two strict criteria: it must contain at least 1500 endemic species of vascular plants and have lost at least 70 percent of its original habitat. (i.e. it is threatened).

1. Looking at the map, where are most of the hotspots concentrated?_____

2. Use your research tools (including the Weblinks identified below) to identify each of the 25 biodiversity hotspots illustrated in the diagram above. For one region that interests you, summarise the characteristics that have resulted in it being identified as a biodiversity hotspot. Attach your summary to this page.

WEB   LINK   LINK

KNOW 201 202 205

© 2015 **BIOZONE** International
ISBN: 978-1-927309-13-1
Photocopying Prohibited

202 How Humans Affect Biodiversity

Key Idea: The activities of an expanding human population are contributing to an increase in extinction rates above the natural level and a local and global reduction in biodiversity. The natural environment provides humans with the resources that sustain us, including food, water, fuel, and shelter. As the human population grows, demand on natural resources increases and land is cleared to build the houses and infrastructure associated with servicing a growing population. As a consequence of human demand, pressure on habitats and their natural populations increases and biodiversity declines. Humans rely heavily on biodiversity for survival, so a loss of biodiversity has a negative effect on us all.

How humans reduce biodiversity

Projections of current human population growth predict the human population will reach between 9 and 11 billion by 2050. This growth will create an increasing demand on natural resources, particularly water, arable land, and minerals.

As the human population increases, cities expand, fragmenting or destroying the natural ecosystems surrounding them. Careful management of urban development and resource use will be needed to prevent local extinctions and loss of biodiversity.

Natural extinction rates for all organisms are estimated to be 10-100 species a year. The actual extinction rate is 100-1000 times higher, mainly due to the effects of human activity. The pool frog (above) is endangered in Britain due to habitat loss.

Most industry depends on the combustion of fossil fuels and this contributes to **global warming**, the continuing rise in the average temperature of the Earth's surface. Global warming and associated shifts in climate will affect species distributions, breeding cycles, and patterns of migration. Species unable to adapt are at risk of extinction.

Eighty percent of Earth's documented species are found in tropical rainforests. These rainforests are being destroyed rapidly as land is cleared for agriculture or cattle ranching, to supply logs, for mining, or to build dams. Deforestation places a majority of the Earth's biodiversity at risk and threatens and stability of important ecosystems.

Demand for food increases as the population grows. Modern farming techniques favour **monocultures** to maximise yield and profit. However monocultures, in which a single crop type is grown year after year, are a low diversity system and food supplies are vulnerable if the crop fails. The UN estimates that 12 plant species provide 75% of our total food supply.

1. The human population is growing at a rapid rate and as a result the demand for resources in increasing. Discuss how human activities are affecting biodiversity on Earth:

_____

_____

_____

_____

_____

_____

_____

Loss of biodiversity

Insects make up 80% of all known animal species. There are an estimated 6-10 million insect species on Earth, but only 900 000 have been identified. Some 44 000 species may have become extinct over the last 600 years. The Duke of Burgundy butterfly (*Hamearis lucina*), right, is an endangered British species.

About 5% of the 8225 reptile species are at risk. These include the two tuatara species (right) from New Zealand, which are the only living members of the order Sphenodontia, and the critically endangered blue iguana. Only about 200 blue iguanas remain, all in the Grand Caymans.

	Total number of species*	Number of IUCN listed species
Plants	310 000 - 422 000	8474
Insects	6 -10 million	622
Fish	28 000	126
Amphibians	5743	1809
Reptiles	8225	423
Birds	10 000	1133
Mammals	5400	1027

* Estimated numbers

The giant panda (above), is one of many critically endangered terrestrial mammals, with fewer than 2000 surviving in the wild. Amongst the 120 species of marine mammals, approximately 25% (including the humpback whale and Hector's dolphin) are on the ICUN's red list.

Prior to the impact of human activity on the environment, one bird species became extinct every 100 years. Today, the rate is one every year, and may increase to 10 species every year by the end of the century. Some at risk birds, such as the Hawaiian crow (right), are now found only in captivity.

Current estimates suggest as many as 47% of plant species may be endangered. Some, such as the South African cycad *Encephalartos woodii* (above), is one of the rarest plants in the world. It is extinct in the wild and all remaining specimens are clones.

2. (a) Comment on the actual extinction rate compared with the estimated background extinction rate: _____

_____

_____

(b) What factor is attributed to this difference? _____

3. The International Union for Conservation (IUCN) has established a Red List Index (RLI) for four taxonomic groups: reef forming corals, amphibians, birds, and mammals. This index focusses on the genuine status of changes. An RLI of 1.0 equates to all species qualifying as Least Concern (unlikely to become extinct in the near future). An RLI of 0 means that all species have become extinct. The figure right shows the trends in risk for the four taxonomic groups currently completed.

(a) Which taxon is moving most rapidly towards extinction risk?

_____

(b) Which taxon is, on average, the most threatened?

_____

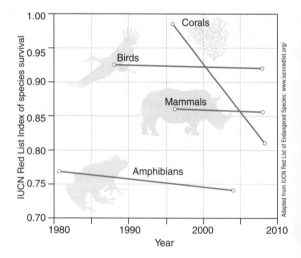

(c) Why would an index like this be useful and how could it help to highlight environmental issues of concern?

_____

_____

_____

4. Of the nearly 45 000 species assessed for the IUCN's red list, nearly 17 000 are threatened with extinction (endangered, critically endangered or vulnerable). The weblinks for this activity provide links to information on four British species. Select one and, on a separate sheet of paper, describe its conservation status, the reasons for its current status, and what is being done to assist its conservation. Attach the summary to this page.

203 Agriculture and Biodiversity

Key Idea: Agricultural systems generally have lower biodiversity than natural ecosystems.

Throughout the world, the intensification of agriculture has been associated with a decline in biodiversity. After the native vegetation has been cleared, soil tillage and burning reduces microbial biomass in the soil, altering soil structure and processes such as decomposition and nutrient cycling. When habitats shrink, populations decline and small isolated populations may not be viable. Habitat fragmentation also disrupts the activity patterns of mobile species, especially those that will not move over open agricultural land. Modern farming practices, such as dependence on mechanisation and a move away from mixed farming operations, have greatly accelerated the decline in biodiversity. In the UK, steps to conserve the countryside, such as hedgerow legislation, policies to increase woodland cover, and schemes to promote environmentally sensitive farming practices are designed to reduce loss of biodiversity.

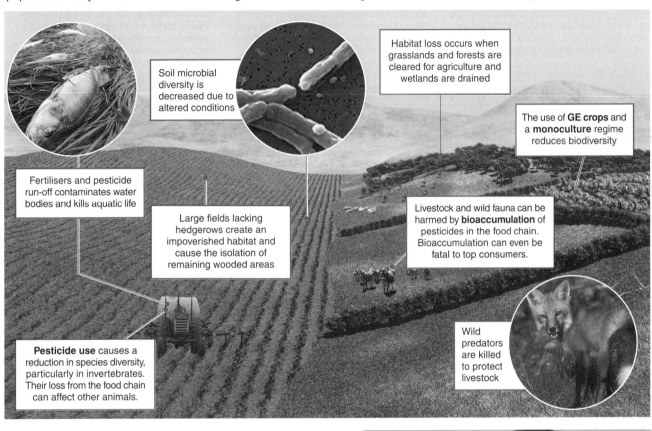

Soil microbial diversity is decreased due to altered conditions

Habitat loss occurs when grasslands and forests are cleared for agriculture and wetlands are drained

The use of **GE crops** and a **monoculture** regime reduces biodiversity

Fertilisers and pesticide run-off contaminates water bodies and kills aquatic life

Large fields lacking hedgerows create an impoverished habitat and cause the isolation of remaining wooded areas

Livestock and wild fauna can be harmed by **bioaccumulation** of pesticides in the food chain. Bioaccumulation can even be fatal to top consumers.

Wild predators are killed to protect livestock

Pesticide use causes a reduction in species diversity, particularly in invertebrates. Their loss from the food chain can affect other animals.

Natural grasslands are diverse and productive ecosystems. Ancient meadows may have contained 80-100 plant species, in contrast to currently cultivated grasslands, which may contain as few as three species. Unfortunately, many of the management practices that promote grassland species diversity conflict with modern farming methods. For example, the extensive use of fertilisers and selective herbicides on pastures favours aggressive species, such as nettles and docks, which out-compete ecologically important species such as orchids and cowslips. Appropriate management can help to conserve grassland ecosystems while maintaining their viability for agriculture.

Wildflower meadow in Britain

1. One solution to the conflicting needs of conserving biodiversity and productivity is to intensively farm designated areas, leaving other areas for conservation. From the farmer's perspective, outline two advantages of this approach:

    (a) _____

    _____

    (b) _____

    _____

    (c) Describe a disadvantage of this management approach: _____

    _____

    _____

LINK   LINK   WEB
206 **205** **203**   KNOW

An increase in urban sprawl and the pressure on farmers to increase productivity are having a dramatic impact on the once common flowering plants of Britain's grasslands. Diversity can be maintained only through careful management and conservation of existing ecosystems.

Grassland conservation is not only important for maintaining plant diversity, many animals rely on these ecosystems for food and shelter. A reduction in the diversity of grassland plant species translates to a reduction in the diversity of other species.

This woodland in Yorkshire, England, is home to numerous species of organisms. Clearing land for agriculture reduces both biodiversity and the ability of the community to adapt to changing environmental conditions. Natural ecosystem stability is decreased as a result.

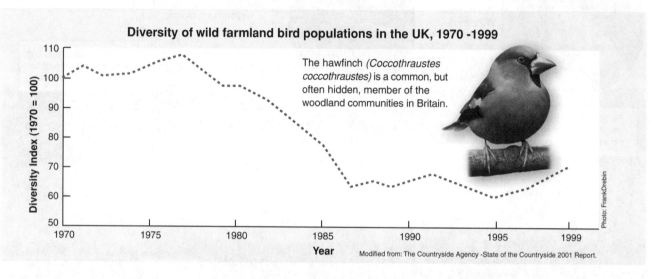

Diversity of wild farmland bird populations in the UK, 1970 -1999

The hawfinch (Coccothraustes coccothraustes) is a common, but often hidden, member of the woodland communities in Britain.

Photo: FrankDrebin

Modified from: The Countryside Agency -State of the Countryside 2001 Report.

2. Populations of wild farmland bird species, because of their wide distribution and position near the top of the food chain, provide good indicators of the state of other wildlife species and of environmental health in general. Over the last 25 years, there has been a marked net decline in the diversity of farmland bird populations (above). However, since 1986, diversity has ceased to decline further and, in recent years, has actually showed an increase.

Suggest two possible reasons for this decline in the diversity of farmland birds (also see the activity on hedgerows):

(a) _____

(b) _____

3. (a) Describe three initiatives local and national government have implemented in an attempt to reverse this decline:

(b) Discuss the role of environmental impact assessments and biodiversity estimates when planning such initiatives:

4. Provide an argument for retaining areas of uncultivated meadow alongside more intensively managed pasture:

204 Climate Change and Biodiversity

Key Idea: Global warming is causing shifts in the distribution, behaviour, and viability of plant and animal species.

Global warming is changing the habitats of organisms and this may have profound effects on the biodiversity of specific regions as well as on the planet overall. As temperatures rise, organisms may be forced to move to areas better suited to their temperature tolerances. Those that cannot move or tolerate the temperature change may face extinction. Changes in precipitation as a result of climate change will also affect where organisms can live. Long term changes in climate will ultimately result in a shift in vegetation zones as some habitats contract and others expand.

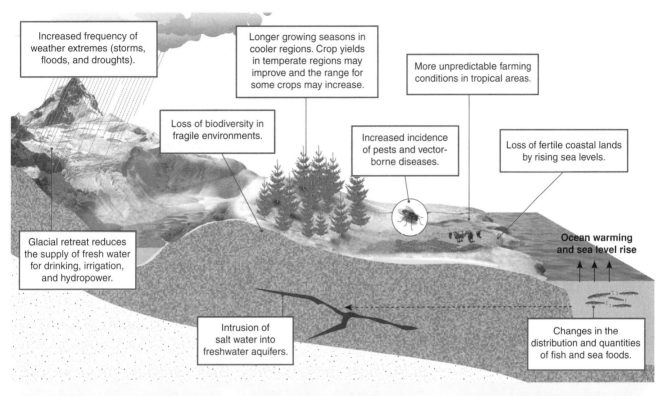

Increased frequency of weather extremes (storms, floods, and droughts).

Longer growing seasons in cooler regions. Crop yields in temperate regions may improve and the range for some crops may increase.

More unpredictable farming conditions in tropical areas.

Loss of biodiversity in fragile environments.

Increased incidence of pests and vector-borne diseases.

Loss of fertile coastal lands by rising sea levels.

Glacial retreat reduces the supply of fresh water for drinking, irrigation, and hydropower.

Ocean warming and sea level rise

Intrusion of salt water into freshwater aquifers.

Changes in the distribution and quantities of fish and sea foods.

Scotland's ancient Caledonian pinewood forests once covered thousands of kilometres of the highlands. Now they are restricted to 180 km², at only four sites. A warmer, wetter climate is predicted for Scotland, and the diversity of lowland flora is expected to increase as southern species move northwards. Species typical of the Caledonian forest, such as one-flowered wintergreen, will be threatened if the forest converts to broadleaved woodland, so conservation of pines will be a priority.

Photo: Walter Siegmund

Studies of the distributions of butterfly species in many countries show their populations are shifting. Surveys of Edith's checkerspot butterfly (*Euphydryas editha*) in western North America have shown it to be moving north and to higher altitudes.

An Australian study in 2004 found the centre of distribution for the AdhS gene in *Drosophila*, which helps survival in hot and dry conditions, had shifted 400 kilometers south in the last twenty years.

Studies of sea life along the Californian coast have shown that between 1931 and 1996, shoreline ocean temperatures increased by 0.79°C and populations of invertebrates including sea stars, limpets and snails moved northward in their distributions.

A 2009 study of 200 million year old plant fossils from Greenland has provided evidence of a sudden collapse in biodiversity that is correlated with, and appears to be caused by, a very slight rise in CO_2 levels.

Effects of increases in temperature on animal populations

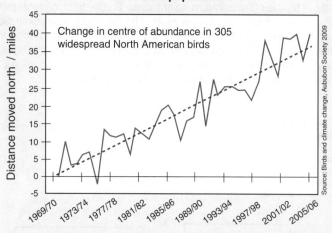

Change in centre of abundance in 305 widespread North American birds

Distance moved north / miles

1969/70 1973/74 1977/78 1981/82 1985/86 1989/90 1993/94 1997/98 2001/02 2005/06

Source: Birds and climate change, Audubon Society 2009

A number of studies indicate that animals are beginning to be affected by increases in global temperatures. Data sets from around the world show that birds are migrating up to two weeks earlier to summer feeding grounds and are often not migrating as far south in winter.

Animals living at altitude are also affected by warming climates and are being forced to shift their normal range. As temperatures increase, the snow line increases in altitude pushing alpine animals to higher altitudes. In some areas of North America this has resulted in the local extinction of the North American pika (*Ochotona princeps*).

Sevenstar public domain

1. Describe some of the likely effects of global warming on physical aspects of the environment: _____

_____

_____

_____

2. (a) Using the information on this and the previous activity, discuss the probable effects of global warming on plant crops:

_____

_____

(b) Suggest how farmers might be able to adjust to these changes: _____

_____

_____

_____

3. Discuss the evidence that insect populations are affected by global temperature: _____

_____

_____

4. (a) Describe how increases in global temperatures have affected some migratory birds: _____

_____

_____

(b) Explain how these changes in migratory patterns might affect food availability for these populations: _____

_____

_____

5. Explain how global warming could lead to the local extinction of some alpine species: _____

_____

_____

_____

205 Why is Biodiversity Important?

Key Idea: Maintaining biodiversity enhances ecosystem stability and functioning and also provides economic and aesthetic benefits to humans.

Ecosystems provide both material and non-material benefits to humans. These benefits, or ecosystem services, are best provided by healthy, diverse systems. As a general rule, high diversity ecosystems are ecologically more stable (constant in character over time) and resistant to disturbance (**resilient**) than systems with low diversity. Maintaining diversity therefore has economic benefits to humans through their use of ecosystem resources and through the generation of income from tourism to ecologically significant areas. Although often discussed as individual benefits, the ecological, aesthetic, and economic reasons for maintaining biodiversity overlap.

Ecological reasons for maintaining biodiversity

Evidence from both experimental and natural systems indicates that the most diverse ecosystems are generally the most stable, most probably because the complex network of species interactions has a buffering effect against change. Maintaining biodiversity is therefore critical to maintaining key ecological functions such as nutrient cycling and water purification.

Ecosystems include many interdependent species (e.g. flowering plants and their pollinators, hosts and parasites). The loss of even one species can detrimentally alter ecosystem dynamics, especially if the species is a keystone species. For example, in the Caledonian forest in Scotland, the Scots pine is key to the survival of many of the species present there. Its loss would affect the survival of those species and compromise the stability of the ecosystem.

Genetic diversity is an important component of ecosystem stability and resilience. A loss of genetic diversity is associated with an increased risk of extinction and a greater chance that an ecosystem will become impoverished and degraded. Genetic diversity effectively represents genetic resources, i.e. those genes in living organisms that may have benefits to humans (e.g. medicinal plants). Once an organism is extinct, those genetic resources are also lost.

Rainforest

Monoculture of soy beans

Rainforests represent the highest diversity systems on Earth. Whilst they are generally resistant to disturbance (resilient), once degraded (e.g. by deforestation), they have little ability to recover. Monocultures, which provide the majority of the world's food supply, represent very low diversity systems and are particularly susceptible to diseases, pests, and disturbance.

Aesthetic reasons for maintaining biodiversity

Many people enjoy looking at, or spending time in areas of natural beauty. Viewing aesthetically pleasing landscapes provides satisfaction and enjoyment to the individual. Nature can also provide inspiration for artists, photographers, and writers, as well as economic benefits from tourism. As countries become more populated and development increases, it becomes more important to maintain and protect natural landscapes as areas of natural beauty. The UK has several programmes designed to protect habitat and landscape for a variety of reasons, including aesthetics.

The images below show two coral reefs. Reef A has high biodiversity, many different species are represented and it is full of colour and life. Reef B is an area of coral bleaching and supports far fewer species. Imagine you were a tourist paying to visit the reef. Which would you rather visit?

A

B

1. What is the most likely reason for high diversity ecosystems being more stable than ecosystems with low biodiversity?

_____

_____

_____

2. Describe two aesthetic benefits of maintaining biodiversity: _____

_____

_____

3. (a) What is a genetic resource? _____

_____

(b) Many medicines are derived from plants. How does tropical rainforest destruction reduce genetic resources?

_____

_____

LINK   WEB
206 205   KNOW

Economic reasons for maintaining biodiversity

A variety of economic benefits (goods and services) are generated by biodiversity. These benefits are commonly called **ecosystem services** and are split into four categories: provisioning, regulating, and cultural services, which directly affect people, and supporting services, which maintain the other three services. The provisioning services are sometimes referred to as goods because they can be sold and their economic value can easily be calculated as they have a monetary value. Estimating the total economic value of total ecosystem services is difficult and contentious, but some estimates place their value at £81 trillion per year.

Provisioning services

(Products obtained from ecosystems)

- Food
- Water
- Fuel wood
- Fibres
- Biochemicals
- Genetic resources

Regulating services

(Benefits obtained from the regulation of ecosystem processes)

- Climate regulation
- Disease regulation
- Water regulation
- Water purification
- Pollination

Food production

Pollination

Ecotourism

Soil formation

Cultural services

(Nonmaterial benefits people obtain from ecosystems)

- Spiritual and religious
- Recreation and ecotourism
- Aesthetic
- Inspirational
- Educational
- Cultural heritage

Supporting services

(Services necessary for the production of all other ecosystem services)

- Soil formation
- Nutrient cycling
- Primary production

The economic cost of soil depletion

Soil depletion refers to the decline in soil fertility due to the removal of nutrients. Some definitions of soil depletion also include the physical loss (erosion) of soil.

The increase of continuous monoculture farming practices has contributed to a rapid loss of nutrients from the soil over the last few decades. Farmers must make an economic choice: spend money on fertilisers to add nutrients back to the soil or do nothing and suffer the economic consequences of low crop yields.

4. The 17th century Irish potato famine is an example of how low biodiversity can threaten our food supply. Farmers planted only one potato variety with limited genetic diversity. Most potato crops were destroyed by the fungal disease late blight and, exacerbated by the political environment at the time, there was widespread famine. How could have this situation have been prevented?

Blight affected potato

_____

_____

_____

5. Summarise the economic benefits of maintaining biodiversity: _____

_____

_____

_____

_____

_____

_____

_____

© 2015 **BIOZONE** International
ISBN: 978-1-927309-13-1
Photocopying Prohibited

206 Hedgerows

Key Idea: Hedgerows provide food, shelter and transport corridors for many species so are important for biodiversity. Since the 1940s, many thousands of kilometres of hedgerows have been removed from the British landscape each year as traditional mixed farms have been converted to farms with larger fields. In addition, neglect and improper management have been responsible for almost half of lost hedgerows every year. Hedgerows require maintenance and management in order to remain viable, yet hedge-laying and trimming skills are rapidly becoming lost. In 1997, legislation was introduced to control the destruction of hedgerows in rural settings. In England and Wales, landowners must apply to the local authority for permission to remove a hedgerow of greater than 20 metres in length, and this can be refused if the hedge is shown to be significant in terms of its age, environmental, or historical importance.

Hedgerows are important because...

- Hedges may support up to 80% of England's birds, 50% of its mammals, and 30% of its butterflies.
- The ditches and banks associated with hedgerows provide habitat for amphibians and reptiles.
- Hedges provide habitat, nesting material and food for birds and mammals.
- Some small mammals, e.g. dormice, once used hay ricks as overwintering habitat. With the loss of hay ricks, hedgerows are virtually their only alternative.
- They act as corridors, along which animals (e.g. pheasants) can safely move between areas of woodland.
- They provide overwintering habitat for predatory insects which move into crops to control pest insects in spring.
- Hedges provide shelter for stock and crops and reduce wind speed, which prevents erosion.
- Hedges act as barriers for windborne pests.

Photo courtesy, Kimberley Mallady

Bjorn Schulz

Hazel dormouse

Hedgerows commonly comprise hawthorn, blackthorn, field maple, hazel, and bramble. A hedgerow is essentially a linear wood and many of the associated plants are woodland species. At least 30 bird species nest in hedges. Hedgerows of different heights are preferred by different bird species, so management to provide a range of hedge heights and tree densities provides the best option for increasing diversity. For example, bullfinches prefer well-treed hedgerows over 4 m tall, whereas whitethroats, linnets, and yellowhammers favour shorter hedgerows (2-3 m) with fewer trees. The hedge base is important for ground-nesting species like the grey partridge. Hedgerows are important habitat for dormice and are used as dispersal corridors linking copses that are too small to support a viable populations on their own. Crucially they also support breeding populations independent of other habitats.

1. From an environmental perspective, describe three benefits of hedgerows to biodiversity:

   (a) _____

   (b) _____

   (c) _____

2. Explain why hedgerows might be regarded as undesirable from the perspective of a modern farmer: _____

   _____

   _____

3. Outline a brief argument to convince a farmer to retain and manage hedgerows, rather than remove them:

   _____

   _____

   _____

   _____

   _____

207 *In-Situ* Conservation

Key Idea: *In-situ* (on site) conservation methods manage ecosystems to protect diversity within the natural environment. A variety of strategies are used to protect at-risk species and help the recovery of those that are threatened. *In-situ* conservation means conservation on site and it focusses on ecological restoration and legislation to protect ecosystems of special value. Ecological restoration is a long term process and often involves collaboration between scientific institutions and the local communities involved. Some examples of *in-situ* conservation methods in the UK are shown below.

Snake's head fritillaries

Pagham Harbour

Starlet sea anemone

National Nature Reserves (NNRs)

The UK has 364 National Nature Reserves (NNRs), which are areas designated as having wildlife, habitat, or natural formations needing protection. NNRs often contain rare or nationally important species of plants or animals. The North Meadow NNR in Wiltshire is home to snake's head fritillaries (*Fritillaria meleagris*) a plant that is now rarely found in the English countryside.

Marine Conservation Zones (MCZs)

The UK has several types of Marine Protected Areas, each giving different levels of protection. Recently, Marine Conservation Zone (MCZ) were added. MCZs aim to conserve the diversity of rare and threatened marine species or habitats. They protect nationally important marine wildlife, habitats, and geology while allowing some sustainable activities within their boundaries. Pagham Harbour, West Sussex was designated a MCZ to protect the seagrass beds, lagoon sand shrimp, Defolin's lagoon snail, and the starlet sea anemone found there.

A case study in *in-situ* conservation

The East Midland Ancient Woodland Project is a government project to restore ancient woodland sites in the Northants Forest District in central England. England was once extensively wooded, but much native woodland was cleared or replanted last century, mostly with Norway spruce. The project, which was launched in 2000, aims to restore ancient woodland sites (those dating back to 1600 or before) to native woodland. The project will focus on key species.

How the project will proceed

▶ Restore plantations of ancient woodland sites to semi-natural woodland.

▶ Remove conifers and exotic broadleaf species.

▶ Expand the size and range of key species.

▶ Restore and manage the woodland to reflect its culture and history, while recognising current uses.

Advantages of *in-situ* conservation

• Species left in the protected area have access to their natural resources and breeding sites.

• Species will continue to develop and evolve in their natural environment thus conserving their natural behaviour.

• *In-situ* conservation is able to protect more species at once and allow them greater space than those in captivity.

• *In-situ* conservation protects larger breeding populations.

• *In-situ* conservation is less expensive and requires fewer specialised facilities than captive breeding.

Disadvantages of *in-situ* conservation

• Controlling illegal exploitation of *in-situ* populations is difficult.

• Habitats that shelter *in-situ* populations may need extensive restoration, including pest eradication and ongoing control.

• Populations may continue to decline during restoration.

Bluebell woodland in Buckinghamshire

In-situ conservation requires a lot of effort initially to restore sites and eradicate pests.

1. Explain why *in-situ* conservation commonly involves both ecosystem restoration and legislation to protect species:

_____

_____

_____

_____

© 2015 **BIOZONE** International
ISBN: 978-1-927309-13-1
Photocopying Prohibited

208 *Ex-Situ* Conservation

Key Idea: *Ex-situ* conservation methods operate away from the natural environment and are useful where species are critically endangered.

Ex-situ conservation is the process of protecting an endangered species outside its natural habitat. It is used when a species has become critically low in numbers or *in-situ* methods have been, or are likely to be, unsuccessful. Zoos, aquaria, and botanical gardens are the most conventional facilities for *ex-situ* conservation. They house and protect specimens for breeding and can reintroduce them into the wild to restore natural populations. The maintenance of seedbanks by botanic gardens and breeding registers by zoos ensures that efforts to conserve species are not impaired by problems of inbreeding.

M. Betley

Above: England is home to a rare sub-species of sand lizard (*Lacerta agilis*). It is restricted to southern heathlands and the coastal sand dunes of north west England. The UK Herpetological Conservation Trust is the lead partner in the action plan for this species and Chester Zoo hosts a captive breeding colony.

Right: A puppet 'mother' shelters a takahe chick. Takahe, a rare rail species native to New Zealand, were brought back from the brink of extinction through a successful captive breeding program.

In New Zealand, introduced predatory mammals, including weasels and stoats, have decimated native bird life. Relocation of birds on to predator-free islands or into areas that have been cleared of predators has been instrumental in the recovery of some species such as the North Island kokako. Sadly, others have been lost forever.

Captive breeding and relocation

Individuals are captured and bred under protected conditions. If breeding programmes are successful and there is suitable habitat available, captive individuals may be relocated to the wild where they can establish natural populations. Zoos now have an active role in captive breeding. There are problems with captive breeding; individuals are inadvertently selected for fitness in a captive environment and their survival in the wild may be compromised. This is especially so for marine species. However, for some taxa, such as reptiles, birds, and small mammals, captive rearing is very successful.

The important role of zoos and aquaria

As well as keeping their role in captive breeding programs and as custodians of rare species, zoos have a major role in public education. They raise awareness of the threats facing species in their natural environments and engender public empathy for conservation work. Modern zoos tend to concentrate on particular species and are part of global programs that work together to help retain genetic diversity in captive bred animals.

D. Eason (DOC)

Above: The okapi is a species of rare forest antelope related to giraffes. Okapi are only found naturally in the Ituri Forest, in the northeastern rainforests of the Democratic Republic of Congo (DRC), Africa, an area at the front line of an ongoing civil war. A okapi calf was born to Bristol Zoo Gardens in 2009, one of only about 100 okapi in captivity.

1. Describe the key features of *ex-situ* conservation methods: _____

_____

_____

_____

2. Explain why some animal species are more well suited to *ex-situ* conservation efforts than others: _____

_____

_____

_____

© 2015 **BIOZONE** International
ISBN: 978-1-927309-13-1
Photocopying Prohibited

LINK   WEB
207 208

KNOW

The role of botanic gardens

Botanic gardens have years of collective expertise and resources and play a critical role in plant conservation. They maintain seed banks, nurture rare species, maintain a living collection of plants, and help to conserve indigenous plant knowledge. They also have an important role in both research and education. The Royal Botanic Gardens at Kew (above) contain an estimated 25 000 species, 2700 of which are classified by the ICUN as rare, threatened, or endangered. Kew Gardens are involved in both national and international projects associated with the conservation of botanical diversity and are the primary advisors to CITES on threatened plant species. Kew's Millennium Seed Bank partnership is the largest ex situ plant conservation project in the world; working with a network in over 50 countries they have banked 10% of the world's wild plant species.

Seedbanks and gene banks

Seedbanks and gene banks around the world have a role in preserving the genetic diversity of species. A seedbank (above) stores seeds as a source for future planting in case seed reserves elsewhere are lost. The seeds may be from rare species whose genetic diversity is at risk, or they may be the seeds of crop plants, in some cases of ancient varieties no longer used in commercial production.

3. Describe three key roles of zoos and aquaria and explain the importance of each:

   (a) _____

   _____

   (b) _____

   _____

   (c) _____

   _____

4. Explain the importance of gene and seed banks, both to conservation and to agriculture: _____

   _____

   _____

   _____

5. Compare and contrast *in-situ* and *ex-situ* methods of conservation, including reference to the advantages and disadvantages of each approach:

   _____

   _____

   _____

   _____

   _____

   _____

   _____

   _____

   _____

   _____

209 Supporting Conservation Through Legislation

Key Idea: The UK adheres to several conservation agreements designed to protect wildlife and habitats.

One of the greatest concerns facing conservationists today is the rapidly accelerating rate at which species are being lost. To help combat this, conservation agreements have been established which typically deal with environmental and conservation issues and are designed to provide long-term protection and conservation priorities for wildlife species and their habitats. Failure to comply with the conditions of the agreement can carry legal or trading implications. The UK has signed up to several European and international conservation agreements, but also has national conservation agreements in place, such as the Countryside Stewardship Scheme, which focuses on arable environments.

International agreements

The UK is a member of several international treaties and conservation agreements between governments designed to conserve biodiversity. Two such agreements are the Rio Convention on Biological Diversity and the Convention of International Trade in Endangered Species (CITES).

Rio Convention on Biological Diversity

The Convention on Biological Diversity became active in 1993. It aims to develop strategies for the conservation and sustainable use of resources while maintaining biodiversity. It has three main goals:

▶ Conservation of biodiversity
▶ Sustainable use of its (biodiversity's) components
▶ Fair and equitable sharing of the benefits arising from genetic resources.

CITES

CITES aims to ensure that trade in species animals and plants does not threaten their survival in the wild. Trade on products are controlled or prohibited depending upon the level of threat to each species. More than 35 000 species are protected under the agreement.

CITES banned trading in ivory (right) or ivory products in 1989. As a result, African elephant populations have been increasing as poachers can no longer sell the ivory.

Domestic agreements

The UK has several conservation agreements in place effective at a national, regional, or community level. The focus of each agreement varies, but in general they all focus on the conservation and preservation of habitat and wildlife.

Most countries have a system of reserved lands focused on ecosystem conservation. These areas aim to protect and restore habitats of special importance and they may be intensively managed through pest and weed control, revegetation, reintroduction of threatened species, and site specific management practices.

Countryside Stewardship Scheme

The main aim of the new Countryside Stewardship Scheme (CSS) is to encourage biodiversity, but water quality and flood management goals are also included. The CSS is run by the Department for Environment, Food and Rural Affairs (Defra). It encourages land owners and farmers to improve the natural beauty and diversity of their land.

Preference is given to those whose actions will benefit the local area (rather than just a single land holding) and benefit wild pollinators, farmland birds, and other wildlife, e.g, sowing flower mixes to provide food for wild pollinators all year round. A financial payment is made if targets are achieved.

1. State the main objectives of the following conservation agreements:

(a) Rio Convention on Biological Diversity: _____

_____

_____

(b) CITES: _____

_____

_____

(c) Countryside Stewardship Scheme: _____

_____

_____

KNOW

210 Chapter Review

Summarise what you know about this topic under the headings provided. You can draw diagrams or mind maps, or write short notes to organise your thoughts. Use the images and hints and guidelines included to help you:

Biodiversity:
HINT: What are the components of biodiversity?

Factors affecting biodiversity:
HINT: How do human activities affect biodiversity?

Why is biodiversity important?
HINT: Include ecological, aesthetic, and economic reasons.

Conservation:
HINT: Summarise strategies for conservation, including legislation.

© 2015 **BIOZONE** International
ISBN: 978-1-927309-13-1
Photocopying Prohibited

211 KEY TERMS: Did You Get It?

1. Students wanted to compare the diversity of insects in a planted barley field and a natural hedgerow. They collected insects from a randomly selected point at each site. Their results are tabulated below.

(a) Describe the relative species richness and species evenness at each site: _____

_____

_____

(b) Complete the two tables by calculating the values for n/N and $(n/N)^2$:

(c) Calculate the Simpson's Index of Diversity (D) for each site and record this in the space provided under each table:

Barley field			
Species	n	n/N	$(n/N)^2$
A	32		
B	78		
C	1		
D	0		
E	0		
F	0		
G	0		
H	0		
I	0		
J	0		
K	85		
L	0		
Total	196		

D =

Under hedgerow			
Species	n	n/N	$(n/N)^2$
A	0		
B	1		
C	2		
D	12		
E	8		
F	9		
G	4		
H	3		
I	2		
J	5		
K	0		
L	7		
Total	53		

D =

(d) Describe the relative diversity of insect species at each site: _____

_____

(e) Give a possible explanation for the difference in the two sites: _____

_____

_____

(f) How could the students have improved their study? _____

_____

_____

_____

2. Describe in words the species richness and evenness of ecosystem A and B (below):

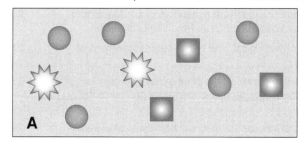

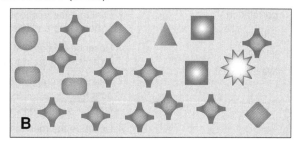

A _____   B _____

_____   _____

Classification and Evolution

Key terms

adaptation

binomial nomenclature

class

classification

continuous variation

convergent evolution

Darwin

differential survival

discontinuous variation

domain (in classification)

evolution

family

fitness

five kingdom classification

fossil record

genotype

genus

interspecific variation

intraspecific variation

kingdom

natural selection

new synthesis

order

phenotype

phylogeny

phylum

polymorphism

population

species

Spearman rank correlation

Student's *t* test

variation

Wallace

Biological classification

Learning outcomes

		Activity number
☐	1 Describe the biological classification of species with reference to the taxonomic hierarchy of kingdom, phylum, class, order, family, genus, and species.	212 213
☐	2 Explain how binomial nomenclature is used to identify species. Describe the advantages of binomial nomenclature and the problems associated with using common names to describe organisms.	212
☐	3 Understand what is meant by a distinguishing feature. Describe the distinguishing features of each kingdom in the five kingdom classification system.	214
☐	4 Describe the evidence that has led to newer classification systems, such as the three domains system. Compare the kingdom and domain systems.	215
☐	5 Describe the relationship between classification and phylogeny.	216

Variation, adaptation, and natural selection

Learning outcomes

		Activity number
☐	6 Describe evidence for the theory of evolution by natural selection, including the contributions of Darwin and Wallace, evidence from the fossil record, and DNA and other molecular evidence (e.g. cytochrome *c*).	217 -226
☐	7 Distinguish between genotype and phenotype. Describe and explain variation in organisms to include both interspecific and intraspecific variation.	227
☐	8 Using examples, distinguish between continuous and discontinuous variation. Describe the contribution of genes and environment to the variation we see in organisms, particularly within species.	227 228
☐	9 Use standard deviation to quantify the spread in a set of data. Use an appropriate statistical test to investigate variation in populations. Suitable examples include:	22 23
	▸ Compare the means of two populations (e.g. males and females) for a phenotypic variable such as hand span, foot length, or resting heart rate (Student's *t* test).	229 230
	▸ Evaluate the relationship between two variables (e.g. hand span and foot length or heart rate and breathing rate) in a population (Spearman rank correlation).	231
☐	10 Describe anatomical (structural), physiological, and behavioural adaptations of organisms to their environment.	232
☐	11 Describe examples to show that different taxonomic groups may show similar adaptations (as a result of convergent evolution), e.g. marsupial and placental ecological equivalents.	233
☐	12 Describe the mechanisms of natural selection, explaining how it can alter the characteristics of a population over time.	234
☐	13 Describe the implications for human populations of the evolution of pesticide resistance in insects and drug resistance in microorganisms.	235-237

212 Classification Systems

Key Idea: Organisms are named and assigned to taxa based on their shared characteristics and evolutionary relationships. Organisms are categorised into a hierarchical system of taxonomic groups (taxa) based on features they share that distinguish them from other taxa. The fundamental unit of classification is the **species**, and each member of a species is assigned a unique two part (binomial) name that identifies it. Classification systems are nested, so that with increasing taxonomic rank, related taxa at one hierarchical level are combined into more inclusive taxa at the next higher level.

Naming an organism

Most organisms have a common name as well a scientific name. Common names may change from place to place as people from different areas name organisms differently based on both language and custom. Scientifically, every organism is given a classification that reflects its known lineage (i.e. its evolutionary history). The last two (and most specific) parts of that lineage are the **genus** and **species** names. Together these are called the scientific name and every species has its own. This two-part naming system is called **binomial nomenclature**. When typed the name is always *italicised*. If handwritten, it should be underlined.

The animal *Rangifer tarandus* is known as the caribou in North America, but as the reindeer in Europe. The scientific name is unambiguous.

1. The table below shows part of the classification for humans using the seven major levels of classification. For this question, use the example of the classification of the European hedgehog on the next page, as a guide.

   (a) Complete the list of the taxonomic groupings on the left hand side of the table below:

	Taxonomic Group	Human Classification
1.	Kingdom	Animalia
2.	Phylum	Chordata
3.	Class	Mammalia
4.	Order	Primates
5.	Family	Hominidae
6.	Genus	Homo
7.	Species	sapiens

   (b) Complete the classification for humans (*Homo sapiens*) on the table above.

2. Construct an acronym or mnemonic to help you remember the principal taxonomic groupings (KPCOFGS):

   Did King Phillip Come Over for Good Spagetti

3. (a) What is the two part naming system for classifying organisms called? Binomial nomenclature

   (b) What are the two parts of the name? Genus and species

4. What are the advantages of a scientific name (as opposed to a common name)? They are universal names

5. What disadvantages can you see that might arise from classification based solely on the appearance of an organism?

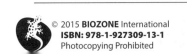
LINK   WEB

213 212   KNOW

Classification of the European hedgehog

The classification for the **European hedgehog** is described below to show the levels that can be used in classifying an organism. Not all possible subdivisions have been shown here (categories as **sub-family** often appear). The only natural category is the **species**, which may be separated into **sub-species**, based on molecular and morphological data.

Kingdom: **Animalia**
Animals; one of five kingdoms

Phylum: **Chordata**
Animals with a notochord (supporting rod of cells along the upper surface)
tunicates, salps, lancelets, and vertebrates

23 other phyla

Sub-phylum: **Vertebrata**
Animals with backbones
fish, amphibians, reptiles, birds, mammals

Class: **Mammalia**
Animals that suckle their young on milk from mammary glands
placentals, marsupials, monotremes

Infra-class: **Eutheria or Placentals**
Mammals whose young develop for some time in the female's reproductive tract gaining nourishment from a placenta
placental mammals

Order: **Eulipotyphla**
The insectivore-type mammals. Once part of the now abandoned order Insectivora, the order also includes shrews, moles, desmans, and solenodons.

20 other orders

Family: **Erinaceidae**
Comprises two subfamilies: the true or spiny hedgehogs and the moonrats (gymnures). Representatives in the family include the Ethiopian hedgehog, desert hedgehog, and the moonrats. The molecular evidence supports the Eulipotyphla being a monophyletic group (a common ancestor and all its descendants) but other classifications are common, e.g. sometimes the order is given as Erinaceomorpha with Erinaceidae as its only family.

4 other families

Genus: *Erinaceus*
One of twelve genera in this family. The genus *Erinaceus* includes four species.

11 other genera

Species: *europaeus*
The European hedgehog. Among the largest of the spiny hedgehogs. Characterised by a dense covering of spines on the back, the presence of a big toe (hallus) and 36 teeth.

3 other species

The advent of DNA sequencing and other molecular techniques for classification has resulted in the reclassification of many species. There is now considerable debate over the classification of species at almost all levels of classification. The now-defunct order, Insectivora, is one example. This order included a range of mammals with unspecialised features. The order was abandoned in 1956 but persisted (and still persists) in many textbooks. Over the years, families were moved out, merged, split apart again and reformed in other ways based on new evidence or interpretations. Do not be surprised if you see more than one classification for hedgehogs (or any other organism for that matter).

European hedgehog
Erinaceus europaeus

© 2015 **BIOZONE** International
ISBN: 978-1-927309-13-1
Photocopying Prohibited

213 Features of Taxonomic Groups

Key Idea: Taxonomy is the branch of science concerned with identifying, describing, classifying, and naming organisms. Taxonomy is the science of classifying organisms. It relies on identifying and describing characteristics that clearly distinguish organisms from each other. Classification systems recognising three domains (rather than five or six kingdoms) are now seen as better representations of the true diversity of life. However, for the purposes of describing the groups with which we are most familiar, the five kingdom system (used here) is still appropriate. The distinguishing features of some major **taxa** are provided in the following pages and examples give an indication of the diversity within each taxon.

SUPERKINGDOM: PROKARYOTAE (Bacteria)

- Also known as prokaryotes. The term moneran is no longer in use.
- Two major bacterial lineages are recognised: the **Archaebacteria** (Archaea) and the more derived **Eubacteria** (Bacteria).
- All have a prokaryotic cell structure: they lack the nuclei and chromosomes of eukaryotic cells, and have smaller (70S) ribosomes.
- Have a tendency to spread genetic elements across species barriers by conjugation, viral transduction, and other processes.
- Asexual. Can reproduce rapidly by binary fission.

- Have evolved a wider variety of metabolism types than eukaryotes.
- Bacteria grow and divide or aggregate into filaments or colonies of various shapes. Colony type is often diagnostic.
- They are taxonomically identified by their appearance (form) and through biochemical differences.

Species diversity: 10 000+ Bacteria are rather difficult to classify to species level because of their relatively rampant genetic exchange, and because their reproduction is asexual.

Eubacteria

- Also known as 'true bacteria', they probably evolved from the more ancient Archaebacteria.
- Distinguished from Archaebacteria by differences in cell wall composition, nucleotide structure, and ribosome shape.
- Diverse group includes most bacteria.
- The **gram stain** is the basis for distinguishing two broad groups of bacteria. It relies on the presence of peptidoglycan in the cell wall. The stain is easily washed from the thin peptidoglycan layer of gram negative walls but is retained by the thick peptidoglycan layer of gram positive cells, staining them a dark violet colour.

Gram positive bacteria

The walls of gram positive bacteria consist of many layers of peptidoglycan forming a thick, single-layered structure that holds the gram stain.

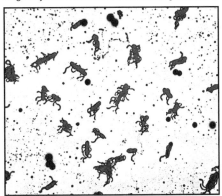

Bacillus alvei: a gram positive, flagellated bacterium. Note how the cells appear dark.

Gram negative bacteria

The cell walls of gram negative bacteria contain only a small proportion of peptidoglycan, so the dark violet stain is not retained by the organisms.

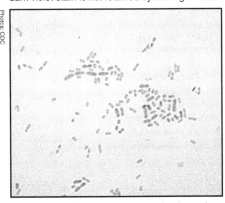

Photos: CDC

Alcaligenes odorans: a gram negative bacterium. Note how the cells appear pale.

SUPERKINGDOM: EUKARYOTAE
Kingdom: FUNGI

- Heterotrophic.
- Rigid cell wall made of chitin.
- Vary from single celled to large multicellular organisms.
- Mostly saprotrophic (ie. feeding on dead or decaying material).
- Terrestrial and immobile.

Examples:
Mushrooms/toadstools, yeasts, truffles, morels, molds, and lichens.

Species diversity: 80 000 +

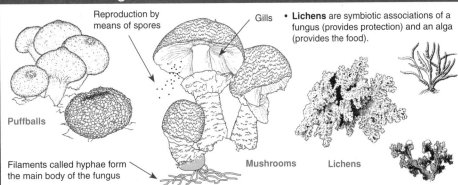

Reproduction by means of spores

Gills

- **Lichens** are symbiotic associations of a fungus (provides protection) and an alga (provides the food).

Puffballs

Filaments called hyphae form the main body of the fungus

Mushrooms   Lichens

Kingdom: PROTOCTISTA

- A diverse group of organisms. They are polyphyletic and so better represented in the 3 domain system.
- Unicellular or simple multicellular.
- Widespread in moist or aquatic environments.

Examples of algae: green, red, and brown algae, dinoflagellates, diatoms.

Examples of protozoa: amoebas, foraminiferans, radiolarians, ciliates.

Species diversity: 55 000 +

Algae 'plant-like' protoctists

- Autotrophic (photosynthesis)
- Characterised by the type of chlorophyll present

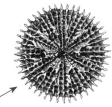

Cell walls of cellulose, sometimes with silica

Diatom

Protozoa 'animal-like' protoctists

- Heterotrophic nutrition and feed via ingestion
- Most are microscopic (5 μm - 250 μm)

Move via projections called pseudopodia

Lack cell walls

Amoeba

Kingdom: PLANTAE

- Multicellular organisms (the majority are photosynthetic and contain chlorophyll).
- Cell walls made of cellulose; food is stored as starch.
- Subdivided into two major divisions based on tissue structure: **Bryophytes** (non-vascular plants) and **Tracheophytes** (vascular plants).

Non-Vascular Plants:

- Non-vascular, lacking transport tissues (no xylem or phloem).
- Small and restricted to moist, terrestrial environments.
- Do not possess 'true' roots, stems, or leaves.

Phylum Bryophyta: Mosses, liverworts, and hornworts.

Species diversity: 18 600 +

Phylum: Bryophyta

Sexual reproductive structures

Flattened thallus (leaf like structure)

Sporophyte: reproduce by spores

Rhizoids anchor the plant into the ground

Liverworts

Mosses

Vascular Plants:

- Vascular: possess transport tissues.
- Possess true roots, stems, and leaves, as well as stomata.
- Reproduce via spores, not seeds.
- Clearly defined alternation of sporophyte and gametophyte generations.

Seedless Plants:

Spore producing plants, includes:
Phylum Filicinophyta: Ferns
Phylum Sphenophyta: Horsetails
Phylum Lycophyta: Club mosses
Species diversity: 13 000 +

Phylum: Lycophyta

Leaves

Club moss

Phylum: Sphenophyta

Leaves

Horsetail

Phylum: Filicinophyta

Large dividing leaves called fronds

Reproduce via spores on the underside of leaf

Rhizome

Adventitious roots

Fern

Seed Plants:

Also called Spermatophyta. Produce seeds housing an embryo. Includes:

Gymnosperms

- Lack enclosed chambers in which seeds develop.
- Produce seeds in cones which are exposed to the environment.

Phylum Cycadophyta: Cycads
Phylum Ginkgophyta: Ginkgoes
Phylum Coniferophyta: Conifers
Species diversity: 730 +

Phylum: Cycadophyta

Palm-like leaves

Cone

Cycad

Phylum: Ginkgophyta

Flat leaves

Ginkgo

Phylum: Coniferophyta

Needle-like leaves

Male cones

Woody stems

Female cones

Conifer

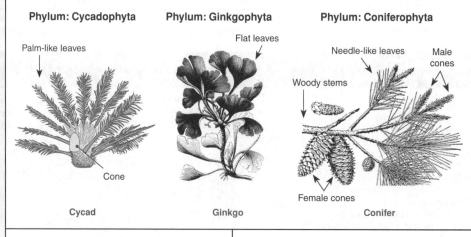

Angiosperms

Phylum: Angiospermophyta

- Seeds in specialised reproductive structures called flowers.
- Female reproductive ovary develops into a fruit.
- Pollination usually via wind or animals.

Species diversity: 260 000 +

The phylum Angiospermophyta may be subdivided into two classes:
Class Monocotyledoneae (Monocots)
Class Dicotyledoneae (Dicots)

Angiosperms: Monocotyledons

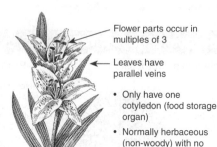

Flower parts occur in multiples of 3

Leaves have parallel veins

- Only have one cotyledon (food storage organ)
- Normally herbaceous (non-woody) with no secondary growth

Lily

Examples: cereals, lilies, daffodils, palms, grasses.

Angiosperms: Dicotyledons

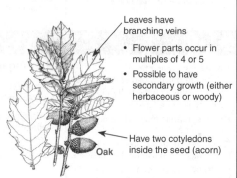

Leaves have branching veins

- Flower parts occur in multiples of 4 or 5
- Possible to have secondary growth (either herbaceous or woody)

Have two cotyledons inside the seed (acorn)

Oak

Examples: many annual plants, trees and shrubs.

Kingdom: ANIMALIA

- Over 800 000 species described in 33 existing phyla.
- Multicellular, heterotrophic organisms.
- Animal cells lack cell walls.

- Further subdivided into major phyla on the basis of body symmetry, development of the coelom (protostome or deuterostome), and external and internal structures.

Phylum: Porifera

- Lack organs.
- All are aquatic (mostly marine).
- Asexual reproduction by budding.
- Lack a nervous system.

Examples: sponges.

Species diversity: 8000 +

Body wall perforated by pores through which water enters

Water leaves by a larger opening - the osculum

Sponge

- Capable of regeneration (the replacement of lost parts)
- Possess spicules (needle-like internal structures) for support and protection

Tube sponge

Sessile (attach to ocean floor)

Phylum: Cnidaria

- Diploblastic with two basic body forms:
  Medusa: umbrella shaped and free swimming by pulsating bell.
  Polyp: cylindrical, some are sedentary, others can glide, or somersault or use tentacles as legs.
- Some species have a life cycle that alternates between a polyp stage and a medusa stage.
- All are aquatic (most are marine).

Examples: Jellyfish, sea anemones, hydras, and corals.

Species diversity: 11 000 +

Some have air-filled floats

Single opening acts as mouth and anus

Polyps may aggregate in colonies

Nematocysts (stinging cells)

Polyps stick to seabed

Brain coral

Jellyfish (Portuguese man-of-war)

Sea anemone

Colonial poly

Contraction of the bell propels the free swimming medusa

Phylum: Rotifera

- A diverse group of small, pseudocoelomates with sessile, colonial, and planktonic forms.
- Most freshwater, a few marine.
- Typically reproduce via cyclic parthenogenesis.
- Characterised by a wheel of cilia on the head used for feeding and locomotion, a large muscular pharynx (mastax) with jaw like trophi, and a foot with sticky toes.

Species diversity: 1500 +

Cilia
Head
Mastax
Foot
Toes

Spines for protection against predators

Lorica

Ovary

Eggs

Bdelloid: non-planktonic, creeping rotifer

Planktonic forms swim using their crown of cilia

Phylum: Platyhelminthes

- Unsegmented. Coelom has been lost.
- Flattened body shape.
- Mouth, but no anus.
- Many are parasitic.

Examples: Tapeworms, planarians, flukes.

Species diversity: 20 000 +

Hooks

Detail of head (scolex)

Liver fluke

Tapeworm

Planarian

Phylum: Nematoda

- Tiny, unsegmented roundworms.
- Many are plant/animal parasites

Examples: Hookworms, stomach worms, lung worms, filarial worms

Species diversity: 80 000 - 1 million

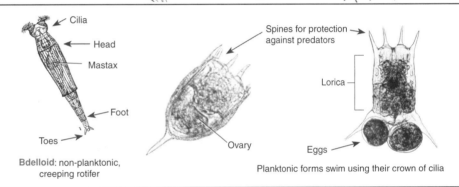

Muscular pharynx   Ovary   Anus

A roundworm parasite

Mouth   A general nematode body plan   Intestine

Phylum: Annelida

- Cylindrical, segmented body with chaetae (bristles).
- Move using hydrostatic skeleton and/ or parapodia (appendages).

Examples: Earthworms, leeches, polychaetes (including tubeworms).

Species diversity: 15 000 +

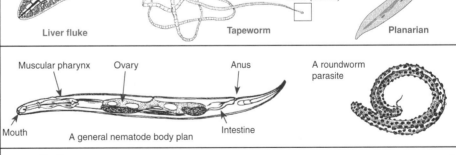
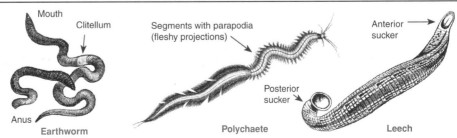

Mouth   Clitellum

Segments with parapodia (fleshy projections)

Anterior sucker

Posterior sucker

Anus   Earthworm   Polychaete   Leech

Kingdom: ANIMALIA (continued)

Phylum: Mollusca

- Soft bodied and unsegmented.
- Body comprises head, muscular foot, and visceral mass (organs).
- Most have radula (rasping tongue).
- Aquatic and terrestrial species.
- Aquatic species possess gills.

Examples: Snails, mussels, squid.

Species diversity: 110 000 +

Class: Bivalvia

Radula lost in bivalves

Mantle secretes shell

Scallop

Two shells hinged together

Class: Gastropoda

Mantle secretes shell

Muscular foot for locomotion

Head

Land snail

Class: Cephalopoda

Well developed eyes

Tentacles with eyes

Squid

Foot divided into tentacles

Phylum: Arthropoda

- Exoskeleton made of chitin.
- Grow in stages after moulting (ecdysis).
- Jointed appendages.
- Segmented bodies.
- Heart found on dorsal side of body.
- Open circulation system.
- Most have compound eyes.

Species diversity: 1 million +
Make up 75% of all living animals.

Arthropods are subdivided into the following classes:

Class: Crustacea (crustaceans)
- Mainly marine.
- Exoskeleton impregnated with mineral salts.
- Gills often present.
- Includes: Lobsters, crabs, barnacles, prawns, shrimps, isopods, amphipods
- **Species diversity**: 35 000 +

Class: Arachnida (chelicerates)
- Almost all are terrestrial.
- 2 body parts: cephalothorax and abdomen (except horseshoe crabs).
- Includes: spiders, scorpions, ticks, mites, horseshoe crabs.
- **Species diversity**: 57 000 +

Class: Insecta (insects)
- Mostly terrestrial.
- Most are capable of flight.
- 3 body parts: head, thorax, abdomen.
- Include: Locusts, dragonflies, cockroaches, butterflies, bees, ants, beetles, bugs, flies, and more
- **Species diversity**: 800 000 +

Myriapods (=many legs)
Class Diplopoda (millipedes)
- Terrestrial.
- Have a rounded body.
- Eat dead or living plants.
- **Species diversity**: 2000 +

Class Chilopoda (centipedes)
- Terrestrial.
- Have a flattened body.
- Poison claws for catching prey.
- Feed on insects, worms, and snails.
- **Species diversity**: 7000 +

Class: Crustacea

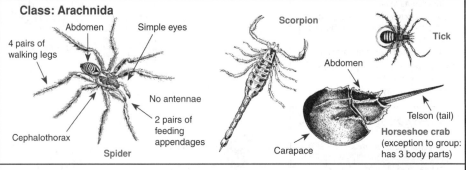

2 pairs of antennae

Cephalothorax (fusion of head and thorax)

Abdomen

Crab

3 pairs of mouthparts

Cheliped (first leg)

Shrimp

Walking legs

Swimmerets

Amphipod

Class: Arachnida

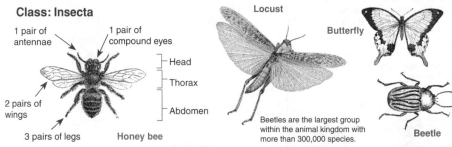

4 pairs of walking legs

Abdomen

Simple eyes

Scorpion

Tick

Abdomen

Cephalothorax

Spider

No antennae

2 pairs of feeding appendages

Carapace

Telson (tail)

Horseshoe crab (exception to group: has 3 body parts)

Class: Insecta

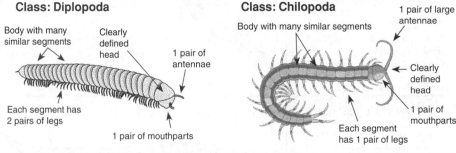

1 pair of antennae

1 pair of compound eyes

Locust

Butterfly

Head

Thorax

2 pairs of wings

Abdomen

3 pairs of legs

Honey bee

Beetles are the largest group within the animal kingdom with more than 300,000 species.

Beetle

Class: Diplopoda

Body with many similar segments

Clearly defined head

1 pair of antennae

Each segment has 2 pairs of legs

1 pair of mouthparts

Class: Chilopoda

Body with many similar segments

1 pair of large antennae

Clearly defined head

1 pair of mouthparts

Each segment has 1 pair of legs

Phylum: Echinodermata

- Rigid body wall, internal skeleton made of calcareous plates.
- Many possess spines.
- Ventral mouth, dorsal anus.
- External fertilisation.
- Unsegmented, marine organisms.
- Tube feet for locomotion.
- Water vascular system.

Examples: Starfish, brittlestars, feather stars, sea urchins, sea lilies.

Species diversity: 6000 +

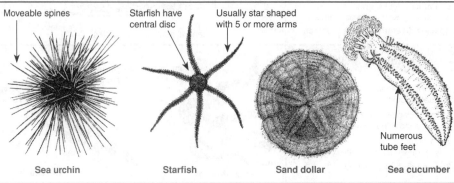

Moveable spines

Starfish have central disc

Usually star shaped with 5 or more arms

Sea urchin

Starfish

Sand dollar

Numerous tube feet

Sea cucumber

© 2015 **BIOZONE** International
ISBN: 978-1-927309-13-1
Photocopying Prohibited

Kingdom: ANIMALIA (continued)

Phylum: Chordata

- Dorsal notochord (flexible, supporting rod) present at some stage in the life history.
- Post-anal tail present at some stage in their development.
- Dorsal, tubular nerve cord.
- Pharyngeal slits present.
- Circulation system closed in most.
- Heart positioned on ventral side.

Species diversity: 48 000 +

- A very diverse group with several sub-phyla:
  - Urochordata (sea squirts, salps)
  - Cephalochordata (lancelet)
  - Craniata (vertebrates)

Sub-Phylum Craniata (vertebrates)
- Internal skeleton of cartilage or bone.
- Well developed nervous system.
- Vertebral column replaces notochord.
- Two pairs of appendages (fins or limbs) attached to girdles.

Further subdivided into:

Class: Chondrichthyes (cartilaginous fish)
- Skeleton of cartilage (not bone).
- No swim bladder.
- All aquatic (mostly marine).
- Include: Sharks, rays, and skates.

Species diversity: 850 +

Class: Osteichthyes (bony fish)
- Swim bladder present.
- All aquatic (marine and fresh water).

Species diversity: 21 000 +

Class: Amphibia (amphibians)
- Lungs in adult, juveniles may have gills (retained in some adults).
- Gas exchange also through skin.
- Aquatic and terrestrial (limited to damp environments).
- Include: Frogs, toads, salamanders, and newts.

Species diversity: 3900 +

Class Reptilia (reptiles)
- Ectotherms with no larval stages.
- Teeth are all the same type.
- Eggs with soft leathery shell.
- Mostly terrestrial.
- Include: Snakes, lizards, crocodiles, turtles, and tortoises.

Species diversity: 7000 +

Class: Aves (birds)
- Terrestrial endotherms.
- Eggs with hard, calcareous shell.
- Strong, light skeleton.
- High metabolic rate.
- Gas exchange assisted by air sacs.

Species diversity: 8600 +

Class: Mammalia (mammals)
- Endotherms with hair or fur.
- Mammary glands produce milk.
- Glandular skin with hair or fur.
- External ear present.
- Teeth are of different types.
- Diaphragm between thorax/abdomen.

Species diversity: 4500 +
Subdivided into three subclasses: Monotremes, marsupials, placentals.

Class: Chondrichthyes (cartilaginous fish)
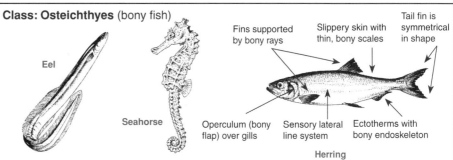

Class: Osteichthyes (bony fish)
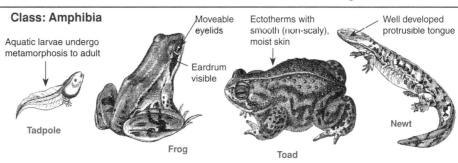

Class: Amphibia
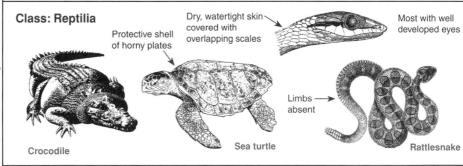

Class: Reptilia
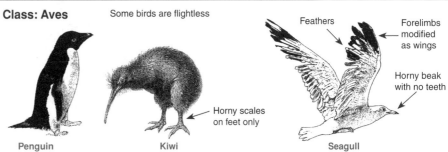

Class: Aves
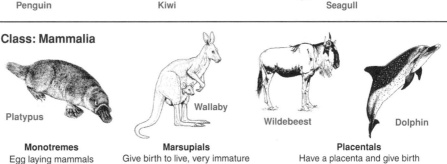

Class: Mammalia

Monotremes Egg laying mammals

Marsupials Give birth to live, very immature young, which then develop in a pouch

Placentals Have a placenta and give birth to live, well developed young

214 Features of the Five Kingdoms

Key Idea: Organisms can be classified into one of five kingdoms on the basis of their distinguishing features. The classification of organisms is based on how biologists believe they are related in an evolutionary sense. Organisms that are closely related will have more features in common than more distantly related organisms. Those features that definitively distinguish one taxon from another are called distinguishing features. Alone, or sometimes collectively, they should define the group. This activity asks you to summarise the distinguishing features of each of the five kingdoms.

1. Distinguishing features of Kingdom **Prokaryotae**:

_____

_____

_____

_____

2. Distinguishing features of Kingdom **Protoctista**:

_____

_____

_____

_____

_____

3. Distinguishing features of Kingdom **Fungi**:

_____

_____

_____

_____

_____

4. Distinguishing features of Kingdom **Plantae**:

_____

_____

_____

_____

_____

5. Distinguishing features of Kingdom **Animalia**:

_____

_____

_____

_____

_____

_____

Staphylococcus dividing

Helicobacter pylori

Red blood cell
Trypanosoma parasite

Amoeba

Mushrooms

Yeast cells in solution

Moss

Pea plants

Cicada moulting

Gibbon

KNOW

© 2015 **BIOZONE** International
ISBN: 978-1-927309-13-1
Photocopying Prohibited

215 The New Tree of Life

Key Idea: The classification of life into specific groups, or taxa, is constantly being updated in light of new information. Taxonomy is the science of classification and, like all science, constantly changing as new information is discovered. With the advent of DNA sequencing technology, scientists began to analyse the genomes of many bacteria. In 1996, the results of a scientific collaboration examining DNA evidence confirmed that life comprises three major evolutionary lineages (domains) and not two as was the convention. The recognised lineages are the Bacteria (formerly Eubacteria), the Eukarya (Eukaryotes), and the Archaea (formerly Archaebacteria). The new classification reflects the fact that there are very large differences between the archaeans and the bacteria. All three domains probably had a distant common ancestor.

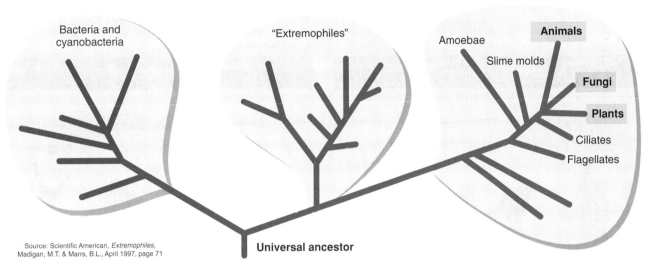

Source: Scientific American, *Extremophiles*, Madigan, M.T. & Marrs, B.L., April 1997, page 71

Domain Eubacteria (bacteria)
Lack a distinct nucleus and cell organelles. Generally prefer less extreme environments than Archaea. Includes well-known pathogens, many harmless and beneficial species, and the cyanobacteria (photosynthetic bacteria containing the pigments chlorophyll a and phycocyanin).

Domain Archaea (archeans)
Closely resemble eubacteria in many ways but cell wall composition and aspects of metabolism are very different. Live in extreme environments similar to those on primeval Earth. They may utilise sulfur, methane, or halogens (chlorine, fluorine), and many tolerate extremes of temperature, salinity, or pH.

Domain Eukarya (eukaryotes)
Complex cell structure with organelles and nucleus. This group contains four of the kingdoms classified under the more traditional system. Note that Kingdom Protoctista is separated into distinct groups: e.g. amoebae, ciliates, flagellates.

The five kingdom world

Before DNA sequencing showed that life was divided into three major domains, taxonomists divided life into five kingdoms based mainly on visible characteristics. This system is still common mainly because it is useful in separating the multicellular organisms that are familiar in our everyday experience. In this system, all prokaryotic organisms are placed in one kingdom (or sometimes two, making six kingdoms) with protoctists (single celled eukaryotes), fungi, plants, and animals being the other four. Clearly, it is not an accurate representation of the evolutionary relationships between organisms. In particular, the Kingdom Protoctista is a diverse collection of organisms that are not necessarily closely related.

In general there are eight taxa (taxonomic groups) used to classify organisms. These are: **domain**, **kingdom**, **phylum**, **class**, **order**, **family**, **genus**, and **species**. An organism's classification is not necessarily fixed, and may change as new information comes to light.

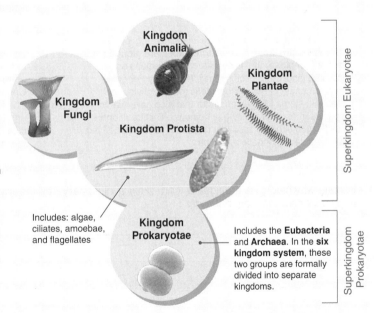

Includes: algae, ciliates, amoebae, and flagellates

Includes the **Eubacteria** and **Archaea**. In the **six kingdom system**, these two groups are formally divided into separate kingdoms.

1. Describe one feature of the three domain system that is very different from the five kingdom classification:

_____

_____

_____

216 Classification and Phylogeny

Key Idea: Classification is the organisation of species into groups (taxa) based on their shared characteristics. The evolutionary history of a species or taxon is its phylogeny. Classification systems aim to accurately reflect phylogeny.

Biological classification today is concerned with organising species (and taxa) in a way that reflects their evolutionary history (phylogeny). Cladistic analysis is one method by which we can construct an evolutionary history for a taxonomic group. Phylogenies constructed using traditional and cladistic methods do not necessarily conflict, but cladistics' emphasis on molecular data has led to reclassifications of a number of taxa (including primates and many plants). In **natural classifications**, all members of the group have descended from a common ancestor (they are **monophyletic**). Molecular evidence has shown that many traditional groups (e.g. reptiles) do not meet this criterion. Popular classifications will probably continue to reflect similarities and differences in appearance, rather than a strict evolutionary history. In this respect, they are a compromise between phylogeny and the need for a convenient filing system for species diversity.

Classification of the "great apes"

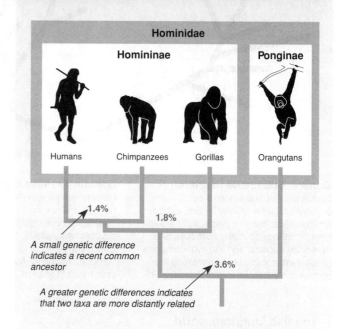

A classical taxonomic view	A cladistic view

A classical taxonomic view

Hominidae — Humans

Pongidae — The 'great apes': Chimpanzees, Gorillas, Orangutans

On the basis of overall anatomical similarity (e.g. bones and limb length, teeth, musculature), apes are grouped into a family (Pongidae) that is separate from humans and their immediate ancestors (Hominidae). The family Pongidae (the great apes) is not monophyletic (of one phylogeny), because it stems from an ancestor that also gave rise to a species in another family (i.e. humans). This traditional classification scheme is now at odds with schemes derived after considering genetic evidence.

A cladistic view

Hominidae

Homininae — Humans, Chimpanzees, Gorillas

Ponginae — Orangutans

1.4% — A small genetic difference indicates a recent common ancestor

1.8%

3.6% — A greater genetic differences indicates that two taxa are more distantly related

Based on the evidence of genetic differences (% values above), chimpanzees and gorillas are more closely related to humans than to orangutans, and chimpanzees are more closely related to humans than they are to gorillas. Under this scheme there is no true family of great apes. The family Hominidae includes two subfamilies: Ponginae and Homininae (humans, chimpanzees, and gorillas). This classification is monophyletic: the Hominidae includes all the species that arise from a common ancestor.

1. Explain why cladistics provides a more likely evolutionary tree for any particular group of organisms than some traditional classification methods:

_____

_____

_____

_____

_____

2. Based on the diagram above, state the family to which the chimpanzees belong under:

   (a) A traditional scheme: _____

   (b) A cladistic scheme: _____

3. What evidence has led to the reclassification of the primates? _____

© 2015 **BIOZONE** International
ISBN: 978-1-927309-13-1
Photocopying Prohibited

217 A Pictorial History of Evolutionary Thought

Key Idea: The modern theory of evolution was developed over many years with contributions by many scientists. Although Charles Darwin is largely credited with the development of the theory of evolution by natural selection, his ideas did not develop in isolation, but within the context of the work of others before him. The modern synthesis of evolution (below) has a long history with contributors from all fields of science. The diagram below summarises just some of the important players in the story of evolutionary biology. This is not to say they were collaborators or always agreed. However, the work of many has contributed to a deeper understanding of evolutionary processes. This understanding continues to develop with the use of molecular techniques and work between scientists across many disciplines.

Find out more!
This timeline has been adapted from the University of California, Berkeley's excellent *Evolution 101* website. Go to the Weblink indicated at the bottom of the page to find out more about the events and the people described.

1900 to present day

1800s

Putneymark

Pre 1800

GEOLOGY - EARTH'S HISTORY -	PALEONTOLOGY - LIFE'S HISTORY -	THE MECHANISMS OF EVOLUTION	DEVELOPMENT AND GENETICS
		Modern evo-devo *Stephen Jay Gould*	
			Genetic similarities *Wilson, Sarich, Sibley, & Ahlquist*
Radiometric dating *Clair Patterson*	Endosymbiosis *Lynn Margulis*	Speciation *Ernst Mayr*	DNA *James Watson & Francis Crick*

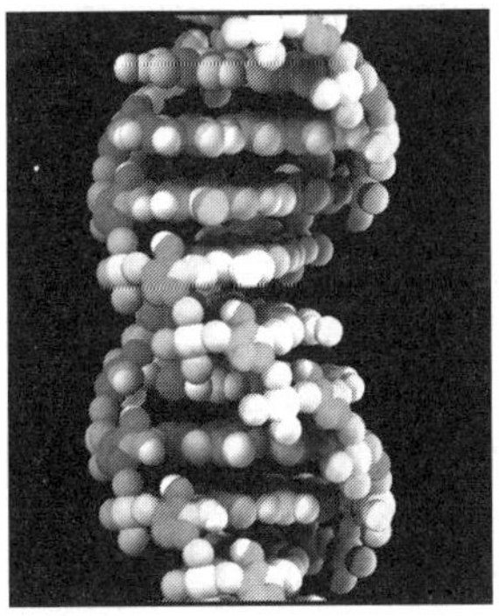

THE MODERN SYNTHESIS OF EVOLUTION
Brought together many disciplines and showed how mutation and natural selection could produce large-scale evolutionary change.
Theodosius Dobzhansky

1900

	Human evolution *Huxley & Dubois*		The founding of population genetics *Fisher, Haldane, & Sewall Wright*
			Chromosomes and mutation *Thomas Hunt Morgan*
	Biogeography *Wallace & Wegener*		
			Early evo-devo *Ernst Haeckel*

Evolution by natural selection
Charles Darwin & Alfred Russel Wallace

		Genes are discrete *Gregor Mendel*	
Uniformitarianism *Charles Lyell*		Chromosomal basis of heredity *August Weismann*	
Biostratigraphy *William Smith*		Evolution *Lamarck*	Developmental studies *Karl Von Baer*

1800

Extinctions *Georges Cuvier*			
Old Earth and ancient life *Comte de Buffon*		The ecology of human populations *Thomas Malthus*	

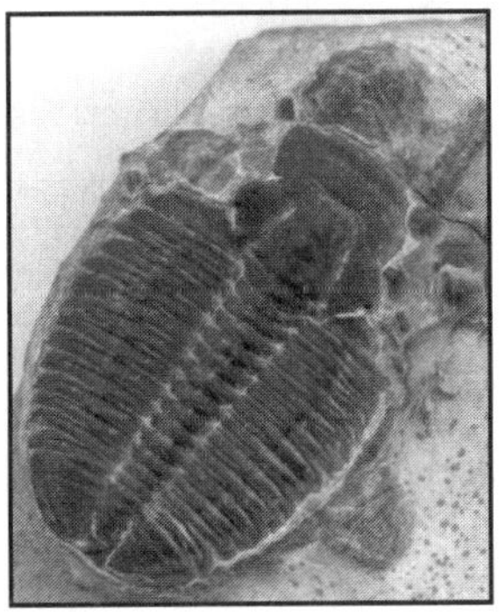

	The order of nature *Carl Linnaeus*		

1700

Fossils and the birth of palaeontology			

Observation and natural theology
Important because it addressed the question of how life works

Comparative anatomy *Andreas Vesalius*			

LINK **219** LINK **218** WEB **217** KNOW

The development of the modern synthesis

Darwin

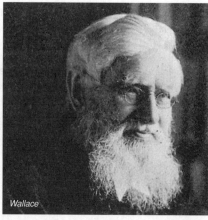

Wallace

Charles Darwin (1809-1882) and **Alfred Russel Wallace** (1823-1913) jointly and independently proposed the theory of evolution by natural selection. Both amassed large amounts of supporting evidence, Darwin from his voyages aboard the Beagle and in the Galápagos Islands and Wallace from his studies in the Amazon and the Malay archipelago. Wallace wrote to Darwin of his ideas on evolution by natural selection, spurring Darwin to publish *The Origin of Species.*

Gregor Mendel (1822-1884) developed ideas of the genetic basis of inheritance. Mendel's *particulate model of inheritance* was recognised decades later as providing the means by which natural selection could occur.

'An inordinate fondness for beetles'

Display: Oxford University Museum of Natural History

Theodosius Dobzhansky (1900-1975) was a Ukrainian who synthesised the ideas of genetics and evolutionary biology and defined evolution as "a change in the frequency of an allele within a gene pool". Dobzhansky worked on the genetics of wild *Drosophila* species and was famously quoted as saying "Nothing in biology makes sense except in the light of evolution".

Ernst Mayr (1904-2005) was a German evolutionary biologist who collaborated with Dobzhansky to formulate the modern evolutionary synthesis. He worked on and defined various mechanisms of speciation and proposed the existence of rapid speciation events, which became important for later ideas about punctuated equilibrium.

Ronald Fisher, **JBS Haldane**, and **Sewall Wright** founded population genetics, building sophisticated mathematical models of genetic change in populations. Their models, together with the work of others like Mayr and Dobzhansky contributed to a refinement and development of Darwin's theory into the **modern synthesis.** Haldane was quoted as saying that the Creator must have "an inordinate fondness for beetles".

The modern synthesis today

James Watson and **Francis Crick**'s discovery of DNA's structure in 1953 revolutionised evolutionary biology. The genetic code could be understood and deciphered, and the role of mutation as the source of new alleles was realised.

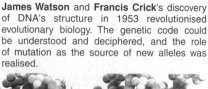

Stephen Jay Gould (1941-2002)

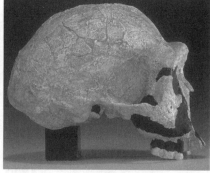

After Haeckel's flawed work on embryology fell out of favour, the evolutionary study of embryos was largely abandoned for decades. However, in the 1970s, **Stephen Jay Gould**'s work on the genetic triggers for developmental change brought studies of embryological development back into the forefront. Today evo-devo is providing some of the strongest evidence for how novel forms can rapidly arise.

In recent decades, DNA hybridisation studies, DNA sequencing and protein analyses have revolutionised our understanding of phylogeny. **Allan Wilson** was one of a small group of pioneers in this field, using molecular approaches to understand evolutionary change and reconstruct phylogenies, including those of human ancestors.

1. Using a separate sheet, research and then write a 150 word account of the development of evolutionary thought and the importance of contributors from many scientific disciplines in shaping what became the modern synthesis. You should choose specific examples to illustrate your points of discussion.

218 The Contributions of Darwin and Wallace

Key Idea: Both Charles Darwin and Alfred Russel Wallace produced theories supported by evidence for evolution by natural selection.

Both Darwin and Wallace collected a wide range of evidence to support their ideas of evolution. Darwin began to formulate his theory of evolution by natural selection during his voyage aboard the *Beagle*, especially with observations of animals in the Galápagos islands. When he returned to England, he

then spent many years gathering more evidence to support his idea that species could change. Wallace spent much time in the Amazon basin and Malay Archipelago collecting specimens for sale to collectors. Through his observations of species during this time, he formulated his own independent ideas of evolution by natural selection and identified the faunal divide known as the Wallace line that separates the Malay Archipelago into two distinct parts.

During the voyage of the *Beagle* Darwin carries out numerous geological surveys, providing evidence of geological changes over long periods of time.

While studying barnacles Darwin finds homologies, the same structure in different species modified for different uses. He also finds evidence for the evolution of distinct sexes.

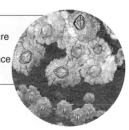

1831 - 1836

putneymark CC 2.0

1847

Collection of Galápagos finches while aboard the Beagle later helps Darwin realise that they evolved from a single ancestor species.

During his explorations of the Amazon and Malay Archipelago, Wallace notes that related species inhabit neighbouring areas.

Evolution by natural selection 1858

In *The Origin of Species*, Darwin argues that natural selection works on the same principles as artificial selection by making comparisons with a range of domesticated animals. Darwin shows unfit species are constantly replaced by fitter ones, thus explaining extinction and the appearance of unknown animals in the fossil record. While in the Malay Archipelago, Wallace develops his ideas on natural selection, writing to Darwin. His ideas are published alongside Darwin's.

Jim Gifford CC 2.0

While exploring the Malay Archipelago, Wallace realised that a line could be drawn through the archipelago separating the fauna that originated from Australia from the fauna of Asian origin.

Wallace explained bright colouration in insects (e.g monarch caterpillars) as a warning to predators of their foul taste and toxic nature.

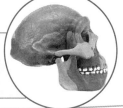

Darwin's book *Fertilisation of Orchids* details how natural selection can explain ecological relationships by coevolution.

Darwin shows how sexual selection plays an important role in evolution of species including humans and birds of paradise in his book *The Descent of Man*.

1862

1871

Wallace proposes species isolating barriers that would prevent hybridisation of species and further drive evolution.

Wallace publishes many books and articles that both defend natural selection and use it to explain other biological phenomena. He also writes about social politics, economics, and astrobiology.

1. What is the importance of long geological time spans in evolution? _____

_____

2. What was the significance of the realisation that the Galápagos finches were all related? _____

_____

3. What important biogeographic ideas did Wallace formulate? _____

_____

_____

© 2015 **BIOZONE** International
ISBN: 978-1-927309-13-1
Photocopying Prohibited

LINK   LINK   WEB

219 **217** **218**   KNOW

The rock pigeon: a versatile progenitor

Photo: JM Garg, CC 3.0, Wikipedia

The rock pigeon or rock dove (*Columba livia*) includes the domestic pigeon (including the fancy pigeons on which Darwin worked) and domestic pigeons which become feral. It is a highly adaptable species and shows a range of phenotypes. Feral pigeons for example show many different plumage colorations.

Pigeon fanciers and selective breeding

"*... from so simple a beginning endless forms most beautiful and most wonderful have been, and are being evolved.*" This quotation closes Charles Darwin's most famous work "*The Origin of Species by Means of Natural Selection*". Most students of biology know of Darwin's voyage aboard *The Beagle*" and his precise and careful documenting of the variety of species he encountered on his travels, to the Galapagos in particular. But the naturalist's careful attention to biological detail extended to his work at home in England. Darwin began to formulate his theory of evolution during his five year voyage aboard *The Beagle*, but this work continued in earnest when he returned home to England and established a home (and research station) at Down House. Darwin delayed publishing his greatest work, fearing ridicule in the deeply religious English society. He wanted to gather more evidence to support his idea that species could change. He found this evidence by studying domesticated species that he knew could be shaped through breeding. Pigeons, rabbits, cabbages, gooseberries; these organisms would become his window into the workings of selection. Thus Darwin became a pigeon fancier. Indeed, the humble pigeon, loved by generations of English people, played a most important part in his work on both 'The Origin of Species' (1859) and 'Variation in Domestication' (1868). He said "*Believing that it is always best to study some special group, I have . . . taken up domestic pigeons.*"

Darwin excelled in careful observation and meticulous record keeping and he was a frequent correspondent with like-minded thinkers. As well as breeding his own pigeons, he managed to secure skins and skeletons from colleagues and acquaintances all over Britain. But Darwin was interested in evolution, not pigeon shows. He wanted a sense of how much variation existed within a single species in nature and saw selective breeding as a "speeded up version" of the process that gave rise to new species in nature. Darwin's pigeon work was much more than a hobby; it was a way to get his point across and to demonstrate the dramatic effects of selection. Darwin skeletonised and meticulously recorded the details of hundreds of specimens and concluded that if artificial selection could produce such diversity over decades, what might natural selection produce over millions of years?

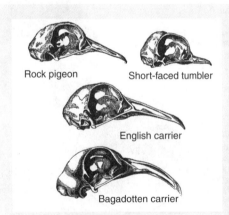

Skulls of various pigeon breeds as drawn by Darwin. Relative sizes accurate. Darwin noted that difference in breed appearance extended even to the skeletal features.
(Charles Darwin/Frances Darwin - out of copyright)

Pouters: This group includes breeds developed for the ability to inflate their crops. The pygmy pouter's bizarre appearance has made it one of the least popular breeds, except in shows.

photos: Jim Gifford, Wikipedia (originally via Flickr)

The fantail is characterised by a fan-shaped tail composed of 30 to 40 feathers; more than most members of the pigeon family, which usually have only 12 to 14 feathers. A feather mutation called silky produces yet another variety.

1. Explain why Darwin sought support for his evolutionary theory from his pigeon breeding work: _____

_____

_____

2. Explain why his findings supported his ideas that species could change over time: _____

_____

_____

_____

_____

_____

© 2015 **BIOZONE** International
ISBN: 978-1-927309-13-1
Photocopying Prohibited

220 Fossils

Key Idea: Fossils are the preserved remains or traces of organisms. They provide a record of the appearance and extinction of organisms over time.

Fossils are the remains of long-dead organisms that have escaped decay and become part of the Earth's crust. For fossilisation to occur, rapid burial of the organism is required (usually in water-borne sediment). This is followed by chemical alteration, where minerals are added or removed.

Fossilisation requires the normal processes of decay to be permanently arrested. This can occur if the remains are isolated from the air or water and decomposing microbes are prevented from breaking them down. Fossils provide a record of the appearance and extinction of organisms, from species to whole taxonomic groups. Once this record is calibrated against a time scale, it is possible to build up a picture of the evolutionary changes that have taken place.

Mould: This impression of a lamp shell is all that is left after the original shell material was dissolved after fossilisation. Jurassic (New Zealand).

Ray structure

Bark

Growth rings largely destroyed

All photos: RA

Ants

Polished amber

Insects in amber: The fossilised resin or gum produced by some ancient conifers trapped these insects (including the ants visible in the enlargement) and hardened about 25 million years ago (Madagascar).

Petrified wood: A cross-section of a limb from a coniferous tree (Madagascar). Petrification (or silicification) occurs when silica from weathered volcanic ash is gradually incorporated into partly decayed wood.

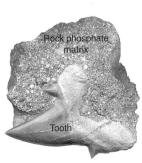

Rock phosphate matrix

Tooth

Shark tooth: The tooth of a shark *Lamna obliqua* preserved in phosphate beds, Eocene (Khouribga, Morocco). This process is called phosphatisation.

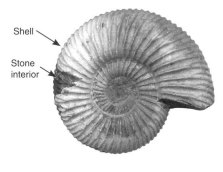

Shell

Stone interior

Ammonite: This ammonite still has a layer of the original shell covering the stone interior, Jurassic (Madagascar).

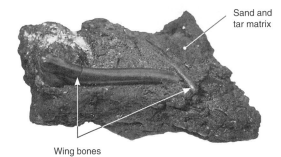

Sand and tar matrix

Wing bones

Bird bones: Fossilised bones of a bird that lived about 5 million years ago and became stuck in the tar pits at la Brea, Los Angeles, USA.

Cast: This ammonite has been preserved by a process called pyritisation, where Iron pyrite replaces hard remains of the dead organisms. Late Cretaceous (Charmouth, England).

Fossil fern: This compression fossil of a fern frond shows traces of carbon and wax from the original plant, Carboniferous (USA).

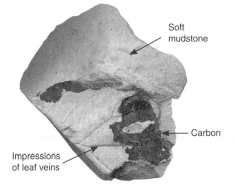

Soft mudstone

Carbon

Impressions of leaf veins

Sub-fossil: Leaf impression in soft mudstone (can be broken easily with fingers) with some of the remains of the leaf still intact (a few thousand years old), New Zealand.

© 2015 **BIOZONE** International
ISBN: 978-1-927309-13-1
Photocopying Prohibited

LINK 223   LINK 222   LINK 221   WEB 220

KNOW

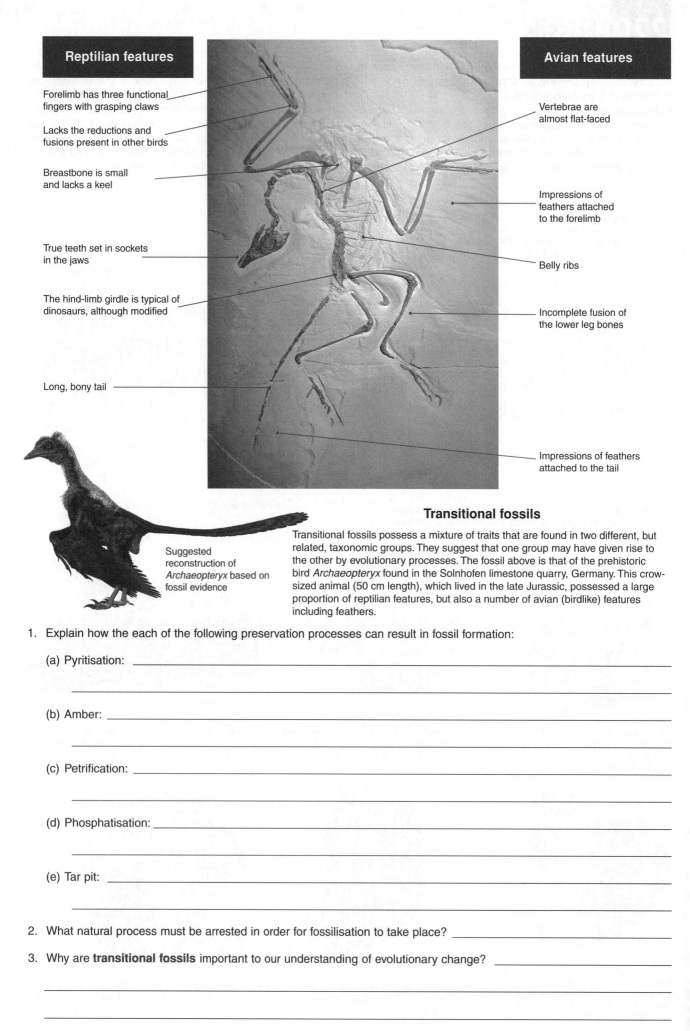

Reptilian features

Forelimb has three functional fingers with grasping claws

Lacks the reductions and fusions present in other birds

Breastbone is small and lacks a keel

True teeth set in sockets in the jaws

The hind-limb girdle is typical of dinosaurs, although modified

Long, bony tail

Avian features

Vertebrae are almost flat-faced

Impressions of feathers attached to the forelimb

Belly ribs

Incomplete fusion of the lower leg bones

Impressions of feathers attached to the tail

Suggested reconstruction of *Archaeopteryx* based on fossil evidence

Transitional fossils

Transitional fossils possess a mixture of traits that are found in two different, but related, taxonomic groups. They suggest that one group may have given rise to the other by evolutionary processes. The fossil above is that of the prehistoric bird *Archaeopteryx* found in the Solnhofen limestone quarry, Germany. This crow-sized animal (50 cm length), which lived in the late Jurassic, possessed a large proportion of reptilian features, but also a number of avian (birdlike) features including feathers.

1. Explain how the each of the following preservation processes can result in fossil formation:

(a) Pyritisation: _____

_____

(b) Amber: _____

_____

(c) Petrification: _____

_____

(d) Phosphatisation: _____

_____

(e) Tar pit: _____

_____

2. What natural process must be arrested in order for fossilisation to take place? _____

3. Why are **transitional fossils** important to our understanding of evolutionary change? _____

_____

_____

221 The Evolution of Horses

Key Idea: The evolution of the horse is one of the most robust examples of evolution documented in the fossil record.

The evolution of the horse from the ancestral *Hyracotherium* to modern *Equus* is well documented in the fossil record. The rich fossil record, which includes numerous **transitional fossils**, has enabled scientists to develop a robust model of horse phylogeny. It is a complex tree-like lineage with many divergences (below), and a diverse array of often coexisting species. The environmental transition from forest to grasslands drove many of the changes observed in the fossil record. These include reduction in toe number, increased size of cheek teeth, and increasing body size.

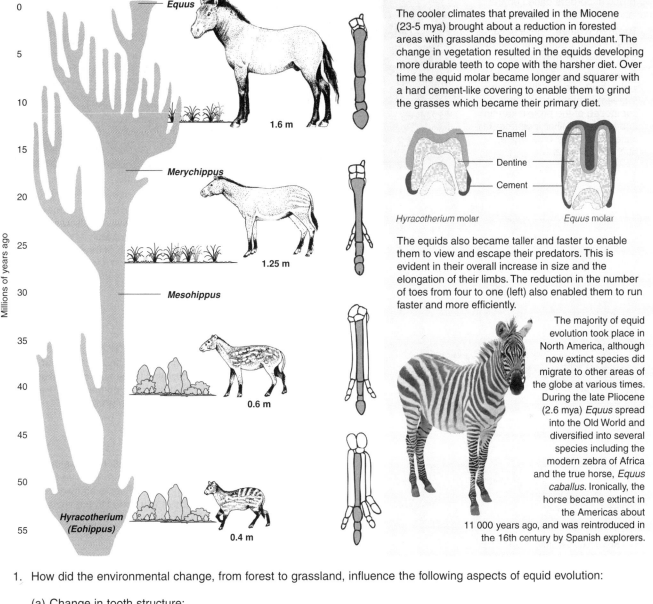

The cooler climates that prevailed in the Miocene (23-5 mya) brought about a reduction in forested areas with grasslands becoming more abundant. The change in vegetation resulted in the equids developing more durable teeth to cope with the harsher diet. Over time the equid molar became longer and squarer with a hard cement-like covering to enable them to grind the grasses which became their primary diet.

Enamel
Dentine
Cement

Hyracotherium molar   *Equus* molar

The equids also became taller and faster to enable them to view and escape their predators. This is evident in their overall increase in size and the elongation of their limbs. The reduction in the number of toes from four to one (left) also enabled them to run faster and more efficiently.

The majority of equid evolution took place in North America, although now extinct species did migrate to other areas of the globe at various times. During the late Pliocene (2.6 mya) *Equus* spread into the Old World and diversified into several species including the modern zebra of Africa and the true horse, *Equus caballus*. Ironically, the horse became extinct in the Americas about 11 000 years ago, and was reintroduced in the 16th century by Spanish explorers.

Equus — 1.6 m
Merychippus — 1.25 m
Mesohippus — 0.6 m
Hyracotherium (Eohippus) — 0.4 m

Millions of years ago

1. How did the environmental change, from forest to grassland, influence the following aspects of equid evolution:

    (a) Change in tooth structure: _____

    _____

    (b) Limb length: _____

    _____

    (c) Reduction in number of toes: _____

    _____

2. Why does the equid fossil record provide a good example of the evolutionary process? _____

    _____

    _____

    _____

LINK   WEB

223   221

222 The Evolution of Whales

Key Idea: The evolution of whales is well documented in the fossil record, with many transitional forms recording the shift from a terrestrial to an aquatic life.

The evolution of modern whales from an ancestral land mammal is well documented in the fossil record. The fossil record of whales includes many transitional forms, which has enabled scientists to develop an excellent model of whale evolution. The evolution of the whales (below) shows a gradual accumulation of adaptive features that have equipped them for life in the open ocean.

Modern whales are categorised into two broad suborders based on the presence or absence of teeth.

▶ **Toothed whales**: These have full sets of teeth throughout their lives. Examples: sperm whale and orca.

▶ **Baleen whales**: Toothless whales, which have a comb-like structure (baleen) in the jaw. Baleen is composed of the protein keratin and is used to filter food from the water. Examples: blue whale, humpback whale.

Orca
Robert Pittman - NOAA

Humpback whale

50 mya *Pakicetus*

Pakicetus was a transitional species between carnivorous land mammals and the earliest true whales. It was mainly land dwelling, but foraged for food in water. It had four, long limbs. Its eyes were near the top of the head and its nostrils were at the end of the snout. It had external ears, but they showed features of both terrestrial mammals and fully aquatic mammals.

45 mya *Rhodocetus*

Rhodocetus was mainly aquatic (water living). It had adaptations for swimming, including shorter legs and a shorter tail. Its eyes had moved to the side of the skull, and the nostrils were located further up the skull. The ear showed specialisations for hearing in water.

Legs became shorter

40 mya *Dorudon*

Dorudon was fully aquatic. Its adaptations for swimming included a long, streamlined body, a broad powerful muscular tail, the development of flippers and webbing. It had very small hind limbs (not attached to the spine) which would no longer bear weight on land.

Hind limbs became detached from spine

Balaena (recent whale ancestor)

The hind limbs became fully internal and vestigial. Studies of modern whales show that limb development begins, but is arrested at the limb bud stage. The nostrils became modified as blowholes. This recent ancestor to modern whales diverged into two groups (toothed and baleen) about 36 million years ago. Baleen whales have teeth in their early fetal stage, but lose them before birth.

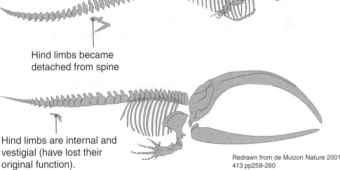
Hind limbs are internal and vestigial (have lost their original function).

Redrawn from de Muizon Nature 2001 413 pp259-260

1. Why does the whale fossil record provide a good example of the evolutionary process? _____

   _____

   _____

2. Briefly describe the adaptations of whales for swimming that evolved over time: _____

   _____

   _____

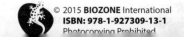
© 2015 **BIOZONE** International
ISBN: 978-1-927309-13-1
Photocopying Prohibited

223 Interpreting the Fossil Record

Key Idea: Fossils provide a record of the appearance and extinction of organisms. The fossil record can be used to establish the relative order of past events.

Fossils provide a record of the appearance and disappearance of organisms over time. Rock layers (**strata**) are arranged in the order of deposition (unless they have been disturbed by geological events). Strata from widespread locations can be correlated because a particular stratum at one location is the same age as the same stratum at a different location. Placing the strata in a sequential (relative) order of past events in a rock profile allows scientists to provide **relative dates** of past events, but it can not provide an absolute date for an event.

The formation of rock strata

The Earth's landscape has been shaped over a very long time through natural geological processes that continue today. Over time, layers of sedimentary rock, ash, or lava were deposited. Newer layers were deposited on top of older layers so that the oldest layers became buried. Layers are (usually) deposited horizontally and remain so unless they have been disturbed by geological processes such as mountain building or erosion.

These strata have been disturbed (tilted).

These strata remain in their original horizontal position.

Gaps in the fossil record

One of the difficulties with interpreting the fossil record is that it contains gaps. Without a complete record, it can be difficult to establish the evolutionary history of a taxon. There are several reasons for gaps in the fossil record, including:

▶ Organisms are only preserved as fossils rarely and many fossils have not been found.

▶ Fossils are often destroyed or distorted through changes in the preservation environment.

▶ Some organisms do not fossilise well. The record is biased towards organisms with hard parts.

Profile with sedimentary rocks containing fossils

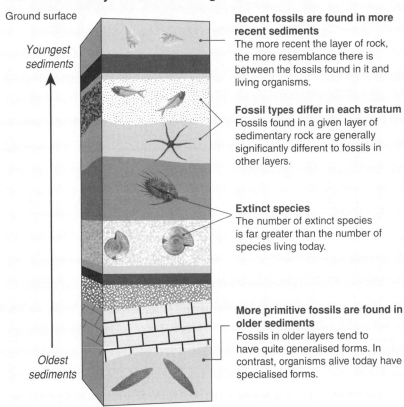

Ground surface

Youngest sediments

Oldest sediments

Rock strata are layered through time

Rock strata are arranged in the order that they were deposited (unless they have been disturbed by geological events). The most recent layers are near the surface and the oldest are at the bottom. Fossils can be used to establish the sequential (relative) order of past events in a rock profile.

Each rock layer (stratum) is unique in terms of the type of rock (sedimentary or volcanic) and the type of fossils it contains.

New fossil types mark changes in environment

In the strata at the end of one geological period, it is common to find many new fossils that become dominant in the next.

Each geological period had a different environment from the others. Their boundaries coincided with drastic environmental changes and the appearance of new niches. These produced new selection pressures resulting in new adaptive features in the surviving species, as they responded to the changes.

Recent fossils are found in more recent sediments

The more recent the layer of rock, the more resemblance there is between the fossils found in it and living organisms.

Fossil types differ in each stratum

Fossils found in a given layer of sedimentary rock are generally significantly different to fossils in other layers.

Extinct species

The number of extinct species is far greater than the number of species living today.

More primitive fossils are found in older sediments

Fossils in older layers tend to have quite generalised forms. In contrast, organisms alive today have specialised forms.

1. Discuss the importance of fossils as a record of evolutionary change over time: _____

_____

_____

_____

2. Why can gaps in the fossil record make it difficult to determine an evolutionary sequence? _____

_____

_____

LINK   WEB
220 **223**   KNOW

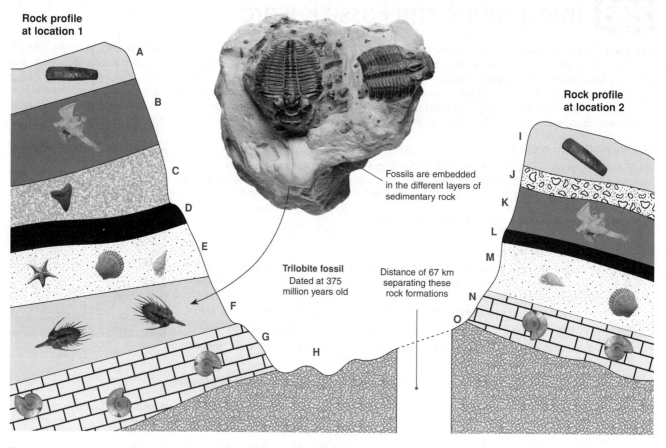

Rock profile at location 1

A
B
C
D
E
F
G
H

Rock profile at location 2

I
J
K
L
M
N
O

Fossils are embedded in the different layers of sedimentary rock

Trilobite fossil
Dated at 375 million years old

Distance of 67 km separating these rock formations

The questions below relate to the diagram above, showing a hypothetical rock profile from two locations separated by a distance of 67 km. There are some differences between the rock layers at the two locations. Apart from layers D and L which are volcanic ash deposits, all other layers comprise sedimentary rock.

3. Assuming there has been no geologic activity (e.g. tilting or folding), state in which rock layer (A-O) you would find:

   (a) The youngest rocks at location 1: ———————— (c) The youngest rocks at location 2: ————————

   (b) The oldest rocks at location 1: ———————— (d) The oldest rocks at location 2: ————————

4. (a) State which layer at location 1 is of the same age as layer M at location 2: _____

   (b) Explain the reason for your answer above: _____

   _____

   _____

5. The rocks in layer H and O are sedimentary rocks. Explain why there are no visible fossils in these layers:

   _____

   _____

   _____

   _____

6. (a) State which layers present at location 1 are missing at location 2: _____

   (b) State which layers present at location 2 are missing at location 1: _____

7. Using radiometric dating, the trilobite fossil was determined to be approximately 375 million years old. The volcanic rock layer (D) was dated at 270 million years old, while rock layer B was dated at 80 million years old. Give the approximate **age range** (i.e. greater than, less than, or between given dates) of the rock layers listed below:

   (a) Layer A: _____ (d) Layer G: _____

   (b) Layer C: _____ (e) Layer L: _____

   (c) Layer E: _____ (f) Layer O: _____

© 2015 **BIOZONE** International
ISBN: 978-1-927309-13-1
Photocopying Prohibited

224 Homologous DNA Sequences

Key Idea: The relatedness of species can be deduced from the differences in their DNA.

DNA-DNA hybridisation (below) provides a way to compare the genomes of different species by measuring the degree of genetic similarity between DNA sequences. More closely related species have fewer differences between their genomes than more distantly related species. This technique gives a measure of 'relatedness' and can be calibrated as a **molecular clock** against known fossil dates. It has been used to help determine the approximate date of human divergence from the apes, which has been estimated to be between 10 and 5 million years ago.

DNA hybridisation

1. DNA from the two species to be compared is extracted, purified and cut into short fragments (e.g. 600-800 base pairs).

2. The DNA of one species is mixed with the DNA of another.

3. The mixture is incubated to allow DNA strands to dissociate and reanneal, forming hybrid double-stranded DNA.

4. The hybridised sequences that are highly similar will bind more firmly. A measure of the heat energy required to separate the hybrid strands provides a measure of DNA relatedness.

DNA homologies today

DNA-DNA hybridisation has been criticised because duplicated sequences within a single genome make it unreliable comparing closely related species.

Today, DNA sequencing and computed comparisons are more widely used to compare genomes, although DNA-DNA hybridisation is still used to help identify bacteria.

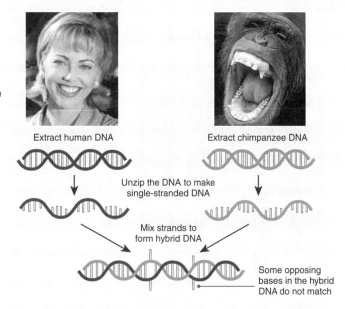

Extract human DNA · Extract chimpanzee DNA

Unzip the DNA to make single-stranded DNA

Mix strands to form hybrid DNA

Some opposing bases in the hybrid DNA do not match

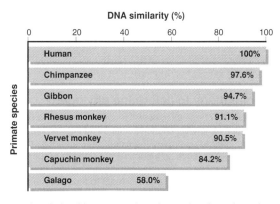

Flamingo · Ibis · Shoebill · Pelican · Stork · New World vulture

The relationships among the New World vultures and storks have been determined using DNA hybridisation. It has been possible to estimate how long ago various members of the group shared a common ancestor.

Similarity of human DNA to that of other primates

DNA similarity (%)

Primate species	DNA similarity (%)
Human	100%
Chimpanzee	97.6%
Gibbon	94.7%
Rhesus monkey	91.1%
Vervet monkey	90.5%
Capuchin monkey	84.2%
Galago	58.0%

The genetic relationships among the primates has been investigated using DNA hybridisation. Human DNA was compared with that of the other primates. It largely confirmed what was suspected from anatomical evidence.

1. Explain how **DNA hybridisation** can give a measure of genetic relatedness between species:

_____

_____

_____

2. Study the graph showing the results of a DNA hybridisation between human DNA and that of other primates.

(a) Which is the most closely related primate to humans? _____

(b) Which is the most distantly related primate to humans? _____

3. State the DNA difference score for:　(a) Shoebills and pelicans:_____　(b) Storks and flamingos: _____

4. On the basis of DNA hybridisation, state how long ago the ibises and New World vultures shared a common ancestor:

_____

LINK　LINK　WEB
226 225 224　KNOW

225 Homologous Proteins

Key Idea: Proteins are the product of gene expression, so an analysis of the differences between the same protein in different taxa gives an indication of species relatedness.

Traditionally, phylogenies were based largely on anatomical traits, and biologists attempted to determine the relationships between taxa based on similarity or by tracing the appearance of key characteristics. With the advent of new molecular techniques, homologies (similarities resulting from shared ancestry) could be studied at the molecular level as well and the results compared to phylogenies established using other methods. Protein sequencing provides an excellent tool for establishing homologies. A protein has a specific number of amino acids arranged in a specific order. Any differences in the sequence reflect changes in the DNA sequence. Commonly studied proteins include blood proteins, such as haemoglobin, and the respiratory protein cytochrome c.

Amino acid differences in haemoglobin

Human beta chain	0
Chimpanzee	0
Gorilla	1
Gibbon	2
Rhesus monkey	8
Squirrel monkey	9
Dog	15
Horse, cow	25
Mouse	27
Grey kangaroo	38
Chicken	45
Frog	67

When the sequence of the **beta haemoglobin chain** (right), which is 146 amino acids long, is compared between humans, five other primates, and six other vertebrates, the results support the phylogenies established using other methods. The numbers in the table (left) represent the number of amino acid differences between the beta chain of humans and those of other species. In general, the number of amino acid differences between the haemoglobins of different vertebrates is inversely proportional to genetic relatedness.

Shading indicates (from top) primates, non-primate placental mammals, marsupials, and non-mammals.

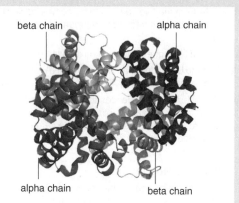

beta chain   alpha chain

alpha chain   beta chain

In most vertebrates, the oxygen-transporting blood protein haemoglobin is composed of four polypeptide chains, two alpha chains and two beta chains. Haemoglobin is derived from myoglobin, and ancestral species had just myoglobin for oxygen transport. When the amino acid sequences of myoglobin, the haemoglobin alpha chain, and the haemoglobin beta chain are compared, there are several amino acids that remain **conserved** between all three. These amino acid sequences must be essential for function because they have remained unchanged throughout evolution.

Using immunology to determine phylogeny

The immune system of one species will recognise the blood proteins of another species as foreign and form antibodies against them. This property can be used to determine the extent of relatedness between species. Blood proteins, such as albumins, are used to prepare **antiserum** in rabbits. The antiserum contains antibodies against the test blood proteins (e.g. human) and will react to those proteins in any blood sample they are mixed with. The extent of the reaction indicates how similar the proteins are; the greater the reaction, the more similar the proteins. This principle is illustrated (right) for antiserum produced to human blood and its reaction with the blood of other primates and a rat.

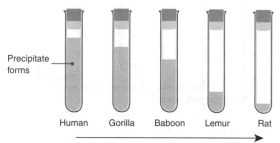

Precipitate forms

Human   Gorilla   Baboon   Lemur   Rat

Decreasing recognition of the antibodies against human blood proteins

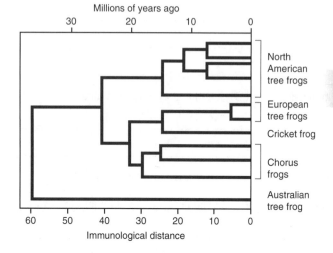

Millions of years ago

North American tree frogs

European tree frogs

Cricket frog

Chorus frogs

Australian tree frog

Immunological distance

The relationships among tree frogs have been established by immunological studies based on blood proteins such as immunoglobulins and albumins. The **immunological distance** is a measure of the number of amino acid substitutions between two groups. This, in turn, has been calibrated to provide a time scale showing when the various related groups diverged.

© 2015 **BIOZONE** International
ISBN: 978-1-927309-13-1
Photocopying Prohibited

Highly conserved proteins

Some proteins are common in many different species. These proteins are called **highly conserved proteins**, meaning they change (mutate) very little over time. This is because they have critical roles in the organism (e.g. in cellular respiration) and mutations are likely to prevent them from functioning correctly.

Evidence indicates that highly conserved proteins are homologous and have been derived from a common ancestor. Because they are highly conserved, changes in the amino acid sequence are likely to represent major divergences between groups during the course of evolution.

Cytochrome C (left) is a respiratory protein located in the electron transport chain in mitochondria.

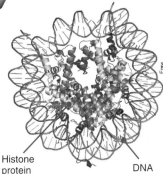

Histones (right) are a family of proteins that associate with DNA and organise it so that it can fit inside the cell nucleus.

Histone protein   DNA

The Pax-6 protein provides evidence for evolution

▶ The Pax-6 gene belongs to a family of genes that regulate the formation of a number of organs, including the eye, during embryonic development.

▶ The Pax-6 gene produces the Pax-6 protein, which acts as a transcription factor to control the expression of certain genes.

▶ Scientists know the role of Pax-6 in eye development because they created a knockout model in mice where the Pax-6 gene is not expressed. The knockout model is eyeless or has very underdeveloped eyes.

▶ The Pax-6 gene is so highly conserved that the gene from one species can be inserted into another species, and still produce a normal eye.

▶ This suggests the Pax-6 proteins are homologous, and the gene has been inherited from a common ancestor.

An experiment inserted mouse Pax-6 gene into fly DNA and turned it on in a fly's legs. The fly developed morphologically normal eyes on its legs!

1. Compare the differences in the haemoglobin sequence of humans, rhesus monkeys, and horses. What do these tell you about the relative relatedness of these organisms?

_____

_____

_____

2. (a) What is a highly conserved protein? _____

_____

(b) What type of proteins tend to be highly conserved? _____

_____

(c) Why are the proteins named in (b) highly conserved? _____

_____

(d) Why are highly conserved proteins good for constructing phylogenies? _____

_____

_____

3. (a) Describe the role of the Pax-6 gene: _____

_____

_____

(b) What evidence is there that the Pax-6 protein is highly conserved? _____

_____

_____

226 The Molecular Clock Hypothesis

Key Idea: The molecular clock hypothesis proposes that mutations occur at a steady rate and that changes in DNA sequences between species can determine phylogeny.

The molecular clock hypothesis states that mutations occur at a relatively constant rate for any given gene. The genetic difference between any two species can indicate when two species last shared a common ancestor and can be used to construct a phylogenetic tree. The molecular clock for each species, and each protein, may run at different rates, so molecular clock data is calibrated with other evidence (e.g. morphological) to confirm phylogeny. Molecular clock calculations are carried out on DNA or amino acid sequences.

In a theoretical example, the DNA sequence for a gene in two species (A & B, right) alive today differs by four bases. The mutation rate for the gene is approximately one base per 25 million years. Based on this rate, it can be determined that the common ancestor for these two species lived 50 mya.

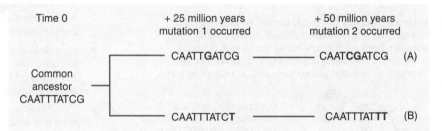

Time 0 — Common ancestor CAATTTATCG

+ 25 million years, mutation 1 occurred: CAATTGATCG

+ 50 million years, mutation 2 occurred: CAAT**C**GATCG (A)

CAATTTAT**CT** — CAATTTAT**TT** (B)

Cytochrome *c* and the molecular clock theory

		1	2	3	4	5	6	7	8	9	10	11	12	13	14	15	16	17	18	19	20	21	22
Human		Gly	Asp	Val	Glu	Lys	Gly	Lys	Lys	Ile	Phe	Ile	Met	Lys	Cys	Ser	Gln	Cys	His	Thr	Val	Glu	Lys
Pig												Val	Gln			Ala							
Chicken				Ile						Val		Val	Gln			Ala							
Dogfish										Val		Val	Gln			Ala							Asn
Drosophila	<<									Leu		Val	Gln	Arg		Ala							Ala
Wheat	<<		Asn	Pro	Asp	Ala		Ala				Lys	Thr	Arg		Ala						Asp	Ala
Yeast	<<		Ser	Ala	Lys			Ala	Thr	Leu		Lys	Thr	Arg		Glu	Leu						

This table shows the N-terminal 22 amino acid residues of human cytochrome *c*, with corresponding sequences from other organisms aligned beneath. Sequences are aligned to give the most position matches. A shaded square indicates no change. In every case, the cytochrome's heme group is attached to the Cys-14 and Cys-17. In *Drosophila*, wheat, and yeast, arrows indicate that several amino acids precede the sequence shown.

The sequence homology of cytochrome *c* (right), a respiratory protein, has been used to construct a phylogenetic tree for some species. Overall, the phylogeny aligns well to other evolutionary data, although the tree indicates that primates branched off before the marsupials diverged from other placental mammals, which is incorrect based on other evidence. Highly conserved proteins, such as cytochrome *c*, change very little over time and between species because they carry out important roles and if they changed too much they may no longer function properly.

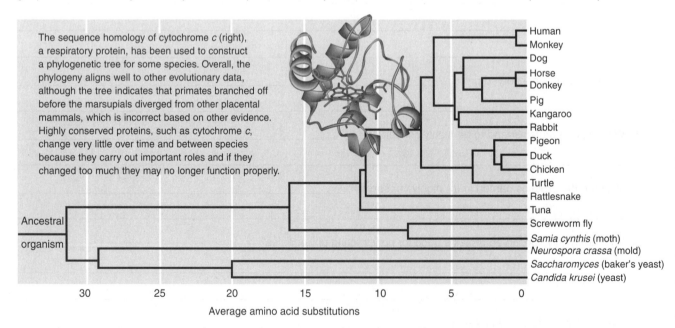

Species (top to bottom): Human, Monkey, Dog, Horse, Donkey, Pig, Kangaroo, Rabbit, Pigeon, Duck, Chicken, Turtle, Rattlesnake, Tuna, Screwworm fly, *Samia cynthis* (moth), *Neurospora crassa* (mold), *Saccharomyces* (baker's yeast), *Candida krusei* (yeast)

Ancestral organism

Average amino acid substitutions: 30, 25, 20, 15, 10, 5, 0

1. Describe a limitation of using molecular clocks to establish phylogeny: _____

_____

_____

2. For cytochrome *c*, suggest why amino acids 14 and 17 are unchanged in all the organisms shown in the table: _____

_____

227 Types of Variation

Key Idea: Variation can occur both within and between species and may be continuous or discontinuous. Variation is affected by both genetics and the environment.

Variation refers to the diversity within and between species. The genetic variation in species is largely due to meiosis and sexual reproduction, which shuffles existing genetic material into new combinations as it is passed from generation to generation. Mutation is also a source of variation as it may create new alleles. Variation gives species more opportunity to adapt to a changing environment because,

at any one time, some individuals will have higher fitness (leave more offspring) than others. Variation in a population can be continuous or discontinuous. Traits determined by a single gene (e.g. ABO blood groups) show discontinuous variation, with a very limited number of variants present in the population. In contrast, traits determined by a large number of genes (e.g. skin colour) show continuous variation, and the number of phenotypes is very large. Environmental influences (differences in diet for example) also contribute to the observable variation in a population.

Sources of variation in organisms

An individual's phenotype (how it looks is the result of interactions between the environment and the genes carried by the individual.

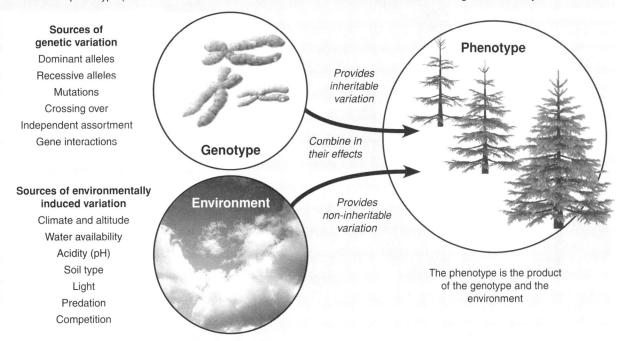

Sources of genetic variation
Dominant alleles
Recessive alleles
Mutations
Crossing over
Independent assortment
Gene interactions

Genotype

Provides inheritable variation

Combine in their effects

Phenotype

Sources of environmentally induced variation
Climate and altitude
Water availability
Acidity (pH)
Soil type
Light
Predation
Competition

Environment

Provides non-inheritable variation

The phenotype is the product of the genotype and the environment

Intraspecific variation

All members of a species differ from each other in some way. Some of this variation can be attributed to the environment in which the individuals developed, but much can be attributed to differences in genetics. An example of variation within a population is shown right. The ladybirds in the photo are all of the same species even though there are many variations in the colouration and number of dots on the carapace. Genetic variation within a species is important in enabling that species to adapt to changes in the environment. For example the darker insects might have an advantage if the prevailing climate became cooler because the dark carapace would absorb more heat from the environment.

Interspecific variation

Tillandsia aeranthos

Phyzome CC 3.0

Tillandsia excelsa

Codiferous CC 3.0

Interspecific variation will always be greater than intraspecific variation. The less related the species, the greater the differences. Although species in the same genus are closely related genetically, they can be morphologically diverse. For example the genus *Tillandsia* (commonly known as air plants) has about 730 species.

1. Explain why interspecific variation is greater than intraspecific variation: _____

   _____

   _____

2. What is the importance of variation within a species? _____

   _____

LINK   LINK
229 228
KNOW

Continuous and discontinuous variation

Variation in populations can be **continuous** (falling somewhere in a continuous distribution, e.g the height of 20 year old male humans) or **discontinuous** (either one thing or the other, e.g red or white flowers). Traits determined by the interaction of many different genes and the environment are called quantitative traits and they show continuous variation. Traits determined by several genes at the most are called qualitative traits. Such traits show discontinuous variation; there are a very limited number of variants in the population, with no gradation between them.

Albinism (above) is the result of the inheritance of recessive alleles for melanin production. Those with the albino phenotype lack melanin pigment in the eyes, skin, and hair.

Comb shape in poultry is a **qualitative trait** and birds have one of four phenotypes depending on which combination of four alleles they inherit. The dash (missing allele) indicates that the allele may be recessive or dominant.

Quantitative traits are characterised by **continuous variation**, with individuals falling somewhere on a normal distribution curve of the phenotypic range. Typical examples include skin colour and height in humans (left), grain yield in corn (above), weight gain in pigs (above, left), and milk production in cattle (far left). Quantitative traits are determined by genes at many loci (polygenic) but most are also influenced by environmental factors.

Single comb	Walnut comb	Pea comb	Rose comb
rrpp	**R_P_**	**rrP_**	**R_pp**

Flower colour in snapdragons (right) is also a **qualitative trait** determined by two alleles. (red and white). The alleles show incomplete dominance and the heterozygote (C^RC^W) exhibits an intermediate phenotype between the two homozygotes.

C^RC^R

3. What is the difference between **continuous** and **discontinuous** variation?_____

_____

_____

4. Identify each of the following phenotypic traits as continuous (quantitative) or discontinuous (qualitative):

   (a) Wool production in sheep: _____   (d) Albinism in mammals: _____

   (b) Hand span in humans: _____   (e) Body weight in mice: _____

   (c) Blood groups in humans: _____   (f) Flower colour in snapdragons: _____

5. On a windswept portion of a coast, two different species of plant (species A and species B) were found growing together. Both had a low growing (prostrate) phenotype. One of each plant type was transferred to a greenhouse where "ideal" conditions were provided to allow maximum growth. In this controlled environment, species B continued to grow in its original prostrate form, but species A changed its growing pattern and became erect in form. Identify the **cause** of the prostrate phenotype in each of the coastal grown plant species and explain your answer:

   Plant species A: _____

   _____

   _____

   Plant species B: _____

   _____

   _____

228 The Effects of Environment on Phenotype

Key Idea: An organism's phenotype is influenced by the environment in which it develops, even though the genotype remains unaffected.

External environmental factors can modify the phenotype encoded by genes. This can occur both during development and later in life. Even identical twins have minor differences in their appearance due to environmental factors such as diet and intrauterine environment before birth. Environmental factors that affect the phenotype include nutrients or diet, temperature, and the presence of other organisms.

The effect of temperature

▶ The sex of some animals is determined by the incubation temperature during their embryonic development. Examples include turtles, crocodiles, and the American alligator. In some species, high incubation temperatures produce males and low temperatures produce females. In other species, the opposite is true. Temperature regulated sex determination may provide an advantage by preventing inbreeding (since all siblings will tend to be of the same sex).

▶ Colour-pointing is a result of a temperature sensitive mutation to one of the melanin-producing enzymes. The dark pigment is only produced in the cooler areas of the body (face, ears, feet, and tail), while the rest of the body is a pale colour, or white. Colour-pointing is seen in some breeds of cats and rabbits (e.g. Siamese cats and Himalayan rabbits).

The effect of other organisms

▶ The presence of other individuals of the same species may control sex determination for some animals. Some fish species, including Sandager's wrasse (right), show this characteristic. The fish live in groups consisting of a single male with attendant females and juveniles. In the presence of a male, all juvenile fish of this species grow into females. When the male dies, the dominant female will undergo physiological changes to become a male. The male and female look very different.

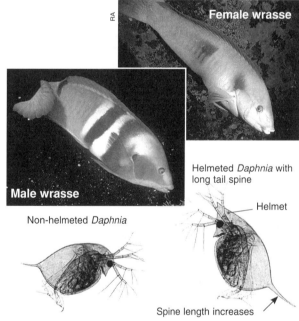

Female wrasse

Male wrasse

Helmeted *Daphnia* with long tail spine

Helmet

Non-helmeted *Daphnia*

Spine length increases

▶ Some organisms respond to the presence of other, potentially harmful, organisms by changing their body shape. Invertebrates such as *Daphnia* will grow a large helmet when a predatory midge larva is present. The helmet makes *Daphnia* more difficult to attack and handle. Such changes are usually in response to chemicals produced by the predator (or competitor) and are common in plants as well as animals.

1. (a) Give two examples of how temperature affects a phenotypic characteristic in an organism: _____

_____

(b) Why are the darker patches of fur in colour-pointed cats and rabbits found only on the face, paws, and tail?

_____

_____

_____

2. How is helmet development in *Daphnia* an adaptive response to environment? _____

_____

_____

LINK   WEB
227 228   KNOW

229 Quantifying Variation Using Student's *t* Test

Key Idea: Differences between two populations can be tested for significance using the Student's *t* test.

The Student's *t* test is commonly used to compare two sample means, e.g. means for a treatment and a control in an experiment, or the means of some measured characteristic between two animal or two plant populations. It is a simple test and useful for distinguishing real but marginal differences between samples. A simple example outlining the steps in the Student's *t* test is provided below. It compares data for a treatment and a control from a hypothetical experiment (the units are not relevant in this case, only the values). The worked example is followed by an exercise in which you will compare heart rate at rest (in beats per minute or bpm) in males and females.

Steps in performing a Student's *t* test

1 **Calculate summary statistics for the two data sets**

Control (A)	Treatment (B)
6.6	6.3
5.5	7.2
6.8	6.5
5.8	7.1
6.1	7.5
5.9	7.3

$n_A = 6$, $\bar{x}_A = 6.12$, $s_A = 0.496$

$n_B = 6$, $\bar{x}_B = 6.98$, $s_B = 0.475$

n_A and n_B are the number of values in the first and second data sets respectively (these do not need to be the same).

$\bar{x}$ is the mean.

s is the standard deviation (a measure of scatter in the data).

2 **Set up and state your null hypothesis (H_0)**

H_0: there is no treatment effect. The differences in the data sets are the result of chance and they are not really different. The alternative hypothesis is that there is a treatment effect and the two sets of data are truly different.

3 **Decide if your test is one or two tailed**

A one-tailed test looks for a difference only in one particular direction. A two-tailed test looks for any difference (+ or –). This tells you what section of the *t* table to consult. Most biological tests are two-tailed. Very few are one-tailed.

4 **Calculate the *t* statistic**

For our sample data above the calculated value of *t* is –3.09. The degrees of freedom (df) are $n_1 + n_2 - 2 = 10$.

Calculation of the *t* value uses the variance which is simply the square of the standard deviation (s^2). You may compute *t* using a spreadsheet but manual computation is not difficult (see opposite). It does not matter if the calculated *t* value is a positive or negative (the sign is irrelevant).

The absolute value of the *t* statistic (3.09) well exceeds the critical value for $P = 0.05$ at 10 degrees of freedom.

We can reject H_0 and conclude that the means are different at the 5% level of significance.

If the calculated absolute value of *t* had been less than 2.23, we could not have rejected H_0.

1. (a) In an experiment, data values were obtained from four plants in experimental conditions and three plants in control conditions. The mean values for each data set (control and experimental conditions) were calculated. The *t* value was calculated to be 2.16. The null hypothesis was: "The plants in the control and experimental conditions are not different". State whether the calculated *t* value supports the null hypothesis or its alternative (consult *t* table below):

_____

_____

(b) The experiment was repeated, but this time using 6 control and 6 "experimental" plants. The new *t* value was 2.54. State whether the calculated *t* value supports the null hypothesis or its alternative now:

_____

_____

2. Explain what you understand by statistical significance:

_____

_____

_____

_____

_____

Table of critical values of *t* at different levels of *P*.

Degrees of freedom	Level of Probability		
	0.05	0.01	0.001
1	12.71	63.66	636.6
2	4.303	9.925	31.60
3	3.182	5.841	12.92
4	2.776	4.604	8.610
5	2.571	4.032	6.869
6	2.447	3.707	5.959
7	2.365	3.499	5.408
8	2.306	3.355	5.041
9	2.262	3.250	4.781
10	2.228	3.169	4.587
11	2.201	3.106	4.437
12	2.179	3.055	4.318
13	2.160	3.012	4.221
14	2.145	2.977	4.140
15	2.131	2.947	4.073
16	2.120	2.921	4.015
17	2.110	2.898	3.965
18	2.101	2.878	3.922
19	2.093	2.861	3.883
20	2.086	2.845	3.850

© 2015 **BIOZONE** International
ISBN: 978-1-927309-13-1
Photocopying Prohibited

DATA

3. The table below presents data for heart rate (beats per minute) in samples of ten males and females from a population.
   (a) Complete the calculations to perform the *t* test for these two samples. The steps are outlined in the right hand column.

x (bpm)		**x − x̄** (deviation from the mean)		**(x − x̄)²** (deviation from mean)²	
Male	**Female**	**Male**	**Female**	**Male**	**Female**
70	69	-2.3	1	5.29	1
74	62	1.7	-6	2.89	36
80	75				
73	66				
75	68				
82	57				
62	61				
69	84				
70	61				
68	77				

$n_A = 10$ $n_B = 10$ | The sum of each column is called the sum of squares | $\Sigma (x − x̄)^2$ $\Sigma (x − x̄)^2$

The number of samples in each data set

Step 1: Summary statistics
Tabulate the data as shown in the first 2 columns of the table (left). Calculate the mean and give the n value for each data set. Compute the standard deviation if you wish.

Males $x̄_A = 72.3$ Females $x̄_B = 68.0$
$n_A = 10$ $n_B = 10$
$s_A = 5.87$ $s_B = 8.47$

Step 2: State your null hypothesis

Step 3: Test is one tailed / two tailed (delete one)

Step 4: Calculating *t*

4a: Calculate sums of squares
Complete the computations outlined in the table left. The sum of each of the final two columns (left) is called the sum of squares.

(b) The variance for males: $s^2_A =$

The variance for females: $s^2_B =$

4b: Calculate the variances
Calculate the variance (s^2) for each data set. This is the sum of squares ÷ by $n − 1$ (number of samples in each data set − 1). In this case the n values are the same, but they need not be.

$$s^2_A = \frac{\Sigma(x − x̄)^2}{n_A − 1} (A) \qquad s^2_B = \frac{\Sigma(x − x̄)^2}{n_B − 1} (B)$$

(c) The difference between the means for males and females

$(x̄_A − x̄_B) =$

4c: Differences between the means
Calculate the difference between the means
$$(x̄_A − x̄_B)$$

(d) $t_{(calculated)} =$

4d: Calculate *t*

$$t = \frac{(x̄_A − x̄_B)}{\sqrt{\frac{s^2_A}{n_A} + \frac{s^2_B}{n_B}}}$$

(e) Determine the degrees of freedom (d.f.)

d.f. $(n_A + n_B − 2) =$

4e: Determine the degrees of freedom
Degrees of freedom (d.f.) = $n_A + n_B − 2$ where n_A and n_B are the number of counts in each of populations A and B.

(f) $P =$

$t_{(critical value)} =$

(g) Your decision is: _____

_____

_____

_____

_____

Step 5: Consult the *t* table
Consult the *t*-tables (opposite) for the critical *t* value at the appropriate degrees of freedom and the acceptable probability level (e.g. P = 0.05).

5a: Make your decision
Make your decision whether or not to reject H_0. If t_{calc} is large enough you may be able to reject H_0 at a lower P value (e.g. 0.001), increasing confidence in the alternative hypothesis.

230 Spearman Rank Correlation

Key Idea: The Spearman rank correlation is a test used to determine if there is a statistical dependence (correlation) between two variables.

The Spearman rank correlation is appropriate for data that have a non-normal distribution (or where the distribution is not known) and assesses the degree of association between the X and Y variables (if they are correlated). For the test to work, the values used must be monotonic i.e. the values must increase or decrease together or one increases while the other decreases. A value of 1 indicates a perfect correlation; a value of 0 indicates no correlation between the variables. The example below examines the relationship between frequency of the drumming sound made by male frigatebirds (Y) and the volume of their throat pouch (X).

Spearman's rank data for frigate bird pouch volume and drumming frequency

Bird	Volume of pouch / cm³	Rank (R_1)	Frequency of drumming sound / Hz	Rank (R_2)	Difference (D) (R_1-R_2)	D^2
1	2550		461			
2	2440	I	473	6	-5	25
3	2740		532			
4	2730		465			
5	3010		485			
6	3370		488			
7	3080		527			
8	4910		478			
9	3740		485			
10	5090		434			
11	5090		468			
12	5380		449			
Based on Madsen et al 2004				ΣD^2		

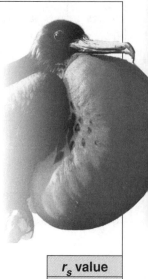

r_s value

Analysing the data

Step one: Rank the data for each variable. For each variable, the numbers are ranked in descending order, e.g. for the variable, volume, the highest value 5380 cm³ is given the rank of 12 while its corresponding frequency value is given the rank of 2. Fill in the rank columns in the table above in the same way. If two numbers have the same rank value, then use the mean rank of the two values (e.g. 1+2 = 3. 3/2= 1.5).

Step two: Calculate the difference (D) between each pair of ranks (R_1-R_2) and enter the value in the table (as a check, the sum of all differences should be 0).

Step three: Square the differences and enter them into the table above (this removes any negative values).

Step four: Sum all the D^2 values and enter the total into the table.

Step five: Use the formula below to calculate the Spearman Rank Correlation Coefficient (r_s). Enter the r_s value in the box above.

$$r_s = 1 - \left(\frac{6\Sigma D^2}{n(n^2-1)} \right)$$

Spearman rank correlation coefficient

Step six: Compare the r_s value to the table of critical values (right) for the appropriate number of pairs. If the r_s value (ignoring sign) is greater than or equal to the critical value then there is a significant correlation. If r_s is positive then there is a positive correlation. If r_s is negative then there is a negative correlation.

Number of pairs of measurements	Critical value
5	1.00
6	0.89
7	0.79
8	0.74
9	0.68
10	0.65
12	0.59
14	0.54
16	0.51
18	0.48
20	0.45

1. State the null hypothesis for the data set. _____

_____

_____

2 (a) Identify the critical value for the frigate bird data: _____

(b) State if the correlation is positive or negative: _____

(c) State whether the correlation is significant: _____

3. In your class, gather data on heart rate (beats per minute measured by carotid or radial pulse) and breathing rate (breaths per minute). Use the Spearman rank coefficient to determine if there is a relationship between these variables. Complete your analysis and staple it to this page.

© 2015 **BIOZONE** International
ISBN: 978-1-927309-13-1
Photocopying Prohibited

231 Adaptation

Key Idea: Adaptations are inherited traits that have evolved and are maintained by natural selection. They have a functional role in an organism's life and enhance an individual's fitness. An **adaptation** (or adaptive feature) is any heritable trait that equips an organism to its functional position in the environment (its niche). These traits may be structural, physiological, or behavioural and reflect ancestry as well as adaptation.

Adaptation is important in an evolutionary sense because adaptive features promote fitness. **Fitness** is a measure of an organism's ability to maximise the numbers of offspring surviving to reproductive age. Genetic adaptation must not be confused with physiological adjustment (acclimatisation), which refers to an organism's ability to adjust during its lifetime to changing environmental conditions.

Ear length in rabbits and hares

The external ears of many mammals are used as important organs to assist in thermoregulation (controlling loss and gain of body heat). The ears of rabbits and hares native to hot, dry climates, such as the jack rabbit of south-western USA and northern Mexico, are relatively very large. The Arctic hare lives in the tundra zone of Alaska, northern Canada and Greenland, and has ears that are relatively short. This reduction in the size of the extremities (ears, limbs, and noses) is typical of cold adapted species.

Arctic hare: *Lepus arcticus*

Black-tail jackrabbit: *Lepus californicus*

Body size in relation to climate

Regulation of body temperature requires a large amount of energy and mammals exhibit a variety of structural and physiological adaptations to increase the effectiveness of this process. Heat production in any endotherm depends on body volume (heat generating metabolism), whereas the rate of heat loss depends on surface area. Increasing body size minimises heat loss to the environment by reducing the surface area to volume ratio. Animals in colder regions therefore tend to be larger overall than those living in hot climates. This relationship is know as **Bergman's rule** and it is well documented in many mammalian species. Cold adapted species also tend to have more compact bodies and shorter extremities than related species in hot climates.

Fennec fox

Arctic fox

The **fennec fox** of the Sahara illustrates the adaptations typical of mammals living in hot climates: a small body size and lightweight fur, and long ears, legs, and nose. These features facilitate heat dissipation and reduce heat gain.

The Arctic fox shows the physical characteristics typical of cold adapted mammals: a stocky, compact body shape with small ears, short legs and nose, and dense fur. These features reduce heat loss to the environment.

Number of horns in rhinoceroses

Not all differences between species can be convincingly interpreted as adaptations to particular environments. Rhinoceroses charge rival males and predators, and the horn(s), when combined with the head-down posture, add effectiveness to this behaviour. Horns are obviously adaptive, but it is not clear if having one (Indian rhino) or two (black rhino) horns is related to the functionality in the environment or a reflection of evolution from a small hornless ancestor.

African black rhino

Great Indian rhino

1. Distinguish between adaptive features (genetic) and acclimatisation: _____

_____

_____

2. Explain the nature of the relationship between the length of extremities (such as limbs and ears) and climate:

_____

_____

3. Explain the adaptive value of a compact body with a relatively small surface area in a colder climate: _____

_____

_____

Snow bunting
(*Plectrophenax nivalis*)

The snow bunting is a small ground feeding bird that lives and breeds in the Arctic and sub-Arctic islands. Although migratory, snow buntings do not move to traditional winter homes but prefer winter habitats that resemble their Arctic breeding grounds, such as bleak shores or open fields of northern Britain and the eastern United States. Snow buntings have the unique ability to molt very rapidly after breeding. During the warmer months, the buntings are a brown colour, changing to white in winter (right). They must complete this colour change quickly, so that they have a new set of feathers before the onset of winter and before migration. In order to achieve this, snow buntings lose as many as four or five of their main flight wing feathers at once, as opposed to most birds, which lose only one or two.

Very few small birds breed in the Arctic, because most small birds lose more heat than larger ones. In addition, birds that breed in the brief Arctic summer must migrate before the onset of winter, often travelling over large expanses of water. Large, long winged birds are better able to do this. However, the snow bunting is superbly adapted to survive in the extreme cold of the Arctic region.

White feathers are hollow and filled with air, which acts as an insulator. In the dark-coloured feathers the internal spaces are filled with pigmented cells.

Less heat is lost from white plumage compared to dark plumage.

Snow buntings, on average, lay one or two more eggs than equivalent species further south. They are able to rear more young because the continuous daylight and the abundance of insects at high latitudes enables them to feed their chicks around the clock.

During snow storms or periods of high wind, snow buntings will burrow into snowdrifts for shelter.

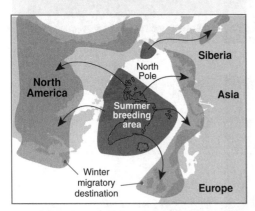

Habitat and ecology: Widespread throughout Arctic and sub-Arctic Islands. Active throughout the day and night, resting for only 2-3 hours in any 24 hour period. Snow buntings may migrate up to 6000 km but are always found at high latitudes. **Reproduction and behaviour**: The nest, which is concealed amongst stones, is made from dead grass, moss, and lichen. The male bird feeds his mate during the incubation period and helps to feed the young.

4. Describe a structural, physiological, and behavioural adaptation of the **snow bunting**, explaining how each adaptation assists survival:

   (a) Structural adaptation: _____

   _____

   _____

   (b) Physiological adaptation: _____

   _____

   _____

   (c) Behavioural adaptation: _____

   _____

   _____

5. Examples of adaptations are listed below. Identify them as predominantly structural, physiological, and/or behavioural:

   (a) Relationship of body size and shape to latitude (tropical or Arctic): _____

   (b) The production of concentrated urine in desert dwelling mammals: _____

   (c) The summer and winter migratory patterns in birds and mammals: _____

   (d) The C4 photosynthetic pathway and CAM metabolism of plants: _____

   (e) The thick leaves and sunken stomata of desert plants: _____

   (f) Hibernation or torpor in small mammals over winter: _____

   (g) Basking in lizards and snakes: _____

232 Adaptation and Convergent Evolution

Key Idea: Evolution in response to similar selection pressures can result in unrelated species appearing very similar.

Convergent evolution (convergence) describes the process by which species from different evolutionary lineages come to resemble each other because they have similar ecological roles, and natural selection has shaped similar adaptations.

It can be difficult to distinguish convergent and parallel evolution, as both produce similarity of form. Generally, similarity arising in closely related lineages (e.g. within marsupial mice) is regarded as parallelism, whereas similarity arising in more distantly related taxa is convergence (e.g. similarities between marsupial and placental mice).

Convergence in swimming form

Not all similarities between species are the result of common ancestry. Selection pressures to solve similar problems in particular environments may result in similarity of form and function in unrelated (or distantly related) species. The development of succulent forms in unrelated plant groups (*Euphorbia* and the cactus family) is an example of **convergence** in plants. In the example (right), the selection pressures of the aquatic environment have produced a similar **streamlined** body shape in unrelated vertebrate groups. Icthyosaurs, penguins, and dolphins each evolved from terrestrial species that took up an aquatic lifestyle. Their general body form has evolved to become similar to that of the shark, which has always been aquatic. Note that flipper shape in mammals, birds, and reptiles is a result of convergence, but its origin from the pentadactyl limb is an example of **homology**.

Analogous structures

Analogous structures (or **homoplasies**) are those that have the same function and often the same appearance, but different origins. The example (right) shows the structure of the **eye** in two unrelated taxa (mammals and cephalopod molluscs). The eye appears similar, but has evolved independently. The **wings** of birds and insects are also analogous structures. The wings have the same function, but the two taxa do not share a common ancestor. *Longisquama*, a lizard-like creature that lived about 220 mya, also had 'wings' that probably allowed gliding between trees. These 'wings' were not a modification of the forearm (as in birds), but highly modified long scales or feathers extending from its back.

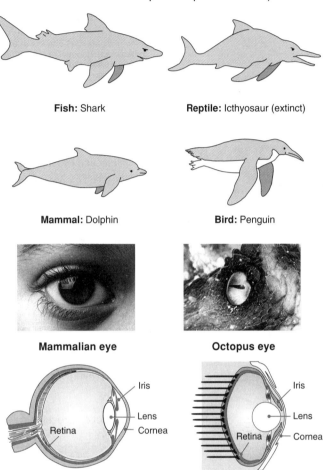

Fish: Shark   **Reptile**: Icthyosaur (extinct)

Mammal: Dolphin   **Bird**: Penguin

Mammalian eye   **Octopus eye**

Iris — Lens — Retina — Cornea   Iris — Lens — Retina — Cornea

1. In the example above illustrating convergence in swimming form, describe two ways in which the body form has evolved in response to the particular selection pressures of the aquatic environment:

   (a) _____

   _____

   (b) _____

   _____

2. Describe two of the selection pressures that have influenced the body form of the swimming animals above:

   (a) _____

   (b) _____

3. When early taxonomists encountered new species in the Pacific region and the Americas, they were keen to assign them to existing taxonomic families based on their apparent similarity to European species. In recent times, many of the new species have been found to be quite unrelated to the European families they were assigned to. Explain why the traditional approach did not reveal the true evolutionary relationships of the new species:

   _____

   _____

   _____

   _____

LINK   WEB
231   232   KNOW

20

4. For each of the paired examples, briefly describe the adaptations of body shape, diet and locomotion that appear to be similar in both forms, and the likely selection pressures that are acting on these mammals to produce similar body forms:

Convergence Between Marsupials and Placentals

Australia

Marsupial and **placental** mammals diverged very early in mammalian evolution (about 120 mya), probably in what is now the Americas. Marsupials were widespread throughout the ancient supercontinent of Gondwana as it began to break up through the Cretaceous, but then became isolated on the southern continents, while the placentals diversified in the Americas and elsewhere, displacing the marsupials in most habitats around the world. Australia's isolation from other landmasses in the Eocene meant that the Australian marsupials escaped competition with the placentals and diversified into a wide variety of forms, ecologically equivalent to the North American placental species.

North America

Some older sources cite this example as one of parallelism, rather than convergence. However, a greater degree of morphological difference than now once separated the ancestors of the placental and marsupial lineages being compared, making this a case of convergence, not parallelism.

Marsupial Mammals   **Placental Mammals**

Wombat	(a) Adaptations: Rodent-like teeth, eat roots and above ground plants, and can excavate burrows. Selection pressures: Diet requires chisel-like teeth for gnawing. The need to seek safety from predators on open grassland.	Woodchuck
Flying phalanger	(b) Adaptations: Selection pressures:	Flying squirrel
Marsupial mole	(c) Adaptations: Selection pressures:	Mole
Marsupial mouse	(d) Adaptations: Selection pressures:	Mouse
Tasmanian wolf (tiger)	(e) Adaptations: Selection pressures:	Wolf
Long-eared bandicoot	(f) Adaptations: Selection pressures:	Jack rabbit

© 1995-2014 **BIOZONE** International
ISBN: 978-1-927173-97-8
Photocopying Prohibited

233 Mechanism of Natural Selection

Key Idea: Natural selection is the evolutionary mechanism by which organisms that are better adapted to their environment survive to produce a greater number of offspring.

Evolution is the change in inherited characteristics in a population over generations. Evolution is the consequence of interaction between four factors: (1) The potential for populations to increase in numbers, (2) Genetic variation as a result of mutation and sexual reproduction, (3) competition for resources, and (4) proliferation of individuals with better survival and reproduction.

Natural selection is the term for the mechanism by which better adapted organisms survive to produce a greater number of viable offspring. This has the effect of increasing their proportion in the population so that they become more common. This is the basis of Darwin's theory of evolution by natural selection.

We can demonstrate the basic principles of evolution using the analogy of a 'population' of M&M's candy.

#1

In a bag of M&M's, there are many colours, which represents the variation in a population. As you and a friend eat through the bag of candy, you both leave the blue ones, which you both dislike, and return them to bag.

#2

The blue candy becomes more common...

#3

Eventually, you are left with a bag of blue M&M's. Your selective preference for the other colours changed the make-up of the M&M's population. This is the basic principle of selection that drives evolution in natural populations.

Darwin's theory of evolution by natural selection

Darwin's theory of evolution by natural selection is outlined below. It is widely accepted by the scientific community today and is one of founding principles of modern science.

Overproduction
Populations produce too many young: many must die

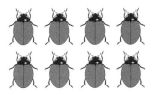

Populations generally produce more offspring than are needed to replace the parents. Natural populations normally maintain constant numbers. A certain number will die without reproducing.

Variation
Individuals show variation: some variations more favourable than others

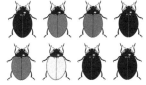

Individuals in a population have different phenotypes and therefore, genotypes. Some traits are better suited to the environment, and individuals with these have better survival and reproductive success.

Natural selection
Natural selection favours the individuals best suited to the environment at the time

Individuals in the population compete for limited resources. Those with favourable variations will be more likely to survive. Relatively more of those without favourable variations will die.

Inherited
Variations are inherited: the best suited variants leave more offspring

The variations (both favourable and unfavourable) are passed on to offspring. Each generation will contain proportionally more descendants of individuals with favourable characters.

1. Identify the four factors that interact to bring about evolution in populations: _____

_____

_____

_____

© 2015 **BIOZONE** International
ISBN: 978-1-927309-13-1
Photocopying Prohibited

LINK **236** LINK **235** LINK **234** WEB **233** KNOW

Variation, selection, and population change

1. **Variation through mutation and sexual reproduction:**
In a population of brown beetles, mutations independently produce red colouration and 2 spot marking on the wings. The individuals in the population compete for limited resources.

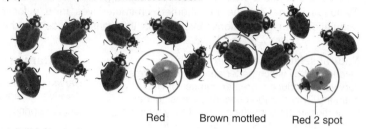

Red   Brown mottled   Red 2 spot

2. **Selective predation:**
Brown mottled beetles are eaten by birds but red ones are avoided.

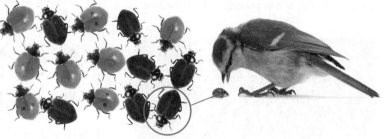

3. **Change in the genetics of the population:**
Red beetles have better survival and fitness and become more numerous with each generation. Brown beetles have poor fitness and become rare.

Natural populations, like the ladybug population above, show genetic variation. This is a result of **mutation** (which creates new alleles) and sexual reproduction (which produces new combinations of alleles). Some variants are more suited to the environment of the time than others. These variants will leave more offspring, as described for the hypothetical population (right).

2. What produces the genetic variation in populations? _____

3. Define evolution: _____

_____

4. Explain how the genetic make-up of a population can change over time: _____

_____

_____

_____

_____

_____

_____

5. Complete the table below by calculating the percentage of beetles in the example above right.

Beetle population	% Brown beetles	% Red beetles	% Red beetles with spots
1			
2			
3			

234 Insecticide Resistance

Key Idea: Insect resistance to insecticide is increasing as a result of ineffectual initial applications of insecticide that only kill the most susceptible insects, leaving the more resistant ones to form a new, more resistant population.

Insecticides are pesticides used to control pest insects. They have been used for hundreds of years, but their use has increased since synthetic insecticides were first developed in the 1940s. When **insecticide resistance** develops, the control agent will no longer control the target species. Resistance can arise through behavioural, anatomical, biochemical, and physiological mechanisms,

but the underlying process is a form of **natural selection**, in which the most resistant organisms survive to pass on their genes to their offspring. To combat increasing resistance, higher doses of more potent pesticides are sometimes used. This drives the selection process, so that increasingly higher dose rates are required to combat rising resistance. This phenomenon is made worse by the development of multiple resistance in some pest species. Insecticides are widely used, so the development of resistance has serious environmental and economic consequences.

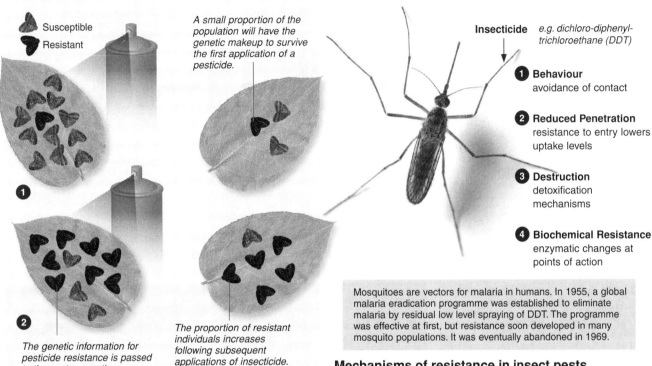

Susceptible
Resistant

A small proportion of the population will have the genetic makeup to survive the first application of a pesticide.

Insecticide e.g. dichloro-diphenyl-trichloroethane (DDT)

1 Behaviour
avoidance of contact

2 Reduced Penetration
resistance to entry lowers uptake levels

3 Destruction
detoxification mechanisms

4 Biochemical Resistance
enzymatic changes at points of action

1

2

The genetic information for pesticide resistance is passed to the next generation.

The proportion of resistant individuals increases following subsequent applications of insecticide. Eventually, almost all of the population is resistant.

Mosquitoes are vectors for malaria in humans. In 1955, a global malaria eradication programme was established to eliminate malaria by residual low level spraying of DDT. The programme was effective at first, but resistance soon developed in many mosquito populations. It was eventually abandoned in 1969.

The development of resistance

The application of an insecticide can act as a potent selection pressure for resistance in pest insects. The insecticide acts as a selective agent, and only individuals with greater natural resistance survive the application to pass on their genes to the next generation. These genes (or combination of genes) may spread through all subsequent populations.

Mechanisms of resistance in insect pests

Insecticide resistance in insects can arise through a combination of mechanisms. (1) Increased sensitivity to an insecticide will cause the pest to avoid a treated area. (2) Certain genes (e.g. the PEN gene) confer stronger physical barriers, decreasing the rate at which the chemical penetrates the cuticle. (3) Detoxification by enzymes within the insect's body can render the pesticide harmless, and (4) structural changes to the target enzymes make the pesticide ineffective. No single mechanism provides total immunity, but together they transform the effect from potentially lethal to insignificant.

1. Give two reasons why widespread insecticide resistance can develop very rapidly in insect populations:

   (a) _____

   (b) _____

2. Explain how repeated insecticide applications act as a selective agent for evolutionary change in insect populations:

   _____

   _____

3. With reference to synthetic insecticides, discuss the implications of insecticide resistance to human populations:

   _____

   _____

   _____

235 The Evolution of Antibiotic Resistance

Key Idea: Current widespread use of antibiotics has created a selective environment for the proliferation of antibiotic resistance in bacterial populations.

Antibiotic resistance arises when a genetic change allows bacteria to tolerate levels of antibiotic that would normally inhibit growth. This resistance may arise spontaneously, through mutation or copying error, or by transfer of genetic material between microbes. Genomic analyses from 30 000 year old permafrost sediments show that the genes for antibiotic resistance are not new. They have long been present in the bacterial genome, predating the modern selective pressure of antibiotic use. In the current selective environment, these genes have proliferated and antibiotic resistance has spread. For example, methicillin resistant strains of *Staphylococcus aureus* (MRSA) have acquired genes for resistance to all penicillins. Such strains are called superbugs.

The evolution of drug resistance in bacteria

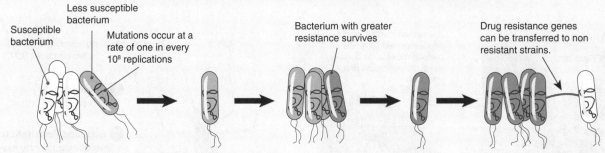

Susceptible bacterium / **Less susceptible bacterium** / Mutations occur at a rate of one in every 10^8 replications / **Bacterium with greater resistance survives** / Drug resistance genes can be transferred to non resistant strains.

Any population, including bacterial populations, includes variants with unusual traits, in this case reduced sensitivity to an antibiotic. These variants arise as a result of mutations in the bacterial chromosome.

When a person takes an antibiotic, only the most susceptible bacteria will die. The more resistant cells remain alive and continue dividing. Note that the antibiotic does not create the resistance; it provides the environment in which selection for resistance can take place.

If the amount of antibiotic delivered is too low, or the course of antibiotics is not completed, a population of resistant bacteria develops. Within this population too, there will be variation in susceptibility. Some will survive higher antibiotic levels than others.

A highly resistant population has evolved. The resistant cells can exchange genetic material with other bacteria (via horizontal gene transmission), passing on the genes for resistance. The antibiotic initially used against this bacterial strain will now be ineffective.

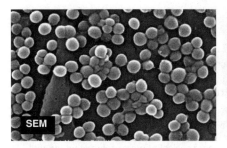

SEM

Staphylococcus aureus is a common bacterium responsible various minor skin infections in humans. MRSA (above) is variant strain that has evolved resistance to penicillin and related antibiotics. MRSA is troublesome in hospital-associated infections where patients with open wounds, invasive devices (e.g. catheters), and weakened immune systems are at greater risk for infection than the general public.

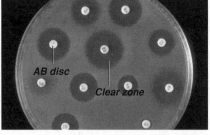

AB disc / Clear zone

The photo above shows an antibiogram plate culture of *Enterobacter sakazakii*, a rare cause of invasive infections in infants. An antibiogram measures the biological resistance of disease-causing organisms to antibiotic agents. The bacterial lawn (growth) on the agar plate is treated with antibiotic discs, and the sensitivity to various antibiotics is measured by the extent of the clearance zone in the bacterial lawn.

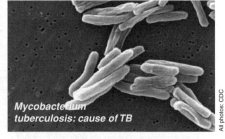

Mycobacterium tuberculosis: cause of TB

All photos: CDC

TB is a disease that has experienced spectacular ups and downs. Drugs were developed to treat it, but then people became complacent when they thought the disease was beaten. TB has since resurged because patients stop their medication too soon and infect others. Today, one in seven new TB cases is resistant to the two drugs most commonly used as treatments, and 5% of these patients die.

1. (a) How does antibiotic resistance arise in a bacterial population? _____

_____

(b) Describe two ways in which antibiotic resistance can become widespread: _____

_____

_____

2. With reference to tuberculosis, discuss the implications to humans of widespread antibiotic resistance:

_____

_____

_____

© 2015 **BIOZONE** International
ISBN: 978-1-927309-13-1
Photocopying Prohibited

236 Chloroquine Resistance in Protozoa

Key Idea: Resistance to antimalarial drugs in *Plasmodium* has spread since their introduction, especially chloroquine.

Chloroquine is an antimalarial drug, discovered in 1934, and first used clinically to prevent malaria in 1946. Chloroquine was widely used because it was cheap to produce, safe, and very effective. Chloroquine resistance in *Plasmodium falciparum* first appeared in the late 1950s, and the subsequent spread of resistance has significantly decreased chloroquine's effectiveness. The WHO drug efficacy update in 2010 showed that when chloroquine is used as the single therapy, it is still effective at preventing malaria in Central American countries where chloroquine resistance has not yet developed. In 30 other countries, chloroquine failure rates ranged between 20-100%. In some regions, chloroquine is still an effective treatment if used in combination with other anti-malarial drugs.

Global spread of chloroquine resistance

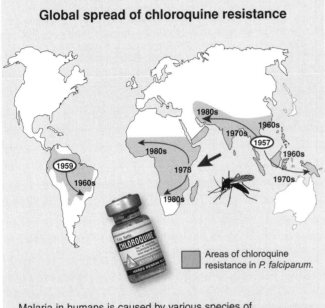

Areas of chloroquine resistance in *P. falciparum*.

Malaria in humans is caused by various species of *Plasmodium*, a protozoan parasite transmitted by *Anopheles* mosquitoes. The inexpensive antimalarial drug **chloroquine** was used successfully to treat malaria for many years, but its effectiveness has declined since resistance to the drug was first recorded in the 1950s. Chloroquine resistance has spread steadily (above) and now two of the four *Plasmodium* species, *P. falciparum* and *P. vivax* are chloroquine-resistant. *P. falciparum* alone accounts for 80% of all human malarial infections and 90% of the deaths, so this rise in resistance is of global concern. New anti-malarial drugs have been developed, but are expensive and often have undesirable side effects. Resistance to even these newer drugs is already evident, especially in *P. falciparum*, although this species is currently still susceptible to artemisinin, a derivative of the medicinal herb *Artemisia annua*.

Recent studies have demonstrated a link between mutations in the chloroquine resistance transporter (PfCRT) gene, and resistance to chloroquine in *P. falciparum*. PfCRT is a membrane protein involved in drug and metabolite transport.

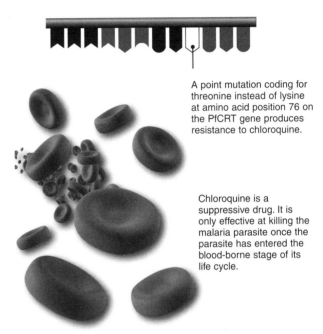

A point mutation coding for threonine instead of lysine at amino acid position 76 on the PfCRT gene produces resistance to chloroquine.

Chloroquine is a suppressive drug. It is only effective at killing the malaria parasite once the parasite has entered the blood-borne stage of its life cycle.

The use of chloroquine in many African countries was halted during the 1990s because resistance developed in *P. falciparum*. Recent studies in Malawi and Kenya have revealed a significant decrease in chloroquine resistance since the drug was withdrawn. There may be a significant fitness cost to the PfCRT mutants in the absence of anti-malaria drugs, leading to their decline in frequency once the selection pressure of the drugs is removed. This raises the possibility of re-introducing chloroquine as an anti-malarial treatment in the future.

1. Describe the benefits of using chloroquine to prevent malaria: _____

_____

_____

2. With reference to *Plasmodium falciparum*, explain how chloroquine resistance arises:

_____

_____

_____

3. Describe two strategies to reduce the spread of chloroquine resistance while still treating malaria:

(a) _____

_____

(b) _____

_____

© 2015 **BIOZONE** International
ISBN: 978-1-927309-13-1
Photocopying Prohibited

LINK
176
KNOW

237 Chapter Review

Summarise what you know about this topic under the headings provided. You can draw diagrams or mind maps, or write short notes to organise your thoughts. Use the images and hints included to help you:

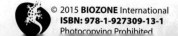

Classification
HINT: Describe features of the five Kingdoms.

Evolution
HINT: Describe the fossil and molecular evidence for evolution.

Natural selection
HINT: Describe the mechanism of natural selection and its importance in resistance to medical drugs.

© 2015 **BIOZONE** International
ISBN: 978-1-927309-13-1
Photocopying Prohibited

238 KEY TERMS: Did You Get It?

1. Test your vocabulary by matching each term to its correct definition, as identified by its preceding letter code. This activity tests your knowledge of the vocabulary used in this and the previous chapter.

adaptation

binomial nomenclature

convergent evolution

discontinuous variation

domain

fitness

fossil record

genotype

natural selection

phenotype

variation

A   The process by which heritable traits in organisms become more or less common in a population as a function of their effect on fitness (differential reproductive success).

B   A feature with a current functional role in the life history of an organism that evolved and is maintained by means of natural selection.

C   Variation characterised by a limited number of discrete phenotypes.

D   The sum total of an organism's observable characteristics or traits.

E   A formal system of naming species of organisms by giving each a Latin name composed of two parts.

F   Evolution in unrelated species occupying similar niches that causes them to arrive at similar structural, physiological and behavioural solutions.

G   The incomplete history of past life recorded in the preserved remains or traces of organisms.

H   The highest taxonomic rank in the revised classification of life based on recognition of prokaryote diversity.

I   The differences observed between individuals within a species and between species as a result of genes and environment.

J   The genetic makeup of an organism.

K   A measure of the ability of an organism to survive and reproduce.

2. Two populations of daisy were found growing in a small valley. One population was found on the south facing slope while the other was found on the north facing slope. Investigators measured the diameter of a sample of the daisy flowers from each population to determine if there was a difference between the two populations. The results are shown below:

Population	Flower diameter / cm										
A	1.3	1.2	1.4	1.5	1.2	1.1	1.0	1.4	1.3	1.3	1.2
B	1.1	1.3	1.1	0.9	0.9	1.3	1.4	0.8	1.3	1.1	1.0

(a) Calculate the mean flower size for population A: _____ Population B: _____

(b) Calculate the standard deviation for population A: _____ Population B: _____

(c) Determine the *t* value for the study: _____

(d) Use a *t*-table to determine if there is a significant difference in flower size between the populations: _____

_____

3. The two plants shown right are unrelated. The left hand image shows a cactus from North America, while the right hand image shows a Euphorbia from Africa. Both these plants live in deserts. Identify the pattern of evolution displayed by these plants an describe the environments associated with the adaptations.

_____

_____

_____

_____

LINK

229 TEST

Image credits

The writing team would like to thank the following people and organisations who have kindly provided photographs or illustrations for this edition:

• PASCO for their photographs of probeware • Habitat news for sampling photos • Dan Butler for the photo of the cut finger • Dartmouth College and Dr Louisa Howard for TEMs of cell structures • Wadsworth Centre (NYSDH) for the photo of the cell undergoing cytokinesis • Ed Uthman • Angela Simpson for the photo of the cockroach trachea • Janice Haney Carr, CDC • Charles Goldberg, University of California, San Diego School of Medicine, for the photograph of a patient with rheumatoid arthritis • Western New Mexico University Department of Natural Sciences /Dale A. Zimmerman Herbarium • The late Stephen Moore for his photos of aquatic invertebrates • Rhys Barrier for black mudfish photos • Dept. of Natural Resources, Illinois, for the photograph of the threatened prairie chicken • Jesse Allen and Robert Simmon (NASA) for the image of deforestation in the Amazon • Frank Drebin for the photo of the hawfinch • Kimberly Mallady for the hedgerow photo • APS for the photo of Theodosius Dobzhansky

We also acknowledge the photographers who have made images available through **Wikimedia Commons** under Creative Commons Licences 2.0, 2.5, or 3.0: • Enwinoseen • Synamorphy • Goran Ekstrom (PLoS) • Olaboy • Jeffery M. Vincour • Dartmouth College • Barfooz and John Grosse • Alison Roberts • Y tambe • Mnoff • Rufino Uribe • Miquel, Vilavella, Shimalov & Torres • FontanaCG • Zephyris • JPbarrass • Matthias Zepper • dsworth center - New York State Department of Health • Nephron • D_kuru • Kelvinsong • Fred Brooks, University of Hawaii • Dr David Midgley • Dr Graham Beards • Artem Topchly • Stefan Goen, Uckermarck • Piet Spaans • Walter Siegmund • Sevenstar • Bjorn Schulz • Micheal Apel • Simon Carey • Cymothoa exigua • Keith Hulburt and Paul Zarucki • M Betley • Keith Evans • NIAD • PLoS • G Dallimore • Kathy Chapman • Jim Gifford • JM Garg • Robert Pittman (NOAA) • Phyzome • Codiferous • C Johnson-Walker

Contributors identified by coded credits:

BF: Brian Finerran (University of Canterbury), **CDC**: Centers for Disease Control and Prevention, Atlanta, USA, **DH**: Don Horne, **DW**: David Wells, **EII**: Education Interactive Imaging, **GW**: Graham Walker, **JDG**: John Green (University of Waikato), **KP**: Kent Pryor, **MPI**: Max Planck Institute for Developmental Biology, Germany **NASA**: National Aeronautics and Space Administration, **NIH**: National Institute of Health, **RA**: Richard Allan, **RCN**: Ralph Cocklin, **TG**: Tracey Greenwood, **WBS**: Warwick Silvester (University of Waikato), **WMU**: Waikato Microscope Unit.

Image libraries:

We also acknowledge our use of royalty-free images, purchased by BIOZONE International Ltd from the following sources: **Corel** Corporation from various titles in their Professional Photos CD-ROM collection; Dollar Photo Club, dollarphotoclub.com; istock photos, istockphoto.com; **IMSI** (International Microcomputer Software Inc.) images from IMSI's MasterClips® and MasterPhotosTM Collection, 1895 Francisco Blvd. East, San Rafael, CA 94901-5506, USA; ©1996 **Digital Stock**, Medicine and Health Care collection; ©**Hemera** Technologies Inc, 1997-2001; © 2005 JupiterImages Corporation www.clipart.com; ©1994., ©**Digital Vision**; Gazelle Technologies Inc.; ©1994-1996 **Education Interactive Imaging** (UK), **PhotoDisc®**, Inc. USA, www.photodisc.com. We also acknowledge the following clipart providers: TechPool Studios, for their clipart collection of human anatomy: Copyright ©1994, TechPool Studios Corp. USA (some of these images have been modified); Totem Graphics, for clipart; Corel Corporation, for vector art from the Corel MEGAGALLERY collection.

Index